THE ROUTLEDGE HANDBOOK OF THE POLITICS OF BREXIT

The surprise decision expressed by the British people in the referendum held in June 2016 to leave the European Union was remarkable. It also presents a "natural experiment" where the exposure of a society to an extraordinary event allows scholars to observe, in real time in the real world, the interaction of variables.

The Routledge Handbook of the Politics of Brexit takes stock of what we know in the social science community about the Brexit phenomenon so far and looks to make sense of this remarkable process as it unfolds. The book asks simple questions across a range of areas and topics so as to frame the debate into a number of navigable "subdiscussions", providing structure and form to what is an evolving and potentially inchoate topic. As such, it provides a systematic account of the background for, the content of, and the possible implications of Brexit.

The handbook therefore does not examine in detail the minutiae of Brexit as it unfolds on a day-to-day basis but raises its sights to consider both the broad contextual factors that shape and are shaped by Brexit and the deeper sources and implications of the British exit from the European Union. Importantly, as interest in Brexit reaches far beyond the shores of the United Kingdom, so an international team of contributors examines and reveals the global implications and the external face of Brexit.

The Routledge Handbook of the Politics of Brexit will be essential reading and an authoritative reference for scholars, students, researchers and practitioners involved in and actively concerned about research on Brexit, British politics, European Union politics, and comparative politics and international relations.

Patrick Diamond is Senior Lecturer at the School of Politics and International Relations, Queen Mary University of London, United Kingdom.

Peter Nedergaard is Professor at the Department of Political Science, University of Copenhagen, Denmark.

Ben Rosamond is Professor at the Department of Political Science, University of Copenhagen, Denmark.

"Diamond, et al. 2018 constitutes the most important reference work that deals with both the sources and implications of Brexit published to date."

Matthias Matthijs and Christina Toenshoff, *Oxford Bibliographies*

"Wow! Almost nothing about Brexit is clear – and that makes this an extraordinary and extraordinarily useful collection. For it contains both all that there is to know about Brexit and all that we need to make sense of it – insofar, that is, as there is sense to be made of it. A wonderful achievement and very highly recommended."

Colin Hay, *Professor of Political Science,*
Sciences Po, Paris

"This is a wide ranging, informative, and up-to-date survey of Brexit and its implications for the United Kingdom, for the European Union, and for countries beyond. Each of the twenty-four chapters provides a state-of-the-art contribution that summarizes the current state of knowledge for students and experts alike."

Gary Marks, *Burton Craige Distinguished Professor,*
UNC-Chapel Hill, and Robert Schuman Fellow, EUI, Florence

"British exit from the European Union has become the defining issue for the UK today. This insightful text tells you everything you need to know, and might not even have known to ask, from the inside and the outside. Remarkable not only for the range of topics considered but also for the depth of analysis of its stellar list of contributors, this book is *the* indispensable guide to Brexit."

Vivien A. Schmidt, *Jean Monnet Professor of*
European Integration, Boston University, USA

"Brexit is a process rather than an event, which has implications which go far beyond the UK itself. With its excellent team of authors this book provides a broad, comprehensive and insightful account of the many different contexts, issues and dilemmas associated with the decision and its consequences. It will be an indispensable source for all students of Brexit."

Andrew Gamble, *Emeritus Professor of Politics, University of*
Cambridge, and Professorial Fellow, University of Sheffield, UK

THE ROUTLEDGE HANDBOOK OF THE POLITICS OF BREXIT

Edited by Patrick Diamond,
Peter Nedergaard and Ben Rosamond

Routledge
Taylor & Francis Group

LONDON AND NEW YORK

First published in paperback 2019

First published 2018
by Routledge
2 Park Square, Milton Park, Abingdon, Oxon OX14 4RN

and by Routledge
711 Third Avenue, New York, NY 10017

Routledge is an imprint of the Taylor & Francis Group, an informa business

British Library Cataloguing-in-Publication Data
A catalogue record for this book is available from the British Library

Library of Congress Cataloging-in-Publication Data
Names: Diamond, Patrick, editor. | Nedergaard, Peter, 1957– editor. | Rosamond, Ben, editor. | Lequesne, Christian, editor.
Title: The Routledge handbook of the politics of Brexit / edited by Patrick Diamond, Peter Nedergaard and Ben Rosamond.
Description: Abingdon, Oxon ; New York, NY : Routledge, 2018. | Includes bibliographical references and index.
Identifiers: LCCN 2018003051 | ISBN 9781138049369 (hardback) | ISBN 9781315169613 (ebook)
Subjects: LCSH: European Union—Great Britain—History—Handbooks, manuals, etc. | Referendum—Great Britain—History—21st century—Handbooks, manuals, etc. | Great Britain—Politics and government—2007—Handbooks, manuals, etc. | Great Britain—Foreign relations—Handbooks, manuals, etc.
Classification: LCC HC240.25.G7 R68 2018 | DDC 341.242/230941—dc23
LC record available at https://lccn.loc.gov/2018003051

ISBN: 978-1-138-04936-9 (hbk)
ISBN: 978-0-367-27808-3 (pbk)
ISBN: 978-1-315-16961-3 (ebk)

Typeset in Bembo
by Apex CoVantage, LLC

CONTENTS

Figures   viii
Tables   ix
Box   x
Contributors   xi
Preface   xiv

1   Introduction   1
    Patrick Diamond, Peter Nedergaard and Ben Rosamond

PART I
Brexit from the inside   13

2   Brexit and the state of the United Kingdom   15
    Daniel Wincott

3   Brexit and the Irish case   27
    Mary C. Murphy

4   Brexit and Scotland   40
    Michael Keating

5   Brexit and the City of London: the revenge of the ultraliberals?   49
    Leila Simona Talani

6   Brexit and the future model of British capitalism   66
    Andrew Baker and Scott Lavery

7 Brexit and British trade policy   80
   Jed Odermatt

8 Brexit and agriculture   92
   Wyn Grant

9 Brexit and higher education and research   103
   Anne Corbett and Claire Gordon

10 Brexit, 'immigration' and anti-discrimination   118
   Adrian Favell and Roxana Barbulescu

11 Brexit and British exceptionalism   134
   Peter Nedergaard and Maja Friis Henriksen

12 Brexit and English identity   147
   Ben Wellings

13 Brexit and the Conservative Party   157
   Richard Hayton

14 Brexit and the Labour party: Euro-caution vs. Euro-fanaticism?
   The Labour party's 'constructive ambiguity' on Brexit and
   the European Union   167
   Patrick Diamond

15 The (anti-)politics of Brexit   179
   Matthew Flinders

PART II
Brexit from the outside   **195**

16 Brexit and the Commonwealth: fantasy meets reality   197
   Peg Murray-Evans

17 Brexit and Britain's role in the world   208
   Oliver Daddow

18 Brexit and the EU as an international actor   223
   Henrik Larsen

19 Brexit and European defence: why more defence does not
   equal more integration   233
   Mikkel Vedby Rasmussen

Contents

20 Brexit and EU financial regulation   244
    Lucia Quaglia

21 Brexit and the European Union: hanging in the balance?   254
    Mads Dagnis Jensen and Holly Snaith

22 Brexit and small states in Europe: hedging, hiding or seeking shelter? 266
    Anders Wivel and Baldur Thorhallsson

23 Brexit and the EU's affiliated non-members   278
    John Erik Fossum

24 Brexit and the future of EU theory   290
    Christian Lequesne

Index   298

FIGURES

9.1 What about applications to Horizon 2020 from the rest of the world?
     Top ten third countries in terms of share of participations in signed
     grant agreements, Horizon 2020 compared with FP7   110
23.1 Patterns of differentiation in the EU   280
23.2 The institutional structure of the European Economic Area Agreement   283

TABLES

5.1	Financial markets share by country	53
5.2	UK share of financial markets	54
6.1	Four power blocs and the emergent political economy of Brexit	73
13.1	Conservative leadership election: result of parliamentary ballots	160
15.1	Five types of anti-politics	181
21.1	A taxonomy for measuring the impact of Brexit on the balance of power in the EU	255

BOX

9.1 Countries in the EU association agreements with the EU higher education
    and research programmes   104

CONTRIBUTORS

Andrew Baker is Professor at the Department of Politics, University of Sheffield, United Kingdom.

Roxana Barbulescu is Academic University Fellow at the Faculty of Education, Social Sciences and Law, University of Leeds, United Kingdom.

Anne Corbett is Senior Associate at LSE Enterprise, London School of Economics and Political Science, United Kingdom.

Oliver Daddow is Assistant Professor at the School of Politics and International Relations, University of Nottingham, United Kingdom.

Patrick Diamond is Senior Lecturer at the School of Politics and International Relations, Queen Mary University of London, United Kingdom.

Peg Murray-Evans is Research Associate at the Department of Politics, University of York, United Kingdom.

Adrian Favell is Chair in Sociology and Social Theory at the School of Sociology and Social Policy, University of Leeds, United Kingdom.

Matthew Flinders is Professor at the Department of Politics, University of Sheffield, United Kingdom.

John Erik Fossum is Professor at the ARENA Centre for European Studies, University of Oslo, Norway.

Claire Gordon is Teaching Fellow at the European Institute, London School of Economics and Political Science, United Kingdom.

Wyn Grant is Emeritus Professor at the Department of Politics and International Studies, University of Warwick, United Kingdom.

Richard Hayton is Associate Professor at the School of Politics and International Studies, University of Leeds, United Kingdom.

Maja Friis Henriksen is Research Assistant at the Department of Political Science, University of Copenhagen, Denmark.

Mads Dagnis Jensen is Associate Professor at Department of Business and Politics, Copenhagen Business School, Denmark.

Michael Keating is Professor and Chair in Scottish Politics at the Department of Politics and International Relations, University of Aberdeen, United Kingdom.

Henrik Larsen is Professor with special responsibilities at the Department of Political Science, University of Copenhagen, Denmark.

Scott Lavery is Research Fellow at Sheffield Political Economy Research Institute, University of Sheffield, United Kingdom.

Christian Lequesne is Professor at the Centre De Recherches Internationales, SciencesPo, Paris, France.

Mary C. Murphy is Lecturer at the Department of Government, University College Cork, Ireland.

Peter Nedergaard is Professor at the Department of Political Science, University of Copenhagen, Denmark.

Jed Odermatt is Postdoc at the Centre of Excellence for International Courts, Faculty of Law, University of Copenhagen, Denmark.

Lucia Quaglia is Professor at the Department of Political and Social Sciences, University of Bologna, Italy.

Mikkel Vedby Rasmussen is Professor and Head of the Department of Political Science, University of Copenhagen, Denmark.

Ben Rosamond is Professor at the Department of Political Science, University of Copenhagen, Denmark.

Holly Snaith was Assistant Professor of Political Science at the University of Copenhagen, Denmark, and is currently an Honorary Fellow of the Aston Centre for Europe, Aston University, United Kingdom.

Leila Simona Talani is Professor at the Department of European and International Studies, King's College London, United Kingdom.

Baldur Thorhallsson is Professor and Head of the Faculty of Political Science, University of Iceland, Iceland.

Ben Wellings is Senior Lecturer in Politics and International Relations, Monash University, Australia.

Daniel Wincott is Professor and Blackwell Chair of Law and Society, School of Law and Politics, Cardiff University, United Kingdom.

Anders Wivel is Professor with special responsibilities at the Department of Political Science, University of Copenhagen, Denmark.

PREFACE

This collection of papers is among the first attempts to produce a systematic academic overview and analysis of the Brexit process that was initiated by the United Kingdom's (UK's) decision to vote to leave the European Union (EU) in June 2016, and the UK Government's subsequent decision to trigger Article 50 of the Lisbon Treaty. We recognise that at this stage, the Brexit process is scarcely complete and that, as a consequence, Brexit is a 'moving target' with no predetermined end point or destination. We nonetheless hope that the outstanding group of scholars who have contributed to this volume have identified among the most important issues and challenges that are set to define the Brexit process in the years and decades ahead of us.

This *Routledge* handbook on the politics of Brexit analyses the UK's imminent departure from the EU along two critical dimensions. The first aspect relates to the *internal* impact of Brexit on the UK's economy, society and politics; how far will the Brexit process transform the economic and social structures of Great Britain in the foreseeable future? To what extent will Brexit lead to a far-reaching overhaul of the British state and the nature of the UK polity, as many adherents of Brexit hope? Will Brexit inevitably encourage the reconfiguration of English, Welsh, Scottish and Irish identities so as to threaten the underpinnings of the UK territorial state? How will particular sectors and arenas of national life – from agriculture to higher education – protect their strategic interests in the aftermath of Great Britain's exodus from the EU?

The second dimension of the volume relates to the *external* context of Brexit; what will be the impact of Brexit on states outside the UK? How will the UK's withdrawal from the treaties affect the balance of power within the EU's political institutions and between member states? Will Europe automatically be a less influential and powerful actor on the global stage? Beyond the EU, how will the Commonwealth countries react to the UK's retreat from the Union, given the anachronistic appeal of the 'Anglosphere tradition' in most Commonwealth nations?

These are among the most important and critical questions relating to the UK's parting from the EU that are discussed. We do not pretend that the treatment offered here is exhaustive; inevitably, there have been issues that we were not able to address in greater detail, from the impact of Brexit on the European social model to future relationships between the EU and the United States. Nevertheless, we very much hope that the handbook will make a compelling contribution to the scholarly debates around these crucial issues in the coming years.

In compiling the book, we would like to express our profound thanks to Maja Friis Henriksen who has provided outstanding research support on the volume, as well as contributing substantively to one of the chapters. We would like to thank Department of Political Science at University of Copenhagen for funding Maja Friis Henriksen as research assistant for this project. At Routledge, our editors Andrew Taylor and Sophie Iddamalgoda have been a source of great help and encouragement throughout. Patrick Diamond would also like to thank Queen Mary, University of London for providing a period of sabbatical leave that helped to ensure the completion of this volume.

Patrick Diamond
Peter Nedergaard
Ben Rosamond
December 2017

1

INTRODUCTION

Patrick Diamond, Peter Nedergaard and Ben Rosamond

Whether 'Brexit' materializes or whether Brexit is ultimately 'hard' or 'soft' in character, the decision taken by the British people in the referendum held in June 2016 to leave the European Union (EU) was a remarkable development from both political and scholarly points of view. Politically, exiting the EU represents easily the most significant realignment of United Kingdom (UK) foreign policy for many decades. In terms of process and consequence, Brexit poses stark challenges. As the only example of a member state opting to leave the EU, Brexit raises huge questions about the future integrity and coherence of the EU itself. Domestically, Brexit poses a series of 'wicked problems' in terms of the UK polity and its politics and policy. The challenges to policymaking and public administration of disentangling the UK from four and a half decades of accumulated EU legislation are immense. Most serious projections suggest that Brexit will have a negative impact upon the UK economy, which in turn provokes the urgent search for viable post-Brexit growth models for the UK. Moreover, Brexit provides a stark reminder of the peculiar character of the UK's plurinational constitutional settlement, not to mention its increased delicacy. Beyond Europe, the prospect of the UK leaving the EU and (very possibly) the Single Market and the Customs Union has wide-ranging and unpredictable implications for the foreign economic policies and domestic politics of a significant number of countries. Actors across the world have attached symbolic value to Brexit. For some, it represents the triumph of a form of sovereign freedom consistent with an open liberal trading order. For others, it signifies nothing less than the dangers of populist demagoguery and the pernicious spread of 'post-truth' politics. Brexit inevitably shapes external views of both the UK and the EU (Oliver 2017).

Of course, social scientists in general and political scientists in particular are interested in these Brexit effects. Changes in the world we study, especially when they are as visible and as obviously significant as Brexit, provoke a flurry of academic activity, often in defiance of the rhythms of normal scholarly time. The scholar's impulse is to seek deeper explanation and understanding of the phenomenon in question, to ask 'Of what is this an instance?' (Rosenau and Durfee 1995), even if the thing we are witnessing seems to be without precedent. Needless to say, different subfields will pose distinct versions of this question and will seek to situate Brexit within a set of pre-existing debates. So for those who have spent time researching the history of UK–EU relations and/or the evolution of British attitudes to European integration, Brexit may come to be seen as the ultimate expression of the UK's status as an 'awkward partner' (George 1994; Wall 2008), or of the fundamental ambivalence of its appropriate foreign policy orientation (Sanders and Houghton 2016; Grob-Fitzgibbon 2016), or of the UK's peculiar orientation to the global economy (Gamble 2005), or of the way in which all of the foregoing have yielded a particularly toxic version of Euroscepticism in the context of the UK (or perhaps, more accurately, England's) distinctive pattern of inter- and intra-party politics (Baker and Schnapper 2015). At the same time, for students of British politics, Brexit is not just about 'Europe'. Brexit touches every aspect of politics and policymaking in the UK – parliamentary politics, public administration, party politics, electoral politics, devolved government, foreign policy, economic policy and so on (Armstrong 2017; Evans and Menon 2017).

If it is now impossible to write about and teach British politics without putting Brexit centre stage, then the same is surely true for EU studies. Here there are two obvious foci for Brexit-related work. The first is the assessment of the impact of British withdrawal from the Union upon the EU's polity, policymaking and politics. Research in the field has a long track record of dealing with these effects in relation to the expansion of the EU to include more member states, but never before have scholars of EU politics been forced to contemplate and assess the institutional, policy and political consequences of a member state (and a large one at that) exiting the Union. The second focal point is the question of the extent to which Brexit is representative or perhaps constitutive of a broader crisis of European integration (Dinan et al. 2017). Of special interest here is the question of whether Brexit can be understood as an instance of European *dis*-integration, perhaps presaging the ultimate collapse of the EU or, if not that, then maybe a new phase where integration becomes more differentiated and the EU itself emerges weakened and less effective (Vollaard 2014, Webber 2014, Rosamond 2016). A strong counter-hypothesis is the idea that Brexit, by removing the EU's primary gadfly, will actually come to be seen as a harbinger of much deeper integration, at least among the core member states (De Witte 2017).

Brexit will clearly occupy a prime place on the research agendas of specialists in EU and British politics for many years. But it also holds important implications for a much broader community of scholarship. For example, Brexit has become a key case for comparative discussions of populist politics and especially in the search for the drivers of the revolt of the so-called left-behinds or losers of globalisation in the rich democracies. There is a good deal of agreement that the result of the Brexit referendum and the election of Donald Trump to the US presidency should be understood as parts of the same political moment (Barnett 2017; Blyth 2016) but there less certainty as to whether Trump and Brexit are best explained in relation to identity or economic variables or through some permutation of the two (see variously Hobolt 2016; Clarke et al. 2017; Inglehart and Norris 2016; Becker et al. 2016; Gidron and Hall 2017). Either way, Brexit would seem to tell us at least two things about the general trajectory of democratic politics in the early decades of the twenty-first century. First, it is suggestive of the presence of an aggressive anti-establishmentarianism at work within mature democracies, characterized by a distrust of elites and the projects and institutions with which elites are associated (Hopkin 2017). Second, Brexit seems to have been propelled by a distinctively populist and plebiscitary understanding of democracy. The reduction of democratic politics to the 'will of the people' (as expressed by a bare majority of the population) can be read as either a very effective campaigning tactic by those Brexiteers who are keen to deliver on the result of the referendum, or it could be taken as indicative of the broader 'hollowing out' of democratic politics (Mair 2013) where established political parties have, in recent decades, become less able to mediate between the imperatives of 'responsible' government on the one hand and the need to represent and channel popular will into the political system on the other.

It is hard to think of a political science subfield or, for that matter, any social science discipline that will remain untouched by Brexit or that will fail to develop its own distinctive debates around Brexit. This book represents a relatively early but – we hope – reflective and systematic contribution to this scholarly conversation. As previously noted, much has been written already about why Brexit occurred, but there have been relatively few attempts to understand the long-term impact of the Brexit process on the UK and on those countries with ties to the UK. In methodological terms, Brexit might even be thought of as a 'natural experiment', where the exposure of a society to an extraordinary political shock or contingent event allows scholars to observe, in real time and in the real world, the interaction of a variety of complex social, political and economic variables. There are obvious dangers in trying to grapple with a rapidly changing analytical object in real time. For example, happenings that might seem vitally important in the eye of the political storm might, in the longer run, turn out to be merely incidental details. Nevertheless, we maintain that Brexit is too important and frankly too interesting to ignore. As we will explain, our approach – while not completely 'future proof' – is designed to put Brexit into broader perspective and to make a meaningful scholarly contribution to a societal and academic conversation that has been on going in advance of and since the referendum.

The overwhelming interest in the Brexit phenomenon amongst the media and decision-makers and within the social scientific community is hardly surprising, but the resulting cacophony demands that we take stock, making sense of this remarkable process as it unfolds. It is increasingly clear that the UK's departure from the EU will have far-reaching consequences for the future shape and cohesion of the UK polity, the UK model of capitalism, UK foreign policy, and Britain's role in the world. It is also important to remember that interest in Brexit reaches far beyond the shores of Britain. Brexit is, of necessity, a key agenda item in capitals around the world. For example, Commonwealth countries that were once integral to the UK's foreign economic policy are anxious to assess the likely impact of the UK's departure from the EU on their domestic economy and politics. It is not just in the UK where it is important to understand both why Brexit came about and how the Brexit process will unfold in years to come.

The rationale of this handbook is to take stock of what we know in the social science community about Brexit so far. Our intention is to be among the first to do so on a large scale. As previously noted, the UK's departure from the EU is self-evidently a moving target, which poses significant challenges for those seeking to produce a 'state-of-the-art' analysis of the Brexit process. Our approach is to ask a very simple question across a range of thematic areas and topics in the chapters: what does Brexit tell us about this topic or area? Inevitably, this question leads our contributors to assess the impact of Brexit on, inter alia, the territorial constitution of the UK, the UK economy, UK policymaking, UK foreign policy, the European Union, international trade and so on. But it is also worth noting that, by analysing Brexit in relation to particular domains of inquiry, we also have the chance to reflect on what we already know about those domains and how Brexit fits into long established scholarly literatures and policy discourses. As such, the handbook will not bury itself in the minutiae of the Brexit negotiations as they unfold on a day-to-day basis. Rather, the volume raises its sights to consider both the broad contextual factors that shape and are shaped by Brexit, as well as the deeper sources and longer-term implications of the UK's exit from the EU.

Our primary criterion for inviting authors to contribute to this handbook has been simple. They are all scholars with a track record of delivering outstanding publications in the relevant areas of concern. For some of our authors, their chapter in this handbook will be one of many contributions that they produce on Brexit. For others, this chapter here may be the only thing that they publish on the politics of the UK's departure from the EU. Our contributors have been recruited on an international scale, since it is obviously vital to explore not only the internal political, societal and economic dynamics of the UK leaving the EU but also the global implications and external dimensions of Brexit. In any case, as previously argued, Brexit is not just about British politics. Like it or not, many scholarly fields are now stakeholders in Brexit.

As far as disciplinary coverage is concerned, the field of political science is, for obvious reasons, well represented among the authors; we hope that the book will be used widely among political scientists and in university political science courses. However, a project such as this must take proper account of contributions from a variety of subfields and disciplines across the political and social sciences. As such, we have recruited expert contributors from the fields of law, political economy, political sociology, international relations, security policy and so on.

Themes and objectives

In this handbook, we want to take stock of the scholarly discussion and debate on the Brexit process. We aim to structure this somewhat inchoate and multifaceted debate into two dimensions to provide a systematic analysis of the background for, as well as the content and the possible implications of, the Brexit process. In order to structure the book, we have divided the contributions into the following key sections:

- *Brexit from the inside.* How does Brexit affect the United Kingdom as a multinational state, especially in terms of its distinctive plurinational territorial compact? How far will Brexit influence the future politics of the UK, and will it lead to far-reaching realignment of the party system? Is it likely that Brexit will lead to the reshaping of the British model of capitalism? How far will Brexit lead to the revival of the 'Anglosphere tradition' in British politics?
- *Brexit from the outside.* How does Brexit affect the political system of the EU as well as various member states of the EU? How will Brexit shape the political system and the institutions of the EU (e.g. the European Parliament and the European Commission)? How will Brexit influence the policies of the EU in key areas such as trade, the internal market, employment and social affairs and agriculture? And how will Brexit change the relationship between the EU and the UK on the one hand, and the United States, Russia and China on the other?

Inevitably, there are important topics that we have not been able to cover specifically, such as the strategic implications of Brexit for the UK's 'special relationship' with the United States (see Wilson 2017) or the gender dimensions of Brexit (see Hozić and True 2017). But it also strikes us that this volume breaks new ground by exploring aspects of Brexit that have been largely neglected in the scholarly literature so far.

The chapters

The first section of the book examines the impact of the Brexit process internally on the polity, economy and society of the UK.

Daniel Wincott assesses the underlying disunity that has framed the debate about the UK's membership of the EU over the last decade. According to Wincott, this discord arises because none of the major political parties have been able to address coherently the European question in British politics. Political divisions have also grown because of the emergence of plural–national identities across the UK, alongside the development of spatial inequalities in economic growth breeding new resentments and material grievances. Wincott examines the multiple challenges that now confront the UK state in the aftermath of the Brexit decision. There is a deep legacy of division and mistrust among citizens following the referendum outcome. There are also growing concerns about the capacity of British public administration and the Civil Service to address the issues raised by Brexit, and meanwhile the decision of British voters to leave the EU is destabilising the territorial and judicial framework of the UK after two decades of intensive constitutional reform. In particular, Brexit is 'set to transform the territorial state' in the years ahead. Moreover, the economic instability that is likely to accompany the UK's transition away from the EU might exacerbate the very geographical, political and social divisions that produced the outcome of the EU referendum in the first place.

In her chapter on Brexit and the Irish case, Mary Murphy looks at the impact of the Brexit vote on the Republic of Ireland, the country outside the UK that is likely to be affected the most by the decision of the British people to leave the EU. After several decades of generally cordial relations between the UK and the Irish Republic, Brexit is likely to create new strains, given both its certain effect on Ireland's domestic economy and its external trade patterns and the constitutional and territorial upheaval implied by the UK ceasing to be an EU member state. The process of the British departure is already fomenting tensions between the north and south of Ireland. In turn, this threatens to imperil the peace process that has brought an end to decades of political violence in Northern Ireland following the signing of the Good Friday Agreement in 1998. The Dublin Government's concern that the UK Government has failed to give proper consideration to the Irish dimension of Brexit is rooted in deep uncertainties about the nature of the border regime after the UK's departure from the EU. The Irish border is the only physical land frontier between the UK and another EU member state. It would be an important space of Brexit with no other factors in play, but, as Murphy shows, the precise configuration of the UK's post-Brexit relationship with the Customs Union and the Single Market is overlain with deep – and arguably intractable – security concerns.

Michael Keating's chapter assesses Scotland's position in the light of the Brexit vote against the backdrop of the 2014 referendum on Scottish independence and the ongoing political tensions between nationalism and unionism in Scotland. In the period following British withdrawal from the EU, England and Scotland are more likely to diverge politically and constitutionally, while the apparatus of the state in Westminster will inevitably struggle to maintain the cohesion of the UK. The disagreement stems not merely from different orientations towards the EU but also from diametrically opposed views of the very nature of the British state. Many supporters of Brexit believe that the Westminster Parliament is 'supreme' and that leaving the EU allows the UK to reclaim its sovereignty. On the other hand, those parties most invested in the process of political devolution argue that the UK is now a 'union of nations' and that the future status of the UK and its relationship with the European Union has to be negotiated between each of the constituent nations. Membership of the EU has enabled the UK to evolve as a multinational state with a shared identity that has contributed since the 1990s to a significant modernisation of the UK's governing arrangements. It is as yet unclear whether Brexit will reverse this process, in so doing imperilling the 400-year-old union between Scotland and England.

Leila Simona Talani's chapter considers the likely impact of Brexit on the City of London. It is widely accepted that the dominance of financial services, the core activity of the City, is the centrepiece of the British model of capitalism. Talani notes that the impact of the UK's departure from the EU will have unpredictable consequences for the City. On the one hand, the City's financial services sector depends on open access to global markets, which Brexit will almost certainly undermine. On the other hand, the UK leaving the EU might be the 'catalyst' for a new phase of liberalisation, including further deregulation of product and capital markets, lower taxes and the retrenchment of the welfare state: 'the revenge of the ultra-liberals'. The paradox, as other authors in this collection note, is that such a shift towards ultra-liberalisation would cut across the political and economic aspirations of many of those who voted for Brexit in the first place – those who sought a retreat from globalisation and a return towards a more protective and even protectionist state.

Andrew Baker and Scott Lavery examine the political-economic implications of the Brexit decision. They argue that Brexit is unlikely to have any fundamental impact on the British model of capitalism. Baker and Lavery emphasise the importance of path dependency on the economic structures of the UK. London is likely to remain a leading financial centre, while the UK will still be characterised by a deregulated and flexible labour market in the aftermath of Brexit. Above all, the British model of capitalism will still be shaped by the established logic of the competition state. Nevertheless, they acknowledge the inevitability of volatility and turbulence in Britain's political economy as a consequence of leaving the EU, while the economic and political outcomes remain uncertain. Baker and Lavery show that heightened economic instability arising from turbulence elsewhere in the global economy or from the Brexit process itself will have unpredictable consequences for the future of British capitalism and for the scope and viability of prospective growth models for the UK. The return to a more protectionist regime from either the left or the right cannot be ruled out.

Jed Odermatt's contribution investigates the long-term consequences of the UK gaining (on the face of it) considerable autonomy over trade policy in the aftermath of Brexit. Supporters of Brexit insist that ceasing to be a member of the EU will enable the UK to regain its historical status as a global trading nation. More pessimistic voices dispute the claim that EU membership was ever an impediment to free trade, and others still note that trade policy in the twentieth century involves considerably more than the exchange of goods and services and the exploitation of comparative advantages. There are certainly serious legal, political and regulatory impediments to the UK playing a 'Global Britain' role, although Odermatt uses his chapter to argue that it is in the mutual interests of both the UK Government and the EU to work together to ensure a stable transition as the UK ceases to be a formal member of the EU trading bloc.

Wyn Grant revisits the controversial topic of the Common Agricultural Policy (CAP) and the impact of Brexit on UK agricultural policy and interest group politics. In the long run, UK farmers will no longer be afforded the protections associated with the CAP. Yet there are those within British agriculture who see Brexit as something of a strategic opportunity rather than a threat for their sector. While agricultural support policies have long been a feature of industrial democracies, there is a feeling that the CAP regime has always been a poor fit for the UK agricultural sector. The impact of the UK's exit on the EU budget might appear to be a catalyst for far-reaching reform of the CAP, but, as Grant contends, a series of incremental adjustments are more likely. CAP reform will remain, in all likelihood, an agonisingly slow process even in the wake of the Brexit vote.

In their chapter on the UK higher education sector, Anne Corbett and Claire Gordon review the impact of the Brexit shock on universities located in the UK. The most immediate question is whether UK universities will, after Brexit, continue to be part of the various EU regimes of research funding and teaching exchange, together with pan-European systems of mutual recognition of degree standards and quality assurance. Corbett and Gordon suggest that, in these respects, precedents suggest that Brexit is most likely to be 'soft'. Corbett and Gordon show that key actors on both sides regard such an outcome as being key to the maintenance of the global pre-eminence of both UK and EU higher education. But Brexit also coincides with moves to fundamentally question the very conception of the university upon which those criteria of excellence rest. With increasing emphasis in the UK on the commodification of higher education and the idea of the higher education 'market', Brexit is likely to accelerate the moves made by the UK not only to develop competitive advantages in relation to higher education but also to use universities as instruments of the UK's new external trade policy.

In Chapter 10, Adrian Favell and Roxana Barbulescu identify the prominent role that migration played in driving the UK's decision to exit the EU. They make the claim that much of the political science literature that seeks to analyse the Brexit vote has uncritically reproduced the logic and discourse of the United Kingdom Independence Party's stance on immigration. The 'problem' of migration and mobility in the UK is principally derived from democratic legitimacy rather than from the economic impact of immigration flows. The chapter predicts that the UK's decision to leave the EU will, in all likelihood, make it harder for key sectors in the British economy, in particular financial services, to attract and retain human capital. Favell and Barbulescu also refer to the fundamental contradiction in the UK Government's position on Brexit where, on the one hand, there is an emphasis on accommodating the preferences of socially conservative working-class voters for lower levels of immigration, while, on the other, the vision of Global Britain enunciated by many prominent supporters of Brexit means the continued acceptance of the free movement of people across borders. Again, as others in the book argue, a renewed phase of ultra-liberalisation in the aftermath of Brexit that leads to a fresh influx of migrants would exacerbate the very tensions that led to the 2016 referendum outcome in the first place.

Peter Nedergaard and Maja Friis Henriksen maintain that the UK's decision to depart from the EU was not merely the product of political contingency but had deep roots in the British polity, British history and British political culture. The UK has been shaped by a conception of 'liberal exceptionalism' that convinced the British, more particularly the English, that the UK was better governed than other comparable states. This abiding faith that Great Britain was superior in its administrative and constitutional practices was augmented by a strong measure of British patriotism rooted in the experience of military victory in major wars from the fifteenth through to the twentieth centuries. Nedergaard and Friis Henriksen make the claim that liberal exceptionalism and patriotism have prevented the UK from cooperating effectively with other states in continental Europe.

It follows that the outcome of the UK leaving the EU is unquestionably a reflection of the distinctive 'English character', as outlined by Ben Wellings in his chapter on Brexit and English identity. The politicisation of English identity in recent years contributed significantly to the referendum outcome. While there has been an understandable focus on the political motivations of the so-called left-behinds, Wellings demonstrates that the desire to break away from the EU was not only animated by material grievances. At root, Brexit has ideational underpinnings emanating from a virulent strain of English nationalism driven principally by the 'defence of British sovereignty', as well as the desire for realignment towards the 'Anglosphere tradition' and the imagined community of Atlanticism. The alliance between these components was fragile and ephemeral but was able to hold together briefly and decisively for the duration of the referendum. Brexit, he suggests, has been peculiarly English in character.

In his chapter on Brexit and the Conservative Party, Richard Hayton outlines the challenge posed by Brexit for the Conservative conception of statecraft. The Conservative Party's political strength throughout the twentieth century has been derived historically from the party's ability to succeed both in the politics of support, namely winning elections, and in the politics of power, namely governing proficiently. Hayton shows how Brexit undermines both the politics of support and the politics of power, potentially fatally weakening the tried and trusted Conservative notion of statecraft. Brexit and the emergence of a more hard line Euroscepticism within the Conservatives has undermined the party's ability to win the support of those who voted to remain in the EU, as demonstrated in the 2017 general election. At the same time, the Brexit process is manifestly creating renewed economic uncertainty, which is undermining growth and living standards, threatening the Conservative Party's enduring reputation for economic competence.

Brexit poses no fewer challenges for the British Labour Party, as Patrick Diamond attests in his chapter. In recent decades, Labour has emerged as the most influential pro-European party in British politics, and in the main Labour campaigned vigorously for the UK to remain an EU member during the 2016 referendum. Nevertheless, there is a tendency to overstate Labour's pro-Europeanism and to underestimate the ambiguity traditionally felt within British social democracy towards the European project. Labour's current leader, Jeremy Corbyn, is a long-standing Eurosceptic on the left of the party. Many traditional Labour supporters voted for Britain to leave the EU in 2016. This situation has compelled Labour to adopt a position of 'constructive ambiguity' in the Brexit process. The party has sought to appeal to both Leave and Remain voters by underlining its commitment to respect the referendum result while calling for a 'softer' Brexit than the Conservative government's position would seem to sanction. Without doubt, Labour managed this balancing act very effectively in the 2017 general election, but it is far from clear that the position of 'constructive ambiguity' is electorally or politically sustainable in the longer term. If Labour were to enter government before the Brexit process was completed, the cohesion of the party would be sorely tested.

Matthew Flinders then examines the impact of so-called anti-politics on the Brexit process, which, he argues, raises fundamental questions about the relationship between representative democracy and political populism. The chapter makes the claim that the Brexit referendum created a 'window of opportunity' in June 2016 through which frustration and disillusionment with the conventional political process – which has arisen in the wake of the financial crisis and the pursuit of austerity policies – could be channelled by populist and nationalist forces in UK politics. While UK-specific factors drove the Brexit vote, Flinders recognizes that the anti-political elements that drove the UK to leave the EU are hardly particular to Britain. Other states in the EU are similarly vulnerable to these anti-political movements, as confirmed by the rising demand for exit referendums in a number of member states.

The second substantive section of the volume reviews the external impact of the Brexit process on countries and regions outside the UK.

Peg Murray-Evans assesses the impact of Brexit on the Commonwealth. She notes that in the discourse of Global Britain, there is a strong emphasis on the potential economic benefits of refocusing UK external trade policy on the emerging market economies of the Commonwealth. The claim promulgated by many advocates of Brexit is that ceasing to be an EU member will enable the UK to pivot away from the relatively stagnant European market to more dynamic Commonwealth markets. Nonetheless, Murray-Evans reveals the potential weakness of this strategy in the light of major changes in the relationship between the UK and the Commonwealth states since the 1970s. Those countries with the most important material ties to the UK such as the African, Caribbean and Pacific states are the least emphasized within the Eurosceptic discourse on the UK's global economic strategy in the wake of Brexit. The negotiation of trade agreements with favoured Commonwealth countries such as India is likely to prove much more difficult and protracted.

Oliver Daddow maintains that the UK's decision to leave the EU has led to the emergence of a more fundamental debate about Britain's role in the world. The UK Government's vision, shared by many leading supporters of Brexit, is of a Global Britain in which the UK regains its influential role on the world stage. Traditionally, the UK has struggled to resolve its European vocation. Since Churchill, the UK has tended to work with a self-image of its foreign policy as positioned at the centre of three circles of influence: Empire, the Anglosphere and Europe. This position accorded only marginal significance to the union with Europe, a stance apparently confirmed by the UK's decision to leave the EU in June 2016. Yet Daddow maintains that it is not yet clear whether Global Britain is even a viable proposition, let alone a desirable goal for the UK in the aftermath of the Brexit vote. The UK is a medium-sized power whose economic importance and geopolitical influence in relative terms has been in long decline, as power has shifted to other regions of and to other actors in the international system.

In Chapter 18, Henrik Larsen examines the role of the EU as an international actor in the wake of Brexit. The chapter begins by restating a long-standing dualism. By leaving the EU, the UK will deprive the Union of the key resources and assets required to pursue an ambitious international policy. On the other hand, the UK has long been sceptical of EU action in the realm of foreign policy. The UK's departure might therefore help the member states of the EU to forge a more ambitious external foreign policy strategy. Nevertheless, Larsen does not foresee major changes in the approaches and practices of EU decision-making in foreign policy. What is more likely is that, in the absence of the UK, the importance of the Franco-German alliance will grow, while it is likely that the situation in Russia and Eastern Europe will become even more important for the EU. As Larsen makes clear, the question of what kind of actor the EU will be in the future is likely to be resolved by broader external dynamics in the emergence of a multipolar world order, notably the impact of the Trump presidency in the United States, Russia's attempted 'destabilisation' of Eastern Europe and the growth of Asian geopolitical power.

Mikkel Vedby Rasmussen's chapter addresses the related question of European defence, seeking to trace the substantive position of the main EU players on defence and how they are likely to react to the reality of Brexit. He shows that the strategic position of Germany, France and the UK on defence policy remains ambivalent and uncertain, a situation underlined by the spending constraints in the defence arena. Furthermore, there has been a significant 'renationalization' of defence policy across the EU in recent years. Aspirations for a common European army are likely to remain unrealizable, despite their salience in Eurosceptic discourse in the UK. A more feasible goal is improved cooperation on defence among EU member states in addressing the strategic challenges posed by Russia, North Africa and the Middle East, as well as stronger EU–US cooperation through NATO to deal with the security challenges of the future. The priority will be the effective pooling of resources. Vedby Rasmussen's punchline is that Brexit is likely to have little impact on European defence. The dependency of European states on the United States means that shifts in American foreign and defence policy are of much greater potential consequence for the EU.

In relation to financial regulation at the European level, Lucia Quaglia demonstrates that Brexit is likely to have a decisive impact, especially in the event of a 'no deal' version of a hard Brexit. Historically, the UK Government has played a key role in winning the case for 'market-friendly' financial regulation, as well as in promoting financial integration across Europe. The City of London has also benefited enormously as one of the world's leading financial centres. Quaglia speculates that, whatever the outcome of the Brexit talks and the nature of the agreement that is reached between the UK and EU member states, the UK is likely to be less integrated with the rest of the European financial sector, while the EU will be a less powerful actor within the international financial system.

Chapter 21 address the potential impact of the Brexit vote on the institutions of the EU itself. Mads Dagnis Jensen and Holly Snaith examine the power shifts that are likely to occur as a consequence of Brexit, taking into account the micro, meso and macro levels of analysis: changes within, between and outside the key EU institutions. They examine the potential shifts in geopolitical power that may arise as a consequence of the Brexit decision. These structural recalibrations in the balance of power, they argue, are likely to take place at three distinct levels: within, between and outside the EU's institutions. Dagnis Jensen and Snaith remind us that, despite its reputation for awkwardness, the UK has over the decades of membership been a key shaper of the EU's institutional order. As such, Brexit will not just alter matters such as voting weights and coalition possibilities within institutions; it also implies a new politics of institutional evolution. Brexit may well lead to increased relative power for either the European Council or the European Commission, depending on how the institutional compromise between intergovernmentalism and supranationalism is eventually recalibrated. Moreover, it is important to remember that internal institutional rebalancing will also have effects on the coherence and viability of EU external actions in the years ahead.

Anders Wivel and Baldur Thorhallsson address the fate of small states in the EU in the light of the decision of the UK to leave the EU by invoking Article 50 of the Lisbon Treaty. The UK ceasing to be a member of the EU poses strategic problems for small states. Historically, small states have benefited from British membership of the EU, since the UK has provided a counterweight to France and Germany, while promoting the causes of intergovernmentalism, Atlanticism and free trade that are often held to be in the strategic interest of small states. Of course, Brexit necessarily affects small states differently. The smaller countries in the EU are nonetheless likely to respond to Britain's departure by adopting one of three key strategies: 'hiding', 'seeking shelter' or 'hedging'. Thus far, hedging appears to be the most likely strategy for small member states to adopt, forging new alliances and coalitions while doing all they can to avoid direct conflict or confrontation with France and Germany.

John Erik Fossum reviews the impact of Brexit on the non-member states that are currently affiliated with the EU. A crucial question to emerge from the Brexit negotiations is whether the UK will make the transition from an EU member to a non-EU member by adopting an existing model of affiliation, for example by becoming a member of the European Economic Area (EEA). Fossum argues that the most likely impact of the Brexit process is for the UK to adopt a model of affiliation that is consistent with a soft Brexit but formally outside EEA arrangements, in practice conforming to many of the rules and norms of EEA membership.

In his contribution, the final chapter in the collection, Christian Lequesne argues that Brexit will compel scholars of European integration to revisit dominant theories and narratives of the integration process. It can no longer be assumed that the EU is destined for ever closer and more harmonious integration and convergence among member states. In particular, Brexit will require analysts of EU institutions and political processes to take domestic politics within member states more seriously, while coming to terms with the various factors that are leading to major disintegration across the EU, in particular the impact of the 'new social cleavages' that have arisen in key member states since the early 1990s and the rise of a virulent strain of anti-politics in Western representative democracies.

Brexit can be understood through the lens of *longue durée* analysis. Equally, it can be seen as something made possible by a quite specific set of conjunctural circumstances. It is a very British phenomenon, but its implications are global and its sources have analogues elsewhere. It is hard to imagine a single study of Brexit that could capture all of that. We hope that this anthology at least demonstrates this multidimensionality of Brexit. The chapters in this book have sought to anchor the discussion of Brexit in established conceptual and empirical literatures. Yet almost every chapter concludes by emphasizing the contingency of the Brexit process, as well as its fundamental uncertainty in terms of outcomes. Of course, this reflects scholarly honesty. There are limits on what we can know, particularly in terms of forecasting a multivariate process like Brexit. But 'uncertainty' is also an accurate descriptor for actors of all kinds – be they politicians or private individuals – caught up in the Brexit whirlwind. If nothing else, the study of Brexit is and must continue to be a study of that uncertainty.

References

Armstrong, K. (2017) *Brexit Time: Leaving the EU – Why, How and When?* Cambridge: Cambridge University Press.

Baker, D. and Schnapper, P. (2015) *Britain and the Crisis of the European Union*. London: Palgrave Macmillan.

Barnett, A. (2017) *The Lure of Greatness: England's Brexit and America's Trump*. London: Unbound.

Becker, S.O., Fetzer, T. and Novy, D. (2016) Who Voted for Brexit? A Comprehensive District Level Analysis, University of Warwick, Centre for Competitive Advantage in the Global Economy. Working Paper Series, No. 305, October. Available at: https://warwick.ac.uk/fac/soc/economics/research/centres/cage/manage/publications/305-2016_becker_fetzer_novy.pdf [Accessed January 5, 2018].

Blyth, M. (2016) Global Trumpism. *Foreign Affairs*, November 16. Available at: www.foreignaffairs.com/articles/2016-11-15/global-trumpism [Accessed January 5, 2018].

Clarke, H.D., Goodwin, M. and Whiteley, P. (2017) *Brexit: Why Britain Voted to Leave the European Union*. Cambridge: Cambridge University Press.

De Witte, B. (2017) The Future of Variable Geometry in a Post-Brexit European Union. *Maastricht Journal of European and Comparative Law* 24(2): 153–157.

Dinan, D., Nugent, N. and Paterson, W.E. (eds.) (2017) *The European Union in Crisis*. London: Palgrave Macmillan.

Evans, G. and Menon, A. (2017) *Brexit and British Politics*. Cambridge: Polity Press.

Gamble, A. (2005) *Between Europe and America: The Future of British Politics*. Basingstoke: Palgrave Macmillan.

George, S. (1994) *An Awkward Partner: Britain in the European Community*. 2nd Edition. Oxford: Oxford University Press.

Gidron, N. and Hall, P.A. (2017) The Politics of Social Status: Economic and Cultural Roots of the Populist Right. *British Journal of Sociology* 68(S1): S57–S84.

Grob-Fitzgibbon, B. (2016) *Continental Drift: Britain and Europe from the End of Empire to the Rise of Euroscepticism*. Cambridge: Cambridge University Press.

Hobolt, S.B. (2016) The Brexit Vote: A Divided Nation, a Divided Continent. *Journal of European Public Policy* 23(9): 1259–1277.

Hopkin, J. (2017) When Polanyi Met Farage: Market Fundamentalism, Economic Nationalism and Britain's Exit from the European Union. *British Journal of Politics and International Relations* 19(3): 465–478.

Hozić, A. and True, J. (2017) Brexit as a Scandal: Gender and Global Trumpism. *Review of International Political Economy* 24(2): 270–287.

Inglehart, R. and Norris, P. (2016) Trump, Brexit, and the Rise of Populism: Economic Have-Nots and Cultural Backlash. HKS Faculty Research Working Paper Series RWP16–026, August. Available at: www.hks.harvard.edu/publications/trump-brexit-and-rise-populism-economic-have-nots-and-cultural-backlash [Accessed January 5, 2018].

Mair, P. (2013) *Ruling the Void: The Hollowing of Western Democracy*. London: Verso.

Oliver, T. (2017) Never Mind the Brexit: Britain, Europe, the World and Brexit. *International Politics* 54(4): 519–532.

Rosamond, B. (2016) Brexit and the Problem of European Disintegration. *Journal of Contemporary European Research* 24(4): 864–871.

Rosenau, J.N. and Durfee, M. (1995) *Thinking Theory Thoroughly: Coherent Approaches in an Incoherent World*. Boulder, CO: Westview Press.

Sanders, D. and Houghton, D.P. (2016) *Losing an Empire, Finding a Role: British Foreign Policy since 1945*. 2nd Edition. London: Palgrave Macmillan.

Vollaard, H. (2014) Explaining European Disintegration. *Journal of Common Market Studies* 52(5): 1142–1159.

Wall, S. (2008) *A Stranger in Europe*. Oxford: Oxford University Press.

Webber, D. (2014) How Likely Is It the European Union Will Disintegrate? A Critical Analysis of Competing Theoretical Perspectives. *European Journal of International Relations* 20(2): 341–365.

Wilson, G.K. (2017) Brexit, Trump and the Special Relationship. *British Journal of Politics and International Relations* 19(3): 543–557.

PART I

Brexit from the inside

2

BREXIT AND THE STATE OF THE UNITED KINGDOM

Daniel Wincott

The outcome of the Brexit referendum in June 2016 – a narrow majority for the United Kingdom (UK) to leave the European Union (EU) – came as a surprise to most commentators and
participants. Even Nigel Farage famously conceded it looks like 'Remain will edge it' as the polls
closed (Cooper and Forester 2016). There had been a diffuse but fairly widespread sense that the
status quo would be retained. This sense prevailed despite the fact that the polls were very tight,
especially if an image of the overall picture was built from analysis of the UK's four 'nations'
(Henderson et al. 2016). In fact, the campaign and result revealed deep disunity among citizens and widespread distrust of authority. Division and distrust were engendered by engrained,
long-standing features of the UK State (Evans and Menon 2017), including the failure of political
parties to articulate and aggregate EU issues, the challenges posed by plural national identities
across the UK and (the role of the State in) the uneven spatial development of the UK economy.

At least for the first eighteen months after the referendum, Westminster party politics seems to
have been caught in a catastrophic equilibrium – the two major party leaders were unable to offer
clear, consistent and compelling plans for Brexit. As prime minister, Theresa May seems to have
focused primarily on maintaining the Brexit-related balance of her Cabinet. Things might have
turned out differently if a pre-referendum Brexit supporter had become prime minister – or if
May's snap general election gambit had met with success. In the autumn of 2017, waves of challenging issues washed over Westminster – from inappropriate and/or abusive behaviour by way of Boris
Johnson's apparently casual aside that jailed UK-Iranian citizen Nazanin Zaghari-Ratcliffe was
'teaching people journalism' to Priti Patel's off-piste meetings with Israeli politicians and officials.
Even then, May's main objective appeared to be a strict maintenance of the Cabinet's Brexit balance.

Particularly after the 2017 general election, Labour leader Jeremy Corbyn's ability to control
his parliamentary colleagues grew stronger. Yet the party's historic electoral base was divided. Its
traditional working-class constituency included many Leave supporters, while Labour's growing
strength was with largely Remain supporting younger and metropolitan voters. Labour's policy
on Brexit was rooted in a commitment to respect the referendum result, while positioning themselves for a somewhat softer Brexit than that pursued by the Conservatives.

The engrained challenges faced by the UK state were widely regarded as fuelling support for
Leave, and, for some, they were deepened by the UK's EU membership. Beyond the immediate
negotiation of Brexit, during the eighteen months after the referendum, difficult issues were
pushed to the sidelines of politics. The sidelining of other issues occurred for reasons of political

sociology, of public administration and, to an extent, of political economy. Identifying major economic challenges and recognizing deep spatial and social inequalities, Theresa May's Industrial Strategy was a partial exception to this rule. Even so, the UK party system only weakly articulated political-sociological divisions over the EU into the State. The lines of party competition were primarily drawn across other issues that did not map onto conflict over the EU. Moreover, the UK is a plurinational and devolved State. The evidence is that, individually and in a variety of combinations, national aspects of identity (British, English, Irish, Northern Irish, Scottish and Welsh) have strong and divergent connections with citizens' attitudes on Brexit (Henderson et al. 2016, 2017). In the referendum's aftermath, there has been little evidence of conciliation or convergence in public attitudes or that underlying issues of distrust, disconnection and division were being addressed.

Turning to public administration, the UK Civil Service has had a high reputation for the quality of its engagement with the EU. But without clear political direction, it cannot function effectively: in the Brexit context, Anand Menon has characterised it as a 'Rolls Royce' public administration 'driven by drunks' (2017). Equally, a long-standing analysis of the central UK State (Bulpitt 1983) and Civil Service (Dunleavy 1991) highlights their preoccupation with metropolitan, high-level policy concerns at the expense of detailed practical work. More generally, the opportunity cost demands of Brexit may mean that political parties, government and public administration do not have the capacity (or 'bandwidth') to take on other priorities – even where, like the Industrial Strategy, they have been explicitly articulated. The en bloc resignation of the Social Mobility Commission in December 2017 dramatised this 'bandwidth' issue (Pickard 2017). Moreover, the Industrial Strategy issues – such as productivity and uneven development – are long-standing 'wicked' problems, difficult to address in any circumstances.

Brexit has also changed the context for the constitutional arrangement of the UK. They are famously 'flexible' – not collected together in a definitive text or set of texts. Since the 1990s, UK constitutional practice had been changing, although arguably without reaching a balance. The constitutional role of the senior courts – especially the Supreme Court – had been growing. EU law played a key role in these developments, as did national-democratic devolution. Brexit unsettled and challenged the foundations on which the new judicial-constitutional role was being built. It poses sharp questions about the future of the UK's territorial constitution, even if the immediate possibility of secession (by Scotland or Northern Ireland) faded in the eighteen months after the referendum. But whatever territorial form the UK may take in the future, Brexit raises the general question of what the constitutional role of the courts will be in the future, an issue that has exercised senior judges (Bowcott 2017; Watts 2017).

The eighteen months after the referendum offered little evidence of momentum towards a reversal of the Brexit decision. Equally, the prospects that the UK might leave the EU with no agreement – the 'hardest' form of Brexit – seemed to recede after the 8 December agreement between the UK and EU to conclude the first stage of the Article 50 negotiations. While the implications of the Joint Report (Gov.UK 2017) on those negotiations continued to be contested, the atmosphere around Brexit seemed to relax. At the time of writing the negotiations seem set to be extended to include a transition period largely based on the current *status quo*. The UK Government's ultimate position is that it will leave the Single Market and Customs Union, which precludes remaining in the European Economic Area (EEA) by joining the European Free Trade Area (EFTA). In principle, EFTA, which includes a court that adjudicates on Single Market matters for Iceland, Norway and Liechtenstein (Baudenbacher 2017), might provide a framework for the softest of UK Brexits. Practically speaking, adding a large State whose relationship to the Single Market has proven contentious would disrupt the existing balance of the EEA. Equally, however, whatever its form, maintaining *any* continuing economic relationship negotiated between the UK and the EU (beyond World Trade Organization rules), including how disputes over its terms would be resolved, raises concerns about legitimacy and seem likely to involve and engage the UK's judiciary.

This chapter's next section discusses the UK's recent constitutional development. It considers the role of EU law in UK constitutional change. After raising a question about the implications of Brexit for UK constitutional jurisprudence, it turns to its possible impact on the territorial dimension of the constitution, including devolution. Then, the analysis will turn to questions of political sociology, addressing issues of party politics and the UK's plurinational character. Finally, the chapter considers how patterns in public administration and political economy shape the prospects for the UK State as it negotiates its way through Brexit.

The EU and the UK constitution

The European Communities Act (ECA) of 1972 occupies a paradoxical position in the historical development of the UK constitution. It was, at once, a legal reassertion of the idea of parliamentary sovereignty and a basis on which that idea could be transformed. A couple of decades earlier, the (then flagging) idea that parliamentary sovereignty was *the* core constitutional principle had been strongly restated by Sir William Wade (1955). Clever ECA drafting made European Community (and later Union) law contingent on the Westminster statute. But the European legal system that the UK joined in the 1970s was not fully developed. The principle that European treaty provisions could have primacy over domestically generated laws and be directly effective in the domestic system *had* been established. But these ideas had not been extended to Directives – a critical form of legislation made under the Treaties. It would be anachronistic to argue that to claim that EU law would inevitably take the shape and form that it subsequently developed.

Over the next twenty or thirty years, what eventually became the EU expanded its policy scope significantly. Alongside that expansion Europe's legal system developed a much more extensive, authoritative and elaborate structure. These changes are not best characterised as an imposition of structures, processes, rules and regulations from the European level on the UK (and other member states). Instead, member state institutions and actors were intimately involved in the construction of the new legal Europe. For example, domestic courts – including those in the UK – played a major role in developing the structure of European law. From a simple organisational point of view, what was initially a single court sitting in Luxembourg could not have unilaterally 'conjured up' a European legal system. Instead, it was interaction and dialogue between the European Court and member states' courts that created the European legal system. In an important sense, this continuing interaction and dialogue *are* the European legal system.

Courts in the UK played a key role in these developments. As a consequence, their position, relative to that of the executive and legislature branches of government, was enhanced, at least on topics that fell within the purview of the EU. Many UK–EU cases were at once landmarks of European law and part of a process of change in the UK's own constitution. The precise nature and interpretation of these developments have been – and remain – contentious. Nevertheless, nearly twenty-five years after the ECA and over forty years after he had reasserted the doctrine of parliamentary sovereignty, Sir William Wade saw a constitutional *revolution* (1996) in a House of Lords decision on *Factortame* (United Kingdom House of Lords Decisions 1990). In other words, for its erstwhile high priest, parliamentary sovereignty had been changed and restricted. Judges had, Wade argued, recognised and were implementing a new basic structure to the constitution.

The senior judiciary seems never fully to have embraced Wade's conception of revolutionary change. Nevertheless, a series of judgements that culminated in the Supreme Court's *HS2* decision – R (Supreme Court UK 2014) – did describe some laws as having a special constitutional status. Any subsequent statute that implies a change in the meaning of an earlier law effectively 'repeals' the earlier 'ordinary' statute. The constitutional implications of so-called constitutional statutes can be repealed only by subsequent legislation that states explicitly its constitutional repeal objective. After *HS2*, a sense was growing that the idea of constitutional statutes had introduced potentially wide-ranging changes. The full extent and implications of this idea had still to be worked through. Nevertheless, the balance had shifted between the judiciary on the one hand and the legislative and executive branches of government on the other.

Discontent about the role played by the Court of Justice of the European Union (CJEU) and the idea of the supremacy of EU law has been a core feature of Euroscepticism in the UK. For those of this disposition, eliminating any role for the CJEU in the UK is a key objective of leaving the EU. The distinct but related question of what the role of the UK's Supreme Court should be after Brexit has been the subject of much less extensive discussion. Should the Supreme Court retain its enhanced position as an interpreter of constitutional statutes? Can it do so? The *Miller* case (Supreme Court UK 2017) focused on the role Westminster should play in relation to the triggering of Article 50 (see also Chapter 4). It *has* received considerable attention. In it, the Supreme Court explicitly repudiated the claim that the ECA or the UK's membership of the EU had changed the underlying principle – the rule of recognition – of the UK Constitution. There is a powerful sense of the Court re-emphasizing Westminster parliamentary sovereignty as a (at times even *the*) core constitutional principle of the UK State. Even so, the notion that the ECA enjoyed some sort of distinctive status, a 'constitutional statute' was not explicitly repudiated. Moreover, according to the majority view, EU law was in itself a source of UK law at least until the UK left the EU. The UK had embarked on a deliberate process of leaving the EU. Westminster legislation was brought forward with the explicit purpose of repudiating the authority of EU law in the UK.

What of the wider ramifications of Brexit for the role of the courts? At one time, the idea of setting legal constraints around the operation of central government had been associated with the political right (see, notably, Hailsham 1976). But nearly twenty years of Conservative government after 1979 transformed the partisan politics of Constitutionalism in the UK. Treatment of certain statutes as constitutional practice grew up around the ECA and the developing structure of EU law. More than a quarter of a century after its enactment, the ECA was joined by a raft of seemingly constitution-changing legislation on human rights and devolution. Perhaps partly inspired by the 'constitutionalisation' of the ECA, legislation was introduced to disperse power from the executive and legislature towards the judiciary and from Westminster and Whitehall to Belfast, Cardiff and Edinburgh. The Human Rights Act (1998) 'domesticated' the European Convention on Human Rights. The process of dialogue triggered between the UK's domestic courts and the European Court of Human Rights echoed that between UK and EU courts. The second major strand of constitutional change – devolution – is considered in more detail shortly.

The senior judiciary has expressed concern about the role of the courts after the EU withdrawal (for example, Watts 2017). Excising the ECA from the UK's statute book will cut away the main pillar on which UK judicial practice developed around constitutional statutes. In contrast to the devolution legislation, the ECA has provided UK judges with an external legal point of reference for constitutional adjudication. The original approach taken by the EU (Withdrawal) Bill implies a broad movement from constitutional European to ordinary domestic law. Its aim was to 'domesticate' the body of EU law by 'retaining' it as Westminster law. Provision was also made to alter these rules, generally through secondary legislation, in order to allow the executive to make rapid legal adjustments to meet emergent issues after Brexit. The Bill also revealed and reflected the breadth and depth of the presence of the EU within the UK. It will not necessarily remove from the statute book all those 'constitutional' elements that had been linked to the EU. Nevertheless, repealing the ECA will transform the courts' constitutional practice. The range of matters it covers will be sharply reduced, and, in general, its foundations seem likely to be weakened.

The UK's territorial constitution

Two interlinked keywords – 'ambiguity' and 'asymmetry' – have always defined the territorial constitution of the United Kingdom of Great Britain and Northern Ireland. The widespread idea that the UK was, in a straightforward sense, a Unitary State can distract our attention from the length and depth of its history of asymmetry (see Mitchell 2011). Nevertheless, a core set of Anglo-British institutions in Whitehall and Westminster has been the ever present kernel central to this Unitary constitutional imaginary. But its influence has ebbed as well as flowed. Arguably, Unitary ideas had a particularly strong influence on how the constitution was understood during the period in the 1970s and 1980s when the UK was first integrating with the EU, under the twin influence of the parliamentary road to socialism and Thatcherism. But these ideas were always hard to reconcile with some aspects of UK territorial governance.

Northern Ireland provides the clearest challenge to any thoroughgoing notion that the UK was politically 'unitary'. The existence of a devolved parliament and government in Northern Ireland for the entire period between 1921 and 1972, followed by direct rule, exemplifies asymmetric differentiation. In addition, the Scottish Office provided devolved administrative arrangements for major areas of domestic policy, including the major social services for the whole period from 1921 to 1998. Both Northern Ireland and Scotland have separate and distinct territorial legal jurisdictions, which endure from before their Unions with Great Britain and England, respectively. By contrast, in legal terms, Wales had been comprehensively integrated with England. The absence of a separate or distinct legal jurisdiction was part of the rationale for the more limited form of devolution dispensed to Wales in 1998.

'Devolution settlement' is the standard code for the arrangements created for Scotland, Wales and Northern Ireland under Labour after 1997. That code is misleading. The idea of a 'settlement' suggests a well defined, agreed and stable set of arrangements. The framework for Northern Ireland does seem well defined and has been confirmed explicitly in international treaties. Plainly, it has not been stable. Devolved government has been suspended on several occasions, including in the period before the Brexit referendum. In Scotland, devolution has been called into question by demands for independence. The population is, in effect, split down the middle on the independence question – and has been governed by the pro-independence Scottish National Party since 2007 (see Chapter 4). Independence was narrowly defeated in the 2014 referendum. In its wake, steps have been taken to devolve significant additional powers to Scotland.

Devolution in Wales has not been marked by the drama attached to Scotland or Northern Ireland. Even so, the history of Welsh devolution has been chronically unsettled. Wales has experienced nearly twenty years of permanent constitutional reform. No fewer than four major Westminster Acts (Government of Wales Acts [GOWA] 1998 and 2006 and the Wales Acts 2014 and 2017) have made fundamental changes to the constitutional basis of devolution in Wales, if repeatedly on a piecemeal basis.

Before Brexit, England was governed by 'Anglo-British' institutions at Whitehall and Westminster. In 2015, some potentially important but little noticed changes were made to Westminster parliamentary practice. They introduced English Votes on English Laws (EVEL). But the basic processes and practices of the state showed a remarkable capacity to carry on as before, perhaps reflecting the fact that England provides something like 85 per cent of the UK's population. 'Carrying on' means that the new realities of devolution to Scotland and Wales introduced nearly two decades earlier had not been fully absorbed into the self-understanding and practices of the Anglo–British State. Politics outside England occupy the attention of the central State only episodically.

These brief remarks show that devolution dispensations in the UK are plainly asymmetrical. With some justification, they have been developed to reflect the particular circumstances of specific parts of the UK. As well as being particular, they are often ad hoc and bilateral; that is, they seem to have developed in response to specific pressures and demands from individual territories. By contrast, only limited and weakly institutionalised State-wide systems of intergovernmental relations have been designed. Even the highest profiles of those – like the Joint Ministerial Committees – have operated intermittently and at times have been completely in abeyance.

Mechanisms have developed to manage the relationships between different sources of legislation across the UK. The overarching 'sovereignty' of the UK Parliament had to be reconciled with primary legislative competence at the devolved level. The convention has been to put Legislative Consent Motions (LCMs) to the devolved legislatures before Westminster makes law in an area of devolved competence. These motions have been used fairly widely and, in general, have not proven particularly controversial. Although the descriptive term 'LCM' is now widely used, these motions are also known as Sewell motions, after the member of the House of Lords who proposed them for the Scottish Parliament. It is characteristic that the means of managing a critical relationship should be both conventional and named for the individual who proposed it. After promises made during the 2014 Scottish independence referendum, LCM processes have been written into devolution statutes. However, this change has not altered their conventional status. They are not justiciable before the courts.

Overall, the sense of a system or scheme for devolution – or conception of the UK as a devolved state – is weakly developed, if not wholly absent. Moreover, there is often disagreement, if not necessarily explicit contestation, as to how devolution is understood. Distinct views are taken at Whitehall and Westminster, in Belfast, Cardiff and Edinburgh, as well as within each of these places.

The complex, weakly institutionalised, ad hoc and asymmetrical character of devolution notwithstanding, in general its practical operation has been remarkably smooth. Devolution benefited from an unusually benign environment while it bedded in. The fact that Labour led the administrations in Cardiff and Edinburgh as well as London was arguably less important than the remarkable growth in public spending for the first decade of devolution. But another factor has to be noted as well. The Civil Service managed the process of devolution with remarkable quiet aplomb. Without detracting from its contribution, the part it played illustrates Civil Service's weaknesses as well as demonstrating its strengths. It ran devolution with Rolls Royce smoothness but did not see thinking through the UK's Constitution as a whole or suggesting future-proofing reforms as part of its task. Its effectiveness in avoiding and managing conflict may have contributed to a wider failure to think through devolution's implications.

The ad hoc, bilateral and asymmetrical character of devolution has added to the historic ambiguity of the UK's territorial constitution. On the one hand, all the Westminster devolution legislation is careful to preserve the 'sovereignty' of the UK Parliament. In that sense, power 'devolved' is power 'retained'. On the other, the devolved institutions are all rooted in authorizing referendums in relevant – typically 'national' – populations. Westminster legislation also refers to the permanence of devolved institutions. The sense of the historic authenticity of these institutions was expressed particularly dramatically, as temporary presiding officer, Winnie Ewing opened the first session of the newly elected Scottish Parliament in 1999. These were her words: 'The Scottish Parliament, which adjourned on the 25th day of March 1707 is hereby reconvened'.

For roughly the first decade of devolution, there was remarkably little recourse to the courts to adjudicate the boundaries of the new territorial constitution. The effective absence of a role for the courts was remarkable when set in the comparative context of multilevel and federal-type states. Partly, it reflected the conventional, unwritten/uncodified nature of the UK 'constitution'. But, as we have seen, starting with the ECA, the notion that some Westminster legislation had a distinctive 'constitutional' character grew up from the mid-1990s. The Westminster devolution statutes were an important element of this development; that is, it emerged alongside and became intertwined with devolution. Perhaps partly as a consequence, more devolution cases started to come before the courts, notably the Supreme Court of the United Kingdom. Perhaps the most striking of these cases were those relating to Wales. They included clear statements about the National Assembly for Wales as a legitimate, democratic source of primary legislation. These cases reflected and reinforced the sense that devolved institutions were a solid and permanent feature of life. The Brexit cases heard in the High Court and Supreme Court during 2016 seem to point in a different direction. Grounded in the idea of (Westminster) parliamentary sovereignty, they may represent a more centralist rebalancing of UK-level constitutional practice.

Political sociology of Brexit: parties, national identities and the State

Two longer-term aspects of the UK political sociology helped to shape the context of the Brexit referendum. The first concerns the treatment of the EU issue by Britain's two largest political parties. As both are basically divided internally over Europe, they have failed to link or to mobilise public attitudes on the issue into the State. Second, these parties have found it difficult to address questions of national identity across the UK, particularly in England. These two are examples of State failure – in the sense that the State has been compromised by or implicated in a deep problem.

For most of the twentieth century, political parties were central to the democratic operation of Western states. These states were, in effect, party democracies or party states. Throughout the history of the UK's membership, both of the main British political parties have been divided over the EU. These divisions have meant that the linkage role of parties and the party system – connecting and aggregating citizens' views on the EU into the UK State – has not operated effectively. The divisions and sense of political disconnection they engender have been a breeding ground for distrust. A tendency (not limited to the UK) for national politicians to shift the blame for unpopular policies onto the EU institutions has further exacerbated distrust.

The weak connection between the people and the State has a spatial or geographic aspect. It is, no doubt, true that invisible differences exist over Brexit between people with, say, similar income, occupations and education who live together in the same particular places (Kaufmann 2016). Nevertheless, the interaction of class, education, income, age, national identity within and across places is poorly articulated, weakly represented by political parties and largely ignored by political science. It is, for example, clear that the Labour Party hierarchy in Wales (solidly committed to Remain in the referendum) lost touch with its traditional heartlands in the South Wales Valleys (some voted Leave by 20-percentage-point margins). Equally, we have little sense of how far citizens in Brexit-backing places – Bleanau Gwent, Bolsover and Bexley; North Antrim, South Holland, West Somerset and East Belfast – share Brexit-related hopes, expectations, fears and concerns. How do the attitudes and values in these places compare to those in West Belfast, North Lanarkshire and Moray? More generally, the relationship of micro-level social and political processes rooted in particular places to the macro-level operation of the State needs to be more closely analysed and better understood.

Citizens' attitudes towards Brexit changed strikingly little during the first eighteen months after the referendum. Some research, including Livermore and Clarkson's (2017) analysis of qualitative 'Brexit Diaries', has detected a measure of movement. They characterise some 14 per cent of the population as 'accepting pragmatists' – Remain voters who were looking to move on. But they categorize three in ten as 'devastated pessimists'. But unless attitudes shift substantially, the UK will face a difficult problem of 'loser's consent' to Brexit. Since the referendum, the parties at Westminster seemed to be stuck in a self-perpetuating equilibrium, with little prospect for reconciliation or winning consent from the losing side.

The UK has a complex pattern of national identities (see also Chapter 12). They are entangled with emergent – and continually changing – constitutional practices across the State. We have seen that the UK has a long history of special arrangements for peripheral nations and territories. The political sociology of Northern Irish politics has always been treated separately from 'British politics', with surprisingly little scholarship addressed to the UK as a whole. 'Within' Britain, the politics of peripheral nations and national identities in Wales and Scotland have received specialist attention, perhaps especially since the advent of democratic devolution at the end of the 1990s. England, however, remains largely out of focus in empirical political science – hidden in plain sight (although an important historically oriented political theory literature *has* developed on England – Aughey 2007, Wellings 2012; Kenny 2014). Overwhelmingly its largest part, England, is effectively conflated with Britain and thus avoids direct interrogation (Henderson et al. 2017).

Powerful and complex patterns of national identification exist across the UK, including England. Most people in the UK have strong – and often multiple – national identities. Mainstream models of electoral politics tend to treat national identification as 'baked in' (more a constant than a variable – Clarke et al. 2017: 146) and as 'nested' (at least in Britain, with Welsh, Scottish and English identities nestled within British identity). Careful analysis shows a rather different picture. British identity seems to operate in a different way in England, as compared to Wales and Scotland (Henderson et al. 2017). Moreover, the balance between multiple identities can shift over time. In short, these identities have political implications – or are available for political mobilization. National parties in Wales and Scotland provide some structure for the mobilization of national identities into politics. On occasion, Englishness has been activated politically – including by the Conservative Party in the UK's 2015 general election (Jeffery et al. 2016). But, so far, English national identity has not been mobilized into the political party structure of Anglo-UK politics. In particular, no political party has systematically sought to be the party of England; still less has that position been achieved. Explicit appeals to Englishness were not a major theme of the 2016 referendum campaign. Nevertheless, the evidence suggests that people who gave priority to English identity were significantly more likely than others to vote to leave the EU (Henderson et al. 2017). The political potential of English identity retains a protean quality. After Brexit, national identities in England and Englishness more generally could prove powerful forces in UK politics.

Brexit, political economy and public administration

The UK economy is marked by starkly uneven spatial patterns. Wealth and income are concentrated in London and the South-East of England, where productivity rates are also much higher than they are across the rest of the UK. These spatial patterns have deep roots – which date back at least to the industrial shock of the Great Depression in the 1930s. The position of heavy manufacturing and extractive industries recovered, to an extent, during the post-war boom years. Throughout this period, however, the UK's economy did not perform as well as our main competitors in Europe and across the Western world – particularly in terms of productivity.

At the start of the 1950s, the UK's level of output per hour worked was below that of the United States on the one hand and a bit above that of France and Germany on the other. The latter two countries were, however, on a steeper improvement path. Both overtook the UK in the late 1960s and caught up with the United States by the early 1990s. 'Relative decline' was the leitmotiv of the UK's anxiety-ridden political classes throughout the post-war 'boom' (Barnett 1986; Weiner 1985). And while a more confident mood came to be reasonably well established by the 1990s (Brivati 2007), the size of the UK's productivity gap with the United States, France and Germany has persisted. Since 2008 and the threat of a global banking collapse, UK productivity levels have stagnated, and the gap with leading competitors has widened (Harari 2017: 8).

Even as its economy experienced fundamental processes of restructuring, the trajectory of UK aggregate productivity figures proved persistently poor. Both the sectoral mix and the spatial balance of the UK economy changed dramatically since the 1950s. Understood as ending the post-war boom, economic shocks during the 1970s hit the manufacturing industry particularly hard. During the 1980s, services came to be consolidated at the UK economy's metropolitan centres. Economic dynamism has come to be concentrated in those cities where the population is comparatively highly educated – particularly in and around London (see also Chapter 5). Those places that were once dominated by extractive and manufacturing industry – as well as remote rural locations and some coastal towns – have not fared well. And the State has mostly retreated from any systematic effort to rebalance the UK economy, which many have regarded as a beyond its scope to achieve.

Brexit has brought questions of productivity, relative decline and uneven spatial development into a sharp focus. By espousing an Industrial Strategy, Theresa May indicated government could and should do – and be seen to do – something active about the performance of the UK economy. These interventions should also make a difference to the impact of overall economic performance for a wider range of people and places. Not all her Conservative colleagues are likely to share this position. For some, including many free trade Brexiteers the Industrial Strategy idea would make the State too large and interfering.

There is a public administration dimension to these issues. The record of the UK State in designing and delivering industrial interventions has not been stellar. One way or another, acute analysts from Bulpitt (1983) to Dunleavy (1991) have observed that the UK's central institutions have sought largely to eschew entanglements with the complexity and messiness of peripheral 'low' politics. Although his argument is pitched at a general theoretical level, Dunleavy's suggestion that bureaucrats prefer to do interesting work in small, elite agencies close to centres of political power chimes in close harmony with the cultural norms that prevail in Whitehall. This disposition provides a weak foundation on which a government might build an Industrial Strategy. Even during those post-war decades when faith in the capacity of the State for economic management was strong, Bulpitt noted a tendency to distance the political-administrative centre from industry. He saw UK Keynesian practice as focused on aggregate demand management, with levers being pulled from the Treasury. Public administrators were not required to roll up their sleeves. After 1979, Industrial Strategy was, for long periods, anathema to central government. As a consequence, it had no place on the palette of skills required of the core Civil Service.

Brexit has triggered a massive learning process within government – about Britain and about its economic relationships with Europe and the wider world.

For example, the Department for Business, Energy and Industrial Strategy (BEIS) has engaged with the pattern of economic activity across the territory of the UK, developing knowledge of the industrial supply chains that run through Britain and that link it into the global economy. By the same token, however, the novelty of this work illustrated how little was known previously in government about the structure of the UK's manufacturing economy.

Conclusions

Eighteen months after the referendum, Brexit had already posed massive challenges to the UK State. It revealed and arguably deepened a disconnection between citizens and the State – and dramatized the failure of political parties to provide an effective linkage mechanism between them. Historically, the two main Britain-wide parties have been integral to a cleavage structure that organised the mass citizenry into politics. Citizens are now divided in other politically significant ways, which cut across party lines and block the effective articulation and aggregation of citizens' values at Westminster, seriously weakening the sense in which the UK approximates to the idea of either parliamentary or party democracy. National identities are one aspect of this disconnection. The existence of distinct peripheral Celtic sub-state nationalisms is reasonably well understood. But nationalisms in the UK's largest country – England – have largely been neglected. Brexit itself was partly shaped by the interplay of Englishness and Britishness (Henderson et al. 2017). There is more to come – politically and institutionally – from the interaction of plural nationalisms in England as well as across the UK.

One tangible, if currently rather distant, possibility associated with Brexit is a change to the territorial boundaries of the UK State, which could involve Scotland and/or Northern Ireland. Even if the UK does hold together within its current boundaries, it cannot remain the same: Brexit is set to transform the territorial State. As originally proposed, the EU (Withdrawal) Bill illustrated and would probably have the effect of entrenching the Anglo-British character of the State's Westminster/Whitehall core. Devolution has always had something of an ad hoc, Heath Robinson quality; it cannot survive Brexit in its current form. That might create an opportunity to reconstruct the UK's territorial constitution on more systematically laid foundations. But the UK State's capacity to think through fundamentals and design a constitutional system is limited. Even the disposition to do so seems alien to the Anglo-British UK tradition. The pressing urgency of Brexit makes a constitutional design project both more important and less likely.

Arguably, the Supreme Court has done more than any other branch of government to decide specific cases on the basis of a devolution system. Together with decisions that discussed 'constitutional statutes', the devolution cases were one leg of an emergent Supreme Court constitutional jurisprudence. By repealing the ECA, Brexit removes what has hitherto been a strong leg of that approach. Possible alternatives can be imagined. They could draw on the kind of partnership developed between the UK Supreme Court and the European Court of Human Rights. Joining EFTA or drawing lessons from its court (Baudenbacher 2017) could provide other models. For anything beyond WTO terms, the febrile atmosphere around Brexit and the UK's ongoing economic relationship with EU makes for a challenging context in which judges will need to decide cases that engage and divide politicians, the media and the wider public.

Finally, the economic context in which all these political issues will have to be addressed may prove challenging. Some pro-Brexit commentators and politicians foresee enticing new economic opportunities for the UK after Brexit. In general, those to take this position are proponents of a free-market, free-trading future for the UK. Its advocates argue that flexibility is a key merit of a free-trade growth model. Whatever its advantages, that flexibility itself – and particularly the transition to a model of this kind – might deepen precisely the social, geographical and political divisions that the Brexit process has revealed and hit some majority-Leave communities especially hard. But most economists argue that Brexit brings with it a likelihood of significant economic difficulty. The response of May's Conservative government – to develop an Industrial Strategy – is a striking reversal of the prior UK orthodoxy. Hitting the targets of that strategy – such as improving productivity and upgrading infrastructure, as well as wider objectives for housing, mental health, injustice and inequality – would transform the UK socially and politically as well as economically. And yet although these problems are well known, solving them is much more difficult. In contrast to the constitutional issue, though, on these questions, certain Whitehall departments – notably BEIS – do seem to be engaging in new ways.

References

Aughey, A. (2007) *The Politics of Englishness*. Manchester: Manchester University Press.

Barnett, C. (1986) *The Audit of War*. London: Macmillan.

Baudenbacher, C. (2017) How the EFT Court Works – and Why It Is an Option for Post-Brexit Britain. *LSE Brexit Blog*, August 25. Available at: http://blogs.lse.ac.uk/brexit/2017/08/25/how-the-efta-court-works-and-why-it-is-an-option-for-post-brexit-britain/ [Accessed December 14, 2017].

Bowcott, O. (2017) UK's New Supreme Court Chief Calls for Clarity on ECJ after Brexit. *The Guardian*, October 5. Available at: www.theguardian.com/law/2017/oct/05/uks-new-supreme-court-chief-calls-for-clarity-on-ecj-after-brexit [Accessed December 14, 2017].

Brivati, B. (2007) *The End of Decline*. London: Politico.

Bulpitt, J. (1983) *Territory and Power in the United Kingdom: An Interpretation*. Manchester: Manchester University Press.

Clarke, H., Goodwin, M. and Whiteley, P. (2017) *Brexit: Why Britain Voted to Leave the European Union*. Cambridge: Cambridge University Press.

Cooper, C. and Forester, K. (2016) EU Referendum: Nigel Farage Says It 'Looks Like Remain Will Edge It' as Polls Close. *The Independent*, June 23. Available at: www.independent.co.uk/news/uk/home-news/eu-referendum-nigel-farage-remain-edge-it-brexit-ukip-a7098526.html [Accessed December 14, 2017].

Dunleavy, P. (1991) *Democracy, Bureaucracy and Public Choice*. Brighton: Harvester Wheatsheaf.

Evans, G. and Menon, A. (2017) *Brexit and British Politics*. Cambridge: Polity Press.

Gov.UK (2017) Joint Report from the Negotiators of the European Union and the United Kingdom Government on Progress during Phase 1 of Negotiations under Article 50 TEU on the United Kingdom's Orderly Withdrawal from the European Union. December 8. Available at: www.gov.uk/government/uploads/system/uploads/attachment_data/file/665869/Joint_report_on_progress_during_phase_1_of_negotiations_under_Article_50_TEU_on_the_United_Kingdom_s_orderly_withdrawal_from_the_European_Union.pdf [Accessed December 14, 2017].

Hailsham, L. (1976) Elective Dictatorship. *The Listener*, October 26, pp. 496–500.

Harari, D. (2017) Productivity in the UK. *House of Commons Library Briefing Paper* No. 06492. Available at: http://researchbriefings.parliament.uk/ResearchBriefing/Summary/SN06492 [Accessed February 7, 2018].

Henderson, A., Jeffery, C., Liñeira, R., Scully, R., Wincott, D. and Jones, R.W. (2016) England, Englishness and Brexit. *The Political Quarterly* 87(2): 187–199.

Henderson, A., Jeffery, C., Wincott, D. and Jones, R.W. (2017) How Brexit Was Made in England. *British Journal of Politics and International Relations* 19(4): 631–646.

Jeffery, C., Henderson, A., Scully, R. and Jones, R.W. (2016) England's Dissatisfactions and the Conservative Dilemma. *Political Studies Review* 14(3): 335–348.

Kaufmann, E. (2016) It's Not the Economy, Stupid: Brexit as a Story of Personal Values. *LSE British Politics and Policy Blog*. Available at: http://blogs.lse.ac.uk/politicsandpolicy/personal-values-brexit-vote/ [Accessed December 14, 2017].

Kenny, M. (2014) *The Politics of English Nationhood*. Oxford: Oxford University Press.

Livermore, S. and Clarkson, T. (2017) *The Brexit Diaries: Engaging with the Public in Brexit Britain*. London: BritainThinks. Available at: http://britainthinks.com/pdfs/The-Brexit-Diaries_engaging-with-the-public-in-Brexit-Britain_170329.pdf [Accessed December 14, 2017].

Menon, A. (2017) Government Confusion over Brexit Means our World Class Civil Service Is Going to Waste: A Rolls Royce Is Being Driven by Drunks. *Prospect*, September 1. Available at: www.prospectmagazine.co.uk/politics/government-confusion-over-brexit-means-our-world-class-civil-service-is-going-to-waste [Accessed December 14, 2017].

Mitchell, J. (2011) *Devolution in the UK*. Manchester: Manchester University Press.

Pickard, J. (2017) Theresa May's Social Mobility Commission Walks Out. *Financial Times*, December 3. Available at: www.ft.com/content/e4426dce-d808-11e7-a039-c64b1c09b482 [Accessed December 14, 2017].

Supreme Court UK (2014) *R (HS2 Alliance) v. Secretary of State for Transport*, January 22. Available at: www.supremecourt.uk/cases/docs/uksc-2013-0172-judgment.pdf [Accessed December 14, 2017].

Supreme Court UK (2017) *R (Miller) v. Secretary of State for Exiting the European Union*, January 24. Available at: www.supremecourt.uk/cases/docs/uksc-2016-0196-judgment.pdf [Accessed December 14, 2017].

United Kingdom House of Lords Decision (1990) *Regina v. Secretary of State for Transport (Respondent) Ex Parte Factortame Limited and Others (Appellants)*, July 26. Available at: www.bailii.org/uk/cases/UKHL/1990/7.html [Accessed December 14, 2017].

Wade, W. (1955) The Basis of Legal Sovereignty. *Cambridge Law Journal* 13(2): 172–197.

Wade, W. (1996) Sovereignty: Revolution or Evolution? *Law Quarterly Review* 112(4): 568–575.

Watts, J. (2017) Brexit: Supreme Court President Calls for Greater Clarity on Legal Ramifications of EU Withdrawal. *The Independent*, August 8. Available at: www.independent.co.uk/news/uk/politics/brexit-latest-european-court-justice-future-eu-exit-lord-neuberger-supreme-court-president-ecj-a7881836.html%3famp [Accessed December 14, 2017].

Weiner, M. (1985) *English Culture and the Decline of the Industrial Spirit.* Harmondsworth: Penguin.

Wellings, B. (2012) *English Nationalism and Euroscepticism: Losing the Peace.* Bern: Peter Lang.

3

BREXIT AND THE IRISH CASE

Mary C. Murphy

Introduction

On 25 June 2016, the day after the UK referendum on European Union (EU) membership, an *Irish Times* headline declared, 'Deep disquiet as vote pushes North[ern Ireland] into "unchartered waters"'. The headline encapsulated the profound sense of dismay felt in Ireland following the UK's unexpected decision to leave the European Union (EU). For Ireland, the UK vote to depart the EU poses acute economic and political challenges. Indeed, such is the magnitude of the Brexit issue for Ireland that the *National Risk Assessment 2017* has identified the UK exit from the EU as a 'strategic geopolitical risk' and a 'strategic economic risk' for Ireland (Department of the Taoiseach 2017). In a foreword to the document, Taoiseach Leo Varadkar notes, 'Brexit represents an overarching theme that could have far-reaching impacts on nearly all aspects of national life' (ibid.). More than any other EU member state, Ireland stands to be most severely affected by their neighbour's decision to sever ties with the EU. The Irish state harbours fundamental concerns about the likely negative impact of Brexit on the economy and about the potential for Brexit to be accompanied by political instability in Northern Ireland.

Ireland and the UK are neighbouring states, but relations between the two have often been acrimonious. A long history of conflict, particularly the Northern Ireland Troubles, contaminated the relationship. Developments from the 1990s onward, however, helped to heal uneasy relations. More recently, the relationship has been not just cordial but friendly. The signing of the 1998 Belfast Agreement was a pivotal moment that helped to placate and stabilise Northern Ireland and in so doing improved relations between the neighbouring states. Importantly, joint membership of the EU was the backdrop against which the peace process evolved and British–Irish relations improved. The UK decision to leave the EU, however, exposed some tension between the two states about the future relationship between the UK and the EU and what this means for Ireland. Perhaps more significantly, it also upset the delicate political equilibrium that supported the path to peace in Northern Ireland. A strong British–Irish relationship underpins the Belfast Agreement. The depth and strength of this relationship, however, is threatened by the UK decision to leave the EU.

The implications for Ireland of the UK leaving the EU are manifold. The precise economic impact is unclear, but such is the extent of Ireland's trading relationship with the UK that any impact is likely to be negative and will affect a variety of sectors. Brexit also potentially entails broader political and territorial implications as it alters the framework within which recent constitutional issues in Northern Ireland were agreed. This may lead to longer-term constitutional and territorial change for both Ireland and the UK.

This chapter examines the history of the British–Irish relationship against the backdrop of shared EU membership. It notes the anticipated impact of Brexit on the Irish economy and on the politics and broader constitutional arrangements on the island of Ireland. It details the Irish Government's approach to the Brexit challenge and notes how Brexit has impacted the tone and tenor of the British–Irish relationship. A perception that the Irish/Northern Ireland dimension was overlooked, neglected and possibly even misunderstood fuelled Irish Government frustration with the UK's approach to Brexit. This prompted an increasingly hard-line approach by the Irish Government under Taoiseach Leo Varadkar on the issue of Brexit and the Irish border. In turn, this led to tensions between the two governments and challenged an important bilateral relationship. The various economic and political dimensions of Brexit have the potential to produce unanticipated and wide-ranging constitutional and territorial changes that impact severely both the UK and its nearest neighbour.

The history of British–Irish relations

For much of the twentieth century, relations between Ireland and the UK were frequently difficult and marred by violence, particularly in Northern Ireland. The 1920 Government of Ireland Act partitioned the island and created a contested territorial arrangement where the six counties of Northern Ireland remained part of the United Kingdom and the remaining twenty-six counties became first the Irish Free State and later the Republic of Ireland. Partition clouded relations between Ireland and the UK for many decades. British Unionists (in the UK and Northern Ireland) supported the policy, but it was strongly opposed by Irish nationalists on both sides of the Irish border. Political contact and cooperation between the UK and Ireland was largely non-existent during this period. Although relations began to thaw during the 1960s with the emergence of a new generation of political leadership in both the Republic of Ireland and Northern Ireland, relations again deteriorated from the early 1970s with the emergence of the civil rights movement in Northern Ireland when the contested territorial question became entangled with issues around equality. The resulting violent conflict crystallised around a constitutional cleavage where unionists favoured Northern Ireland remaining part of the UK and nationalists supported a united Ireland. These opposing constitutional positions infiltrated all aspects of Northern Ireland politics and society, creating long-term division and hostility between communities and also between the UK and the Republic of Ireland. Relations between the two states remained tense throughout the 1970s and 1980s. Interestingly, however, the key forum for Irish–British contact and cooperation during this time was within the EU.

On 1 January 1973, the UK and the Republic of Ireland joined the then European Economic Community (EEC). Ireland's decision to seek membership of the EU was heavily influenced by the UK's decision. Substantial Irish dependency on the UK market effectively required Ireland to follow the UK's lead and seek membership of the Community. The decision was also influenced by a new and younger generation of Irish politicians who sought to consolidate Irish statehood through a process of economic and social modernisation. EU membership was seen as instrumental to this objective. Ireland's experience of the EU has been decidedly different from that of its neighbour. Originally one of the poorest and least developed of EU member states, the Republic of Ireland has, on the whole, benefited from membership of the EU. Participation in the single European market, access to the Common Agricultural Policy (CAP) and receipts from EU structural funding helped to transform the Irish economy. Today, Irish living standards are recovering following the post-2008 economic crisis and are currently above the EU average. Public support for Ireland's EU membership has typically been high. All of the main political parties and social partners are broadly supportive of the EU, and there is no strong Irish Eurosceptic movement. The overall Irish experience of the EU and positive Irish attitudes towards the EU contrast starkly with the UK's more fractious and testy relationship.

Contrasting attitudes towards the EU, however, was not an obstacle to the softening of relations between the UK and Ireland from the 1990s. This thawing of relations came as a consequence of closer collaboration and cooperation between the two states on the Northern Ireland question. Attempts to address the conflict became more emphatic from the late 1980s onward and culminated in the signing of the 1998 Belfast Agreement. The Agreement was a blueprint for peace in Northern Ireland. It created novel power-sharing institutions and included agreement on contested areas of public policy. New cross-border and cross-national institutions nurtured links between Northern Ireland, the Republic of Ireland and other parts of the UK. EU membership allowed for the border between north and south to soften to the point of invisibility and so facilitated close economic and political connections between the Republic of Ireland and the UK, as envisaged in the Belfast Agreement. Membership of the Single Market, free movement and engagement with EU institutions supported cooperation and contact between the neighbouring states. The resulting network of economic, political, social, cultural and psychological linkages aided and encouraged a fledgling peace process. The EU also played an important role in practically supporting moves towards peace in Northern Ireland by encouraging state-level agreement, committing Peace funding, and facilitating regional-level empowerment (see Hayward and Murphy 2012). Collectively, all of these domestic and European developments permitted a shift in the tone and tenor of British–Irish relations to produce constructive cooperation based on respectful relations. The altered relationship between the UK and Ireland has also been instrumental in terms of sustaining the peace process after 1998 when sporadic crises threatened to derail it. Successive UK and Irish prime ministers (and senior Cabinet members) maintained a close interest in Northern Ireland affairs and were available to engage with parties when necessary. In these instances, a strong British–Irish relationship was pivotal in stabilising the region. This more cordial, cooperative and collaborative relationship, however, has been bruised by the UK decision to leave the EU – a decision that involves immense economic and political consequences for Ireland, north and south.

Brexit and the British–Irish economic relationship

Ireland's original decision to join the EU was heavily influenced by the UK decision to seek membership. Irish reliance on UK markets meant that EU membership was imperative in order to safeguard Ireland's economy. EU membership, however, was also seen as a means for Ireland to diversify its trade relations and so to lessen its economic dependency on the UK. Over four decades later, Ireland is considerably less dependent on the UK. However, the magnitude of its economic linkages with Britain remain substantial, and so the economic ramifications of Brexit are potentially significant.

In 2015, 13.9 per cent of goods and 18 per cent of services were exported from Ireland to the UK. Approximately 25 per cent of all Irish imports emanated from the UK. Some sectors are more heavily impacted than others. The *National Risk Assessment 2017* notes that sectors including agri-food, retail, tourism, fishing and energy face 'critical risks' (Department of the Taoiseach 2017: 14). Various studies have pointed to the negative macroeconomic impact of Brexit on the Irish economy with estimates of the effect ranging from a reduction in GDP between 0.5 per cent and 3 per cent (see Bergin et al. 2016: 3). The most comprehensive analysis of the impact of Brexit on Ireland considers the complete macroeconomic impact under three alternative scenarios over the medium term. This study confirms that:

> Ireland will be particularly badly impacted by Brexit. Depending on the scenario considered, the level of Irish output ranges to between 2.3 and 3.8 per cent below what it otherwise would have been.
>
> *(ibid.: 10)*

The future status of the border between Northern Ireland and the Republic of Ireland is central to how Irish economic interests will fare post-Brexit. The two economies are highly interdependent. Cross-border trade is significant, labour markets are integrated and many industries operate on an all-island basis. The establishment of a hard border would severely challenge existing economic activities and relationships.

Dire predictions about the impact of Brexit for Ireland have motivated the Irish Government and the Irish business community to examine means of exploiting the economic opportunities that may arise from Brexit. Continued Irish membership of the EU means that Ireland will retain its attractiveness as a location for foreign direct investment. Irish business is working to diversify its trading profile by boosting trade links with other parts of the EU and other parts of the world and by encouraging increased investment. The relocation of business from the UK (particularly from London and particularly in the financial services) may also be to Ireland's benefit. However, even the most positive assessments do not view these opportunities as being sufficient to fight off the net negative impact of Brexit on Ireland.

Brexit will also impact on the movement of people between the Republic of Ireland and the UK. In 2015, visitors from the UK accounted for 41 per cent of overseas trips to Ireland by non-residents (Central Statistics Office 2016). This ease of movement between the two states predates UK and Irish membership of the EU. The Common Travel Area (in existence since 1922) has allowed Irish and UK citizens the right to live, study and work in either state. It means that Irish and UK citizens have access to various benefits and services in both countries. The CTA plays a significant role in facilitating the Irish–UK trade relationship. But it is also particularly important for Northern Ireland as it facilitates an open border between the two parts of the island. This means that those living along the border (and elsewhere) can move freely between the two jurisdictions – a freedom that is seen as central to livelihoods, identity and political aspiration and that is particularly important in terms of satisfying Irish nationalist identification with the Republic of Ireland.

The most visible impact of Brexit for Ireland will be on the economy, trade and free movement. These economic issues intersect with politically charged concerns about the status of the border between north and south and about the future of relationships within Northern Ireland, on the island of Ireland and between the UK and Republic of Ireland. The multilayered and complex web of interconnectedness between the two islands has been underpinned by membership of the EU. Removing that support block risks collapsing a series of not just economic gains but also important political achievements that have been fundamental to the attainment of peace and stability on the island of Ireland.

The British–Irish political and constitutional landscape after Brexit

Brexit presents pronounced political, constitutional and diplomatic challenges for the Republic of Ireland, and it has brought contested constitutional issues into sharp focus in Northern Ireland. The UK exit from the EU changes the political and constitutional conversation in Northern

Ireland because it removes an important shared feature of the UK and Irish political landscape. Brexit also exposes highly sensitive political complexities for the island of Ireland, which have the potential to fracture political relationships between Ireland and the UK and to destabilise Northern Ireland politics.

The 1998 Belfast Agreement is the anchor of the Northern Ireland peace process. It is based on a multiparty agreement between a majority of Northern Ireland's political parties and an international agreement between Britain and Ireland. The document underpins the establishment of power-sharing institutions in Northern Ireland and contains provisions for dealing with policing, prisoners and the decommissioning of weapons. It also contains important principles in relation to civil, cultural and human rights, and future constitutional preferences. The fact of Irish and UK membership of the EU facilitated the inclusion of important guarantees in the Agreement. These included an open border between Northern Ireland and the Republic of Ireland through membership of the single European market. The significance of cross-border freedom brings economic benefits but also political and symbolic advantages too. It enables an ease of association with the Republic of Ireland that facilitates the expression of nationalist identity. The Agreement also created cross-border institutions and bodies that give institutional recognition and meaning to a series of economic, political and cultural connections between Northern Ireland and the Republic of Ireland. East–West bodies that have a variety of policy remits also exist and allow for mutually beneficial policy objectives to be explored and pursued. Joint EU membership means that all of these cross-border and cross-national institutions often cooperate on EU policy issues (see Murphy 2014). This demonstrates the subtle political benefits of shared EU membership for relations on the island of Ireland and between the UK and Republic of Ireland.

The Agreement is also notable for guaranteeing the right of Northern Ireland citizens to self-identity as Irish and/or British. Because of joint UK and Irish membership of the EU, either classification of citizenship guarantees EU citizenship. The Irish Government has expressed serious concerns about how Brexit challenges the legal, political and human rights arrangements contained in the Belfast Agreement – an agreement that Ireland is legally party to. Equally significant is how Brexit potentially undermines confidence in the Agreement as a basis for Northern Ireland's hard won peace. The former secretary of state for Northern Ireland, however, is not persuaded that Brexit threatens the durability of the Belfast Agreement. In his evidence to the House of Lords European Union Committee report, *Brexit: UK–Irish Relations* (2016: 41), James Brokenshire stressed that 'the Government stood behind its commitments in the Belfast/ Good Friday Agreement, and "in our judgement the EU referendum does not change that at all". This difference of interpretation between the UK and Republic of Ireland is an increasingly troubling aspect of the fallout from Brexit. When the Irish and British analysis of an issue that affects Northern Ireland is not shared, it complicates and undermines the prospect of resolving that issue (see Tannam 2017).

The principle of consent is a fundamental aspect of the Belfast Agreement. It provides that there will be no change in the status of Northern Ireland until such time as a majority favour change. The UK decision to leave the EU is at odds with the preference of the majority in Northern Ireland – 55.8 per cent of Northern Ireland voters voted for the UK to stay in the EU. This majority is comprised of overwhelming nationalist support and approximately one-third support among unionists (Murphy 2016: 849). The majority Northern Ireland vote and the very strong nationalist preference for Remain are overridden by the slim UK majority vote in favour of Brexit. Concerns exist about how this complies with the consent principle enshrined in the Belfast Agreement.

Addressing the Irish border issue in the context of Brexit means grappling with a series of economic, political and security challenges. Administering, managing, policing and ultimately minimising the border between north and south presents a considerable challenge for the EU, the UK and Republic of Ireland. Suggestions that the frontier be controlled and managed using advanced technology have not been met with enthusiasm. Irish Foreign Affairs Minister Simon Coveney has objected to such plans:

> What we do not want to pretend is that we can solve the problems of the border on the island of Ireland through technical solutions like cameras and pre-registration and so on. That is not going to work.
>
> *(BBC News 2017: 1)*

Other proposals that advocate the status quo or suggest that Northern Ireland remain within the European Economic Area (EEA) may be practically feasible, but they are nevertheless politically problematic because they effectively mean moving the land border between the UK and Ireland to the Irish Sea. Such ideas are synonymous with calls for 'special status' for Northern Ireland being urged by Sinn Féin and the Social Democratic and Labour Party (SDLP). These plans are unacceptable to unionists, who view such a move as fundamentally undermining the integrity of the UK. The Irish Government has not explicitly proposed a special or unique arrangement for Northern Ireland but has been steadfast in its commitment to avoiding the imposition of a hard border with Northern Ireland.

The Irish Government's pronouncements on Brexit are in contrast to the relative silence of the Northern Ireland administration. The Northern Ireland Executive did not produce a position paper on the EU referendum or on Brexit. This was because of differences around the power-sharing table. Nationalists supported the UK remaining in the EU during the referendum campaign. Following the Leave result, they called for a special deal for Northern Ireland. In contrast, a majority of unionists favoured a UK exit from the EU and do not support special arrangements for Northern Ireland. The collapse of the Northern Ireland Executive in early 2017 meant that there was no forum for the parties to agree on how Northern Ireland might face the challenge of Brexit. Perhaps even more worrying however, was the fact that the prolonged absence of an Executive demonstrated the tenuous nature of the peace accord in Northern Ireland.

The achievement of permanent peace and reconciliation in Northern Ireland has been. A number of legacy issues remain unresolved, including dealing with the past, parading and the status of the Irish language. There are also persistent concerns about respect for equality in Northern Ireland and fundamental differences between the parties in relation to the introduction of same-sex marriage. Attempts to address and resolve these outstanding difficulties soured relations between the two political blocs. An unrelated financial scandal,[1] which nevertheless brought lingering political anxieties to the fore, culminated in the suspension of the Northern Ireland Assembly in early 2017. Election results also contributed to some destabilisation of relations between unionists and nationalists. Nationalist political representation in the Northern Ireland Assembly increased following the 2017 Assembly elections. However, this electoral trend was arrested following the 2017 Westminster election, which recorded gains for Northern Ireland's largest unionist political party, the Democratic Unionist Party (DUP). A surprising national election outcome was to play out well for the DUP party. An electoral gamble by Prime Minister Theresa May failed to pay off. The Conservative Party sustained losses, and the prime minister was forced to seek support from Northern Ireland's pro-Brexit unionist party. The DUP agreed to shore up Theresa May's minority government, but the party's new role propping up the British Government was met with dismay by Irish nationalists, who saw the alliance as being antithetical to nationalist interests. The benevolence of the UK Government on the Irish question was also called into question given their reliance on unionist support. In a further twist, the general election also reduced nationalist representation in Westminster. The smaller nationalist party, the SDLP failed to return an MP, while Sinn Féin's tally of MPs increased by three. The loss of SDLP representation however, meant that there was no Irish nationalist voice in Westminster. This is because the Sinn Féin Party follows an abstentionist policy and so refuses to take its seats in the House of Commons. These shifting electoral arrangements challenged central planks of the peace process, namely the UK as a benign force and nationalists having equal input and status to the political system. The Irish Government was attuned to these difficulties and consistently eager that the British Government take more serious heed of how Brexit and other internal developments produced a destabilising effect on Northern Ireland politics and Irish interests.

The precariousness of Northern Ireland's political situation and the unsettling effect of Brexit reopened some old political vestiges. A possible reimposed physical border between Northern Ireland and the Republic of Ireland would be redolent of the worst days of the Northern Ireland conflict. It may involve the installation of customs points and checkpoints, which would likely act as a reminder of division and conflict. A physical border would be practically and psychologically difficult for border communities in particular (see Hayward 2017). There would be security implications too. Earlier border constructions were frequently targets for paramilitary attacks. In sum, the establishment of any form of border control system would signal a backwards step for relations on the island of Ireland. In the worst-case scenario, Brexit may provoke a sinister response from dissident groups, which could fatally undermine peace in Northern Ireland and undo years of economic and political progress.

In its *Position Paper on Northern Ireland and Ireland*, the UK Government (2017) outlined its commitment to safeguard the Belfast Agreement and stability in Northern Ireland. The document, however, was heavy on aspiration and weak on detail. The British Government proposed ideas that were dismissed as 'wishful thinking' by the EU and deemed unsatisfactory by the Irish Government. The UK also rejected calls for special treatment for Northern Ireland and were supported in this position by Northern Ireland's unionist community.

The paucity of workable ideas emanating from the UK about how to deal with Brexit, in particular about how to manage the Ireland/Northern Ireland dimension, came to a head in late 2017. Plans to proceed to phase two of negotiations between the UK and the EU were temporarily derailed when the DUP strongly objected to an initial deal between the UK and the EU that included provisions to effectively keep Northern Ireland in the Single Market and Customs Union after Brexit by keeping EU regulations in place. This form of proposed special treatment for Northern Ireland was unacceptable to unionists for the way in which it threatened to separate Northern Ireland from the rest of the UK by creating distinct arrangements for the region. The conclusion of phase one Brexit negotiations was eventually reached in mid-December 2017 when the European Council deemed that 'sufficient progress' had been made to allow for phase two negotiations on the future UK–EU trading relationship to commence in early 2018. This decision to agree on the movement to phase two negotiations was based on a Joint Report agreed on between the UK Government and EU negotiators on 8 December 2017 following consultation with the DUP. The report included a section on 'Ireland and Northern Ireland' and contained a number of commitments in relation to the Irish dimension to Brexit. These included the protection of the 1998 Belfast Agreement, a commitment to North–South cooperation and the avoidance of a hard border. It is intended that the objective to prevent a hard border will be achieved through agreement on the new EU–UK relationship. In the event that this cannot be achieved, the UK Government has committed to ensuring that no new regulatory barriers will be erected between Northern Ireland and the rest of the UK, unless these are consistent with the Belfast Agreement and agreed to by the Northern Ireland Executive and Assembly.

The Joint Report is heavily focused on commitments and principles with little detail in relation to how such pledges might be secured and upheld. Reflecting the priority afforded to Ireland and Northern Ireland, phase two negotiations include a distinct strand focused on fleshing out detailed arrangements to give effect to the commitments contained in the Joint Report. The report has been criticised for its vagueness, ambiguity and lack of detail. Key issues were to some extent 'fudged' to allow the negotiations to proceed to the next phase.

Brexit also reopened debates in the UK about the UK's constitutional future. Shortly after the referendum result, the Scottish National Party (SNP) called for a second Scottish independence referendum, a development with the potential to challenge the very unity of the UK. In Ireland, questions about the future cohesion of the UK have opened up a space for those who see Brexit as an opportunity to further a united Ireland agenda. Some Irish nationalists have been emboldened by Brexit to more seriously consider the rationale for Irish unity. The push for a border poll (i.e. referendum on Irish unity) has been led by Sinn Féin. The issue was also addressed by the Oireachtas Joint Committee on the Implementation of the Good Friday Agreement (2017), which examined the effect of Brexit on Ireland and included consideration of what Ireland would need to do to facilitate Irish unity in the event that the people of Northern Ireland supported constitutional change. The main political parties, including Fine Gael and Fianna Fáil, have also lately been more outspoken about the possibility of a united Ireland. Fianna Fáil is expected to publish a white paper on Irish Unification in 2018 and is planning to field candidates in future Northern Ireland elections. A more detailed and vocal discussion of a future united Ireland by Ireland's larger mainstream political parties is unsettling for unionists. The constitutional status quo, which favours unionist preferences, is less secure than it was pre-Brexit. In short, the political narrative around the UK's constitutional future has shifted. In the post-Brexit period, it includes the discussion of constitutional options and possibilities that enjoyed only marginal and peripheral support before the referendum vote but that now have broader appeal.

The likelihood of imminent constitutional change on the island of Ireland is low. Unlike Sinn Féin, other Irish political parties have not called for a referendum on the issue of Irish unity. This is because public opinion polls suggest that there is currently no majority support for such a prospect. Of course, this may conceivably change in the event that Brexit delivers negative results. Developments external to Northern Ireland, including the detail of the UK–EU exit package, a further growth in electoral support for Sinn Féin (North and South) and (unknown) economic shocks may also impact voter preferences. Northern Ireland's constitutional status quo is no longer as assured as it was pre-Brexit, and this is disturbing a delicate political settlement between two communities who are still not fully reconciled.

For Northern Ireland – a post-conflict society in transition – Brexit provoked anxiety about the political and constitutional status quo. The implications are potentially far-reaching. Not only might economic progress be stalled, but peace and stability on the island of Ireland are also at risk. The Irish Government has been working assiduously to stave off these threats and to protect Ireland's vital national and nationalist interests.

Brexit and the pursuit of Irish priorities

The Irish Government's preference for the softest possible Brexit is not shared by the British Government. Whereas the Irish Government favours continued UK membership of the Customs Union and Single Market, the British Government appears to have rejected this scenario. In the aftermath of the referendum vote, therefore, the Irish Government has been focused on limiting the worst impact of Brexit in two key areas: the Irish economy and the Northern Ireland peace process.

The Irish Government has identified four priorities for Ireland during the negotiation stages:

- Minimising the impact on trade and the economy.
- Protecting the Northern Ireland peace process.
- Maintaining the Common Travel Area.
- Influencing the future of the European Union.

(Irish Government 2017: 4)

Irish diplomatic forces and resources were extensively mobilised to advance and protect Irish interests during the Brexit negotiations. Irish Government figures actively pursued the Irish cause in Brussels and across various European capital cities (over 400 engagements to date). Officials and politicians worked to inform and educate their fellow Europeans about the impact of the UK exit from the EU on Ireland. This involved outlining and explaining the consequences of Brexit for the Irish economy and for the Northern Ireland peace process. This strategy aimed to furnish the remaining EU27 with information and to contextualise Irish fears about the political ramifications of Brexit for the island of Ireland. Between 2016 and 2017, the Irish Government convened seven Cabinet committee meetings on Brexit, and cross-departmental work streams were established. Additional staff were also recruited to key agencies, including Bord Bia (Irish Food Board), the Industrial Development Authority (IDA) and Enterprise Ireland, in order to support businesses affected by Brexit. Many of these state agencies highlight Ireland as a place of trade, tourism and investment. They are focused on insulating Ireland from the negative impact of Brexit by working to diversify Ireland's trading relations. The government was particularly attentive to the agri–food sector – the 2017 budget made €150 million available in loans to Irish farmers via a low-cost scheme. The cheap availability of finance helped Irish farmers to withstand the impact of sterling currency fluctuations following the referendum result.

A further significant development was the creation of the All-Island Civic Dialogue, which meets in plenary and sectoral format. An initiative of former Taoiseach Enda Kenny, the All-Island Civic Dialogue brings together civil society, interest groups, civil servants and politicians to identify, discuss and analyse what Brexit means for specific sectors and how those challenges can be met. The initiative has an explicitly all-island dimension and seeks to capture perspectives from both Northern Ireland and the Republic of Ireland. Unionists, however, were quick to dismiss the initiative and did not engage with the process of the consultation and deliberation that the All-Island Civic Dialogue sought to nurture.

Irish efforts to protect Irish interests returned some early and important successes. UK Prime Minister Theresa May's letter to European Council President Donald Tusk in March 2017, triggering Article 50, made specific reference to Ireland and to protecting the peace process in Northern Ireland. This echoed one of the twelve principles contained in the UK Government's white paper on exiting the EU (see HM Government 2017). References to Northern Ireland's special position were also contained in a European Council note issued on 31 March and in a European Parliament Resolution issued after Article 50 was triggered. The resolution:

urges that all means and measures consistent with European Union law and the 1998 Good Friday Agreement be used to mitigate the effects of the United Kingdom's withdrawal on the border between Ireland and Northern Ireland; insists in that context on the absolute need to ensure continuity and stability of the Northern Ireland peace process and to do everything possible to avoid a hardening of the border.

(European Parliament 2017)

A further significant development was the Irish Government's success at the 29 April 2017 EU summit in achieving an EU declaration recognising the potential for Irish unification. The declaration allows Northern Ireland automatic membership of the EU in the event of unification. One commentator characterised this as a 'stunning diplomatic coup' (Collins 2017) won on the back of an extraordinary diplomatic effort by the Taoiseach, government ministers and officials.

The EU's commitment to Irish interests was articulated during an address to the Joint Houses of the Irish Oireachtas (Parliament) in May 2017 by Chief EU Brexit Negotiator Michel Barnier, who said:

> I want to reassure the Irish people: in this negotiation Ireland's interest will be the Union's interest. We are in this negotiation together and a united EU will be here for you.
>
> *(Barnier 2017)*

Barnier's address also demonstrated an understanding of the myriad ways in which the reimposition of a hard border on the island of Ireland may undo years of economic progress and peace building. As a former European Commissioner with responsibility for the EU's PEACE programme, Barnier is well acquainted with Northern Ireland's journey away from conflict. His address noted how the EU facilitated the lifting of borders, strengthened dialogue between communities in Northern Ireland and supported the Belfast Agreement. In his address, Barnier committed that 'nothing in this negotiation should put peace at risk' (ibid.).

The same message was reiterated in the EU's *Guiding Principles for the Dialogue on Ireland/Northern Ireland* (European Commission 2017a), which placed a heavy emphasis on protecting 'the gains of the peace process and of the Good Friday Agreement (Belfast Agreement) in all its parts' (p. 2). The document was clear that, in terms of proposing solutions to the border issue, the onus was explicitly on the UK. Dealing with the Irish border issue is regarded as a unique aspect of the wider Brexit challenge and not one that might predetermine solutions in the context of wider discussions about the future of the UK–EU relationship. Jean Claude Juncker further reiterated EU support for the 1998 Agreement by alluding to partial EU ownership of the Northern Ireland peace process, which he claimed was 'a major achievement of European, and British and Irish policy-making' (Rae 2017).

The combination of these statements and positions suggests strong acknowledgement and awareness of specific Irish and Northern Ireland issues at the EU level and considerable resolve in protecting these interests. Notwithstanding the lack of detail in the EU–UK Joint Report agreed on in December 2017, the EU's approach to negotiations with the UK prioritised achieving some agreement on the status of the border between Northern Ireland and the Republic of Ireland post-Brexit before substantive negotiations on the future UK–EU trading relationship.

Brexit and the British–Irish relationship: pressures and prospects

The Irish Government's approach to Brexit altered following the installation of Leo Varadkar as Taoiseach in mid-2017. A previously soft diplomatic stance hardened. Borne out of Irish frustration about the UK's perceived failure to fully appreciate the seriousness and the sensitivities of Brexit for Ireland, north and south, the taoiseach stated:

> We do not think it's in the interests of Northern Ireland or the United Kingdom that there should be an economic Border between our two countries or on our island and we're not going to be helping them [the UK] to design some sort of Border that we don't believe should exist in the first place.
>
> *(Leahy and Minihan 2017)*

There is some measure of consensus that Brexit will have an economic impact on the UK (and also the EU, the Republic of Ireland and Northern Ireland). It is the scale and magnitude of the impact, however, that is disputed by Brexiteers and Remainers. The constitutional impact of Brexit for the UK, however, reveals even less consensus. Those in favour of Brexit in Northern Ireland view the UK exit from the EU as a project in protecting and buttressing the national sovereignty of the British state. Those who oppose Brexit (Northern Ireland nationalists and the Irish Government) harbour fears about its economic consequences and its impact on the Northern Ireland peace process. The fact of disagreement between the British and Irish administrations is not problematic in itself, but, when it is accompanied by poor communication and megaphone diplomacy on issues affecting Northern Ireland, it signals that the resilience of the British–Irish relationship is under pressure. Brexit has contributed to a discernible tension in the British–Irish relationship. Diverging views about how to confront the Brexit challenge have divided the two administrations at a time when agreement and consensus are essential to stabilising Northern Ireland. One of the hallmarks of Northern Ireland's peace process has been a joint British–Irish approach to various issues and sporadic crises. The apparent weakening of this approach does not bode well in terms of dealing constructively with the very complex political and economic challenges facing Northern Ireland and the Republic of Ireland as a consequence of Brexit.

One form of constitutional change that does not enjoy support in Ireland is a so-called Ir-exit, that is, an Irish exit from the EU. Brexit has prompted some discussion in Ireland of the possibility of Ireland leaving the EU (see Coughlan 2017; Bassett 2017). There is little official or public appetite for such a prospect. Irish support for the EU is among the highest of any member state, and Ireland is the most optimistic about the future of the EU (see European Commission 2017b). Moreover, none of the larger political parties or social partners in Ireland are supportive of an Irish exit. Nevertheless, in the broader European context and in the longer term, Brexit will challenge some of the fundamentals of Ireland's relationship with the EU. The UK exit from the EU alters the balance of interests within the Union. Following Brexit, Ireland will lose an important ally at the European table. Irish and UK interests certainly do not converge on all issues, but there are certain policy areas where Ireland and the UK share similar views. As the EU moves on from Brexit, its agenda is likely to include proposals for deeper cooperation on defence, Schengen and the Eurozone (see more in Chapters 19 and 20). For a number of these issues, the UK and Ireland would have been united in their opposition to change. For example, in his 2017 State of the European Union address, Commission President Jean Claude Juncker outlined plans to pursue tax harmonisation, a move that Ireland is opposed to. The state's ability to successfully oppose the introduction of a Common Consolidated Corporate Tax Base (CCCTB), however, is compromised by the UK exit from the EU. Ireland's relationship with the EU looks set to be tested as new policy issues become perceivable. The direct territorial and constitutional implications of these developments are limited, but there may be important longer-term political ramifications that affect the Irish party system and the relative strength of political parties. Such developments may indirectly prompt a more detailed national conversation around EU membership, Irish unity and Ireland's constitutional future. Even after Brexit, UK/Irish constitutional and territorial questions may continue to create animation and agitation on the two islands.

Conclusion

For Ireland, the UK exit from the EU represents a critical moment. Brexit potentially threatens peace, prosperity and stability on the island of Ireland. The Irish Government harbours serious concerns about the economic, political, security, social, cultural and psychological implications of Brexit for Ireland, most especially for Northern Ireland. The absence of a functioning regional Executive and Assembly limited the extent to which Northern Ireland contributed to the Brexit process. Recent electoral outcomes diminished nationalist representation in Westminster and elevated the influence of unionism. Against this backdrop, the Irish Government became increasingly bellicose in its approach to Brexit and sought to loudly voice its concerns about the implications of the UK's EU exit for the island of Ireland. Ireland was supported in its approach by senior EU figures and by a series of EU positions and negotiating guidelines.

The Irish Government's primary concern is about what form a hard or soft border between the UK and Ireland will take, how it will be managed and policed and where that border might be. The Government's opposition to the reimposition of any sort of border between north and south is motivated by both political and economic factors. In short, the Irish Government expressly supports the UK remaining in the Customs Union and Single Market. The British Government's obfuscation in relation to what type of Brexit it favours and how it might pursue that preference has frustrated the Irish Government, which perceives poor levels of British understanding of, and responsiveness to, legitimate Irish concerns. From this perspective, Irish fears about how Brexit has the potential to reawaken old political insecurities and lead to political instability in Northern Ireland were not fully appreciated by the British Government (at least during phase one negotiations). The implications of Brexit-related developments for the UK's constitutional future are similarly underestimated.

The robustness of the British–Irish relationship is tested by the UK decision to leave the EU. Relations between the two states shifted and cooled as differences of outlook and interpretation became more pronounced. These developments happened at a time when Northern Ireland's devolved institutions were suspended and the political situation there was tenuous. The delicate political accommodation in Northern Ireland was achieved in the context of shared membership of the EU, an arrangement that provides a common legal and policy framework for various forms of cross-border cooperation. The peace process in Northern Ireland was also underpinned by a strong cooperative and collaborative British–Irish relationship. Both of these pillars of the political and constitutional settlement on the island of Ireland are challenged by the UK decision to exit the EU. The 'far-reaching impacts' of Brexit identified by Taoiseach Leo Varadkar loom large over Ireland's economic, political and constitutional future.

Note

1   First Minister and DUP leader Arlene Foster was implicated in a political scandal concerning the Renewable Heat Incentive (RHI) scheme, which it is alleged was mismanaged to the tune of stg£400 million. The first minister's refusal to step aside while an investigation was carried out triggered the resignation of the former Sinn Féin deputy first minister, the late Martin McGuinness, amid concerns about accountability, respect and equality. The collapse of the Northern Ireland Assembly and the suspension of devolution followed.

References

Barnier, M. (2017) Address to Both Houses of the Oireachtas. *Leinster House*, Dublin, May 11. Available at: https://ec.europa.eu/ireland/news/eu-chief-negotiator-michel-barnier-addresses-both-houses-of-the-oireachtas_en [Accessed November 1, 2017].

Bassett, R. (2017) After Brexit, Will Ireland Be Next to Exit? *Policy Exchange Report*, June. Available at: https://policyexchange.org.uk/wp-content/uploads/2017/07/After-Brexit-will-Ireland-be-next-to-exit-1.pdf [Accessed November 1, 2017].

BBC News (2017) Brexit: Coveney Says 'Tech Alone Will Not Solve Border Issue', July 17. Available at: www.bbc.com/news/world-europe-40637851 [Accessed November 1, 2017].

Bergin, A., Rodriguez, A.G., Inerney, N.M., Morgenroth, E. and Smith, D. (2016) Modelling the Medium to Long Term Potential Macroeconomic Impact of Brexit on Ireland. *ESRI Working Paper* No. 548, November. Available at: www.esri.ie/pubs/WP548.pdf [Accessed November 1, 2017].

Central Statistics Office (CSO) (2016) Brexit-Ireland and the UK in Numbers, December 20. Available at: www.cso.ie/en/releasesandpublications/ep/p-biun/biun/ [Accessed November 1, 2017].

Collins, S. (2017) Kenny Has Delivered on First Round of Brexit Talks. *Irish Times*, April 27. Available at: www.irishtimes.com/opinion/stephen-collins-kenny-has-delivered-on-first-round-of-brexit-talks-1.3062157 [Accessed November 1, 2017].

Coughland, A. (2017) *Why Brexit Should Be Accompanied by Irexit (Ireland Exit)*. London: The Bruges Group.

Department of the Taoiseach (2017) National Risk Assessment 2017: Overview of Strategic Risks. *Department of the Taoiseach*, Dublin. Available at: www.taoiseach.gov.ie/eng/Publications/Publications_2017/National%20Risk%20Assessment%202017%20-%20Overview%20of%20Strategic%20Risks.pdf [Accessed November 1, 2017].

European Commission (2017a) Guiding Principles Transmitted to EU27 for the Dialogue on Ireland/Northern Ireland. TF50 (2017) 15, September 6. Available at: https://ec.europa.eu/commission/sites/beta-political/files/guiding-principles-dialogue-ei-ni_en.pdf [Accessed November 1, 2017].

European Commission (2017b) Public Opinion in the European Union. Standard Eurobarometer 87, Spring 2017. Available at: http://ec.europa.eu/commfrontoffice/publicopinion/index.cfm/Survey/getSurveyDetail/instruments/STANDARD/surveyKy/2142 [Accessed November 1, 2017].

European Parliament (2017) Joint Motion for a Resolution. European Parliament Resolution 2017/2593(RSP), April 10. Available at: www.europarl.europa.eu/sides/getDoc.do?pubRef=-//EP//TEXT+MOTION+P8-RC-2017-0237+0+DOC+XML+V0//EN [Accessed November 1, 2017].

Hayward, K. (2017) *Bordering on Brexit: A Report Prepared for the Irish Central Border Area Network (ICBAN)*. Belfast: Queen's University. Available at: www.qub.ac.uk/brexit/Brexitfilestore/Filetoupload,781170,en.pdf [Accessed January 9, 2018].

Hayward, K. and Murphy, M.C. (2012) The (Soft) Power of Commitment: The EU and Conflict Resolution in Northern Ireland. *Ethnopolitics* 11(4): 439–452.

HM Government (2017) The United Kingdom's Exit from and New Partnership with the European Union. Cm 9417, February. Available at: www.gov.uk/government/uploads/system/uploads/attachment_data/file/589191/The_United_Kingdoms_exit_from_and_partnership_with_the_EU_Web.pdf [Accessed November 1, 2017].

House of Lords European Union Committee (2016) Brexit: UK–Irish Relations. 6th Report of Session 2016–2017, HL Paper 76, December 12. Available at: https://publications.parliament.uk/pa/ld201617/ldselect/ldeucom/76/76.pdf [Accessed November 1, 2017].

Irish Government (2017) Brexit: Ireland's Priorities. Available at: https://merrionstreet.ie/en/EU-UK/Key_Irish_Documents/Government_Approach_to_Brexit_Negotiations.pdf [Accessed January 10, 2017].

Joint Committee on the Implementation of the Good Friday Agreement (2017) Brexit and the Future of Ireland: Uniting Ireland and Its People in Peace and Prosperity. 32/JCIGFA/02, August. Available at: www.oireachtas.ie/parliament/media/committees/implementationofthegoodfridayagreement/jcigfa2016/Brexit-and-the-Future-of-Ireland.pdf [Accessed November 1, 2017].

Leahy, P. and Minihan, M. (2017) Varadkar's Comments on Brexit Are a Sharp Message to London. *Irish Times*, July 29. Available at: www.irishtimes.com/news/politics/varadkar-s-comments-on-brexit-are-a-sharp-message-to-london-1.3170367 [Accessed January 9, 2018].

Murphy, M.C. (2014) *Northern Ireland and the European Union: The Dynamics of a Changing Relationship*. Manchester: Manchester University Press.

Murphy, M.C. (2016) The EU Referendum in Northern Ireland: Closing Borders, Re-Opening Border Debates. *Journal of Contemporary European Research (JCER)* 12(4): 844–853.

Rae, S. (2017) Exclusive Audio: 'My European Tax Plans Are Not Anti-Irish' Insists Juncker. *Irish Independent*, September 16. Available at: www.independent.ie/irish-news/politics/exclusive-audio-my-european-tax-plans-are-not-antiirish-insists-juncker-36137506.html [Accessed November 1, 2017].

Tannam, E. (2017) Cracks Are Beginning to Appear in the British–Irish Relations. *LSE Brexit Blog*, July 26. Available at: http://blogs.lse.ac.uk/brexit/2017/07/26/cracks-are-beginning-to-appear-in-british-irish-relations/ [Accessed November 1, 2017].

UK Government (2017) Policy Paper: Northern Ireland and Ireland – Position Paper. *Northern Ireland Office and Department for Exiting the European Union*, August 16. Available at: www.gov.uk/government/publications/northern-ireland-and-ireland-a-position-paper [Accessed November 1, 2017].

4

BREXIT AND SCOTLAND

Michael Keating

Scotland and Europe

Brexit has exposed the differences between two radically different conceptions of the UK's largely unwritten constitution. The first is the Westminster view, according to which Parliament is supreme and can do anything except bind itself. The devolution of power, whether to the European Union, the nations of the UK or to local government, represents nothing more than the lending of authority that can be taken back at any time. The other conception is that of the UK as a union of nations that have come together at various stages of their development but without surrendering their own identities and political traditions. In this view, there is no single UK people or *demos*, nor is there shared *telos*, or final destiny for the Union. It is, rather, negotiated and renegotiated over time and is interpreted differently in its component parts. Britishness, rather than being a single thing, is a family-resemblance concept whose meaning varies across the constituent nations. So English people might feel a single national identity, variously articulated as English or British, often without making a distinction between the two, while Scots can feel dual identities, as British and Scottish in various proportions. There is a legal/constitutional dimension to this, expressed in the idea that the Westminster view of sovereignty is alien to Scottish legal traditions and was not part of the Union compact of 1707 (MacCormick 1999).

Devolution from 1999 gave substance to this Scottish constitutional tradition, drawing on two legacies. One is the existing principle of the Scottish right to self-determination, recognized even by staunch unionists like Margaret Thatcher (1993) and John Major (1992) who, even while opposing devolution, agreed that, if it really insisted, Scotland could leave the union. The other is the idea that the Scottish Parliament is not merely the creature of Westminster but results from the popular referendum of 1997, as an expression of constituent power.

A persistent argument of Eurosceptics has been that the EU is incompatible with the UK's constitutional order based on parliamentary supremacy and omnicompetence. The aim of Brexit was to restore power to Westminster or, in some formulations, the British people. If we regard the constitution in the second way, however, there is a deep compatibility between the UK and the EU. Both are plurinational unions without a unitary *demos* or shared *telos*, organized in a rather asymmetrical fashion and leaving key questions about where sovereignty lies in abeyance. If there is a sovereignty doctrine, it is based on 'post-sovereign' ideas of pooled and shared authority (MacCormick 1999; Keating 2001).

This is not to say that Europe has always been popular in Scotland. In the referendum of 1975, Scotland voted to remain in the EEC by a smaller majority than in England. The Scottish National Party (SNP) (apart from a small minority) was hostile to Europe as an infringement of national sovereignty and even more remote than Westminster. Labour, then the dominant party in Scotland, was largely opposed, as was most of the trade union movement. A change occurred in the mid-1980s. Jacques Delors, at his address to the Trades Union Congress, persuaded Labour of the merits of a social Europe. The SNP was converted to the policy of independence in Europe as a way of dealing with the externalities of independence and guaranteeing market access, inspired by the example of the small member states. More recently, they have combined this with proposals to retain close links with the UK. Indeed, during the 2014 independence referendum campaign, they claimed that Scotland was in six unions (political, monarchical, monetary, security, European and social) and only proposed to withdraw from the political one (Keating and McEwen 2017). There is a long history of such 'independence-lite' as it has become known. Demands for home rule before the Second World War were mostly placed in the wider context of Empire. This has now been replaced by Europe. While nationalists pressed for independence in Europe, sections of the Labour Party in Scotland were converted to the Europe of the Regions movement as a way of accommodating devolution.

Even as the SNP made a connection between independence and Europe, however, they never quite convinced the public of the link. Repeated studies have failed to show any connection between support for independence and for European integration. It does seem that, at the extremes, very strong Scottish nationalists and very strong British nationalists in Scotland are Eurosceptic, but these are few in number. More important is a strong clustering in the middle of both nationalist–unionist and Europhile–Eurosceptic axes, where moderate pro-European attitudes link to support for more devolution. Research on the Scottish independence referendum of 2014 showed that, while during the campaign there was a movement from No to Yes, underlying attitudes shifted very little (Liñeira et al. 2017). It was, rather, that significant numbers of voters saw a Yes vote as the best way to get to their preferred outcome of enhanced devolution. This suggests that most Scots are content to live with multiple levels of government and that the number who want all the sovereignty to be in one place is rather small. It seems that 17 per cent of Scots voted Yes to independence and Leave the EU (Prosser and Fieldhouse 2017). To that we might perhaps add some 3 per cent who are against any devolution and voted Leave. This would give only 20 per cent of 'sovereigntists'. That is consistent with historic interpretations of the union as a pact to be renegotiated periodically. Such an interpretation does not depend on Scots being Europhiles; the evidence has consistently shown them just a bit less Eurosceptic than the English.

Devolution since 1999 has occurred entirely during UK membership of the EU and the European Single Market and has been profoundly affected by it. In a very specific way, the Scottish Parliament is obliged to work within EU law (and also the European Convention on Human Rights), and its legislation can be struck down by any court if it is not compliant. Most challenges to devolved competences have been made in relation to European law rather than the Scotland Act itself. Brexit means that, at a minimum, the clauses in the Act binding the Scottish Parliament in this way will have to be repealed. Several key competences of the Scottish Parliament, notably in agriculture, fisheries, the environment and parts of justice and home affairs, are also EU competences, which has resulted in a double loss of power. The competences are Europeanized, but, because the UK is the member state, it is the UK that negotiates over these matters in the Council of Ministers. Scotland, with the other devolved nations, provides an input through the Joint Ministerial Committee (Europe) (JMC), the only JMC that has had a continuous existence, and Scottish ministers are invited to join the UK Council delegation. In a broader sense, Europe has provided a discursive space for ideas of shared sovereignty and a multilevel constitutional order to thrive. For the SNP, this has allowed them to reframe independence as less threatening and even to appropriate the language of union (Keating and McEwen 2017), while Labour, while in government, was able to work across European networks, giving devolution an external dimension without threatening the UK union.

The Brexit campaign

During the Brexit referendum campaign, Scottish political opinion and civil society were broadly in favour of Remain. The SNP government joined the Remain campaign not just in Scotland but across the United Kingdom. There were few dissidents, although it subsequently emerged that a handful of leading nationalists had voted Leave. Scottish Labour was largely in favour, with a small Leave minority. The Conservatives, too, were largely pro-Remain, notably their leader Ruth Davidson, who became a prominent Remain campaigner at the UK level.

A notable difference between Scotland and many parts of England has been the salience of the issue of migration and free movement. Public opinion about migration has been a little more liberal than in most parts of the UK, but the big difference is in the way that it has been framed by political leaders. From the early 2000s, a consensus emerged that Scotland had an emigration rather than an immigration problem and that, for economic and demographic reasons, it needed more people. Successive Labour/Liberal Democrat and SNP governments encouraged migration and integration, even though this is a reserved matter. Conservatives were largely in agreement.

The result of this broad consensus was a 62 per cent vote to remain, against just 47 per cent in England and Wales. It had been suggested that there might be divergent majorities across the UK, but a 15 per cent difference came as a surprise and opened up a series of constitutional issues.

The first is the democratic nature of the Brexit mandate. Before the referendum, the SNP had suggested that Brexit should require concurrent mandates across the four nations, a suggestion that had received no support in London. They had also insisted that, if Scotland voted to remain but was taken out of the EU against its will, this would provide a moral case and a mandate for another independence referendum. Such an outcome would provide the 'material change in circumstances' that they claimed would allow them to revisit the 2014 referendum in which Scots had voted 55–45 to remain in the UK. In the immediate aftermath of the Brexit vote, First Minister Nicola Sturgeon declared that another referendum was 'very likely'. The Conservative, Labour and Liberal Democrat Parties were united in their view that the issue had been settled in 2014 for a generation and that Brexit made no difference. This created an acute dilemma. Scots had voted in successive referendums to remain in both the UK and the European Union. Indeed during the 2014 independence referendum, unionists had warned that the only way Scotland could remain within the EU was to vote against independence (Keating 2017). Having done that, they now found that it was the other way round.

Since devolution is so deeply embedded in Europe, Brexit has highly destabilizing affects and cannot leave the devolution settlement untouched. There are three ways of resolving the issue, none of which is straightforward: independence, recentralization and differentiation.

Independence

At the time of the 2014 independence referendum, there was a debate about whether and how Scotland would be allowed to join the EU. As this was a central part of the independence prospectus, it was an important issue, although not critical in the vote (Keating 2017). EU officials including Commission President José Manuel Barroso and Council President Herman Van Rompuy had talked down Scotland's prospects. At one point, Barroso had even declared that it might be impossible for Scotland ever to join the EU, even though the UK had pledged to respect the referendum result and Scotland was already compliant with the admission criteria. Unionists in Scotland limited themselves to saying that Scotland would have to leave and then face a long and difficult process to get back in. They also suggested that unnamed other member states would veto Scottish membership. This was clearly a reference to Spain, although the Spanish Government, while very worried that Scotland would set an example for Catalonia, never actually threatened a veto.

In the aftermath of the Brexit referendum, most of this hostility disappeared, although other member states did not go out of their way to recognize Scotland's position. The Spanish foreign minister said that Spain would not veto Scottish membership (ABC News 2017). The practical difficulties, however, remained formidable. Scotland could not negotiate with the EU before becoming independent, meaning that it might indeed have to spend a time outside, although some transitional arrangements could be possible.

The main difficulty, however, is that, with Scotland inside the EU and the rest of the UK outside, there would be a hard EU border between Scotland and England. This is the very thing that the policy of independence in Europe was designed to avoid. Scotland's trade with the rest of the UK is some four times the size of its trade with the EU27 so any trading barriers could be serious. This is not an argument that Brexiteers could plausibly make, of course, as they were assuring the public that trade with the EU would continue to thrive but was an issue for Remainers. There were also some Leave voices emerging in Scotland, even within the SNP itself. SNP veterans Jim Sillars and Alex Neil, architects of the independence-in-Europe idea in the 1970s, supported Brexit, pointing to the EU's hostility during the 2014 referendum and its treatment of the small member state of Greece. Fishers vocally insisted that there should be no return to the Common Agricultural Policy, while pro-Leave farmers still demanded the end of EU regulations (if not of subsidies).

Another possibility is that Scotland could opt for membership of the European Economic Area (EEA). In that case, it would be within the Single Market but be able also to negotiate a free trade agreement with the United Kingdom. It would also be outside the Common Fisheries Policy, a contentious point in Scotland. On the other hand, negotiating EEA membership might be no less complex than getting into the EU, and it would mean that Scotland, like Norway, would have to accept Single Market policies without having any role in making them

Attitudes to independence and to Europe continued to be separate so that the expected bounce in support for independence in the aftermath of the referendum failed to materialize. About 30 per cent of SNP supporters voted for Brexit, concentrated in the same working-class and post-industrial areas that had voted most strongly for independence in 2014. Support for independence remained more or less at its 2014 level, with small numbers of people moving in each direction and cancelling each other out (REFS). As elsewhere in the UK, many Remain supporters were resigned to leaving and feared that an independence referendum would add further uncertainty and risk.

First Minister Nicola Sturgeon nevertheless decided to take the initiative and in March 2017 proposed a referendum to be held between the autumn of 2018 and the spring of 2019. The Scottish Government conceded that, as in 2014, this would require the agreement of the UK Government but did succeed in getting the Scottish Parliament to agree to make such a request, with the support of the SNP and Greens. The other parties remained opposed. Again, there was no bounce in public support, and the process was overtaken by the snap UK general election of June 2017. The Scottish Conservatives seized the opportunity to use the election as a referendum on not having a referendum. Most of their campaign leaflets talked about nothing else, while those of the SNP studiously avoided mentioning it. Ironically, it was the Conservatives, who talked endlessly about the referendum, who accused the SNP of obsessing about it. The Conservative strategy worked. Although they won the largest number of Scottish seats, the SNP vote fell, and they lost twenty-one of their previous fifty-five constituencies. The Conservatives, with 13 seats, put in their best performance since the 1980s. This took the independence referendum off the table at least in the short run, as the SNP leadership conceded.

Recentralization

The Brexit slogan 'take back control' promised a return of powers from the EU back to the United Kingdom. For some, this was linked to the restoration of parliamentary sovereignty. Other Brexiteers, after the referendum, argued that it was a sovereign decision of the British people, so that even Parliament was bound by the result. This was not a strictly legal matter, and the argument in the Miller case at the Supreme Court was rather whether parliamentary law or the royal prerogative was the mechanism to give effect to the referendum. The argument for the people having the last word was, rather, based on convention and democratic principle. Whether it was to the people or to Parliament that sovereignty was being restored, the assumption was that the United Kingdom is a unitary state, with sovereignty located in one place. As previously noted, this is inconsistent with the alternative Scottish conception of the UK as a union in which sovereignty is shared. This issue has arisen in relation to two issues. The first is what the role of Scotland and other devolved units should be in negotiating Brexit. The second is what will happen to those competences that are currently shared between the EU and the devolved level.

The UK Government's line has been that Brexit is a matter of foreign affairs and thus falls within its own exclusive competence. It agreed to listen to the devolved administrations as consultees, on the same basis as other interests. This was not enough for the devolved governments in Scotland and Wales, who argued that they had a democratic mandate and broad responsibilities in relation to negotiations effecting devolved matters but also to the wider Scottish and Welsh interest. In response, the UK Government set up a Joint Ministerial Committee (European Negotiations) representing itself and the devolveds, which was intended to have a regular round of meetings and provide a devolved input. It was largely modelled on the existing Joint Ministerial Committee (Europe), which provides the devolved governments with an input to regular EU policymaking, except that in that case the devolveds have the opportunity to participate as part of the UK delegation. The Scottish and Welsh Governments complained that they were not informed of key policies and white papers in advance, that other papers were delivered late and that nothing of substance was discussed at the plenary meetings. The proposal to have regular JMC (EN) meetings to coincide with the four-week rounds of Brexit negotiations did not materialize.

Instead, the devolved governments pressed for meaningful involvement. The Welsh Government demanded a seat in the room for all negotiations and a seat at the table where Welsh devolved matters were concerned. The Scottish Government was outspoken on its lack of input to the negotiations but uncharacteristically reticent on the details of what it wanted. It is as though it was reluctant to engage in the detail of Brexit, as that would entail accepting the end. Participation in the process would also involve discretion and confidentiality, which might constrain its ability to speak out.

The 1999 Scotland Act establishing the Scottish Parliament is based on a 'reserved powers' model, according to which any power not explicitly reserved to the centre is devolved. Yet it also allows Westminster to legislate in devolved fields and unilaterally to change the allocation of powers. To deal with the resulting confusion, a convention (named the Sewel Convention after the responsible minister) was introduced, that the UK Parliament would not 'normally' legislate in devolved matters without the consent of the Scottish Parliament. In the aftermath of the Scottish independence referendum, following pledges by the unionist parties to entrench devolution, the convention that Westminster would not legislate in devolved matters without consent was incorporated into statute by the Scotland Act (2016); the Wales Act (2017) did the same in Wales. It was also understood that Sewel applied to changes to the powers of the devolved assemblies, and the convention has consistently been applied to that.

Brexit, however, puts this into question. Withdrawal from the EU requires, at the minimum, that those clauses obliging Scotland and the other devolved territories to respect EU law be repealed. Normally this would require a legislative consent motion. There was a preliminary test of this in the Miller case, which was joined by the Scottish Government to argue that triggering Article 50 would require the consent of the devolved legislatures. The UK Government and the Supreme Court could have argued against this on narrow grounds, that the matter concerned relations with the EU, which is a reserved matter, or that the situation was not 'normal'. Instead, the UK Advocate General argued, and the Court agreed, that the Sewel Convention was not binding at all. In one sense, this was telling us what we already knew: that the Sewel is not enforceable in the courts. Yet the implications are wider, since the Court was effectively saying that the convention is a mere matter of political convenience and thus not effective at all. This is to ignore the role of conventions as the basis of much of UK constitutionalism in the absence of a superior form of law. Unlike its counterpart in Canada, the Court was refusing to enter into constitutional reasoning, confining itself to the letter of the law and the doctrine of parliamentary sovereignty. So, after twenty years of a federalizing tendency, reinforced by developments after 2014, it was insisting on the fundamentally unitary nature of the UK constitution.

The issue arose again in relation to those competences that are currently shared between the EU and Scotland. The legal position is that, following Brexit, if nothing else were done, those competences would revert to the devolved legislatures as they are not reserved in UK law. On this matter, the UK Government's (2017b) position departed from the written law and invoked a more general principle that currently the devolved governments 'are responsible for implementing the common policy frameworks set by the EU' rather than making policy. So, 'when the UK leaves the EU, the powers which the EU currently exercises in relation to the common frameworks will return to the UK' (ibid.). Yet no 'decisions' currently taken by the devolved governments will be brought back to Westminster (May 2017); indeed, they might gain powers (UK Government 2017a).

This interpretation was strongly disputed by the Scottish and Welsh Governments, who insisted that these powers belonged to them as right and could not unilaterally be taken back by Westminster without violating existing understandings of devolution. As the UK Government currently has no competence in these fields, that would require an amendment to the devolution statutes in order to take back the powers, and this in turn would engage the Sewel convention. For the UK, this appears to be a matter of convenience, while for the devolved governments it is a matter of principle, revealing a big gap in understandings of the constitution. The devolved governments also argue that there is a big practical difference between policy frameworks set in Europe (after discussion among twenty-eight governments) and policy frameworks dictated by the UK central government for the devolveds.

After some months of wrangling, a consensus emerged that there will need to be some UK-wide frameworks in the absence of European ones and a linkage between the UK and devolved levels. Agricultural support and fisheries management are devolved, but international agreements in these fields are reserved. If future international trade agreements include agriculture, there will be a need for provisions on permissible levels of support and subsidy. Agreements in fisheries will include the management of stocks. There will need to be arrangements for a level playing field across the UK in industrial aid and agriculture support. Environmental policy spills over the borders of the UK nations, calling for cooperation.

The question is about what form these frameworks will take and who will be responsible for making them. At one end is the position of the Welsh Government, which has argued that devolved competences should remain devolved and that common frameworks, where necessary, should be negotiated among the four UK nations. This would be done through a UK Council of Ministers modelled on the EU Council of Ministers. Another suggestion has been that the UK would lay down broad frameworks for policy, while leaving the powers otherwise devolved. The UK Government has recently been suggesting that this would merely reproduce the existing arrangements, in which the devolved bodies are bound by EU frameworks. They implement rather than make policy and would not therefore lose powers.

The proposals in the European Union (Withdrawal) Bill were at the other end of the spectrum from the Welsh suggestion. A category of 'retained EU law' is created, and it was proposed that *all* EU such law revert to Westminster. Ministers suggested that, at a later stage, some powers may again be devolved. In order to achieve this, the Withdrawal Bill amends the devolution statutes for Scotland, Wales and Northern Ireland.

This is a development of great constitutional import as the first general rolling back of devolution since the process started twenty years ago. It triggered the Sewel Convention, and the UK Government accepted that it will seek Legislative Consent Motions. This tests the Sewel Convention to its limits. The Scottish and Welsh Governments indicated that they will not recommend consent, meaning that the motions would be voted down in the Scottish Parliament and in the National Assembly for Wales. Relying on the Supreme Court judgement in Miller and the wider doctrine of parliamentary sovereignty, the UK Parliament could simply ignore this.

Differentiation

The UK devolution settlement is highly asymmetrical. Scotland has led the way on legislative powers, with Wales catching up in stages. The Northern Ireland process has its own dynamics, while in England there is no legislative devolution at all. One way of resolving the Brexit issue could potentially be to allow the individual nations of the UK to find their own accommodation with Europe. This would represent a deepening of devolution and its extension to the external domain, a radical change in the design and workings of the state. There is broad agreement that something will have to be done about Northern Ireland's border and its overall relationship with the Irish Republic in order to secure the gains of the peace settlement, but the Democratic Unionist Party insists that this must not entail a differentiated settlement. So far, nobody has been able to square that circle.

In the case of Scotland, there has been one proposal. In December 2016, the Scottish Government (2016) published *Scotland's Place in Europe*. This listed a set of options in order of priority. The first was for the whole of the UK to remain in the EU, an outcome effectively ruled out by the referendum vote. The second was for the UK to remain in the Single Market and Customs Union, also ruled out by the UK Government's interpretation of the vote. The third was a differentiated settlement for Scotland. The last resort was a new independence referendum, allowing Scotland to join the EU as a member state.

The differentiated option would allow Scotland to remain in the Single Market even if the rest of the UK departed. It would give Scotland a status analogous to that of the European Economic Area (EEA); indeed, Scotland might formally become part of the EEA. As with the EEA, agriculture and fisheries would be excluded. If the UK were to leave the EU Customs Union (as it has declared it will), Scotland would also leave, remaining in a customs union with the UK.

This would allow it to avoid tariffs and rules of origin on trade in goods between Scotland and the rest of the UK and thus obviate the need for a physical border. There would be full access to the Single Market in services and provision for the free movement of workers between Scotland and the EU27. Scotland would participate in European social provisions, in academic exchange and research and in aspects of EU Justice and Home Affairs policies.

These proposals are legally and technically feasible, although they do pose challenges. Being in a customs union with the UK and in the Single Market with the EU could be complex. Retaining a customs union with the UK could remove the need for physical checks on goods traded between Scotland and England. There would, however, need to be rules governing the treatment of goods entering the UK from EU countries, depending on whether they were destined for Scotland or for England and Wales (we leave Northern Ireland aside here as it too might have a differentiated settlement). The Scottish Government concedes that there would have to be certification as to the final point of sale of such goods. There would also have to be rules of origin if intermediate goods were passing through England and Wales en route for Scotland.

There would be a virtual border in services to the degree that EU and UK rules diverged after Brexit. This could be avoided by double compliance rules to ensure that Scottish services were compliant with both UK and EU regulations.

Free movement of workers between Scotland and the EU would require controls to ensure that EU workers did not come into Scotland in order to cross the border to work in England. This is not an insuperable problem since a similar mechanism operates in the Schengen area for third country nationals with the right to work in one member state but not in another. It would be monitored at the place of work rather than at the border. There would also have to be provisions to define a Scottish worker for the purposes of rights to work in member states of the EEA.

In order for Scotland to remain compliant with Single Market regulations, the Scottish Parliament and Government would require new competences across a wide range of Single Market matters that are currently reserved to Westminster. Brexit would thus result in a radical decentralization of the United Kingdom.

The Scottish Government conceded that it could not propose anything directly to the EU so that its proposals could advance only if the UK Government incorporated them into its own negotiating position. In the event, it refused to entertain any territorial differentiation on Brexit.

A rather different line has been taken by some politicians and observers who argue that Brexit might provide an opportunity for Scotland to a gain new powers as competences transferred from the EU are brought home and perhaps supplemented by others. Brexiteers within the SNP see this as a medium-term strategy to avoid a premature independence referendum, which they could lose. From a very different perspective, Gallagher (2017) has argued that more powers could strengthen devolution and allow Scotland to follow EU policy lines where it chose on various issues. The UK Government's position, however, does not seem to envisage anything like that.

Stands Scotland where it did?

Immediately after the 2016 referendum, it appeared that Scotland was headed for a new status as an independent country within the European Union. That option is still open. To the extent that the UK achieves a soft Brexit, the Scottish grievance may be allayed, but the opportunity for independence will be enhanced. At the limit, a UK remaining in the Single Market and Customs Union would reinstate the original independence-in-Europe argument by providing a market framework for secession. The result of the 2017 general election represented a setback for this strategy, but it might return.

Developments in 2017, however, pointed to recentralization as the consequence of Brexit. The Supreme Court (2017) judgement in Miller may not have created anything new by way of law but did affirm that devolution is, at root, little more than the delegation of power, which can be revoked unilaterally at any time. The proposals in the Withdrawal Bill to take back competences to Westminster betrayed a centralizing tendency and a denial of the federalizing implications of Brexit. On the other hand, it succeeded in uniting the Scottish Government (controlled by the SNP) and the Welsh Government (controlled by Labour) in opposition, while even the Scottish Conservatives expressed their unease.

Differentiation has made little progress, as the UK Government is simply not interested. Even when there is a broad consensus in Scotland and few technical obstacles, as on migration and freedom of movement, the UK has been adamant.

The devolution settlement of 1999 was based upon an act of the Westminster Parliament, underpinned by a series of conventions, which appeared gradually to entrench the position of the Scottish Parliament within the constitution, and on a series of abeyances that kept difficult questions of sovereignty off the political agenda. These survived the test of an independence referendum in 2014, which avoided any breach of constitutional order. They may not, however, be strong enough to survive the test of Brexit. Without common membership of the EU and involvement in the European project more broadly, England and Scotland may be pulled into different geopolitical and economic orbits, while the Westminster Government struggles to reimpose a unitary order.

References

ABC News (2017) Spain Makes Clear Position on Gibraltar's Post-Brexit Future. *The Associated Press*, April 2. Available at: http://abcnews.go.com/amp/Politics/wireStory/uk-leader-reassure-gibraltar-brexit-process-46523210 [Accessed December 15, 2017].

Gallagher, J. (2017) Scotland and Brexit: The Last Thing Nicola Sturgeon Wants Is Indyref2. *Blogs LSE*, January 3. Available at: http://blogs.lse.ac.uk/brexit/2017/01/03/scotland-and-brexit-the-last-thing-nicola-sturgeon-wants-is-indyref2/ [Accessed January 20, 2018].

Keating, M. (2001) *Plurinational Democracy: Stateless Nations in a Post-Sovereignty Era*. Oxford: Oxford University Press.

Keating, M. (2017) The European Question. In: Keating, M. (ed.), *Debating Scotland: Issues of Independence and Union in the 2014 Referendum*. Oxford: Oxford University Press.

Keating, M. and McEwen, N. (2017) The Scottish Independence Debate. In: Keating, M. (ed.), *Debating Scotland: Issues of Independence and Union in the 2014 Referendum*. Oxford: Oxford University Press.

Liñeira, R., Henderson, A. and Daleney, L. (2017) Voters' Response to the Campaign. In: Keating, M. (ed.), *Debating Scotland: Issues of Independence and Union in the 2014 Referendum*. Oxford: Oxford University Press.

MacCormick, N. (1999) *Questioning Sovereignty: Law, State and Nation in the European Commonwealth*. Oxford: Oxford University Press.

Major, J. (1992) Foreword by the Prime Minister. In: Secretary of State for Scotland, *Scotland and the Union*. Edinburgh: HMSO.

May, T. (2017) *A Global Britain*. Speech by Prime Minister Rt Hon Theresa May MP. Lancaster House, January 17.

Prosser, C. and Fieldhouse, E. (2017) *A Tale of Two Referendums: The 2017 Election in Scotland*. British Election Study. Available at: www.britishelectionstudy.com/bes-findings/a-tale-of-two-referendums-the-2017-election-in-scotland/#.WeoCaDb9O7M [Accessed December 15, 2017].

Scottish Government (2016) *Scotland's Place in Europe*. Edinburgh: Scottish Government.

Thatcher, M. (1993) *The Downing Street Years*. London: HarperCollins.

UK Government (2017a) *European Union (Withdrawal) Bill*. London: UK Government.

UK Government (2017b) *Legislating for the United Kingdom's Withdrawal from the European Union*. London: UK Government.

UK Supreme Court (2017) *Judgment on the Application of Miller and Another) (Respondents) v Secretary of State for Exiting the European Union (Appellant)*. London: UK Supreme Court.

5

BREXIT AND THE CITY OF LONDON

The revenge of the ultraliberals?

Leila Simona Talani

Introduction

On 23 June 2016, British citizens finally voted for Brexit, opening new questions about what model will British capitalism be following in the future. The discussion about the nature of British capitalism is a long-standing one and revolves around the notion of British "exceptionalism" (see Chapter 11).

The economic, political and social domination of the City of London over any other British socio-economic actors has traditionally been at the core of the debate about "British exceptionalism". Starting from a definition of the City as the locus of merchant or commercial practices, scholars (Nairn 1977; Longstreth 1979; Anderson 1964, 1966, 1968; Talani 2012) have pointed out how these activities guarantee the prosperity of the City itself as separated from the performance of British economy as a whole. In particular, the success of the City has always been detached from the risks associated with the involvement in productive enterprises, thanks to the "short-termism" stemming from its mainly commercial nature. Finally, the enduring hegemony of the City of London in the history of British capitalism cannot be separated from its peculiar ties with the Treasury and the Bank of England, often considered at the roots of its "pragmatic adaptation" (Longstreth 1979).

This chapter will explore how this "pragmatic adaptation", relying on the friendly regulatory and economic policies enacted by the British Government, will help the City of London adapt to the challenges of globalisation and the changing nature of British relation with the EU.

The main argument is that "pragmatic adaptation", as favoured by the British institutional establishment, has been since long the secret of the City's ability to maintain its hegemonic position, both domestically and globally. This is, for example, clear when looking at the way in which the City has been able not only to survive, but also to strengthen its position after the Global Financial Crisis. Moreover, any policy of deregulation and liberalisation following from globalisation, as analysed in the section on "Globalisation and the Future of the City of London", is likely to enhance the success of the City. But is Brexit going to limit the integration of the City in the global political economy? Or, on the contrary, will it trigger ultraliberal policies that will further consolidate its power?

To answer these questions, the chapter is structured in four parts: "What is pragmatic adaptation?", "Pragmatic Adaptation and the Success of the City of London after the Global

Financial Crisis", "Globalisation and the Future of the City of London", and "Brexit and the City: the revenge of the ultraliberals?".

In the first section, the theoretical foundations of the notion of pragmatic adaptation are explored and discussed with reference to the relevant literature. In the second part, the success of the City of London during and after the Global Financial Crisis is analysed with reference to the notion of pragmatic adaptation. The third section will explore the challenges and opportunities that globalisation poses to the City of London. In the final section, the author discusses how the City of London is likely to use pragmatic adaptation to respond to the challenges of Brexit and how this will affect the British economic structure, especially in the case of an "hard" Brexit.

What is "pragmatic adaptation"?

The notion of "pragmatic adaptation" is interconnected with the long-lasting debate about the nature of British capitalism and the "exceptionalism" of its development.

In the most widely accepted explanation, exceptionalism coincides with British traditionalism. As such, any aristocratic, pre-industrial elements still evident in British polity are seen as only symbolic and legitimatory in meaning and do not correspond to any effective divisions within the British capitalist class (Stanworth and Giddens 1974: 100).

However, there is also an alternative, more controversial interpretation of these notions; an interpretation rooted in Anderson's and Nairn's seminal works on the subject.[1] According to this interpretation, traditionalism is still at the core of modern British ideology, not only symbolically but also as directly impacting the structure and performance of the British economy, as it is based on the hegemony of those fractions of British capitalism that recognize it as their ideological point of reference. According to Anderson (1964, 1966, 1968, 1987), the exceptionalism of British society is represented by the dual nature of British capitalism, that is, the separateness of the financial fraction of capital and the industrial one and the dominance of the former over the latter. This is reflected in the persistence of aristocratic, pre-industrial forms in the organization of the civil and political society, as the British financial and banking elite is recognized as the carrier of feudal, aristocratic cultural and social values.

On the other hand, the British capitalist structure is also characterised by the existence of a hegemonic position of the capitalist bloc as a whole, as opposed to the non-hegemonic though self-conscious bloc of the working class. Here the concept of hegemony is defined in Gramscian terms as the "dominance of one social bloc over another, not simply by means of force or wealth, but by a total social authority whose ultimate sanction and expression is a profound cultural supremacy" (Anderson 1964: 39).

Thus, according to this interpretation, the present equilibrium in England remains a capitalist one but within the capitalist class itself, one economic and consequently social component is hegemonic. This component is the financial sector, or, in other words, the City of London. The City is not only a dominant economic and social actor but, together with its political referents (the Treasury and the Bank of England), is deemed responsible for the British economic decline from the second half of the nineteenth century onward. Indeed, within this conceptualization, the crisis of British industry is explained as the logical outcome of a long subordination of the needs of productive capital to the economic interests and preferences of the City of London (Longstreth 1979).

The main criticisms of this interpretation are based on two points: first, the definition of the City and consequently of the nature of the relations between the City and the industry; second, the City–State connections.

The most important problem concerns the conceptualization of the City and the identification of the specific relationship between the British financial sector and the industry as historically developed. For many authors interested in the subject (Aaronvitch 1961; Overbeek 1980), the City is simply the centre of British finance capital, that is, in the Marxist definition, the direct involvement of banking capital in the means by which surplus value is created. A number of objections are raised by other scholars against this conceptualization of the City (Ingham 1984; Strange 1971), and an alternative definition has been proposed, which puts much more emphasis on a clear identification of the City's economic activities.

Whereas many of the City's activities are "financial" in a broader sense as they make money capital available to the productive sector by means of the markets, they mainly comprise commercial practices. Thus, the role of the City's firms as intermediaries in the provision of finance indistinctly to domestic or international players should be understood as that of a commercial entrepôt, giving rise to services income (Longstreth 1979).

Consequently, the City should not be simply defined as the locus of British finance capital or in terms of the identification of its constituent companies. It should instead be conceptualized as the institutional structure of short-term exchanges in commodities, securities, money and services. This definition allows, on one hand, to link the apparently unrelated activities of investment banking, foreign exchange dealing, securities dealings and more and, on the other hand, to account for the City's uniqueness in the world. British exceptionalism is thus ontologically connected to the exceptionalism of the "City of London" (ibid.; Ingham 1984, 1988, 2002).

This leads to the second point related to the conceptualization of the City of London: its continued hegemony in the twentieth century despite its own economic difficulties, the decline of Britain as an economic power and the related dismissal of sterling as a leading international currency. How was this possible? Longstreth (1979) convincingly identifies the capacity of the City of London to constantly adapt to new situations as one of the keys to account for its enduring success.

By defining the City of London through the commercial practices and exchanges that take place within, it is possible to understand more clearly why its survival and success have always relied on its "pragmatic adaptation" strategy. Indeed, it is far easier to quickly adapt to changing economic circumstances if your activities are mainly commercial in nature than if you have engaged in long-term productive investment. This, in turn, needs a level of flexibility and direct control of the levers of economic policymaking and regulation that could be guaranteed only by a very close relationship with some key state institutions: the Bank of England and the Treasury (ibid.).

In conclusion, the main element of British exceptionalism is given not so much by the persistence of a traditional, pre-modern polity, as is the case in Britain, but by the fact that this polity is economically, politically and socially dominated by the City and its social and political allies. Moreover, the City is characterized, or defined, not as the centre of the "finance capital" but as the locus of merchant or commercial practices, ranging from insurance to brokerage activities, from trading in secondary markets to providing professional services. These activities, while on one side limit to a great extent the expansion of British productive sector, on the other side guarantee the prosperity of the City itself as separated from the performance of British economy as a whole, in particular from the risks associated with the involvement in any productive enterprises (so called "short-termism"). Finally, the explanation of British exceptionalism cannot be related only to the establishment, defence and exploitation of the Empire but is also determined by the interactions and dialect relations between the City, the Treasury and the Bank of England, which have guaranteed, over the course of the centuries, its "pragmatic adaptation".

In the next section, we will explore how this "pragmatic adaptation", relying on the friendly regulatory and economic policies enacted by the British Government, has helped the City's revival and ultimate success in the period after the Global Financial Crisis. This will help in understanding how the City has already been able to emerge victorious from an extremely serious crisis, created within the same financial sector, thanks to the proactive role played by the British institutional system.

Pragmatic adaptation and the success of the City of London after the Global Financial Crisis

Within the context of "pragmatic adaptation", this section reviews British economic policymaking during and after the Global Financial Crisis to verify to what extent the City's special relation with the Bank of England and the Treasury confirmed and enhanced the hegemonic position of the City of London within the British capitalist structure, as well as globally.

This section will try to assess whether the financial crisis that hit the global economy unexpectedly in August 2007, producing consequences comparable to the ones experienced in the 1930s, has put under discussion the hegemonic position of the City of London in the domestic and international context.

It is not here the place to address the theories relating to the causes and consequences of the Global Financial Crisis (Talani 2010). It is worth noting, however, that the crisis, although originating from the U.S. housing and mortgaging markets, found very fertile ground in the uncontrolled possibility of the financial markets to develop and sell new financial instruments that allowed the banking sector to greatly expand their capacity to extend loans and provide mortgages even to the least solvent clients. Therefore, the idea that finance was doomed after the crisis was very widespread (Bishop 2009).

In the UK in particular, it was felt that the financial sector could not be the main specialization of Britain any longer; the country will have to find a new one. Many British analysts, in the immediate aftermath of the Global Financial Crisis insisted on the changes that the Crisis would have not only on the British economic strategy but more importantly on the structure of the British economy itself. It seemed almost inevitable that the role of the financial sector would decline, although it did not clearly emerge what would take its place. Further, the centrality of the City of London as the "European" financial capital or as a global financial power was felt to have been put in danger by the crisis (ibid.).

But what was the actual impact of the crisis on the City of London? Lord Adair Turner, the Financial Service Authority chairman, during the tragic week of October 2008 told *The Guardian* that "the days of soft-touch regulation were over, warning the City that higher-paid regulators would ask tougher questions in the wake of the credit crisis".[2] However, by now it is clear that the consequences of the crisis have been felt mainly by the workers of the British and the global financial sector. The International Labour Organization (ILO) estimates total announced layoffs of 325,000 between August 2007 and February 2009 (International Labour Organization 2009: 14). This figure underestimates the real number of jobs lost given that not all institutions announced their employment decisions in advance; in addition, it does not include independent mortgage brokers, other independent contractors or the myriad of small financial firms that were likely to disappear as a consequence of the crisis.

Furthermore, it seems clear that the loss of jobs experienced by the City of London parallels similar layoffs in all the other major financial centres. This means that the position of the City of London as one of the most important global financial players does not seem to have been put under discussion. Moreover, much of the restructuring that led to the rationalization of the workforce, including some nationalizations, was the result of consolidations based on mergers and acquisitions that actually enhanced the overall importance of the financial sector globally and within the UK (Talani 2010). Indeed, there is no evidence that the City of London lost its market share and leadership in the European financial sector.

To prove this point, it is enough to look at the data. In 2014, seven years after the start of the crisis, the City was still contending the primacy of financial markets and activities only with New York (Table 5.1). Moreover, the outlook for many of those markets and activities had

Table 5.1 Financial markets share by country (%)

	UK	US	Japan	France	Germany	Singapore	Hong Kong	Others
Cross–border bank lending (Sept. 2014)	17	11	11	8	8	3	4	38
Foreign Exchange Turnover (Apr. 2013)	**41**	19	6	3	2	6	4	19
Exchange–traded derivatives, number of contracts traded 2014	6	**36**	2	–	10	–	1	45
Interest rate OTC derivatives turnover (Apr. 2013)	**49**	23	2	7	4	1	1	13
Marine insurance net premium income	**26**	5	7	4	4	1	1	53
Fund management (as a source of funds, end 2013)	8	**46**	7	3	2	–	1	33
Hedge funds assets, (end 2013)	18	**65**	2	1	–	1	1	12
Private–equity investment value (2013)	13	**53**	2	5	2	1	–	24

Bold: Market leader

Source: TheCityUK calculations and estimates

actually improved after 2008. This was the case, for example, for the foreign exchange turnover, for OTC derivatives turnover, for marine insurance and premium income and for private equity investment (Table 5.2).

Moreover, the City was actually able to cash in on the Global Financial Crisis. For example, unstable exchange rates may and do actually represent a substantial source of revenue for the City of London. Indeed, the volume of foreign exchange trading surged to record levels at the outset of the credit crisis. Rate cutting from central banks and high volatility in exchange rates (increasing by more than 50 per cent in the dollar/pound exchange rate market in 2009 with respect to 1 September 2007) caused a flight from emerging market currencies to "safe-haven" currencies such as the US dollar (Investment Fund Services Limited 2009).

Global bank revenues from foreign exchange trading benefited from relatively strong trading volumes since the start of the credit crisis and from higher commissions that resulted from a widening of foreign exchange trading spreads. The UK was the main geographic centre for foreign exchange trading with nearly 36 per cent of the global total in April 2009. Average daily turnover on the UK's foreign exchange market totalled $1,269 billion in April 2009, with a further $81 billion traded in currency derivatives (ibid.).

Overall, the City not only survived the blow, but it could be argued that it turned it at its advantage. What was the role of the British institutional system in allowing this to happen? How did "pragmatic adaptation" take place in these rather difficult circumstances for the financial sector?

It is impossible in this context not to notice that, without the intervention of the PM of the day, Mr Gordon Brown, the City would have had a much tougher time escaping the consequences of its own behaviour. In reality, his role was pivotal in addressing the crisis not only at the domestic but also at the global level, as the following account of the events at the peak of it shows.

Table 5.2 UK share of financial markets (%)

	1992	1995	1998	2001	2004	2007	2010	2012	2013	2014
Cross-border bank lending	16	17	20	19	20	18	18	18	17	17
Foreign exchange turnover	27	30	33	31	32	35	37	–	41*	–
Exchange traded derivatives	12	12	11	7	7	6	6	7	6	6
Interest rate OTC derivatives turnover	–	27	36	35	42	44	46	–	49*	–
Marine insurance net premium income	24	21	14	18	19	17	20	22	26	–
Fund management (as a source of funds)	–	–	8	8	8	9	8	8	8	–
Hedge funds assets	–	–	–	9	20	20	19	18	18	–
Private equity investments	–	–	–	6	13	7	17	10	13	–

Source: TheCityUK calculations and estimates

*April 2013

On 4 October 2008, Brown attends an emergency summit in Paris to discuss the crisis with his French, German and Italian counterparts. On 7 October, the Icelandic Internet bank Icesave blocks savers from withdrawing money, and the following day Icesave accounts are declared in default. This move triggers the Financial Services Compensation Scheme to return 100 per cent of savers' money. The same day, the British Treasury announces what amounted to a £500 billion bank rescue package to stop the country's financial system from melting down. Most bank shares fall again. At 12 p.m., the Bank of England, the US Federal Reserve and the European Central Bank all cut half a point off their key interest rates in the first unscheduled rate moves since the aftermath of 9/11. At first, stock markets calm after the turmoil.[3] The FTSE 100 jumps 61 points by midday. Banks continue to recover following the UK government's £500 billion rescue plan announced the previous day. However, the London market fails to hold on to early gains. With Wall Street in decline yet again on the 10th, the FTSE 100 closes 8.85 per cent lower at 3932.1 – a 381.7-point fall, destroying about £89.5 billion of the value of Britain's biggest companies. This is the worst daily fall since the crash of 1987. On 11 October, Alistair Darling, the then chancellor of the Exchequer, attends meetings in Washington with the G7 finance ministers and the International Monetary Fund (IMF). The G7 comes up with a five-point plan, which includes spending billions of taxpayers' money to rebuild the global banking system and reopen the flow of credit.[4]

On the 12th, Gordon Brown travels to Paris where European officials are desperate to prevent a continent-wide meltdown of the banking sector. He succeeds in persuading the EU's core countries to adopt a plan along the lines of his £500 billion banking system bail-out.[5] On the 13th, the 15 members of the Eurozone, led by Germany and France, unveil large, coordinated plans along British lines to provide their banks with capital funding. In the meantime, the British Government announces it will put £37 billion of emergency recapitalisation into the Royal Bank of Scotland, HBOS and Lloyds TSB. In a move that, according to the newspapers of the time "fundamentally changes the nature of banking",[6] Gordon Brown announces that the Government was left with the only choice to nationalize, that is, take a majority shareholding of both the Royal Bank of Scotland (RBS) and Halifax Bank of Scotland (HBOS), fearing that they would collapse otherwise. Lloyds TSB is also bailed out with taxpayer money in exchange for shares, while Barclays manages to avoid state intervention by raising about £7 billion. Overall, more than £50 billion of taxpayers' money are invested in banks in return for shares in the heat of the crisis. Thus, the government, which had already nationalized Northern Rock and Bradford & Bingley, is able to keep four of the country's biggest lenders under its control.[7] The prospect of governments pumping vast sums into banks on both sides of the Atlantic is welcomed by financial markets.[8]

Concluding, it seems that the Treasury decision to pump an enormous amount of public money into the global financial markets saved the day for the City of London, thus confirming the City–State nexus and shifting the burden of the crisis to the middle classes and lower strata of society through the ensuing austerity. Incidentally, precisely the imposition of austerity has been recognized by many as the root of the decision of the UK to leave the EU in 2016, thus directly connecting "pragmatic adaptation" with Brexit (Callinicos 2016; Anderson 2017).

There is, however, the possibility that things can get worse for London as a financial centre. A threat that the circumstances that have allowed London to thrive in the last few decades may be put under discussion through a radical tightening of financial service regulation. The success of the City of London has always been determined by its ability to adapt to the changing environment. Therefore, in the absence of regulatory constraints, its markets and institutions will certainly be able to react to any changing situation. However, it is precisely this capacity to change quickly and react to the changing global environment that could be put under discussion by adopting strict financial markets and banking sector regulation, possibly by the EU.

Will this happen?

The need for global economic governance of the banking and financial sector has been advocated in a number of international forums. In the United States, the Obama administration scored an unexpected victory in favour of more regulation with the passing of the Dodd–Frank Wall Street Reform and Consumer Protection Act in July 2010. At the European level, the partial creation of the European Banking Union and the adoption of the single rulebook for all financial actors of the EU could represent a threat for the future regulatory autonomy of the British banking and financial sector.

However, in the new British regulatory environment, following the events of October 2008, controls are still in the hands of the Bank of England especially after the Chancellor of the Exchequer of the coalition Government announced the abolition of the Financial Services Authority (FSA). Thus, the new system retains the in-house structure of control for the City of London and banking supervision. So which are the challenges that the City of London will have to face in the future? Will Globalisation affect the primacy of the British financial sector both internally and externally?

This is the subject of the following section.

Globalisation and the future of the City of London

Globalisation is one of the most hotly debated topics within the social sciences and certainly one that has captured our imagination when looking toward the future. Globalisation is not only the present but also the future of politics and economics, and no discussion regarding future scenarios can avoid addressing it.

How will globalisation affect the future of the City of London? Will financial globalisation signal the end of the City's hegemony, or will it guarantee its future success?

Questions related to how globalisation affects domestic actors cannot be disentangled from a more general and in-depth analysis of globalisation and its definitions.

The notion of globalisation is not without controversy both within the academic debate and in the wider public discourse. Despite the great success of this concept in recent decades, there is still some degree of confusion about its definition, and the discussion is still open about precisely how globalisation modifies the capacity of the state to intervene in the domestic and global economies (Busch 2008: 5).

However, it is possible to classify positions adopted by scholars into three broad groups, alongside the three traditional approaches to international relations/international political economy (IR/IPE) (Dicken 1999: 5): First, those who deny outright the very existence of the phenomenon of globalisation (Hirst and Thompson 1999a, 1999b; Thompson 1993); second, those who recognize it but tend to give only a quantitative definition of globalisation (Held and McGrew 2000; Holm and Sørensen 1995: 3); third, those who adopt a qualitative definition (Mittleman 2000; Hay and Marsh 2000; Dicken 1999, 2003).

In this section, we shall deal with each of these approaches to the definition of globalisation and their consequences for the future of the City of London both inside and outside the EU.

Let us start from a classical quantitative view of financial globalisation. This has been well summarized by Cohen:

> Financial globalisation (or internationalization) refers to the broad integration of national markets associated with both innovation and deregulation in the postwar era and is manifested by increasing movements of capital across national frontiers. The more alternative assets are closely regarded as substitutes for one another, the higher the degree of capital mobility.
>
> *(Cohen 1996: 269)*

Adopting this definition, capital mobility becomes the constituent element of financial globalisation (Obstfeld and Taylor 2004). In macroeconomic terms, the problem is called the "inconsistent quartet" (Padoa-Schioppa 1994), the "unholy trinity" (Cohen 1996) or the "trilemma" (Obstfeld and Taylor 2004: 29) and posits that in an economic environment characterized by free capital movement, national monetary autonomy becomes an alternative to keeping stable exchange rates. The case rests on the argument that complete capital liberalisation (as implied by the quantitative definition of financial globalisation) and exchange rate stability (as necessary, in theory, for international trade to continue unhindered) are incompatible with divergent national monetary policies.

Although in macroeconomic terms this argument is certainly sound (or, at the least, I am not in a position to criticize it), the British case is relevant in highlighting how financial globalisation did not particularly decrease the power of the City of London as defined here. The main point is that in the trade-off between the stability of exchange rates and autonomous monetary policy, some domestic actors (notably the City of London) might still prefer the latter, as they have demonstrated in their position toward joining the Euro area (Talani 2010). This happens for some concurring reasons.

Some sectors, like financial services, though perfectly integrated at the regional level might still prefer to keep autonomous monetary policy decision-making at the national level. In particular, setting the interest rates at a higher level than other financial centres represents a relevant competitive advantage in attracting short- and very short-term capital. This, of course, is harmful for industrial activity. However, here the issue becomes one of power relations between domestic economic sectors or interest groups. In the context of globalisation, the issue is also influenced by the extent to which the industrial sector is actually relying on domestic production as opposed to production abroad (Dicken 2003).

To conclude the discussion of how the British financial sector will gain from globali-sation at the macro level, it is not unlikely that London will be on the winning side of speculative practices (Guth 1994; Lilley 2000). Following is just one example. In 2008, the FSA was compelled to pass emergency rules banning the short-selling[9] of UK bank shares in the City of London after the practice brought the HBOS share price to a collapse.[10] Well known City operators are believed to have profited from short-selling sub-prime mortgages and betting against HBOS.[11] Hedge funds in the City of London are said to have made at least £1 billion in profits by shorting HBOS shares in June and July 2008, fuelled by City rumours that the bank was in financial distress. At one point in June of that year, a single fund, Harbinger Capital, traded more than 3 per cent of all HBOS shares. Harbinger was run by Philip Falcone, a former Barclays trader who earned £1.7 billion in 2007 alone.[12]

It is, however, at the micro level (i.e. at the level of sectoral and domestic interest group anal-ysis) that we see how the City of London can gain from globalisation.

As Cohen correctly states, "owners of mobile capital thus gain influence at the expense of less fortunate sectors including so-called national capital as well as labor" (Cohen 1996: 286).

How does this happen? To answer this question, it is necessary to adopt a domestic politics (or inside-out) approach to the international political economy.

Assuming that globalisation is defined in quantitative terms as "growing global trade and financial flows" (Frieden and Rogowski 1996: 26), by applying the Heckscher–Ohlin/Stolper–Samuelson approach, it is possible to derive some interesting propositions about the distributional consequences of globalisation. This would imply a rise in the domestic prices of goods whose production is intensive in the given country's abundant factors and a fall in the prices of those goods intensive in scarce factors. In this context, globalisation would benefit the owners of abundant factors and disadvantage those who own scarce factors (ibid.: 37). Therefore, as developed countries are characterized by an abundance of capital and a shortage of unskilled labour, globalisation favours capitalists and skilled labour while unskilled labour is at a disadvantage (ibid.: 40). This is relevant for our domestic politics analysis of who wins and who loses from globalisation as the City of London is composed exclusively of capital and skilled labour and has everything to gain from liberalisation from this perspective.

There are, however, two further dimensions that strengthen the argument that the City of London is certainly on the winning side of globalisation. First, we must consider that, on the basis of this analysis, the power of an interest group to assert its preferences is directly related to its capacity to move, which in turn depends on the mobility of its factor. If an interest group is able to credibly threaten leaving the country, its bargaining power increases. Therefore, globalisation reduces the capacity of the government to disregard the preferences of the most mobile factor, which is capital – and financial capital in particular – and increases the negotiation and political power of the owners of such capital: to wit, the City of London (Keohane and Milner 1996: 19; Busch 2008: 8).

Moreover, adopting a sectoral rather than a factorial type of analysis through the application of the specific factors approach (also known as Ricardo–Viner), the result is even more clearly supportive of the view that the British banking sector has everything to gain from globalisation (Frieden and Rogowski 1996: 38).

This perspective suggests that factors like land, labour or capital are normally used for a specific activity or production, and therefore only price changes in their specific activity or pro-duction (not in all of the uses of the factors) will affect them. To apply it to the case of the UK, if capital is used specifically for banking and financial transactions when the terms of trade in banking change, only the banking sector will gain, not all capital. Overall, the application of the Ricardo–Viner variant implies:

> That the benefits of globalisation will vary with the specificity of the relevant actors' assets.
> That the most competitive sectors will gain more.
> That political pressure will happen at the sectoral rather than at the factorial level.

There is no doubt that financial capital is an abundant factor in the UK. Therefore, to the extent to which the City remains competitive internationally, a high degree of openness is guaranteed, and no unwanted regulation is imposed, it will improve its position not only with respect to labour but also, more importantly given the approach adopted here, with respect to industrial capital.

Let us now address the question from the perspective of a qualitative definition of globalisation. Technological change is at the core of the qualitative definition of globalisation, bringing about changes in the productive and financial spheres (Dicken 2003: 85).

It is technology, therefore, that produces financial globalisation, defined here as the existence of around-the-clock access to financial transactions all over the world (ibid.: 443).

Susan Strange identified the three most important technological changes that have produced financial globalisation: computers, chips and satellites:

> Computers have made money electronic . . . by the mid-1990s computers had not only transformed the physical form in which money worked as a medium of exchange, they were also in the process of transforming the systems by which payments of money were exchanged and recorded.
>
> *(Strange 1998: 24)*

Chips (microprocessors) have allowed for the credit card revolution and the "smart card" revolution as well (Cohen 2001). Finally, satellites are the basis of global electronic communication (Dicken 2003: 85–120).

It is impossible not to understand the implications on financial services in terms of increase in productivity, of patterns of relationships and linkages between financial firms and clients and within the financial community, and of velocity and turnover of investment capital and capacity to react to international events immediately (ibid.: 443).

Even more importantly, the competitive advantage has now moved to the technological infrastructure. Even the technological superiority of cable infrastructure could represent a substantial competitive advantage making physical location actually much more relevant in the globalisation era. Indeed, a study by the European Central Bank concluded that the undersea cables are a critical factor in determining the competitive strength of financial centres, especially the City of London.[13]

As a consequence, there is now consensus in the literature that financial globalisation has "made geography more, not less, important" (ibid.: 59; Coleman 1996: 7).

On the one hand, some financial products contain information that is the result of long, well established business relationships, and this remains the case with financial globalisation. Equities, domestic bonds and bank loans have indeed a large amount of embedded domestic information (Coleman 1996: 7).

Thus, despite the significant emphasis on financial globalisation, the location of global financial power has remained surprisingly unchanged and concentrated in a handful of urban centres, namely New York, London and, to a more limited extent, Tokyo. This concentration is unparalleled in any other kind of industry, and it is also extremely stable (Dicken 2003: 462).

In fact, London is the more broadly based financial centre, and its position does not seem to have changed in the last decade – the decade of globalisation. If anything, with respect to many of its main markets and services, its position has improved. If globalisation is clearly benefitting the British financial sector, how likely is this to be put under discussion by Brexit? This is a question we will try to address in the next section.

Brexit and the City: the revenge of the ultraliberals?

There is the possibility, that, if openness is reduced, as, for example, by closing the European Single Market to the UK as a consequence of a Brexit, all the advantages of globalisation for the City of London could be offset.

This might explain why, at the onset, the City of London was against Brexit. Indeed, the City of London Corporation has openly supported Britain remaining in the EU.

A survey of 147 UK-based financial services firms found 40 per cent chose the UK over other centres because of access to the EU. Eighty-one per cent of 98 fintech start-up businesses, published by Innovate Finance, voted to stay in the EU, this was comparable to the survey conducted by Tech London Advocates in 2015.[14]

Not a single financial trade association has been favourable to Brexit in the debate leading to the 2016 referendum, and the representatives of major City institutions such as Lloyds of London, the London Stock Exchange, Aviva, Goldman Sachs, HSBC, Barclays, Prudential, RSA, Standard Life and Santander have all expressed their institutions' wish that Britain would decide to remain in the EU.

The reasons were initially very clear. If the UK stays in the Single Market, the institutions based in the City have a passport to operate everywhere else in the EU without the need to have separate businesses in other countries, with all that this means in terms of different authorisation processes, regulation as well as staffing costs.[15]

However, as a hard Brexit, that is, an exit not only from the EU but also from the Single Market, becomes more likely, it seems that the City's institutions have adapted themselves to the changing situation through their traditional "pragmatic adaptation". This will take the form of moving all EU services to other EU member states with the aim of keeping their passporting rights. As in the case of the announcement made by Deutsche Bank in March 2017, if Britain were to leave the Single Market, thus losing passporting rights granted to EU members, banks will probably have to turn their London branches into subsidiaries, which would require capital, and move their EU booking hub to an EU financial centre.[16]

Frankfurt could emerge as a winner in a similar race, with Standard Chartered, Nomura, Sumitomo Mitsui and Daiwa Securities picking the city as their EU hub in the year after the Brexit vote, while Citigroup, Goldman Sachs and Morgan Stanley were considering the same location.

However, as Bill Blain, a strategist at Mint Partners in London, says: "They can move as many trading and investment assets to Frankfurt as they want, but the gravitational centre of the European financial universe will remain in London for some time – whatever Brexit we get."[17]

Also Irish authorities claim they achieved deals with more than a dozen London-based banks and finance houses to move some of their operations to Dublin in preparation for Brexit, with US bank JP Morgan buying a landmark office building in Dublin and Bank of America Merrill Lynch, which already has a presence in Dublin, speaking of expanding in the city.[18]

Still, one year after the referendum, experts, such as Mr Kieran Donoghue, head of international financial services at Ireland's Industrial Development Authority, were convinced that the mass exodus from London that was once feared is unlikely to materialise.[19]

In his words: "This is a sensitive event for the financial services, they don't really want to leave decades of infrastructure in London, for them to leave is a disruption to business and a cost. . . . We do not think that London is going to disappear, but the industry will move to a more decentralised model".[20]

Even more clearly: "Essentially there are going to be three or four centres in Europe that are going to grow in size, but not to the point that London becomes irrelevant."[21] This statement is very consistent with the preceding analysis on the geographical concentration effects of globalisation for financial services.

Moreover, the size of the EU market for the City of London shall not be overestimated. Indeed, the Brexit impact papers published by the European Parliament make clear how, in 2015, only 23 per cent of the UK financial services revenues derived from activities relating to the EU.[22] That is to say that the remaining 77 per cent was related to activities outside the EU.

Finally, so far London does not seem to have lost its capacity to attract the especially technologically sensitive financial industry. Reuters reports that over half a billion dollars were poured into British financial technology companies in the first half of 2017. This accounts for over a third more than the same period last year, as the trade body Innovate Finance claimed in July 2017. This is a clear sign that the fast growing fintech sector is betting on a post-Brexit favourable environment. UK-based fintech start-ups pulled in $564 million of venture capital investment in the first six months of the year 2017, more than half of which came from outside Britain. That was up 37 per cent from the first half of 2016 and put Britain in third place globally for fintech investment, behind the United States and China.[23]

Fintech is a sector ranging from mobile payment apps to digital currencies like bitcoin and one that the government considers as key for future economic growth. Therefore, the British Government has identified fintech as a priority area, saying it provides 60,000 jobs and contributes around $9 billion to the economy. In the first six months of 2017, the global investment in fintech was $6.5 billion. Of this, just over half went into US start-ups and around $1 billion into China. A third of the investment into British fintech came from venture capital firms based in the United States.[24]

The main reasons for this renewed confidence in the British economy post-Brexit are, according to Abdul Haseeb Basit, head of Finance and Strategic Projects at Innovate Finance: "Britain's prowess in both conventional finance and technology, as well as light-touch regulation, its pro-business culture and even the fact that it is Anglophone make it difficult for other centres to compete, though many – such as Berlin and Paris – are trying".[25] He also claimed that:

> while passporting rights – which give firms licenced in one EU country the right to trade freely in any other – had been a big concern for investors after Brexit, those worries had eased. Even if Britain loses passporting rights, that would affect only 20 percent of the almost 300 startups that are members of Innovate Finance.[26]

The real worry was that access to highly skilled workers would dry up when Britain leaves the EU as an estimated 30 per cent of the sector's workers are foreigners and most of them from the EU.

In the words of Basit: "Talent is the number one concern, and has been consistently since the referendum – we test [our members on] that every three to six months. So that's been fairly consistent – it's been a worry and until we have more certainty around that, it will remain a worry".[27]

Moreover, according to Basit: "There is a lot of competition in the investment space – there's a lot of capital available and it's looking for good companies to invest in. . . . Were they to not invest in UK companies, they feel like they might miss an opportunity. The appetite is still strong."[28]

It seems thus that the competitive advantages secured so far by the City of London as a global financial centre, such as its technological infrastructure and its high concentration of financial expertise, will be difficult to be put into question by Brexit.

It might even be argued that Brexit could enhance the competitive position of the British financial centre in the era of globalisation, as it will actually require precisely those kind of policies that further enhance the City's hegemonic potential domestically and internationally: liberalisation and deregulation.

It is indeed becoming increasingly clear that, were it to happen, a hard Brexit could actually work for the UK, providing that a specific set of policies are adopted, policies that go precisely in the direction of the kind of Thatcher-style measures strongly supported by the so-called ultra-liberals, the free-marketeers of the City.

Indeed, the two chancellors, Philip Hammond and previously George Osborne, have already hinted at this, when they underlined the structural changes that the British economic model would need post-Brexit. Even Jeremy Corbyn seems very aware of the risk that Brexit poses in terms of moving towards an ultra-liberal, hyper-globalized capitalist system. Moreover, this is certainly in line with Theresa May and her Cabinet's claim that Brexit will make the UK more, not less globalized.[29]

As almost verbatim claimed in the press, in order to keep Britain competitive in the global economy post-Brexit, it will have to "adapt", and the UK's economic model will need to be reset.[30] Britain will have to become a sort of Hong Kong or Singapore of Europe. It will be the completion of Mrs Thatcher City's revolution, and it may be no coincidence that almost all of the Brexiteers are hard-line nostalgic Thatcherites.[31]

So which are those measures, and how are they likely to shape the future of the City outside the EU? Or, put in another way, how will "pragmatic adaptation" unfold in the case of a hard Brexit?

First of all, the British Government will have to declare the adoption of unilateral free trade. By reducing tariffs on all imports to the UK of both goods and services, the country can easily benefit from lower global prices, in exchange for no tariffs and no control on imported goods. According to Her Majesty's Revenue and Customs (HMRC), routine customs declarations could be made electronically and goods cleared at ports in seconds.[32]

This, of course, will undermine the productive base of the country, thus exacerbating further the divide between finance and industry already at the core of the British capitalist system, as analysed when talking about "British Exceptionalism". As during the Thatcher era, the losers will be workers, who will have to endure much higher unemployment and a reduction of the welfare system as the economy adjusts.

Contrary to expectations, migration will not necessarily decrease post-Brexit, as the competitiveness and productivity of the City of London and of the British economy as a whole will have to be maintained by allowing the migrants in. However, migration quotas and skills will now be controlled by the British Government, with far less rights in the case of EU migrants.[33] This more, not less open door on migration, will almost certainly depress domestic wages, in line with traditional supply-side neo-liberal approaches to the labour market and to increased competitiveness, but in contrast to the initial expectations of Brexit.[34]

The same aim of increasing global competitiveness in line with the imperatives of neo-liberal globalisation will produce a further liberalisation of labour and environmental laws, finally freed from the check and balances of the European institutions, especially the European Court of

Justice. An echo of this possibility is to be identified in the debate surrounding the so-called Brexit bill.[35] Flexibility of labour markets will be facilitated by the loss of control by supranational institutions and will be justified as the only way to gain global market shares after leaving the EU trade area.[36]

This links to two further neo-liberal measures that could improve the attractiveness of the UK in the global environment and that have already been advocated by leading Tory politicians: tax cuts and reduction of state intervention in the economy.[37]

In line with theories of the competitive State (Cerny 1995), attracting business in the age of globalisation, especially when capital is very mobile, as in the case of financial capital, requires low taxes, a light-touch regulatory environment, the rule of law and political stability. The UK will need to be able to offer all this once outside the EU because it will not be able anymore to be the gateway to the largest regional trade bloc. It will therefore need to reorientate the incentives it needs to offer foreign investors in a much more liberal way. However, lower taxes will reduce public spending, and more spending for infrastructure will further decrease the share of public expenditure going to the welfare state, including the National Health Service, education and benefits. Again the lower strata of society will be the main losers of such a move, whereas the City of London will benefit not only from the new, more favourable regulatory environment but also from the increase in the use of insurance services to substitute for the demise of the welfare state.

The direction of British economic structure change as a consequence of Brexit seems, therefore, unlikely to be towards social democracy and, even less, socialism, and more towards an exasperated form of neo-liberal globalisation, the only one that, it is claimed, could guarantee some prosperity to the country outside the EU and also the one that the City of London always favoured to maintain its global competitiveness and its domestic hegemony.[38]

Indeed, the City is already positioning itself in this debate. TheCityUK report published in July 2017 suggests that: "Britain will lose its status as Europe's top financial centre unless it keeps borders open to specialist staff, improves infrastructure and expands links with emerging economies".[39]

Conclusion

Summing up, what really counts for the prosperity of the City is a relaxed regulatory environment, which, of course, can be guaranteed by a friendly government post-Brexit.

However, this is a necessary but not sufficient condition for the City to maintain its hegemony both domestically and internationally in the globalisation era.

The second, vital condition is open access to markets globally. This could be jeopardised by a Brexit as it is highly unlikely the EU will grant the UK similar conditions of access to its markets as if it were still a member of the club. However, Brexit could also represent the catalyst for the adoption of ultra-liberal policies, ranging from a liberalisation of labour and environmental laws, import tariffs and controls and low taxes to the diversion of public funds from the welfare state to infrastructures.

This would enhance the capacity of the City to attract investment globally at the expense of the living and working conditions of the lower strata of society, as the debate about the passing of the Brexit bill has demonstrated. Will this be the future of the UK? Will the revenge of the ultra-liberals happen? It will all depend on whether the City–state nexus will hold post-Brexit. It seems, though, that the City's pragmatic adaptation strategy has already started.

Notes

1 See Perry Anderson, "Origins of the Present Crisis", *New Left Review (NLR)* 23, January–February 1964: 26–53; Tom Nairn, "The Twilight of the British State", *NLR* 101–102, February–April 1977: 3–61; W.D. Rubinstein, "Wealth, Èlites and the Class Structure of Modern Britain", in *Past and Present* 76, August 1977: 99–126; Frank Longstreth, Frank, "The City, Industry and the State", in Crouch, Colin, (ed.), *State and Economy in Contemporary Capitalism*, London: Croom Helm, 1979: 157–191, The most important contributions to this debate were Tom Nairn, "The British Political Elite", *NLR* 23, January–February 1964: 19–25, and Perry Anderson, 'Origins of the Present Crisis', *NLR* 23, January–February 1964: 26–53; Tom Nairn, 'The English Working-Class', *NLR* 24, March–April 1964a: 43–57; Tom Nairn, 'The Nature of the Labour Party', *NLR* 27 and 28, September–October and November–December 1964b: 38–65 and 33–62. Sequels included Perry Anderson, 'Socialism and Pseudo-Empiricism', *NLR* 35, January–February 1966: 2–42, and 'Components of the National Culture', *NLR* 50, July–August 1968: 3–5; Tom Nairn, 'The Fateful Meridian', *NLR* 60, March–April: 1970: 3–35, Perry Anderson, "The Figures of Descent", in *NLR*, 161, January–February 1987: 20–77.
2 See "Banking Crisis Timeline", *The Guardian*, 30 October 2008. Available at www.theguardian.com/business/2008/oct/08/creditcrunch.marketturmoil [Accessed September 11, 2017].
3 Ibid.
4 Ibid.
5 Ibid.
6 See Andrew Porter, James Kirkup and Gordon Rayner, "Financial Crisis", *The Telegraph*, 12 October 2008. Available at: www.telegraph.co.uk/finance/financialcrisis/3185120/Financial-crisis-HBOS-and-RBS-to-be-nationalised-in-50-billion-state-intervention.html [Accessed September 8, 2017].
7 Ibid.
8 Ibid.
9 Short-selling is selling borrowed shares in the hopes that their price will fall and that they can be bought back at a profit later on.
10 The ban was then lifted in January 2009.
11 See *The Guardian*, various issues.
12 See James Kirkup, "Protect Bank Shares from Short-Selling, Ministers Told', *The Telegraph*. Available at: www.telegraph.co.uk/news/uknews/2977387/Protect-bank-shares-from-short-selling-ministers-told.html [Accessed June 28, 2010].
13 See *Financial Times*. Available at: www.ft.com/content/56ad41e6-617a-11e7-8814-0ac7eb84e5f1 [Accessed July, 26, 2017].
14 City of London, How We Make Decisions, n.d. Available at: https://www.cityoflondon.gov.uk/about-the-city/how-we-make-decisions/Pages/default.aspx [Accessed on February 17, 2018].
15 Ibid.
16 See Steve Arons, William Canny Donal Griffin and Ruth David, "Brexit: Deutsche Bank Said to Be Switching from London to Frankfurt", *Independent*. Available at: www.independent.co.uk/news/business/news/brexit-latest-news-deutsche-bank-london-frankfurt-uk-leave-eu-switch-a7826361.html [Accessed on July 26, 2017].
17 Ibid.
18 Ibid.
19 Ibid.
20 Ibid.
21 Ibid.
22 See European Parliament, "Brexit: The United Kingdom and EU Financial Services". Available at: www.europarl.europa.eu/RegData/etudes/BRIE/2016/587384/IPOL_BRI%282016%29587384_EN.pdf [Accessed on December 21, 2017].
23 See Chris Skinner, "Fintech: $6.5 Billion Invested in the First Half of 2017", The Finanser. Available at: https://thefinanser.com/2017/07/fintech-6-5-billion-invested-first-half-2017.html/ [Accessed on August 1, 2017].
24 Ibid.
25 See Abhinav Ramnarayan and Anjuli Davies, "Exclusive: Banks Dealing EU Sovereign Debt May Be Dragged out of London", Reuters. Available at: http://uk.reuters.com/article/us-britain-eu-primary-dealers-idUKKBN1AB10U [Accessed on July 26, 2017].
26 Ibid.

27 Ibid.

28 Ibid.

29 See "Brexit: UK Will Not Cut Taxes, says Philip Hammond", BBC News. Available at: www.bbc.com/news/uk-politics-40771900 [Accessed on August 1, 2017].

30 See Sean O'Grady, "Surviving Hard Brexit Will Require Sacrifices Not Seen Since the Second World War", *The Independent*. Available at: www.independent.co.uk/voices/brexit-david-davis-free-trade-migration-labour-laws-low-taxes-a7845421.html [Accessed on August 1, 2017].

31 Ibid.

32 Ibid.

33 Ibid.

34 Ibid.

35 See Polly Toynbee, "The Brexit Bill Is Cataclysmic. Only a Swerve Will Save Us", *The Guardian*. Available at: www.theguardian.com/commentisfree/2017/sep/05/brexit-bill-government-negotiations-labour [Accessed on September 11, 2017].

36 See Sean O'Grady, "Surviving Hard Brexit Will Require Sacrifices Not Seen Since the Second World War", *The Independent*. Available at: www.independent.co.uk/voices/brexit-david-davis-free-trade-migration-labour-laws-low-taxes-a7845421.html [Accessed on August 1, 2017].

37 Ibid.

38 Ibid.

39 See "A Vision for a Transformed, World-Leading Industry", TheCityUK. Available at: www.thecityuk.com/research/a-vision-for-a-transformed-world-leading-industry/ [Accessed on August 1, 2017].

References

Aaronvitch, S. (1961) *The Ruling Class*. London: Lawrence & Wishart.

Anderson, P. (1964) Origins of the Present Crisis. *New Left Review* No. 23, January–February 1964, pp. 26–53.

Anderson, P. (1966) Socialism and Pseudo-Empiricism. *New Left Review* No. 35, January–February 1966, pp. 2–42.

Anderson, P. (1968) Components of the National Culture. *New Left Review* No. 50, July–August 1968, pp. 3–57.

Anderson, P. (1987) The Figures of Descent. *New Left Review* No. 161, January–February 1987, pp. 20–77.

Anderson, P. (2017) Why the System Will Still Win. *Le Monde diplomatique*. Available at: https://mondediplo.com/2017/03/02brexit [Accessed September 11, 2017].

Bishop, G. (2009) Britain's Eternal Vulnerability: Sterling. In: Bishop, G., Buiter, W., Donnelly, B. and Hutton, W. (eds.), *10 Years of the Euro: New Perspectives for Britain*. London: John Stevens, Sarum Colourview.

Busch, A. (2008) *Banking Regulation and Globalisation*. Oxford: Oxford University Press.

Callinicos, A. (2016) Brexit: A World-Historic Turn. *International Socialism*, June 27. Available at: http://isj.org.uk/brexit-a-world-historic-turn/ [Accessed September 11, 2017].

Cerny, P. (1995) Globalisation and the Changing Logic of Collective Action. *International Organization* 49(4): 595–625.

Cohen, B.J. (1996) Phoenix Risen: The Resurrection of Global Finance. *World Politics* 48(2): 268–296.

Cohen, B.J. (2001) Electronic Money: New Day or False Dawn? *Review of International Political Economy* 8: 197–225.

Coleman, W.D. (1996) *Financial Services, Globalisation and Domestic Policy Change*. London: Palgrave Macmillan.

Dicken, P. (1999) *Global Shift, Transforming the World Economy*. London: Paul Chapman Publishing.

Dicken, P. (2003) *Global Shift: Reshaping the Global Economic Map in the 21st Century*. Thousand Oaks, CA: Sage Publications.

Frieden, J. and Rogowski, R. (1996) The Impact of the International Economy on National Policies: An Analytical Overview. In: Keohane, R.O. and Milner, H.V. (eds.), *Internationalization and Domestic Politics*. New York: Cambridge University Press, pp. 25–47.

Guth, M.A. (1994) *Speculative Behavior and the Operation of Competitive Markets under Uncertainty*. Aldershop: Avebury Ashgate Publishing.

Hay, C. and Marsh, D. (2000) *Demystifying Globalisation*. London: Palgrave Macmillan.

Held, D. and McGrew, A. (2000) *The Global Transformations Reader*. Cambridge: Polity Press.

Hirst, P. and Thompson, G. (1999a) *Globalisation in Question*. 2nd Edition. Cambridge: Polity Press.

Hirst, P. and Thompson, G. (1999b) The Tyranny of Globalisation: Myth or Reality? In: Buelens, F. (ed.), *Globalisation and the Nation State*. Broadheath: Edward Elgar.

Holm, H.H. and Sørensen, G. (1995) *Whose World Order? Uneven Globalisation and the End of the Cold War*. Boulder, CO: Westview Press.

Ingham, G. (1984) *Capitalism Divided*. Hampshire: Macmillan Education Ltd.

Ingham, G. (1988) Commercial Capital and British Development: A Reply to Michael Barratt Brown. *New Left Review* No. 172, November–December 1988, pp. 45–65.

Ingham, G. (2002) Shock Therapy in the City. *New Left Review* No. 14, March–April 2002, pp. 152–158.

International Labour Organization (2009) *The Impact of the Financial Crisis on Finance Sector Workers*. Geneva, February 24–25. Available at: www.ilo.org/wcmsp5/groups/public/@dgreports/@dcomm/documents/meetingdocument/wcms_103263.pdf [Accessed January 20, 2018].

Investment Fund Services Limited (IFSL) (2009) Foreign Exchange 2009. Available at: www.thecityuk.com/media/2193/CBS_Foreign_Exchange%202009.pdf [Accessed June 28, 2010].

Keohane, R.O. and Milner, H.V. (eds.) (1996) *Internationalization and Domestic Politics*. Cambridge: Cambridge University Press.

Lilley, P. (2000) *Dirty Dealing: The Untold Truth about Global Money Laundering*. London: Kogan Page.

Longstreth, F. (1979) The City, Industry and the State. In: Crouch, C. (ed.), *State and Economy in Contemporary Capitalism*. London: Croom Helm, pp. 157–191.

Mittleman, J.H. (2000) *The Globalisation Syndrome: Transformation and Resistance*. Princeton, NJ: Princeton University Press.

Nairn, T. (1977) The Twilight of the British State. *New Left Review* No. 101–102, February–April 1977, pp. 3–61.

Obstfeld, M. and Taylor, A.M. (2004) *Global Capital Markets: Integration, Crisis and Growth*. Cambridge: Cambridge University Press.

Overbeek, H. (1980) Finance Capital and the Crisis in Britain. *Capital and Class* 11, Summer 1980: 98–109.

Padoa-Schioppa, T. (1994) *The Road to Monetary Union in Europe: The Emperor, the Kings and the Genies*. Oxford: Clarendon Press.

Rubinstein, W.D. (1977) Wealth, Èlites and the Class Structure of Modern Britain. *Past and Present* No. 76, August 1977, pp. 99–126.

Stanworth, P. and Giddens, A. (1974) *Elites and Power in British Society*. Cambridge: Cambridge University Press.

Strange, S. (1971) *Sterling and British Policy*. London: Oxford University Press.

Strange, S. (1998) *Mad Money*. Manchester: Manchester University Press.

Talani, L.S. (2010) *The Global Crash*. London: Palgrave Macmillan.

Talani, L.S. (2012) *Globalisation, Hegemony and the Future of the City of London*. London: Palgrave Macmillan.

Thompson, G. (1993) *The Economic Emergence of a New Europe?* Broadheath: Edward Elgar.

6

BREXIT AND THE FUTURE MODEL OF BRITISH CAPITALISM

Andrew Baker and Scott Lavery

Introduction

No area of public policy will be left untouched by the UK's vote for Brexit. As outlined in this handbook, from foreign policy to welfare, from the UK's devolution settlement to its international trade orientation, Brexit is likely to produce profound change across multiple policy domains. Brexit also raises broader questions about the future trajectory of British capitalism. Since joining the European Economic Community (EEC) in 1973, the UK's economic model has become increasingly integrated into the political and economic structures of the European continent. The EU's Single Market provides a reservoir of demand for the UK's competitive financial and business services sectors. Membership of the Single Market has facilitated migration from EU member states into the UK labour market. British production hubs have become deeply integrated into EU supply chains. At its core, the UK's exit from the EU threatens to uproot and reconfigure these relations. Moreover, the Leave vote was in part at least due to voters disaffected and left behind by poor UK economic performance since the financial crisis (Goodwin and Heath 2016), suggesting the British model of capitalism might be experiencing its own particular form of crisis, with Brexit as one specific manifestation of this. In this chapter, we assess the extent to which Brexit is likely to lead to *continuation* of or a *rupture* with the UK's prevailing model of capitalism (MOC).

Questions of continuity and change have long preoccupied analysts of advanced capitalist economies (Hay 1999; Streeck and Thelen 2005; Thelen 2009). Within comparative political economy, scholars typically distinguish between distinct 'models' or 'varieties' of capitalism (Albert 1993; Hall 1986; Hall and Soskice 2001). The MOC literature insists that global economic transformation impacts differentially upon national states (Coates 2001). Domestic institutional environments, embodied in distinct labour, capital and product markets and regulatory regimes, mediate international economic pressures in divergent ways (Hall 1986). Over time, these institutional configurations produce distinct incentive structures for firms, workers and public officials. MOC are therefore 'path dependent': they tend to endure over time even under conditions of rapid global change. On this understanding, moments of 'rupture' are relatively rare. But they are not unheard of. Social, economic and political pressures can generate perceptions of a need for change amongst a critical mass of actors regarding appropriate distributional and regulatory arrangements. New forms of persuasive struggle between elites and mass publics evolve as a consequence (Widmaier et al. 2007), and Brexit should be understood in this context.

In this chapter, we assess the extent to which Brexit might represent one such moment of decisive 'rupture' with the UK's prevailing MOC. The UK's MOC is distinguished by its large internationalised financial centre, its flexible labour market regime and the promotion of market competitiveness across a range of social domains by successive UK Governments (Lavery et al. 2017). The UK's MOC is both dynamic and dysfunctional. It generates high levels of employment and draws in large inflows of international capital. At the same time, it generates a number of profound imbalances. The City's position as a central hub of global finance exposes the UK to downturns in international credit conditions, has pushed up the UK's real exchange rate, encodes a lending bias towards property and other financialized rent extraction activities, often at the expense of productive activities, and contributes to concentrations of wealth and economic activity in both geographical (London-centrism) and social terms (Christensen et al. 2016).

In light of these dysfunctionalities, a growing body of scholars and practitioners argue that the UK's MOC is beset by a 'finance curse' (Christensen and Shaxson 2013; Christensen et al. 2016; Baker and Wigan 2017). The 'finance curse' concept draws on the notion of a resource curse that is said to have blighted many developing economies dependent on mineral extractive industries (Karl 1997; Ross 1999). One of these is a form of Dutch disease, involving a suspicion that financial sector growth raises local prices (including property in the south-east) but particularly the exchange rate, making it harder for alternative tradeable sectors to compete in world markets (Christensen and Shaxson 2013: 19). The finance curse generates numerous economic imbalances, including 'brain drain' from non-financial sectors, rent extraction over productive investment and high levels of wealth and income inequality. Crucially, these pathologies are productive of volatile and unpredictable politics. Brexit is one manifestation of this dynamic insofar as it embodies a mass public reaction to the negative everyday lived experiences of British capitalism since the 2008 global financial crash (Hopkin 2017; Thompson 2017). Brexit embodies inter alia a public response to wide-scale migration and its sociocultural effects; low and stagnating wages; rising inequality; austerity-induced falling living standards; perceptions of an excessive degree of regulatory centralisation prioritising the concerns and interests of large multinational corporations; remote and unresponsive elites; as well as the damaged reputation of the EU as a political entity following poor handling of its own banking and debt crisis.

The chapter assesses the extent to which Brexit might precipitate a rupture with the UK's dysfunctional MOC and its associated finance curse. In the first section, we identify the core features of the UK's MOC. In the second section, we outline the ways in which EU membership has shaped and sustained the UK's MOC in the recent past. In the third section, we consider two scenarios where Brexit generates either a rupture with or a deepening of the UK's MOC. In the fourth section, we emphasise the conflictual and contradictory politics of Brexit. We present a two-by-two matrix as a device for understanding the conflicted political economy of Brexit, identifying four significant but fluid 'power blocs' seeking to shape the Brexit process within the UK state and society. While our analysis leans more towards an enduring status quo as far as the UK's model of capitalism is concerned, based on current political trajectories, we note that some evidence and interpretations point to Brexit as a catalyst for a rebalancing. Such a scenario cannot be discounted altogether, but any rebalancing will also have to be politically driven rather than simply being a self-correcting economic phenomenon, and this is where the primary difficulty lies.

The UK's model of capitalism

The UK's MOC is distinguished by a number of core features. First, through the City of London, the UK plays host to *one of the world's largest financial centres* (see also Chapter 5). The City is distinguished by its highly internationalised character (Baker 1999; Los et al. 2017). The City can be understood as a geographically clustered institutional structure of commercial financial trading, advisory and intermediation practices using ever more innovative techniques to deliver income and fees for practitioners (Ingham 1984: 60; Talani 2012: 26). It acts as the headquarters to some of the world's largest international banks and also contains numerous financial sub-sectors – such as asset management, investment banking, clearing, insurance, hedge funds and fintech – which together comprise a complex ecosystem of advanced producer services (Sassen 2011). In terms of its size, the City dwarfs alternative European financial hubs (Faulconbridge 2004). The City's position as a key nodal point within global finance also ensures that it is deeply interconnected with other 'global cities' (Taylor 2004). In particular, the intersection of the City with US banking power comprises a distinctive 'City-Wall Street' nexus, which has been a key driver of financial globalisation since the late 1980s (Green 2013; Wójcik 2013).

The City has had a profound and long-standing impact on the development of the UK's domestic political economy (Ingham 1984). Economic activity associated with the City generates 12 per cent of UK income tax receipts and 15 per cent of corporation tax revenue (James and Quaglia 2017: 8). In terms of employment, the City sustains a large number of highly paid jobs directly in finance but also within a wider ecosystem of advanced producer services and related ancillary industries (Sassen 2011). In terms of the UK's trade position, the City contributes to the UK's balance of payments, generating a £71 billion trade surplus, along with professional services in 2015 (Dörry 2017). However, the dominance of the City within the UK's model of capitalism has also generated a series of developmental pathologies and dysfunctions (Christensen et al. 2016). So-called light touch financial regulation and intense competitive pressures between banking institutions drove a huge expansion in balance sheets throughout the 2000s (Bell and Hindmoor 2015; Thompson 2013). This, combined with high levels of private debt held by UK households, has acted as a drag on growth and has rendered the UK susceptible to a downturn in international credit conditions (Christensen et al. 2016; Crouch 2009). The absence of institutions encouraging long-term investment means that bank lending has been skewed towards residential and commercial property over productive investment (Engelen et al. 2011). Furthermore, capital inflows to the City has generated upward pressure on the UK's real exchange rate, undermining goods exports, squeezing industrial output and exacerbating regional inequities. Economic development in the UK is therefore simultaneously reliant upon but also impeded by the City's position as a hub of global finance.

The second key feature of the UK's model of capitalism is its *flexible labour market regime*. Since the early 1980s, a series of highly restrictive trade union laws have been passed in order to enhance managerial control over the workforce. As a result, UK workers today encounter the fourth lowest level of employment protection of any OECD state. Economic growth has also overwhelmingly been generated by the services sector, which experiences both low levels of unionisation and a tendency to generate low-productivity jobs, in particular in relation to the manufacturing sector. The result is that whilst the UK sustains a number of well paid sectors and professions, large swathes of the UK labour market are subject to high levels of precariousness, low pay and in-work poverty. These trends have intensified since the 2008 crisis. Over this period, real wages collapsed (Green and Lavery 2015). Furthermore, new legislation designed to further intensify the 'flexible' labour market regime was introduced in this period. Fees for employment tribunals were increased, preventing workers from seeking recompense for managerial malpractice (Heyes and Lewis 2015). These processes have consolidated the UK MOC's reliance on low-pay work. Low productivity, stagnant living standards and volatile anti-systemic politics have been the result (Hopkin 2017).

The third feature of the UK's model of capitalism is the role which successive governments – and the UK's financial and monetary authorities – have played in advancing marketization and commodification. In Phil Cerny's terms, the UK embodies a *'competition state' par excellence.*

Far from 'receding' as a result of globalisation, the UK state has been qualitatively reconfigured, oriented towards supporting and promoting the extension of competitive market forces (Jessop 2002). In macroeconomic terms, this has involved core state agencies – such as HM Treasury and the Bank of England – seeking to secure 'credibility' with international capital markets through tight fiscal discipline and counter-inflationary monetary policy (Baker 1999; Roberts 2011). The UK state has also adopted a proactive role in advancing 'workfare policies' that combine welfare residualism with increasingly punitive conditionality attached to welfare provision (Peck 2001). This logic – introduced incrementally by the Major government, extended under New Labour and expanded through the Coalition's sanctions regime – was designed with the explicit objective of channelling labour market outsiders into work with the goal of reducing wages in the aggregate. Throughout the 2000s, these 'competition state' policies were paralleled by an expansion of state expenditure on public services, in particular on the National Health Service and education under New Labour (Gamble 2010). Limited forms of redistribution through the tax and benefit system served to limit in-work poverty and constrain income inequality during this period. However, the Coalition's adoption of austerity and its attempt to eliminate the budget deficit primarily through public expenditure cuts reversed many of these transitory gains (Lavery 2017b).

The European Union and the UK's model of capitalism

Since the signing of the Single European Act, the UK's model of capitalism has been shaped in important ways by its position inside the European Union. The EU's Single Market – originally driven by the Thatcher government and key UK policymakers – significantly reduced non-tariff barriers between member states through enhanced regulatory convergence, 'mutual recognition' and the extension of qualified majority voting to a wide range of policy areas. As the world's largest single trading bloc, the Single Market has acted as an important outlet for UK exports, particularly from the UK's competitive financial and professional services sectors. For example, in 2016, 30 per cent of financial services exports were directed towards the EU27 whilst the UK emerged as the EU's de facto 'investment banker' (James and Quaglia 2017). In specific financial sub-sectors, the City has excelled. For example, the City clears 75 per cent of euro-denominated derivatives and accounts for 85 per cent of the EU's hedge funds and 42 per cent of its private equity financing (Quaglia 2016b: 7). The Single Market also provides an important outlet for the export of manufactured goods from the UK to the EU. Fifty-six per cent of the UK's pharma-ceuticals exports, 51 per cent of its automotive exports and 27 per cent of its aerospace exports have typically been destined for the Single Market (CBI 2013). The geographical proximity of the EU to the UK and the deep integration of intra-European supply chains have underpinned these close trading relations. For example, between 2000 and 2010, regions outside of London and the South East saw their dependence on EU demand for the export of goods and services increase substantially (Los et al. 2017: 789).

EU membership has also underpinned the UK's flexible labour market regime in a variety of respects. The extension of EU competence over social and employment policy has long been viewed by business and the Conservative Party as a threat to the UK's flexible labour market. The ambition to create a supranational 'floor' of employment rights – exemplified by Delors's vision of a 'Social Europe' – has been a particular bugbear of the British neo-liberal right. However, in practice EU integration has tended to intensify pressures on European social welfare regimes whilst leaving the UK's liberal labour market model relatively intact (Hyman 2008; Scharpf 2010). In fact, EU integration has positively reinforced the UK's flexible labour market regime in a number of respects. The free movement of labour – one of the 'four freedoms' of the Single Market – has provided the UK labour market with access to over 500 million EU nationals. As a result, highly skilled workers have poured into the UK and in particular to London (Ryan and Mulholland 2014: 3). At the same time, high levels of 'low-skilled' EU migrants have entered the UK labour in recent decades. The Blair government's decision in 2004 to eschew transitional controls on inflows of labour from the Central and Eastern European 'accession' states was crucial here. The Treasury noted that the inflow of workers would act as a brake on wage growth and inflation in the UK (Thompson 2017: 238). As such, UK business models within high-wage sectors such as finance and business services and in low-wage sectors such as agriculture, retail and hospitality have increasingly come to depend on labour from EU member states. The UK's status as a low-wage service and assembly economy, outside of highly skilled sectors, was consequently reinforced by integration into the EU labour market.

Unfettered 'access' to the Single Market has not been the only way in which EU membership has served to prop up the UK's MOC. The capacity of UK policymakers to influence and actively *shape* the rules of the Single Market has also been a central element of the relation between British capitalism and EU integration. In particular, UK policymakers and business groups have attempted to 'defend and extend' a liberalising agenda within the EU by utilising the UK's position as powerful member state (Lavery 2017a). In the field of EU social and employment policy, for example, the UK secured an 'opt-out' from a directive designed to limit the length of the working week, and UK business associations effectively defended this derogation at the EU level. Although the institutional set-up of the EU embodies a structural bias towards 'negative' or 'market' integration (Scharpf 2010), at key moments UK policymakers have mobilised to curtail the development of the 'social Europe' agenda. Similarly, the Treasury and powerful actors from within the City collectively assumed a proactive position in shaping Juncker's 2014 Capital Markets Union (CMU) agenda (CBI 2015; TheCityUK 2015). For example, a quarter of responses to the Commission's 2015 CMU consultation were from UK-based financial firms, whilst the then commissioner for CMU – UK national Jonathan Hill – convened regularly with the City on the topic (European Commission 2017; Quaglia 2016a). In this way, successive UK governments have aimed to shape EU legislation in the image of the UK's MOC, promoting liberalisation through a 'selective' Europeanism organised around key government departments' strategic objectives (Baker 2005).

Brexit as structural shift: an end to the UK's finance curse?

The one certainty facing UK capitalism is that the conflicts and contingencies unleashed by Brexit make the future deeply uncertain. Material aspects of the UK's model of capitalism are directly challenged by the prospect of leaving the EU. The prospect of reduced access to the Single Market is already changing the incentives and calculations facing transnational financial firms currently located in the City of London (see also Chapter 5). Meanwhile, the European Central Bank and the Commission have sought to bring the Euro clearing business back within its own jurisdictional competence as political hostility to the UK from EU institutions and governments is on the rise (Stafford 2017). Adjustments to freedom of movement will qualitatively change the UK's labour market and the regime for governing it, reducing access to pools of European labour in both low-skilled and scarce-skill sectors. A combination of wage pressures and sterling depreciation (currently around 15 per cent) promise to contribute to creeping inflationary pressures. While the UK retains a clear ideological commitment to tariff free trading agreements, market access and modern trade politics revolve around complex legal agreements governing recognition of other jurisdictions' product standards. Brexit will necessitate a huge process of renegotiating such agreements involving a jurisdictional transfer of authority and with it significant medium-term trading uncertainties. In summary, Brexit increases uncertainty surrounding the three core features of the UK's model of capitalism: the role and status of the City of London;

the highly flexible mobile labour market that was able to attract and take advantage of both low- and highly paid workers from across Europe; and the terms on which the UK is inserted into the production and financial structures of the global political economy, including the terms on which it does business with the rest of the world.

Amidst this great uncertainty, it may be unwise to attempt to predict the impact of Brexit on the future trajectory of the UK's model of capitalism. Nonetheless, two possible scenarios for the future of UK capitalism and its associated finance curse can be outlined briefly. The first scenario views Brexit as a moment of structural transformation that – through a process of currency devaluation and capital flight – leads to a *reconfiguration* of the UK's MOC. A number of prominent macroeconomists have countenanced this scenario. The IMF's former director for Europe Ashoka Mody has pointed to the City's role as a magnet for financial and property flows from around the world, especially from dollar surplus states like Russia, China and the Gulf countries. This led to extended bank leverage and an overvaluation in Sterling of 20–25 per cent on a trade-weighted basis prior to Brexit (Evans-Pritchard 2016; Kaminska 2016).[1] In Mody's diagnosis, the UK's political economy has been characterised by a bank–property nexus that left the rest of the economy to suffer with only 1.5 per cent of loans going to manufacturing. According to Mody, Brexit breaks the political economy lock of elites wedded to banking and financial interests, albeit by accident, by reducing the potential attractiveness of the City as a financial centre (due to leaving the Single Market) and through a 15 per cent devaluation in Sterling, leading to a rebalancing away from finance (Evans-Pritchard 2016). The former governor of the Bank of England, Mervyn King, while not going as far as Mody in calling for further falls in sterling to a rate of $1.15, compared to the current rate of $1.30, has also claimed that a lower exchange rate, lower house prices and higher interest rates would be welcome side effects of Brexit, producing a better balanced UK economy with a lower current account deficit (Conway 2016). A similar view has been expressed by Paul Krugman, who stated that:

> Pre-Brexit, Britain was obviously experiencing a version of the so-called Dutch disease. In its traditional form, this referred to the way natural resource exports crowd out manufacturing by keeping the currency strong. In the UK case, the City's financial exports play the same role. So their weakening helps British manufacturing – and, maybe, the incomes of people who live far from the City and still depend directly or indirectly on manufacturing for their incomes. . . . [A] weaker pound shouldn't be viewed as an additional cost from Brexit, it's just part of the adjustment. And it would be a big mistake to prop up the pound.
>
> *(Krugman 2016)*

In this scenario, Brexit forces a 'rebalancing' of the UK away from its destabilising reliance on financial service exports and credit-fuelled growth. However, this 'rebalancing thesis' is not without its problems. These analyses largely emerge from model-based macroeconomics, and many of its advocates assume 'rebalancing' will be a quasi automatic, self-adjusting and market-led process, in turn placing too much stress on the depreciation of the pound as a market signal (see Krugman 2016). Problems in the UK run rather deeper and manifest themselves in persistent underperformance in productivity that shows no signs of abating (Haldane 2017). This chapter has already noted how the UK is weak in terms of a coherent integrated skills or training strategy (see the reliance on high net EU migration), but infrastructure problems also abound, including the harnessing of technology to boost productive capacity, London-centric transportation networks and questionable R&D practices. Furthermore, the UK's tradeable goods exports are deeply integrated into EU supply chains. This means that the potential export boost generated by devaluation is significantly curtailed by the inflated cost of importing from the Single Market. Far from producing a 'rebalancing' of the UK's model of capitalism and an alleviation of its finance curse, Brexit could instead erode living standards, increase pressure on the public finances and even *augment* the Treasury's dependence on tax revenues from the City.

This is where the second scenario emerges: one where Brexit *deepens* the UK's financial-ised model of capitalism and intensifies its exposure to the finance curse. In this scenario, the interlocking symptoms of the finance curse reinforce one another. These include brain drain as finance attracts the best and the brightest, depriving other sectors of their talents (Kneer 2013); a crowding out or vacuum cleaner effect as the financial sector disproportionately attracts surplus capital (Haldane 2012); financialisation and rent extraction, with financial activities and logics taking precedence over other forms of activity and generating systemic risk with the potential to induce recessions and retard growth when there is 'too much finance' (Arcand et al. 2015); uneven geographical development as a metropolitan hub sucks in talent and resources; asset inflation, wage disparities and rising inequality, in which access to asset ownership becomes difficult for many; and finally a form of multifaceted political capture in which a well connected financial sector comes to dominate public debate on economic policy and regulation and has disproportionate political influence, so that financial sector promotion and protection become a core state priority and government officials are reluctant to take corrective action due to easy rents (Baker 2010).

Under these conditions, the structural dominance of finance within the UK's model of cap-italism produces an intensification of the UK's existing growth model. The City, now excluded from the EU's financial regulatory architecture, consolidates its position as a lightly regulated 'offshore' centre, drawing in speculative global capital flows whilst further undermining the UK's productive base. This process would potentially produce important spillover effects into other spheres of UK capitalism. The UK's flexible labour market regime – now unencumbered by the (limited) protections associated with EU employment law – intensifies as the government attempts to reduce wage costs and lessen the inflationary impact of devaluation. The UK's 'com-petition state' orientation is increased, as the Treasury enacts cuts to corporation and income tax in an attempt to induce external investment. In sum, Brexit produces an intensification of the UK's existing MOC in this scenario. For libertarian proponents of a 'global Brexit', this opportu-nity to cast aside 'burdensome' regulations and limitations on international trade is the standout prize of leaving the EU. For those of a more critical orientation, the deepening of the UK's existing MOC increases the UK's exposure to the finance curse and intensifies all the deleterious social, political and economic effects associated with this developmental form.

Brexit and political agency: rival power blocs and the future of the UK's model of capitalism

Brexit presents clear material challenges to UK capitalism. As the preceding scenarios suggest, two relatively extreme 'Brexit futures' can be identified: one that generates a *rupture* with and one that *deepens* the UK's MOC. But both of these scenarios assume that the UK's MOC will adjust in quasi automatic fashion to the economic impact of Brexit. However, sudden 'shocks' of this form are always mediated and shaped by political actors. Models of capitalism are not reified structures. They are at all times underpinned and sustained by underlying 'power blocs' or 'coalitions of social forces' (Baccaro and Pontusson 2016: 200). Brexit's impact on the UK's future MOC is therefore contingent and subject to highly fluid forms of negotiation, contestation and political construction. In what follows, we tentatively identify four con-tending 'power blocs' that are currently attempting to shape the political economy of Brexit (see Table 6.1). The 'power blocs' we identify are not exhaustive. Instead, the two-by-two

Table 6.1 Four power blocs and the emergent political economy of Brexit

Attitude towards European Union

		Continuity	Change
Continuity		**A** **Business as usual** City of London lobby (TheCityUK/ City of London Corporation) HM Treasury/Bank of England Business lobby groups (e.g. CBI) Elements of Conservative Cabinet Parliamentary Labour Party 'moderates' Sections of Civil Service Liberal Democrats	**B** **'Singapore on Thames'** Elements of Conservative Cabinet 'Globalist' Conservative backbench MPs Hedge funds UKIP elites and funders Deregulatory libertarian think tanks (Economists for Brexit, Institute of Economic Affairs, Adam Smith Institute)
Change		**C** **Soft reformism** Elements of Labour Party Shadow Cabinet 'Soft Brexit' Labour MPs Bulk of Labour Party membership Trades Union Congress Devolved administrations (Holyrood/Welsh Assembly)	**D** **Protectionist-interventionist-populist blocs** Elements of Labour Party left Radical rank and file trade unions Populist right forces – residual UKIP vote Some leftist commentators, including Larry Elliott

Position on UK Capitalism (vertical axis label)

matrix seeks to capture in heuristic form the broad coalitions of powerful public and private actors in the UK that presently seek to articulate particular visions of Brexit and pathways for the UK's future MOC.

The first power bloc, outlined in quadrant A, is classified as the *business as usual* coalition. This bloc embodies a synthesis of corporate interests, government departments and backbench MPs who together seek to limit the 'damage' that Brexit might cause to the UK's MOC and in particular its financial sector. Financial lobby groups and powerful interests within the City sit at the centre of this coalition (James and Quaglia 2017). The primary government department responsible for setting UK Government economic policy, HM Treasury, effectively acts as the City's agent in Westminster. Following the financial crash, the Treasury, in conjunction with a group of City notables published the Bischoff Report that instigated a streamlining of City pro-motional and advocacy activities under one roof in the creation of TheCityUK. The Treasury has representation in TheCityUK, while TheCityUK is represented in the Treasury's own high-level group. This was an instance of the British state shaping the organisational and advocacy structures of a key industry, ensuring that the City had a coherent analytical arm and a public policy voice that were structurally entwined with the most senior levels of British economic policymaking, effectively creating a bolstered City–Treasury nexus at the heart of British development strategy and economic policymaking, at precisely the point when the City looked at its most politically vulnerable for decades (Baker and Wigan 2017: 12). The central narrative pushed by this business-as-usual power bloc is that the 'City is indispensable' for UK growth and tax revenues. Protecting its international position is therefore advanced as a key Brexit objective, ensuring that UK political parties face few incentives to actively instigate trajectory change (Baker and Wigan 2017). This City–Treasury nexus – which also enjoys support from some 'Remain' Tory MPs, the rump of the Labour PLP but not its leadership, as well as the Liberal Democrats – seeks to maintain as much continuity in UK relations with the EU and in the current UK model of capitalism, centred around protecting the role of the City. This coalition would have preferred no Brexit and will no doubt be working to minimise the degree of change that ensues. Historically, this bloc has formed the core nexus of power at the heart of the British state and economy (Ingham 1984). However, the capacity of the City to mobilise to shape the Brexit process in line with its interests has been markedly weakened for a range of political reasons (James and Quaglia 2017; Thompson 2017).

The second power bloc that can be identified is classified as the *Singapore on Thames* coalition, located in quadrant B. This bloc seeks to initiate a sharp break with EU's apparently overbearing regulatory architecture in order to *deepen* the UK's deregulated MOC. This group is supported by large swathes of the Conservative Party membership and backbench MPs, including senior members of the current Cabinet, maverick business interests and the libertarian wing of the United Kingdom Independence Party (UKIP). Brexit and the referendum process revealed that the City itself is increasingly divided as a political actor. In addition to an establishment City closely entwined with the Treasury, there is a far more aggressive and renegade City that favoured Brexit and provided a source of funding for UKIP. Examples include Andy Brough, star fund manager at Schroders, hedge fund manager Crispin Odey of Odey Asset Management, Christopher Mills of hedge fund JO Hambro and Stuart Wheeler of IG group (Dennys 2013). Party leader Nigel Farage made an explicit point of targeting the hedge fund industry for funding and frequently claimed that City support for his party was a function of excessive EU financial regulation such as the financial transaction tax proposal, which he described as a 'deliberate assault on the City'. This coalition is libertarian in inclination and includes links to Robert Mercer, a billionaire US hedge fund owner who put his Cambridge Analytica and Aggregate IQ data harvesting companies at the disposal of the Leave campaign (Cadwalladr 2017). This loose collection of renegade libertarians view Brexit as an opportunity to further reduce red tape and regulatory oversight, while pursuing lower taxes and further deregulation in a so-called Singapore-on-Thames model (CITYPERC 2017). Support for this view is also evident in many of the public positions of libertarian think tanks, such as the Institute of Economic Affairs (IEA) and the Adam Smith Institute. Freed from the shackles of EU oversight, this coalition is attempting to accentuate the dominant features of UK capitalism, intensifying its 'competition state' orientation whilst levelling down on environmental and employment standards (Fox 2017).

The third power bloc that can be identified seeks to maintain a high degree of proximity to the EU but differs from the first two blocs insofar as it seeks to initiate a decisive break with the UK's existing MOC. This power bloc – the *soft reformism* coalition – includes a large part of the Labour shadow Cabinet, some of the Parliamentary Labour Party, the Trade Unions Congress, as well as the Scottish and Welsh devolved administrations. There are, of course, internal tensions within this power bloc. For example, survey evidence suggests that 80 per cent of the Labour membership is in favour of continued membership of the Single Market. The Labour leadership have only recently softened their position on access to the single market, possibly because MPs in heavily leave constituencies have felt compelled to talk of ending free movement. Ambiguities therefore abound in the Labour position as it seeks to appease contradictory elements in its social base of support. For example, during the referendum, the party leadership campaigned on a platform of 'remain and reform', borne out of a view that, while the EU afforded some protections for British workers, the EU needed to develop a stronger social dimension, which had in recent times begun to be overshadowed by the promotion of market competitiveness and liberalization. Moreover, while the Labour leadership wanted to change and challenge the complexion of the EU, the positions adopted by factions of the Conservative Party and talk of a so-called hard Brexit, have caused the party's leadership to call for more continuity in the UK's relationship with the Single Market.

The final quadrant D we characterise as the *protectionist-interventionist-populist bloc*. This comprises a diverse array of forces, ranging from the Eurosceptic Labour left to those elements of UKIP that have aimed (unsuccessfully) to capture the blue-collar vote through a mix of economic populism and anti-immigrant rhetoric. Insofar as the Labour leadership tends towards a hard Brexit in order to end free movement, it also flirts with this political terrain, as well as some sympathies for more interventionist economic policies it may allow. These forces share a protectionist-interventionist objective of repatriating powers in order to bring about a profound break with both the institutional structures of the EU and to fundamentally restructure the UK's social and economic fabric. On the left, this implies overcoming the EU's 'state aid' rules, for example, which – it is claimed – limits the ability of the state to intervene in the economy (Guinan and Hanna 2017). It is also a position that has been articulated by *The Guardian* newspaper's economics correspondent, Larry Elliott, arguing that a more radically socialist programme would be illegal under EU law (Elliott 2017). On the right, control over borders is identified as the essential means through which jobs for 'British' workers and public services can be protected. Polanyian 'double movement' arguments invoking Brexit as a social revolt against the logic of remote and unfettered markets have consequently been made (Hopkin 2017). The populisms of the left and right within quadrant D arguably embody distinct faces of this 'double movement'. The ability of this bloc to precipitate a hard Brexit and a profound restructuring of the British economy is questionable. In organisational terms, the Eurosceptic left remains in the minority within the Labour Party (both parliamentary and among the broader membership, though not irrelevant with some sympathy from the current leadership), while UKIP's pivot towards Northern constituencies has ultimately failed. Furthermore, the structural dependence of the UK's MOC on investment flows and trade with the Single Market ensures that there are strong pressures that militate against a sharp 'cliff edge' break with the EU. The protectionist-populist bloc will continue to shape Brexit debates because they remain a potentially potent electoral group, but they are unlikely to have a decisive influence.

Conclusion

Our two-by-two matrix of rival blocs and coalitions simplifies the complex political economy of Brexit. Nonetheless, it does help us to visualise emerging conflicts between distinct positions and how rival coalitions are attempting to realise their vision for the future of UK capitalism in relation to Brexit. The situation is, of course, further complicated because the agents involved are still interpreting the rapidly evolving and complex legal, financial, economic and political terrain of the UK after Brexit, and their positions will continue to evolve as a consequence. The strategic positioning of the four power blocs is therefore fluid rather than fixed, and there is likely to be some criss-crossing and movement among the quadrants over time. Nonetheless, as a heuristic

device, our 'power bloc' typology underscores one key truth about the emerging political economy of Brexit: that the future trajectory of the UK's MOC is not preordained. *Politics* will play a
key role in shaping the future of the UK's economic model, and UK politics has been unpredictable for some time. The balance of forces between the four power blocs will be crucial. There is
no way to confidently predict which centre of power, if any, is likely to prevail. That said, a few
cautionary notes are in order by way of conclusion.

As argued earlier in this chapter, we take issue with those commentators who anticipate that Brexit will precipitate a sudden *rupture with* or rapid *deepening of* the UK's MOC.
Macroeconomists who argue that sterling devaluation could initiate a 'rebalancing' of
the UK's MOC away from finance understate the extent to which UK export sectors
are deeply integrated into EU supply chains and overstate the extent to which structural
economic transformation can occur as a result of quasi automatic adjustment to price
signals (this has been borne out so far – the sterling depreciation that has taken place
since the 2016 referendum does not as yet appear to have produced much rebalancing).
Rebalancing the UK's MOC towards greater productivity and manufacturing, including
better levels of pay in non-financial sectors would be a long and arduous process to
which there are many political barriers. Conversely, insurgent libertarian forces – such
as the Singapore-on-Thames coalition – who agitate for a low-tax, hyper-competitive
and deregulated UK MOC – find themselves aligned against considerable forces pushing
for greater continuity, though they could win isolated victories by shaping Conservative
Party policy. Business-as-usual coalitions with considerable resources will continue to
argue for a high degree of regulatory harmonisation with the EU after Brexit. Pronounced public fatigue with fiscal austerity and deteriorating public services also means
public appetite for a smaller state and reduced public investment and social protections
is likely to be limited.

The most likely outcome of this messy and complex terrain is a further iteration of the British tradition of muddling through, represented by a circle crossing the quadrants A, B and C.
The City's centrality in global finance may experience a period of turbulence and uncertainty,
but it is unlikely to lose its position as a leading global financial centre. In an era of low trade
union membership, growing employment in precarious service sectors and rising automation,
the UK's flexible labour market regime is in the short term unlikely to be subjected to a radical
upheaval. Furthermore, the 'competition state' orientation of the UK Government shows no sign
of abating, at least under the present Conservative government. For these reasons, the *continuity* of
the UK's financialised MOC, rather than its sudden transformation, seems the more likely prospect, as is evident in efforts to construct a transitional regime of post-Brexit UK–EU relations.
Further economic deterioration in the aftermath of a chaotic Brexit, including a global slow-
down, could lead to growing demands for protectionist policies on the left and right. At the same
time, the current government's need to navigate a hung parliament means that it is far from stable
and a further general election and party leadership challenges cannot be ruled out. A Corbyn-led
administration may even invoke some of the logics of quadrant D in their negotiations and public
utterances. Brexit will reduce volumes and terms of trade in the medium term, and with it falls
in investment, lower growth and likely labour market bottlenecks in both high- and low-pay sectors. In turn, this will increase fiscal pressures on the state, weaken tax revenues and may increase
fiscal and current account deficits. Economic turbulence, political volatility and deepening social
unrest may well mount. The UK's MOC is not being systematically re-engineered after Brexit,
not least because it is very difficult to simultaneously challenge political, institutional, social and
economic supports. Changing trajectory to a different model of economic and social relations
cannot be accomplished at the flick of a switch. For politicians, especially in uncertain times, there

is a certain comfort in familiarity. Swirling hostile economic conditions and volatile political conditions, global and national, do, however, continue to make Brexit and its consequences for UK capitalism highly unpredictable and deeply politically contested.

Note

1   These calculations are based on IMF measures of real effective exchange rates.

References

Albert, M. (1993) *Capitalism against Capitalism*. London: Whurr.

Arcand, J.L., Berkes, M. and Panizza, U. (2015) Too Much Finance? *Journal of Economic Growth* 20(2): 105–148.

Baccaro, L. and Pontusson, J. (2016) Rethinking Comparative Political Economy: The Growth Model Perspective. *Politics and Society* 44(2): 175–207.

Baker, A. (1999) Nebuleuse and the 'Internationalization of the State' in the UK? The Case of HM Treasury and the Bank of England. *Review of International Political Economy* 6(1): 79–100.

Baker, A. (2005) The Political Economy of the UK Competition State: Committed Globalism, Selective Europeanism. In: Stubbs, R. and Underhill, G.R.D. (eds.), *Political Economy and the Changing Global Order*. Oxford: Oxford University Press, pp. 408–418.

Baker, A. (2010) Restraining Regulatory Capture? Anglo-America, Crisis Politics and Trajectories of Change in Global Financial Governance. *International Affairs* 86(3): 647–663.

Baker, A. and Wigan, D. (2017) Constructing and Contesting City of London Power: NGOs and the Rise of Noisier Financial Politics. In: *Economy and Society*. London: Taylor & Francis Online. Available at: http:// dx.doi.org/10.1080/03085147.2017.1359909 [Accessed November 7, 2017].

Bell, S. and Hindmoor, A. (2015) Taming the City? Ideas, Structural Power and the Evolution of British Banking Policy amidst the Great Financial Meltdown. *New Political Economy* 20(3): 454–474.

Cadwalladr, C. (2017) The Great British Brexit Robbery: How our Democracy Was Hijacked. *The Guardian*, May 7. Available at: www.theguardian.com/technology/2017/may/07/the-great-british-brexit-robber y-hijacked-democracy [Accessed November 7, 2017].

CBI (2013) *Our Global Future: The Business Vision for a Reformed EU*. London. Available at: www.cbi.org.uk/ global-future/ [Accessed November 7, 2017].

CBI (2015) *The Business Vision for a Capital Markets Union in Europe*. London: CBI.

Christensen, J. and Shaxson, N. (2013) The Finance Curse: How Oversized Financial Centres Attack Democracy and Corrupt Economies. *Tax Justice Network*. Available at: www.taxjustice.net/cms/upload/ pdf/Finance_Curse_Final.pdf [Accessed November 7, 2017].

Christensen, J., Shaxson, N. and Wigan, D. (2016) The Finance Curse: Britain and the World Economy. *The British Journal of Politics and International Relations* 18(1): 255–269.

CITYPERC (2017) A Singapore on Thames? Post-Brexit Deregulation in the UK. Available at: www.city. ac.uk/__data/assets/pdf_file/0005/356558/CPRMay2017.pdf [Accessed December 21, 2017].

TheCityUK (2015) Capital Markets Union: The Perspective of European Growth Companies. Available at: www.thecityuk.com/research/capital-markets-union-the-perspective-of-european-growth-compan ies/ [Accessed November 7, 2017].

Coates, D. (2001) *Models of Capitalism: Growth and Stagnation in the Modern Era*. Hoboken, NJ: Wiley.

Conway, E. (2016) Lower Pound a Welcome Change. *Sky News*, October 11. Available at: http://news.sky. com/story/lower-pound-a-welcome-change-says-former-bank-chief-lord-king-10612690 [Accessed November 7, 2017].

Crouch, C. (2009) Privatised Keynesianism: An Unacknowledged Policy Regime. *British Journal of Politics and International Relations* 11(3): 382–399.

Dennys, H. (2013) City Firms Switching from Tories to UKIP. *Daily Telegraph*, May 24, 2013. Available at: www.telegraph.co.uk/finance/newsbysector/banksandfinance/10079115/City-firms-switching-from-Tories-to-UKIP-says-Nigel-Farage.html [Accessed November 7, 2017].

Dörry, S. (2017) The Geo-Politics of Brexit, the Euro and the City of London. *Geoforum* 85: 1–4.

Elliott, L. (2017) Why the Moaning? If Anything Can Halt Capitalism's Fat Cats Its Brexit. *The Guardian*, July 21. Available at: www.theguardian.com/commentisfree/2017/jul/21/capitalism-fat-cats-brexit-leaving-eu [Accessed November 7, 2017].

Engelen, E., Erturk, I., Froud, J., Johal, S., Leaver, A., Moran, M. and Nilsson, A. (2011) *After the Great Complacence: Financial Crisis and the Politics of Reform*. Oxford: Oxford University Press.

European Commission (2017) Meetings with Organisations and Self-Employed Individuals. *European Commission Website*. Available at: http://ec.europa.eu/transparencyinitiative/meetings/meeting.do?host=ebb93164-c494-436e-b965-e367adbcae32&d-6679426-p=1 [Accessed March 10, 2017].

Evans-Pritchard, A. (2016) Britain Should Embrace Weaker Pound. *Daily Telegraph*, October 10. Available at: www.telegraph.co.uk/business/2016/10/10/currency-guru-says-pound-slide-liberates-uk-from-malign-grip-of/ [Accessed November 7, 2017].

Faulconbridge, J.R. (2004) London and Frankfurt in Europe's Evolving Financial Centre Network. *Area* 36(3): 235–244.

Fox, J. (2017) Understanding the UK's Strange Singapore Envy. *Bloomberg View*, April 10. Available at: www.bloomberg.com/view/articles/2017-04-10/understanding-the-u-k-s-strange-singapore-envy [Accessed November 7, 2017].

Gamble, A. (2010) New Labour and Political Change. *Parliamentary Affairs* 63(4): 639–652.

Goodwin, M.J. and Heath, O. (2016) The 2016 Referendum, Brexit and the Left Behind: An Aggregate-Level Analysis of the Result. *The Political Quarterly* 87(3): 323–332.

Green, J. (2013) *The Political Economy of the Special Relationship: British Development and American Power*. Toronto: York University.

Green, J. and Lavery, S. (2015) The Regressive Recovery: Distribution, Inequality and State Power in Britain's Post-Crisis Political Economy. *New Political Economy* 20(6): 1–30.

Guinan, J. and Hanna, T. (2017) Lexit: The EU Is a Neoliberal Project, So Let's Do Something Different When We Leave It. Available at: www.newstatesman.com/politics/brexit/2017/07/lexit-eu-neoliberal-project-so-lets-do-something-different-when-we-leave-it [Accessed December 21, 2017].

Haldane, D. (2012) A Leaf Being Turned. Speech at Friend's House, Euston, London, October 29. Available at: www.bis.org/review/r121031f.pdf [Accessed November 7, 2017].

Haldane, D. (2017) Producity Puzzles. Speech at London School of Economics, March 20. Available at: www.bankofengland.co.uk/publications/Documents/speeches/2017/speech968.pdf [Accessed November 7, 2017].

Hall, P.A. (1986) *Governing the Economy: The Politics of State Intervention in Britain and France*. Oxford: Oxford University Press.

Hall, P.A. and Soskice, D. (2001) *Varieties of Capitalism: The Institutional Foundations of Comparative Advantage*. Oxford: Oxford University Press.

Hay, C. (1999) Continuity and Discontinuity in British Political Development. In: Marsh, D., Buller, J., Hay, C., Johnston, J., Kerr, P., Mcanulla, S. and Watson, M. (eds.), *Postwar British Politics in Perspective*. Hoboken, NJ: Wiley, p. 264.

Heyes, J. and Lewis, P. (2015) Employment Protection Legislation and the Growth Crisis. In: Green, J., Hay, C. and Taylor-Gooby, P. (eds.), *The British Growth Crisis: The Search for a New Model*. Basingstoke: Palgrave Macmillan, pp. 221–241.

Hopkin, J. (2017) When Polanyi Met Farage: Market Fundamentalism, Economic Nationalism, and Britain's Exit from the European Union. *The British Journal of Politics and International Relations* 19(3): 465–478.

Hyman, R. (2008) Britain and the European Social Model: Capitalism against Capitalism? *Institute for Employment Studies*, November 2008. Available at: www.employment-studies.co.uk/system/files/resources/files/wp19.pdf [Accessed November 28, 2017].

Ingham, G.K. (1984) *Capitalism Divided? The City and Industry in British Social Development*. New York: Schocken Books.

James, S. and Quaglia, L. (2017) Brexit and the Limits of Financial Power in the UK. *Global Economic Governance Programme*, May. Available at: www.bsg.ox.ac.uk/sites/www.bsg.ox.ac.uk/files/documents/GEG%20WP%20129%20-%20Brexit%20and%20the%20City_James%26Quaglia.pdf [Accessed November 28, 2017].

Jessop, B. (2002) *The Future of the Capitalist State*. Cambridge: Polity Press.

Kaminska, I. (2016) Brexit and Britain's Dutch Disease. *Financial Times*, October 12. Available at: https://ftalphaville.ft.com/2016/10/12/2177179/brexit-and-britains-dutch-disease/ [Accessed November 7, 2017].

Karl, T.L. (1997) *The Paradox of Plenty: Oil Booms and Petro States*. Berkeley, CA: Berkeley University Press.

Kneer, C. (2013) Finance as a Magnet for the Best and Brightest: Implications for the Real Economy. De Nederlandsche Bank, Working Paper No. 392. Available at: www.dnb.nl/binaries/Working%20Paper%20392_tcm46-296166.pdf [Accessed November 7, 2017].

Krugman, P. (2016) Notes on Brexit and the Pound. *New York Times*, October 11. Available at: https://krugman.blogs.nytimes.com/2016/10/11/notes-on-brexit-and-the-pound/ [Accessed November 7, 2017].

Lavery, S. (2017a) British Business Strategy, EU Social and Employment Policy and the Emerging Politics of Brexit. *SPERI Paper* No. 39, pp. 1–20. Sheffield: University of Sheffield.

Lavery, S. (2017b) The Legitimation of Post-Crisis Capitalism in the United Kingdom: Real Wage Decline, Finance-Led Growth and the State. *New Political Economy* 23(1): 1–19.

Lavery, S., Quaglia, L. and Dannreuther, C. (2017) The Political Economy of Brexit and the UK's National Business Model. *SPERI Paper* No. 41, pp. 1–57. Sheffield: University of Sheffield.

Los, B., Mccann, P., Springford, J. and Thissen, M. (2017) The Mismatch between Local Voting and the Local Economic Consequences of Brexit. *Regional Studies* 51(5): 786–799.

Peck, J. (2001) *Workfare States*. New York: Guilford Press.

Quaglia, L. (2016a) European Union Financial Regulation, Banking Union, Capital Markets Union and the UK. *SPERI Paper* No. 38, pp. 1–21. Sheffield: University of Sheffield.

Quaglia, L. (2016b) European Union Financial Regulation, Banking Union, Capital Markets Union and the UK. Available at: www.policy-network.net/publications_download.aspx?ID=9489 [Accessed December 21, 2017].

Roberts, A. (2011) *The Logic of Discipline: Global Capitalism and the Architecture of Government*. Oxford: Oxford University Press.

Ross, M.L. (1999) The Political Economy of the Resource Curse. *World Politics* 51(2): 297–322.

Ryan, L. and Mulholland, J. (2014) Trading Places: French Highly Skilled Migrants Negotiating Mobility and Emplacement. *Journal of Ethnic and Migration Studies* 40(4): 584–600.

Sassen, S. (2011) *Cities in a World Economy*. London: Sage Publications.

Scharpf, F.W. (2010) The Asymmetry of European Integration, or Why the EU Cannot Be a 'Social Market Economy'. *Socio-Economic Review* 8(2): 211–250.

Stafford, P. (2017) City's Clear Relief Tempered as EU Details Examined. *Financial Times*, June 15, 2017. Available at: www.ft.com/content/7e6f7954-50e7-11e7-a1f2-db19572361bb [Accessed November 7, 2017].

Streeck, W. and Thelen, K. (2005) Introduction : Institutional Change in Advanced Political Economies. In: Streeck, W. and Thelen, K. (eds.), *Beyond Continuity: Institutional Change in Advanced Political Economies*. Oxford: Oxford University Press, pp. 1–39.

Talani, L.S. (2012) *Globalization, Hegemony and the Future of the City of London*. Basingstoke: Palgrave Macmillan.

Taylor, P. (2004) *World City Network: A Global Urban Analysis*. London: Routledge.

Thelen, K. (2009) Institutional Change in Advanced Political Economies: First Annual Lecture of the BJIR. *British Journal of Industrial Relations* 47(3): 471–498.

Thompson, H. (2013) UK Debt in Comparative Perspective: The Pernicious Legacy of Financial Sector Debt. *British Journal of Politics and International Relations* 15(3): 476–492.

Thompson, H. (2017) Inevitability and Contingency: The Political Economy of Brexit. *The British Journal of Politics and International Relations* 19(3): 434–449.

Widmaier, W.W., Blyth, M. and Seabrooke, L. (2007) Exogenous Shocks or Endogenous Constructions? The Meanings of Wars and Crises. *International Studies Quarterly* 51(4): 747–759.

Wójcik, D. (2013) The Dark Side of NY-LON: Financial Centres and the Global Financial Crisis. *Urban Studies* 50(13): 2736–2752.

7

BREXIT AND BRITISH TRADE POLICY

Jed Odermatt

Introduction[1]

One of the economic arguments in favour of the United Kingdom leaving the European Union was that the UK would regain control over its trade policy. The EU, it was argued, had failed to enter into trade deals with important economies including the United States, Japan, India, ASEAN and Mercosur (Vote Leave 2016; Department for Exiting the European Union 2017). Unencumbered by EU membership, this argument goes, the UK would be free to strike trade deals with countries around the globe. Not only would these be concluded more quickly than those negotiated by the EU but would also be more suited to British interests. British Prime Minister Theresa May made these arguments during her speech at Lancaster House, setting out the UK's key negotiating priorities for Brexit. She argued that trade as a percentage of GDP had stagnated since the UK joined the EU, and "[t]hat is why it is time for Britain to get out into the world and rediscover its role as a great, global, trading nation" (May 2017b). According to this view, leaving the European Union would allow the UK to become a trading nation, renewing its links with the Commonwealth and creating closer ties with emerging markets in Asia and beyond.

Whether such a vision of a 'Global Britain' will become a reality remains to be seen. It is unclear whether any increased trade from new trade agreements would make up for the consequences of the UK's exit from the Single Market, especially given the size and importance of the EU for the British economy. The premise that the UK's trade is hindered by EU membership should also be questioned. Its access to the Single Market makes Britain a desirable destination, and the UK benefits from the bargaining power that comes from membership of an economic bloc consisting of the economies of 28 Member States.

This chapter does not aim to discuss these economic arguments. Rather, it focuses on the legal and practical issues that arise from the UK gaining autonomy over its trade policy. As UK Secretary for International Trade Liam Fox pointed out in a speech to the first meeting of the UK–US Trade and Investment Working Group: "Our challenge is not primarily economic, but practical and political" (Fox 2017). The chapter gives an overview of some of these challenges and identifies ways in which they could be addressed.

The chapter is divided into three main sections. The first section discusses the fate of existing trade agreements upon the UK's withdrawal from the EU. It discusses whether the UK will continue to be bound by EU agreements after Brexit and how the UK may seek to ensure stability and certainty during a period of transition. It also discusses the issues that arise regarding the UK's membership in the World Trade Organization (WTO). The second section then turns towards the UK's future trade relationship with the EU. Although different models have been discussed, it appears the most likely option is that the UK will enter into a free trade agreement (FTA) with the EU with transitional arrangements in place during the interim. This raises questions about the design of such an agreement. The final section then discusses the UK's trade with the rest of the world. This also gives rise to new questions, such as the timing of negotiations, the types of agreements to be concluded and the scope of their coverage. These three issues – the fate of pre-Brexit agreements, the EU–UK FTA and trade agreements with non-EU countries – are inexorably linked. The type of trade agreements the UK will negotiate with non-EU states, for instance, will depend on the type of agreement concluded between the EU and the UK. The phased approach to Brexit negotiations, whereby the practical arrangements for the UK's withdrawal are discussed before any future trade relationship, may make it more difficult to adopt the practical measures necessary to ensure a smooth transition.

Pre-Brexit trade agreements

Challenges of Brexit

Since the UK joined the European Economic Community (EEC) in 1973, the UK has not had an independent trade policy. The UK has always had the power to encourage trade and investment. UK Trade & Investment (UKTI), for example, dealt with trade promotion, helping British businesses to gain access to international markets and to attract foreign direct investment. The new Department for International Trade (DIT) has taken over this role. Yet upon the UK's departure from the Union, DIT will take over many of the responsibilities that previously fell within the EU's Common Commercial Policy (CCP), an area where the EU has exclusive competence. In addition to the negotiation of trade agreements, DIT and other government departments will be tasked with the responsibilities previously exercised by the EU institutions, such as the Directorate General for Trade (DG Trade). This includes, for example, international representation on trade issues in various international forums. While most of this will involve participation in negotiations and dispute settlement in the WTO context, it also includes the UK's involvement in informal bodies (e.g. G20) and standard-setting bodies dealing with trade-related issues (e.g. Codex Alimentarius Commission). Beyond these international engagements, the UK will have to be prepared to take trade remedies, such as anti-dumping action, in response to action that causes injury to a domestic industry. The UK Government aims to establish a new Trade Remedies Organization in order to investigate and respond to incidents of unfair trade (Mance 2017b). The UK will also have to develop policy in areas related to trade, such as sanctions policy and export controls. Regaining autonomy over trade policy involves much more than the negotiation of trade agreements.

This transition – from having almost no autonomous trade policy to a being in a position to negotiate trade agreements with the EU and the rest of the world – will pose practical challenges for the UK Government. Given that the UK Civil Service has very little experience and expertise in trade negotiations, the UK Government has sought to hire and train negotiators in the DIT and other departments to address this gap. DIT appointed Crawford Falconer, New Zealand's former ambassador to the World Trade Organization, as the chief trade negotiation adviser (Department for International Trade 2017). In addition to recruiting and training talent in DIT, a further challenge will be to implement trade policy across other relevant departments, including the Department for Exiting the European Union (DExEU).

Existing EU trade agreements

As an EU Member State, the UK is currently covered by international agreements entered into by the EU. First, there are agreements to which the EU is a party but not the individual Member States (EU-only agreements). The UK is bound by EU-only agreements by virtue of EU law, specifically Article 216(2) of the Treaty on the Functioning of the European Union (TFEU) (2012). Second, there are agreements to which both the EU and the Member States are parties (mixed agreements). What will be the fate of these agreements upon the UK's withdrawal from the EU?

The UK will no longer be bound by EU-only agreements after withdrawal. This is because the UK will be neither an EU Member State nor a contracting party in its own right (Van der Loo and Blockmans 2016). These agreements usually include a territorial application clause that sets out that they apply to the area in which EU law is applied, which will no longer include UK territory after Brexit. One could make the argument, however, that the UK could continue to be bound by such agreements upon Brexit by way of succession. According to this argument, the EU entered into commitments 'on behalf' of the UK, and these commitments would then flow back to the UK upon its exit from the Union. Lorand Bartels has made this argument in relation to the WTO Government Procurement Agreement (World Trade Organization 2014), a plurilateral agreement that includes the EU as a party but not the UK. He argues that "on leaving the EU, the UK will succeed to the GPA in its own right, in accordance with rules of customary international law on the succession of States to treaties, and practice under the GATT 1947, which 'guides' the WTO" (Bartels 2016a: 18). This succession argument is based in part on the practice of the dissolution of unions and federations (ibid.: 19). There is very little international practice of states leaving an international organization, however, especially one like the EU that has its own independent international obligations. Whereas there is customary international law applicable to the succession of states to treaties, there is no such developed practice in relation to the departure from international organizations.

One approach would be to apply, by analogy, the customary rules of state succession, which are reflected in the Vienna Convention on Succession of States in Respect of Treaties (United Nations 1978). Yet this can only take us so far, since this treaty applies with respect "to the effects of a succession of States in respect of treaties between States" (Article 1). It is not clear why rules of succession developed in the context of state succession would be applicable to a sovereign state leaving an international organization. The cited practice relating to succession of trade agreements relies on examples of the dissolution of unions of states, not to economic integration organizations such as the EU. In his report on succession in respect of treaties, Humphrey Waldock (1972) cautioned against treating economic organizations as unions of states: "there are some hybrid unions which may appear to have some analogy with a union of States but which do not, in the opinion of the Special Rapporteur, form part of the present topic. . . . One such hybrid is EEC [European Economic Community]." For the purposes of succession, the EEC was to be dealt with as an intergovernmental organization rather than being analogous to unions of states. There are relevant differences between instances of state succession and a state leaving an international organization. In situations of state succession, there is a change in sovereign authority over a territory, including instances of decolonization, secession, state dissolution or merger. The law of state succession, one of the most disputed fields of international law, was developed in relation to these types of scenarios (Shaw 2014: 695) and is concerned with ensuring continuity and stability in treaty relations.

Adam Łazowski and Ramses Wessel (2017: 13) also point to some "serious flaws" with the succession argument. The first obstacle is that EU-only agreements do not include the UK or the other Member States as a contracting party. Second, these agreements are often structured in a bilateral way, or include commitments that can only be effectively exercised within the EU framework. This means that it might prove difficult to apply these agreements to the context of the UK as a separate, non–EU party. These arguments are not necessarily fatal to the succession theory. Just because it might prove difficult to disentangle the UK's obligations from the EU context does not mean that such an exercise could not be carried out. The other argument against succession is that it denies the EU's status as a separate and distinct legal entity in international law. Since the EU is an autonomous actor with legal personality, they argue that "it is difficult to hold on to the idea that the EU acted on behalf of its Member States." (ibid.). The EU is not bound by the international obligations of its members. Likewise, EU Member States are no longer bound by agreements entered into by the EU once they have formally left the organization.

The analysis differs with regard to mixed agreements, since the UK is a party to these agreements alongside the EU. Whether these obligations continue to apply to the UK depends on how the agreement in question defines the 'contracting parties'. In many instances, the UK's status as a contracting party is tied to its membership of the EU. This is the case, for instance, when an agreement applies to the "EU and its Member States." Many mixed agreements are structured in a bilateral manner, with the EU and its Member States on one side and the other State or group of States on the other (Van der Loo and Blockmans 2016). Yet in other instances, the UK is clearly a contracting party in its own right, and its status is in no way connected to EU membership. This is most often the case for multilateral mixed agreements (Van der Loo and Wessel 2017: 736). In these situations, the UK will remain bound by international obligations.

Since international law provides no clear answers, the fate of EU agreements should be addressed within the withdrawal agreement to be negotiated by the EU and UK. For example, it could set out a list of agreements to which the UK would continue to be bound post-Brexit. This 'continuity strategy' would allow the UK (and the EU) to decide which agreements remain applicable to the UK immediately after its departure (Cremona 2017: 251). This will depend on practical issues, such as whether the agreement can be applied outside the context of EU membership. Such a strategy cannot take place unilaterally, however, since other parties to the agreement should agree to this change in status. In this case, a protocol should be adopted to allow the UK to continue as a separate, non–EU party and to make any appropriate modifications to take into account the UK's status. This would follow the practice of when new states join the EU, where a protocol amends the agreement allowing the participation of the new Member State. The continuity strategy has the benefit of ensuring some stability for the UK, the EU and their trading partners. Such a strategy could apply for a transitional period, in which the UK would decide whether to replace its former EU agreements.

The European Council guidelines appear to support this continuity strategy. The Guidelines accept that, after withdrawal, the UK will no longer be bound by agreements concluded by the EU or by the EU and the Member States acting jointly. Yet they also point to the need for continuity, setting out that the European Council:

> expects the United Kingdom to honour its share of all international commitments contracted in the context of its EU membership. In such instances, a constructive dialogue with the United Kingdom on a possible common approach towards third country partners, international organisations and conventions concerned should be engaged.
>
> *(European Council 2017)*

This suggests that the UK will not have a completely 'clean slate' after Brexit but may remain bound by certain obligations undertaken in the EU context.

WTO

Another preliminary issue that must be addressed is the UK's position in the WTO after Brexit. The UK was a founding member of the General Agreement on Tariffs and Trade (GATT) and is a WTO member alongside the EU. The UK will continue to be a WTO member and exercise its rights and obligations of WTO membership upon Brexit. It will remain bound by the multilateral WTO agreements, such as the Agreement on Trade-Related Aspects of Intellectual Property Rights (TRIPS). Yet there are areas where the UK's obligations will need to be updated to reflect the UK gaining autonomy over trade policy. This is because, since the EU has exclusive competence in CCP, these rights have been exercised by the EU, not the UK. Both the EU and the UK will wish to resolve some of these issues relatively quickly. The so-called WTO option is considered to be the default position if there is no EU–UK trade agreement in place by the date of Brexit. This is far from an ideal outcome – it has been described as "the cold hard floor on which the UK will splat down if no safety net is in place in time" (Green 2017). Non-EU states will want to know the details of the UK's position in the WTO before any trade negotiations take place, since WTO rules act as a baseline for future negotiations (Cremona 2017: 264). The UK's status within the WTO should therefore be clarified before its trade relationships with the EU and with other states can be determined.

Of the many WTO issues that arise from Brexit, the one that has received the most attention from trade lawyers has been the issue of WTO schedules. These schedules set out the maximum tariff that applies to a good or class of goods in relation to each WTO member. The UK does not currently have its own individual schedules covering trade in goods and services because these are currently shared with the EU. The question, then, is which rates will apply in respect to the UK once it is no longer an EU member. The position of the UK Government and many trade lawyers is that the UK could simply 'cut and paste' the EU schedules, thereby replicating the previous situation to the UK context (Blitz and Donnan 2016). The DIT has indicated that it aims to replicate as far as possible the UK's position under the EU, thereby allowing greater certainty and continuity. Others have argued that this could not be achieved so easily, since it would involve negotiations between the UK, EU and other WTO members in order to accept new schedules (Hillman and Horlick 2017: 6). In some fields, it may not be easy to unbundle the EU and UK shares. For instance, this would be more complex regarding agricultural goods covered by tariff-rate quotas (TRQs), which rise in steps along with the volume of imports. There is no simple rule or formula for dividing 'shared' quotas (Bartels 2016b). However, as previously discussed in relation to succession, just because untangling these obligations would be complicated does not meant that it could not be carried out.

This also gives rise to the question of whether the new schedules would need to be accepted by the WTO membership, the concern being that the UK's trading relationships would be under an effective veto by other WTO members. There were initial fears that the UK would be subject to complicated and protracted negotiations in the WTO upon Brexit, spurred in part by comments by WTO Director General Roberto Azevêdo before the Brexit vote warning of these complications (Donnan 2016). Such fears and concerns seem to have subsided, however. The division of the EU schedules should be viewed as a technical exercise rather than as an opening for political negotiations. This does not mean, however, that the WTO will not be a ground for politics (Ungphakorn 2016). As with the continuity strategy previously discussed, other WTO members may protest these changes if they believe they would cause economic harm. The resolution of this issue will depend not only on the application of legal doctrine but also on the willingness of other WTO members to support the positions of the UK and the EU. As such, the EU and UK will be involved in a diplomatic exercise to ensure that the UK and EU commitments can be disentangled without having a negative effect on the rights of any third parties.

As the UK gains autonomy over its trade policy, it will also find that its freedom of manoeuvre is also limited by its WTO membership. The UK must ensure that its domestic rules comply with WTO law and that new trade agreements comply with those commitments (Messenger 2017). It is unlikely that these WTO commitments will be as politically contentious as EU law or the dispute settlement mechanism as controversial as the EU Court of Justice. The UK consistently argues that it supports free trade and a rules-based system of trade governance in which the WTO plays a central role.

Trade with the EU

Article 50(2) of the Treaty on European Union sets out that the Union is to negotiate and conclude with the leaving state an agreement setting out "arrangements for its withdrawal, taking account of the framework for its future relationship with the Union" (Treaty on European Union 2012). This is widely understood to mean that there will be two separate agreements: a 'divorce' agreement that addresses the immediate consequences of the UK's withdrawal (the UK's financial obligations, rights of UK and EU citizens, the border with Ireland etc.) and an agreement relating to the future relationship between the EU and the UK. Whereas the withdrawal agreement is to be negotiated within the two-year period (unless extended), there is no such time limit applicable to the future relationship agreement. Nonetheless, the British Government maintains that it will conclude a future relationship agreement by the time the UK officially leaves the EU. Given these time constraints and the political deadlock that has already appeared during the negotiations, it is unlikely that a comprehensive trade agreement could be concluded without some kind of transitional period to prevent a 'hard landing' on the Brexit date.

Non-FTA options

The British electorate voted in favour of leaving the Union, but it did not decide upon the type of relationship the UK should have with the EU upon withdrawal. A number of possible options are available, each of which differs in terms of how closely aligned the UK wishes to remain to the EU. At one end of the spectrum are options that envisage the UK remaining in the Customs Union and Single Market (the so-called soft Brexit). The UK Government has rejected these options since they would leave the UK "half-in, half-out" (May 2017b). This rigid position appears to be based more on ideological grounds related to regaining sovereignty than solid economic arguments. At the other end of the spectrum is having 'no deal' in place by the time of withdrawal, which would mean a fallback to WTO rules. This option is also unacceptable given the economic impact that such a sudden change would have. Between these extremes are various models, the details of which are discussed extensively elsewhere (House of Commons International Trade Committee 2017).

There has been much more discussion recently of possible transitional arrangements that would ease the UK's exit, for example, the option of the UK rejoining the European Free Trade Association (EFTA) (Waterfield 2017). The EFTA option has become more appealing as the UK Government realizes the need for transitional arrangements in order to avoid a 'cliff edge' moment for British businesses (Cooper and von der Burchard 2017). EFTA already has a number of free trade agreements in place. Moreover, it is also not a political union in the same way as the EU, which may be more appealing to the UK. A report of the House of Commons International Trade Committee called upon the government to explore potential benefits of EFTA membership (House of Commons International Trade Committee 2017, para. 23).

At the time of writing, the UK Government still showed a strong preference for concluding a comprehensive trade agreement with the EU. Such an agreement, moreover, would seek not to replicate any of the 'models' of other countries but to develop an agreement suited to the UK (May 2017b).

Free trade agreement with the EU

Article 50 TEU does not require the EU or the leaving state to enter into an agreement on their future arrangements, only stating that the withdrawal agreement should be negotiated "*taking account* of the framework for its future relationship with the Union". It is clearly in the interests of both sides to conclude such a treaty, yet there is disagreement upon what kind of agreement this will be.

The first issue relates to when negotiations on a future relationship agreement could start. The UK was originally in favour of starting negotiations of the withdrawal agreement and future relationship agreement simultaneously. Brexit Secretary David Davis stated that the timetable for the Brexit talks would be the "row of the summer" (Mance 2017a). The EU position was that any trade talks could only begin once substantial progress had been made on preliminary exit issues. The sequencing of the negotiations is closely tied to the negotiation strategy of each side – the UK clearly believes it would have a better hand if all issues are discussed together rather than in discrete blocks. The phased approach, as promoted by the EU, would make it very difficult to achieve a trade agreement within the two-year period, making it more likely that the UK will accept an 'implementation period' or 'transitional arrangements'. In order to facilitate this smooth transition, the UK will seek to retain current customs arrangements with the EU for a number of years, yet it is unclear how this will work in practice (Pickars et al. 2017).

Another question relates to what a future relationship agreement would include. The UK seeks a "deep and special partnership between the UK and the EU, taking in both economic and security cooperation" (May 2017a). Yet an agreement could include many other issues besides trade and security cooperation, such as cooperation in the fields of science and education. The future arrangements between the EU and the UK may take the form of multiple agreements. This could consist, for example, of a comprehensive FTA in parallel with bilateral agreements in other areas of cooperation such as security, free movement and education. WTO law would prevent agreements on specific sectors, however, since an FTA should cover 'substantially all trade' (Cremona 2017: 255). The European Council guidelines also set out as a core principle that "[p] reserving the integrity of the Single Market excludes participation based on a sector-by-sector approach" (European Council 2017, para. 1). What would be the benefit of multiple agreements? First, focusing on trade to the exclusion of other issues could speed up the conclusion of any agreement. Another benefit is that it could allow the agreement to be concluded as an EU-only agreement, which would mean that it would not have to involve the 27 individual Member States, which would also slow down the process. Recent CJEU jurisprudence including *Opinion 2/15* on the EU–Singapore FTA may support this approach. The CJEU held that a number of fields belonged to the exclusive competence of the EU, including intellectual property, competition, public procurement, sustainable development, transport and transport services. As such, it appears that an EU–UK FTA could be concluded so that does not include the individual Member States as parties.

Given that the UK is already an EU Member State, some have argued that this makes the negotiation of an EU–UK trade deal relatively straightforward. Liam Fox stated, for instance, that "[n]ever before have two parties seeking a new trade agreement begun with the advantages of complete regulatory equivalence and a zero tariff environment" (Fox 2017). It is true that the EU and UK will start from a position of tariff-free market access and a high level of regulatory convergence. After Brexit, however, it will be difficult to retain this common 'regulatory space'. Upon leaving the EU, the UK will no longer be bound by EU law. While the Repeal Bill seeks to retain much of the EU *acquis* in British law, there is no way to ensure that British regulation will remain compatible with EU standards after that. One option would be to have a mechanism to monitor regulatory divergence. The EFTA surveillance authority, for example, monitors compliance with EEA rules in Iceland, Liechtenstein and Norway. The UK is unlikely to accept any form of external supervision given that one of the primary aims of Brexit was to regain control of its laws. This would mean that the EU and UK would no longer form a harmonized regulatory space. An EU–UK FTA would therefore not reproduce elements of EU membership in a new form but will probably resemble the type of relationship the EU has with other non-EU members, such as the EU–Canada Comprehensive Economic and Trade Agreement (CETA). Given the existing close links between the UK and European markets, including integrated supply chains, this loss of a common regulatory space could have a negative impact on EU–UK trade.

Another issue of concern is the 'red lines' that both the EU and UK have set out, which limit the possibilities for compromises and innovative solutions. On the EU side, the European Council Guidelines firmly state that a non-member cannot have the same rights as a member if it does not agree to live up to same conditions. This is widely interpreted to mean that the UK would need to accept continued free movement of EU citizens and the jurisdiction of the CJEU to continue to access the Single Market. On the UK side, the position of the government is equally firm that it cannot accept such arrangements that would simply replicate EU membership in a new form. One area where such non-negotiable red lines may prove difficult to reach an agreement is on the issue of dispute settlement. Both the UK and EU agree that a future relationship agreement should include some form of dispute settlement in order to provide legal certainty and to enforce its terms, yet there is sharp disagreement on what this would entail. Since the UK is adamant that it must remain outside the CJEU jurisdiction, it would reject a trade agreement that involves CJEU supervision. On the other hand, an agreement that establishes a new form of dispute settlement, such as a hybrid court or panel, would unlikely be accepted by the EU. This is because the CJEU would likely find that such arrangements violate the autonomy of the EU legal order if they allow for that body to interpret EU law, even indirectly.

A position paper released by the UK Government on "Future Customs Arrangements" sets out that the UK seeks customs arrangements that secure "the freest and most frictionless trade possible in goods between the UK and the EU" (HM Treasury et al. 2017: 2). The paper sets out two possible arrangements. The first is a "highly streamlined customs arrangement", whereby the EU and UK trade as third parties but would continue some of the existing agreements between the UK and the EU. The second approach is for a new customs "partnership" with the EU, which would entail the UK aligning (or 'mirroring') its approach to the customs border so that there is no need for a UK–EU customs border. The UK acknowledges that this is an innovative and untested approach (ibid.: 10) and that there may be challenges reconciling these approaches with the UK's independent trade policy. The position paper is light on details and sets out objectives and ideas rather than any concrete solutions. It recognizes that the shape of any future customs arrangement will depend largely on the outcome of negotiations in other areas, including the UK–EU trade agreement and the goal of ensuring there is no hard border between the UK and Ireland. The paper is much more open to transitional arrangements, speaking of "a time-limited interim period" in order to prevent a cliff-edge scenario (ibid.: 2). This would allow the EU and UK time to implement any new arrangements, which may include new technology-based solutions, and give businesses time to adjust. It is unlikely, however, that the UK could allow new trade agreements with third countries to enter into force while interim arrangements are in effect.

Although the UK wants "frictionless" trade with the EU post-Brexit, this will be difficult to reconcile with the UK's desire to leave the Customs Union and pursue a fully independent trade policy. Even the scenarios set out in the position paper would require new solutions that would produce more red tape (Pickard and Toplensky 2017).

Trade with the rest of the world

While it is important for the UK to continue trading with EU countries after Brexit, the UK already has trade agreements beyond Europe in its sights. As Prime Minister May outlined in her Lancaster speech, a Global Britain must "get out into the world and rediscover its role as a great, global, trading nation" (May 2017b). This also comes with practical questions and challenges.

When can the UK begin negotiations on a trade agreement with a third country? The UK cannot legally conclude any agreement until it officially is no longer an EU member (House of Commons International Trade Committee 2017, para. 164). Yet there might be some flexibility about what the UK is entitled to do before that date. Given that securing a trade agreement can take several years of negotiation and then ratification, the UK will want the opportunity to begin preliminary talks soon. It could be argued that the UK is legally prevented from even participating in such talks before Brexit, since this would breach the UK's duty of sincere cooperation under EU law. There is no reason for a rigid approach to this issue. The UK has now officially activated Article 50 by notifying its intent to withdrawal, and while EU law continues to apply with respect to the UK, its obligations should be understood in light of its status as a withdrawing member. Allowing the UK to enter into preliminary talks with third countries would not necessarily undermine the EU's international position in other trade negotiations and could even allow a smoother transition. As Cremona (2017: 265) argues, such an approach would be legally defensible because it gives "a practical expression to the duty of cooperation working in a post-notification transitional context." The question, then, is at which point 'preliminary talks' are considered prohibited 'negotiations'?

From a practical perspective, third states may not wish to enter into negotiations with the UK until the other preliminary issues previously discussed – EU trade agreements, WTO schedules, the future EU–UK relationship – have been more or less settled. In the meantime, DIT has begun to prepare the ground for such preliminary discussions with non-EU countries.

The next question is which countries or group of countries the UK would prioritise. Given its finite resources and experience, DIT must decide where to focus its attention. Such decisions will likely be shaped as much by politics, history and geography as by hard economic interests. As discussed, the UK's first priority, in order to allow a smooth transition, should be those countries with whom the EU has existing trade agreements. The Brexit White Paper stresses that the UK will seek "continuity" in its trade and investment relationships that are now covered by EU FTAs (Department for Exiting the European Union 2017, para. 9.11), a strategy referred to as "grandfathering" EU trade agreements (House of Commons International Trade Committee 2017, para. 150).

Beyond this, Prime Minister May has outlined the Government's desire to enter trade agreements with "old friends and new allies from outside Europe" (May 2017b). In the first place, connecting with "old friends" would mean entering into agreements with countries in the Commonwealth including Australia, New Zealand, India and Canada. There is also a strong desire to enter talks with the United States. Although President Barack Obama had stated previously that Brexit would put the UK to the 'back of the queue' in trade talks, it is unclear whether this has changed under the Trump administration. President Donald Trump has indicated his intention to begin trade talks with the UK, but the United States may still prefer to strike an agreement with the EU first, since it is the far larger and more important market (Barber 2017). In addition to "old friends", the UK has also shown a desire to "increase significantly its trade with the fastest growing export markets in the world" (May 2017b) and has mentioned China, Brazil and the Gulf States as potential partners.

In addition to deciding which countries to enter into discussions with, the UK must also decide the type of agreements to pursue and what they will cover. In recent years, the EU has focused on large and complex 'mega regional' trade agreements that aim at deep integration between markets, such as the Transatlantic Trade and Investment Partnership (TTIP). The UK might follow a different approach, focusing less on deep integration between developed economies (covering e.g. investment, services, public procurement etc.) and more on trade agreements focusing on a more limited range of issues.

Conclusion

The UK's decision to leave the EU is often presented as a decision by 'little Britain' to retreat from the world. Viewed this way, leaving the EU is about escaping from the realities of globalisation and a desire to increase protectionism. Yet since the Brexit vote, Prime Minister May has sought to reframe Brexit in the opposite light, arguing that Brexit is about rediscovering the UK's role as a Global Britain. According to this vision, Brexit not only allows the UK to regain its sovereignty, it also allows it to reengage with the partners beyond Europe: "the United Kingdom – a country that has so often been at the forefront of economic and social change – will step up to a new leadership role as the strongest and most forceful advocate for business, free markets and free trade anywhere in the world" (May 2017c). Even if such ambitions are realized, they entail numerous legal, practical and political complications. This chapter has discussed some of the possible challenges and the ways in which they could be addressed. It is in the interests of all parties to address these issues soon. Rather than deal with them in isolation, the different aspects of UK trade policy should be dealt with together, since they are related to other issues of withdrawal. Trade is also an area in which both the UK and EU have a strong interest in working together to support a smoother transition. Trade should not be considered a separate topic for future discussion but as a high priority to ensure continuity and certainty for businesses in Europe, the UK and the rest of the world.

Note

1   This article was last updated 31 August 2017.

References

Barber, T. (2017) The EU and UK's Race for a US Trade Deal. *Financial Times*, April 26, 2017. Available at: www.ft.com/content/f6be0ac8-2a73-11e7-bc4b-5528796fe35c [Accessed August 25, 2017].

Bartels, L. (2016a) The UK's Status in the WTO after Brexit. In: Schütze, R. and Tierney, S. (eds.), *The United Kingdom: 'Federalism' Within and Without*. University of Cambridge Faculty of Law Legal Studies Research Paper Series. Available at: https://papers.ssrn.com/sol3/papers.cfm?abstract_id=2841747 [Accessed August 25, 2017].

Bartels, L. (2016b) Understanding the UK's Position in the WTO after Brexit: Part II: The Consequences. *International Centre for Trade and Sustainable Development*, September 26, 2016. Available at: www.ictsd. org/opinion/understanding-the-uk-0 [Accessed August 25, 2017].

Blitz, J. and Donnan, S. (2016) Liam Fox Opens Talks with WTO over Terms of Membership. *Financial Times*, December, 2016. Available at: www.ft.com/content/97d1c8ce-bb0b-11e6-8b45-b8b81dd5d080 [Accessed August 25, 2017].

Cooper, C. and von der Burchard, H. (2017) UK Drifts Closer to a Norway-Style Brexit Transition. *Politico*, August 3, 2017. Available at: www.politico.eu/article/brexit-eea-negotiation-transition-uk-drifts-closer -to-norway-style [Accessed August 25, 2017].

Cremona, M. (2017) UK Trade Policy. In: Dougan, M. (ed.), *The UK after Brexit: Legal and Policy Challenges*. Cambridge: Intersentia, pp. 247–265.

Department for Exiting the European Union (2017) The United Kingdom's Exit from and New Partnership with the European Union White Paper, May 15, 2017. Available at: www.gov.uk/government/

publications/the-united-kingdoms-exit-from-and-new-partnership-with-the-european-union-white-paper [Accessed August 25, 2017].

Department for International Trade (2017) DIT Appoints Crawford Falconer as New Chief Trade Negotiation Adviser. Available at: www.gov.uk/government/news/dit-appoints-crawford-falconer-as-new-chief-trade-negotiation-adviser [Accessed August 25, 2017].

Donnan, S. (2016) WTO Warns on Tortuous Brexit Trade Talks. *Financial Times*, May 25, 2016. Available at: www.ft.com/content/745d0ea2-222d-11e6-9d4d-c11776a5124d [Accessed August 25, 2017].

European Council (2017) *Guidelines Following the United Kingdom's Notification under Article 50 TEU*. Note, XT 20004, April 29, 2017.

Fox, L. (2017) *Liam Fox Champions Global Free Trade*. Speech at the AEI during his US Visit for the First Meeting of the UK–US Trade and Investment Working Group, July 24, 2017. Available at: www.gov.uk/government/speeches/liam-fox-champions-global-free-trade [Accessed August 25, 2017].

Green, D. (2017) Brexit and the Issue of the WTO Schedules, February 28, 2017. Available at: http://blogs.ft.com/david-allen-green/2017/02/28/brexit-and-the-issue-of-the-wto-schedules/ [Accessed August 25, 2017].

Hillman, J. and Horlick, G. (2017) Introduction. In: Hillman, J. and Horlick, G. (eds.), *Legal Aspects of Brexit: Implications of the United Kingdom's Decision to withdraw from the European Union*. Washington, DC: Institute of International Economic Law, pp. 1–8.

HM Treasury, HM Revenue and Customs and Department for Exiting the European Union (2017) Policy Paper: Future Customs Arrangements: A Future Partnership Paper, August 15, 2017. Available at: www.gov.uk/government/publications/future-customs-arrangements-a-future-partnership-paper [Accessed August 29, 2017].

House of Commons International Trade Committee (2017) UK Trade Options Beyond 2019, March 7, 2017. Available at: https://publications.parliament.uk/pa/cm201617/cmselect/cmintrade/817/817.pdf [Accessed August 25, 2017].

Łazowski, A. and Wessel, R.A. (2017) The External Dimension of Withdrawal from the European Union. *Revue des Affaires européennes*. Available at: www.utwente.nl/en/bms/pa/research/wessel/wessel122.pdf [Accessed August 25, 2017].

Mance, H. (2017a) David Davis Warns Brexit Timetable Will Be 'Row of the Summer'. *Financial Times*, May 14, 2017. Available at: www.ft.com/content/01396086-38ae-11e7-821a-6027b8a20f23 [Accessed August 25, 2017].

Mance, H. (2017b) Job Advert Reveals Surprise Plans for New Trade Authority. *Financial Times*, August 2, 2017. Available at: www.ft.com/content/78201a5e-77a2-11e7-a3e8-60495fe6ca71 [Accessed August 25, 2017].

May, T. (2017a) *Article 50 Notification Letter 2017*. London: 10 Downing Street, March 29, 2017. Available at: www.gov.uk/government/uploads/system/uploads/attachment_data/file/604079/Prime_Ministers_letter_to_European_Council_President_Donald_Tusk.pdf [Accessed October 30, 2017].

May, T. (2017b) The Government's Negotiating Objectives for Exiting the EU: PM Speech. Available at: www.gov.uk/government/speeches/the-governments-negotiating-objectives-for-exiting-the-eu-pm-speech [Accessed August 25, 2017].

May, T. (2017c) Speech to the 2017 World Economic Forum, January 19, 2017. Available at: http://nordic.businessinsider.com/theresa-may-davos-speech-full-text-2017-1?r=UK&IR=T [Accessed October 30, 2017].

Messenger, G. (2017) Membership of the World Trade Organization. In: Dougan, M. (ed.), *The UK after Brexit: Legal and Policy Challenges*. Cambridge: Intersentia, pp. 225–245.

Pickard, J. and Toplensky, R. (2017) Brexit Customs Plan Threatens to Increase Obstacles to Trade. *Financial Times*. Available at: www.ft.com/content/25e8643c-81b4-11e7-a4ce-15b2513cb3ff [Accessed August 29, 2017].

Pickars, J., Tetlow, G. and Beesley, A. (2017) UK Looks to Retain Brussels Customs Deal. *Financial Times*, August 2015. Available at: www.ft.com/content/f6be0ac8-2a73-11e7-bc4b-5528796fe35c.www.ft.com/content/b58ca3b6-811c-11e7-a4ce-15b2513cb3ff [Accessed August 25, 2017].

Shaw, M. (2014) *International Law*. 7th Edition. Cambridge: Cambridge University Press.

Treaty on European Union (TEU) (2012) Official Journal C326, October 26, 2012. Available at: http://eur-lex.europa.eu/legal-content/EN/TXT/HTML/?uri=CELEX:12012M/TXT&from=DA [Accessed September 6, 2017].

Treaty on the Functioning of the European Union (TFEU) (2012) Official Journal C326, October 26, 2012. Available at: http://eur-lex.europa.eu/legal-content/EN/TXT/HTML/?uri=CELEX:12012E/TXT&from=EN [Accessed September 6, 2017].

Ungphakorn, P. (2016) Nothing Simple about UK Regaining WTO Status Post-Brexit. *International Centre for Trade and Sustainable Development*, June 27, 2016. Available at: www.ictsd.org/opinion/nothing-simple-about-uk-regaining-wto-status-post-brexit [Accessed August 25, 2017].

United Nations (1987) Vienna Convention on Succession of States in Respect of Treaties, August 23. Available at: http://legal.un.org/ilc/texts/instruments/english/conventions/3_2_1978.pdf [Accessed September 6, 2017].

Van der Loo, G. and Blockmans, S. (2016) The Impact of Brexit on the EU's International Agreements. *Centre for European Policy Studies*. Available at: www.ceps.eu/publications/impact-brexit-eu's-international-agreements [Accessed August 25, 2017].

Van der Loo, G. and Wessel, R. A. (2017) The Non-Ratification of Mixed Agreements: Legal Consequences and Solutions. *Common Market Law Review* 54(3): 735–770.

Vote Leave (2016) Briefing: Trade, Investment and Jobs Will Benefit If We Vote Leave. Available at: www.voteleavetakecontrol.org/briefing_trade.html [Accessed August 25, 2017].

Waldock, H. (1972) Fifth Report on Succession in Respect of Treaties. *Yearbook of the International Law Commission* 18(2). U.N. Doc. A/CN.4/SER.A/1972/Add.1.

Waterfield, B. (2017) European Court of Justice President Koen Lenaerts Offers European Free Trade Association as Solution to Brexit Conundrum. *The Times*, August 9, 2017. Available at: www.thetimes.co.uk/article/european-court-of-justice-president-koen-lenaerts-offers-european-free-trade-association-as-solution-to-brexit-conundrum-dnwf83zxw [Accessed August 25, 2017].

World Trade Organization (2014) Agreement on Government Procurement: Text of the Agreement. Available at: www.wto.org/english/tratop_e/gproc_e/gpa_1994_e.htm [Accessed October 30, 2017].

8

BREXIT AND AGRICULTURE

Wyn Grant

Introduction: the Common Agricultural Policy

The Common Agricultural Policy (CAP) has been a cornerstone of the European Community since its formation. It was the earliest policy to be developed and has continued to be an influence on the business decisions taken by farmers. It remains the largest single component of the European Union (EU) budget at 39 per cent of the total. In the 2014–2020 financial framework period, €400 billion will be spent on the CAP. The EU considers that it has provided safe and secure food for European citizens at affordable prices with increasing attention being paid to its environmental impact. Given the size of the CAP budget and an anticipated net reduction of 8 per cent in EU revenues following Brexit, adjustments to the scope and form of the CAP will be a major agenda item for the EU.

Attitudes towards the CAP in the UK have been largely negative. From a UK Government perspective, the CAP has been a major factor in ensuring that the UK has been a net contributor to the EU budget, given that the UK has fewer farmers as a percentage of the working population than most other member states. The UK Government has sought to reform the CAP to make it more efficient and reduce its budgetary impact but has found it difficult to win support for change from a sufficient number of other member states. Farmers have become reliant on subsidies paid to them under the CAP, with the payments making the difference between operating at a loss or a profit for the majority of them. However, they resent the form filling associated with obtaining the subsidies and what they see as a regulatory burden emanating from the EU, which may have influenced the voting behaviour of some of them in the referendum on British membership.

Criticisms of the CAP

In assessing the CAP, it has to be remembered that it was devised in a very different decision-making environment. Its originators could remember the severe shortages of food in Europe in the years after the end of the Second World War. The Cold War context of the late 1950s meant that concerns about food security remained prominent, with European countries unable to produce sufficient food to feed their populations. Food security remains a central concern of advocates of the CAP, although the emphasis today is on price volatility in global markets rather than on interruptions to supply as a result of war.

Nevertheless, the CAP was provided with contradictory objectives in the Treaty of Rome with no priority ordering of these objectives. These objectives have not been revised in subsequent treaties, although it should be noted that the implicit policy objectives have changed, particularly in the direction of some 'greening' of the CAP. New policy instruments have also been devised to replace earlier instruments that led to a number of problems such as large surpluses of certain products held in storage.

Five objectives of the CAP are set out in Article 39(1) of the Treaty of Rome, and insofar as they have an underlying theme, it is the maximisation of production in order to provide food security. Indeed, such a productionist agenda was also the organising principle of the UK's landmark 1947 Agriculture Act. The first objective was concerned with increasing agricultural productivity through the promotion of technical progress and the optimum utilisation of factors of production, especially labour. Technical progress has been achieved, but it was not so much the result of EU policy as of technical innovations, which were then adopted and marketed by multinational companies. The mechanisation of EU agriculture, which brought big productivity gains, was still under way at the end of the 1950s. By 2017, the most advanced equipment had become very sophisticated, making extensive use of information technology, for example downloading data to combine harvesters. There have also been substantial advances in veterinary drugs and agrochemicals. Labour was shed as farming became more capital intensive.

The second objective was to ensure a fair standard of living for the agriculture community, in particular by increasing the individual earnings of persons engaged in agriculture. There was a concern that the disparity between urban and rural incomes in Europe might become a source of social unrest and offer a reservoir of support for extremist political movements. The gap between agricultural and other incomes was not eliminated and remains a source of concern for policymakers. However, agricultural subsidies are an inefficient mechanism for tackling this problem, particularly given that it is estimated that the distribution of subsidies follow a Pareto rule with 80 per cent of the payments going to 20 per cent of farmers (European Commission 2017: 18).

The third objective was to stabilise markets. Agricultural markets are subject to cyclical price fluctuations, in part because of the effect of weather on supplies. However, the use of intervention pricing to provide a floor to the market encouraged farmers to overproduce as they knew there would be a market for their produce above the marginal cost of production. This led to the infamous 'butter mountains' and 'wine lakes' that were difficult to dispose of.

The fourth objective was to ensure security of supply, and this has been achieved in the sense that exports have increased and imports of temperate products have been reduced. There is a surplus of exports over imports. This, however, has partly been achieved by raising high external tariff barriers. These have had an impact on the fifth objective, ensuring that supplies reached consumers at 'reasonable' prices. Much depends on what one thinks is a reasonable price, but tariff protection has certainly pushed prices of food in the EU above world market prices, although less so in recent years.

The CAP has been reformed, in large part in response to budgetary and international trade negotiation pressures. At one point in the 1970s, it accounted for over 70 per cent of the EU budget, and it threatened to break the budget in the early 1980s, leading to a number of changes in the regime for the dairy sector, in particular the imposition of quotas to restrain production. The MacSharry reforms, produced in response to the Uruguay Round trade negotiations, were an important step forward, introducing a system of area-based subsidies in the arable sector.

These reforms were taken a step further through reforms introduced by Commissioner Franz Fischlerler (1996–2004) in 2003. 'These reforms are assessed by many experts as the most radical reforms of the CAP since its creation' (Swinnen 2008: 1). A central change was the introduction of the Single Farm Payment (SFP), now known as the Basic Payment, on the basis of historical entitlements. This decoupled a large share of CAP support from production and meant that farmers were no longer incentivised to overproduce in order to claim their subsidy payments. Over 70 per cent of the CAP budget is accounted for by these direct payments.

Two new policy instruments, cross-compliance and modulation, were introduced.

> Cross-compliance requirements ensure that the SFP is only paid to farmers who abide by a series of regulations relating to the environment, animal welfare, plant protection and food safety. Modulation refers to the shift of funds to rural development policies . . . by reducing transfers to the larger farms.
>
> *(ibid.: 2)*

One of the criticisms made of the CAP was that it led to an intensification of production that led to environmental damage, for example the impacting of soils by heavy machinery or water pollution resulting from the run-off of fertilisers and pesticides. Attempts have been made to make the policy more environmentally friendly, such as through a system of agri-environmental payments, although their effectiveness has been questioned. In particular, it has been argued that even after the reforms introduced in 2013, the new environmental prescriptions are so diluted that they are unlikely to benefit biodiversity (Pe'er et al. 2014). What remains absent from the policy is any attempt to tackle climate change, although agriculture remains a significant contributor through the use of fossil fuels by machinery and methane emissions from cattle. The introduction of a third pillar relating to climate change was produced in the most recent reform round but was quickly dropped, probably in response to representations from the agribusiness lobby.

One of the issues with some of the environmental measures is that they have imposed significant transaction costs on farmers without having a substantial impact on environmental outcomes. The 'three crop' requires farms of more than 30 hectares to grow at least three crops to counteract the effects of monoculture on biodiversity:

> The crop diversification greening measure is a scandalous waste of resources. Not only does the EU notionally spend €6 billion annually on this measure for virtually no environmental or other impact (as we will see). It is also a very complex measure to administer, requiring significant changes in the computer systems of the paying agencies to track individual cropping patterns and thus adding to the administrative costs of making payments to farmers.
>
> *(Matthews 2015)*

This became an issue in the referendum campaign, with farmers resenting what they saw as interference in farm business decisions.

The European Commission takes the somewhat Panglossian view that '[f]armers provide a stable and high-quality food supply produced in a sustainable way at affordable prices for more than 500 million Europeans while respecting the requirements for animal health and welfare, environmental protection and food safety' (European Commission 2017: 17). However, it also admits, 'In some cases, these payments do not contribute to the structural development of the sector but tend to increase land prices that may hinder the entry of young farmers into the market' (ibid.: 18). Despite claims of enhanced competitiveness, the policy is really aimed at sheltering farmers from competition.

How farmers voted in the referendum

A myth has been embedded that farmers voted overwhelmingly for Brexit. However, this view is largely based on a series of *Farmers Weekly* polls that were not based on a sample but on self-selected responses. Thus, if Brexiteers were stronger in their beliefs, they might be more likely to respond. Some cite anecdotal evidence of the number of pro-Brexit posters seen in farmers' fields, but they may again reflect their stronger commitment whereas Remain voters might have been more inclined to see their vote as the lesser of two evils.

This does not mean that nothing can be learnt from these polls. The latest online poll shows that of 1,400 active farmer respondents, 54 per cent voted to leave and 44 per cent voted to remain. 28 per cent thought they would be better off as a result of Brexit and 41 per cent thought they would be worse off (21 per cent about the same). Even among those who voted to leave, there has been a decline in optimism.

Horticulture was the only sector in which more farmers voted to remain than leave. The sector is highly dependent on migrant labour from the EU. Unsurprisingly, those sectors that have received little or no support from the CAP were most likely to vote Leave (poultry, pigs, potatoes). The pig meat sector incurs heavy transaction costs in meeting EU environmental regulations. More than half of the farmers in Scotland, Wales and Northern Ireland voted to leave, although they are particularly reliant on subsidies.

It is important to note that farmers often voted on the basis of the same concerns as the public in general rather than agricultural policy. Those who wanted to leave were concerned about issues such as loss of sovereignty and migration. Those who voted to remain were more concerned about market access and loss of support.

During the referendum campaign, the writer addressed a number of meetings of farmers on Brexit with an estimated total attendance of 600. Straw polls conducted at the end of each meeting indicated majority support for the Remain option. Since then, I have sought the views of well connected farmers for their views on patterns of voting.

The general view was that livestock farmers were more likely to vote for Brexit as they felt constrained by what they saw as EU regulations. The *Farmers Weekly* poll shows that support for Brexit was particularly strong in the south-west, a livestock region. However, there is anecdotal evidence that some arable farmers voted for Brexit because they felt constrained by the EU pesticides regime, e.g., restrictions on neonicotinoids and a possible ban on glyphosate, a popular weed killer. However, they now realize that if the UK wants to export grains to the EU, it would have to abide by EU regulations.

The impact of Brexit on UK agriculture

This is very sensitive to the nature of the final deal achieved, and a number of alternative scenarios are considered here. However, there is no doubt that whatever deal is finally achieved, the impact will be considerable. That is why the UK Government is proposing to introduce a new Agriculture Bill to set the framework for a new domestic agricultural policy. This promises to be as significant as the 1947 Agriculture Act.

This section focuses on three key areas of impact: subsidy payments, external trade relations, and migrant labour. This does not exhaust the range of possible impacts, for example the UK will need to consider what sort of domestic regime it needs to create for the regulation of pesticides and how this will relate to the EU regime. There are also implications for the relationship between the UK Government and the devolved administrations and the need for a framework for agricultural policy across the UK. The Scottish Government has emphasized that any such framework should not be imposed but should be the outcome of negotiation.

> Data from the Farm Business Survey for 2014/15 for England show a very considerable dependence on the SFP Scheme and other payments, albeit in a year which was not a good one for many farms commercially. Across all farm types, the Single Farm Payment Scheme accounted for 56 per cent of total income and agri-environment and other payments for a further 15 per cent.
>
> *(Farmer Scientist Network 2016: 12)*

However, these figures fall within the estimated range of EU subsidies making up 'between 50 and 60 per cent of farm income in the UK as a whole'. Farmers in the devolved administrations are, however, more reliant on payments from the EU, 'which account for 87 per cent of total farming income in Northern Ireland, 80 per cent in Wales, and three quarters of total incoming from farming in Scotland' (House of Lords 2017: 58).

Arable farms, dairy farms and mixed farms are particularly dependant on these payments to turn a profit. 'Three sectors were less reliant on these payments: specialist pigs (20 per cent in total; horticulture, 17 per cent in total; and specialist poultry, eight per cent in total)' (Farmer Scientist Network 2016: 12). It should also be noted that average figures across all farm types, for the farms included in the Farm Business Survey, and that the situation of individual farms may vary considerably. For example, the level of debt carried by a farm business could affect its ability to survive without existing subsidies, as could diversification into other activities, such as on farm tourism, or farmhouse food processing, such as specialist cheeses and high-value ice cream. However, most of the 'low hanging fruit' from such diversification activities has been taken up.

The potential impact on an individual farm may be illustrated by using the so-called Meadow Farm model for a family-run 154-hectare beef, sheep and arable holding developed by Andersons Farm Business Consultants. The pre-referendum projection for 2017 was a production loss of £166 per hectare, offset by subsidies of £188 per hectare, giving a business surplus of £22 per hectare. They compared hard and soft Brexit scenarios (no access to the Single Market and continued access). Under soft Brexit, with subsidies assumed to fall by one-third by 2025 from present levels, the production loss is £131 per hectare, offset by subsidies of £139, giving a small business surplus of £8 per hectare. Under hard Brexit, subsidies are assumed to fall to one-third of present levels (this looks like a more realistic figure), producing a production loss of £240 per hectare, which a subsidy of £71 per hectare, leading to a loss of £170 per hectare (Grant 2017).

A rapid withdrawal of these subsidies would be very disruptive for the farm sector. Accordingly, the UK Government initially undertook to maintain them until the end of the current EU budgetary period. Following the 2017 general election, this was extended until 2022, providing farmers with a longer adjustment period. After then, it is anticipated that the Basic Payment will be withdrawn, although it may be phased out over a period of years. New types of support payment are anticipated, and the form these might take is discussed later in the chapter.

The UK is a substantial net importer of agricultural products. The National Farmers Union of England and Wales (NFU) places considerable emphasis on low levels of domestic self-sufficiency as a justification for continued subsidies on food security grounds. The value of food, feed and drink exports from the UK in 2015 was £18.0 billion, while the value of imports was £35.1 billion. 'The UK – which often likes to think of itself as a meat producer – actually imports more beef, poultry, pork and lamb than it exports' (Lang et al. 2017: 26). There have been concerns that in an attempt to secure trade deals with third countries after Brexit, the UK will sacrifice agricultural protection not just in terms of tariffs but also allowing in goods such as meat produced with beef hormones in the United States, which are currently restricted in the EU. Member states that supply the UK market are in terms of order by value: the Netherlands (but this includes some transit goods), Ireland, France, Germany, Spain and Italy. They will wish to retain access to the UK market without the imposition of tariff or non-tariff barriers, and this does give the UK some leverage in negotiations.

On average, 80 per cent of the UK's agricultural exports go to the EU (House of Lords 2017: 13). Depending on the form that Brexit took, UK exporters could face tariff barriers. However, 'Non-tariff barriers could be equally if not more disruptive to trade in agricultural products and food' (ibid.: 77). These include rules of origin, pre-shipment inspections and label-ling. 'Significant divergence in the regulatory frameworks in the UK and the EU, by creating non-tariff barriers, could make it more difficult to continue to trade agri-food products after Brexit' (ibid.: 79).

The effects of a change in trading relationships with the EU would vary by farm sector. The sheep meat sector is particularly vulnerable. About a third of sheep meat is exported, the UK being the largest sheep meat exporter in the EU. Ninety-five per cent of the exports go to EU countries, principally France, followed by Germany. A potential threat is a free trade agreement with Australia that increased sheep meat imports from there (imports from New Zealand are anticipated to remain similar to current levels). 'If UK sheep meat was subject to tariffs when entering the EU, it would result in product from the UK becoming uncompetitive in our main markets, potentially leading to a collapse in export volumes' (Agriculture and Horticulture Devel-opment Board 2016: 20). This could be devastating for the viability of the sector that is particu-larly important in upland areas where there are few alternative forms of farming.

Exports to the EU are important for the dairy sector in terms of disposing of surplus milk:

> The eventual deal between the UK and EU will be of key importance for the UK dairy industry. The EU currently provides the home for the majority of UK exports and milk production is expected to return to growth over the coming years, production of commodity products is likely to grow.
>
> *(ibid.: 13)*

This is a sector in which trade with Ireland is important, although it should be noted that Ireland is also the dominant supplier of imported beef accounting for 70 per cent of the market. 'Any imposition of tariffs on UK exports to the EU could cause particular issues for the cross-border trade with Ireland. As indicated above, large volumes of milk are exported from the UK for processing in the Irish Republic' (Agriculture and Horticulture Development Board 2017: 13).

A report produced by the Agriculture and Horticulture Development Board (AHDB) on prospects for the grain sector after Brexit emphasizes that the global grain trade is driven by competitiveness. It is a high-volume, low-margin business, dominated by relatively few multi-nationals. The UK generally produces a surplus of grain for export but is a small player in a big market. In the past four seasons, the UK exported 11 per cent of its wheat and 17 per cent of its barley crop. Competition for barley export business is likely to get tougher in future. There is no doubt that the UK faces tough competition from lower-cost producers with higher outputs (ibid.). The report also notes that loss of preferential treatment in relation to the EU market is likely to mean loss of access agreements with non-EU countries such as Morocco and Algeria in the absence of new access arrangements and probably tariffs.

'[It] is clear that EU migrants make up a substantial proportion of the workforce across all agricultural sectors in the UK' (House of Lords 2017: 68). The horticulture sector in particular is almost entirely reliant on seasonal migrant labour. With near full employment, it is not possible to recruit from local workers who, in any case, are unwilling to undertake what is monotonous and arduous work.

For a long time, the need for migrant labour was met by the Seasonal Agricultural Workers Scheme (SAWS). In 2003/2004 there were 25,000 places on the scheme. In 2005, this was reduced to 16,250 following the accession of eight East European states to the EU. From 2008, the scheme was open only to workers from Bulgaria and Romania (A2). The number of places had to be increased by 5,000 after labour shortages in 2007 and 2008, which saw crops left in the ground and produce having to be imported to fill supermarket shelves. The scheme came to an end in 2013 when A2 workers no longer had any restrictions on where they could work in the EU.

Many of those who came under the scheme were students in search of summer work with no intention of settling permanently. They were also interested in improving their English language skills, and the better producers organised classes for them. Brexit has already had an effect on the supply of migrant labour, with employers encountering difficulty in recruiting all the workers they need with an estimated fall of 17 per cent in numbers recruited in 2017. In part, this is because of a fall in the value of the pound, which makes working in the UK less financially attractive. It is also because of a perception that they are less welcome in the UK than before the referendum. The obvious policy solution would be to restore a version of the SAWS scheme, but the Government has so far been unwilling to do so, arguing that labour problems in the sector have been exaggerated and could be dealt with by new technology or recruiting more local labour.

Post-Brexit scenarios

There is a considerable number of post-Brexit scenarios, particularly in relation to future trade relationships. The number of possible options discussed here has been limited to reduce complexity. It should be noted that there is likely to be some kind of transitional arrangement, so the impact on agricultural trade is not likely to be immediate.

A number of scenarios are possible, even desirable, but unlikely to be achieved for political reasons. It is assumed that the UK remaining within the Customs Union and Single Market is politically unlikely to happen. If that did happen, there would be relatively little disruption to current relationships. If the UK had a customs arrangement with the EU similar to that of Turkey, it would not cover agriculture.

There has been some revival of interest in the 'Norwegian' solution in which Britain remained in the European Economic Area (EEA). The CAP regime as such is not included in the EEA, so there would be scope for a distinctive domestic agricultural policy. However, such an arrangement involves accepting EU regulations while having a limited influence on them.

The drawback of having to accept a considerable body of EU law without the ability to shape it also applies to the 'Swiss' solution. Switzerland is in the European Free Trade Area (EFTA) but not in the EEA. It has a series of bilateral treaties negotiated with the EU on a case-by-case basis. Like Norway, Switzerland is able to sustain one of the highest levels of agricultural support in the world. However, the relationship has encountered difficulties recently, particularly over migration issues, and the EU would not see it as an acceptable model.

Some Remain supporters would like to see the UK stay within the Customs Union or at least have some kind of associate membership of it. British agricultural exports would be able to move freely within the EU. It would also overcome the potential problem of a 'hard' border interrupting the substantial agricultural trade between the north and south of Ireland. From the point of view of supporters of a 'hard' Brexit, Britain would have to maintain the Common External Tariff (CET), which would remove the possibility of driving down food prices through cheap imports. Farmers would, of course, wish to maintain the CET. It would also mean that the UK would not be able to negotiate new free trade agreements with countries elsewhere in the world.

A free trade agreement (FTA) with the EU after Brexit is the UK's preferred solution. However, agriculture is unlikely to be the UK Government's priority in the negotiation of any such agreement. They are likely to be more concerned with the fate of financial services and industries such as pharmaceuticals, aerospace and motor vehicles, all of which account for a higher proportion of GDP and rely on integrated supply chains. Agriculture and food processing also rely on integrated supply chains that are more vulnerable to interruptions at borders because of the perishable nature of food. It is possible that a free trade agreement would involve some tariff and non-tariff barriers for agriculture.

Less has been heard of the 'no deal is better than a bad deal' since the 2017 general election, although it was always probably more of a negotiating tactic than a desired policy outcome, leaving aside the preferences of hard-line supporters of Brexit. However, it is quite possible that the negotiations with the EU will not reach a successful conclusion, leaving the UK to trade with the EU on World Trade Organization (WTO) terms. 'Many of our agricultural producers, and our food manufacturers, would incur substantial costs associated with tariff and non-tariff barriers when exporting to the EU, with sectors such as pig and sheep meat at particular risk' (House of Lords 2017: 34).

Even with an FTA the UK would have to separate its WTO schedules from those of the EU. The UK would have to make commitments consistent with the WTO Agreement on Agriculture in the areas of tariffs and tariff rate quotas (TRQs), domestic support and export subsidies. TRQs allow the imposition of lower tariffs up to a quantitative limit. 'Reaching agreement on dividing the EU's [TRQs] could be challenging, not least because the proposed reallocation will be open to negotiation by WTO members, not only the EU' (ibid.: 76).

The UK is also covered by the EU's so-called Amber Box commitment, which relates to domestic support measures considered to distort production and trade. How the UK manages to secure a share of the EU's Amber Box commitment could constrain the future development of domestic agricultural policy. 'There is no precedent for splitting . . . the Amber Box entitlement and in our view the Minister was over-confident that other WTO members would accept such a split. (ibid.: 25–26). It is evident that here and in other areas of future trade relationships, the UK is entered uncharted territory with many uncertainties and risks to the current pattern of trade.

Designing a domestic agricultural policy

Brexit does offer an opportunity to design a domestic agricultural policy tailored to UK needs, but whether that opportunity can be seized is open to question.

> There is a risk that future policy will be constrained by the legacy of past policies and practices. Whilst a transition arrangement between current and future policies is both sensible and inevitable, it is important to grasp this opportunity to remake our rural development and agricultural policies and to avoid 'lock-in' to unsustainable practices.
> *(Gravey et al. 2017: 5)*

It is open to question whether the UK Government has sufficient capacity to devise a coherent domestic agricultural policy in the time frame available. The responsible department, the Department for Environment, Farming and Rural Areas (Defra), has seen a hollowing out of its capacity. Its budget was reduced in real terms by 30 per cent in real terms from 2010/2011 to 2015/2016. In the summer of 2017, it advertised for 30 new recruits in its policy and communication departments to meet the challenges of Brexit and the UK taking back control of its agricultural policy, but this was rather late in the day. Problems arising from the lack of expert staff have been enhanced by rapid ministerial turnover.

A number of new policy instruments have been floated in a debate about agricultural policy after Brexit that was only just getting under way in 2017. There is a broad consensus that support will move 'up the hill' to more marginal upland farms and that there will be a greater emphasis on the provision of public goods, particularly environmental measures. In that connection, there has been an emphasis on paying farmers for providing what are called 'ecosystem services', for example afforestation, upstream water storage, maintaining peatlands and so on. However, payment for ecosystem services has not been used in practice, and there is uncertainty about how one would strike a fair and realistic price.

Other measures might focus on 'precision farming', such as the use of drones to survey crops and inform fertiliser and agrochemical applications. This could involve funds being made available for investment in capital equipment and for training. However, what is clear is that the total sum of money made available for agricultural support payments would be reduced at a time when there are many other politically well supported demands on public expenditure. Farm subsidies have long been a target of the Treasury as inefficient and market distorting.

Devolution presents a difficult set of challenges. There is already substantial policy differentiation. The SFP was implemented differently in the four territories; there are separate rural development programmes for each of the four territories reflecting different priorities; and there are differences in animal health and welfare polices such as the treatment of bovine TB. The Scottish Government introduced a policy on the bovine viral diarrhoea (BVD) that had potential implications for agricultural trade (McEldowney et al. 2013: 85–86). The Scottish Government has initiated 'recoupled' policies to support livestock farming in remoter areas. Greer (2017: 4) comments:

> Broader trade relations and overall funding seem likely to remain within a UK framework, but a key issue is the scope for policy variation allowed to the territories. If this increases – for instance on the distribution of subsidies and the nature of regulation – then there is the possibility of the emergence of 'un-level playing fields' and differentiation in the treatment of farmers across the UK.

Implications for the EU

The EU will lose about 8 per cent of its current income after Brexit and is thinking about how to adjust to this loss. Given that the CAP accounts for a large slice of the EU budget, it is at the forefront of concerns. In its Reflection Paper', the European Commission (2017) sets out its initial thinking about possible responses. In terms of what it has to say about agriculture, it is an interesting mix of sticking to old orthodoxies and some signs of new thinking.

The document admits, 'There is a growing call for the policy to focus further on the provision of public goods, such as safe and healthy food, nutrient management, response to climate change, protection of the environment and its contribution to the circular economy' (European Commission 2017: 24). Measures to tackle climate change have been a serious omission in the current policy. There is also recognition of the need to encourage farmers to invest in new technologies, which is forming part of the UK debate on a new domestic agricultural policy.

It is pointed out that this is the only area of EU policy managed with the member states without an element of national co-financing. The document therefore envisages 'the introduction of a degree of national co-financing for direct payments in order to sustain the overall levels of current support' (ibid.: 24). This will not go down well in countries such as France and Germany, which benefit from the current distribution of CAP funds. It would, however, benefit countries such as Malta and Romania where small farms predominate, so there is potentially a redistributive effect among member states.

There is also reference to reducing direct payments for large farms that have already been subject to some capping. The risk here is that it is the larger farms that are more internationally competitive, but then supporting competitiveness has never been a central objective of the CAP.

It is suggested that one scenario is that there should be a new 'focus on farmers under special constraints, e.g., small farms, mountainous areas and sparsely populated regions' (ibid.: 3). This is consistent with current policy directed at so-called Less Favoured Areas. Again, care will be needed to ensure that the chosen policy instruments do really tackle problems such as rural depopulation. For example, improving rural broadband might be a more effective way of stimulating new economic activity rather than propping up farms that lack viability.

Conclusions

There are considerable complexities and uncertainties surrounding UK agricultural policy after Brexit. However, agriculture could be one of the sectors hardest hit by Brexit, depending on the eventual settlement that is reached. British farmers will certainly receive lower levels of support, and they will lose the political cover provided by farmers in other member states where agriculture constitutes a larger part of GDP or has deep cultural roots as in France.

Brexit does provide an opportunity as well as a threat. However, the debate about designing a new domestic agricultural policy has been slow to get off the ground, in part because of a lack of leadership by government. Contributions are, however, being made by farm organizations, academic and consultants.

The departure of the UK will put new pressures on the EU budget in which the CAP is by far the biggest single item. The EU is starting to consider the adjustments that might have to be made to the CAP. However, this is not being taken as an opportunity to rethink the purposes of the CAP. What seems to be envisaged is a series of incremental adjustments to current policy, although there may be some prospect of initiatives on climate change. The slow progress of CAP reform provided ammunition for those who wanted to leave the EU, although agriculture was not prominent in the referendum debate.

References

Agriculture and Horticulture Development Board (2016) What Might Brexit Mean for UK Trade in Agricultural Products? Available at: www.ahdb.org.uk/documents/Horizon_Brexit_Analysis_Report-Oct2016.pdf [Accessed July 5, 2017].

Agriculture and Horticulture Development Board (2017) Post-Brexit Prospects for UK Grains. Available at: www.ahdb.org.uk/documents/Horizon_Brexit_Analysis_june2017.PDF [Accessed July 5, 2017].

European Commission (2017) Reflection Paper on the Future of EU Finances. Available at: https://ec.europa.eu/commission/sites/beta-political/files/reflection-paper-eu-finances_en.pdf [Accessed July 5, 2017].

Farmer Scientist Network (2016) The Implications of 'Brexit' for UK Agriculture: A Report for the Yorkshire Agricultural Society. Available at: http://yas.co.uk/uploads/files/YAS_FSN_Brexit_-_Full_Report.pdf [Accessed July 5, 2017].

Grant, W. (2017) The Future of Pillar 1 Subsidies: An Update Provided for the Brexit Working Party of the Yorkshire Agricultural Society. Available at: http://yas.co.uk/uploads/files/Paper_1_The_Future_of_Pillar_1_Subsidies_by_Prof_Wyn_Grant.pdf [Accessed July 5, 2017].

Gravey, V., Brown, I., Farstad, F., Hartley, S.E., Hejnowicz, A.P., Hicks, K. and Burns, C. (2017) Post-Brexit Policy in the UK: A New Dawn? Agri-Environment. *University of York*. Available at: www.york.ac.uk/media/yesi/researchoutputs/Brexit%20Agri-Environment%20Brief.pdf [Accessed July 5, 2017].

Greer, A. (2017) Devolution Aspects of Brexit and Agriculture: An Update Provided for the Brexit Working Party of the Yorkshire Agricultural Society. Available at: www.farmerscientistnetwork.co.uk/uploads/files/Paper_4_Devolution_aspects_of_Brexit_and_Agriculture_by_Prf_Alan_Greer.pdf [Accessed July 6, 2017].

House of Lords (2017) Brexit: Agriculture. *European Union Committee*, 20th report of Session 2016–17. Available at: https://publications.parliament.uk/pa/ld201719/ldselect/ldeucom/3/3.pdf [Accessed December 12, 2017].

Lang, T., Millstone, E. and Marsden, T. (2017) A Food Brexit: Time to Get Real. Available at: https://www.sussex.ac.uk/webteam/gateway/file.php?name=foodbrexitreport-langmillstonemarsden-july2017pdf.pdf&site=25 [Accessed August 16, 2017].

Matthews, A. (2015) Scrap the Crop Diversification Greening Requirement and Find a Sensible Replacement. *CAPReform.eu blog*. Available at: http://capreform.eu/scrap-the-crop-diversification-greening-requirement-and-find-a-sensible-replacement/ [Accessed July 5, 2017].

McEldowney, J., Grant, W. and Medley, G. (2013) *The Regulation of Animal Health and Welfare*. Abingdon: Routledge.

Pe'er, G., Dicks, L.V., Visconti, P., Arlettaz, R., Báldi, A., Benton, T.G., Collins, S., Dieterich, M., Gregory, R.D., Hartig, F., Henle, K., Hobson, P.R., Kleijn, D., Neumann, R.K., Robijns, T., Schmidt, J., Schwartz, A., Sutherland, W.J., Turbé, A. and Scott, A.V. (2014) EU Agricultural Reform Falls on Biodiversity. *Science* 344(6188): 1090–1092. Available at: www.researchgate.net/profile/Raphael_Arlettaz/publication/262886978_Agriculture_policy_EU_agricultural_reform_fails_on_biodiversity/links/541c502c0cf2218008c6154c/Agriculture-policy-EU-agricultural-reform-fails-on-biodiversity.pdf [Accessed December 12, 2017].

Swinnen, J.F.M. (2008) Introduction. In: Swinnen, J.F.M. (ed.), *The Perfect Storm: The Political Economy of the Fischler Reforms of the Common Agricultural Policy*. Brussels: Centre for European Policy Studies, pp. 1–8.

9

BREXIT AND HIGHER EDUCATION AND RESEARCH

Anne Corbett and Claire Gordon

Introduction

As the referendum votes rolled in on 23–24 June 2016, the commiserations of the European higher education and research sector for their British colleagues were unfeigned. The day after the referendum, the biggest stakeholder, the European University Association, spoke for many when it said that UK universities would always be part of the family.[1] It was a significant statement: the EUA represents many of the university community's leaders across forty-seven countries, countries that between them have 4,000-plus institutions and some 19 million students. The university presidents who make up the body have since reiterated their commitment to working together to ensure that the long-standing research and exchange relationships among Europe's universities, including the British, continue.[2] The European Students Union (ESU), representing 15 million students in forty-five national unions of students (NUS) in thirty-eight countries, declared itself in solidarity with UK students, fearing the decision would jeopardise all young people's future.[3]

But more than eighteen months on, there is a question as to whether UK higher education and research systems and those of the European sector will diverge further or whether each side has discovered, as the dust settled, that they can continue do business much as before. At the time of writing, Prime Minister Theresa May's government was still bent on taking the UK out of the Single Market and the Customs Union, while promising to work for continued cooperation in science and research and continued participation in the programmes Horizon 2020 and Erasmus+ until the end of the current financial cycle in 2020.

This chapter looks at two issues: the reactions in the university sector across the EU to Brexit and the UK's attempted global turn to overcome some of the vote's domestic consequences.

The European higher education and research world has come a long way since the 1960s and 1970s. These were years that saw the first steps to construct European higher education cooperation (Corbett 2005). The popular Erasmus programme, created in 1987 to promote student mobility and cooperation, has continued to expand its remit and its global reach to cover many forms of mobility and cooperation in the education sphere. Education cooperation was significantly boosted by the Treaty of Maastricht (1992), which defined how the EU could act to help raise the quality of the European dimension in education. The Treaty of Amsterdam (1997) marked a step towards treating research as more than an adjunct to an Industrial Strategy (Chou 2014). The Union was given the objective of strengthening its scientific and technological bases by achieving a European research area in which researchers, scientific knowledge and technology might circulate freely.

The Bologna Declaration of 1999 started as a new political process to create a European Higher Education Area in which higher education systems would become compatible and comparable by voluntary means. By 2015, Bologna had forty-eight countries, key stakeholders and the Commission as the 49th member providing most of the resources. Bologna has succeeded in establishing agreed frameworks of quality assurance and degree recognition that are something of a global model. It also provides incentives to enhance cooperation and use Bologna as a learning platform. The Lisbon Agenda launched in 2000 made it possible to move from cooperation to incentive-funded and targeted coordination across the range of its education and training. The Commission has given substance to this with various versions of a modernisation agenda, reflecting a shifting context in which efficiency was the talisman to more societal concerns.

Higher education and research (HER) are now recognised as having strategic importance within the EU in its search for growth that is sustainable and inclusive (European Commission 2010). Research and higher education feature strongly, along with employment and environmental concerns, with the EU seeing close and effective links between education, research, and innovation as three sides of the 'knowledge triangle', an essential construct for global competitiveness.[4]

Notable authorities argue that the rationale for EU action in this sphere is primarily economic. It ranges from a desire for greater efficiency, to the necessity of savings for survival, to acquire greater visibility in regional or national competition, and to raise quality and consolidate systems (Teixeira 2013).[5] Such is the EU's diversity that in countries such as Poland, this strategy is one of necessity driven by fragmentation and/or demographic decline. In the countries of South-East Europe, the drive has been to work for a general consolidation of the systems in line with the criteria of the European Higher Education Area.

We have argued elsewhere that the economic rationale is not the only one for EU action (Corbett and Gordon 2016). The EU sustained a values-based approach to the development of research and education in three ways: through the fundamental principles enshrined in EU law of non-discrimination between citizens and freedom of movement; through the embedding over time of higher education and research initiatives into a broader policy agenda; and through the institutionalisation of education and research through programmes of research collaboration, education and engagement: notably the research framework programmes, currently Horizon 2020, and the mobility and educational cooperation programme, Erasmus+. (See Box 9.1.)

Box 9.1 Countries in the EU association agreements with the EU higher education and research programmes

Horizon 2020

Horizon works with a structure of programme countries and associated countries that negotiate an association agreement linked to their circumstances.

• Iceland • Norway • Albania • Bosnia and Herzegovina • the former Yugoslav Republic of Macedonia • Montenegro • Serbia · Turkey • Israel • Moldova • Switzerland • Faroe Islands • Ukraine • Tunisia • Georgia • Armenia

Erasmus + programme

The Erasmus+ programme works within a structure of programme countries and partner countries. The EU programme countries are the EU27 and their overseas territories and dependencies, the countries of the EEA (Norway, Iceland and Liechtenstein) and Turkey and the former Yugoslav Republic of Macedonia. Partner countries operate under specific agreed conditions.

There is objective evidence that the EU is currently a world leader in terms of its global share of researchers (22 per cent) and its scientific output. This puts the EU collectively ahead of China (19.1 per cent) and the United States (16.7 per cent). As great a distinction is to have formed a globally important science hub in which talent can flow between countries without visas or point systems and that can assemble constellations of cutting-edge labs, industry and small businesses to tackle major challenges at both the global and local levels through the European Research Area (Galsworthy and Davidson 2015). At any one time, top teams may be collaborating with institutions in any one of 170 countries. The education programmes are open to many parts of the world and/or to researchers who bring their talents to Europe (Marie Skłodowska–Curie Programme [MSCP] for early career researchers). The European Institute of Technology (EIT) and its associated Knowledge and Information Centres (KICs) have a similarly open approach in linking universities and business. This is achieved with now substantial funds for research. Almost 50 per cent of the EU's total budget has a research element attached. This covers not just the core research policy but also research in other policy sectors, notably the cohesion funds and particular policy sectors such as agriculture and security. But education as such remains a poor relation accounting for less than 1 per cent of the total EU budget.

The impact of Brexit on European HE and research

Ninety per cent of people working in higher education voted Remain in the referendum. Their alarm was patent on the day of the results. Their fear: that this would mean the end of freedom of movement and citizenship rights incorporated in the Treaty and on which, in many cases, their jobs and indeed their job satisfaction depended. These were issues that the UK higher education sector itself had not taken seriously before the referendum, focussed as it was on its economic implications (Corbett 2016b). But the citizen reaction chimed with the EU's negotiating team strategy, which was to deal with the divorce from Treaty obligations, only secondly to sort out the future UK–EU27 relationship.

It took the Brexit vote to give political weight to the view that the Treaty rights to study, work and live abroad were personally precious for thousands of individuals in the higher education and research (HER) sector and that their abolition would be destructive to family as well as professional life. The Government's inability to say what it wanted to achieve created massive insecurity for individuals as to what their status would be past the exit date of 29 March 2019 (Education Select Committee 2017). It initially left students and those already on research grants in the dark about whether they would be able to complete their courses or their research contracts. It cast a long shadow of whether non-UK nationals would continue to find UK universities as attractive a place to study as they had been for decades.

There have been many anecdotal reports of EU staff and their families finding themselves victims of xenophobia and of EU research opportunities involving top-ranking British scientists having diminished or gone by default. As the air cleared, it looked as if Brexit was having a differential effect. Only research-strong universities appeared to be maintaining their attraction for EU academics. There have been some weighty press reports that the expected restrictions on freedom of movement has led to an exodus of EU27 researchers from the UK.[6] The prospect of EU students having to pay full foreign student (higher) fees after the exit is widely seen as likely to exacerbate the trends to pick and choose. There is also resentment on the Continent that a walkout of UK, as a net contributor to the EU budget, will significantly diminish the research budget available to the EU27.[7] The UK is seen as a key player in a field in which partners from several countries are involved as a matter of course. Collaboration is seen as a matter of principle and of necessity. Projects associated with the major challenges of tomorrow, such as climate change and Europe's aging society and disease, need access to data sets that are beyond the capacity of a single member state to assemble. UK researchers have also consistently topped the league in winning the prestigious grants of the European Research Council for both early career and advanced research.[8]

The UK's universities are one of the top destinations for international researchers and part of the European draw for students worldwide.[9] The UK's approach to quality assurance, although not universally admired, has been widely seen as providing lessons from which other European university systems have benefitted. Another often cited example is the UK's drawing power for young academics and researchers in search of more opportunities for creativity and achievement than they tend to get under a traditional continental pattern where professors exert control over knowledge creation. There are also attitudes that earn the UK respect: a low tolerance of corruption is one of them (Pruvot and Estermann 2017).

Hence there is general lobbying within the European policy area to ensure that the UK will at least achieve an associate status. The EUA has been assiduous in lobbying Brussels to make the links between the UK's aspirations for a continued place in science programmes, which UK Prime Minister Theresa May has several times declared she desires.[10]

In a key statement made in Florence in May 2017, the EU's chief negotiator, Michel Barnier, explicitly recognised the HER case: 'EU policy is important in creating networks and exchanges between universities in all 28 countries'. The solution to the problems of continued cooperation in higher education, however, were for discussion 'down the line' in the second, trade-related phase of the negotiations. What Barnier indicated was that the UK could decide to continue to support university networks and projects as a third country after Brexit. 'This would require a different legal and financial framework'.[11] Thomas Jørgensen, the senior policy adviser on Brexit at the European University Association, has written that it is widely recognised that higher education and research is a sector where there are technical solutions that can be managed independently of the outcome of the ongoing negotiations.[12] This would not be as good a situation as at present. But the UK can expect to negotiate association agreements for Horizon 2020 and Erasmus+ and their successors. It will cost money. It excludes the UK from a policymaking role. It does, however, maintain UK–EU links.

National interests: competing and compensation-seeking

The education and research interests of the EU27 themselves have been largely ignored in the sectoral Brexit debate. The UK basks in its global achievements with its leading universities in the global top ten rankings (Corbett 2016a). But in the last two decades, enormous efforts have been made in most European systems to make their universities more competitive as almost all have become more integrated at the European and global levels. The high-prestige awards of the European Research Council show that the UK, which does so well, is in fact one of a trio of successful countries, the others being the Netherlands and Germany.[13] OECD statistics on international student mobility as a proxy for attractiveness show that though the UK, like other English-speaking nations, does well, the nations of Europe are highly attractive too, notably Germany and France.[14]

The global ranking systems underline that Europe has a solid base of high-quality universities that make their presence felt.[15] The relevant cut-off point reflecting Europe's high overall standing is the first 200 in the rankings – out of the world's 20,000 or so universities. But some countries may be striving for more. Excellence systems, having been rejected for a long time as unfair in a system as a whole, are now part of the higher education strategy of West European countries, including France, Germany, the Netherlands and Russia, a big and historic player.

The university systems of Eastern Europe have a particular concern. EU policy tends to exacerbate the brain drain from these countries. In theory, the EU balances the excellence policies that drive competitiveness with capacity-building policies that build cohesion and solidarity through the regional cohesion funds. This strategy has taken three main forms: performance-based funding, which has led to increased differentiation within systems, mergers to build on strengths and excellence schemes, to focus on a few. But taking the example of where holders of the prestigious European Research awards choose to study, the gap between East and West is stark. Award winners from Eastern Europe overwhelmingly go to the 'golden triangle' countries of the UK, Germany and France (Teixeira 2013).

As we will suggest shortly, there is a new impetus behind the development of EU education and research policy that will lead to old questions such as these rising up on the agenda again. However, as time drags on and clocks go on ticking, we can expect to see more assertive efforts on the part of other EU university systems to take advantage of Brexit. French President Emmanuel Macron has taken a lead; he has been upfront about his desire to get French academics working overseas to return. His eyes have been on UK and US universities in particular (Corbett 2016b).

How Brexit might affect the international relations of higher education and research

Our second question for this chapter is how Brexit might change the United Kingdom's relationships with countries beyond the European Union in the higher education and research sector and the viability of such proposals.

As in other UK policy domains, in the lead-up to and in the wake of the June 2016 referendum, there was no clear policy or plan of action for UK higher education and research, just a broad recognition of the world-class standing of the sector, its important contribution to the UK economy and the need to maintain this. While supporters of the Leave Campaign and some members of the government have emphasized the legal possibility for developing and strengthening the UK's already existing links in higher education and research beyond Europe, much of the focus of the sector has been concentrated on seeking concrete ways to maintain existing relationships with Europe, a position favoured by European institutions as well as university leaders (as discussed earlier in this chapter). While there has certainly been some sectoral support for expanding and building international relationships, the preference has been to achieve this through continuing to build on existing European projects and programmes, networks and relationships.

So what are the possible options for increased internationalisation of UK higher education and research, including the opportunities and challenges linked to the development and expansion of the UK's international relationships in the United States, China and India? To ask the question raises issues about the very notion of internationalisation, which is variously defined in the literature, as well as the different rationales and logics that might underpin it (De Wit et al. 2012; Knight 2017). The discussion about possibilities for internationalisation intersects with evolving UK Government policy in which the place of HER has moved up the agenda (evidenced by Theresa May's inclusion of science and innovation as one of the twelve key points in her Brexit plan[16]) and has also been increasingly linked to logics of commercialisation, competition and financial gain. This poses tensions for some to alternative visions of the purpose of higher education and research. However, the challenges and opportunities for building future international relationships beyond Europe raises a complex set of issues around regulatory frameworks and the alignment and transferability of qualifications, questions about intellectual property rights and technology transfer, as well as uncertainty about the future attractiveness of the UK HE and research space, given the potential loss of its leading role as a bridge into European networks and exchange programmes in education and research.

This section explores how the UK's relationship to the European higher education and research space has fostered the development of international relationships. It then turns to explore existing and recently established initiatives, which have linked UK universities, researchers and students to international networks and higher education settings. In so doing, we consider the government emphasis on the expansion of the UK's international higher education and research relationships through their integration into a new generation of post-Brexit free trade agreements, the increased focus on commercialisation and on the linking of the outputs of research to Industrial Strategy. This direction of travel dates back at the very least to the 2010 Browne Report, which led to a narrowing of government funding for UK HER with a strong focus on STEM subjects.

These different dimensions are not necessarily mutually exclusive, but they may be underpinned by differing logics and therefore raise questions about the role and purpose of the university in the post-Brexit era. Thus, the latest indications from government suggest that it will seek to retain as full as possible access to EU research and education funding and networks, but its post-Brexit priority is for broader international expansion and commercialisation.[17] It is an irony that the questions of mobility and migration revealed as a thorny Brexit issue could prove to be major stumbling blocks in negotiations with partners beyond Europe.

UK HE and research: the international context[18]

The UK higher education and research space is already highly international. So the question in the post-Brexit context really concerns how to maintain and strengthen the UK's relative outstanding global position, a point that was underlined in the report of Education Select Committee (ESC) Hearings on Brexit and higher education (Education Select Committee 2017). Before considering the possibilities for building the UK's international relationships, we provide some illustrative background as contextual information about the nature and size of UK involvement in HE beyond Europe.

At home, the UK is the second most popular worldwide destination for international students after the United States. In 2015–2016, there were 438,010 international students studying in the UK with the highest number, 94,150, coming from EU countries (this is based on data from the top ten EU countries) followed by some 91,000 coming from China, and 16,000–17,000 coming from Malaysia, United States, HK China, India and Nigeria. International students contribute hugely to the UK economy. In 2014–2015 alone, £10.8 billion worth of export earnings were generated from international students. Meanwhile, students continue to be included in the UK migration figures, despite evidence that the British public and many in Prime Minister May's government do not agree with this position and support the continuation of equally high numbers of international students coming to study in the UK. The continuing uncertainty over the status of EU students, future visa conditions and fee structures looms large over the sector and makes forward planning difficult. It is hard to predict whether a decline in EU students coming to study in the UK will open the doors to more non-EU students, given changes in visa provision, or whether the UK will become a less attractive proposition if it loses its bridge into Europe status. NUS Education Officer Sorana Vieru, (2016–2017), in her oral evidence to the ESC Hearing at UCL on 25 January 2017, highlighted the value that EU students bring – 'challeng[ing] perspectives, enrich[ing] the overall university experience and help[ing] home students develop new views' (Gordon 2017).

The UK academic community is no less diverse and highly mobile. Twenty-nine per cent of all academic staff in UK universities hail from overseas, including (including 16.9 per cent from EU/European Economic Area). Marie-Skłodowska Curie Actions and Erasmus+ mobility schemes have enabled over 10,000 academics to travel overseas within and outside the EU, while UK higher education institutions (HEIs) have welcomed 13,464 academics from overseas.

Overall, approximately 27,400 UK students had the opportunity to study abroad in 2015–2016 with 53 per cent studying in other EU countries, 18 per cent in the United States and 11 per cent in Asia. Evidence suggests that students who have studied or worked abroad as part of their degree are 24 per cent less likely to be unemployed six months after graduation compared with their less mobile peers (Universities UK International 2017).

The UK educational brand is buoyant overseas. Over 700,000 students now study for UK higher education qualifications outside the UK, the overwhelming majority from countries beyond the EU with the largest numbers in Malaysia, China and Singapore (Universities UK British Council 2016). There are twice as many students studying on UK university courses outside the UK as there are inside it. Given the 81 per cent increase in the number of UK HE transnational students since 2008–2009 with 99 per cent of students based outside Europe, this is likely to be an area for future growth. It is worth noting, however, that questions about quality assurance, degree transferability, comparability of experience and fairness have been levelled by some critics of practices in the UK transnational education space (Walters 2017).

Internationalisation through Europe: a bridge between Europe and world?

As previously suggested, the UK's connectedness to the European higher education and research has in part heightened its attractiveness to overseas partners. The evidence demonstrating the UK's position as a heavy hitter in higher education and research in Europe suggests that remaining connected with Europe as closely as possible while pursuing more outward expansion would be the best and most rational option for a post-Brexit UK.

In terms of research leadership and collaboration, thirteen of the UK's top twenty partners are EU member states, and one in six Horizon 2020 projects to date have been coordinated by the researchers in the UK, mainly based at UK universities. But we should note that partners beyond the EU figure prominently in EU funding programmes. They include the United States, Canada, China and Australia, as can be seen in the graph in Figure 9.1 on the top ten third-countries in terms of shares or participation in signed Horizon 2020 grant agreements compared with FP7. In all, seventy-three third countries participate in Horizon 2020 programme, underlining its global reach.

Significantly, a June 2017 Universities UK position paper called for continued access to Erasmus+, together with enhanced investment 'to grow other international mobility opportunities' (Universities UK 2017b). The paper underlined the way in which participation in EU schemes such as the Marie Skłodowska–Curie Programme enables universities not only to welcome skilled researchers from Europe but also to create strategic partnerships with leading institutions worldwide. The vision is clearly one of the United Kingdom as bridge between Europe and the wider world.

Internationalisation: expanding beyond Europe with Europe

Encouraged by government, UK universities have been building research and education links beyond Europe for a number of years. The Research Council UK has offices in China, India and the United States. There are a range of funds seeking to promote international research and innovation partnerships, including the Global Innovation Initiative Fund and Newton Fund, as well as a range of educational cooperation schemes for bringing overseas scholars and future leaders to study in the UK, such as the Chevening Global Award Programme. As part of the broader push towards internationalization, a significant number of UK universities have established joint degree or franchised programmes with higher education institutions beyond Europe and/or set up overseas campuses for the education of their own students or with the purposes of attracting

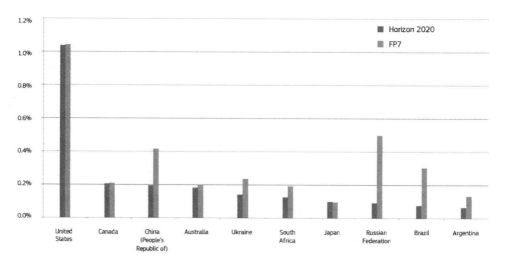

Figure 9.1 What about applications to Horizon 2020 from the rest of the world? Top ten third countries in terms of share of participations in signed grant agreements, Horizon 2020 compared with FP7

Source: European Union, 2015 ©: https://ec.europa.eu/programmes/horizon2020/sites/horizon2020/files/horizon_2020_first_results.pdf

international students. There is also a well established tradition of international students undertaking distance learning degrees with the University of London International Programmes and Open University being leaders in this field (Universities UK British Council 2016). It is also likely that there will be a greater push from overseas universities to establish their own campuses in the UK. These initiatives look set to be accelerated. Nevertheless, the challenges and time frames involved in setting up and institutionalising these relationships in both the research and educational spheres should not be underestimated. Nor should the competition from other English-speaking providers such as the United States, Australia and Canada, as well as newer entrants to the market such as China, Singapore, Malaysia and South Korea (British Council 2012).

The extent of the partnerships and the financial sums involved to date have been small scale, suggesting that a continuation of the current incremental approach to development and expansion might not be sufficiently effective. The complexity of growing international partnerships has also come to the fore. Key issues relate to freedom of movement and visa restrictions and how to ensure transferability of credit and degree qualifications, as well as agreement over intellectual property rights. The UK's international relationships with overseas research partners and higher education institutions will not be able to quickly match the level of integration in education and research that has been achieved with the EU.

The most sustained efforts with the United States, India and China to boost partnerships in higher education and research have a mixed record. Data from the Research Councils UK's (RCUK) US office, established in 2007, shows a number US-led joint initiatives, including work with the US Department of Defense, the US National Science Foundation (NSF) and the US Department of Energy. Comparison studies have demonstrated that UK and US approaches to technology transfer are broadly similar, a contrast with some of the UK's other potential partners. That the two countries share similar challenges might bode well for the development of future joint initiatives.[19] However, to date as suggested by Kemp and Humfrey in an investigation into US–UK higher education partnerships, only a limited number of UK institutions have been successful at growing excellent, high-profile strategic partnerships with US research-led universities. Kemp and Humfrey conclude that across the UK HER sector, activities have tended to be 'ad hoc' and that 'the UK and its institutions are under-investing in the US relationship' compared to other key partners, a consequence potentially of the importance of the UK's relationship with its European partners (Kemp and Humfrey 2010). The United States itself is not exclusively focussed on the UK. It has been keen to diversify and enhance its international outreach and cooperation particularly in the Asia-Pacific region. The United Kingdom, notwithstanding the excellence of its HER sector, is not 'the only game in town'.

As regards educational exchange, approximately 52,000 US students come to the UK on a yearly basis to study for entire degrees in UK universities or for a study period as part of their US degree, resulting in an annual turnover from US–UK higher education of over £1 billion. Will the UK remain as attractive a destination for US students with the loss of its gateway position into Europe, let alone the ever growing supply of English language degree options offered by European institutions, and other English-speaking providers?

In the case of India, a number of initiatives have been introduced in recent years to support the development of research and education cooperation between the UK and India. Further to a visit by Tony Blair in 2005, the UK India Education & Research Initiative (UKIERI) has been funding collaborative activity between India and the UK in academic leadership, research and skills. The programme was launched in April 2006 based on co-funding from the UK and Indian Governments with the aim of delivering a 'step change' in educational relations between India and the UK, so that the two countries become each other's partner of choice in education. During this period, over £35 million has been jointly committed to the initiative.[20] The British Government, through the efforts of RCUK India office, together with the Government of India and other third parties, has invested over £230 million in 140 co-funded research programmes and involved over 100 industry partners since the RCUK office was established in 2008.

Theresa May's visit to India in November 2016, however, provided a stark warning that a crude concentration on the economics of higher education is not a winning policy. India and other countries see the UK's higher education and immigration policies as inextricably linked. Prime Minister Modi highlighted the key immigration challenge involved. His message was neatly encapsulated in a Universities UK statement that 'you want our trade, but not our children' (Stern 2017). Already the UK's restrictive immigration policy on the availability of Tier 2 visas has led to a more than 50 per cent decline in Indian international students studying in the UK since 2010 when the post-work study visa option was closed off.[21] In short: immigration is likely to bedevil any future trade negotiations with the UK that include clauses relating to higher education and research.

RCUK China, established in 2007, was the first RCUK overseas office to be set up, a signal of the potential the UK Government has seen for the growth and development of research cooperation between the two countries. Over the past ten years, more than £220 million has been co-invested by the Research Councils and Chinese partners involving more than 150 academic institutions and over 120 businesses.[22] Cooperation has included supporting the establishment of joint centres, which bridge research communities across both countries and disciplines and a range of activities to promote knowledge exchange and to increase bilateral collaboration including forty Summer Schools and over fifty UK–China workshops. As concerns student education, Chinese students form almost 20 per cent of the total number of international students coming to the UK (Corbett 2016a). And the trend towards fostering deeper ties with UK higher education institutions, research and business looks set and is underlined by the analysis and recommendation of a Confederation of British Industry report November 2016 entitled 'Bridges to the Future', though the sponsoring of the report also highlights a trend towards commercialisation in the HE sector (CBI 2016).

This array of initiatives notwithstanding, the sector continues to be concerned. Universities UK has called on the government to develop a more 'joined up . . . strategic', 'cross-government approach to supporting in international research collaboration' (Adams 2017). UK universities are only too aware that a piecemeal approach to building international relationships with HER beyond Europe, whether by bottom-up university initiatives or existing government-sponsored programmes, will not be enough to maintain the global standing of the sector in a post-Brexit world.

While there are signs that the UK Government sees building these international research and education relationships as integral to the broader post-Brexit development of UK relations with foreign governments and businesses, this potentially welcome strategic approach appears to be linked to the commercialization potential.[23] The Government's 2017 Industrial Strategy green paper called on UK universities to carve out a more proactive role within new free trade agreements (FTAs). This line of thinking to take advantage of the competitive global higher education market has been echoed elsewhere in government. Former Undersecretary for State Mark Garnier noted at the International Higher Education Forum in March 2017 that the Department for International Trade intended to build the country's success in exporting education and had recruited its own HE specialist to 'support the sector's global ambitions'. Meanwhile a recent briefing from the UCL-IOE Centre for Global Higher Education also explicitly argues for the incorporation of higher education and research cooperation in the FTAs, which will have to be negotiated in the wake of Brexit (Highman 2017). This positioning and approach raises many questions for the HER, many of whom have opposed what is seen as the creeping marketization and commercialisation of sector (a strand of opinion eloquently voiced by Stefan Collini (2012).

Do all these initiatives amount to a changed set of international relations? The solutions currently advocated cannot easily replicate the infrastructure and synergies of UK's engagement with Europe. A Universities UK report underlines sectoral scepticism towards post-Brexit solutions. 'Specific analysis of FTAs' impacts on cooperative activities under research and education are not readily available' (Universities UK 2017a). Beyond the time taken to negotiate a free trade agreement or other forms of cooperation agreement, the Universities UK report highlights the familiar challenges of obtaining academic credit from home institutions for courses taken abroad. Evidence points to credits taken abroad being scaled down when students return home, a lack of professional staff to effectively manage programmes, and changes in academic staff. There has been no sign that government recognises these difficulties.

Academic research also highlights the problem of regulation in the sector. In a discussion of the application of Christopher Hood et al.s' (2004) work on different regulatory modes (contrived randomness, mutuality, rivalry and oversight) to higher education, Martin Lodge underlined a dynamic of 'growing marketization . . . coupled with growing hierarchical oversight' in certain countries. He also pointed to the 'the growing internationalised nature of positional competition among universities moving increasingly beyond national boundaries' (Lodge 2015). The trend towards increased oversight in the HE sector in England and Wales is visible, with the establishment of the new Office for Students and an amalgamated United Kingdom and Republic of Ireland. These domestic trends in regulation, together with the new funding challenges and the possible declines in staff and student recruitment in the wake of Brexit, mean that the pressures on the higher education and research sector are likely to be reinforced in the coming years.

In line with this, some researchers point to another layer of complexity: the diverse systems and interests of each potential partner country: 'each negotiation will be different because partners differ so much in their own regulation and commitments (and objectives in the UK as well). Academic system harmonisation or clear agreements on mutual recognition of modules/degrees are important for student mobility' (Universities UK 2017a). Bologna, in which the UK will continue to participate, might offer some salutary lessons and useful regulatory models emphasizing the continued role for systems of relations underpinned by mutuality and contrived randomness to support such developments.

However, it is clear is that the EU may continue to provide an effective bridge even in the post-Brexit circumstances. As Universities UK suggests to government, 'given that the UK and EU are already fairly well integrated in education and qualifications, serious thought should be given to preserving those links and aligning other FTAs with them' (Universities UK 2017a).

Looking forward: associate status?

In concrete terms, three options present themselves. These can be summed up as the Norway option, the Swiss option and the default to WTO rules. As a member of EFTA and the EEA, Norway enjoys membership of the Single Market, access to research funding and the Erasmus+ programme, in exchange for freedom of movement and payments to the EU budget but no control over the rules. This would deliver the UK the closest thing to the status quo but with limited formal voice. Meanwhile, in the case of Switzerland, which is a member of EFTA but not of the EEA, access to the EU market is governed by a series of bilateral agreements. For education and research, this tailored association includes participation in research programmes in exchange for free movement for academics and students. It not only has limited influence over the design of European-led research programmes but also some significant cost implications. This worked under the FP7 (2007–2013) programme, but Switzerland was temporarily barred from Horizon 2020 when its 2014 referendum opposed freedom of movement. It has since been fully readmitted into the funding programme. The third and least desirable option, but the most likely, given the current line taken by the UK Government, would be the default to WTO rules if the negotiations conclude without agreement and the need to negotiate special association agreements – that is, as Michel Barnier said to the UK Government early in the proceedings, 'third country' status (as previously discussed).

However, the rhetorical commitment to reaching a positive and workable solution among the HER community remains largely undiminished and may yet yield surprises. As the negotiations have stumbled on, passing the first veto point of the divorce deal, it is likely that we will hear more of a settlement for the higher education and research sector being a pragmatic technical challenge rather than a political one. In European quarters, this is combined with the recognition of the greater imperative for the European project to move on, with or without the UK.

The ambitious vision laid out in the November 2017 European Commission Communication on 'Strengthening European Identity through Education and Culture' highlights this shift (European Commission Communication 2017). The Communication outlined a series of proposals for strengthening the European higher education and research space, including moves towards increased mutual recognition of HE and school diplomas, as well as study abroad periods, the further expansion of the Erasmus+ scheme, the introduction of an EU student card and the development of so-called truly European universities'. Coupled with this, bold proposals for boosting language learning and the development of digital and entrepreneurship capabilities have also been placed on the table. This also suggests a shift to greater EU political leadership in this sphere, as evidenced by the advocacy of Council Recommendations to back these policy ideas, in contrast to the Bologna dependency on the intergovernmental communiques of the Bologna process.

With education, a national-level prerogative and the Commission not in a position to propose legally binding actions, the key question is whether the necessary political will and backup is present to take these initiatives forward. Twenty-five years post-Maastricht, the EEA may be about to experience a new lease on life, aided by the ambitions of President M. Emmanuel Macron to get his peers to accept a network of twenty European excellence universities, a not too subtle bid to provide an alternative pole to the UK's big four of Oxford, Cambridge, Imperial and University College London.

Conclusions

This chapter has suggested that Brexit negotiations relating to higher education and research, which will come to the fore in stage two of the negotiations, are likely to focus on EU willingness to give the UK the associate status that would open up access to EU programmes, subject to defined conditions. We have indicated that European sector actors would be seeking to keep the bridges open to their UK colleagues.

At the same time, the signs are that European universities are in for a period of closer collaboration, spurred on by the combination of the EU strategy for 2021–2028, a more ambitious Bologna process emerging as it celebrates twenty years of existence and signs of the political will championed by Emmanuel Macron with its implicit underpinning that Brexit is a university opportunity for Europe.

We can conclude that, whatever happens, there is a historical legacy to the UK's membership of the EU that spills over into higher education and research. The EU leads the world in producing ways to link countries with different languages and histories and different patterns of intellectual formation together. But will the UK, in its attempts to go global more effectively, be building on or jettisoning the common regulatory instruments and collaborative experience of its EU years? To the extent UK is distancing itself from the EU, the challenge becomes greater of making the potentially conflicting drivers of competition/collaboration and commercialisation development work together.

The endgame for higher education and research will not be negotiated in isolation. Many other things will be happening at the same time, as the waves move outwards from the Brexit policy shock. In understanding the impact of Brexit, it is also important to take into account the potential for unforeseen events to shape outcomes. Were UK public opinion to shift against Brexit – and there are some precursor signs that it might – the whole political landscape would change. Eighteen months plus post the referendum, we are no closer to an answer to the question, which is of critical academic, as well as personal interest to many of those in the university sector: how close will the UK and the EU remain once Brexit has taken place?

Notes

1 EUA press statement July 22, 2016. Available at: www.eua.be/activities-services/news/newsitem/2016/07/22/universities-uk-statement-european-university-leaders-call-for-continued-collaboration-after-brexit-vote [Accessed December 1, 2017].

2 See EUA Brexit fact sheet at: www.eua.be/activities-services/news/newsitem/2016/12/02/new-eua-brexit-factsheet-the-uk-in-european-research-and-student-mobility [Accessed December 11, 2017].

3 According to the ESU. Available at: www.esu-online.org/?news=esu-stands-in-solidarity-with-uk-students-in-expressing-disappointment-over-brexit-outcome [Accessed December 11, 2017].

4 European Commission, Knowledge Triangle and Innovation, n.d. Available at: http://ec.europa.eu/education/policy/higher-education/knowledge-innovation-triangle_en [Accessed February 10, 2018]

5 Prof Teixeira kindly made data from his current research available to us.

6 Higher Education Statistics Agency (HESA). Available at: www.hesa.ac.uk/data-and-analysis/staff [Accessed February 10, 2018].

7 Times Higher Education (September 13, 2017) quotes Professor Kurt Deketelaere, secretary-general of the League of European Research Universities, which represents twenty-three research-intensive universities throughout Europe, as saying that UK's exit from the EU means that, for the first time, "really difficult decisions" will have to be made over how the EU spends its budget because, overall, the UK is a

net contributor to the EU budget, with ramifications for research. Available at: www.timeshighereduca-tion.com/features/how-will-brexit-shape-european-research-landscape [Accessed February 10, 2018].

8 European Research Council statistics quoted in Times Higher Education. Available at: www.timeshighereducation.com/features/how-will-brexit-shape-european-research-landscape [Accessed February 10, 2018].

9 OECD on characteristics of international student mobility. Available at: www.keepeek.com/Digital-Asset-Management/oecd/education/education-at-a-glance-2017_eag-2017-en#page286 [Accessed February 10, 2018].

10 Theresa May, Lancaster House speech, 17 January 2017. Available at: www.gov.uk/government/speeches/the-governments-negotiating-objectives-for-exiting-the-eu-pm-speech; Theresa May, Florence, 22 September 2017. Available at: www.gov.uk/government/speeches/pms-florence-speech-a-new-era-of-cooperation-and-partnership-between-the-uk-and-the-eu [Accessed December 1, 2017].

11 Speech by Michel Barnier at the 7th State of the Union Conference, European University Institute, Florence, 5 May 2017. Available at: http://europa.eu/rapid/press-release_SPEECH-17-1236_en.htm [Accessed December 1, 2017].

12 According to Thomas Jørgenson. Available at: www.universityworldnews.com/article.php?/story+2017091914025079 [Accessed February 10, 2018].

13 A good source on this question is the Royal Society evidence to a 2015 House of Lords inquiry. Available at: www.Parliament.uk/business/committees/committees-a-z/lords-select/science-and-technology-committee/inquiries/parliament-2015/eu-relationship-and-science/ [Accessed February 10, 2018].

14 According to the OECD. Available at: www.keepeek.com/Digital-Asset-Management/oecd/education/education-at-a-glance-2017_eag-2017-en#page286 [Accessed December 1, 2017].

15 According to THE Global Rankings. Available at: www.timeshighereducation.com/world-university-rankings/2018/world-ranking#!/page/0/length/25/sort_by/rank/sort_order/asc/cols/stats [Accessed December 1, 2017].

16 The Government's Negotiating Objectives for Exiting the EU: PM Speech. Available at: www.gov.uk/government/speeches/the-governments-negotiating-objectives-for-exiting-the-eu-pm-speech [Accessed September 17, 2017].

17 See UK Sets Clear Objectives for Continued Science Success. Available at: www.gov.uk/government/news/uk-sets-clear-objectives-for-continued-science-success [Accessed September 24, 2017].

18 Much of the data in this section is drawn from Universities UK, International Higher Education in Facts and Figures 2017. Available at: www.universitiesuk.ac.uk/policy-and-analysis/reports/Pages/international-facts-figures-2017.aspx [Accessed September 17, 2017].

19 According to the University Knowledge Exchange. Available at: www.hefce.ac.uk/media/HEFCE,2014/Content/Pubs/Independentresearch/2016/University,KE,framework,Good,practice,in,technology,transfer/2016_ketech.pdf [Accessed December 1, 2017].

20 According to UK–India Education. Available at: www.ukieri.org/program-background.html [Accessed February 10, 2018].

21 See Manoj Ladwa, It's Time to Recognize the Truth – A Trade Deal with India Means Concessions on Immigration. *New Statesman*, July 28, 2017. Available at: www.newstatesman.com/politics/staggers/2017/07/its-time-recognise-truth-trade-deal-india-means-concessions-immigration [Accessed November 25, 2017].

22 Grace Lang, Influence through Impact: 10 Years of the UK Research Councils in China. Foreign & Commonwealth Office, September 14, 2017. Available at: https://blogs.fco.gov.uk/jacksmith/2017/09/14/influence-through-impact-10-years-of-the-uk-research-councils-in-china/ [Accessed December 11, 2017].

23 According to the Universities UK, Domestic Policy Change, n.d. Available at: www.universitiesuk.ac.uk/policy-and-analysis/brexit/Pages/domestic-policy-change.aspx [Accessed December 1, 2017].

References

Adams, J. (2017) International Research Collaboration after the UK Leaves the European Union: A Report from Digital Science Consultancy for Universities UK. *Universities UK*. Available at: www.universitiesuk.ac.uk/policy-and-analysis/reports/Documents/2017/international-collaboration-uk-post-exit.pdf [Accessed December 1, 2017].

British Council (2012) The Shapes of Things to Come: Higher Education Global Trends and Emerging Opportunities to 2020. Available at: www.britishcouncil.org/sites/default/files/the_shape_

of_things_to_come_-_higher_education_global_trends_and_emerging_opportunities_to_2020. pdf [Accessed January 8, 2018].

Chou, M.-H. (2014) The Evolution of the European Research Area as an Idea in European Integration. In: Chou, M.-H. and Gornitzka, A. (eds.), *Building the Knowledge Economy in Europe: New Constellations in European Research and Higher Education Governance.* Cheltenham: Edward Elgar, pp. 27–50.

Collini, S. (2012) *What Are Universities For?* Harmondsworth: Penguin.

Confederation of British Industry (CBI) (2016) Bridges to the Future: The Role of Universities in UK–China Relationship. Available at: www.cbi.org.uk/index.cfm/_api/render/file/?method=inline&fileID= BBC0D1C0-84C7-43F6-89A72E3C3D46D2B0 [Accessed December 1, 2017].

Corbett, A. (2005) *Universities and the Europe of Knowledge: Ideas, Institutions and Policy Entrepreneurship in European Union Higher Education, 1955–2005.* Basingstoke: Palgrave Macmillan.

Corbett, A. (2016a) But We Can't Do It Alone: The Future of British Universities. *London School of Economics and Political Science.* Available at: http://blogs.lse.ac.uk/brexit/2016/09/21/but-we-cant-do-it-alone-the-future-of-british-universities-post-brexit/ [Accessed November 25, 2017].

Corbett, A. (2016b) Research and Higher Education: UK as International Star and Closet European? *Political Quarterly* 87(2): 166–173.

Corbett, A. and Gordon, C. (2016) The Impact of Exiting the European Union on Higher Education Inquiry. *Education Selection Committee Hearings*, HC683. Available at: www.parliament.uk/business/ committees/committees-a-z/commons-select/education-committee/inquiries/parliament-2015/brexit-impact-higher-education-16-17/ [Accessed November 25, 2017].

De Wit, H., Deca, L. and Hunter, F. (2012) Internationalization of Higher Education: What Can Research Add to the Policy Debate? [Overview Paper]. In: Curaj, A., Matei, L., Pricopie, R., Salmi, J. and Scott, P. (eds.), *The European Higher Education Area: Between Critical Reflections and Future Policies.* London: Springer. Available at: https://link.springer.com/content/pdf/10.1007%2F978-3-319-20877-0.pdf [Accessed December 1, 2017].

Education Select Committee (2017) The Impact of Exiting the European Union on Higher Education Inquiry. *Education Selection Committee Hearings*, HC683. Available at: www.parliament.uk/business/ committees/committees-a-z/commons-select/education-committee/inquiries/parliament-2015/brexit-impact-higher-education-16-17/ [Accessed November 25, 2017].

European Commission (2010) Europe 2020: A Strategy for Smart, Sustainable and Inclusive Growth Targets. Available at: http://ec.europa.eu/eu2020/pdf/COMPLET%20EN%20BARROSO%20%20%20007%20 -%20Europe%202020%20-%20EN%20version.pdf [Accessed December 11, 2017].

European Commission Communication (2017) Strengthening European Identity through Education and Culture. Available at: https://ec.europa.eu/commission/sites/beta-political/files/communication-strengthening-european-identity-education-culture_en.pdf [Accessed November 25, 2017].

Galsworthy, M. and Davidson, R. (2015) Debunking the Myths about British Science after an EU Exit. *London School of Economics and Political Science.* Available at: http://blogs.lse.ac.uk/brexit/2015/12/05/ debunking-the-myths-about-british-science-after-an-eu-exit/ [Accessed November 25, 2017].

Gordon, C. (2017) It's Time Students Take to the Barricades over Brexit. *London School of Economics and Political Science.* Available at: http://blogs.lse.ac.uk/brexit/2017/09/11/its-time-students-take-to-the-barricades-over-brexit/ [Accessed November 25, 2017].

Highman, L. (2017) Brexit and the Issues Facing UK Higher Education. *Centre for Global Higher Education.* Available at: www.researchcghe.org/perch/resources/publications/brexit-and-the-issues-facing-uk-higher-education.pdf [Accessed November 25, 2017].

Hood, C., Oliver, J., Peters, G.B. and Colin, S. (2004) *Controlling Modern Government: Variety, Commonality and Change.* Cheltenham: Edward Elgar.

Kemp, N. and Humfrey, C. (2010) UK-US Higher Education Partnerships: Realising the Potential. *British Council.* Available at: www.britishcouncil.us/sites/default/files/uk-us_higher_education_partnerships_ executive_summary_0.pdf [Accessed December 1, 2017].

Knight, J. (2017) Key Concepts and Element in Internationalisation of Higher Education: A Handbook. Available at: www.handbook-internationalisation.com/ [Accessed November 25, 2017].

Lodge, M. (2015) Regulating Higher Education: A Comparative Perspective. In: Black, J., Boggs, A.M., Fry, H., Hillman, N., Jackson, S., King, R. and Lodge, M. (eds.) and Underwood, S., *The Regulation of Higher Education.* Discussion Paper, Centre for Analysis of Risk and Regulation, No. 77. Available at: http:// www.lse.ac.uk/accounting/Assets/CARR/documents/D-P/Disspaper77.pdf [Accessed December 1, 2017].

Pruvot, E.B. and Estermann, T. (2017) University Autonomy in Europe: The Scorecard 2017. *European University Association.* Available at: http://eua.be/Libraries/publications/University-Autonomy-in-Europe-2017.pdf?sfvrsn=4 [Accessed December 1, 2017].

Stern, V. (2017) Brexit: Challenges and Opportunities. *Blog Post, Universities UK*. Available at: www. universitiesuk.ac.uk/blog/Pages/Brexit-challenges-and-opportunities.aspx [Accessed December 1, 2017].

Teixeira, P.N. (2013) The Tortuous Ways of the Market: Looking at the Integration of Higher Education from an Economic Perspective. In: Kleine, M., Monastiriotis, V., White, J. and Gattermann, K. (eds.), *LSE 'Europe in Question'*, 56/2013, Discussion Paper Series. London.

Universities UK (2017a) Can Free Trade Agreements Enhance Opportunities for UK Higher Education after Brexit? Available at: www.universitiesuk.ac.uk/policy-and-analysis/reports/Documents/2017/ international-collaboration-uk-post-exit.pdf [Accessed December 1, 2017].

Universities UK (2017b) What Should Be the Government's Priorities for Exit Negotiations and Policy Development to Maximise the Contribution of British Universities to a Successful and Global UK? *Briefing Paper, Universities UK*. Available at: www.universitiesuk.ac.uk/policy-and-analysis/brexit/ Documents/brexit-briefing-final-june.pdf [Accessed December 1, 2017].

Universities UK British Council (2016) The Scale and Scope of UK Higher Education Transnational Education. *Joint Report*. Available at: www.britishcouncil.org/sites/default/files/scale-and-scope-of-uk-he-tne-report.pdf [Accessed December 1, 2017].

Universities UK International (2017) Gone International: Mobility Works. Available at: www.universitiesuk. ac.uk/policy-and-analysis/reports/Documents/International/GoneInternational2017_A4.pdf [Accessed January 7, 2018].

Walters, J. (2017) International Student Mobility and Transnational Education: New Geographical Imaginaries Post-Brexit. *Academic Mobility and Brexit, SRHE Higher Education Policy Network Event*. London, October 2017.

10

BREXIT, 'IMMIGRATION' AND ANTI-DISCRIMINATION

Adrian Favell and Roxana Barbulescu

Introduction

However it is interpreted, no one will deny that central to the causes and consequences of Brexit have been migration and the European Union's foundational commitment to the free movement of persons. The dust had barely begun to settle on the result before a host of academic commentators had stepped forward to identify "EU immigration" as a – if not *the* – decisive factor behind the Leave vote.

Our contribution to this volume examines what lies underneath the "EU immigration" hypothesis that has become such a dominant interpretation. To speak of "EU immigration" is a legally as well as sociologically inadequate view of free movement and population in the UK and Europe. In a first section, we sketch some of the key political science sources on the EU referendum, showing how these works have in effect uncritically confirmed and reproduced a reading of EU immigration and Brexit uncomfortably close to the one promoted by the UK Independence Party's leading figure, Nigel Farage. In the second, we introduce into a debate dominated by specialists of public opinion and electoral analysis, the view of migration scholars: facts about immigration, migration, mobilities and free movement in the UK, as well as facts about the dynamics and effects of migration and the European labour market in a comparative European context. As a political issue, the "democratic" effects of migration need to be separated from its economic and demographic drivers. Each has its own potential sustainability in any given context. As we will show, in the UK, the problem with migration and mobility is strictly one about its popular democratic sustainability, not its economic or demographic features – particularly when viewed comparatively. In a third section, we consider the evolution of legal and policy responses to the Brexit vote, as political leaders wrestled with reconciling the needs of a porous, highly transnational economy and society with the false, nationally bounded understanding of "the people". This talks us through the details of former Prime Minister David Cameron's fateful deal on EU migration before the vote, to the consequences after it, and to the unfolding of the ongoing negotiation over the UK's exit. The conclusion then speculates on the likely scenarios for migration in a post-Brexit Britain.

Who or what is "EU immigration"?

It is widely accepted that the calling of the Brexit referendum was directly linked to inner turmoil in the British Conservative Party over Euroscepticism and to the threat from the right posed by the UK Independence Party (UKIP) – notably after the 2012 European elections (see Chapter 13).

UKIP had long advocated a stop on EU migration to the UK, an issue it saw at the heart of British sovereignty and a mobilising factor for working-class voters. After the vote, pioneering scholarship on UKIP (Ford and Goodwin 2014) was extended to suggest that peripheral and impoverished voters, who were mostly former Labour voters – in many discussions referred to as "the left-behind" – had converted their transfer of support to UKIP into a Leave vote at the referendum (Goodwin and Heath 2016; Goodwin and Milazzo 2017; Ford and Goodwin 2017). Polling and early analysis – including the widely cited Ashcroft surveys (Ashcroft 2016) – meanwhile had quickly discovered that "immigration" and "sovereignty" were indeed the most stable likely causes of such voting; the most likely suspects being the more than 3 million "uncontrolled" foreign EU nationals in the UK as residents (in early 2017, the figure was said to be as high as 3.7 million; see Vargas-Silva 2017). "Immigration" has also been widely affirmed as the key factor in Euroscepticism across Western Europe (Kriesi et al. 2008; Toshkov and Kortenska 2015; de Vries 2018). Other scholars questioned the emphasis on social class rather than values, but did not question the focus on "immigration" (Kaufmann 2016; Inglehart and Norris 2016). This mode of thinking further solidified with the first definitive book-length analysis of the referendum, with "immigration" again seen as a key pillar of the Leave vote (Clarke et al. 2017).

The cumulative effect of this powerful consensus of leading scholars propelled to centre stage the idea that a hitherto silenced or marginalised white working class had managed to articulate a majority anti-immigration voice through the referendum (notably in the work of electoral specialist Evans and his various associates; i.e., 2016a). This argument became a core part of what will likely be regarded as a definitive statement on Brexit and British politics (Evans and Menon 2017). In 2015, Evans and a different co-author had published a short blog piece on how what they labelled "EU immigration" was likely to determine the outcome of the upcoming referendum (Evans and Mellon 2015). The key part of the argument was how the rising "immigration" of EU origin tracked trends in growing percentages of people willing to vote Leave, converting the hitherto low salience of the EU as a political issue in the UK into a central concern. The referendum then became the moment this would be expressed. Crucial in the run-up to the referendum was what Evans referred to as the "incontrovertible fact" that from 2013 "mass EU immigration" had become the largest component of migration to the UK, around half of a total net figure of about 320,000 (Evans 2016b). In the wake of the vote, the stark and simple 2015 thesis was elevated to the status of uncanny foresight – joining voices across the political spectrum blaming the defeat on Tony Blair and his open border, cosmopolitan policies of the 1990s and early 2000s (Coleman 2016; Goodhart 2017).

Remarkably, the debate amongst public opinion and electoral specialists has taken place with little attention to what this "immigration" of EU nationals *in fact* is – both legally and sociologically. We may all agree that the surveys suggest that the British population (or more, accurately, the English) tend to perceive the 3 million-plus resident non-national Europeans as "immigrants" – at least when they are asked directly how they feel about "immigrants". The implication is that Nigel Farage was right to say – as in the notorious poster unveiled in London a week before the referendum – that Britain had reached a "breaking point" on its willingness to accept immigration from the EU. He pictured this "immigration" as hordes of swarthy-looking men from somewhere East swarming over a border in Central Europe. But who or what were Leave voters really thinking of? Was there really a "mass" aggregate of "EU immigration" causally determining political and policy outcomes?

It is a normative not an empirical choice to prioritise the receiving society as the primary jurisdiction of this migration. This is indeed a question of "sovereignty", as Farage would say. Foreigners are always present in contemporary globalised societies, in very large numbers. Their status is determined by a variety of legally and economically determined means. Counting some of these movers as an "immigrant" is what a receiving nation state does routinely in order to assert its sovereign power over a numerically tiny part of the overall population who are daily crossing its borders. EU freedom of movement of persons, however, blurs precisely this enactment of sovereignty, as a very large number of EU citizens may be present in Britain well beyond the short term of a "tourist" visit – or even the OECD's standard one-year criterion of migration. Evans and others use international passenger survey data about such "long term migrants", which estimates numbers on the basis of small samples and unreliable statements by those entering about their intentions to stay. However numerous, these EU citizens remain indeterminate as migrants or movers in terms of ultimate jurisdiction, without *any* obligation to become an "immigrant" – at least not until they cross some legal line that indicates a genuine settlement. On this, a willingness to take permanent resident status or, better, to seek naturalisation would seem the obvious objective criterion in order to count someone as an "immigrant". Yet Evans and others provide no evidence as to what proportion of the total claimed 3.7 million EU residents or the 160,000 or so net annual "EU immigrants" are really *immigrants* in this sense. Moreover, they offer no recognition at all of the enormous heterogeneity of this population. EU nationals in the UK include very high numbers of professional, skilled and human capital–rich workers. Until very recently, at least half have been West European; they are mostly younger and more educated than their British counterparts, and are difficult to distinguish from the high numbers of students and tourists in the country (Rienzo and Vargas-Silva 2017; Gordon et al. 2007). All these categories of people are foreigners presently legally on British soil. But they are not all automatically "immigrants". Echoing Farage's sweeping exaggerations, the Brexit scholarship has also relied on dubious assumptions about an aggregate "mass immigration" to sustain its findings.

Evans and Mellon claim, "Actual immigration rates are the key to understanding levels of concern about immigration" (2015). The truth is the reverse. Public concern about "immigration" has been used to confirm and reproduce false academic measures, categorisations and representations of "immigration". As Nando Sigona put it poignantly (being one of them), EU nationals in the UK woke up one morning in June 2016 to discover a border had passed over them (Gonzales and Sigona 2017: 2); they had, overnight, become "EU immigrants" – just as Farage had labelled them. In the days to come, they discovered their own colleagues using the same language and same methodological nationalist assumptions about mobile populations. A Hobbesian notion of sovereignty reasserted its power to "name": to normatively classify, identity and delimit the "true" British population and those "foreign" to it, regardless of the functional reality of its global and regionally integrated economy and society or the heterogeneous "face" that its mobile and migrant populations in fact had. With the Brexit vote, economy and demography were reduced to "democracy".

Needless to say, no "democratic" vote should be allowed to determine the scientific understanding of how in fact economy and demography work in a porous global society; nor should it be allowed to pre-empt law and determine the formal status of foreigners present on a territory or to mischaracterise populations sociologically. Academic interpretations and statistical constructions bear some responsibility for confirming rather than contesting the misrepresentations that drove the Leave vote.

Economy and demography versus politics

Membership of the EU meant, of course, that the UK had to accept consequences for migration more generally. Regarding migration internal to the EU, the free movement of persons is one of the foundational tenets of the EU's Single Market. This entails the right of any EU national to live and work freely in the UK under certain conditions, notably to be protected from disadvantage (i.e., discrimination) on the basis of their foreign nationality. Protection against discrimination in the UK on the basis of gender, sexuality, age, race or disability has been strongly inscribed in national law and practice for decades. Introducing non-discrimination by nationality was thus a dramatic extension of these equality principles. For example, in the job market: non-national EU residents had the same equal claims as nationals; to discriminate against foreign EU nationals if they were the best qualified person – that is, to view them as an "immigrant" with a lesser claim than a "national", such as insisting they need to get prior authorisations (i.e., a "visa") before consideration – becomes the equivalent of discriminating against someone on the basis of race, gender or disability. This is a line that is very heavily policed in British organisations and institutions. Britain's attractiveness to free movers in the EU as well as the host population's advanced sensibility in applying non-discrimination norms in questions of employment, in access to education and in the private sphere – i.e., in rentals or buying a house – made it arguably the *most* effectively Europeanised member state on this dimension (that is, in a "horizontal" sociological sense; see Favell and Guiraudon 2011).

Britain has always been noted as a very "good" member of the EU in terms of compliance to freedom of movement norms, and British of all stripes have never been shy in using their free movement rights abroad (especially retirement migration and property investment in the South of Europe; Benson and O'Reilly 2009). They now number 1.4 million, with very high numbers in Spain and France. Back home, flying in the face of the UK's universally assumed Euroscepticism and its so-called cultural "exceptionalism" (Evans et al. 2016; Dennison and Carl 2016), the British were in fact "hyper-European" in terms of "fair play" towards EU foreigners. This has been something that cannot be so well claimed in other "advanced" North European countries: for example, in terms of some kinds of employment in France, Denmark, or Germany, or of access to housing in Netherlands or Sweden. British attitudes towards the regulation and functioning of free market principles and implementation of non-discrimination norms, in fact, put it at the heart of European political values, very close to the liberal view of the EU Commission and its views on the normative goals of Europe (Gerhards 2007; Manners 2002).

On migration to the UK from *outside* the EU (extra-EU migrants), however, Britain has been notorious for how, over the years, it has negotiated a very long string of opt-outs on migration and borders, such that it was largely insulated from much of the Europeanisation (in a vertical policy sense) of EU immigration policy. Britain has been part of the Dublin convention on asylum but was not part of Schengen. It avoided most of the consequences of the Syrian refugee crisis. It also has a bespoke free movement accord with Ireland as part of the Common Travel Area, which has become a very difficult element in Brexit negotiations. The EU's concerns over the rights of third-country nationals, common border policing and security, visa regimes, neighbourhood cooperation, or immigrant integration thus have not and do not impinge much upon British sovereign control over its own immigration policies – again, to be clear, for migrants from outside the EU.

Under the pressure of UK politics, from Labour to Conservative administrations, the UK's immigration policy towards the rest of the world has been rigorously tough and mean for decades and increasingly so in recent years – arguably tougher than any close neighbour apart from Denmark. It imposes caps on numbers (including students and nurses), it has successively tightened access for family members, discriminates against spouses, sets high economic thresholds on proving independent means and is only averagely open to high-skilled migrant visas (Ruhs and Anderson 2010; Briddick 2015). These factors all impose discrimination or simply exclusion on the chances of foreign workers in the British labour market, however much they are objectively "needed".

Both the Conservative and Labour Parties campaigned on a ticket to reduce overall immigration in the general elections in 2015 and 2017, committing themselves to draconian (and completely unrealistic) upper number limits that even included students (the most obvious source of high-skilled selective migration). The commitment to the symbolic threshold of 100,000 net migrants annually has not been met for twenty years (Cohen 2017). In setting these state-sanctioned targets, the scope of the British migration system has already been transformed from one that selects according to regulated market allocations to one that reduces migration by top-down state intervention, dedicated above all to letting in *fewer* people, regardless of talent or skill. The goal of Brexit will be to impose this immigration policy on all migration in the country. Understanding British immigration policy to the rest of the world is indeed key to the question of "EU immigration" and Brexit because the current prime minister, Theresa May, was the chief architect of this policy while at the Home Office; it is this construct that has determined the Government's view of EU migration after Brexit.

The reality was that Britain did not need to leave the EU to achieve this level of "independence" on immigration policy. That is not to say that its external borders are airtight. In fact, by all visible accounts, because of the deregulated nature of parts of the economy, there are very significant numbers of black market workers in the UK, working in low-end hospitality, services, domestic and care work, sex work, agriculture and construction and so on.

Brexit will not change much of Britain's already independent immigration policy, therefore, although it will change the supply–demand dynamics because of the way extra-EU migration and intra-EU migration are related. Without doubt, EU membership *did* have a dramatic effect on this migration and other forms of spatial mobility to the UK from Europe. It is not clear how much the Labour Party intended it, but their policies of the early 2000s on EU accession certainly did lead to a transformation of population in the UK (Regout 2016). This was qualitative as much as quantitative. Labour gambled on further extending and deepening British porousness to global flows and mobilities of all kinds, which date back to the "big bang" trade policies of the Thatcher era. This inevitably created an "addiction" to labour migration, as Chancellor Gordon Brown's Britain became from the late 1990s to the mid-2000s, becoming the most open migrant labour market and economy in Europe. The opening to East Europeans with the 2004 accession and afterward, however, effected a signal change on the potential of satisfying the rampant British economy's demand for migration. From sources for immigration that were predominantly non-European, non-white, lower skilled and substantially irregular, there could be a shift to a new source of regulated, skilled migrants from Eastern Europe, who – it may have been thought – would be much more likely to *not* settle long term or cause "ethnic" frictions because of their (white) race, (Christian) culture and easy access to back-and-forth lifestyles in their home countries, especially on cheap airlines like Ryan Air (Favell 2009).

The opening of British borders to the freedom of movement of persons after accession in 2004 was also part of the British geopolitical commitment to Eastern Europe – the French, for example, were much less keen on Eastern enlargement. Britain, in effect, aligned with Germany on weighing the opportunities of enlargement over the risks. It was widening rather than deepening. The effects were certainly dramatic. With only Sweden and Ireland joining the UK in opening the doors unreservedly to free movement from new member states, and other EU member states imposing sometimes lengthy barriers of up to seven years to full accession, it became a kind of natural experiment in varieties of labour market, border regimes and migration selection/sorting mechanisms.

The percentage of East Europeans interested in moving West was high (albeit always massively exaggerated, especially by German and Austrian demographers; see Kupiszewski 2002). Notoriously, though, it was heavily underestimated in Britain by advisors to the government (Dustmann et al. 2003). What was estimated at around 50,000 became well over half a million in the first two years, mainly from Poland. Overall, following the enlargement, 3 million people have moved from the Central and Eastern states to the West European states (Barbulescu et al. 2015). Over a third have come to Britain. While Germany was open to comparable numbers to the UK, it kept Central and Eastern European movers in subordinate statuses, perpetuating a dual economy for migrant workers. In France, foreign workers have been routinely excluded by both formal and informal means, in both labour market and welfare state access; it is now slowly moving towards more liberal policies. The Netherlands and Scandinavia were also long able to restrict access to the labour market for foreign skilled workers through unionisation and limited recognition of foreign credentials (Favell 2014).

Given this range of labour market conditions, the basic migrant supply, the choice of destination, and the demand of a booming UK economy under New Labour, the selection effects for the UK were astonishing. The supply was overwhelmingly "positive" in normative economists' terms (what critical scholars label "neo-liberal"): young, mobile, skilled, human capital rich, and well organized in transnational migration practices (Garapich 2008). Poland and later Romania and the Baltics were all a significant source of well qualified, skilled, and/or highly motivated workers. This has had large effects on multiple sectors of the British economy: in services, hospitality, care, but also education, health care, and finance, all of which had access to a pool of talent wider than any of their European neighbours. A large-scale study following the accession of the A8 countries found that employers characterized the increased labour supply very broadly as young, both male and female and prepared to do "entry level jobs", as well as those bringing skills. Employers observed that skilled workers were available at lower pay relative to their skill, either because their qualifications were not recognized or because they wanted to work abroad in an English language-speaking environment, seen as a gateway to the world (Ruhs and Anderson 2010: 84). The enlargement helped workers from these countries move more freely between jobs and therefore gain access to better work (Ruhs 2018). At the same time, there was in effect a brain drain from Poland and Romania to the UK via the remarkably open British university sector (Moros anu 2016), as well as jobs in finance and other high-end services (Csedö 2008). By 2015, 40 per cent of all new jobs in the UK university sector were being taken by EU citizens (Times Higher Education Supplement 2016). As a result, 17 per cent (33,735) of academic staff at UK universities are from other EU member states, with the majority concentrated in research-intensive universities (Universities UK 2017b). East European migration was only adding to a sizeable booming West European professional migration since the late 1990s, which was largely invisible to everyone except employers. On all points, the British economy collected the benefits. In terms of economic theory, this was a model migration system from the receiving point of view (Drinkwater et al. 2009). Britain was selecting at the high end; even among the lower-skilled, Polish migration was weighted towards entrepreneurial business activities and complementary roles in the economy. These highly transnational migrants and their families benefitted at home and abroad: capital was flowing back to Poland, driving growth there. If any economy in Europe fitted neoclassical economist George Borjas's model of the EU and free movement (Borjas 1999), it was the Poland–UK migration system in the 2000s.

The 2008 financial crisis hit the UK less than other parts of Europe. There was an uptick in net migration after 2010, and certainly numbers and types of migration diversified under the pressure of poverty migration from some sending countries (Lafleur and Stanek 2016). Even then, if one were to focus on a substantial part of this "new" new migration – Southern Europeans – it would be found to be overwhelmingly young, economically mobile and able to find work in the UK. London continued to attract the majority of EU citizens arriving to UK, retaining up to a third of all new arrivals; recent waves of Europeans, particularly those from the new member states, tended to be somewhat more dispersed (Vargas-Silva 2016). This uneven distribution certainly meant that the benefits and costs were not divided evenly among different parts of the country – a significant factor in the polarisation of the Brexit vote. There has also been a marked tendency of employers and entrepreneurs to go "off-the-books" in employment practices in agricultural and construction work, relying increasingly on the informality and flexibility of transient East European low-skilled workers (Morris 2014). "Posted" workers also can avoid the free movement anti-discrimination norms, working at rates under the legal minimum. These practices drew increasing media attention and sparked growing anger in some provincial regions.

Even so, and despite the ever ramped-up attempts to restrict and lock out non-European migrants in UK immigration law and policy in the last two decades, it was not until 2015 that intra-EU migration to the UK exceeded extra-EU migration. The proportion of the two groups still remains close to 3:5 among the 8 million resident non-nationals; the vast majority of the further 5 million immigrant new British citizens (i.e., those born outside the UK who have naturalised) were born *outside* the EU.

At the beginning of 2017, entries from the European Union in the UK still made up for half of the total net entries of non-citizens of about 320,000 net growth each year – certainly a very substantial population growth by any European standards. After this, EU migration to the UK fell off. As of the first quarter of 2017, 2.4 million of the total 3.7 million EU born were reported to be in work (Vargas-Silva 2017: 3–5). Given this is primarily a labour-driven migration, it is perhaps not surprising that Europeans have had higher employment rates than those born in the UK. Male workers born in the EU15 (mostly West Europeans) had only a slightly higher employment rate than the males born in the UK (78 per cent to 74 per cent). On the other hand, Eastern and Central Europeans from the newer member states – A8 and A2 residents – had higher employment rates than both than EU15 and UK nationals; indeed, they were higher than for any other categories or nationalities, highlighting the strong implantation of the new mobility from the EU in the British labour market. In 2015, (male) employment rates for A8 residents stood at 91 per cent, whereas for A2 residents it was a slightly lower 89 per cent per cent, a solid +17 per cent and +15 per cent higher than for British-born males, respectively (Rienzo 2016: 4). Similarly, employment rates for women were higher for A8 and EU14 than for those born in UK.

The British Labour Force shows that there has been an important shift in terms of the numbers of workers *amongst* those born in EU countries. If before the accession of A8 countries in 2004, 85 per cent of the EU-born workers were born in the EU15, starting with 2011 and with the raise in the volume of the post-enlargement mobility, most EU-born workers were indeed A8 workers. By the first quarter of 2017, 58 per cent of total EU born workers were from A8 and A2 countries (Vargas-Silva 2017: 5ff). This clearly had potential selection effects: the nature of British demand for workers may have been shifting in a more low-end direction.

Employment rates only give a crude indication of effects on the economy. The best economic analyses offer absolutely no support for the "EU immigration" hypothesis. It has been repeatedly shown that the net fiscal effects of EU migration to the UK have been substantially positive in the aggregate (Dustmann and Frattini 2014). With Brexit looming, it has also been repeatedly shown that any reversal of Britain's openness to migrant workers will have substantially negative effects on the economy (Portes 2013, 2016). Britain's demographic profile would also be negative were the children of these migrants not counted as "British" (Grant 2015). EU workers were clearly visible to poor and marginalised English populations in agricultural and coastal locations, but there was little to suggest they were taking low-end jobs that the heavily benefits-reliant English population in these locations would be willing to accept. At the same time, many areas of England with next to no EU citizens present voted to Leave; among those who voted to leave but who had never voted substantially for UKIP were also some constituencies with very high South Asian populations (Ehsan 2017). The analyses of so-called benefits tourism by poor EU movers also showed the cost of migration to be a media-spun myth. A 2013 study found that, although newspapers were claiming there were over half a million EU unemployed, these gross figures included students, pensioners, non-working mothers and other family members. Forty-three per cent of the UK national population is "not working" in this sense, compared to 30 per cent of the EU national population. There were, in fact, at the time about 100,000 EU nationals unemployed, and about 60,000 were claiming job support allowance, with much lower rates for disability and other benefits to which they are equally entitled (Portes 2014).

The only reasonable conclusion that can be drawn from comparative economic and demographic analyses is that high levels of mobile and flexible EU workers in an open global economy, without necessarily a long-term settlement in the UK, made for both an economically and a demographically sustainable population system, which positioned the UK to great advantage in the EU during the 1990s and 2000s. Britain's problem with "EU immigration", given its hugely difficult management of non-EU immigration, was strictly a political problem – "Great" British democracy was unable to handle the growth dynamics and the social transformation it implied.

The path to Brexit

The EU referendum was prefigured by quite desperate negotiations to solve these political problems by then Prime Minister David Cameron, to secure concessions or British opt-outs on aspects of the legal framework of EU freedom of movement. Harassed by UKIP's rise and the right wing of his own party, he pursued a solution to the "migration equation" (Barker et al. 2015) that might reconcile the contradiction between the growing political unsustainability of the UK's commitment to freedom of movement with the continuance of an open "neo-liberal" style economic regime structurally dependent on higher levels of migration than its neighbours (see Parker 2017 on the left wing version of this dilemma). During the coalition years (2010–2015), Cameron was vulnerable above all else to successive governments' unrealistic commitments on limiting annual aggregate numbers of net migrants in the UK economy. He was also vulnerable to any downturn in the economy in both receiving *and* sending contexts that might affect the transnational mobility of migrants (i.e., migrants having to give up on coming-and-going patterns and instead settling) or that might affect positive selection effects (i.e., the possible growth of poverty migration from Southern Europe – however implausible Britain might be as a generous welfare state haven). Neither he nor any Conservatives felt confident trying to make the positive case on economic or demographic sustainability.

Instead, Cameron played the welfare spongers card: basically creating a phantasm of welfare benefits abuse among "immigrants" in order to justify both tightening the rules and a political deal on modifying freedom of movement with the EU. Observers could also read how these tendencies were targeted in fact at something else (Anderson 2013; Tyler 2010): austerity towards the much higher numbers of UK nationals dependent on the welfare system. By instigating normative or moralised ideas about "bad" "immigrants" who could be denied parity with "good" citizens, the government could reinforce and align attempts to exclude other "bad" citizens, who were full national members of the polity, from the full citizenship and welfare rights it guarantees under the usual norms of social citizenship. In other words, the unemployed, the homeless, the mentally or physically disabled, single mothers and so on could also be positioned as "unworthy" of citizenship, analogous to Roma beggars or Polish families with too many children. Yet this rollback of the classic Marshallian ideas of inclusive citizenship was not limited to the UK. Much of the incremental restrictions being brought in by the British state in these years was not at all out of line with the restrictionism of both European Court of Justice jurisprudence or the tightening of bureaucratic practices being developed in other countries (Menendez 2014; Everson 2014).

So Cameron was not so much out of step with EU colleagues in seeking a four-year delay on welfare entitlement or a ceiling on absolute numbers in an "emergency brake" on EU migrants to the UK. It was a "Deal" as Donald Tusk tweeted. It could have worked as a selling point for the Remain campaign, but it did nothing to silence the political lies circulating about "EU immigrants". Without any kind of positive discourse about the 3-plus million, the nature of their presence and involvement in the labour market in Britain, and the sheer marginality of even the best economic analysis, Cameron's solution to the migration equation was too little too late. In any event, the deal was defunct with the Brexit vote; instead, Article 50 would be triggered, and henceforth instead of negotiating over a small amendment to freedom of movement of persons in Europe, Britain would be negotiating every single line of its world trade agreements on the freedom of movement of capital, goods, services and persons – the entire infrastructure of its place in global capitalism. In the meantime, Britain was left with its current legal commitment to freedom of movement and 3-plus million residents plus EU non-nationals facing an expiry date on their right to even be present on UK soil. And so now they became an object of negotiation – and of blatant, undignified horse-trading – on preliminary agreements before even the trade negotiations could begin. Moreover, in one fell swoop, the UK had landed 1.4 million of its own citizens living in the EU in their own serious status problems – on a reciprocal hiding to nothing.

Unlike their counterparts in the UK, British populations abroad are predominantly non-independent older residents who highly dependent on transnational benefits agreements and overseas health care – so unlike Britain's youthful and mobile EU populations. They are also hugely reliant on cheap airline mobility, effortless banking and the goodwill of rural and coastal populations tolerating their often brazenly colonial lifestyles (King et al. 2000). The population of Gibraltar, at least, realised this; voting 96 per cent to Remain despite historical volatility over the status of the municipality in Spain. Back home, the British voted to strip themselves of the cross-border citizenship rights they had enjoyed – albeit unconsciously – for decades. Brexit would inevitably devalue British citizenship internationally in terms of equal, reciprocal access to other states (Kochenov 2016, 2018). It seemed to concern Brexit voters very little, so confident were they with their colonial birthright: one lady was quoted as saying that EU citizenship meant nothing to her because "British people had been able to live and work and travel anywhere they wanted to in the world for centuries now". Rule Britannia, indeed.

British negotiators, however, were certainly conscious of this potential devaluing. One of May's redlines has been the untrammelled right of British to continue to be able to live, work and move freely around Europe (as will, of course, non-British EU citizens, excepting in the UK); this would be something like exiting the club but retaining all membership benefits. On the other side, with "EU immigration" being credited with playing a key role in the Brexit vote, the EU's ongoing commitment to the freedom of movement of persons has become an article of faith sitting awkwardly at the core of the ongoing negotiations. In its purest sense, non-discrimination by nationality is the economic commitment of a member state to a de-nationalised European-scale labour market, regulated not by national sovereignty but by a legal affirmation of the claims of post-national membership, albeit incomplete (notably over voting rights). For Brexit to *mean* Brexit (in May's stentorian phraseology), it must in some sense *end* these practices of non-discrimination. The British abroad and EU nationals in Britain *must*, in this logic, face discrimination again as foreigners and "immigrants".

On the face of it, then, as a two-way negotiation, the EU as well as the UK have been keen on the retention of rights for their citizens but equally keen on ending the ones of citizens of the other side. With the European Commission as the named guardian of the freedom of movement, the EU insisted that the 3-plus million EU nationals in the UK who have made use of these rights in good faith should not lose the right to remain or enjoy equal treatment when the UK is no longer an EU member. On the other hand, the UK entered the negotiations with not one but two objectives: firstly, to repatriate some control over *who* among the 3-plus million Europeans would still be able to come to work and live in the UK after Brexit, which will entail discrimination by nationality; and secondly, to safeguard the existing rights of UK citizens across the EU member states, including voting rights – assumed basically as a national birthright.

To break the deadlock of the negotiation, in June 2017 Theresa May proposed a "settled status" for all EU citizens living in the UK, which would give access to the same rights including "healthcare, education, benefits and pensions". "Settled status" was a UK neologism for permanent residency status that has existed as an option for EU nationals since 2004, although it has never been mandatory and was largely ignored by them. However, since 2015, it has been needed before naturalisation can be applied for or before children have access to British *ius soli* citizenship. Procedures regarding "settled status" have been cumbersome, expensive and weighted towards making access difficult: proof of several years physical presence in the UK is required, and the processing costs have risen steadily to well over £2,000 out of pocket per applicant. It can be assumed that the final goal of these procedures is to impose the same tough treatment and restrictions on any new EU migration after Brexit as exist already for immigration from outside the EU, as well as being as exclusionary as possible to those already in the UK.

In the event, negotiations on the post-Brexit rights of EU nationals in the UK and British nationals in the EU concluded on 8 December 2017 (European Commission and UK 2017a, 2017b; European Commission 2017). The document was strongly formulated in terms of reciprocity between the two parties, although more attention was given to specifying the conditions for residency of EU nationals in the UK. The document was, at first glance, a breakthrough, as it largely confirmed the existing rights of EU nationals and their family members who are "legally" residing in the UK. Yet as Peers (2017) has noted, "legally" here is an ambiguous notion. Most EU nationals have resided in the UK for many years, sometimes decades, without being checked and without applying for permanent residence. It could instead mean only those who hold or are able to gain formal residency from the Home Office. The reality on the ground here is salutary. In a position paper of an organisation defending the rights of EU nationals, it was reported there has been a 29 per cent rejection rate and a 10 per cent error rate in applicants for permanent residence (The 3 Million 2017). Even more alarmingly, women are less likely to secure their residence due to their irregular work histories and over-representation in unpaid work (Shutes and Walker 2017). Overall, about a third of those who apply cannot secure permanent residence to retain their right to remain or work in the UK. Many EU nationals, in fact, have been advised by their lawyers not to apply, as they do not meet the conditions and by applying they would put their residency in danger. These people would become subject to immigration control under British law after Brexit Day. Concerning family member of EU nationals, meanwhile, only those related to EU nationals at the time of the exit would enjoy the same rights (i.e., not those who get married or who are born afterward). The EU for its part was concerned about the conditions under which the UK would confirm the rights of EU nationals and the oversight of the European Court of Justice and international human rights obligations. It continued to baulk at confirming the rights of British citizens to continue to enjoy free movement outside their country of residence, since it does not want to allow an exiting state to cherry-pick benefits without membership.

Britain has wanted to make all resident EU nationals go through an assessment process, including those who have already taken a permanent residence certificate under EU regulations. While both the UK and the EU reserve the right to ask residents to reapply for their status after Brexit Day, it was Britain that announced this, thereby setting its own terms and conditions on the so-called settled status, which will bring EU nationals under British immigration law (UK Government 2017a). UK Government can also demand EU nationals to take part in mandatory civic integration tests that before Brexit applied only to migrants from outside the EU (see Barbulescu 2015, forthcoming). Leaders of the Brexit negotiations had promised simplified procedures to confirm existing rights for the EU nationals in the UK.

Furthermore, the UK has been successful in instrumentalising the safeguards attached to freedom of movement that seek to protect member states from so-called rights abuse by EU nationals. For example, homelessness is seen to be a sufficient condition for "rights abuse", which thereby allows Britain to remove many EU nationals. A first likely target will be those Roma EU nationals visible in large British cities. After Brexit Day, Britain would be able to introduce additional requirements. This is likely to include removal of those with a criminal record as part of the transfer from EU to national immigration law. This transfer will undoubtedly also imply systematic administrative checks and differentiation between wanted and unwanted workers. Ordinary EU nationals would thus become subject to the "hostile environment" to immigration that May has pursued since she was home secretary. Effectively, the NHS, employers, landlords, universities and banks would now need to formally check the residence status of EU nationals, reporting those who do not have it. All of these points fly in the face of existing anti-discrimination norms (Guardian 2017).

Ironically, if Brexit is forcing EU nationals to become "immigrants" in future, then naturalisation becomes the one key option for lowering the cost of the daunting insecurity for them in the UK, as well as for British citizens in the EU. A large proportion of EU nationals in the UK never wanted to naturalise, but maybe they will now see it as a simple instrumental calculation. A 2006 study found that only about a quarter of East Europeans expressed an intention to settle (Anderson et al. 2006). Europeans made up only 11 per cent of total naturalisations in 2016, despite the fact that the potential eligible population is in the order of millions. Put another way, the rate of annual naturalisation of EU nationals is under 10 per cent of their annual net inflow. Now needing to secure their status, naturalisations by EU citizens have increased by a third from 2015 to 2016 and will clearly continue to increase as borders close and free moving transnational family options are rendered more difficult.

In this sense, Brexit can only increase immigration; over 3 million mobile and flexible EU citizens will be forced to choose to stay and settle, to become the "immigrants" Farage, May and others had said they were. The prospect of 3-plus million overnight naturalisations without any emotional commitment to the country implies administrative chaos; the numbers that might stay permanently will certainly be far larger than it would have been. This is not a bad thing for diversity in the UK, its population structure or its economy – far from it. But it is diametrically the opposite of what Leave voters wanted to see happening.

Conclusion

What may be the consequences down the road for Britain after Brexit? In terms of migration, the selection effects are already visible. Britain has committed an international public relations disaster; the best and the brightest are already considering their options elsewhere. The City is already haemorrhaging businesses and talents. UK universities have become less attractive, and Brexit has tarnished their "world-class" claims. Brexit will hit all kinds of industries and their personnel dynamics, even though the post-Brexit vote crash of the pound has been a boon for tourism and some services.

Britain, too, always had an advanced reputation for multi-ethnic, multiracial, cosmopolitan diversity; this surely will change. The naked racialisation of the Brexit campaign has been a shock, especially the suspicion that the EU vote was driven substantially by anti-Muslim prejudice. EU movers will become visible "immigrants" like everyone else and subject to the same draconian and iniquitous immigration regime as non-EU nationals. The labour market will be state controlled through visas, quotas-based employment channels and bureaucratic logic, rather than market demand. Discrimination by nationality will return according to some colonial/racial hierarchy – in which we like Danes, are not so keen on Spanish, please no Romanians and definitely not Turks. It is likely to be far less competitive or selective and implies a huge amount of governmental red tape (and costs) to control and pattern something that was hitherto left to employers to determine via market selection. There may be some formal preference for UK nationals imposed in the job market – effectively state-sanctioned discrimination against foreigners, in the name of some fictional nation in which less qualified, less motivated and less worldly British workers always get the job.

This is all good news for Paris, Amsterdam, Frankfurt and Berlin. These locations will already sound hugely attractive to capital; free movers will follow. Many British abroad have been scuttling to adopt new nationalities. What about the global effects? Here the UK faces a dramatic Scylla and Charybdis. To put into effect the kind of state-controlled mechanisms on the labour market that might protect UK workers, improve their pay (relative to foreigners) or incentivise them to take up all the jobs they have been refusing to take – that is, Theresa May's peculiarly socialistic ideas of drawing the working class to the nationalist conservative side – clearly will kill the golden goose: the global neo-liberalism that has made Britain such an open, performative yet inequitable economy in the last two decades.

Since the socialist island option is highly unlikely – and very likely not at all sincere in Conservative Party circles – Britain may instead throw itself open to the four winds, making open trade deals with anyone wanting access to its shores. Much has been made of how a post-Brexit "Global Britain"– the "Empire 2.0" mission of Boris Johnson and others (Andrews 2017) – would look to fill new demand by a competitive points-based system for new immigration on the model of Canada or Australia. Even leaving aside the naïve analogy with the population structure of these small, highly diverse and capacious immigrant economies that are much better equipped at policing borders, there seems very little appetite for the mentality shift in British politics that a truly open "global" immigration policy based on competition for talent would entail. Brexiteers may talk the bravado of being open for global business, but they will baulk at what this could mean in terms of population change. As Hix, Kaufmann and Leeper have shown recently (2017), in fact Brexit voters dislike extra-EU migrants rather *more* than so-called EU immigrants.

This leaves a dilemma; free movement of capital, goods and services necessarily entails the movement of people. For the UK to keep its present economy and position within the North Atlantic region and globally, the immigrant economy must persist, and demand must continue to drive it. Absent of regulated, legal EU migration, these structural necessities are likely to produce higher numbers of illegal, unregulated, low-end migrants (something like the United States today), through a proliferation of sordid but highly profitable illegal entry points – from Europe and beyond. British who see the UK glowingly as the 51st state should be careful of what they wish for: the US–Mexican border and the politics surrounding Latin American migration in the United States make up one of the least edifying migration systems in the world (Massey et al. 2002; De Genova 2010). This "global" future is one that is the opposite of what Leave voters predominantly voted for: of even higher levels of foreign ownership of Britain, more migration, higher inequalities, much more offshoring and partial exiting – for the richest few – and likely massive further political tensions among the less well off and "left-behind".

The new migrations that follow Brexit may thus yet be even more spectacular in their effects and consequences – unless the British economy collapses, and migrant demand with it, as it exits global trade agreements and capital takes flight. The dominantly positive effects of the well regulated EU migrations of the 1990s and 2000s, hinged on complementarity and positive selection during an era of economic success and social inclusion, might then be presented in a much better political light.

References

The 3 Million (2017) The 'Hostile Environment' (and Why the 3 Million Opposes Settled Status), December 10. Available at: www.the3million.org.uk/hostile-environment [Accessed December 12, 2017].

Anderson, B. (2013) *Us and Them: The Dangerous Politics of Immigration Control.* Oxford: Oxford University Press.

Anderson, B., Ruhs, M., Spencer, S. and Rogaly, B. (2006) *Fair Enough? Central and East European Migrants in Low-Wage Employment in the UK.* Oxford: Joseph Rowntree Foundation. Available at: www.compas.ox.ac.uk/2006/pr-2006-changing_status_fair_enough/ [Accessed December 12, 2017].

Andrews, K. (2017) Building Brexit on the Myth of Empire Ignores our Brutal History. *The Guardian*, March 7. Available at: www.theguardian.com/commentisfree/2017/mar/07/building-brexit-on-myth-of-empire-ignores-history-at-our-peril [Accessed December 12, 2017].

Ashcroft, M. (2016) How the United Kingdom Voted on Thursday . . . and Why, June 24. Available at: https://lordashcroftpolls.com/2016/06/how-the-united-kingdom-voted-and-why/ [Accessed December 12, 2017].

Barbulescu, R. (2015) Inside Fortress Europe: The Europeanisation of Immigrant Integration and Its Impact on Identity Boundaries. *Politique Européenne* 47(1): 24–44.

Barbulescu (forthcoming) *Migrant Integration in a Changing Europe. Immigrants, Co-ethnics and European Citizens.* Notre Dame Indiana: University of Notre Dame Press.

Barbulescu, R., Lafleur, J.-M. and Stanek, M. (2015) Intra-European Mobility: Patterns of Immigration Flows and Policies. In: *Western Europe 2016.* London: Routledge, pp. 35–39.

Barker, B., Foy, H. and Parker, G. (2015) Cameron's Migration Equation. *Financial Times*, June 19, p. 5.

Benson, M. and O'Reilly, K. (eds.) (2009) *Lifestyle Migration: Expectations, Aspirations and Experiences.* London: Routledge.

Borjas, G. J. (1999) *Economic Research on the Determinants of Immigration: Lessons for the European Union.* Washington, DC: World Bank.

Briddick, C. (2015) Fortress Europe: Cause or Consequence of Europe's 'Migrant Crisis'. *The London School of Economics and Political Science*, August 28. Available at: http://blogs.lse.ac.uk/eurocrisispress/2015/08/28/fortress-europe-cause-or-consequence-of-europes-migrant-crisis/ [Accessed December 12, 2017].

Bridget, A., Ruhs, M., Spencer, S. and Rogaly, B. (2007) *Migrants' Lives beyond the Workplace: The Experience of Central and East Europeans in the UK.* Oxford: Rowntree Foundation. Available at: www.compas.ox.ac.uk/2007/pr-2007-changing_status_eastern_europeans-2/ [Accessed January 14, 2018].

Clarke, H.D., Goodwin, M. and Whiteley, P. (2017) *Brexit: Why Britain Voted to Leave the European Union.* Cambridge: Cambridge University Press.

Cohen, R. (2017) Fear Trumps Facts: Why Theresa May Is Sticking with Her Migration Cap. *The Conversation*, May 31. Available at: https://theconversation.com/fear-trumps-facts-why-theresa-may-is-sticking-with-her-migration-cap-78125 [Accessed December 12, 2017].

Coleman, D. (2016) Uncontrolled Immigration Means Finis Britanniae. *Standpoint*, June. Available at: www.standpointmag.co.uk/node/6525/full [Accessed December 12, 2017].

Csedö, K. (2008) Negotiating Skills in the Global City: Hungarian and Romanian Professionals and Graduates in London. *Journal of Ethnic and Migration Studies* 34(5): 803–823.

De Genova, N. (2010) The Deportation Regime: Sovereignty, Space and the Freedom of Movement. In: De Genova, N. and Peutz, N. (eds.), *The Deportation Regime.* Durham, NC: Duke University Press, pp. 33–65.

Dennison, J. and Carl, N. (2016) The Ultimate Causes of Brexit: History, Culture and Geography. *LSE British Politics and Policy*, July 28. Available at: http://blogs.lse.ac.uk/politicsandpolicy/explaining-brexit/ [Accessed December 12, 2017].

de Vries, C. (2018) *Euroscepticism and the Future of European Integration.* Oxford: Oxford University Press.

Drinkwater, S., Eade, K. and Garapich, M. (2009) Poles Apart? EU Enlargement and the Labour Market Outcomes of Immigrants in the United Kingdom. *International Migration* 47(1): 161–190.

Dustmann, C., Casanova, M., Fertig, M., Preston, I. and Schmidt, C.M. (2003) The Impact of EU Enlargement on Migration Flows. Immigration and Nationality Directorate of the UK, Online Report 25/03. London: Home Office. Available at: http://discovery.ucl.ac.uk/14332/1/14332.pdf [Accessed December 12, 2017].

Dustmann, C. and Frattini, T. (2014) The Fiscal Effects of Immigration to the UK. *The Economic Journal* 124(580). London: University College London.

Ehsan, R. (2017) Inside the British Asian Vote – and Why It Contains a Few Surprises. *The Conversation*, February 16. Available at: http://theconversation.com/inside-the-british-asian-brexit-vote-and-why-it-contains-a-few-surprises-72931 [Accessed December 12, 2017].

European Commission (2017) Communication from the Commission to the European Council (Article 50) on the State of Progress of the Negotiations with the United Kingdom under Article 50 of the Treaty on European Union, December 8. Available at: https://ec.europa.eu/commission/publications/communication-commission-european-council-article-50-state-progress-negotiations-united-kingdom-under-article-50-treaty-european-union_en [Accessed December 8, 2017].

European Commission-UK (2017a) Joint Report from the Negotiators of the European Union and the United Kingdom Government on Progress during Phase 1 of Negotiations under Article 50 TEU on the United Kingdom's Orderly withdrawal from the European Union, December 8. Available at: https://ec.europa.eu/commission/publications/joint-report-negotiators-european-union-and-united-kingdom–government–progress–during–phase–1–negotiations–under–article–50–teu–united–kingdoms–orderly–withdrawal–european–union_en [Accessed December 8, 2017].

European Commission-UK (2017b) Joint Technical Note Expressing the Detailed Consensus of the UK and EU Positions on Citizens' Rights, December 8. Available at: https://ec.europa.eu/commission/publications/joint-technical-note-expressing-detailed-consensus-uk-and-eu-positions-respect-citizens-rights_en [Accessed December 8, 2017].

Evans, G. (2016a) The British People Are Perceptive: Immigration and the EU. In: Cowley, P. and Ford, R. (eds.), *More Sex, Lies and the Ballot Box*. London: Biteback Publishing.

Evans, G. (2016b) Why British People Voted to Leave the EU. *BBC Parliament Debate*, July 5. Available at: www.youtube.com/watch?v=p_maX5wJQAQ [Accessed December 12, 2017].

Evans, G. and Mellon, J. (2015) Immigration and Euroscepticism: The Rising Storm. *UK in a Changing Europe*, December 18. Available at: http://ukandeu.ac.uk/immigration-and-euroscepticism-the-rising-storm/ [Accessed December 12, 2017].

Evans, G. and Menon, A. (2017) *Brexit and British Politics*. Cambridge: Polity Press.

Evans, G., Noah, C. and Dennison, J. (2016) European but Not European Enough: The Causes and Consequences of Brexit. Available at: www.academia.edu/29503724/EUROPEAN_BUT_NOT_EUROPEAN_ENOUGH_THE_CAUSES_AND_CONSEQUENCES_OF_BREXIT [Accessed December 12, 2017].

Everson, M. (2014) A Citizenship in Movement. *German Law Journal* 15(5): 965–983.

Favell, A. (2009) Immigration, Migration and Free Movement in the Making of Europe. In: Checkel, J. and Katzenstein, P. (eds.), *European Identity*. Cambridge: Cambridge University Press, pp. 167–189.

Favell, A. (2014) The Fourth Freedom: Theories of Migration and Mobilities in 'Neo-Liberal' Europe. *European Journal of Social Theory* 17(3): 275–289.

Favell, A. and Guiraudon, V. (eds.) (2011) *Sociology of the European Union*. Basingstoke: Palgrave Macmillan.

Ford, R. and Goodwin, M. (2014) *Revolt on the Right: Explaining Support for the Radical Right in Britain*. London: Routledge.

Ford, R. and Goodwin, M. (2017) A Nation Divided. *Journal of Democracy* 28(1): 17–30.

Garapich, M. (2008) The Migration Industry and Civil Society: Polish Immigrants in the United Kingdom before and after EU Enlargement. *Journal of Ethnic and Migration Studies* 34(5): 735–752.

Gerhards, J. (2007) *Cultural Overstretch? Differences between Old and New Member States of the EU and Turkey*. London: Routledge.

Gonzales, R. and Sigona, N. (eds.) (2017) *Within and beyond Citizenship: Borders, Membership and Belonging*. London: Routledge.

Goodhart, D. (2017) *The Road to Somewhere: The Populist Revolt and the Future of Politics*. London: Hurst.

Goodwin, M. and Heath, O. (2016) The 2016 Referendum, Brexit and the Left Behind: An Aggregate Level Analysis of the Result. *The Political Quarterly* 87(3): 323–332.

Goodwin, M. and Milazzo, C. (2017) Taking Back Control? Investigating the Role of Immigration in the 2016 Vote for Brexit. *The British Journal of Politics and International Relations* 19(3): 450–464.

Gordon, I., Travers, T. and Whitehead, C. (2007) *The Impact of Recent Immigration on the London Economy*. London: School of Economics and Political Science, Report for City of London.

Grant, S. (2015) Looking a Gift Horse in the Mouth: Analyzing the UK Fertility Boom amidst the New Hopes and Realities of Immigration, Fertility Behaviours and Nationalist Futures. Paper presented at the 22nd International Conference for Europeanists, Sciences Po, July 8–10. Paris.

Guardian (2017) Post-Brexit Immigration: 10 Key Points from the Home Office Document, September 5. Available at: www.theguardian.com/uk-news/ng-interactive/2017/sep/05/post-brexit-immigration-10-key-points-from-the-home-office-document [Accessed December 12, 2017].

Hix, S., Kaufmann, E. and Leeper, T. (2017) UK Voters, Including Leavers, Care More about Reducing Non-EU Than EU Migration. *LSE EUROPP*, May 30. Available at: http://blogs.lse.ac.uk/europpblog/2017/05/30/uk-voters-including-leavers-care-more-about-reducing-non-eu-than-eu-migration/ [Accessed December 12, 2017].

Inglehart, R. and Norris, P. (2016) Trump, Brexit and the Rise of Populism: Economic Have-Nots and Cultural Backlash. Faculty Research Working Paper Series, Harvard Kennedy School, September 2. Available at: https://research.hks.harvard.edu/publications/workingpapers/Index.aspx [Accessed December 12, 2017].

Kaufmann, E. (2016) It's Not the Economy, Stupid: Brexit as a Story of Personal Values. *The London School of Economics and Political Science*, July 7. Available at: http://blogs.lse.ac.uk/politicsandpolicy/personal-values-brexit-vote/ [Accessed December 12, 2017].

King, R., Warnes, T. and Williams, A. (2000) *Sunset Lives: British Retirement Migration to the Mediterranean*. London: Bloomsbury Publishing.

Kochenov, D. (2016) Argentinisation of British Citizenship: Don't Overstay Your 90 Days on the Continent. *The London School of Economics and Political Science*, June 28. Available at: http://blogs.lse.ac.uk/brexit/2016/06/28/argentinisation-of-british-citizenship-dont-overstay-your-90-days-on-the-continent/ [Accessed December 12, 2017].

Kochenov, D. (2018) Misguided 'Associate EU Citizenship' Talk as a Denial of EU Values. Testimony on EU Citizenship law in front of the Rights and Liberties committee of the European Parliament. https://verfassungsblog.de/misguided-associate-eu-citizenship-talk-as-a-denial-of-eu-values/

Kriesi, H., Grande, E., Lachat, R., Dolezal, M., Bornschier, S. and Frey, T. (2008) *West European Politics in the Age of Globalization.* Cambridge: Cambridge University Press.

Kupiszewski, M. (2002) How Trustworthy Are Forecasts of International Migration between Poland and the European Union? *Journal of Ethnic and Migration Studies* 28(4): 627–645.

Lafleur, J.-M. and Stanek, M. (eds.) (2016) *South-North Migration of EU Citizens in Times of Crisis.* Amsterdam: Springer.

Manners, I. (2002) Normative Power Europe: A Contradiction in Terms. *Journal of Common Market Studies* 40(2): 235–258.

Massey, D.S., Durand, J. and Malone, N. (2002) *Beyond Smoke and Mirrors: Mexican Immigration in an Era of Economic Integration.* New York: Russell Sage Foundation.

Menendez, A.J. (2014) Which Citizenship? Whose Europe? The Many Paradoxes of European Citizenship. *German Law Journal* 15(5).

Moros anu, L. (2016) Professional Bridges: Migrants' Ties with Natives and Occupational Advancement. *Sociology* 50(2): 349–365.

Morris, L. (2014) Analysing Status Diversity: Immigration, Asylum, and Stratified Rights. In: Morris, L. (ed.), *Routledge International Handbook of Diversity Studies.* London: Routledge.

Parker, O. (2017) Critical Political Economy, Free Movement and Brexit: Beyond the Progressive's Dilemma. *British Journal of Politics and International Relations* 19(3): 479–496.

Peers, S. (2017) The Beginning of the End? Citizens' Rights in the Brexit 'Sufficient Progress' Deal. *EU Law Analysis*, December 9. Available at: http://eulawanalysis.blogspot.jp/2017/12/the-beginning-of-end-citizens-rights-in.html?m=1 [Accessed January 14, 2018].

Portes, J. (2013) The Economic Implications for the UK of Leaving the European Union. *National Institute Economic Review* No. 226/F4. Available at: www.niesr.ac.uk/sites/default/files/commentary.pdf [Accessed December 12, 2017].

Portes, J. (2014) Benefits Tourism: The Facts. *The Guardian*, June 7. Available at: www.theguardian.com/commentisfree/2013/oct/14/benefit-tourism-facts-european-commission-report [Accessed December 12, 2017].

Portes, J. (2016) Immigration, Free Movement and the EU Referendum. *National Institute Economic Review* 236(1): 14–22.

Regout, S. (2016) *European Union, States and Markets: The Transitional Period to the Free Movement of Workers for the 2004 EU Enlargement.* Université Libre de Bruxelles: PhD Thesis.

Rienzo, C. (2016) Characteristics and Outcomes of Migrants in the UK Labour Market. In: *The Migration Observatory.* University of Oxford: COMPAS. Available at: www.migrationobservatory.ox.ac.uk/resources/briefings/characteristics-and-outcomes-of-migrants-in-the-uk-labour-market/ [Accessed December 12, 2017].

Rienzo, C. and Vargas-Silva, C. (2017) Migrants in the UK: An Overview. In: *The Migration Observatory.* University of Oxford: COMPAS. Available at: www.migrationobservatory.ox.ac.uk/wp-content/uploads/2017/02/Briefing-Migrants_UK_Overview.pdf [Accessed December 12, 2017].

Ruhs, M. (2018) 'The Impact of Acquiring EU Status on the Earnings of East European Migrants in the UK: Evidence from a Quasi-Natural Experiment' in *British Journal of Industrial Relations*, first view https://doi.org/10.1111/bjir.12223

Ruhs, M. and Anderson, B. (eds.) (2010) *Who Needs Migrant Workers? Labour Shortages, Immigration and Public Policy.* Oxford: Oxford University Press.

Shutes, I. and Walker, S. (2017) Gender and Free Movement: EU Migrant Women's Access to Residence and Social Rights in the U.K. *Journal of Ethnic and Migration Studies* 44(1).

Times Higher Education Supplement (2016) EU Nationals Fill Four in Ten New University Jobs in England, March 10. Available at: www.timeshighereducation.com/news/eu-nationals-fill-four-10-new-university-jobs-england [Accessed December 12, 2017].

Toshkov, D. and Kortenska, E. (2015) Does Immigration Undermine Public Support for Integration in the European Union? *Journal of Common Market Studies* 53(4): 910–925.

Tyler, I. (2010) Designed to Fail: A Biopolitics of British Citizenship. *Citizenship Studies* 14(1): 61–74.

UK Government (2017a) Assessment of EU Nationals in UK: What You Need to Know, April 7. Available at: www.gov.uk/guidance/status-of-eu-nationals-in-the-uk-what-you-need-to-know#assessment-of-settled-status-applications [Accessed January 14, 2018].

Universities UK (2017b) Survey Reveals Impact of Brexit Vote on EU University Workforce, July 31. Available at: www.universitiesuk.ac.uk/news/Pages/Survey-reveals-impact-of-Brexit-vote-on-EU-university-workforce.aspx [Accessed December 12, 2017].

Vargas-Silva, C. (2016) Geographical Distribution and Characteristics of Long-Term International Migration Flows to the UK. In: *The Migration Observatory*. University of Oxford: COMPAS. Available at: www.migrationobservatory.ox.ac.uk/resources/briefings/geographical-distribution-and-characteristics-of-long-term-international-migration-flows-to-the-uk/ [Accessed December 12, 2017].

Vargas-Silva, C. (2017) EU Migration to and from the UK. In: *The Migration Observatory*. University of Oxford: COMPAS. Available at: www.migrationobservatory.ox.ac.uk/resources/briefings/eu-migration-to-and-from-the-uk/ [Accessed December 12, 2017].

11

BREXIT AND BRITISH EXCEPTIONALISM

Peter Nedergaard and Maja Friis Henriksen

Introduction[1]

Throughout history, Europe and the rest of the world have benefited greatly from the British[2] *Sonderweg* (i.e. the will to take a different path than the majority). Although typically not appreciated in the short term,[3] the British propulsion towards wealth-production, innovation and cultural expression have long spread worldwide and continue to do so. So-called British exceptionalism has thus far primarily had positive effects on other countries (see also Ben Wellings' Chapter 12, which alludes to English exceptionalism, and Tilford [2017] and Triandafyllidou [2017]). No one knows whether this will be the case regarding the new and pivotal step when Britain 'goes solo' and 'Brexits' after more than four decades of EU membership.[4]

Despite their reputation for doing things differently, the British Brexit decision came as a surprise to many politicians and citizens within and outside Europe. How could the Britons withdraw from a project that, despite its drawbacks, has been the primary collaboration and problem-solving forum for European countries for sixty years? On top of which comes the relative British success in terms of shaping key EU projects for the last twenty years, including the Single Market and EU enlargement, while at the same time carving out advantageous deals for the UK in the field of financial services. This chapter presents a political and historical explanation of this paradox aimed at establishing a more nuanced understanding of Brexit.

Many journalists and researchers (e.g. Birrell 2016; Glencross 2016; Moravcsik 2017) have pointed out how Brexit was based on a short-term miscalculation by Prime Minister (PM) David Cameron, who, according to this interpretation, thought that he would be able to shut down the EU-critical flank in the Conservative Party by ensuring a majority for continued EU membership once and for all. The project failed miserably, obviously, and the blame – if relevant – can arguably be placed on Cameron's shoulders. But this interpretation cannot stand alone. As a matter of fact and despite a questionable 'remain' campaign (Glencross 2016: 35f), this interpretation cannot explain *why* the UK historically has been part of the reluctant flank of EU members[5] and what actually led to the 2016 referendum questioning EU membership itself. Albeit important, it is not sufficient to examine the election campaign alone without making allowance for deeper, underlying explanatory factors in order to understand the causes behind Brexit. This chapter argues that these causes are historically rooted and were plainly known even before the British EU membership itself.

This observation is supported by a statement famously made by French President Charles de Gaulle, who appeared to have a premonition of the problems relating to the impending British EU membership already in the 1960s. Acting on his feelings, de Gaulle vetoed British membership on the grounds that the UK was not politically or constitutionally suited to full EU membership. In 1963, de Gaulle explained:

> England in effect is insular, she is maritime, she is linked through her interactions, her markets and her supply lines to the most diverse and often the most distant countries; she pursues essentially industrial and commercial activities, and only slight agricultural ones. She has, in all her doings, very marked and very original habits and traditions.
>
> *(Spectator 2016)*

This chapter follows this track by drawing on the historical perspective and answering the follow questions: From where does the willingness to take a different path than the rest of Europe originate? What does this British 'exceptionalism'[6] consist of? And which parts of history are relevant when trying to understand Brexit in depth?

To answer these questions, twelve British exceptionalisms over the last nearly 1,000 years will be covered. As we will show, from this perspective, Brexit is not so surprising after all.

Obviously, establishing causal relationships throughout history is exceedingly difficult. This chapter must therefore be taken with a grain of salt. But despite the unavoidable uncertainty concerning historical analyses, the previous history is nonetheless worth considering and possibly provides the most powerful analytical tool available when trying to understand the British resignation. The following sections will outline the twelve British exceptionalisms.

1   Common law

The last invasion of the British Isles took place in 1066. Before that, weak state formations meant that the isles were exposed to repeated invasions at the hands of the Romans, Frisians, Saxons, Angles and Jutes – and last but not least the Danish and Norwegian Vikings (Campbell 1985: 59f; Mayr-Harting 1985: 55f). This all came to an end in 1066, when the Norman William the Conqueror (ruled 1066–1087) won the Battle of Hastings over the previous Anglo-Saxon rulers and initiated the development of a new, much stronger British state (Bates 1985: 66). In the wake of the Norman conquest of England, a reform of the legal system was carried out. Henry II (ruled 1154–1189) introduced a system whereby royal judges travelled the country and took up cases locally (Maddicott 1985: 97). To support this work, a systematic recording procedure was introduced. This constituted the basis for the English Common Law system, which later became an independent legal tradition adopted by most British colonies (Daniels et al. 2011; Warren 1985: 100f). Common Law means, among other things, that an offense in the past must provide the same sentence in the present. The key element is the notion of precedent created by previous convictions (Berkeley 2010). The contemporary British legal system stands in contrast to the tradition of acts and judgements resting on general law principles (the Civil Law tradition) characterising the continental European legal tradition.

The pragmatic Common Law system establishes the first example of British (or rather English and Welsh) exceptionalism, which should be understood in relation to the legal doctrine in other parts of Europe. This entails a British legal system with a distaste for grandiose thought and might challenge the legitimacy of EU legal practice – especially regarding the juridical foundation of the EU itself: the Treaties of the European Union, which are fundamentally more inclined to the doctrine in continental Europe than in the UK. This also relates to how the EU cooperation as manifested by these treaties is shaped by actual 'constitutions',[7] which stands in contrast to the British tradition of having no such (Maddicott 1985: 97). In that sense, the EU cooperation is far more formalised than in the UK.

2   Early tradition of power-sharing

Henry II's son, Richard (Lion's heart) (reigned 1189–1199) continued to consolidate the Kingdom of England. After Richard's sudden death in 1199, John 'Lackland'[8] took over the throne (1199–1216), which marked the beginning of the English downturn. England lost her possession of France, which had belonged under England since the time of William the Conqueror (Maddicott 1985: 94). At home, the aristocracy increasingly opposed the unfortunate king and his expensive attempts at rescuing the lost land on the other side of the English Channel. The English nobility staged a revolt and forced the king to issue the Magna Carta (Latin for 'Large Letter') (ibid.: 97), markedly limiting the king's power. Among other things, he was paralysed regarding taxation, the right to dispose of the goods of deceased underpinnings and the imprisonment of 'free men' (*Liber Homo*) without law and judgements (Warren 1985: 102), albeit the latter applied only to noble vassals and the like.

Around the year 1350, the Liber Homo concept attained broader meaning in English case law. At the same time, the Magna Carta also protected the merchants, who, 'in accordance with ancient and lawful customs',[9] were to have unlimited access to travel within and outside of England. They were also exempted from all charges except in times of war and if they belonged to the country waging war on the English nation.[10]

From the thirteenth century onward, the Magna Carta meant that the English monarch could no longer rule the country at his own discretion (ibid.). Whereas a French king much later could claim, '*L'état, c'est moi*' ('The State, that's me'), the Magna Carta prevented the English king from doing so. England was no longer a place for monolithic power blocks. Any attempt at collecting power in one place is against British tradition, and gradual integration in the EU – historically implemented by treaties – has often been cited as challenging the legitimacy of British EU membership (MacShane 2016: 36). Related to the aforementioned exceptionalism of legal practice, the supremacy of EU law[11] – a bearing principle of the EU legal system since the van Costa versus ENEL case of the European Court of Justice in 1964 (Nedergaard 2005: 115) – has been a thorn in the side of British EU sceptics from the very beginning (Mustad et al. 2012: 65; Nedergaard 2005: 351–363). Accordingly, the recapture of the supremacy of British legal practice is frequently mentioned as a windfall from leaving the EU, an argument especially prevalent in the Leave campaign during the 2016 referendum.[12] It was therefore hardly surprising when, early in the resignation process (even before triggering Article 50), PM Theresa May announced her plans to end 'the supremacy of EU lawmakers' by preparing the Great Repeal Bill.[13] To many British EU sceptics, the EU is perceived as exactly *the* monolithic power block that they tried to suppress by issuing the Magna Carta (MacShane 2016).

3   The Parliament's role and deliberation

Under Edward I (ruled 1272–1307), it became commonplace to summon representatives from all of the districts for deliberation. In practice, this applied to barons and knights from the rural areas and merchants and citizens from towns and cities (Maddicott 1985: 97f, 107). These deliberations were called a 'parliament' – a place of speech after the French-Norman word, *parler* (Mustad et al. 2012). During this time, the notion that the highest underpinnings of the state had the right to formalised participation in the governing of the kingdom spread. In 1257, the king became obliged to promise that Parliament (both the House of Lords, i.e. the peerage, and the House of Commons, i.e. the locally elected citizens) should approve any new taxes that the king wished to introduce (Maddicott 1985: 98). New taxes requiring parliamentary approval meant that it gained a strength without precedent in any other country; yet another exceptionalism was born.

Today, even though the countries of the European mainland have gained their own lengthy parliamentary traditions, the British Parliament still retains a number of peculiarities. The most striking of these might be the tone of communication in the House of Commons, the lower house, which is far more proactive and vociferous than the controlled tone of debate in the parliaments of continental Europe. In this regard, the British Parliament has preserved many of its characteristics since its ancient beginnings in the early 1300s; indeed, the British Parliament still satisfies the actual meaning of the word 'parliament' in the most deliberate sense. The delibe-rate forum of debate is underpinned by the structural setting of both chambers of the British Parliament, with members seated on benches and facing each other after the arrangement in St Stephen's Chapel,[14] instead of facing the chairman, as in other European parliaments. In that sense, the European Parliament evidently has more similarities with the parliamentary traditions of continental Europe with than those of Britain.

4   The oversea focus

England's main enemy in the 1500s was Spain. Both countries had strong navies, and the con-flict culminated in war after the Spanish ambassador in London attempted to overthrow the Protestant Elisabeth I (ruled 1558–1603) and replace her with the Catholic Mary Stuart (Hilton 1985: 146). The conspiracy was discovered, Mary executed and the ambassador expelled. In response, Spain equipped an armada to sail against England (Fernández-Armesto 1988). England destroyed the first such Spanish fleet in 1587. And when the Spanish sailed a new armada of more than 130 vessels to England the next year, the English again won convincing victories. Hereinafter, 'Britannia ruled the waves'[15] right up until the twentieth century (Marshall 1998: 5; Rodger 1998: 169). This was partly due to English technological and professional excellence. The English navy was far ahead of the Spanish in terms of manoeuvrability, cannons and crew, meaning that they were able to defend themselves against their outer enemies exclusively with the fleet (Reynolds 1992: 8). In contrast to countries on the continent, England could therefore refrain from having to finance a standing army and a great military apparatus with high taxes. On the European continent, the latter formed the background for the establishment of absolute and autocratic monarchies.[16] This was avoided in England, once again bringing us back to a new English exceptionalism.

An army was later established as a standing military force under Charles II (ruled 1660–1685) – albeit with primary focus on the Royal Navy. This overseas military force is perceived as the vital factor in the rise of the British colonial Empire in the eighteenth century (ibid.). Despite highly prioritising the military in the national budget today,[17] the UK stood out as the primary opponent in recent discussions regarding the establishment of a standing EU army and close EU defence cooperation. In this regard, then British Secretary of State for Defence Michael Fallon underpinned the strong British assessment of the NATO cooperation by declaring that 'it is up to NATO to defend Europe, not the EU' (Emmott and Siebold 2016: 1). Some debaters point out how the British engagement in NATO should be understood in connection with the UK self-perception as being an international rather than a regional military capacity, wherefore NATO is perceived as a more appropriate military collaborator than the EU (Allison 2015). Even though most European countries are engaged in NATO today, most do not perceive a regional European army and the transatlantic NATO cooperation as antagonistic – including NATO itself (Emmott and Siebold 2016). But the UK does. This refusal therefore points in the direction of symbolic value. British withdrawal from the EU will effectively remove one of the hindrances to achieving the goal of an EU army, and initiatives to furthering EU integration will presumably be taken.

5   The prioritising of property rights

Turning back in history, political developments around the year 1700 led the Parliament at Westminster to become the crucial power in Britain. In this sense, the British Government became the first parliamentary government in the world (Maddicott 1985: 97ff). However, only a minority of the nobility, idlers and a few other groups were obliged to vote in and be elected to the House of Commons (ibid.). British parliamentarianism gradually became more democratic through electoral reforms between 1832 and 1918 (Hilton 1985: 53f). In the longer term, the political system – with gradually introduced parliamentarianism – came to create the ideal framework for the first breakthrough of a capitalist economy in the shape of an industrial revolution (Payne 1985). The cause: the parliament was a strong defender of the securing of private property rights, thereby establishing yet another exceptionalism.

This exceptionalism is easily related to the promotion of negative liberty in Isaiah Berlin's (1969) terminology. This concept refers to the freedom of the individual from being governed by the authority of others and is often associated with British thinkers such as John Locke, Thomas Hobbes and Adam Smith. In contrast, continental European theorists like G. W.F. Hegel, Jean-Jacques Rousseau and Karl Marx primarily promoted thoughts of the opposite: positive liberty.[18] Even though the concepts of liberty are often intertwined in practice, they function as analytical tools separating how states – here, European parliaments – perceive their role *relative* to their population. Through not being clear-cut, the British Parliament has historically ensured the absence of intervention in individual life, whereas continental European parliaments have primarily focused on guaranteeing positive rights of citizens (Berlin 1969: 131).

Individual rights are also secured differently in the UK than on the European mainland. Most European countries affirm individual rights in a constitution, but a striking British peculiarity is the tradition of having no such institution (Mustad et al. 2012: 65); instead, individual rights are defined in provisions and passed in Parliament. The British Parliament therefore traditionally possessed an exceptional freedom of manoeuvre, which became limited by British EU membership. The British constitution remains unwritten, however, and the Magna Carta has served as the nearest approximation (Maddicott 1985: 97), even though constitutional historians such as Vernon Bogdanor (2009) would argue that the UK now has a written constitution as a result of reforms since 1997 (albeit not codified in a single document). Nevertheless, the constitutional flexibility of the UK provides Parliament with extensive flexibility – under European legislation (ibid.). The crucial role of Parliament and the tendency of the EU to limit it have not passed quietly. As former Labour politician and Minister for Europe Denis MacShane (2016) incisively writes in his book on Brexit, 'The British like their parliament, but no other' (p. 151).

6   Social class defined by its capital

The idlers (or the capitalist class) emerged as a financially powerful group in Britain. In particular, trade increasingly flourished from the seventeenth century onward (Loades 1985: 179f), which was supported by an efficient infrastructure with cheap transport on inland waterways, and merchants were protected by the Magna Carta (as mentioned) (Griffin 2010: 18f).

The growing trade resulted in ever stronger competition in many areas, which in turn forced a streamlining of many professions and heightened productivity (ibid.: 178). Trade brought goods to where capital gains were highest. Through this – and what Adam Smith called the 'invisible hand' (1759) – capitalists' cultivation of their own interests thereby benefitted general society economically. The result: an emerging British class as a merger of the merchant class and parts of the nobility (especially the gentry class), which first and foremost amounted to something due to its accumulated capital. This development ran contrary to the situation on the European continent, where feudal privileges continued and constituted obstacles to financial expansion and social mobility (Brouwer 2016: 130). This class of shareholders and entrepreneurs was a major contributing factor to the world's first industrial revolution, in Britain, which once and for all changed the country and subsequently the rest of the world.

The early existence of a social class defined by its capital paved the way for the industrial revolution, but the legacy from this early economic development remains evident. The UK, the metropole of London in particular,[19] remains the financial centre of Europe and hosts a huge number of financial institutions.[20] This leading financial position is primarily the result of an investment-friendly environment with the easiest establishment conditions and among the lowest taxes in Europe (Collinson 2017; Santander 2017) (see also Chapter 5 of Laila Talani and chapter 20 of Lucia Quaglia). With Brexit, PM May's spokesperson declared her willingness to abandon 'European economy with European style taxation' and turn UK into a low-tax, low-regulation haven if Britons are denied access to the Single Market (Bienkov 2017: 1).[21] Here, the liberal British *Sonderweg* becomes strikingly evident. However, the UK is afraid of losing its exceptionalism as a financial hub (and in contrast to most other exceptionalisms) due to Brexit.

7 The innovative, industrial revolution

The world's first industrial revolution occurred in England. Unfolding in the late eighteenth and early nineteenth centuries, it radically transformed British society financially, socially and culturally (Payne 1985: 270). The already market-oriented, capitalistic society – with strong respect for property rights – became the ideal setting for an industrial revolution (Beckett 1985: 225). Among other things, the Britons had access to a well developed bank and credit system (Brouwer 2016: 119), meaning that it was far easier to obtain capital for new investments than elsewhere in Europe.

In addition, the traditional English textile manufacturing industry flourished in the UK, with roots stretching back to the Middle Ages. This industry was easily developed and became the engine of the first phase of industrialisation (Griffin 2010: 90ff). While the raw material was initially wool, it was replaced by imported cotton from the colonies in North America in the second phase of the industrial revolution. One of the other factors triggering the industrial revolution was a successful combination of natural resources and new inventions (ibid.: 86f; Beckett 1985: 225, 272), including the invention of the steam engine – powered by British coal – and various automatic spinning machines (ibid.: 97ff). The early industrial revolution – and the transforming effect on British society – constitutes a further UK exceptionalism.

The fact that industrialisation came first in the UK also meant that it was here that the first implications developed in the form of a poor working class, which was analysed and described by, among others, Friedrich Engels and Charles Dickens. The British working class dominated areas like the Northeast of England, South Wales and the Glasgow area in Scotland. These were the first areas to be targeted in the 1970s by the EU industrial policy for deindustrialised areas, albeit with little success. To have the first areas in the world dominated by rundown industrial production also represents a form of British exceptionalism. During the 2016 referendum, the British rust belt was overwhelmingly in favour of Brexit, although it should also be noted that the more prosperous south of England also voted leave.

8   Gradual promotion of voting rights

Industrialisation in the eighteenth and nineteenth centuries triggered developments with political consequences, including increasing political unrest and major social disorder (Rose 1985: 276ff). In the wake of the French Revolution, the political establishment sought to avoid violent riots[22] by reforming the election system and extending the right to vote to more groups in society (Thomas 1985: 283f). A reform[23] was implemented in 1832, which, according to the established politicians, extended voting rights for as many 'responsible' and 'enlightened' Britons as possible (ibid.: 278). Still, the establishment advocated for a parliament to represent the property rights of the wealthier groups rather than the entire population. This meant that working–class men still could not vote. Nevertheless, electoral reform in 1867[24] doubled the electorate to include one-third of all adult males and all household patriarchs in the urban areas (Matthew 1985: 256). In 1884,[25] further steps were taken to include the majority of all male rural workers (ibid.: 258), 60 per cent of the UK's total adult male population now being able to vote. With the large electoral reform in 1918,[26] all adult males (now only with the exception of criminals and mental patients) had voting rights, as well as women over age 30 (Robbins 1985: 295).

The gradual expansion of voting rights from 1832 to 1918 is a distinctive feature of the UK. In the rest of Europe (with the exception of countries like the Netherlands and Denmark), the countries usually experienced dramatic and revolutionary shifts in the political direction from quasi democracy towards democracy. The extreme gradualism of the British introduction to democracy is yet another British exceptionalism. It also means that the popular vote is not seen as a potential destroyer of the stability of the entire political system to the same degree as in countries like Italy, Germany and France.

9   The eternal conqueror

In the twentieth century, Britain fought and won two world wars along the front rows of the battlefield. In both cases, victory was far from certain. Prior to the First World War (1914–1918), the UK fell into conflict with Germany (Lowe 1985). The two main reasons for this were German colonial activity since the late 1800s, which threatened the British Empire, and the matter of the German fleet in the North Sea, which challenged the supremacy of the Royal Navy in the area (ibid.: 312; Reynolds 1992: 22).

During the First World War, the ground on the front quickly froze along a line in northern France (ibid.: 313), where hundreds of thousands of British soldiers fell to German machinegun fire. The British soldiers also fell due to their insufficient training, which was partly due to Britain's history of not having a standing army, in contrast to Germany. The front first moved after the United States joined the war in 1917, helping to ensure British victory.

The Britons entered the Second World War after Hitler attacked Poland on 1 September 1939, although this effort first began in earnest almost eight months later. From July to October 1940, the Battle of Britain – aerial warfare intended to pave the way for a German invasion – played out in southern England (Lowe 1985: 316). Britain ultimately prevailed by an extremely narrow margin. The political and military turning point in the Second World War was again the American decision to join the fray (in December 1941), which – together with the strong effort of the Soviet Union – meant British victory in 1945. In 1948, Winston Churchill held a famous speech where he introduced the idea that the UK was the only country among free nations and democracies that had a great part of 'three great circles': the first being the British Commonwealth and Empire, the second the English-speaking world and the third a 'United Europe'. (However, according to Churchill, the UK should not belong to the core of this last circle; see more in Chapter 17).

Yet another British exceptionalism is about the self-awareness achieved from clutching victory in two world wars from the jaws of defeat. After these victories, even stronger self-assertive waves reigned in the UK.

10 Peaceful dismantling of the Empire

In the post-war period, the British Empire was the world's greatest, numbering approximately one-third of the world's population (Reynolds 1992: 8f). Geographically, the Empire stretched around the entire planet,[27] 'the empire on which the sun never set', as Britons proudly declared.

The Empire was dismantled gradually and relatively quietly after the Second World War (Reynolds 1992: 31; Robbins 1985: 289f), giving rise to independent states.[28] Most of the former colonies remained members of the intergovernmental Commonwealth of Nations,[29] which today numbers fifty-two countries,[30] many of which have retained the British monarch as their formal head of state. The peaceful dismantling of its massive Empire also distinguishes the UK from the rest of Europe,[31] and one should not underestimate the impact of this colonial history on British patriotism (Mustad et al. 2012: 95ff; Reynolds 1992: 8ff).

If the UK managed to rule one-third of the world's population personally, why should Britons accept being subordinated to a distant EU regulator? And why could a UK with strong relationships with so many countries around the globe not establish new relationships? Such questions seem to be the talk of the town. Now as then, the British do not appear to be afraid of standing on their own two feet.

11 Flexible political control

The British parliamentary system is often called a 'Westminster system', consisting of very few constitutional conditions, the UK having no actual constitution. In addition, the UK electoral system is based on first-past-the-post majority voting (Mustad et al. 2012: 67), which usually produces a clear parliamentary majority. Combined, this enables the UK to switch political course quickly if a newly elected government wishes to do so. The government usually enjoys a single-party majority in the House of Commons, although the newest political development marks a surprising breach with the tradition of parliamentary majority ruling. The 2017 general election, called by PM May to ensure a stronger mandate for the Brexit negotiations, shockingly backfired, the Conservatives losing their absolute majority.[32] This is only the third time since the election of 1929[33] that the UK has experienced a 'hung parliament', which in British parlance refers to an undesirable parliamentary development.[34] Although interesting, this state of parliament is rather rare, and the majority tradition remains prominent. Overall, the British political system is able to rapidly change track when only one party is holding the reins of power. Such a situation occurred in 1979, when Margaret Thatcher took over from Labour and immediately set a new political course, which is further outlined in the next section.

The ability to manoeuvre like a speedboat and not a supertanker, like other consensus-oriented European countries, is yet another British exceptionalism and further helps explain why the UK is the first – and thus far only – member state to resign from the EU.

12 Neoliberalism's country of birth

After rising to power in 1979, Thatcher implemented a specific economic philosophy, called 'neo-liberalism' (Mustad et al. 2012: 79). The code words in this philosophy were 'privatisation' and the 'promotion of market forces'. One of Thatcher's two major sources of inspiration was economist and Nobel Prize winner Friedrich von Hayek,[35] who published a wide range of writings, including *Individualism and Economic Order* in 1948, where he asserted that societal problems were solved far more effectively if the governments left the economy to 'the market's spontaneous order' (cf. Adam Smith's 'invisible hand', previously mentioned); state intervention only exacerbated problems. Hayek argued that the state's primary task is to establish the basis of a well functioning market economy (Hayek 1967: 38).

Neo-liberalism has strongly influenced the political development in many countries around the world. It succeeded in the UK in the sense that it boosted the national economic growth above the EU average after 1979, whereas it had formally languished below average.[36] Even Labour governments (under Tony Blair and Gordon Brown) have therefore generally respected the neo-liberal management philosophy, and the economic adjustments, which are very prominent in the EU (e.g. fiscal policy targeting), thus stand out for many Britons as representing exactly the opposite of the neoliberal recommendations (Mustad et al. 2012: 79). Contrarily, many continental European countries – and the EU itself – seem to be much more inspired by interventionist fiscal management thought (Horowitz 1997).

Conclusion

Many analysts and journalists have preferred making Brexit a question of unfortunate calculations made by David Cameron to solve conflicts within the Conservative Party. And this undoubtedly played a role. However, it would be overly simplistic to use this to explain Brexit as a whole. As argued in this chapter, Brexit also has far more ancient roots, manifested throughout this chapter in terms of British exceptionalisms, even though not all exceptionalisms have pointed in the Brexit direction (the financial sector exceptionalism, for example, points in the opposite direction).

Despite being relatively diverse, some overall lines seem to pervade the twelve exceptionalisms presented in this chapter. The most striking manifestations of such lines are represented by two 'isms'. If broadly used, the doctrines of liberalism, representing the first of these lines, are evident in how Britain conducts law and judgements, in the establishment and practice of democracy, in relation to the role of the British Parliament, in the decentralisation of power, and in the decline of the king's power. Last but not least, liberalism is especially perceptible in the economic expansion of interventions and investments characterising much of British history. Although playing a crucial role in this history, liberalism itself does not offer much better tools in comprehending what led to Brexit. As is evident in the exceptionalisms presented here, liberalism characterises a way of thinking that diffuses into administrative practices of all kinds, whether juridical, democratic, cultural or economic. However, an awareness that these administrative practices constitute remarkable differences from other countries – and faith in one's own practices as best – must be necessary conditions for abandoning interstate cooperation. In this regard and when combined with patriotism as the second pervading line, liberalist exceptionalism stands much stronger. Combined, these two concepts may help us explain the actual outcome of the 2016 referendum in greater detail.

In itself, patriotism also permeates the 12 exceptionalisms. Winning the Spanish war in the 1500s and two world wars in the twentieth century, not to mention ruling the seas for centuries, boosted British patriotism and resulted in a great colonial empire and massive economic engine. More importantly and concerning Brexit specifically, patriotism crystallises into an awareness of own peculiarities. Nevertheless, patriotism is not only about the country under scrutiny – in our case the UK. Exceptionalism – emotionally manifested as patriotism – never becomes relevant without comparison to other countries. The argument of the UK as being characterised by twelve exceptionalisms was never formed when considering the UK alone. Other countries are required to serve as 'constitutive others' (Houtum 2002: 44). This is an analytical point as well as one of practical meaning: Brexit could become a reality only if Britons were aware of their peculiarities, that they believe to be something first and foremost in themselves – and not necessarily due to their EU membership.

Together, patriotism and liberalism provide strong incentive to withdraw from close cooperation with continental Europe. If assuming the broad understanding of liberalism, the British legal system, the practice of democracy, the role of the parliament, the decentralisation of power and financial market management – the way of administrating British society, generally speaking, has historically proven its applicability, especially when measured in terms of economic growth. When further believing in the correctness of this administration compared to the structure of continental Europe, which is clearly different from the UK's in at least twelve regards.

If accepting the historical perspective is the underlying premise of this chapter, Brexit happened partly due to differences in the administrative practices between the UK and the European mainland, as described by twelve exceptionalisms and partly due to emotional ideas of the British people being first and foremost something unto themselves: a nation historically capable of standing on its own feet.

Notes

1 This chapter is an extended version of an article in the Danish social science journal, *Raeson*, 2016 3: 8–11.
2 The first exceptionalisms of this chapter are English exceptionalisms. Thereafter, they are British exceptionalisms. We alternate between the two.
3 The British reluctance towards the EU collaboration has caused great frustration during the British membership period. An example of this is described in Philip Stephens' article, 'Brexit: Europe Loses Patience with London', *Financial Times*, October 18, 2012.
4 The UK entered the EU in 1973, together with Denmark and Ireland.
5 The British EU reluctance has been evident in European Parliament elections, where the anti-EU party, United Kingdom Independent Party (UKIP), won the largest share of British seats in the European Parliament in the 2014 election (approximately 28 percent of the votes).
6 Throughout this chapter, 'exceptionalism' is taken to mean the 'belief that something is exceptional', that is, unusual or atypical to the general phenomenon or development. This definition is in accordance with the *English Oxford Dictionaries*, found on https://en.oxforddictionaries.com/definition/exceptionalism [Accessed July 19, 2017].
7 Understood here as primary documents on which an institution – not only a state – rests.
8 'Lackland' refers to the loss of the duchy of Normandy to King Philip II of France in the thirteenth century.
9 The quote is taken from the English translation of the original Magna Carta text found on www.bl.uk/magna-carta/articles/magna-carta-english-translation [Accessed July 15, 2017].
10 Ibid.: §41.
11 A principle that ensures that European law prevails in conflicts between European and national law.
12 The argument to take back supremacy over British law was one of prominent Leave promoter Boris Johnson's main arguments for Brexit. Available at: www.telegraph.co.uk/opinion/2016/03/16/boris-johnson-exclusive-there-is-only-one-way-to-get-the-change/ [Accessed February 10, 2018].
13 The Great Repeal Bill is a proposal to annul the 1972 European Communities Act (see endnote 12), which allows parliament to sort out unwanted items of EU legislation. Available at: http://ca.reuters.com/article/topNews/idCAKBN16X0ZJ-OCATP [Accessed February 10, 2018].
14 The original home of the House of Commons until it burned down in 1834.
15 'Rule, Britannia' by James Thomson.
16 E.g. in France and Prussia.
17 For instance, Britain is meeting NATO's 2 per cent target. Available at: www.bbc.com/news/uk-politics-38971624 [Accessed February 10, 2018].

18 According to the *Stanford Encyclopedia of Philosophy*. Available at: https://plato.stanford.edu/entries/liberty-positive-negative/ [Accessed February 10, 2018].

19 More precisely, since the Bank of England moved here in 1734, London county, 'The City of London', has been a European commercial centre.

20 London ranks highest on the Global Financial Centres Index (GFCI), ahead of New York (no. 2) and Singapore (no. 3).

21 However, other members of the Tory cabinet, like Philip Hammond, have argued that the UK would remain broadly 'European' in its economic model.

22 E.g. the 1819 Peterloo Massacre.

23 More specifically, the (first) Parliamentary Reform Act of 1832.

24 (Second) Reform Act of 1867.

25 With the Third Reform Act of 1884.

26 The Fourth Reform Act of 1918.

27 The British Empire included India and was well entrenched in Australasia and Southern Africa.

28 The decolonisation process started in 1947, when India and Pakistan became independent.

29 With the significant exception of the United States.

30 According to the Commonwealth web page. Available at: http://thecommonwealth.org/member-countries [Accessed February 10, 2018].

31 Especially compared to empiricist France, where the Battle of Algiers encapsulated a more brutal decolonisation.

32 Before the 2017 general election, the Conservatives had a seventeen-seat majority. The election left them with 317 of 650 seats, eight seats shy of a parliamentary majority.

33 The 1929 elections resulted in the last hung parliament for many years to come, the other hung parliaments resulting in 1974, 2010 and 2017.

34 After the 2010 election resulted in a hung parliament, the government asked for an alternative vote system to avoid this situation in the future. However, 70 per cent opposed (Mustad et al. 2012: 68).

35 The other inspiration source was Milton Friedman.

36 Today, according to Eurostat, the UK has a GDP per capita approximately 20 per cent above the EU average. Available at: http://ec.europa.eu/eurostat/statistics-explained/index.php/GDP_per_capita,_consumption_per_capita_and_price_level_indices [Accessed February 10, 2018].

References

Allison, G. (2015) Britain's Defence Relationship with the European Union. *UK Defence Journal.* Available at: https://ukdefencejournal.org.uk/britains-defence-relationship-with-the-eu/ [Accessed July 19, 2017].

Bates, D. (1985) Government and Politics 1042–1154: The Norman Conquest and the Anglo-Norman Realm. In: Haigh, C. (ed.), *The Cambridge Historical Encyclopaedia of Great Britain and Ireland.* Cambridge: Cambridge University Press.

Beckett, J.V. (1985) The Economy: Towards Industrialization. In: Haigh, C. (ed.), *The Cambridge Historical Encyclopaedia of Great Britain and Ireland.* Cambridge: Cambridge University Press, pp. 225–229.

Berkeley (2010) The Common Law and Civil Law Traditions. *The Robbins Collection.* Available at: www.law.berkeley.edu/library/robbins/pdf/CommonLawCivilLawTraditions.pdf [Accessed July 15, 2017].

Berlin, I. (1969) *Four Essays on Liberty.* New York: Oxford University Press.

Bienkov, A. (2017) Theresa May 'Stands Ready' to Turn Britain into a Tax Haven after Brexit. *Business Insider,* January 16, 2017. Available at: www.businessinsider.com/theresa-may-stands-ready-to-turn-britain-into-a-tax-haven-after-brexit-2017-1?r=UK&IR=T&IR=T [Accessed July 19, 2017].

Birrell, I. (2016) Boris, 'Brexit' and Cameron's Miscalculation. *The Wall Street Journal Asia,* March 4, 2016. Available at: http://search.proquest.com.ep.fjernadgang.kb.dk/docview/1770825422/fulltext/B8FF-B198EB5D4029PQ/1?accountid=13607 [Accessed July 19, 2017].

Bogdanor, V. (2009) *The New British Constitution.* London: Bloomsbury.

Brouwer, M. (2016) *Governmental Forms and Economic Development: From Medieval to Modern Times.* Amsterdam: Springer.

Campbell, J. (1985) Government and Politics 409–1042: Saxons and Scandinavians. In: Haigh, C. (ed.), *The Cambridge Historical Encyclopaedia of Great Britain and Ireland.* Cambridge: Cambridge University Press.

Churchill, W.S. (1950) Conservative Mass Meeting: A Speech at Llandudno, 9 October 1948. *Europe Unite: Speeches 1947; 1948.* London: Cassell, pp. 416–418.

Collinson, P. (2017) Tax on Test: Do Britons Pay More Than Most? *The Guardian*, May 27, 2017. Available at: www.theguardian.com/money/2017/may/27/tax-britons-pay-europe-australia-us [Accessed July 19, 2017].

Daniels, J., Trebilcock, M.J. and Carson, L.D. (2011) The Legacy of Empire: The Common Law Inheritance and Commitments to Legality in Former British Colonies. *The American Journal of Comparative Law* 59(1): 111–178.

Emmott, R. and Siebold, S. (2016) Britain's Fear of European Army Muddles EU Defense Plan. *Reuters*, September 27, 2016. Available at: www.reuters.com/article/us-eu-defence-idUSKCN11X00G [Accessed July 19, 2017].

Fernández-Armesto, F. (1988) *The Spanish Armada: The Experience of War in 1588*. Oxford: Oxford University Press.

Glencross, A. (2016) *Why the UK Voted for Brexit: David Cameron's Great Miscalculation*. London: Palgrave Macmillan.

Griffin, E. (2010) *A Short History of the British Industrial Revolution*. London: Palgrave Macmillan.

Hayek, F.A. von (1967) The Legal and Political Philosophy of David Hume. In: *Studies in Philosophy, Politics, and Economics*. Chicago: University of Chicago Press, pp. 106–121.

Hilton, B. (1985) Government and Politics 1783–1846: England, Scotland and Wales. In: Haigh, C. (ed.), *The Cambridge Historical Encyclopaedia of Great Britain and Ireland*. Cambridge: Cambridge University Press.

Horowitz, I.L. (1997) British Exceptionalism. *Modern Age* 66–73, Winter, pp. 66–72.

Houtum, H. van (2002) Borders of Comfort: Spatial Economic Bordering Processes in and by the European Union. *Regional & Federal Studies*. Abingdon: Routledge, pp. 37–68.

Loades, D.M. (1985) Warfare and International Relations. In: Haigh, C. (ed.), *The Cambridge Historical Encyclopaedia of Great Britain and Ireland*. Cambridge: Cambridge University Press.

Lowe, P. (1985) Warfare and International Relations: Empire, Commonwealth, Community. In: Haigh, C. (ed.), *The Cambridge Historical Encyclopaedia of Great Britain and Ireland*. Cambridge: Cambridge University Press, pp. 312–320.

Macshane, D. (2016) *Brexit: How Britain Left Europe*. London: I.B. Tauris & Co.

Maddicott, J.R. (1985) Medieval Empire: England and Her Neighbours 1154–1450: Overview. In: Haigh, C. (ed.), *The Cambridge Historical Encyclopaedia of Great Britain and Ireland*. Cambridge: Cambridge University Press, pp. 94–141.

Marshall, P.J. (1998) Introduction. In: Marshall, P.J. (ed.), *The Oxford History of the British Empire: The Eighteenth Century*. Oxford: Oxford University Press, pp. 1–27.

Matthew, H.C.G. (1985) Government and Politics 1846–1901: Free Trade, Franchise and Imperialism. In: Haigh, C. (ed.), *The Cambridge Historical Encyclopaedia of Great Britain and Ireland*. Cambridge: Cambridge University Press, pp. 255–260.

Mayr-Harting, H. (1985) Saxons, Danes and Normans 409–1154. In: Haigh, C. (ed.), *The Cambridge Historical Encyclopaedia of Great Britain and Ireland*. Cambridge: Cambridge University Press, pp. 54–63.

Moravcsik, A. (2017) Capsule Review: Why the UK Voted for Brexit: David Cameron's Great Miscalculation. *Foreign Affairs*, May/June 2017 Issue. Available at: www.foreignaffairs.com/reviews/capsule-review/2017-04-14/why-uk-voted-brexit-david-cameron-s-great-miscalculation [Accessed July 19, 2017].

Mustad, J.E., Rahbek, U., Sevaldsen, J. and Vadmand, O. (2012) *Modern Britain: Developments in Contemporary British Society*. Frederiksberg: Samfundslitteratur.

Nedergaard, P. (2005) *Organiseringen af Den Europæiske Union: Bureaukrater og Institutioner: EU-forvaltningens effektivitet og legitimitet. Et dansk perspektiv*. Copenhagen: Handelshøjskolens Forlag.

Payne, P.L. (1985) The British Economy: Growth and Structural Change. In: Haigh, C. (ed.), *The Cambridge Historical Encyclopaedia of Great Britain and Ireland*. Cambridge: Cambridge University Press, pp. 269–275.

Reynolds, D. (1992) *Britannia Overruled: British Policy & World Power in the 20th Century*. London: Longman Group UK.

Robbins, K. (1985) From Empirical Power to European Partner 1901–1975. In: Haigh, C. (ed.), *The Cambridge Historical Encyclopaedia of Great Britain and Ireland*. Cambridge: Cambridge University Press, pp. 288–337.

Rodger, N.A.M. (1998) Sea-Power and Empire, 1688–1793. In: Marshall, P.J. (ed.), *The Oxford History of the British Empire: The Eighteenth Century*. Oxford: Oxford University Press, pp. 169–183.

Rose, M.E. (1985) Society: The Emergence of Urban Britain. In: Haigh, C. (ed.), *The Cambridge Historical Encyclopaedia of Great Britain and Ireland*. Cambridge: Cambridge University Press, pp. 276–281.

Santander Tradeportal (2017) United Kingdom: Foreign Investment. Available at: https://en.portal.santandertrade.com/establish-overseas/united-kingdom/foreign-investment [Accessed July 19, 2017].

Smith, A. (1759) An Inquiry into the Nature and Causes of the Wealth of Nations. Available at: www.econlib.org/library/Smith/smWN.html [Accessed January 5, 2018].

Spectator (2016) Charles de Gaulle Knew It: Britain Does Not Belong in the EU, May 1, 2016. Available at: https://blogs.spectator.co.uk/2016/05/charles-de-gaulle-knew-it-britain-does-not-belong-in-the-eu/ [Accessed July 19, 2017].

Thomas, W.E.S. (1985) Culture: Revolution, Romanticism and Victorianism. In: Haigh, C. (ed.), *The Cambridge Historical Encyclopaedia of Great Britain and Ireland.* Cambridge: Cambridge University Press, pp. 282–287.

Tilford, S. (2017) The British and Their Exceptionalism. *Centre for European Reform*, d. 3. maj. Tilgængelig på. Available at: www.cer.eu/insights/british-and-their-exceptionalism [Accessed December 29, 2017].

Triandafyllidou, A. (2017) New British Exceptionalism: No Longer in Competition for the Best and the Brightest? *Blogs LSE*, December 13, 2017. Available at: http://blogs.lse.ac.uk/brexit/2017/12/13/new-british-exceptionalism-no-longer-in-competition-for-the-best-and-the-brightest/ [Accessed December 29, 2017].

Warren, W.L. (1985) Government and Politics: England 1154–1272. In: Haigh, C. (ed.), *The Cambridge Historical Encyclopaedia of Great Britain and Ireland.* Cambridge: Cambridge University Press, pp. 100–104.

12

BREXIT AND ENGLISH IDENTITY

Ben Wellings

Introduction

By treating Brexit as an extended event that pre- and post-dated the referendum of 2016, this chapter analyses the links between Euroscepticism and a politicised English identity. Expressions of this identity were grounded in the imperatives of a historically informed understanding of English nationalism in its traditionally integrative and novel secessionist guises. The historical imperative of *English* nationalism – the ideas that inform the traditions that shape responses to political dilemmas – should be understood as one primarily conditioned by a defence of *British* sovereignty. The integrative element of this nationalism results in an instinctive, if weakening commitment to the Union amongst the English even if political elites remain wedded to the idea of a United Kingdom. However, as a result of resistance to European integration, English nationalism developed a secessionist dimension unheard of in its previous history but that was nevertheless grounded in long-standing notions of English exceptionalism that connected England to parts of the world beyond Europe.

This chapter argues that the political project to withdraw from the European Union combined material and political grievances with ideational narratives conditioned by the historical construction of English nationalism. By analysing Brexit with reference to a politicised English identity, this chapter seeks to take analysis of Brexit beyond the 'left-behind' thesis as the dominant explanation for the vote to leave the European Union in 2016 and to explore how Brexit was 'made in England' (Henderson et al. 2017). Crucially it was narratives resting on English political traditions that made leaving the EU seem not only desirable but also possible – and gave Brexit its distinctly English character.

Identity and nationalism

When considering the relationship between English identity and Brexit, it is important to note that 'identity' is not always a stable mode of being but is a contested and discursive way of understanding one's place in the world (Özkırımlı 2005: 30). It is comprised of a set of ideas and ideologies that help relate an individual to other individuals and self-defining human groups. Identity becomes politicised when it becomes a means of mobilising individuals and groups to attain collective goals in situations of political dilemma and genuine social choice (Hay 2007).

When confronted with such dilemmas, political traditions inform responses to the problem that presents itself providing legitimacy to the chosen course of action by creating a sense of continuity at moments of change (Bevir and Rhodes 2006; Bevir et al. 2013).

One of those groups mobilised to attain collective goals is the nation, which encompasses diverse political traditions and ideologies. Nationalism is generated as a response to economic, political and social change by providing a sense of psychological security at an otherwise insecure moment of disruption (Nairn 2003 [1981]: 336). By seeking political mobilisation in order to respond to and alter material conditions of inequality and oppression, nationalists make ideational claims to 'identity, territory and jurisdiction' (Hearn 2006: 6). In so doing, nationalists invoke the nation to attain collective goals, usually defined by the self-conscious nationalists but that must resonate with the broader population to gain support. The process and politics of European integration, in addition to the policies that brought about 'globalisation', accelerated the type of change that helped create sentiment receptive to a nationalist critique in England ahead of the Brexit referendum. This sentiment was notable amongst disadvantaged groups in the developed economies of the world, not least in England, but was not confined to them alone.

Thus, although nationalists make claims about commonality and continuity, they are driven by attempts to manage complex and often disconcerting change. In order to mobilise popular support, nationalists must rhetorically overcome divisions within the political community that would otherwise undermine their claims to represent the general will of the people. Such claims may be specious. Yet this imperative requires the creation of contingent alliances between elites – people like Boris Johnson and Nigel Farage who we might label 'posh populists' – and a broad section of the political community, even though the goals and agendas of each might ultimately differ.

Once constituted, nationalism has two major functional elements: its integrative and disintegrative aspects. The first element leads to reform-oriented and unification nationalisms, the second to separatism (Breuilly 2001: 39–42). Nationalism is often associated with its disintegrative (or secessionist) tendencies. But its integrative capacities are an important day-to-day (or 'banal') part of life in developed liberal democratic polities (Billig 1995), providing the legitimation for wealth redistribution (Miller 1995) and reinforcing understandings of the collective self in relation to others (Sumartojo 2017). Identity and nationalism thus link citizens to the state and form an important element of the 'input' legitimacy of a polity.

Politicised English identity

The salience of secessionist nationalism in Scotland from 2011 to 2017 should not distract us from the equally important politicisation of Englishness that occurred in the decade before the Brexit vote. Articulations of a politicised Englishness offered an explanation of England's place in the UK and the UK's place in the world. In this way, politicised Englishness framed and informed both Euroscepticism and the search for an alternative to membership of the EU, projects that linked popular discontent with elite objectives. Importantly, we should not expect English nationalism to take the form of its Scottish counterpart in setting itself first and foremost against the United Kingdom. Certainly, discontent with the devolution settlement grew notably in England from 2007, whereby discontent with the political and financial consequences of devolution drove English sentiment away from support for the constitutional status quo (Wyn Jones et al. 2012: 9).

Instead, English nationalism was more usually expressed as the integrationist variant of nationalism, conditioned by its dominant imperative: the defence of British sovereignty. Support for 'English Votes for English Laws' (EVEL) was framed by this English political tradition. Data from the British Election Study gathered in 2015 showed that only 13 per cent of respondents wanted to see a separate English Parliament, with only 3 per cent wanting England to be independent of the UK, whereas 56 per cent wished to resolve the dilemma of England's political representation by dealing with English-only legislation at Westminster but with only English MPs voting on such matters (British Election Study 2017).

Despite its increasing salience in the decade before 2016, this English defence of British sovereignty was historically conditioned. The historic emergence of nationalism in England at a time of imperial expansion inclined English national consciousness towards affective support for polities larger than England itself, notably the United Kingdom and the British Empire (Kumar 2003: 34). The need to legitimise the United Kingdom and the British Empire created an enduring political tradition that linked British status, nationality and citizenship to the wider categories of Empire and Commonwealth that Andrew Gamble has described as 'Anglo-Britishness' (Gamble 2016: 359). The success of these two polities in the eighteenth and nineteenth centuries and their endurance in the first half of the twentieth century produced a sense of 'greatness' and assumptions about England's place in the world refracted through the UK and – until its dissolution – the Empire (Bryant 2003). It was this that informed the content of English nationalism, closely aligning narratives of Englishness with the symbols of the British state (Wellings 2002).

Thus the politicisation of English identity required the disentangling of English and British identities. Existing in a unitary United Kingdom, England could easily be portrayed as a cultural and sporting category with no political counterpart: as Robin Mann and Steve Fenton argued, before the 1990s, at a political level there was really 'nothing to be English about' (Mann and Fenton 2017). Increasing and hardening levels of Euroscepticism coupled with growing disaffection with the devolution settlement in the UK were the two elements that combined to reveal a politicised Englishness where one had been hard to discern before the 1990s. Importantly, the Eurosceptic driver of this politicised identity preceded that of devolution. Devolution was a necessary condition in the revelation of English nationalism, but the content was shaped beforehand by a Eurosceptic defence of British sovereignty with its support concentrated in England.

Nevertheless, when devolution renewed the so-called West Lothian Question in the late 1990s, Derry Irvine famously asserted that the best way to answer the question about England's constitutional status was to stop asking it. Thus it appeared at the beginning of the twenty-first century that no one would 'speak for England'. Yet Irvine's comment raised an important point about the questions social scientists ask about sub-state nationalisms and the answers they find thereby (Jeffery and Wincott 2010). Part of the problem in identifying what Susan Condor labelled the 'missing backlash' anticipated in the late 1990s (Condor 2012: 83) was that analysts were searching for the secessionist variant of nationalism opposed to the UK rather than looking for its integrationist expressions or secessionist arguments aimed at withdrawal from the EU. Another still was that official data-gathering agencies, notably the Office for National Statistics, were slow to see English identity as a discrete category worthy of collection: the 2011 census was the first to add a question about English identity.

In the absence of popular campaigns seeking English self-government, it seemed as if Englishness remained in Arthur Aughey's characterisation a 'mood not a movement' (Aughey 2010: 506). Yet it was in this context of emerging calls for recognition of English identity as a separate category at the turn of the decade that important research by the Future of England Survey (FoES) was released. This survey research generated useful large-scale data on England as a discrete political community. The survey team's key finding was that a politicised Englishness existed and was driven by three issues: 'devo-anxiety', immigration and Euroscepticism (Wyn Jones et al. 2013: 17–22). Importantly, those who identified most strongly as English were most dissatisfied with the political status quo – and that included the EU (ibid.: 19). By 2016, this dissatisfaction had gone beyond passive complaint into active politicisation. 'English national identity', concluded the research team, 'was mobilised by the Brexit question' (Henderson et al. 2017: 632).

At the same time, political sociologists, notably Michael Skey (2012) and Charles Leddy-Owen (2014), published qualitative research that also indicated the existence of a politicised Englishness that articulated discontent with the political status quo. Significantly, all authors linked the emergence of a politicised English identity to the increasing precariousness of the respondents' economic situation. This was exactly the type of social change that theorists of nationalism suggested should generate politicised identities from a group of people whose voice was accorded little importance by the neo-liberal logic of the governing elites and whose expressions of nationhood diverged from the official nationalism promoted by state agencies and their supporters.

Unlike the constitutional questions animating Scottish nationalism in the 2000s, debates framed by expressions of English nationhood focused on immigration and multiculturalism. Where debates within the frame of English nationhood took on a constitutional hue were in regard to the UK's relationship with the European Union. Yet these issues were linked to migration (or, more accurately, free movement of labour) by the increasingly influential UK Independence Party (UKIP) especially after the European Parliament (EP) elections of 2009. This – coupled with the increasing self-identification of BME groups to see themselves as 'more British than English' (Wyn Jones et al. 2012) – meant that, with some notable exceptions such as the Blue Labour and Red Shift initiatives within the Labour Party alongside Billy Bragg's 'progressive patriotism', progressives in England were uncomfortable with the label of 'English', preferring 'Britishness' as a more inclusive concept (Bragg 2006; Kiss and Park 2014: 61–94). Even though Ed Milliband attempted to address Englishness within the framework of Britishness in 2012, this discomfort or even hostility on the left to Englishness as a political category was illustrated by the Rochester-gate affair of 2014. Other than the campaign pledge to make St George's Day a public holiday during the 2017 general election, Jeremy Corbyn avoided the issue. The political consequence of this avoidance meant that debates about English nationhood were conducted in an idiom and on issues of the right's choosing. Euroscepticism was one such issue, sustained and legitimised by narratives of English nationalism.

English nationalism and Euroscepticism

This survey and sociological work complemented research stemming from historically informed enquiry that sought to illuminate continuities in the articulations of nationhood in England. The line of interrogation in this body of research was not so much concerned with what self-consciously English people thought about their constitutional status or about other peoples in the UK and the EU. Instead, it focused on which political traditions and ideologies the English and those who spoke in their name drew upon to explain their collective place in the United Kingdom and the world. Scottish secessionism played an important part in generating a politicised Englishness, as we have noted. But it was resistance to European integration that pushed the newly politicised English back onto a defence of British sovereignty, creating powerful links between expressions of English nationalism and Euroscepticism (Wellings 2012).

This was why Krishan Kumar, Arthur Aughey and Michael Kenny began their analyses with the content of what they referred to respectively as English identity, Englishness and English nationhood. For Kumar, England's identity was conditioned by the political need to not destabilise the Empire. This imperative led to a posture of political quiescence until the 1990s (Kumar 2003: 34). For Aughey, the politics of Englishness was conditioned by traditions of behaviour that might be temporary but were certainly not arbitrary (Aughey 2007: 7–8). For Kenny, English nationhood was an encompassing meta-tradition transcending the politics of left and right and that held the potential (as yet unrealised) for inclusive forms of citizenship (Kenny 2014: 241).

Kumar, Aughey and Kenny's research directed attention onto which polities, ideologies and political traditions were available to the English when faced with political dilemmas. Yet seeking to analyse the claims made about and within the frames provided by the political traditions that, taken collectively, constituted English identity posed problems. During the formative period of nationalism in the nineteenth and twentieth centuries, England was always linked with other nations and polities. Its dominant narratives blurred with those of other extant and emergent polities. Its constitutive ideologies rested heavily on transnational narratives that connected it to a world larger than England itself (Wellings 2002). England's political traditions were rarely England's alone.

The most salient of England's dilemmas, which its enmeshed traditions were asked to resolve, was membership of the EU. Previously there had been little explicit linkage in analyses of English identity and Euroscepticism (Colls 2006; Mandler 2006). Emerging research on Euroscepticism suggested that this political phenomenon was not simply a product of intra-party competition on the margins of European politics. Nick Startin and Simon Usherwood sought to illustrate the 'persistent and embedded' nature of Euroscepticism throughout the EU (Usherwood and Startin 2013: 10). At an ideational level beyond the structuring elements of the post-war British economy (Gifford 2014), Euroscepticism aligned with older narratives of English nationalism. This alignment with older traditions of English nationalism helped explain the persistent and embedded nature of resistance to European integration in England.

In this light, the Englishness of Brexit beyond the majority vote to leave in England became apparent in the mutually reinforcing narratives of English nationalism and Euroscepticism via a defence of British sovereignty in the face of deepening European integration. This link between English nationalism and Euroscepticism was a persistent feature of resistance to European integration in England. A defence of parliamentary sovereignty ('taking back control' in contemporary parlance) was always at the core of resistance to European integration across both major parties. Labour anti-Marketeers sought to defend British sovereignty in the 1960s and 1970s to protect British socialism from the EEC. The clearest lineage between attempts to articulate an English nationalism and resistance to European integration came from Enoch Powell in the 1960s and 1970s (Wellings 2013). What became known as Powellism was a mixture of policies advocating low taxation, free trade, anti-immigration and repatriation, as well as resistance to European integration, all based on the English traditions that sustained a defence of parliamentary sovereignty.

Calls for withdrawal from European Communities on the left of politics waned after 1983 but began to coalesce amongst the Thatcherite wing of the Conservatives between Margaret Thatcher's Bruges Speech in 1988 and the final ratification of the Maastricht Treaty in 1993. The idea and policies of 'social Europe' and the advent of New Labour's 'third way' politics under Tony Blair silenced without fully eradicating what was now called Euroscepticism on the left, particularly with reference to the Single Currency. This new expression of the defence of British sovereignty gained increasing support on the right of British politics, however. The corrosive effect of this new factionalism within the Conservatives on the Major government of 1992–1997 is well documented. What was novel compared to the anti-Market sentiment of the 1970s was that this political phenomenon coincided with a cultural defence of British sovereignty that rested heavily on the memory of the Second World War, notably the 'beef wars' of 1996 and the novel profusion of St George's flags at Euro96. This trend was sustained in intensity for a decade and more and fitted well with the type of popular, cultural expressions of nationhood that precede political mobilisation (Hutchinson 2005: 45). What this signalled was that the English were no longer an invisible or silent majority in a plurinational state.

Yet in contrast to the situation in Scotland and Wales, neither main party wished to harness this English identity for political ends. The period of New Labour government and Conservative opposition from 1997 to 2010 was important for the politics of English identity and Euroscepticism in two regards (Hayton 2012). Firstly, it was a time of significant source of division within the Conservatives over how to position the UK towards the EU and what level of integration should be accepted and advocated. Secondly, devolution and the Conservatives' electoral struggles outside of England meant that Euroscepticism became a preoccupation in English public life. Meanwhile the New Labour government found it hard to articulate an English identity within its multicultural framing of nationality. Gordon Brown's later emphasis on Britishness also added to a sense revealed by subsequent survey research that the English were not given political or ideational representation in a devolved and multicultural United Kingdom (Henderson et al. 2016). This was allied with a collapse in trust of party politics and politicians in the wake of the Global Financial Crisis and the parliamentary expenses scandals at the end of the decade. In this situation, referendums were suggested as a mechanism that would restore trust in democracy and recreate a healthy engagement between citizen and politics (Wellings and Vines 2016).

Scottish politics became an important comparator to England at this juncture. This was not in the sense that the English outside of London were demanding home rule as the Scots had in the 1990s. The important comparator was in attitudes towards European integration. For the Scottish National Party, the EU became the facilitator of an economically viable independence within the EU and for Unionists a means of persuading voters in 2014 to vote to stay in the UK (because a vote for independence would jeopardise Scotland's membership of the EU). Consequently, membership of the EU enjoyed broad support in Scotland amongst nationalists *and* unionists. Attitudes towards European integration were very different in England whereby Conservative 'hard' Eurosceptics and UKIP supporters successfully framed the EU as a constraint on the UK's independence.

Furthermore, following devolution, England became a political community by default without any party articulating a specifically English form of politics. A newly politicised English identity filled this void. By the time of the 2014 elections to the European Parliament, the content of English nationalist discourse was simultaneously both integrationist and secessionist with ultimately successful yet politically exhausting efforts to keep the UK united in the face of Scottish secessionism and increasing calls to leave the EU from parties who found their main support in England. The general election of 2015 reinforced the picture of politicised national identities in the UK. A Scottish National Party–dominated Scotland faced a Conservative majority in England. UKIP built on its success in the 2014 EP elections and won 3.9 million votes (a vote share of 14.1 per cent in England compared to 1.6 per cent in Scotland), adding an element of unpredictability to the political balance in England.

UKIP's success as an insurgent party also helped explain David Cameron's earlier decision to commit to a referendum on EU membership. The result of the Brexit referendum in 2016 appeared to confirm national divisions and further outline England's emergence as a distinct political community. Scotland voted 62–38 to remain in the EU, whereas England voted 53–47 to leave. This is not to say that this simple majority can be taken as clear evidence of the Englishness of Brexit even if it is easy to suggest that the English vote to leave took the rest of the UK out of the EU. Wales also returned a majority to leave. Education – a good indicator of wealth and status – was the main correlate with a vote to leave the EU. The picture in England was complicated by the majority in favour of Remain in London and a diversified vote in the south of England. England recorded both the highest vote of anywhere in the UK to remain in the EU (Lambeth on 79 per cent) and the highest vote to leave (Boston on 76 per cent). In the 2017 "Brexit" general election, Labour – despite its ambiguous position on access to the Single Market – picked up Conservative and Lib Dem Remain voters, and this realignment contributed to its surprise gains.

Building on long-standing analyses of the essentially regressive nature of English nationalism (Nairn 2003 [1981]) and more recent research on support for radical right parties in Britain

(Ford and Goodwin 2014), an explanation for Brexit established itself in the wake of the vote. The vote was explained as a revolt by those left behind by the benefits of globalisation. Yet these explanations – important though they were – captured only part of the reason for support for Brexit. A vote to leave the EU was not the same as a vote for UKIP even if many Leave voters had supported UKIP at an election in the previous six years (Evans and Mellon 2016a). Although 3.6 million people voted for UKIP in England in the 2015 general election, 15.1 million people in England voted to leave the EU the following year. Jonathan Evans and Geoffrey Mellon (2016b) took issue with Ford and Goodwin's depiction of a typical radical right voter as a disaffected white working-class male in his fifties and pointed out that UKIP's party membership was more white collar than often assumed (ibid.: 464). Immediately after the referendum, Benjamin Hennig and Danny Dorling (2016: 20) argued that:

> The outcome was frequently – and erroneously – blamed on the working class in the North of England. However, because of the differential turnout and the size of the denominator population, most people who voted to Leave – by absolute numbers – lived in the South of England.

This emphasis on the south of England is important. In this area, political grievances could not be channelled into demands for regional devolution within the UK. Even in places such as the North East and North West where regional identities were strong, attempts to establish regional governance were defeated, most notably with the voting down of the North East Assembly in 2004. But grievances in the south of England had to be channelled elsewhere. In 2016, this case the target for such grievances was not the UK but the EU.

In order to bridge the gap between committed Brexiteers and potential Leave voters, the majority of who were likely to be in England, the Brexit campaign had to be conducted in a national register uniting the two Leave campaigns. The three-word slogan 'Take back control' could be read on two levels: the first being a critique of the EU's 'democratic deficit' and a restoration of trust in politics (the constitutional argument) and the second being a mechanism to keep out foreigners (the xenophobic argument). The tone of the campaign was within the frames laid down by the English Euroscepticism that had re-emerged since the 1990s: representative democracy, arguments about free trade and global influence that rested heavily on memories of empire and, although never reaching the intensity of the mid-1990s, war memory. The English register was taken as the British norm, despite the campaigns being different in each of the constituent parts of the United Kingdom. The defence of British sovereignty – taking back control – was the meta-narrative that underpinned this unstated English national register masked by the rhetoric of Britishness.

After Brexit: the Anglosphere alternative

The vote to leave the EU should not be seen as a victory for so-called Little Englanders. With its historic connections to other parts of the world, English nationalism was persistently 'global'. Unionism remained one of the 'wider categories of belonging' that informed political English-ness, growing popular disaffection with the devolution settlement notwithstanding. Yet ideas for an alternative to membership of the European Union were informed by another of England's wider categories of belonging that drew on a persistent lineage of thought in British politics. Since its return to prominence in the twenty-first century, this ideological current went under the name of the Anglosphere.

Brexit should not be understood as the referendum of 2016 alone but as a protracted political event that pre- and post-dated the referendum. Thus, in analysing Brexit from the perspective of English identity, we need to be mindful of the alternatives to European integration suggested by Eurosceptics and the interrelationship between such alternatives and dominant traditions in England's political identities. Importantly, we should take heed of Arthur Aughey's warning not to suffer from 'Singapore syndrome': we should not face all our explanatory guns in the wrong direction and see English nationalism as generated by responses to political developments within the United Kingdom alone (Aughey 2013: 115). Understanding the affinities between Euroscepticism and English nationalism is an important step in that direction. But Aughey's imperial metaphor was apt because another significant element in English identity is what we might call the English-speaking peoples and the Commonwealth traditions. Examining this element of a politicised English identity allows us to comprehend the link between popular disaffection in England with Brexit as an elite project that attempted to legitimise a radical policy departure within the frames of England's national past.

Such an analysis builds on Krishan Kumar's appeal to analyse English identity 'from the outside in' (Kumar 2003: 17). If English nationalism helps explain the 'embedded and persistent' nature of Euroscepticism in the UK, then the Anglosphere helps explain what John Fitzgibbon, Benjamin Leruth and Nicholas Startin have identified as Euroscepticism's 'transnational' potential too (Fitzgibbon et al. 2017); although in this case in an 'extra-European' rather than 'pan-European' guise. The Anglosphere's great appeal after 2016 was that it offered reassuring continuity in the wake of the great rupture caused by the vote to leave and held out the promise of help from trusted friends and allies in what was presented as an hour of national renewal.

This tendency to re-engage with partners from the other four 'core' states of the Anglosphere (the United States, Canada, Australia and New Zealand) survived the Iraq War and accelerated with William Hague's emphasis on cooperation with 'traditional allies' (a category that did not include the EU) when foreign secretary from 2010 to 2013. The result of the 2016 referendum forced the inchoate ideology of the Anglosphere up the political agenda but linked it to Brexit rather than just the 'soft Euroscepticism' articulated by Hague. The Anglosphere project had three important supporters in May's post-referendum Cabinet, all of whom survived the 2017 general election in place: Boris Johnson, David Davies and Liam Fox.

Anglosphere countries were held up as exemplars during the referendum campaign referendum. For Michael Gove, the United States was an exemplar of what an aspirational independent nation could become. For Leave EU campaigners, Australia appeared to show that asylum-seeking migrants could be stopped at the borders (even if its much touted points-based immigration system served to increase Australia's population, not reduce it). Norman Lamont thought that Canada showed how an independent UK could have a free trade agreement with the EU, an idea developed by David Davis after June 2016. All of these countries had the unstated advantage of falling within the 'kith and kin' notion of English belonging and were higher in status than Norway, Iceland or Lichtenstein, which were also held up as models for Britain's post-Brexit relationship with the EU, reinforcing the English sense of 'greatness' as the UK left the EU.

Beyond such exemplary politics, Anglosphere arguments couched in the frames of English nationalism simultaneously created a sense of incompatibility with the European Union and commonalities with other English-speaking peoples. It would be a mistake to see support for the Anglosphere as simply 'Empire 2.0', as Matthew Parris suggested (Parris 2017). Certainly intellectual lineages with forms of British imperialist thought are clearly discernible, as Duncan Bell has shown (Bell 2006). Such ideas only breached the surface in fits of absent-mindedness, such as the debate about President Barack Obama's Kenyan ancestry during the referendum campaign. Amongst Brexiteers, empire was usually remembered positively for having left a legacy of free trade amongst former Dominions where the correct relationship between states and markets was understood and who stood with Britain in its hour of need in 1940–1945. Of course, memories of these events and developments could differ, even if a common narrative of 'liberty' that underpinned the Anglosphere ideology could bridge any differences amongst the ideas of supporters across the 'core' Anglophone states. It was the English-speaking peoples, after all, who were credited with 'inventing freedom' (Hannan 2013), freedom the English were encouraged to vote for on 23 June 2016. In this teleology, Britain's membership of the EU was a mere interregnum before the restoration of un-mediated trade and diplomatic ties with true friends. The Anglosphere was not only a tradition that offered an analytical point of departure for resolving England's main dilemma but one that offered a political destination too (Wellings and Baxendale 2015: 123).

Conclusion

This chapter has shown that the political project to withdraw from the EU combined material and political grievances with ideational narratives conditioned by the historical construction of English nationalism. A defence of British sovereignty and a need to legitimise the extent and operation of that sovereignty historically conditioned the traditions of thought and practice informing English nationalism. Support in England for Brexit fitted this pattern laid down by the historical formation and trajectory of English nationalism, a nationalism that was always shaped and informed by its 'wider categories of belonging', which did not include Europe in a sufficiently affective way. Unionist projects before and after the referendum blurred the distinction between England and Britain and the articulation of alternatives to EU membership suggesting international realignment towards Anglosphere states and economies. Thus, an elite project aimed at an economic reorientation away from the EU and informed by the Anglosphere tradition in British politics was sustained by popular English disaffections. This temporary alliance resulted in political movement that was unified briefly but decisively by the device of a referendum. Therein lay the peculiar Englishness of Brexit.

References

Aughey, A. (2007) *The Politics of Englishness*. Manchester: Manchester University Press.

Aughey, A. (2010) Anxiety and Injustice: The Anatomy of Contemporary English Nationalism. *Nations and Nationalism* 16(3): 506–524.

Aughey, A. (2013) Review: English Nationalism and Euroscepticism. *Scottish Affairs* 83(1): 115–118.

Bell, D. (2006) *The Idea of Greater Britain: Empire and the Future of World Order, 1860–1900*. Princeton, NJ: Princeton University Press.

Bevir, M., Daddow, O. and Hall, I. (2013) Introduction: Interpreting British Foreign Policy. *British Journal of Politics and International Relations* 15(2): 163–174.

Bevir, M. and Rhodes, R. (2006) *Governance Stories*. Abingdon: Routledge.

Billig, M. (1995) *Banal Nationalism*. London: Sage Publications.

Bragg, B. (2006) *The Progressive Patriot: A Search for Belonging*. London: Bantam Press.

Breuilly, J. (2001) The State and Nationalism. In: Hutchinson, J. and Guibernau, M. (eds.), *Understanding Nationalism*. Cambridge: Polity Press, pp. 32–52.

British Election Study (2017) Preferences for English Powers – English Votes for English Laws. Available at: www.britishelectionstudy.com/graph/?id=13739#.WbCMxmUqakg [Accessed September 7, 2017].

Bryant, C. (2003) These Englands, or Where Does Devolution Leave the English? *Nations and Nationalism* 9(3): 393–412.

Colls, R. (2006) *Identity of England*. Oxford: Oxford University Press.

Condor, S. (2012) Understanding English Public Reactions to the Scottish Parliament. *National Identities* 14(1): 83–98.

Evans, G. and Mellon, J. (2016a) Are Leave Voters Mainly UKIP? *British Election Study*. Available at: www.britishelectionstudy.com/bes-impact/are-leave-voters-mainly-ukip-by-jonathan-mellon-and-geoffrey-evans/#.WbCFVGUqakh [Accessed September 7, 2017].

Evans, G. and Mellon, J. (2016b) Working Class Votes and Conservative Losses: Solving the UKIP Puzzle. *Parliamentary Affairs* 69(2): 464–479.

Fitzgibbon, J., Leruth, B. and Startin, N. (2017) *Euroscepticism as a Transnational and Pan-European Phenomenon: The Emergence of a New Sphere of Opposition.* Abingdon: Routledge.

Ford, R. and Goodwin, M. (2014) *Revolt on the Right: Explaining Support for the Radical Right in Britain.* Abingdon: Routledge.

Gamble, A. (2016) The Conservatives and the Union: The 'New English Toryism' and the Origins of Anglo-Britishness. *Political Studies Review* 16(3): 359–367.

Gifford, C. (2014) *The Making of Eurosceptic Britain.* 2nd Edition. Farnham: Ashgate.

Hannan, D. (2013) *Inventing Freedom: How the English-Speaking Peoples Made the Modern World.* New York: Broadside Books.

Hay, C. (2007) *Why We Hate Politics.* Cambridge: Polity Press.

Hayton, R. (2012) *Reconstructing Conservatism? The Conservative Party in Opposition, 1997–2010.* Manchester: Manchester University Press.

Hearn, J. (2006) *Rethinking Nationalism: A Critical Introduction.* Basingstoke: Palgrave Macmillan.

Henderson, A., Jefferey, C., Liñeira, R., Scully, R., Wincott, D. and Wyn Jones, R. (2016) England, Englishness and Brexit. *The Political Quarterly* 87(2): 187–199.

Henderson, A., Jefferey, C., Scully, R., Wincott, D. and Wyn Jones, R. (2017) How Brexit Was Made in England. *British Journal of Politics and International Relations* 19(4): 631–646.

Hennig, B. and Dorling, D. (2016) In Focus: The EU Referendum. *Political Insight* 7(2): 20–21.

Hutchinson, J. (2005) *Nations as Zones of Conflict.* London: Sage Publishing.

Jeffery, C. and Wincott, D. (2010) The Challenge of Territorial Politics: Beyond Methodological Nationalism. In: Hay, C. (ed.), *New Directions in Political Science: Responding to the Challenges of an Interdependent World.* Basingstoke: Palgrave Macmillan, pp. 167–188.

Kenny, M. (2014) *The Politics of English Nationhood.* Oxford: Oxford University Press.

Kiss, Z. and Park, A. (2014) National Identity: Exploring Britishness. In: Park, A., Bryson, C. and Curtice, J. (eds.) *British Social Attitudes: The 31st Report.* London: NatCen, pp. 61–77.

Kumar, K. (2003) *The Making of English National Identity.* Cambridge: Cambridge University Press.

Leddy-Owen, C. (2014) 'It's True, I'm English . . . I'm Not Lying': Essentialised and Precarious English Identities. *Ethnic and Racial Studies* 37(8): 148–166.

Mandler, P. (2006) *The English National Character: The History of an Idea from Edmund Burke to Tony Blair.* New Haven, CT: Yale University Press.

Mann, R. and Fenton, S. (2017) *Nation, Class and Resentment: The Politics of National Identity in England, Scotland and Wales.* Basingstoke: Palgrave Macmillan.

Miller, D. (1995) *On Nationality.* Oxford: Oxford University Press.

Nairn, T. (1981) *The Break-Up of Britain: Crisis and Neo-Nationalism.* London: Verso.

Özkırımlı, U. (2005) *Contemporary Debates on Nationalism: A Critical Engagement.* Basingstoke: Palgrave Macmillan.

Parris, M. (2017) Empire 2.0 Is a Dangerous Post-Brexit Fantasy. *The Australian*, March 25. Available at: www.theaustralian.com.au/news/world/the-times/empire-20-is-a-dangerous-postbrexit-fantasy/news-story/c9b0b14c901285fd0c320cad388a6628 [Accessed July 17, 2017].

Skey, M. (2012) 'Sod Them, I'm English': The Changing Status of 'Majority' English in Post-Devolution Britain. *Ethnicities* 12(1): 106–125.

Sumartojo, S. (2017) Making Sense of Everyday Nationhood: Traces in the Experiential World. In: Skey, M. and Antonsich, M. (eds.), *Everyday Nationhood: Theorising Culture, Identity and Belonging after Banal Nationalism.* London: Palgrave Macmillan, pp. 197–214.

Usherwood, S. and Startin, N. (2013) Euroscepticism as a Persistent Phenomenon. *Journal of Common Market Studies* 51(1): 1–16.

Wellings, B. (2002) Empire-Nation: National and Imperial Discourses in English Nationalism. *Nations and Nationalism* 8(1): 95–109.

Wellings, B. (2012) *English Nationalism and Euroscepticism: Losing the Peace.* Oxford: Peter Lang.

Wellings, B. (2013) Enoch Powell: The Lonesome Leader. *Humanities Research* 19(1): 33–45.

Wellings, B. and Baxendale, H. (2015) Euroscepticism and the Anglosphere: Traditions and Dilemmas in Contemporary English Nationalism. *Journal of Common Market Studies* 53(1): 123–139.

Wellings, B. and Vines, E. (2016) Populism and Sovereignty: The EU Act and the In-Out Referendum Debate, 2010–15. *Parliamentary Affairs* 69(2): 309–326.

Wyn Jones, R., Lodge, G., Henderson, A. and Wincott, D. (2012) *The Dog That Finally Barked: England as an Emerging Political Community.* London: Institute for Public Policy Research.

Wyn Jones, R., Lodge, G., Jeffery, C., Gottfried, G., Scully, R., Henderson, A. and Wincott, D. (2013) *England and Its Two Unions: A Nation and Its Discontents.* London: Institute for Public Policy Research.

13

BREXIT AND THE CONSERVATIVE PARTY

Richard Hayton

Introduction

The vote for Brexit poses a fundamental challenge to Conservative statecraft, the most profound the party has faced since Edward Heath's administration secured entry to the EEC in 1973. The referendum result was the central failure of David Cameron's premiership, prompting his immediate resignation. It exposed the limitations of his efforts to modernise his party (Kerr and Hayton 2015) but also reflected deeper tensions that have animated Conservative politics throughout the democratic era. This chapter analyses these utilising Andrew Gamble's (1974) conceptual framework of the politics of power and the politics of support. In his seminal text, *The Conservative Nation*, Gamble argued that the Conservatives have traditionally sought to balance the demands of electoral politics with a desire to uphold the prevailing politics of power (through which the state reflects the interests of capital). The need to cultivate a politics of support that does not challenge the fundamentals of the economic system explains the 'Conservative wish to base their appeal to the electorate on a national rather than a class perspective', most famously articulated through the language of 'One Nation' conservatism (ibid.: 18). It also helps account for the historic reputation of the party as one willing to compromise in order to secure power and its self-image as a party of practical government rather than ideology. Managing the process of leaving the European Union raises the possibility of a major conflict between the politics of power and the politics of support. If the party leadership can navigate a way through this hostile terrain, Brexit may be recorded by history as an exemplar of Conservative statecraft. However, the process is unlikely to be a smooth one and threatens to destabilise British politics and cause ructions in the Conservative Party for years to come.

This chapter explores this firstly by exploring the politics of support, arguing that, since the Thatcher era, the Conservatives have become a largely Eurosceptic party and by considering the implications of this for the party leadership. It then moves on to consider the politics of power, which it is argued will likely have a restraining effect on the politics of support, tempering the form of Brexit the Conservatives are able to pursue while in office. Should the party find itself in opposition before the Brexit process is completed, however, it is likely to resort to an even harder Euroscepticism under a leader committed to an uncompromising Brexit. The conclusion outlines several possible scenarios as to what might unfold.

The politics of support

The politics of support, Gamble (1974: 6) tells us, 'takes place in three main arenas – Parliament, the party organization, and the mass electorate'. An aspiring party leader needs to be capable of mustering the support of parliamentary colleagues and securing the backing of the party membership, before they have the opportunity attempt to win over the public at a general election. When David Cameron stood for the party leadership in 2005, he did so in the context of three consecutive electoral defeats that the Conservatives had suffered at the hands of Tony Blair's Labour (see also Chapter 14). He consequently found a party reasonably receptive to his message that it must 'change to win'. However, mindful perhaps of the rejection of the pro-European Ken Clarke in the leadership elections of 1997 and 2001, Cameron realised there were limits to the degree of change that the party would be willing to accept, with Europe being the touchstone issue for many of his fellow MPs and party members. He therefore sought to burnish his own Eurosceptic credentials by promising that, if elected, he would withdraw Conservative MEPs (members of European Parliament) from the European People's Party grouping in the European Parliament – something he eventually did in 2009 (Hayton 2012: 73). Cameron's strategy for managing the European question was therefore embedded before he even won the party leadership. He sought an accommodation with his party's Euroscepticism and, to downplay the salience of the issue, did not seek a confrontation with it. As Lynch (2015: 188) argues, as Leader of the Opposition, 'Cameron approached the EU issue primarily in relation to the politics of support' rather than in consideration of the wider politics of power he would come to face in government. As such, he continued the trend set by his predecessors (William Hague, Iain Duncan Smith and Michael Howard) in offering a 'harder but quieter' stance on European integration (Bale 2006: 388).

Given he achieved his primary objective of returning the Conservatives to power after thirteen years in opposition, we can credit Cameron's handling of the EU issue prior to the 2010 election with some success. Although he did nothing to challenge his party's Eurosceptic orientation, he was able to reduce the profile of the issue sufficiently so that it did not scupper his wider attempt to detoxify the Conservative brand through modernisation (Hayton 2012). It can also be argued that in some ways Cameron linked his European policy with modernisation, for example through his call for the EU 'to focus on globalisation, global warming and global poverty' (Lynch 2015: 189). Critically, in terms of the politics of support, the Conservatives appeared relatively united under Cameron, helping re-establish their reputation for governing competence as Labour's was hit by the 2008 crash.

This approach was accordingly carried forward by Cameron into government, where it would have far-reaching consequences. The dominance of the politics of support in driving Conservative policy towards the EU is critical for understanding the pathway to Cameron's decision to offer an in/out referendum. In the first of Gamble's arenas, Parliament, Cameron had to manage a large group of increasingly restive Eurosceptic members of the Parliamentary Conservative Party (PCP), as part of his wider efforts to hold together a Coalition with the Liberal Democrats. October 2011 saw the largest ever rebellion on the issue of Europe, as eighty-one Conservative backbenchers flouted a three-line whip to support a motion calling for a referendum on EU membership (Cowley et al. 2016: 110). This came despite the Coalition legislating in 2011 for a 'referendum lock' on the ratification of any treaty transferring powers to the EU (Menon and Salter 2016: 1301). A further mutiny over Europe saw the government defeated in October 2012, when Labour joined with fifty-three Conservative rebels in support of an amendment calling for the EU budget to be cut (ibid.: 111). In 2013, 'faced with what would have been an enormous rebellion', the government allowed backbenchers a free vote on amendment to the Queen's Speech voicing regret at the absence of a referendum bill (ibid.: 112). The degree of division over the issue was illustrated by Cameron's extraordinary decision to allow ministers to abstain on the measure, leaving it to Labour and Liberal Democrat votes to ensure that the motion was defeated.

Analysis of the PCP in the 2010–2015 parliament confirms the depth of Eurosceptic feeling it contained. Three-quarters of Conservative MPs could be classified as Eurosceptics, with around a third of that number identified as 'hard' Eurosceptics favouring withdrawal from the EU (Heppell 2013: 345). Cameron also had to contend with widespread Euroscepticism in the second arena: the party organization. Here, a 2013 survey of party members found some 70.8 per cent favouring withdrawal from the EU, although 53.6 per cent were willing to back remaining after a renegotiation of the terms of membership (Bale and Webb 2016: 126). Eurosceptic sentiment could also be identified as a threat to the Conservatives in the third arena of the mass electorate. Under the leadership of Nigel Farage, the UK Independence Party (UKIP) made significant advances in the opinion polls, particularly following the unpopular March 2012 budget (which was labelled an 'omnishambles'). The fact that the Conservatives were in Coalition with the Liberal Democrats created political space to their right, which UKIP were keen to exploit, and fuelled pressure within the Conservative Party for Cameron to try and counter their appeal (Lynch and Whitaker 2016: 128). This (historically unusual) competition on the right of British politics was illustrated by survey data suggesting that more than half of Conservative Party members – who it could reasonably be assumed would have a high degree of loyalty to the party – regarded themselves as possible UKIP voters (Webb and Bale 2014: 964). As UKIP support increased throughout the 2010 parliament, it appeared that this surge was largely at the expense of the Conservatives: estimates by pollsters in early 2013 suggested that at least half of UKIP's supporters had voted Conservative at the previous general election (Webb and Bale 2014: 963). Cameron acknowledged that UKIP and intra-party divisions were key factors in his decision to offer an in/out EU referendum (Laws 2016: 237; Ford and Goodwin 2017: 23).

In the light of the referendum result, Cameron's approach to managing the European issue has been widely criticised. Menon and Salter, for example, argue that the UK has historically been quietly effective at shaping outcomes at the EU level in ways that suited British interests but that this was hardly ever trumpeted to a domestic audience to make the case for membership:

> Rather than challenging the sceptics in his own party, the Prime Minister had pandered to them, to the point of claiming that he would reconsider his support for British membership if his renegotiation demands were not met. Small wonder, then, that shifts in the Union that suited the UK were hardly mentioned. An awful lot was going to rest on the outcome of the renegotiation.
>
> *(Menon and Salter 2016: 1306)*

On this reading, Cameron's strategy of managing the European issue almost exclusively in terms of the politics of support was fatally flawed, as, although it helped secure an unexpected outright victory in the 2015 general election, it undermined his ability to make a powerful argument for remaining in the EU on principle during the referendum campaign. Rather, by suggesting that he would be willing to contemplate leaving the EU if he failed to secure satisfactory renegotiated terms of membership, he implied that the existing arrangements were unacceptable and should be rejected. When the deal he came back with was strikingly similar to the existing terms, his 'pirouette from potential Brexiteer to committed campaigner for Remain lacked credibility' (Menon and Salter 2016: 1308). The journalist Polly Toynbee (2016) commented: 'Cameron enters the "in" campaign having spent his entire decade as party leader undermining support for it. He deserves to lose, but we have to hope to God he doesn't'. The perceived failure of Cameron's negotiating strategy helps explain the fact that 144 Conservative MPs – a higher number than had been widely anticipated – eventually backed the Leave campaign. This number came particularly from the more socially conservative wing of the PCP where the most vociferous critics of Cameron's leadership could be found (Heppell et al. 2017).

The politics of support continued to dominate Conservative Party activity in the aftermath of the referendum result. His credibility in pieces, David Cameron immediately resigned, but as he did so, he stressed that the outcome of the vote 'must be respected' (Cameron 2016). This set the tone for the leadership election that followed, with none of the contenders questioning the wisdom of the decision the country had just taken or suggesting that it might in any way be revisited. This was most effectively captured by Theresa May, who, although she had sided with Remain during the referendum, rapidly declared that 'Brexit means Brexit' (May 2016b). May presented herself as the candidate best placed to competently deliver Brexit and to reunify the Conservatives. Her overwhelming victory in the ballot of Conservative MPs (Table 13.1) suggested that she had successfully reached out across the ideological divide over Europe, perhaps helped by the fact that her campaign for the leadership was run by a prominent campaigner for Brexit, Cabinet Minister Chris Grayling. However, analysis of the result indicated that, although May had eventually attracted the support of around a third of the Conservative MPs who had publicly backed the Leave campaign, divisions over Europe were still the key determinant of voting behaviour. In the second round of voting, May attracted the overwhelming support (91 per cent) of MPs who had opposed Brexit, with the bulk of the pro-Brexit bloc dividing between the two Brexiteer candidates, Michael Gove and Andrea Leadsom (Jeffery et al. 2017).

Under the party's leadership election rules, the top two candidates should have then progressed to a ballot of the full party membership, but Leadsom withdrew, recognising that it would be difficult for her to lead the PCP having won the support of only a quarter of MPs. This decision was greeted with relief by May's supporters, in recognition of the fact that the depth of Eurosceptic feeling amongst the wider membership meant that a May victory was far from certain. However, it left the new prime minister open to the charge that she lacked the legitimacy that a full endorsement from her party would have provided, and she faced calls from Labour and the Liberal Democrats for an early general election.

May fleshed out her position on Brexit in a speech to the Conservative Party conference in October. This again illustrated the extent to which the politics of support continued to drive policymaking in this area. Dismissing the notion of a 'soft' Brexit, the prime minister argued that: 'We are going to be a fully-independent, sovereign country, a country that is no longer part of a political union with supranational institutions that can override national parliaments and courts' (May 2016a). She also made it clear that the outcome of the Brexit process must involve

Table 13.1 Conservative leadership election: result of parliamentary ballots

	First ballot		Second ballot	
	MPs	%	MPs	%
May	165	50.2	199	60.5
Leadsom	66	20.1	84	25.5
Gove	48	14.6	46	14.0
Crabb★	34	10.3	–	–
Fox	16	4.9	–	–

★Withdrew after first ballot voluntarily.

regaining 'control' over immigration and hailed the first steps in forging new trade deals with countries outside the EU. The speech won warm applause from the conference delegates and placated backbenchers growing restless for Article 50 to be triggered – something she pledged to do by the end of March 2017. However, the stance adopted by May effectively ruled out continued membership of either the Single Market or the Customs Union before the negotiations had formally begun, significantly reducing her room for manoeuvre in the politics of power.

The politics of power

The politics of power and the politics of support are deeply interlinked. Theresa May's basic Brexit strategy was to mobilise the politics of support to give her leverage in the politics of power. Her sole argument for calling the 2017 general election, her central contention to the electorate, was that the mandate derived from a big election victory would strengthen the UK's hand in the negotiations with the EU. This approach was blown apart by the election result, which deprived the Conservatives of their majority and left the government dependent on a confidence and supply agreement with the Democratic Unionist Party (DUP) of Northern Ireland. May's catastrophic miscalculation led rapidly to the reopening of divisions within the Conservative Party and to widespread doubts about her capacity to conclude the negotiations successfully. It is likely that we will witness the reassertion of the politics of power and that this will fuel intra-party rifts.

As Gamble (1974: 208) explains, whereas in the political market the key function of political parties is the mobilization of electoral support, 'in the politics of power the function of parties is to be an instrument of government, and thereby to reconcile their supporters in the political nation to the existing state'. In this formulation, the state is conceived as the site where a consensus is reached between economic interests and political forces. Traditionally, the Conservative Party has sought to uphold the prevailing politics of power and then 'appealed for support on the basis of national, not class issues its capacity to provide national leadership and its identification with national institutions' (ibid.). At times, however, when the established consensus has been deemed inadequate to the interests of capital, it has played a leading role in challenging and recasting it. The most striking instance of this occurred in the Thatcher era. Brexit is an acutely problematic issue for the Conservatives as it brings the politics of support into conflict with the politics of power, but also as the latter is divided over the role of the EU in relation to the UK's Anglo-liberal political economy and how to respond to the referendum outcome.

For the far left who came to advocate 'Lexit', European integration has been a vehicle for embedding neo-liberalism and de-politicising economic management through a rules-based system elevated above the democratic control of individual nation states (Gifford 2016: 780–782). This viewpoint is reinforced by some on the right who advocated membership of the EU on the grounds that it gave the UK not only unhindered access to European markets but substantial influence in setting the rules of the game governing them. Arguably successive British Governments have 'proved remarkably successful' at shaping European policy frameworks towards their preferences (Menon and Salter 2016: 1300). Ironically, given the association of Euroscepticism with Thatcherism, the most integrationist measure agreed by any UK Government was the Single European Act (SEA) signed by Margaret Thatcher in 1986. However, the SEA (which created the Single Market and significantly extended qualified majority voting to enable the harmonisation of regulatory standards) played a vital role in embedding an agenda of liberalisation in the EU, to the advantage of key sections of British capital, not least the City of London (see more in Chapter 5). As Scott Lavery (2017: 707) argues, business support for EU membership was premised not just on membership of the Single Market: 'the capacity to shape EU legislation was also a crucial strategic consideration'. The vote for Brexit consequently 'generates a series of dilemmas from the perspective of British capital' as the previous strategy of seeking to 'defend and extend a liberalising agenda' is no longer available to business lobbyists (ibid.: 707).

The general election result immediately prompted business groups to call on the government to soften its stance on Brexit and to reconsider its position in relation to leaving the Single Market and the Customs Union (Savage 2017). Divisions within the Conservative Party were also soon on public display, with the Chancellor of the Exchequer Philip Hammond (2017) telling the City that the government must 'do a Brexit deal that puts jobs and prosperity first' and raising the possibility of extended transitional arrangements. If the vote to leave the EU could be interpreted as politics prevailing over economics (Jensen and Snaith 2016), the election aftermath appeared to signal the resurgence of the imperative of political economy. However, identifying the interests of business and capital, or rather how these might be best protected outside of the European Union, is not a simple task. While a so-called soft Brexit retaining membership of the Single Market and the Customs Union would alleviate concerns over market access, it would also leave the UK as a 'rule taker', potentially vulnerable to the encroachment of EU regulation that might undermine British interests. Research suggests this would be unacceptable to key business organisations, including the CBI and representatives of the financial sector (Lavery 2017: 708). Politically, any Brexit deal that preserved the jurisdiction of the European Court of Justice (ECJ) on any long-term or far-reaching basis in the UK would be fiercely opposed by much of the Conservative Party, even if a majority could be found for it in the House of Commons.

Disagreement on the right over the location of core UK economic interests also manifests itself in debates over political economy. Chris Gifford (2016: 792) argues that the UK elites have 'constructed the United Kingdom as a distinctive Eurosceptic political economy' in opposition to the project of European integration, particularly in response to the Economic and Monetary Union (EMU). As a consequence, in the referendum, no serious case for European integration was advanced. Rather, the key divide was 'between those who consider that British power, and its neo-liberal political economy, is augmented by opposition from within the EU or those who advocate complete withdrawal' (ibid.: 785). Following the referendum, the debate, in terms of the politics of power, concerns not only how a 'smooth' Brexit can be achieved, which does not cause a crisis of business confidence and an economic downturn, but also how competitive advantage can be retained by the UK economy, especially as the EU might seek to restrict the activities of the City of London, which some regarded as damaging to the Eurozone (Thompson 2017: 439). While some Conservatives favour retaining something as close to Single Market membership as possible (essentially a continuation strategy), others envision a 'Global Britain' carrying the torch for economic freedom and striking free trade deals around the world.

The notion of Global Britain was embraced by Theresa May (2016a) and is a key element of the government's Plan for Britain setting out its objectives for Brexit. Indeed, in the text of the prime minister's speech launching that plan, the phrase 'Global Britain' appears eleven times and 'global' a further half dozen, as May (2017) promised, 'A country that reaches out to old friends and new allies alike. A great, global, trading nation. And one of the firmest advocates for free trade anywhere in the world'. However, this concept is not a new one in Conservative circles – the Global Britain group, which campaigned for withdrawal from the EU, was founded in 1997 by amongst others Lord Pearson (who later left the Conservative Party to join UKIP). The ideology behind the Global Britain view is one of hyperglobalist Euroscepticism: 'the legacy of the exercise of hegemony in the global economy in the 19th century through an "open seas" policy which emphasised free trade and free movement of capital and labour' (Baker et al. 2002: 422). From this standpoint, European integration is opposed as an essentially protectionist, regionalist project, placing unwelcome restrictions on neoliberalism both domestically and internationally. The globalist view, by contrast, contains a nostalgic appeal to Britain's 'great' past but also links strongly to 'Atlanticism' (ibid.). Proponents of Anglo-America and the Anglosphere were prominent in the Leave campaign and continue to be at the forefront of calls for a 'hard' or in some cases even a unilateral Brexit, willing to countenance withdrawal from the EU with no exit deal. For some, the argument goes beyond free trade and is also a cultural one, in which the English-speaking world is viewed as sharing essentially the same liberal values. This leads some to endorse an integrative political union to rival the EU between Canada, Australia, New Zealand and the UK – 'CANZUK' (Lilico 2017).

Encompassing as it does cultural ties, international relations and a political economy perspective, the Anglosphere 'furnishes staunch Eurosceptics with a ready-made vision of a post-EU future' (Bell 2017). However, there is little to suggest that the idea commands widespread popular support or that the electorate would wish to swap freedom of movement with the EU for a similar arrangement with a more far-flung collection of countries in CANZUK. As such, it highlights the disjuncture between the Euroscepticism of much of the Conservative Party elite (with its concerns about national sovereignty, political economy and trade) and the more populist variant, mobilised in the referendum campaign primarily around the issue of immigration. While business organisations have generally been supportive of freedom of movement as a feature of the UK's flexible labour market, controlling immigration was the single biggest driver of the vote for Brexit (Clarke et al. 2017). Conservative hopes of marginalising UKIP as a significant electoral threat on their right flank in the light of Brexit are reliant on a settlement that allows them to claim that they have re-established 'control' of immigration. However, without a radical improvement in productivity, a sizeable reduction in immigration looks likely to harm UK economic competitiveness and growth. The issue of immigration is likely therefore to be the source of a major conflict between the politics of support and the politics of power.

Conclusion

As Philip Lynch has argued, 'For more than 50 years, European integration has posed significant problems for Conservative statecraft in both the politics of support and the politics of power' (2015: 186). Brexit represents the culmination of a long-standing difficulty for the party, an ideological clash that has threatened its unity and plagued successive leaders. For a brief interlude, following the referendum and the election of Theresa May as Conservative Party leader, it appeared as if the three-decade-long warfare within the party over Europe might have finally come to an end, with the vast bulk of the PCP endorsing her leadership and swinging into line behind her assertion that 'Brexit means Brexit'. Following the 2017 general election however, it is difficult to foresee how May (or her successor) can navigate a path to Brexit that can command the support of the House of Commons while also satiating the demands of the hard-core Eurosceptics in the Conservative Party.

In the politics of support, it is vital to the Conservatives to be seen to deliver on Brexit, as the party's electoral fortunes are now heavily dependent on Brexit supporters. Exit polls at the 2017 election found that 68 per cent of those who voted Conservative said they had voted Leave in the referendum, whereas 64 per cent of Labour voters and 78 per cent of Liberal Democrat voters had voted Remain (Ashcroft 2017). Looking at it the other way, the Conservatives attracted the support of some 60 per cent of Leavers but only 25 per cent of Remainers. Seventy per cent of Conservative voters were enthusiastic about Brexit, saying they wanted to see it happen 'as soon as possible', with just 7 per cent resistant to it. By contrast, only a third of Labour voters wanted to get on with Brexit swiftly, with 43 per cent saying they would still like it prevented if possible. The Conservative strategy of targeting the UKIP vote enjoyed considerable success: of those who had voted UKIP in 2015, some 57 per cent backed the Conservatives in 2017, while 18 per cent voted Labour and 19 per cent stuck with UKIP (ibid.). It leaves the electorate polarized, however, and the Conservatives poorly positioned to reach across the divide to Remain voters.

In the politics of power, the Conservatives also face considerable problems, with powerful business interests pressing the government to prioritise macroeconomic stability and address sectoral concerns. Here the government faces competing and at times contradictory demands, whether that be prioritising the retention of 'passporting' rights for the City of London or the availability of seasonal migrant labour in agriculture. While the primacy of the UK's neoliberal growth model remains largely unchallenged in Conservative circles, disagreements exist over how this can be best sustained post-Brexit. For some, such as the Economists for Free Trade campaign group, Brexit is an opportunity for a further bout of neo-liberalism, reorientating the UK's economy towards global free trade – quite possibly with unilateral tariff-free access to the UK market, combined with tax cuts and deregulation (Worth 2017).[1] Others by contrast want to retain or closely reproduce existing trade arrangements with the EU such as the Customs Union, either for a transitional period or indefinitely.

The contingency of political events makes any attempt to foresee the eventual outcome of the Brexit process futile. Nonetheless, an appreciation of the politics of the Conservative Party outlined in this chapter looks set to be crucial to understanding whatever ultimately materialises. While the party remains nominally united in the objective of delivering Brexit, there is no settled view as to what form it should take or what could be realistically achieved. The emerging conflict between the politics of support and the politics of power looks set to pose major difficulties in party management terms for the Conservative leadership and threatens the electoral coalition the party mobilised at the 2017 general election. More broadly, the government's perilous position in the House of Commons, lacking an overall majority, leaves it highly vulnerable to parliamentarian rebellions. While the DUP are committed to Brexit and their ten MPs are 'likely to prove a solid and reliable voting bloc', the same cannot be said of the Conservative backbenches (Tonge 2017: 413).

A stark illustration of this came in December 2017, when Theresa May suffered her first parliamentary defeat over Brexit. Eleven Conservative MPs backed an amendment tabled by former Attorney General Dominic Grieve to the European Union (Withdrawal) Bill, asserting Parliament's right for a 'meaningful vote' on any Brexit deal struck by the government with the EU. While the rebels insisted that they were not acting to block the UK's withdrawal from the EU, their move was widely interpreted as increasing pressure on the government to strike a softer Brexit deal that might attract cross-party support. Following this vote and facing the prospect of another parliamentary defeat, the government also backed down on its intention to set in legislative stone the UK's departure date from the EU, accepting an amendment to the legislation allowing MPs to alter it later on. The emergence of this relatively small but well organised and determined group of rebellious Conservative Remainers provides a new dimension to intra-party divisions over Europe, where traditionally it has been the hard-core Eurosceptics who have caused problems for the party leadership. If anything, in the early stages of the Brexit process, it has been the rebels on the Remain side that have caused the government the most problems rather than the Brexiteers. Even the agreement struck with the EU in December 2017 on the terms of the UK's departure, which included a 'divorce bill' running to some £39 billion and the promise to 'maintain full alignment' with EU internal market rules in the absence of an agreed solution to the Irish border issue, was largely welcomed by Conservative Brexiteers. It was instead left largely to Leave campaigners from outside of the Tory party, most vocally Nigel Farage, to condemn the deal as a 'humiliation' (quoted in Hope and Rothwell 2017).

The acquiescence of the Brexiteers within the Conservative Parliamentary Party is strictly conditional, however, and underpinned in significant part by the fear that should Theresa May fall, pressure for another general election would rise, possibly paving the way to a Corbyn-led

Labour government. That could, in turn, lead to sustained pressure for a second referendum or alternatively a form of soft Brexit, which would be unacceptable to Conservative Leavers. May's continued tenure in Downing Street is therefore dependent on her carrying forward the Brexit process within the broad parameters she set early in her premiership of leaving the Customs Union and the Single Market, as well as the jurisdiction of the ECJ. As the details of a possible future relationship with the EU are negotiated and begin to emerge, the prime minister will come under intense pressure from the Brexit wing of her party not to compromise overly on those principles. The outcome of the 2017 general election therefore leaves Theresa May's government seeking to perform an incredibly delicate balancing act to ensure the passage of its legislation and deliver Brexit. The behaviour of the Labour Party in Parliament is likely to be crucial (see Chapter 14). If Labour seeks alliances with Conservative rebels to derail the Brexit process, the situation could rapidly become unmanageable for the government. In such circumstances, the only option might be to appeal directly for a mandate from the people via another referendum or general election, but given recent experience, the Conservatives' enthusiasm for either prospect is likely to be non-existent. Ironically, Theresa May's best ally in all of this might yet prove to be Jeremy Corbyn.

Note

1   See for example Economists for Free Trade. Available at: www.economistsforfreetrade.com/about/ [Accessed December 15, 2017].

References

Ashcroft, M. (2017) How Did This Result Happen? My Post-Vote Survey. *Lord Ashcroft Polls*, June 9. Available at: http://lordashcroftpolls.com/2017/06/result-happen-post-vote-survey/ [Accessed December 15, 2017].

Baker, D., Gamble, A. and Seawright, D. (2002) Sovereign Nations and Global Markets: Modern British Conservatism and Hyperglobalism. *British Journal of Politics and International Relations* 4(3): 399–428.

Bale, T. (2006) Between a Soft and a Hard Place? The Conservative Party, Valence Politics and the Need for a New 'Eurorealism'. *Parliamentary Affairs* 59(3): 385–400.

Bale, T. and Webb, P. (2016) Not as Bad as We Feared or Even Worse Than We Imagined? Assessing and Explaining Conservative Party Members' Views on Coalition. *Political Studies* 64(1): 123–142.

Bell, D. (2017) The Anglosphere: New Enthusiasm for an Old Dream. *Prospect*, January 19. Available at: www.prospectmagazine.co.uk/magazine/anglosphere-old-dream-brexit-role-in-the-world [Accessed December 15, 2017].

Cameron, D. (2016) EU Referendum Outcome: PM Statement, June 24, 2016. GOV.UK. Available at: www.gov.uk/government/speeches/eu-referendum-outcome-pm-statement-24-june-2016 [Accessed December 15, 2017].

Clarke, H., Goodwin, M. and Whiteley, P. (2017) *Brexit: Why Britain Voted to Leave the European Union*. Cambridge: Cambridge University Press.

Cowley, P., Stuart, M. and Trenner-Lyle, T. (2016) The Parliamentary Party. In: Peele, G. and Francis, J. (eds.), *David Cameron and Conservative Renewal: The Limits of Modernisation?* Manchester: Manchester University Press, pp. 105–120.

Ford, R. and Goodwin, M. (2017) A Nation Divided. *Journal of Democracy* 28(1): 17–30.

Gamble, A. (1974) *The Conservative Nation*. London: Routledge.

Gifford, C. (2016) The United Kingdom's Eurosceptic Political Economy. *British Journal of Politics and International Relations* 18(4): 779–794.

Hammond, P. (2017) Mansion House 2017: Speech by the Chancellor of the Exchequer, June 20. GOV. UK. Available at: www.gov.uk/government/speeches/mansion-house-2017-speech-by-the-chancellor-of-the-exchequer [Accessed December 15, 2017].

Hayton, R. (2012) *Reconstructing Conservatism? The Conservative Party in Opposition, 1997–2010*. Manchester: Manchester University Press.

Heppell, T. (2013) Cameron and Liberal Conservatism: Attitudes within the Parliamentary Conservative Party and Conservative Ministers. *British Journal of Politics and International Relations* 15(3): 340–361.

Heppell, T., Crines, A. and Jeffery, D. (2017) The United Kingdom Referendum on European Union Membership: The Voting of Conservative Parliamentarians. *Journal of Common Market Studies* 55(4): 673–952.

Hope, C. and Rothwell, J. (2017) How Europe and the UK Reacted to the Brexit Deal: 'We Can Now Move on to the Next Stage of Humiliation'. *Daily Telegraph*, December 7. Available at: www.telegraph.co.uk/news/2017/12/08/brexit-deal-nigel-farage-says-deal-not-acceptable-business-leaders/ [Accessed January 18, 2018].

Jeffery, D., Heppell, T., Hayton, R. and Crines, A. (2017) The Conservative Party Leadership Election of 2016: An Analysis of the Voting Motivations of Conservative Parliamentarians. *Parliamentary Affairs*, DOI: 10.1093/pa/gsx027.

Jensen, M. and Snaith, H. (2016) When Politics Prevails: The Political Economy of a Brexit. *Journal of European Public Policy* 23(9): 1302–1310.

Kerr, P. and Hayton, R. (2015) Whatever Happened to Conservative Party Modernisation? *British Politics* 10(2): 114–130.

Lavery, S. (2017) 'Defend and Extend': British Business Strategy, EU Employment Policy and the Emerging Politics of Brexit. *British Journal of Politics and International Relations* 19(4): 696–714.

Laws, D. (2016) *Coalition: The Inside Story of the Conservative–Liberal Democrat Coalition Government*. London: Biteback Publishing.

Lilico, A. (2017) Why CANZUK Is Britain's Best Hope after Brexit. *CapX*, January 23. Available at: https://capx.co/why-canzuk-is-britains-best-hope-after-brexit/ [Accessed December 15, 2017].

Lynch, P. (2015) Conservative Modernisation and European Integration: From Silence to Salience and Schism. *British Politics* 10(2): 185–203.

Lynch, P. and Whitaker, R. (2016) Continuing Fault Lines and New Threats: European Integration and the Rise of UKIP. In: Peele, G. and Francis, J. (eds.), *David Cameron and Conservative Renewal: The Limits of Modernisation?* Manchester: Manchester University Press, pp. 121–138.

May, T. (2016a) Britain after Brexit: A Vision of a Global Britain, Speech to the Conservative Party Conference. *Press Conservative*, October 2. Available at: http://press.conservatives.com/post/151239411635/prime-minister-britain-after-brexit-a-vision-of [Accessed December 15, 2017].

May, T. (2016b) Theresa May's Launch Statement: Full Text. *Conservative Home*, June 30. Available at: www.conservativehome.com/parliament/2016/06/theresa-mays-launch-statement-full-text.html [Accessed December 15, 2017].

May, T. (2017) The Government's Negotiating Objectives for Exiting the EU: PM Speech. *GOV.UK*, January 17. Available at: www.gov.uk/government/speeches/the-governments-negotiating-objectives-for-exiting-the-eu-pm-speech [Accessed December 15, 2017].

Menon, A. and Salter, J. (2016) Brexit: Initial Reflections. *International Affairs* 92(6): 1297–1318.

Savage, M. (2017) Big Business Leaders Press Theresa May to Rethink Hard Brexit. *The Observer*, June 18. Available at: www.theguardian.com/politics/2017/jun/17/business-pressure-may-hard-soft-brexit-eu-single-market [Accessed December 15, 2017].

Thompson, H. (2017) Inevitability and Contingency: The Political Economy of Brexit. *British Journal of Politics and International Relations* 19(3): 434–449.

Tonge, J. (2017) Supplying Confidence or Trouble? The Deal between the Democratic Unionist Party and the Conservative Party. *Political Quarterly* 88(3): 412–416.

Toynbee, P. (2016) David Cameron Deserves to Come out of the EU Referendum with No Credit. *The Guardian*, February 18. Available at: www.theguardian.com/commentisfree/2016/feb/18/david-cameron-eu-referendum-no-credit-conservative-europe-ashamed [Accessed December 15, 2017].

Webb, P. and Bale, T. (2014) Why Do Tories Defect to UKIP? Conservative Party Members and the Temptations of the Populist Radical Right. *Political Studies* 62: 961–970.

Worth, O. (2017) Reviving Hayek's Dream. *Globalizations* 14(1): 104–109.

14

BREXIT AND THE LABOUR PARTY

Euro-caution vs. Euro-fanaticism?
The Labour party's 'constructive ambiguity' on Brexit and the European Union

Patrick Diamond

Introduction

Over the last two decades, the UK Labour party has been viewed as among the most pro-European parties in British politics. Although Labour argued for withdrawal from the European Community (EC) during the early 1980s, it then shifted position as the Conservatives increasingly embraced a virulent strain of Euroscepticism. By 1997, Labour was evincing a policy of explicit support for British membership of the European Union (EU). The argument that the UK should become a 'leading player' in Europe was an animating theme of the Blair premiership. Having supported the case for the UK remaining in the EU during the 2016 referendum, Labour's pro-European credentials as a 'socially liberal, internationalist party' were well established. Labour is the 'anti-Brexit' party in UK politics, a stance affirmed at the 2017 general election.

Yet the argument of this chapter is that the British Labour party has usually approached the issue of European integration cautiously and pragmatically. Labour will not seek to oppose Brexit in principle; where it does advance the case for a soft Brexit,[1] the party will retain the political space and room for manoeuvre to shift its position as circumstances change. It is important to remember that the British Labour party's stance on European integration has historically been one of 'Euro-caution' rather than 'Euro-fanaticism'. As Andrew Gamble and Gavin Kelly (2000: 3) attest, there are institutional and historical factors that meant the Labour party has had an uneasy relationship with the European project since the Second World War. The political traditions of the party and the social composition of Labour's electoral base mean that the leadership has struggled to provide a coherent defence of the UK's membership of the EU (Gaffney 1991). Since the 2016 referendum, Labour adopted a position of 'constructive ambiguity' on Europe that allowed the party to surpass expectations and perform well in the 2017 election yet that stance could come under pressure were Labour to enter government before the Brexit negotiation process was complete in the spring of 2019.

So why is Labour's position on Brexit of any consequence? After all, the party was defeated in 2017; despite doing considerably better than many political analysts predicted, Labour was condemned to another five years in opposition, by which time the Brexit process should have been concluded. The Labour party's position on Brexit does matter. In the wake of the general election on 8 June 2017, the Conservative Party does not have an absolute majority in the House of Commons and will have to cooperate with other parties to pass parliamentary legislation. The May government will not be in a position to force through its own preferred Brexit arrangement by executive prerogative. Guy Verhofstadt, one of the lead EU negotiators, argued that Labour ought to be formally included in the Brexit talks as the official opposition. The party's Brexit position is also important because it is far from certain that Theresa May's government will last the full five years of the parliament: splits within the Conservative Party emanating from the Brexit process alongside the fragile political authority of the prime minister may lead to an early election, resulting in Jeremy Corbyn's elevation to the premiership were the Conservative Party to be defeated (see also Chapter 13). Labour would then need to have its own negotiating strategy and vision of Britain's relationship with the EU in place.

Finally, the Labour Party's Brexit standpoint is significant because of the potential impact of Brexit on the structure of the UK political system, in particular the cohesion of the major parties. It appears to be the case that 'Brexit has strong potential to destabilise what is already a fragmenting and shaky party system' (Clarke et al. 2017: 228). There has been speculation that divisions over European policy within Labour's ranks might lead to the formation of a breakaway party (Helm 2017). In 1981, four prominent Labour politicians (including former European Commissioner Roy Jenkins) left the Labour party to form the Social Democratic Party (SDP) after Labour formally supported British withdrawal from the EC. A rupture within Labour led by a faction that did not believe the party was providing sufficiently rigorous opposition to Brexit would have major consequences for the future dynamics and shape of British politics.

In considering the Labour party's changing stance on Brexit, this chapter is structured in the following way. The first section of the chapter examines the political culture and traditions of Labour in shaping the party's outlook on European integration after 1945. It is certainly the case that Labour's formal position on Europe shifted during the 1980s and early 1990s: the policy of withdrawing from the EC was abandoned, and in key areas, notably the incorporation of social and employment rights, the party became a 'Euro-enthusiast'. But it is questionable whether underlying attitudes in the party towards European integration were fundamentally altered. When Labour entered government in 1997, the long-standing position of 'Euro-caution' still prevailed among the party's elite; the leadership were sensitive to the electoral constraints on European policy, as the majority of British voters had never been reconciled to EU membership, while there was considerable hostility to the UK joining the single currency.

The next section of the chapter addresses Labour's European policy under Jeremy Corbyn's leadership of the party from September 2015, alongside the stance that Corbyn has adopted in the aftermath of the 2016 referendum. Despite a long track record of principled opposition to the EU, Corbyn has acted prudently on Europe since becoming leader, paying attention to the need to preserve party unity and shore up Labour's electoral coalition. The tone of the 2017 election manifesto and the pronouncements on the Brexit negotiations by Corbyn and his Shadow Chancellor John McDonnell have been less supportive of a so-called soft Brexit than many Labour parliamentarians would have liked; but Corbyn's tentative approach is hardly inconsistent with the 'Euro-cautious' strategy adopted by past Labour leaders. The chapter then addresses Labour's position on Brexit in the lead-up to the conclusion of negotiations with the EU in March 2019.

The chapter utilises a variety of primary sources, including party policy documents and manifestos, as well as the speeches of leading Labour politicians. The theoretical approach assumes that party debates on Europe are 'structured' by a range of 'complex historical and institutional factors' (Gamble and Kelly 2000: 2; Gaffney 1991; Schnapper 2015).

The Labour tradition on Europe

The Labour party leadership since the Second World War have adopted a pragmatic 'realist' view of Europe as a consequence of their party's ambivalence about the Community and their awareness of the electoral constraints under which the party is operating. The central issue for Labour's leaders since 1945 has been about whether internationalism entails full participation in the EC or whether such values mean remaining apart from Europe to engage in a variety of international alliances, particularly through the Commonwealth (Schnapper 2015) (see also Chapter 16). That conundrum relates to the fundamental question of whether or not, politically, the UK perceives itself to be part of the continent of Europe (Bogdanor 2017). In the aftermath of the Second World War, Clement Attlee and Ernest Bevin were adamantly opposed to Britain joining any federal association that was intended to strengthen the political unity of Europe. The post-war Labour government: 'wanted nothing to do with a customs union that would compromise the UK's imperial role'; Bevin insisted that Britain was 'not just another European country' (Callaghan 2007: 172).

In the late 1950s and 1960s, Hugh Gaitskell and Harold Wilson began to develop a more positive approach to British participation in the EC, while underlining their reservations about European integration. Gaitskell warned about subjugating 'a thousand years of British history', although he was not opposed to membership of the Community in principle; Wilson railed against the terms of entry negotiated by Harold Macmillan in 1961; Wilson infamously denounced the EC as 'an arid, sterile and tight trading bloc against the East' (cited in Callaghan 2007: 247). Yet Wilson was soon forced to acknowledge that in the face of relative economic decline, it might be necessary for Britain to join the EC, while ensuring that safeguards were in place to protect Commonwealth states. The 1975 referendum was intended by the then prime minister to preserve party unity in the renegotiation process, while there was no attempt to convert the labour movement to the cause of EC membership (George and Haythorne 1993). In the words of John Callaghan (2007: 282), 'The Labour party was by no means committed to a European future'.

Subsequent Labour leaders have been similarly 'hard-headed', willing where necessary to assert British national interests. The most successful political leaders over the last forty years have retained the ability to 'finesse' their approach to Europe, shifting their position as political and economic circumstances have changed (Bogdanor 2017). James Callaghan maintained a cautious view of proposals for monetary integration in the late 1970s against the backdrop of recession in the British economy, aware of the shift to the left underway in the British labour movement. Neil Kinnock adopted a more positive stance on Europe, moving Labour away from the 1983 'suicide note' manifesto of Michael Foot's leadership, which had called for unilateral withdrawal from the EC. Even Kinnock trod cautiously, however; there were limits to how far the party was prepared to go in embracing the cause of European integration. For example, Labour's Policy Review in 1990 merely expressed qualified support for the EC, employing distinctly ambiguous and coded language (Gaffney 1991). For most of the period since 1940, the Labour party has sustained a hard-nosed position of 'Euro-caution' (George and Haythorne 1993: 1).

John Smith and then Tony Blair's leadership was to some extent 'outliers' since Smith and Blair were prepared to make an explicit argument in favour of 'sovereignty pooling' and the pursuit of common European interests. By the mid-1990s, Gamble and Kelly (2000: 1) contend that Labour was 'clearly a pro-European party'. It is nevertheless striking that Labour's leaders remained cautious about major aspects of European integration. Blair claimed that he would put Britain at the heart of

Europe after decades of ambivalence and mistrust, but this ambition had not been realised by the end of his premiership (Riddell 2005). There were concerted efforts in European security and defence following the Anglo-French summit at Saint Malo in December 1998; Blair also made a passionate case for economic and social reform in Europe, which he placed at the heart of the agenda for the UK presidency of the EU in the second half of 2005. Nevertheless, the 2003 invasion of Iraq, the defining act of the Blair premiership, created new divisions in Europe; by siding with the US President George W. Bush, the British prime minister squandered his political capital with key member states, particularly France and Germany, while the damage to his standing among UK voters made it even harder for Blair to make the case for constructive engagement in Europe; by April 2004, under pressure from ministers in his own Cabinet, Blair conceded the case for a referendum on ratification of the Lisbon treaty (Bulmer 2008).

Moreover, as prime minister, Blair was clearly aware of the electoral constraints he faced over EU policy and the reticence of the UK electorate; as a consequence, his ministers frequently sought to 'de-politicise' the European issue (Bulmer 2008: 598). Even in the heyday of Labour's pro-Europeanism, the 1997 manifesto demanded 'urgent reform' of the Common Agricultural Policy (CAP) (see Chapter 8), 'greater openness and democracy' in the EU's institutions alongside, 'retention of the national veto over key matters of national interest such as taxation, defence, security, immigration' (cited in Bulmer 2008: 600). During the 1997 election campaign, Blair had written an article for the Eurosceptic newspaper, *The Sun*, entitled 'Why I Love the Pound', in which he claimed: "Labour will have no truck with a European super-state. We will fight for British interests and to keep our independence every step of the way . . . I am a British patriot" (cited in Opperman 2008: 174).

The Labour government's stance on the single currency emphasised a 'rules-based' approach with five key 'tests' that would ensure that the case for entry was primarily based on the economic merits (Bulmer 2008). After the success of the Conservative Party's 'save the pound' campaign in the 1999 European elections, the Labour government quickly backed away from UK membership of the Eurozone (Gamble and Kelly 2000). In government, Labour was forced to recognise that overtly pro-European policy positions were potentially an 'electoral liability'; it was better to defuse the European issue by 'delegating' key decisions to voters, and 'deferring' contentious issues wherever possible (Opperman 2008: 170–172). As a consequence, the Blair governments were criticised for the 'missed opportunities' in framing a more constructive approach to Europe (Smith 2005). An adviser to the prime minister on European affairs lamented in December 2003:

> We desperately need to find a means of changing the psychology of the European debate here. Increasingly in the Party, Europe is seen as a problem and we are running scared of the Tories and the anti-European press. The pro-European cause is seen as in retreat before the forces of anti-Europeanism. Our posture has become wholly defensive. Our MEPs are in despair. We present a grossly distorted picture of European economic performance. This cannot go on. But you are the only person who can stop it.
>
> *(Liddle 2003)*

Following Blair's departure in 2007, Labour swung even further towards Euro-caution. Gordon Brown and Ed Miliband both opposed UK membership of the single currency and were unenthusiastic about the prospect of rewriting the EU's constitutional treaties; Brown was perceived to be much less pro-European than Blair; he found negotiations over the EU budget as Chancellor of the Exchequer particularly tiresome, fearing damage to his domestic political standing; Brown was even more conscious of the electorate's antipathy towards EU institutions (Bulmer 2008). Brown had also presided over the apparently successful modernisation of Britain's domestic economic policymaking institutions; he was less enthusiastic about the 'external discipline' that would be imposed by joining the Euro and was more sceptical of Europe's economic performance in comparison to the 'Anglo-American' states (Gamble and Kelly 2000). Miliband succeeded Brown in 2010 and blamed the rise of Euroscepticism in the UK on the failings of the EU; as leader, he made few speeches on Europe; moreover, Miliband was attracted to 'Blue' Labour ideas that articulated populist working-class hostility to Europe, particularly over the issue of immigration (Schnapper 2015: 169).

The tepid position adopted on European integration by Brown and Miliband was consistent with the party's culture and traditions. Labour was a relatively insular party that had little engagement with socialist and social democratic parties in continental Europe since its inception at the beginning of the twentieth century. The Labour party was a predominantly working-class movement heavily influenced by the trade unions; it inherited a streak of nationalist and even chauvinistic working-class 'social imperialism' that perceived Britain to be inherently superior to other countries (George and Haythorne 1993; Sassoon 1996). While pro-Europeanism always had a marginal position within Britain's national culture, British socialism was positioned as a 'beacon' to the rest of the world (Gaffney 1991). After 1945, the Labour leadership was committed to Britain playing a *global*, not merely a European role, a 'third force' between the United States and Soviet Russia where, 'the British would assume a position of leadership because of their special characteristics as a people' (Brivati cited in Schnapper 2015: 160).

By the 1990s, it was recognised that there were limits to any strategy of 'socialism in one country', but Labour's nascent pro-Europeanism was always vulnerable to Britain's political culture, which remained fundamentally 'suspicious' of the EC (Gaffney 1991: 19). Having lost four consecutive general elections, the leadership of the Labour party was determined to retain its political room for manoeuvre, in case the public mood swung aggressively against EC membership (Gaffney 1991). Despite his pro-European credentials, after 1997 Blair continued to define Britain as a world power rather than as a medium-sized European state, a 'bridge' between the United States and the EU; this position did not suggest that under Labour, Britain had discovered a settled European vocation; Brown referred to Britain's 'uniquely rich, open and outward-looking culture' and its 'distinctive set of British values' (cited in Schnapper 1991: 161). Both leaders insisted that in an era of globalisation, worldwide alliances were as important to Britain as EU membership (Vickers 2011). Brown in particular argued that if the Union were to survive in a more competitive and dynamic world faced with the threat of rising powers such as China and India, EU member states ought to become more like Britain in their flexibility and 'light-touch' regulation of capital, labour and product markets.

Europe has therefore been 'constructed ambiguously' in the Labour party's discourse; the party struggled to make a consistent argument in favour of European integration, while intellectually Labour has remained cautious about EU membership (Schnapper 2015: 159–160). The leadership have never made the case that European integration would make it easier to enact social democratic policies such as progressive taxation and higher public spending in Britain or to fashion a reformed model of British capitalism (Gamble and Kelly 2000). While the party's elite recognised that joining the EC had been beneficial for the UK economy since the mid-1970s, EU membership was perceived to create problems due to the functional inadequacy of European institutions (Schnapper 2015). Since the 1990s, Britain has been besieged by a more Eurosceptic media combined with rising support for the UK Independence Party among working-class voters which have served to entrench Labour's 'soft Euroscepticism' (Schnapper 2015). This was the context through which the party confronted the spectre of Brexit in 2017.

Labour's European policy under Jeremy Corbyn

As a consequence, Jeremy Corbyn's approach to handling Labour party policy on EU membership since becoming leader in September 2015 has been less of a dramatic break with the past than was anticipated by many commentators (Blitz 2017). Corbyn's background is certainly on the so-called 'hard left' of Labour politics: leading politicians on the left such as Tony Benn adopted a vocally anti-European stance in the late 1970s and early 1980s. Benn, a key influence on Corbyn throughout his career, argued that membership of the EC would weaken British national sovereignty, preventing the implementation of a radical socialist economic programme in the UK. Indeed, Benn exhibited strident hostility to the European project throughout this period: "I loathe the Common Market. It's bureaucratic and centralised, there's no political discussion, officials control Ministers, and it just has a horrible flavour about it" (cited in George and Haythorne 1993: 2).

In foreign policy, the Labour left subscribed to an 'internationalist' worldview that favoured strategic alliances around the world with countries that had values in common with socialist Britain. Rhiannon Vickers claims that Labour's tradition of internationalism meant 'a desire to transcend national boundaries to find solutions to international issues' (cited in Schnapper 2015: 158). The party's outlook on the left was suspicious of giving primacy to relations with other EC countries, which were seen as pro-Atlanticist and bound up with membership of the North Atlantic Treaty Organization (NATO). Earlier in his career, the evidence suggests that Corbyn subscribed to the orthodox position of the Labour left that the EC was essentially a capitalist club. Elements of left Euroscepticism lived on into the 1990s, particularly in the ardent opposition among a minority group of the Parliamentary Labour Party (PLP) to European monetary integration and the prospect of Britain joining the single currency.

Yet despite a track record of hostility to the EU, left Euroscepticism has not been the position that defined Corbyn's stance on Europe since his victory in 2015. The left's goal of an alternative strategy of national economic reconstruction and protectionism was abandoned by the late 1980s. Certainly, Corbyn's tone and rhetoric on Europe stressed the need for major reforms of the EU's institutions. Labour's leader attacked the lack of democratic accountability in the decision-making structures of Europe, arguing that the EU had done too little to protect its citizens from the negative impact of globalisation on jobs and labour standards. During the 2015 Labour leadership campaign, Corbyn asserted:

> The EU also knowingly, deliberately maintains a number of tax havens and tax-evasion posts around the Continent – Luxembourg, Monaco and a number of others. I think we should be making demands: universal workers' rights, universal environmental protection, end the race to the bottom on corporate taxation, end the race to the bottom in working wage protection.
>
> *(cited in Shipman 2016: 63)*

Furthermore, Corbyn insisted that the free movement of labour from the accession countries since 2004 may have had a detrimental impact on the wages and living standards of low-paid British workers. During the referendum campaign, Corbyn offered only a 'lukewarm endorsement' of EU membership, refusing to articulate 'a clear and compelling case' for Remain; the Labour leader's 'half-hearted approach' arguably had an impact on the eventual outcome since, 'together with the Conservative divisions, [this] eroded the strength of the cues given by the major parties' to their more committed supporters (Clarke et al. 2017: 149).

The Labour leader was, nevertheless, anxious to distinguish his position from the isolationist rhetoric of leading Conservative politicians; Corbyn was aware that the majority of Labour members, including those who joined after he became leader, were generally 'pro-European' and wanted Britain to remain in the EU. At the Labour Party Conference in 2015, the party had approved a resolution affirming Labour's support for remaining in the EU (Shipman 2016). During the referendum, Corbyn announced that while he was not a fanatical supporter, he would still give the Union 'seven out of ten'; on balance, he accepted that the UK had benefited from EU membership. A recent survey for the Economic and Social Research Council (ESRC) party members project revealed that 68.4 per cent of the current Labour membership would support a second referendum on EU membership, while 66 per cent wanted the UK to remain a full member of the European Single Market (Asthana 2017). The trade unions were, on the whole, strongly in favour of the UK staying in the EU: since Jacques Delors addressed the annual conference of the Trade Union Congress (TUC) in 1989, British unions came to associate Europe with a strong social and employment rights agenda. Indeed, there was much speculation that former Greek Finance Minister and leading left radical Yanis Varoufakis also played a key role in persuading Corbyn of the merits of EU membership (Shipman 2016).

Corbyn was still heavily criticised for his low-key approach in the campaign. Senior figures within the Remain camp reported that the Labour leader appeared lethargic and disinterested in the result, refusing to put the full weight of the Labour party machine behind the Remain cause; Corbyn's Director of Strategy and Communications Seumus Milne was allegedly obstructive, while his team only wanted their leader to do party rallies, which meant minimal broadcast media coverage (ibid.). In the immediate aftermath of the referendum result, Corbyn's 'lacklustre' performance led to political turbulence and a leadership challenge from within the PLP. Backbench MPs were incandescent about their leader's apparent failure to persuade lifelong Labour voters to support EU membership (ibid.).

Yet it must be recognised that Corbyn and his advisers were aware of the electoral constraints under which his party was operating; opinion polls indicated that the referendum outcome was likely to be close and that around a third of Labour voters were intending to vote leave. Corbyn would have inflicted serious damage on the party's electoral prospects had it appeared that Labour was unwilling in principle to accept a Leave outcome. After all, Wilson had remained aloof during the 1975 referendum campaign (Callaghan 2007). Moreover, the party had been scarred by the experience of fighting the referendum on Scottish independence in 2014 alongside the pro-Unionist Conservatives; during the 2016 referendum, Labour sought to keep its distance from the Tories for fear of being labelled as 'collaborators' with David Cameron's party. This tactic contributed to the perception that Corbyn and the Labour leadership were 'half-hearted' in their approach. However, it is unlikely many other Labour leaders would have behaved differently in the circumstances.

The consequence of Corbyn's cautious approach became apparent following the result of the 2017 general election; on the face of it, the result was a vindication of Corbyn's strategy. The British Election Study (BES) indicated that Labour was the party chosen by those who voted Remain in 2016 that sought 'revenge' for the referendum outcome; at the same time, Labour held onto most of its seats in 'leave-supporting' areas of the Midlands and the North of England. Why did those who voted Remain in 2016 support the Labour party at the 2017 general election? The straightforward answer is that those voters had nowhere else to go; the Liberal Democrats had been damaged since leaving the Coalition government in 2015 (Clarke et al. 2017). In Scotland, the post-independence referendum landscape meant that many voters were not prepared to vote for the Scottish National Party (SNP). The softer tone adopted by the Labour party on Brexit by Corbyn and his shadow minister for Brexit, Keir Starmer, accepted the referendum result but called for a new partnership between Britain and Europe that guaranteed the right of EU nationals to continue to reside in the UK after March 2019. This stance was enough to convince Remain voters to transfer their support to the Labour party.

Labour's Brexit stance to 2019

Since the election in June 2017, Labour has maintained its position of ambiguity on Brexit. There was concerted pressure within the PLP for the leadership to explicitly adopt a 'soft Brexit' policy (which in practice meant that the UK remained a member of the EU Single Market with a Customs Union arrangement); some commentators expressed their frustration that the 'socially liberal, internationalist Labour party' was 'siding' with the nationalist Conservative Party (Tilford 2017). But the leadership refused to change the party's position; Corbyn's team were mindful of the fragility of Labour's electoral coalition. Although the party had succeeded in galvanising support of younger voters in 2017, often those most opposed to leaving the EU, Labour performed the worst in those constituencies with a high proportion of Leave voters, often the former industrial areas outside the South of England (Clarke et al. 2017). Labour MPs in Northern and Midlands marginal seats were determined that Labour should acknowledge the hostility to freedom of movement and EU membership in its own former industrial and urban heartlands (Tilford 2017). According to former Europe Minister Denis McShane, 'Many Labour MPs remain frightened of losing the white working-class vote in old mining and metalworking constituencies in the Midlands and the North. In poor, post-industrial areas there are not yet many votes in being pro-European' (cited in Blitz 2017). For Corbyn, the fragility of Labour's electoral alliance crossing the traditional divides of geography, class and demography increases the attraction of a cautious and pragmatic approach. As Clarke et al. (2017: 150) write, 'Brexit and the closely linked issue of immigration had cut directly across the political geography of the Labour party'. In striking that stance, Corbyn was not breaking decisively with the approach to Europe adopted by previous Labour leaders.

During the 2017 election campaign, Labour stated that it believed in a 'jobs-first' Brexit, which meant retaining the benefits of Single Market membership and the Customs Union, without formally being a member of either association. The 2017 Labour party manifesto was clear that '[L]abour accepts the referendum result and that a Labour Government will put the national interest first' (Labour 2017: 24). The central aim of the Brexit negotiation should be 'retaining the benefits of the single market and the customs union'; Labour promised to 'immediately guarantee existing rights for all EU nationals while acknowledging that 'freedom of movement will end when we leave the EU'; the UK's involvement in EU initiatives such as Erasmus, Horizon 2020 and membership of the European Medicines Agency and Euratom (European Atomic Energy Community) would be retained (ibid.: 24–25) (for more on Horizon 2020, see Chapter 9). Moreover, Keir Starmer indicated that Labour would be prepared to accept the jurisdiction of the European Court of Justice (ECJ) in return for continuing access to certain institutional arrangements (Blitz 2017). The workplace protections and social rights stipulated in EU law would also be retained, while Labour would ensure there would be 'no hard border' between Northern Ireland and the Republic. Yet in late 2016, Shadow Chancellor John McDonnell made Labour's acceptance of the Brexit outcome explicit: "It is time we were all more positive about Brexit; Labour wants to see an ambitious Brexit Britain. . . . [W]e must not try to re-fight the referendum or push for a second vote" (Simons 2016).

The position that Corbyn has adopted on the Brexit negotiations is redolent of Harold Wilson's approach in the early 1970s; there is general agreement with the thrust of the Conservative

Government's policy, while criticism is focused on the 'Tory terms' of departure. Corbyn stressed repeatedly that Labour fully accepted the verdict of the British people that the UK should leave the EU. Yet Corbyn sought to emphasise dividing lines that might differentiate Labour's stance on Brexit from that of the May government. First, the Labour party emphasised that 'no deal' with the EU was an unacceptable outcome since it would inflict severe structural damage on the UK economy. Shifting unilaterally to World Trade Organization (WTO) rules would have a massive shake-out effect with negative repercussions for growth and jobs. The second division with the Conservative government was that Labour would guarantee the right to remain in the UK for all EU nationals currently residing in Britain. The government equivocated on this issue for fear of breaking its promise to reduce migration into the UK. Corbyn's team accepted that freedom of movement would cease and that high levels of immigration since the early 2000s have been socially and economically disruptive but sought to avoid blaming or 'scapegoating' migrant communities. The third dividing line between the May government and the Labour Party was that Labour ministers would negotiate to ensure that Britain continued to benefit from access to the EU Single Market and Customs Union, even if the UK could not remain a full member of either. But there was still confusion in the Labour party. In July 2017, Labour's Shadow Brexit Secretary Keir Starmer refused to rule out Britain staying in the Single Market after Brexit and signalled that a Labour government would be prepared to compromise on freedom of movement; in an interview on the BBC *Andrew Marr Show*, John McDonnell then contradicted Starmer's position, insisting that it was 'not feasible' for the UK to remain in the Single Market after Brexit as this would involve, 'not respecting the referendum' (Mason and Asthana 2017). If the UK were to remain in the Single Market or if the UK were merely to become a member of the European Economic Area (EEA), Britain would be required to make budgetary contributions while accepting all of the *acquis* that it would have no formal capacity to influence as a non-member (Bogdanor 2017).

By late August 2017, however, Labour appeared to have shifted its position unequivocally towards a so-called soft Brexit with the UK remaining in the Single Market and Customs Union. *The Observer* newspaper reported that:

> Labour would seek to keep Britain in the single market and a customs union during a transitional period, and possibly in the longer term. . . . It represents a pragmatic shift towards the only conceivable transitional arrangement Britain should be seeking, and puts clear water between the two main parties for the first time. Theresa May's Government insists that in 2019 Britain must leave both the single market and customs union.
>
> *(The Observer 2017)*

As a consequence, Labour would abandon its position of, 'conscious incoherence . . . having a foot in both camps'; the party has begun to shift its thinking because, as Andrew Rawnsley (2017) notes, 'Mr Corbyn is more of a politician than his detractors or his admirers often acknowledge . . . [H]e can do pragmatism and triangulation as well as any of the other grubby compromisers in the rough old trade'. Labour was forced to recognise that some of its voters were overwhelmingly hostile to Brexit; at the same time, to expose divisions within the minority Conservative government when the EU (Withdrawal) Bill was debated in the House of Commons, the party's stance on Brexit needed to be much clearer (Helm 2017). Starmer (2017) talked of 'a new progressive partnership' with the EU, 'based on our common values and shared history', in which the priority for a Labour government would be 'to retain the benefits of the customs union and the single market'.

It is still the case that 'the party's new position remains vague about the final destination it wants for Britain' (Rawnsley 2017). Moreover, the fundamental difficulty for the Labour party is that in preaching the virtues of a 'soft' Brexit, it is signing up to a model of association for the UK that arguably has all the disadvantages and none of the advantages of EU membership (Bogdanor 2017; Thompson 2017). It is unlikely that the position of a Labour government would be much easier during the Brexit negotiation process than the predicament currently facing Prime Minister May and her team. The Labour leadership argue that it has better relationships with key European governments and that the party's more constructive approach to Europe would make the negotiations less fraught. But the same fundamental dynamics apply, whichever of the major parties is in power. EU member states will not agree to a deal for Britain that makes non-membership of the Union attractive for other states. The UK is further disadvantaged because any final deal with the EU has to be agreed by the European Parliament, which is traditionally more integrationist (Bogdanor 2017). The power imbalance between the UK and the other EU states in the negotiations makes Britain's position particularly problematic: while Europe would be damaged by a chaotic UK departure, the impact of 'no deal' for the British economy would be potentially catastrophic. Moreover, any agreement that meant the UK remains in the European Single Market would require Britain to accept freedom of movement, while becoming a 'rule taker' complying with laws and regulations over which the Britain government had no formal influence.

Conclusion

It is often said by academic and political commentators that the Labour party has been compelled to 'face both ways' on Brexit, appealing to electoral constituencies that have diametrically opposing views of European integration and the case for continuing British membership of the EU. The implicit divide in the party's support is neither unusual nor novel: it is the predicament that has faced the Labour party for the last four decades. As leader since 2015, Corbyn has stuck to the pragmatic, Euro-cautious stance of previous leaders of his party. In its approach to European integration, Labour is positioned as defending British national interests to protect its own electoral position; even in the New Labour era, 'every effort was made to ensure European policy did not put at risk the [party's] parliamentary majority' (Bulmer 2008: 615).

As a consequence, since the referendum result, Labour continued to tread carefully in defining its position on Brexit. The Tories are often perceived to be the party that is most fundamentally split over UK membership. Yet Labour is at least as torn as the Conservatives (see also Chapter 13). One influential commentator rightly concluded that Labour is 'as divided over Brexit as the Conservatives. Perhaps more so' (Blitz 2017). The Brexit process is evidently threatening to the Labour party's social democratic objectives; there are some who fear that leaving the EU will trigger a 'race to the bottom' in social and environmental standards, with the UK poised to become a neo-liberal, deregulated offshore state akin to Singapore. Yet Labour is unlikely to rush towards overt opposition to Brexit for fear of alienating its own natural supporters.

When Britain joined the EC in the 1970s, it was accepted that domestic politics would have to adapt to Community membership, whatever the constitutional and political strains this imposed on the UK. Four decades later, the leadership of both the Conservative Party and the Labour Party have concluded that British politics can no longer 'accommodate' EU membership and that the 'absence of sovereignty on immigration' has become an unacceptably high price to pay for access to the core continental European market (Thompson 2017: 12f). Labour's newly constructed 'soft' Brexit approach explicitly acknowledges that the UK is now seeking an economic union with the EU, and that the aspiration of political integration and 'sovereignty pooling' voiced by the minority Euro-fanatic pro-European wing of the party has been firmly cast to one side.

Fundamentally, Labour has been unable to build a new 'domestic consensus' on European policy over the last four decades; in the face of the hostile media and a sceptical public, Labour ministers sought to reduce the salience of the European question, while containing the political management risks associated with key European issues (Bulmer 2008; Opperman 2008). In so doing, however, Labour has limited its ability to reshape UK public opinion on the EU. It therefore seems unlikely that the Labour party will be able to turn the tide on the referendum outcome of June 2016. At best, Labour will try to exploit the Conservatives' disarray through legislative manoeuvres in the House of Commons; but if the party wins power before the Brexit negotiations are complete, Labour's claim that it can deliver a 'softer', more 'progressive' Brexit than the present Conservative government will be sorely tested. Moreover, Labour will be obliged to spell out in concrete terms the long-term relationship it envisages between Britain and the EU while keeping the party united. The evidence so far indicates this will not be an easy task.

Note

1   A soft Brexit is commonly defined as the UK including Northern Ireland continuing to be a member of the EU Single Market and a customs union arrangement after Great Britain ceases to be a member of the EU in March 2019.

References

Asthana, A. (2017) Big Majority of Labour Members 'Want UK to Stay in Single Market'. *The Guardian*, July 24. Available at: www.theguardian.com/politics/2017/jul/17/most-labour-members-want-uk-to-remain-in-single-market [Accessed December 15, 2017].

Blitz, J. (2017) Jeremy Corbyn Is a Brexit Bystander. *The Financial Times*, June 29. www.ft.com/content/ca398c00-5cbb-11e7-b553-e2df1b0c3220 [Accessed December 15, 2017].

Bogdanor, V. (2017) Britain and the EU: In or Out – One Year On. *Gresham College Lecture*, June 21.

Bulmer, S. (2008) New Labour, New European Policy? Blair, Brown and Utilitarian Supranationalism. *Parliamentary Affairs* 61(4): 597–620. Oxford: Oxford Academic.

Callaghan, J. (2007) *The Labour Party and Foreign Policy*. London: Routledge.

Clarke, H., Goodwin, M. and Whiteley, P. (2017) *Brexit: Why Britain Voted to Leave the European Union*. Cambridge: Cambridge University Press.

Gaffney, J. (1991) Labour Party Attitudes and Policy towards Europe: Socialism, Nationalism and British Political Culture. European Community Studies Association Second International Conference, May 22–24. Fairfax, VA: George Mason University.

Gamble, A. and Kelly, G. (2000) The British Labour Party and Monetary Union. *Western European Politics* 23(1): 1–25. London: Routledge.

George, S. and Haythorne, D. (1993) *The British Labour Party*. Sheffield: University of Sheffield Paper.

Helm, T. (2017) As Labour Becomes Party of Soft Brexit, Hard Battles Lie Ahead. *The Observer*, August 26. Available at: www.theguardian.com/politics/2017/aug/26/labour-soft-brexit-jeremy-corbyn-theresa-may [Accessed December 15, 2017].

Labour (2017) For the Many, Not the Few: The Labour Party Manifesto 2017. Available at: https://labour.org.uk/wp-content/uploads/2017/10/labour-manifesto-2017.pdf [Accessed December 15, 2017].

Liddle, R. (2003) Europe. *Confidential Memorandum to the Prime Minister*, December 18.

Mason, R. and Asthana, A. (2017) Labour Would End Free Movement but Not 'Sever Ties' with the EU, Starmer Says. *The Guardian*, April 25. Available at: www.theguardian.com/politics/2017/apr/24/labour-vows-to-rip-up-and-rethink-brexit-white-paper [Accessed December 15, 2017].

The Observer (2017) The Observer View on Labour's New Brexit Policy, August 26. Available at: www.theguardian.com/commentisfree/2017/aug/26/the-observer-view-on-labours-new-brexit-policy [Accessed December 15, 2017].

Opperman, K. (2008) The Blair Government and Europe: The Policy of Containing the Salience of European Integration. *British Politics* 3(2): 158–182. London: Palgrave MacMillan.

Rawnsley, A. (2017) Can Labour's Change of Course over Brexit Change Britain's Fate? *The Observer*, August 26. Available at: www.theguardian.com/commentisfree/2017/aug/26/can-labours-change-of-course-over-brexit-change-britains-fate [Accessed December 15, 2017].

Riddell, P. (2005) *The Unfulfilled Prime Minister*. London: Politicos.

Sassoon, D. (1996) *One Hundred Years of British Socialism: The West European Left in the Twentieth Century.* London: I.B. Tauris & Co.

Schnapper, P. (2015) The Labour Party and Europe from Brown to Miliband: Back to the Future. *Journal of Common Market Studies* 53(1): 157–173. University Association for Contemporary European Studies and Wiley.

Shipman, T. (2016) *All Out War: The Full Story of How Brexit Sank Britain's Political Class.* London: William Collins.

Simons, N. (2016) John McDonnell Says UK Must Be 'Positive' about Brexit and Pledges Labour Will Not Block Article 50. *The Huffington Post*, November 15. Available at: www.huffingtonpost.co.uk/entry/john-mcdonnell-says-uk-must-be-positive-about-brexit-and-pledges-labour-will-not-block-article-50_uk_582afe8be4b09ac74c53d0cd [Accessed December 15, 2017].

Smith, J. (2005) A Missed Opportunity? New Labour's European Policy 1997–2005. *International Affairs* 81(4): 703–721. London: Chatham House.

Starmer, K. (2017) No 'Constructive Ambiguity': Labour Will Avoid Brexit Cliff Edge for UK Economy. *The Guardian*, August 26. Available at: www.theguardian.com/commentisfree/2017/aug/26/keir-starmer-no-constructive-ambiguity-brexit-cliff-edge-labour-will-avoid-transitional-deal [Accessed December 15, 2017].

Thompson, H. (2017) Revisiting Groundhog Day: Theresa May's Search for an EU 'Yes'. *Juncture* 24(10): 7–13.

Tilford, S. (2017) The Limits to Labour's 'Constructive Ambiguity' over Brexit. *CER Insight*, July 6. London: Centre for European Reform.

Vickers, R. (2011) *The Labour Party and the World, Volume 2: Labour's Foreign Policy 1951–2009.* Manchester: Manchester University Press.

15

THE (ANTI-)POLITICS OF BREXIT

Matthew Flinders

Introduction

This chapter explores the relationship(s) between anti-political sentiment and Brexit. It makes three core arguments. The first is that anti-political sentiment was a critical underlying factor in explaining the decision to leave the EU. The vote for Brexit was delivered largely by the 'left-behind', a term describing a range of social groups who share a sense of marginalization, insecurity and frustration and who feel that mainstream politics has to a large extent abandoned them. In this regard, the European Union arguably provided a lightning rod that absorbed not only long-standing national insecurities about the pooling of sovereignty but also a more recent set of democratic anxieties fuelled by rapid social change. And yet none of these social changes or the growth in anti-political sentiment are unique to the UK (see Fawcett et al. 2017). The second argument is therefore that (counter-intuitively) Brexit should not be interpreted as a distinctively 'British' issue but as a critical case in the analysis of a set of social trends that raise fundamental questions about the relationship between populism and democracy. That is not to say that there are not distinctively British dimensions to the Brexit phenomenon; the UK has always been an 'awkward partner' in the EU (see George 1998) and remains the only member state to vote to leave (so far). But it is in teasing apart the relationships between Brexit and anti-political sentiment – or what is termed 'the (*anti*-) politics of Brexit' – that this chapter contributes to a set of broader questions concerning the 'life and death of democracy' (Keane 2009). The final argument is that in many ways it is the unfolding of the post-referendum politics of Brexit that reveals most about anti-political sentiment and the recalibration of representative politics.

The challenge for the political and social sciences, however, is that understanding the relationship(s) between Brexit and anti-politics is the intellectual equivalent of being charged with untangling a vast Gordian knot of complex, multifaceted, interwoven and densely layered factors. The approach to this challenge adopted in this chapter is to begin by unravelling the concept of 'anti-politics' in order to identify a number of component strands that, in turn, highlight how different actors might seek to create, amplify or funnel different types of anti-political sentiment for instrumental reasons (the focus of the first section). Put slightly differently, anti-politics can be conceived as a powerful political resource if those utilising its potency can retain 'outsider' status while maintaining a certain level of credibility or potential governing competence. This, in turn, demands a sophisticated understanding of the drivers of democratic dissatisfaction and the ability to couch a campaign strategy within carefully calibrated parameters. The second section moves from the sphere of 'politics as theory' to that of 'politics as practice' and suggests that a constellation of factors came into alignment in the UK that offered a very specific 'window of opportunity' through which frustration could be channelled around the issue of EU membership.

Understanding anti-politics

Even the most cursory glance at the titles of recent texts on democracy and public attitudes to politics suggests that a problem exists. Books including *Democracy in Crisis* (Papadoplous 2013), *Ruling the Void* (Mair 2013), *New Democracies in Crisis* (Blokker 2014), *The Crisis of Social Democracy in Europe* (Keating & McCrone 2016), *Global Capitalism and the Crisis of Democracy* (Harris 2016), *The New Totalitarian Temptation* (Huizinga 2016), *Four Crises of American Democracy* (Roberts 2017) – to highlight just a few of the leading texts – paint a consistent picture of democratic decline, discontent and disengagement. Everyone appears to be 'against' something – *Against Elections* (Van Reybrouk 2016), *Against Democracy* (Brennan 2016); prophesising 'the end' of something else – *The End of Representative Politics* (Tormey 2015), *The End of Politicians* (Hennig 2017), *The End of British Politics* (Moran 2017), *The End of Europe* (Kirchick 2017); or using the prefix 'post' to encapsulate a state of democratic flux – *Post-Democracy* (Crouch 2004), *Post-Political* (Wilson and Swyngedouw 2014), *Post-Truth* (Ball 2018). And yet what this broad seam of scholarship shares is a common focus on the concept and emergence of anti-political sentiment and the challenges it presents to established modes of democratic governance. Put slightly differently, this anti-political sentiment provides the broader international sociopolitical context in which Brexit occurred.

And yet in terms of exploring the linkage between Brexit and anti-political sentiment – or more accurately the possible linkage*s* [plural] or the *(anti-)politics of Brexit* – it is necessary to acknowledge that 'anti-politics' is an umbrella concept beneath which a range of public attitudes or political practices that share some relationship with the rejection of mainstream politics are commonly grouped. Moreover, it is in teasing-apart some of these constituent strands that a more focused and contextualised understanding of Brexit is arguably achievable. This, in turn, underlines how a focus on Brexit as a specific issue or decision-making process risks overlooking the manner in which it was arguably symptomatic of a far deeper democratic challenge and therefore should not be dismissed as a 'British issue'. Indeed, a sharper understanding of comparative politics and the existence of long-term trends might have made both the rise of UKIP and the Brexit vote far less surprising than it appeared to many commentators (including academics). Indeed, with the benefit of hindsight, works such as Cass Mudde's (2004) writing on the 'populist zeitgeist', Peter Mair's (2007) study on 'political opposition and the European Union' and Pippa Norris's *Radical Right* (2009) all contained significant insights that now appear incredibly pertinent to contemporary analyses. But in terms of moving forward and assessing the Brexit–anti-politics linkage, Table 15.1 attempts to deconstruct the concept of anti-politics in order to identify dominant variants or sub-strands.

The benefit of Table 15.1 is that it provides some sort of heuristic framework or organising perspective that facilitates a degree of analytical purchase on a complex topic. Three immediate insights are worth noting. First, the five types of anti-politics are clearly not discrete conceptual containers and might more accurately be interpreted as concentric circles with significant areas of overlap. Populist anti-politics (AP1) and Alternative anti-politics (AP3), for example, have clear elements of similarity, and populist parties are clearly seeking to promote an alternative way of 'doing' politics. And yet at the same time, AP1 and AP3 tend to be very different in terms of their ambitions, democratic ethos, structures and campaigning tools. Secondly, the value of this five-type framework lies in the manner in which it not only highlights the existence of subtle

Table 15.1 Five types of anti-politics

Type	Root	Essence	Response	Tools
AP1 – *External* *anti-politics*	Populism	Anti-elitist denigration of 'mainstream' politics for failing though a combination of inefficiency and self-interest, combined with an emphasis on pandering to 'them' instead of concentrating on 'us'	*'Drain the swamp!'* Rhetorical commitment to remove existing politicians while legitimating the evisceration of traditional checks and balances through recourse to arguments concerning 'the people'; often combined with nationalism and veiled xenophobia	'Insurgent' political parties, charismatic leaders, pitchfork politics, appeals to the simplicity and common sense of ordinary people; top-down in emphasis
AP2 – *Internal* *anti-politics*	Technocracy	Pro-elitist emphasis on the benefits of de-politicising public functions in order to 'take the politics out' of decision-making; an emphasis on 'output-based legitimacy' (i.e. 'what works') rather than 'process-focused' legitimacy	*'Take the politics out!'* The widespread devolution of powers and responsibilities to a plethora of arm's-length bodies with elected politicians having a directive oversight function (steering, not rowing)	Bureaucratic hyperactivity, scientisation, technocracy, patronage, etc.; generally horizontal in emphasis
AP3 – *Active* *anti-politics*	Alternative	Alternative political movements seeking to demonstrate new ways of 'doing' politics; generally advocating 'deeper' forms of public engagement alongside a reappraisal of the political-economy of contemporary capitalism	*'There is an alternative!'* An emphasis on the existence of alternative forms of social organisation, notably in relation to both democratic politics and the economy	Protests, direct action, new modes of political expression and participation; often digitally based and with a bottom-up or even leaderless emphasis

(Continued)

Table 15.1 (Continued)

Type	Root	Essence	Response	Tools
AP4 – *Passive* *anti-politics*	Apathy	Generally anti-political and anti-politician but disengaged and disinterested when it comes to active engagement of a positive or negative type	*'They are all the same!'* An emphasis on withdrawal, possibly with elements of rational choice (stealth democrats)	Non-voting, non-engagement, etc.; spectatorial emphasis
A5 – *Fundamental* *anti-politics*	Rejection	Democratic *de*-consolidation in the form of a rejection of the underlying values and principles of democratic politics in any form Whereas the other forms of anti-politics (1–4) are generally based on an assumed level of underpinning 'regime legitimacy', fundamental anti-politics is cynical about the value of democracy as a political system.	*'Democracy is over-rated!'*	Support for 'strong leaders' unencumbered by the checks and balances of democracy; possibly combined with support for more authoritarian forms of rule

differences in the drivers or foci of political disaffection, even given that they are all united by a shared rejection of the status quo, but also in the manner in which it suggests that different actors might seek to create, amplify or funnel different types of anti-political sentiment for instrumental reasons and in doing so may target very different constituencies (in a demographic rather than psephological sense). And yet the funnelling of anti-politics as a political resource has not been the focus of sustained analysis, especially in relation to the response or accommodation strategies of mainstream parties. Not only does this insight create the intellectual space and analytical tools through which to undertake an original study of Brexit, it also illuminates a range of related issues that might assist that analysis and not least the manner in which different forms of anti-politics may exist in an almost self-fulfilling, self-sustaining quasi-parasitical relationship. For example, external anti-political pressure (i.e. AP1) may encourage politicians to seek to minimise the sphere of responsibility for which they can be held directly to account by seeking to delegate powers and responsibilities beyond their direct control (i.e. AP2, internal anti-politics). And yet the logic of that internal delegation to arm's-length or supranational actors (i.e. the hollowing out of national democracy) is likely to further inflame external (populist) anti-politics pressures that highlight the existence of an insulated governing elite, or what Frank Vibert (2007) terms 'the rise of the unelected'. Such concerns are clearly relevant to the analysis of Brexit in the sense that the institutions of the European Union were always designed to embrace a rather technocratic and elitist approach to governance legitimated on the basis of a rather tenuous chain of delegation through elected politicians at the national level. It is for exactly this reason that the analysis of European governance has tended to produce allegations of a 'democratic deficit' that explain a number of institutional reforms (notably the introduction of direct elections to the European Parliament in 1979) and has sustained an intellectual debate for decades (e.g. Moravcsik 2002; Follesdal and Hix 2005).

The question then becomes one of explaining exactly *why* the UK's membership of the European Union became such a politically salient issue at a very specific point in time (i.e. why it was 'a constitutional moment'). In this regard, the main argument of this chapter is that the European Union became something of a lightning rod through which UKIP and other promoters of Brexit were able to channel or funnel a broader set of social frustrations. However, in order to make this argument and to fully understand the *(anti-)politics* of Brexit, it is necessary to try and comprehend what lies beneath anti-politics in the sense of the main drivers of democratic dissatisfaction.

Broadly conceived, there are two interrelated theses regarding the recent emergence of powerful currents of anti-political sentiment. The *economic inequality perspective* emphasises two basic issues. Firstly, for the first time since the industrial revolution, standards of living are falling. In most developed democracies, the median income has remained stagnant over the past twenty-five years, leading to increasing inter-generational pressures that focus upon the position of younger people (see Piketty 2014; Piketty et al. 2016). The second issue is increasing economic insecurity and decreasing levels of social protection. The emergence of the 'gig economy' with its emphasis on mobility and flexibility, alongside very limited or negligible workers' rights, is reminiscent of Zygmunt Bauman's writing on 'liquid modernity' (2000); whereas the specific employment effects are encapsulated in Guy Standing's influential work (2014) on *The Precariat: The New Dangerous Class*. The critical element is that these precarious workers are generally the young, the poor and the less educated who increasingly feel 'left behind' by mainstream politics and politicians. Moreover, an emphasis on immigration and identity provides the pivot to a complementary *cultural backlash thesis*. The problem with democracy from this perspective is not just that living standards are now declining from one generation to another but also that the growth in immigration and the role of supranational organisations are perceived to be responsible. During the economic boom of the 1950s and 1960s, large numbers of immigrants were attracted and encouraged to come to Europe but did not pose a threat to national identity for the reason that governments told their citizens that the newcomers were temporary visitors and jobs were relatively plentiful.

By the 1970s and 1980s, millions of immigrants had not returned home but had in fact gained the right to permanent residence and full citizenship and therefore demanded to be treated as full members of their country. During the 1990s, the free movement that came with membership of the European Union began to create tension, and with the benefit of hindsight the 2004 decision by Tony Blair's government to allow unfettered access to the UK for citizens of the eight Central and East European EU newcomers appears to have had a dramatic impact. Most other member states imposed transitional restrictions of up to seven years, and if the UK had done this, then the level of inward migration would have been negligible. Cas Mudde (2004) is correct to highlight the manner in which the rise of anti-political right-wing populists in Europe began before the Global Financial Crisis and cannot therefore be attributed to a simple economic inflection point. and yet it is equally true to suggest that 'post-crisis' politics nurtured anti-political sentiment and more specifically a cultural backlash against those post-war, post-industrial, post-materialist values (cosmopolitanism, feminism, culturalism, environmentalism etc.) that were to some extent and to many people synonymous with the European project. The 'cultural escalator' (Inglehart and

Norris 2016) appeared to have gone into reverse in many countries as commitment to progressive values waned. Or, put more accurately, those 'pockets of resistance' to progressive social dynamics that had always existed but had generally been cushioned by economic growth suddenly grew. 'The silent revolution of the 1970s', Inglehart and Norris conclude (2016: 5), 'appears to have spawned an angry and resentful counter-revolutionary backlash today.'

The question this leaves us with is the extent to which it is possible to forge a relationship between the drivers of anti-political sentiment outlined in this section and the Brexit phenomenon in the UK. This forms the focus of the next section.

The (anti-)politics of Brexit

The previous section explored the concept of anti-politics in order to provide the foundations for this section's more detailed exploration of the (anti-)politics of Brexit. The main aim of this section is to substantiate the argument that anti-political sentiment was a critical underlying factor in explaining the decision to leave the EU. This, in turn, flows into this chapter's second argument and the suggestion that, although Brexit relates to a specifically British political phenomenon, it should not be regarded as an exclusively British issue. Indeed, it might more accurately be interpreted as the most extreme case of institutional rupturing due to a set of underlying sociocultural forces that are actually common across an increasing number of advanced liberal democracies. The successes of the Swiss People's Party, the Austrian Freedom Party, the Sweden Democrats, Greece's Golden Dawn, the Danish People's Party, the Northern League in Italy, Jobbik in Hungary, the Alterative for Germany, the National Front in France, not to mention populist leaders in Latin America or the election of Donald Trump in the United States, suggests that a variety of compressional and constructive anti-political pressure points have emerged in the form of 'new' or 'insurgent' parties (for a discussion, see European Council on Foreign Relations 2016) – parties, furthermore, that all shared a set of 'strikingly similar slogans and tropes' (Mounk 2014: 31), that revolved around linking immigration to economic austerity, expressing outrage against the status quo and 'professional' politicians, promoting nationalist hubris and proffering simple solutions to complex problems. The challenge, however, for parties seeking to manufacture or benefit from anti-political sentiment is that it can sometimes exist at a fairly abstract nebulous or ethereal level, with different parts of society reacting against markedly different sociopolitical frustrations. Put slightly differently, the existence of anti-political sentiment on its own is unlikely to generate change without the existence of (1) some form of trigger point, (2) an institutional carrier (in the sense of a political party or social movement), (3) a constitutional entrepreneur (in the sense of a committed and high-profile individual) and (4) a lightning rod (to provide a clear focus or target).

In the case of the UK, it is possible to argue that the dynamics of context, agency and structure came into alignment in a manner that created a very specific window of opportunity. In the post-crisis 'age of austerity', anti-political sentiment had increased and was visible through a number of authoritative social surveys (Jennings and Stoker 2016). The social context was therefore ripe for an institutional carrier with the capacity to harness this social disquiet, and in the British case, the 'carrier' role of the United Kingdom Independence Party (UKIP) cannot be overstated. The Conservative Party's 2015 manifesto commitment to renegotiate EU membership and then hold a referendum provided the trigger, while Nigel Farage played a key role as a constitutional entrepreneur who was able to position himself as a populist *non-politician* politician in a manner that chimed with the cultural backlash (previously discussed). As Alan Finlayson (2017) has noted, Brexit became a campaign of 'anti-political politics organised around resentment at past losses and scepticism about promised futures'. The sense of a loss of tradition, a mythical integrity, an eviscerated global status, a romanticised past plus a nativist and nationalist anxiety were all set against the perceived excesses of a distant European elite. The weakness in the response of the mainstream parties, politicians and Remainers was arguably their failure to grasp *why emotions matter*. Against a backdrop of economic austerity and cultural anxiety, the political appeal of the rhetorical emphasis placed by both UKIP and the Leave campaign on 'putting Britain first', 'taking back control', 'strengthening borders' and 'saving money' tapped into a powerful source of emotive desire. This desire may not have been 'rational' from the point of view of a scientific, evidence-based analysis, but the emergence of 'expert rejection' underlined the manner in which emotions trump rationality. If you feel scared, threatened, alienated, pessimistic, trapped or unloved, then no matter how many times you are told such feelings are irrational, the feelings remain true. As J. D. Taylor argues in his wonderful book, *Island Story* (2016), 'Politics has never been a matter of reason, but of feeling', and in this regard it is possible to suggest that UKIP possessed a far more sensitive emotional antennae than the mainstream parties.

Understanding the relationship between anti-political sentiment and Brexit therefore hinges on the existence of long-standing suspicions vis-à-vis the European project plus concerns regarding immigration within British society that arguably, taken together, created a particularly fertile political environment. In terms of understanding these relationships, a critical pivot point came in January 2010 when then British Prime Minister David Cameron announced a target to 'cap' net immigration to tens of thousands, but at no point in the subsequent six years did he get even close to this target and just four weeks before the Brexit referendum, the Office for National Statistics announced that 630,000 people had moved to the UK in 2015. The government had set a very public target that it simply could not achieve. Worse still, every three months the Office for National Statistics (ONS) published a new report that constantly reminded the public of the government's failure. In this context, the EU provided an almost perfect lightning rod for a range of social frustrations despite the fact that many of them arguably had very little to do with the EU (the majority of immigrants were non-EU citizens).

The key intellectual reference point that links this argument with the broader international issues discussed in the previous section is Robert Ford and Matthew Goodwin's *Revolt on the Right* (2014), which illustrates that anti-political sentiment aimed at a 'Westminster elite' was a major driver of the UKIP vote. Note that this was *a* major driver, not *the* major driver, as anti-immigrant sentiment formed the most salient issue for supporters, but to a large extent this became almost synonymous with anti-European sentiment, which, in turn, overlaid a deeper sense of cultural anxiety and dissatisfaction about Britain's general direction, its identify and traditional ways of life. This highlights the complex and multilayered quality of any understanding of the relationship(s) between Brexit and anti-politics, but in this context the 'common sense' framing of established parties (and their politicians) by UKIP as corrupt, complacent and out of touch resonated with the world view of increasingly large sections of the public. UKIP's (political) seeds therefore fell into a particularly receptive and fertile (social) soil in the run-up to the Brexit referendum of June 2016. But at the core of UKIP's strategy was the realisation by Nigel Farage that the nature of British society was changing in ways that reflected elements of both the *economic inequality perspective* and *the cultural backlash theory* (previously discussed) and therefore created significant opportunities for a party that could turn anti-political sentiment into a political resource and propelling force (i.e. as an institutional carrier or platform). As Matthew Goodwin and Caitlin Millazzo (2015: 5) note:

> Away from the headlines and the day-to-day battles in Westminster, he saw his party as a ship on the ocean – a vessel that was being pushed forward by deeper currents that lay hidden below the surface of British politics. And several currents were pushing him on.

The distinctive element, however, was the way in which the UKIP 'offer' drew support from both the left and the right of the political spectrum. What had been seen by many on the right as the weakening of traditional conservatism had created a significant layer of disenchanted, older and socially more conservative grass-roots Tories who seemed to resonate with the cultural backlash theory. This was reflected in preferences around reducing immigration, withdrawing from the EU, and halting the spread of cosmopolitan liberal values, such as same-sex marriage, single-sex shortlists and the celebration of ethnic diversity. These were the traditional Tories – or 'cultural conservatives' as Paul Webb and Tim Bale (2014) labelled them – who felt disconnected from the modern party and felt that the world, *their* world, was in some ways under attack and that the EU represented the institutional manifestation of a set of progressive social values that were being imposed by a distant and disconnected elite. And yet there was a second rump of disaffected democrats at the other end of the political spectrum in the form of the gap that appeared to have emerged between the Labour Party and its traditional working-class base. There existed a simmering anger and resentment among blue-collar workers, and indeed non-working or 'in-and-out-of work' people, who felt marginalized by the impact of globalisation, anxious about the erosion of traditional ways of life and forgotten by a Labour Party that had itself, many people felt, become detached from its working-class roots and had ceased to represent or truly understand them (the history and complexities of which have often been misunderstood but are clarified by Evans and Mellon (2016) and Ford and Goodwin (2016)).

This brings both the economic inequality thesis and the cultural backlash theory back into focus. In relation to the former, the rising 'precariat' as a 'new and dangerous class', as described by Guy Standing (2016), were receptive to the arguments of campaigners who promised that leaving the EU would forge greater economic growth, save huge amounts of public money and facilitate greater social protection. These are the individuals and communities that exist within a 'gig economy' defined by the prevalence of hyper-mobility, short-term contracts and limited worker rights or protections. But there was also a very clear cultural dimension in the sense of a reaction against what was perceived to be the mockery by the Labour Party of traditional working-class sentiments and values, such as patriotism and flying the flag of St George. Added to this was a sense that a set of externally imposed progressive values that many people felt had almost defined the expression of any concern about immigration as by definition racist. In this context the common sight of Nigel Farage – cigarette in one hand, pint of beer in the other, his 'every pub is a parliament' mantra – who was willing to talk about immigration and its impact on British society offered a stark contrast to the perceived emergence of a cadre of elite professional politicians within the Labour Party.

The argument here is that UKIP adopted a very specific strategic selectivity in terms of its campaign strategy that acted as a critical vent for those underlying social pressures that mainstream parties appeared to be overlooking or ignoring. Moreover, the more the mainstream parties and established political class dismissed UKIP as a motley collection of 'fruitcakes and loonies and closet racists mostly' (as David Cameron described the party during a radio interview in 2006), the more this simply appeared to confirm UKIP's arguments regarding the existence of a condescending and detached political elite. UKIP offered a voice and a home for the 'ordinary' voter and the disenchanted masses, and by 2014 UKIP was the most significant new independent party in post-war English politics. As such, UKIP exerted a powerful 'blackmail effect' upon the mainstream parties, public discourse and the media that came to a head with the Brexit referendum. The results of the vote revealed a society that had become, when it came to the EU and immigration, divided not by traditional partisan cleavages but by social class, age and geography. Put simply, Leave achieved greatest support within communities that were more economically disadvantaged than average, where levels of education were low, where the local population was predominantly white and amongst those who felt disillusioned with mainstream politics. Households with incomes of less that £20,000 per year were more likely to vote Leave than the wealthiest households, as were the unemployed, people in low-skilled roles and with no qualifications. As research by the National Centre for Social Research reveals, support for Leave was 30 per cent higher amongst those with school-level qualifications than it was for people with a degree; 20 per cent higher among those aged 65 than those aged 25; and 10 per cent higher amongst those earning less than £20,000 per year than it was among those with incomes above £60,000 per year. It is estimated that of those people who did not vote in the 2015 general election but did turn out for the referendum, 60 per cent voted to Leave (see Swales 2017; see also J. Curtice 2017). 'They delivered a sharp blow to what they had long perceived to be a self-serving, out-of-touch political class who did not understand the daily lives of the people they served', the Hansard Society's Fourteenth Audit of Political Engagement (2017: 11) concludes, 'working in a democratic system that failed to address their interests or those of their family'.

One critical element of the Brexit vote with direct implications for anti-political sentiment revolves around the engagement of young people. Surveys had consistently revealed that younger people tended to be far more cosmopolitan in outlook and therefore more likely to vote Remain, and yet this was also the main demographic group that surveys also suggested was most apathetic about mainstream politics and therefore most unlikely to vote. In the event, post-referendum polling suggests that around 64 per cent of young people (18–39) who were registered to vote did cast their ballot with broadly a 2:1 ratio in favour of Remain (75 per cent amongst 18- to 24-year-olds, 56 per cent amongst 25- to 49-year-olds). Turnout was, however, around 80 per cent for those aged 55–64 and close to 90 per cent for those aged 65, with both demographic groups holding a strong preference for Brexit (see Sloam and Ehsan 2017). At base, what the referendum highlighted arguably had less to do with the European Union per se and more to do with highlighting the existence of an increasingly fractured and divided society. This is reflected almost perfectly in the electoral geography of the results and the manner in which the highest levels of support for Leave correlated with communities that possessed low income, education and skill profiles – Great Yarmouth, Mansfield, Ashfield, Stoke-on-Trent, Doncaster, Rotherham and the like – and where UKIP had for some time been gaining support. The contrast with the strong Remain communities could hardly be starker – Islington, Edinburgh, Cambridge, Oxford, Richmond and so on – are all affluent, highly educated and diverse parts of the country. Fifteen of the twenty 'least educated' areas voted to leave, while all of the twenty 'most highly educated areas' voted to remain. Of the twenty youngest local authorities, sixteen voted to remain, but out of the twenty oldest, nineteen voted to leave.

'Groups in Britain who have been "left behind" by rapid economic change and feel cut adrift from the mainstream consensus', Matthew Goodwin and Oliver Heath conclude, 'were most likely to support Brexit. These voters face a "double wammy"' (2016: 3). While their lack of qualifications put them at a significant disadvantage in the modern economy, they are also being further marginalized in society by the lack of opportunities they face in their low-skilled communities. 'This will make it extremely difficult for the left-behind to adapt and prosper in the future' (ibid.). Therefore, to a large extent, the factors that helped explain the rise of UKIP and, critically, the rise of anti-political sentiment also help explain why the British voted for Brexit. In essence, the referendum, or more specifically its result, magnified a deeper set of social, geographic and cultural divides that parties like UKIP have been actively cultivating for many years (see Jennings and Stoker 2016). And yet the existence of these divisions is by no means exclusive to the UK, and this is reflected in the rise of nationalist populism across Western Europe and also in survey evidence suggesting widespread support for national referendums in a range of countries (see Stokes et al. 2017). The next and final section develops this argument by looking at the changing 'politics of anti-politics' in the post-Brexit referendum period.

Anti-politics and the future of British and European Union politics

The core and main argument of this chapter is that the Brexit vote in the UK cannot be reduced to a particularly 'British' phenomenon and might more usefully be interpreted as the structural manifestation of a set of underlying social forces that are increasingly visible in a range of supposedly 'consolidated' democracies. The fact that these forces erupted in such dramatic form in the UK should not distract analysts from decoding Brexit as much as a protest vote against mainstream politics and not simply as a specific vote on future membership of the European Union. Similarly, immigration provided the headline rationale amongst Brexiteers for voting to leave, but this in itself veiled a deeper sense of government failure and political disillusionment. Therefore, the 'island story' possibly has just as much to say about the future of the European Union and representative democracy in an increasingly interdependent, hyper-fluid and technologically driven world than it does about British politics per se. As such, the aim of this final concluding section is to very briefly locate this chapter's focus on the (anti-)politics of Brexit within just three larger themes or debates. The first is a focus on how the Brexit referendum cast a long shadow over the subsequent general election of 2017 in ways that continue to speak to the theme of anti-politics. The second issue locates this chapter's focus on Brexit within the wider rise of nationalist populism across Western Europe. The final theme is a focus of on the risks of this trajectory in terms of democratic de-consolidation and the erosion of diffuse support for the principles and values of democratic politics.

It could be argued that it remains far too early to fully understand the relationship between Brexit and anti-politics (for the UK, other members and the European project itself) because the social and political reverberations are likely to consume much of the next decade. However, it is possible to suggest that the spillover consequences of Brexit have had very direct and tangible impacts upon British politics due to the manner in which it framed the 2017 general election (GE2017). Prime Minister Theresa May called the election in order to secure a 'strong and stable' platform within British politics from which she could lead the Brexit negotiations. The British public, however, refused to provide her with this mandate, and the reason for this is of direct relevance to this chapter's focus on anti-politics. First, with the decision to leave the EU agreed after the 2016 general election the raison d'être for UKIP all but evaporated. In May 2017, UKIP went into the local elections with 145 local councillors and came out with just one. At the general election, just weeks later, the party lost its single MP and secured just 1.8 per cent of the national vote (a decline of 10.8 per cent compared with the 2015 general election). The collapse of UKIP takes us back to Table 15.1 and to a consideration of the strategic selectivity employed by the party in the years running up to the 2016 referendum. This revolved around the aggressive deployment of a raw populism that laid the roots of almost every social evil at the door of the European Commission or other institutions. It was therefore a strategy that funnelled frustration and used the EU as little more than a lightning rod. To some extent the political space on which UKIP had set out its stall had all but disappeared, which in turn raises issues about the need for populist parties to adopt a broad platform of discontents, in much the same way that a mainstream party must attract the support of a cross-section of society.

The critical element of the election, however, was that Theresa May adopted a very hard Brexit stance in a clear attempt to attract former UKIP voters into the Tory fold. And yet at exactly the same moment Jeremy Corbyn re-framed the Labour Party as a broad platform for anti-establishment, anti-elite, anti-austerity politics and through this was able to connect with a large cross-section of 'active anti-political' citizens and groups (i.e. AP3) while also managing to invigorate many people that had previously been passively disengaged (i.e. AP4). The opening lines of Corbyn's first speech of the 2017 campaign made this clear:

The dividing lines in this election could not be clearer from the outset. . . . It is the establishment versus the people and it is our historic duty to make sure that the people prevail. . . . We don't fit in their cosy club. We're not obsessed with the tittle-tattle of Westminster or Brussels. We don't accept that it is natural for Britain to be governed by a ruling elite, the City and the tax-dodgers, and we don't accept that the British people just have to take what they're given, that they don't deserve better.

(Corbyn 2017: 1)

In many ways Corbyn offered a new platform for those who felt 'left behind' in the coastal areas of Eastern England and post-industrial parts of Northern England while also being able to maintain the support of the suburban middle classes and ethnic minorities and to energise younger people to actually cast their vote. The result was a glorious defeat in which the Labour Party increased its vote share by 9.5 per cent (from 2015) and secured 262 seats in the House of Commons (an increase of 30), a result that condemned the Conservatives to leading a minority government. Two elements of this 'Labour surge' are critical to this chapter's focus on the (anti-)politics of Brexit. First and foremost, many former UKIP voters did not return to the Conservative Party as was widely expected. In fact, around a fifth of previously UKIP voters switched support to the Labour Party, and this was generally related to a welfare-based and redistributive agenda (see Ashcroft 2017). Many who had felt left behind returned to the Labour fold, but in this regard they were not alone. A second core feature of GE2017 was a 'youthquake' in the sense that turnout amongst young people increased dramatically. More than half those aged 18–24 turned out to vote (an increase of 16 per cent on 2015), with 60 per cent voting for Labour according to the analysis of Ipsos-MORI (see C. Curtice 2017). Younger voters were also far more supportive of the European Union, and therefore the Labour Party's softer stance on Brexit offered some form of corrective to the hard Brexit stance of the Conservatives. But the main point is that the Labour Party played an explicitly anti-political game and through this was able to build a broad coalition of previously disengaged or disaffected democrats, which explains the shift back towards a two-party system (for a detailed analysis, see Flinders 2018). It is also likely that the strongly hard-Brexit stance taken by the PM, combined with her promise to be a 'bloody difficult women' in negotiations and in her attack upon the 'bureaucrats of Brussels', increased the determination of Remain-inclined voters, who for one reason or another did not vote in the referendum, to go to the polls at GE2017. David Denver (2017) therefore suggests that the election outcome might be characterised as the 'revenge of the Remainers'.

But actually, the more worrying element of the relationship between Brexit and GE2017 is the manner in which both rested, to a large extent, on populism and the funnelling of frustration in the sense of tapping into anti-political sentiment as almost little more than a political commodity or resource to be sown, inflamed, cultivated and then harvested for partisan electoral gain. Brexit was a right-wing populist punch quickly followed by a left-wing populist punch in the form of the Labour surge under Jeremy Corbyn. From a democratic perspective, UKIP's rise was arguably disconcerting, but such concerns were to some extent allayed by the fact that it was so clearly a populist insurgency by an outsider party *against* the mainstream. A Labour victory in 2017 might have given more cause for concern due to the manner in which a mutant or hybrid form of left-wing populism would have infiltrated a core mainstream party. Anyone wanting to understand this argument in more detail would be well served by reading John Lukacs's *Democracy and Populism* (2006), as it underlines how populism is fuelled by the cultivation of fear and hatred that inevitably tends to eviscerate public confidence in democratic politics and is therefore ultimately destructive.

The benefit of this concluding focus on what might be termed 'the perils of playing with populism' allows this chapter's focus on the (anti-)politics of Brexit to be located within the rise of nationalist populism across Western Europe. Put very simply, populist nationalism is a dangerous ideology due to the manner in which it denies the inevitable inefficiencies of democratic politics and offers simple solutions to complex problems that generally revolve around the demonization of a scapegoat community in either a professional (bankers, politicians etc.) or ethnic group (gypsies, asylum seekers, immigrants etc.). The problem with nationalist populism is that it has the unfortunate habit of 'assuming that human beings can be classified like insects and that whole blocks of millions or tens of millions of people can be confidently labelled as "good" or "bad"', as George Orwell wrote in his essay 'Notes on Nationalism' in 1945 (republished in 2018). It is an essentially self-defeating and divisive ideology that fits within and feeds upon broader narratives regarding the 'age of anger' (Mishra 2017) at a historical point that is almost defined by super-wicked problems that can be addressed only through international cooperation. The (*anti-*) politics of Brexit is therefore just one strand of a far wider international phenomenon defined in terms of liberal democracy coming 'under attack from angry and energised democratic majorities' (Fukuyama 2016). The barb, twist or sting in this account of contemporary democratic change, however, exists in relation to the challenge this poses for the future of liberal democracy.

Since the turn of the millennium, a rather benign interpretation has been offered by a large number of scholars who broadly suggest that what the available data reveals is less of a democratic crisis and more a fluctuation in patterns of participation (e.g. Hibbing and Theiss-Morse 2002; Norris 2011; Merkel 2014). This interpretation draws succour from the existence of studies that appear to highlight that, although levels of 'specific support' for political parties, political institutions or political processes may be in decline in many countries, public confidence in the *underlying values and principles* of democratic politics remains strong. Phrased in the language of David Easton's (1965) well known distinction, levels of 'specific support' or 'governmental legitimacy' may have significantly declined, but levels of 'diffuse support' or 'regime legitimacy' remain strong. But what happens if anti-political sentiment deepens to erode the levels of underlying 'diffuse support'? What happens – paraphrasing Juan Linz and Alfred Stepan (1996) – if democracy is no longer regarded as 'the only game in town' for an increasing number of critical citizens? Brought back within the case of Brexit, what happens to confidence in democratic politics when the far-fetched expectations that were fuelled by the Leave campaign in 2016 remain unfulfilled? Might the manner in which prominent Brexit campaigners backtracked within just hours of the vote from the specific commitments they had been only too happy to make during the campaign in relation to immigration control – and therefore from the financial benefits to public services that were promised would arise from voting Leave – lead to a significant Brexit backlash against politics at some point in the future?

The reason these questions matter in the context of analysing the (*anti-*)politics of Brexit is that evidence has recently been published that offers a more malign interpretation of the rise in anti-political sentiment to which this chapter has related. For example, recent analysis of World Values Survey data (1995–2014) suggests that a process of democratic *de*-consolidation is occurring in many advanced liberal democracies and that levels of diffuse support for the values of liberal democracy are eroding. 'What we find is deeply concerning', Foa and Mounk (2016: 7) argue:

> Citizens in a number of supposedly consolidated democracies in North America and Western Europe have not only grown more critical of their political leaders. Rather, they have also become more cynical about the value of democracy as a political system, less hopeful that anything they do might influence public policy, and more willing to express support for authoritarian alternatives. The crisis of democratic legitimacy extends across a much wider set of indicators than previously appreciated.[1]

This study has not gone without challenge (see Voeten 2017; Alexander and Welzel 2017; Norris 2017; see also, Foa and Mounk 2017a, 2017b), but it does suggest that the emergence of a new and potentially more dangerous variant of anti-political sentiment (A5, Table 15.1). Similar arguments have been made about British politics. '[T]hese findings support the claim of rising discontentment among citizens, and of the withdrawal of diffuse support' Jennings et al. (2017: 757) argue:

> We can be clear that there was no golden age of democracy, as a degree of public scepticism about the political system appears to have been present throughout. We are also able to come down against the 'trendless fluctuation' thesis for Britain, at least if the full post-war period is considered.

The paradox of populism, however, is that in adopting explicitly negative, cynical and anti-political platforms for instrumental reasons, politicians may themselves unwittingly serve to advance the *de*-consolidation of democracy that is beginning to be identified. This might, in the long term, be one of the most alarming insights of the (*anti-*)politics of Brexit.

Note

1   Readers might be interested in listening to BBC Radio 4's Analysis Programme on 'Democracy at Risk' that features an interview with Yascha Mounk. Available at: www.bbc.co.uk/programmes/b08y02x0 [Accessed February 14, 2018].

References

Alexander, A. and Welzel, C. (2017) The Myth of Deconsolidation: Rising Liberalism and the Populist Reaction. *Journal of Democracy*, April 28 (updated June 26). Available at: www.journalofdemocracy.org/online-exchange-"democratic-deconsolidation" [Accessed January 18, 2018].

Ashcroft, M. (2017) Hid Did This This Vote Happen? *Lord Ashcroft Polls*, June 9. Available at: https://lordashcroftpolls.com/2017/06/result-happen-post-vote-survey/ [Accessed January 18, 2018].

Ball, J. (2018) *Post-Truth: How Bullshit Conquered the World*. London: Biteback Publishing.

Bauman, Z. (2000) *Liquid Modernity*. Cambridge: Polity Press.

Blokker, P. (2014) *New Democracies in Crisis?* Abingdon: Routledge.

Brennan, J. (2016) *Against Democracy*. Princeton, NJ: Princeton University Press.

Corbyn, J. (2017) Jeremy Corbyn First Speech of the 2017 General Election Campaign, Held April 20. Available at: https://global.ilmanifesto.it/corbyn-speech-general-election/ [Accessed February 14, 2018].

Crouch, C. (2004) *Post-Democracy*. Cambridge: Polity Press.

Curtice, C. (2017) How Britain Voted at the 2017 General Election. *YouGov*, June 13. Available at: https://yougov.co.uk/news/2017/06/13/how-britain-voted-2017-general-election/ [Accessed January 18, 2018].

Curtice, J. (2017) Why Leave Won the UK's EU Referendum. *Journal of Common Market Studies* 55(1): 19–37.

Denver, D. (2017) The Results: How Britain Voted. In: Tonge, J., Leston-Bandeira, C. and Wilks-Hogg, S. (eds.), *Britain Votes 2017*. Oxford: Oxford University Press.

Easton, D. (1965) *A Systems Analysis of Political Life*. New York: Wiley.

European Council on Foreign Relations (2016) *The World According to Europe's Insurgent Parties*. London: ECFR.

Evans, G. and Mellon, J. (2016) Working Class Votes and Conservative Losses: Solving the UKIP Puzzle. *Parliamentary Affairs* 69(2): 464–479.

Fawcett, P., Flinders, M., Hay, C. and Wood, M. (eds.) (2017) *Anti-Politics, Depoliticization and Governance*. Oxford: Oxford University Press.

Finlayson, A. (2017) Brexitism. *London Review of Books* 39(10): 22–23.

Flinders, M. (2018, forthcoming) The (Anti-)Politics of the General Election: Funnelling Frustration in a Divided Democracy. *Parliamentary Affairs* No. 71(suppl.): 222–236.

Foa, R. and Mounk, Y. (2016) The Democratic Disconnect. *Journal of Democracy* 27(3): 5–17.

Foa, R. and Mounk, Y. (2017a) The End of the Consolidation Paradigm: A Response to Our Critics. *Journal of Democracy*, April 28 (Updated June 26). Available at: http://docplayer.net/59303853-The-end-of-the-consolidation-paradigm.html [Accessed January 18, 2018].

Foa, R. and Mounk, Y. (2017b) The Signs of Deconsolidation. *Journal of Democracy* 28(1): 5–15.

Follesdal, A. and Hix, S. (2005) Why There Is a Democratic Deficit in the EU: A Response to Majone and Moravcsik. *European Governance Papers (EUROGOV)* No. C–05–02. Available at: http://edoc.vifapol.de/opus/volltexte/2011/2454/pdf/egp_connex_C_05_02.pdf [Accessed January 18, 2018].

Ford, R. and Goodwin, M. (2014) *Revolt on the Right: Explaining Support for the Radical Right in Britain (Extremism and Democracy)*. London: Routledge.

Ford, R. and Goodwin, M. (2016) Different Class? UKIP's Social Base and Political Impact: A Reply to Evans and Mellon. *Parliamentary Affairs* 69(2): 480–491.

Fukuyama, F. (2016) US against the World? Trump's America and the New Global Order. *Financial Times*, November 11. Available at: www.ft.com/content/6a43cf54-a75d-11e6-8b69-02899e8bd9d1 [Accessed January 20, 2018].

George, S. (1998) *An Awkward Partner: Britain in the European Community*. 3rd Edition. Oxford: Oxford University Press.

Goodwin, M. and Heath, O. (2016) The 2016 Referendum, Brexit and the Left Behind. *Political Quarterly* 87(3): 323–332.

Goodwin, M. and Milazzo, C. (2015) *UKIP*. Oxford: Oxford University Press.

Hansard Society (2017) Audit of Political Engagement 14. *The 2017 Report*. Available at: https://assets.contentful.com/xkbace0jm9pp/1vNBTsOEiYciKEAqWAmEKi/c9cc36b98f60328c0327e313ab37ae0c/Audit_of_political_Engagement_14__2017_.pdf [Accessed January 18, 2018].

Harris, J. (2016) *Global Capitalism and the Crisis of Democracy*. Atlanta: Clarity Press.

Hennig, B. (2017) *The End of Politicians: Time for Real Democracy*. London: Unbound.

Hibbing, J.R. and Theiss-Morse, E. (2002) *Stealth Democracy: Americans' Beliefs about How Government Should Work*. Cambridge: Cambridge University Press.

Huizinga, T. (2016) *The New Totalitarian Temptation: Global Governance and the Crisis of Democracy in Europe*. New York: Encounter Books.

Inglehart, R. and Norris, P. (2016) Trump, Brexit and the Rise of Populism. Presidential Plenary, 24th World Congress. IPSA, Poland.

Jennings, W., Clarke, N., Moss, J. and Stoker, G. (2017) The Decline in Diffuse Support for National Politics. *Political Opinion Quarterly* 81(3): 748–758.

Jennings, W. and Stoker, G. (2016) The Dimensions and Impact of Political Discontent in Britain. *Parliamentary Affairs* 69(4): 876–900.

Keane, J. (2009) *The Life and Death of Democracy*. London: Simon & Schuster.

Keating, M. and McCrone, D. (2016) *The Crisis of Social Democracy in Europe*. Edinburgh: Edinburgh University Press.

Kirchick, J. (2017) *The End of Europe: Dictators, Demagogues, and the Coming Dark Age*. New Haven, CT: Yale College.

Linz, J. and Stepan, A. (1996) *Problems of Democratic Transition and Consolidation*. Baltimore: Johns Hopkins Press.

Lukacs, J. (2006) *Democracy and Populism: Fear and Hatred*. New Haven, CT: Yale University Press.

Mair, P. (2007) Political Opposition and the European Union. *Government & Opposition* 42(1): 1–17.

Mair, P. (2013) *Ruling the Void: The Hollowing of Western Democracy*. New York: Verso.

Merkel, W. (2014) Is There a Crisis of Democracy? *Democratic Theory* 1(2): 11–25.

Mishra, P. (2017) *Age of Anger: A History of the Present*. London: Penguin Books.

Moran, M. (2017) *The End of British Politics?* New York: Palgrave Macmillan.

Moravcsik, A. (2002) In Defence of the Democratic Deficit. *JCMS: Journal of Common Market Studies* 40(4): 603–624.

Mounk, Y. (2014) Pitchfork Politics: The Populist Threat to Liberal Democracy. *Foreign Affairs* 93(5): 27–36.

Mudde, C. (2004) The Populist Zeitgeist. *Government & Opposition* 39(4): 541–563.

Norris, P. (2009) *Radical Right*. Cambridge: Cambridge University Press.

Norris, P. (2011) *Democratic Deficit*. Cambridge: Cambridge University Press.

Norris, P. (2017) Is Western Democracy Backsliding? Diagnosing the Risks. *Journal of Democracy*, April 28 (Updated June 26, 2017). Available at: www.journalofdemocracy.org/sites/default/files/media/

Journal%20of%20Democracy%20Web%20Exchange%20-%20Norris_0.pdf [Accessed January 18, 2018].

Orwell, G. (2018) [1945] *Notes on Nationalism*. London: Penguin. Available at: http://orwell.ru/library/essays/nationalism/english/e_nat [Accessed January 18, 2018].

Papadoplous, Y. (2013) *Democracy in Crisis? Politics, Governance and Policy (Political Analysis)*. Cambridge: Cambridge University Press.

Piketty, T. (2014) *Capital in the Twenty-First Century*. Cambridge, MA: Harvard University Press.

Piketty, T., Saez, E. and Zucman, G. (2016) Distributional National Accounts. NBER Working Paper No.22945. Available at: https://eml.berkeley.edu/~saez/Piketty-Saez-ZucmanNBER16.pdf [Accessed January 18, 2018].

Roberts, A. (2017) *Four Crises of American Democracy*. Oxford: Oxford University Press.

Sloam, J. and Ehsan, M.R. (2017) YouthQuake: Young People and the 2017 General Election. *Intergenerational Foundation*. Available at: www.if.org.uk/wp-content/uploads/2017/11/Youth-Quake_Final.pdf [Accessed January 18, 2018].

Standing, G. (2014) *The Precariat: The New Dangerous Class*. London: Bloomsbury Publishing.

Stokes, B., Wike, R. and Manevich, D. (2017) Post-Brexit, Europeans More Favourable toward EU. *Pew Research Center*. Available at: www.pewglobal.org/2017/06/15/post-brexit-europeans-more-favorable-toward-eu/ [Accessed January 18, 2018].

Swales, K. (2017) *Understanding the Leave Vote*. London: NatCen Social Research.

Taylor, J.D. (2016) *Island Story*. London: Watkins Media.

Tormey, S. (2015) *The End of Representative Politics*. Cambridge: Polity Press.

Van Reybrouk, D. (2016) *Against Elections*. London: Penguin Random House UK.

Vibert, F. (2007) *The Rise of the Unelected: Democracy and the New Separation of Powers*. Cambridge: Cambridge University Press.

Voeten, E. (2017) Are People Really Turning away from Democracy? *Journal of Democracy*, April 28 (updated June 26, 2017). Available at: www.journalofdemocracy.org/sites/default/files/media/Journal%20of%20Democracy%20Web%20Exchange%20-%20Voeten_0.pdf [Accessed January 18, 2018].

Webb, P. and Bale, T. (2014) Why Do Tories Defect to UKIP? Conservative Party Members and the Temptations of the Populist Radical Right. *Political Studies* 62(4): 961–970.

Wilson, J. and Swyngedouw, E. (2014) *The Post-Political and Its Discontents: Spaces of Depoliticisation, Spectres of Radical Politics*. Edinburgh: Edinburgh University Press.

PART II

Brexit from the outside

16

BREXIT AND THE COMMONWEALTH

Fantasy meets reality

Peg Murray-Evans

Introduction

In a speech at the inaugural Commonwealth Trade Ministers' Meeting on 9 March 2017, UK Secretary of State for International Trade Liam Fox (2017b) highlighted the Commonwealth's 'vast pool of talent and resources that can help transform the world' and argued that through this organisation 'we – some of the world's oldest and most resilient friendships and partnerships – can provide the leadership that will guarantee the opportunities that the next generation deserve to have'. The launch of a Commonwealth Trade Ministers Meeting and the optimistic tone struck by Fox's speech reflected an important strand in British Eurosceptic discourse in the lead-up to and aftermath of the referendum on UK membership of the European Union (EU) on 23 June 2016. This discourse centred on the idea that reinvigorated economic relations between Britain and its fifty-two former colonies in the Commonwealth could provide a basis for a renewed global role for the UK in the wake of Brexit. Many commentators are quick to dismiss this idea as the 'ultimate Eurosceptic fantasy' (Bagehot's Notebook 2011), pointing out the Common-wealth's fragmentation and diversity, its limited clout on the global stage and its small economic significance to the UK in comparison to the EU. However, this is to underplay the significance of the Commonwealth as part of the ideological driving force of Brexit, as well as its place in the government's vision for a so-called Global Britain.

In this chapter, I argue that a quite specific vision of the role of the Commonwealth in Brit-ain's external economic relations – one that prioritises links with certain old 'friends' while stress-ing the economic opportunities to be found in Commonwealth emerging markets – informs the UK's current approach to the grouping. I suggest that this vision intersects with the material realities of Britain's trade relationships with Commonwealth countries, which have shifted dra-matically since the end of the Second World War and in particular since Britain's accession to the European Economic Community (EEC) in 1973. Significantly, these historic shifts mean that the Commonwealth countries with the biggest ongoing stake in retaining old trading links with the United Kingdom – small developing countries in Africa, the Caribbean and Pacific – are accorded the least emphasis in prominent British discourses about Commonwealth renewal. Tensions between the role of the Commonwealth in UK political discourse and the material realities of trade relations with the group will therefore be played out as the government's post-Brexit trade policy is enacted.

The chapter proceeds in three main sections. The first highlights the important place of the Commonwealth in contemporary Eurosceptic discourse. The second considers trajectories of UK–Commonwealth relations since 1945 in historical perspective. The third brings these two strands together in order to outline the likely future of UK–Commonwealth relations in the context of Brexit. The chapter draws the conclusion that the prominence of the Commonwealth within imaginaries of Brexit and Global Britain is likely to shape UK external relations in important ways but that these will be refracted through existing trajectories of the relationships between the UK and Commonwealth countries, which are in many ways only partially understood by prominent Eurosceptic discourses.

The Commonwealth in Brexit discourse: imagining Global Britain

The Commonwealth as an idea has its origins in the latter part of the nineteenth century when the British Empire began to cede autonomy to Canada, Newfoundland (not yet part of the Canadian Confederation), Australia, South Africa and New Zealand. These territories were granted the status of 'dominions' by the Balfour Declaration in 1926, and the term "British Commonwealth of Nations" was coined to reflect the new independence of parts of the Empire (Dilley 2016). During the early part of the twentieth century, the British Government debated the proper form that economic relations with the Commonwealth should take. Proponents of Britain as a free-trading exemplar argued for an open orientation towards those inside and outside the Commonwealth. Others – most prominently Liberal Unionist Secretary of State for the Commonwealth Joseph Chamberlain – favoured the creation of an "imperial preference" that would exclude those outside the Commonwealth (Kenny and Pearce 2017). Chamberlain's protectionists were defeated (Bell 2017), but the idea of the imperial preference returned and was enacted at the British Empire Economic Conference in 1932, partly in response to the growing global tide of protectionism that came in the wake of the Great Depression. This conference set in place a loose network of bilateral preferences amongst the members of the Commonwealth following the principle "home producers first, Empire producers second, and foreign producers last" (Richardson 1936: 138).

Britain's imperial economic system remained in place in one form or another until the UK joined the EEC in 1973. At this point, the UK had to end the imperial preference system in order to accept the Community's common external tariff. This choice has been framed by prominent Eurosceptics and campaigners for Brexit like Boris Johnson as a moment of "betrayal" (see Murray-Evans 2016), in which associations with Britain's "true friends" (Hannan 2015) in the Commonwealth were abandoned in favour of a future in Europe. This notion of betrayal applied particularly to the old dominions, which had enjoyed privileged access to the UK market even after their independence and would cease to do so as a result of UK accession to the EEC.

This betrayal narrative has been extended to encompass not just the claimed abandonment of Britain's historic friends and allies but also the betrayal of putative long-standing principles and traditions of British foreign economic policy. Britain's imperial history, it is claimed by contemporary Commonwealth enthusiasts, is characterised by a normative commitment to an expansive and ambitious vision of global liberalism, free trade and democracy (see Davis 2016; Fox 2017b). By contrast, the European continent is widely held by British Eurosceptics to embody a political culture that is authoritarian, bureaucratic, statist and protectionist (Kenny and Pearce 2015). Boris Johnson cited "protectionist forces" (cited in Ross et al. 2016) within the European Union as key barriers to free trade on the part of the UK, while Davis (2016) suggested that the UK must be "unshackled" from the EU in order to "focus policy on trading with the wider world." Furthermore, Eurosceptics frequently claim that there is a group of 'Anglosphere' countries that are closer to the UK in terms of political culture and values than the states of continental Europe (Wellings and Baxendale 2015; Kenny and Pearce 2015). This imagined community of English-speaking liberal nations usually includes Australia, Canada, New Zealand and the United States. The notion of the Anglosphere is linked to older British imperial projects based on "race" (Kenny and Pearce 2017) that sought to create an 'imperial federation' or 'Greater Britain' that would include the UK and the 'white' dominions (ibid.; 2017; Wellings 2017; Guardian 2016; Adler-Nissen et al. 2017).

This narrative therefore casts the UK's EU membership as an "aberration" (Hannan 2015) in the context of Britain's long history as a free-trading liberal nation. Further, the invocation of the Commonwealth by British Eurosceptics is not just an expression of imperial nostalgia but is also linked to a forward-looking agenda that seeks to identify economic opportunities for Britain outside the EU (see Wellings 2016, 2017). Here, the argument goes that, in the context of digital communication and cheap air travel, geography is being dissolved while ties of shared language, culture, history and institutions can provide the anchoring for Britain's global role outside the EU (Hannan 2015; Bounds 2016; Roberts 2016). In this way, the Commonwealth is cast as providing an opportunity to not only recoup any trade losses that are incurred as a result of Brexit but to expand Britain's global trading horizons.

The combination of imperial nostalgia and a forward-looking economic agenda within contemporary Commonwealth discourse has also shaped its geographic focus. While the Commonwealth as an institution includes fifty-three states, the focus of Commonwealth discourse in the UK is generally significantly narrower. Most frequently at the centre of this vision are three of the old dominions – Australia, New Zealand and Canada – that are also central to the long-standing British imperial desire to unite the far-flung English-speaking and predominantly white former colonies in a political and economic alliance. More instrumentally, Commonwealth enthusiasts often explicitly invoked other large or relatively developed Commonwealth countries during and after the referendum campaign, alongside the claim that these would provide the markets of the future for UK exports. Here, the most frequently cited country was India, but others like South Africa, Malaysia and Singapore were also prominent. What is clear is that other members of the Commonwealth – in particular the forty mostly very small developing economies in Africa, the Caribbean and Pacific – were accorded significantly lower priority in this narrative than the old dominions and the larger or relatively developed markets within the Commonwealth.

Commonwealth enthusiasm is reflected in the current government's foreign economic policy discourse and practice. From the relative fringes of David Cameron's coalition government from 2010 to 2015, key Commonwealth enthusiasts Boris Johnson, David Davis and Liam Fox were promoted by new Prime Minister Theresa May to the three most important Brexit-oriented ministerial positions in the wake of the referendum – respectively, secretaries of state for Foreign and Commonwealth Affairs, Exiting the European Union and International Trade. May herself also embraced the role of the Commonwealth in her speech launching her vision for 'Global Britain' in January 2017. She referenced the Commonwealth as a marker of Britain's "unique and proud global relationships" as well as the importance to the UK of "close friends and relatives" in Commonwealth countries (May 2017). Meanwhile, the actions of the Department for International Trade (DIT) has thus far largely reflected the selective approach to the Commonwealth that can be identified in Eurosceptic discourse. Secretary of State for International Trade Liam Fox visited Canada, Australia and New Zealand for trade talks in the year after the referendum. He also travelled to India, Singapore and Malaysia. Fox talked up the possibility of free trade agreements with African countries and made promises that developing countries' trading relationships with the UK will not be adversely affected by Brexit (Coates and Leroux 2017), yet these countries appear to be significantly less of a priority when measured in terms of UK ministerial time and travel. Indeed, the first visit to any African, Caribbean or Pacific Common-wealth country by a DIT minister came more than a year after the Brexit vote when Lord Price visited South Africa and Namibia in July 2017 (Department for International Trade 2017b). The key substantive point here is that the Commonwealth is an important part of contemporary Eurosceptic discourse in Britain and that this appears to be shaping the current government's approach to external economic policy, albeit in a way that is uneven and selective.

The UK and the Commonwealth after Empire: historical trajectories

Commonwealth enthusiasts in Britain are often criticised for their romanticised view of Britain's imperial history and their obscuring of its brutality and exploitation. These arguments have been convincingly rehearsed elsewhere (see, inter alia, Andrews 2017; Blitz 2017; Tharoor 2017; Rachman 2017). In this section, I turn instead to the more recent history of UK–Commonwealth relations. Since the end of the Second World War, these relationships have been transformed in ways that do not align with the priorities of Commonwealth enthusiasts previously set out.

The introduction of the imperial preference in 1932, along with the rise of protectionism elsewhere in the world, saw the proportion of British exports destined for the Commonwealth rise from 41 to 47 per cent between 1932 and 1936 (Dilley 2016). With European economies in ruins, British trade with the Commonwealth peaked in the decade immediately after the Second World War (ibid.). However, this was to be the highpoint before a long decline in the significance of the Commonwealth as a British export destination that began even before Britain's accession to the EEC in 1973. New trade opportunities emerged rapidly as Europe was reconstructed. From 1957 – when the Treaty of Rome was signed by the six original members of the EEC – to 1972, the share of British exports destined for the six grew from 14 to 23 per cent. By the same year, exports to the Commonwealth had fallen from their high of 49 per cent in 1953 to just 18 per cent (ibid.). Britain's first application to join the EEC in 1961 was in part prompted by a growing awareness of the limited trade opportunities offered by the Commonwealth and Britain's declining influence in the organisation as its membership widened to include a large number of newly independent states in Africa and Asia (Murray-Evans 2016: 491). Although the fate of the Commonwealth had been a much discussed and contentious issue in the debate about Britain's EEC accession, by the early 1970s it was clear to most observers that there were no real alternatives and that Britain's economic future lay in Europe (Wellings and Baxendale 2015).

The UK's accession to the EEC had differentiated consequences for the members of the Commonwealth (see also Murray-Evans 2016).[1] The Treaty of Rome had established a system of 'association' that granted preferential access to the EEC market to exports from the African former colonies of the six original member states. The six allowed some but not all of the Commonwealth countries to join this arrangement. Australia, Canada and New Zealand were excluded on the grounds of their relative affluence. The six were also concerned about admit-ting the developing countries of the Asian Commonwealth given the size and diversity of the economies of India and Pakistan, which they feared would dilute the benefits of preferences for existing African beneficiaries (Ravenhill 2004: 120; Winand et al. 2015: 105). These countries were also excluded from the apex of the EEC system of preferences but were instead granted less generous preferential market access via the Generalised System of Preferences (GSP) and a series of commercial agreements. The twenty-one Commonwealth countries located in Africa, the Caribbean and Pacific at that time were, however, integrated into the EEC's most generous set of preferences for former colonies, having been deemed to share similar production structures with the existing African associates. The Lomé Convention that set the terms of this relationship in 1975 was at least as generous as the imperial preference, in particular in its granting of one-way preferences to what was now known as the African, Caribbean and Pacific (ACP) group of countries (see Murray-Evans 2016: 492–3).

Discussions of the consequences of UK accession to the EEC for the Commonwealth have tended to focus on the old dominions – in particular, Australia, New Zealand and Canada. For these countries, accession ultimately meant a loss of preferential access to the UK market. However, British accession to the EEC had been on the cards since the early 1960s, and these countries had already begun to diversify their export destinations well before 1973. Between 1964 and 1973, the proportion of exports to the UK had fallen from 49 to 25 per cent in the case of New Zealand, from 21 to 8 per cent in the case of Australia and from 16 to 7 per cent in the case of Canada (Simoes and Hidalgo 2011). In the period since British accession to the EEC, these countries have become progressively more focused on trade with their respective regions. Australia and New Zealand's exports are now strongly concentrated in Asia and the Pacific, while Canada's main export destinations are China and the United States (ibid.). In each case, the UK remains the most important European market for these countries, but at its most significant it absorbs less than 4 per cent of global exports (in the case of New Zealand), while the significance of other EU markets has grown in comparison (ibid.). UK exports to these destinations have also fallen significantly as a proportion of the total, with Canada and Australia now receiving just over 1 per cent of UK exports while only 0.2 per cent is destined for New Zealand.

The Commonwealth countries of South Asia – Bangladesh, India, Pakistan and Sri Lanka – had privileged access to the EEC market under the GSP and a series of commercial arrangements. Yet this did not halt the decline of the UK as an export destination for India. Where the UK received a 20 per cent share of Indian exports in 1964, this had fallen to 10 per cent by 1973 and further to 5.1 per cent by 1985. At the same time, India's new preferential access to the EEC market after 1971 saw exports to other EEC destinations rise. By the 1990s, however, Indian exports to all EU destinations were declining as trade with alternative markets in Asia and the Middle East – and China in particular – began to grow rapidly (ibid.). British exports to India also declined from already low levels in the 1960s to less than 1 per cent in the 1970s. Liberalisation reforms and early signs of increasing GDP growth meant that India began to become an attractive market for Europe in the 1990s. The EU made India a "top priority" in its New Asia Strategy launched in 1994 (Winand et al. 2015: 146) and began negotiations for a 'comprehensive' free trade agreement with India in 2007 but has yet to reach agreement. India's share in the UK's global exports has risen slightly since the early 1990s but by 2015 remained at a lowly 1.3 per cent (Simoes and Hidalgo 2011). The other South Asian Commonwealth countries barely registered as UK export destinations in 2015, each receiving less than 0.2 per cent of UK exports (ibid.). The UK was a rather more important export destination for these countries, receiving 5.6, 9.4 and 9.9 per cent of global exports from Pakistan, Sri Lanka and Bangladesh, respectively, in 2015 (ibid.).[2]

Commonwealth countries in Africa, the Caribbean and Pacific benefitted from the most generous treatment by the EEC after UK accession. The Lomé Convention remained in place until 2000, when, following adverse legal rulings under the GATT, it was replaced by the Cotonou Agreement. This launched negotiations for a series of free trade agreements between the EU and regional groups of ACP countries. The negotiations for these Economic Partnership Agreements (EPAs) proved highly controversial from the perspective of the ACP (see Heron and Murray-Evans 2017). These negotiations have led to a patchwork of trade arrangements across Africa, the Caribbean and Pacific in which some countries and regions have signed EPAs while others make use of unilateral duty-free access to the EU market under a scheme, Everything but Arms (EBA), which is open to UN-designated least developed countries (LDCs) only (see Heron and Murray-Evans 2016). Under these schemes, almost all of the ACP retains preferential access to the EU market in one form or another. The ACP Commonwealth countries have long been of only marginal significance as UK export markets, and, like the old dominions, their significance has declined over the course of the UK's EU membership. In 2015, two of the ACP countries – South Africa and Nigeria – accounted for 0.8 and 0.4 per cent of UK global exports, respectively (Office for National Statistics 2017). The remaining thirty-eight ACP Commonwealth members as a group received less than 1 per cent of total UK exports (ibid.).

Significantly, however, pockets of dependence on the UK as an export market remain amongst ACP Commonwealth countries, at least in part as a result of their ongoing preferential arrangements with the EU. According to the Commonwealth Secretariat (2016: 3), in 2015 the UK absorbed 16 per cent of the goods exports of Commonwealth developing countries. All of the five Commonwealth countries that are most dependent on the UK as an export market – Botswana, Belize, Seychelles, Mauritius and Saint Lucia – are also ACP countries that currently enjoy preferential access to the EU market via an Economic Partnership Agreement (ibid.). In a number of ACP countries, particular sectors or industries have important historic and continuing links to the UK market. These include bananas from Saint Lucia, sugar from Fiji and Belize, vegetables from Kenya and beef from Botswana (ibid.: 8).

The key points from this section are as follows. Despite the claims of Commonwealth enthusiasts that geography has become insignificant in the contemporary global economy, absent the ties of empire, the trade patterns of the UK and its former colonies have for the most part become much more regionally focused. The UK's membership of the EU is, of course, a large part of the explanation for its own increasingly close trade relationship with its neighbours, but the same has also been true for other Commonwealth countries whose reliance on the UK has declined while their focus on trade partners closer to home has become more significant. This is less the case for some of the small developing Commonwealth countries – mostly in Africa, the Caribbean and Pacific – for whom historic trade links with the UK remain more significant, not least because in most cases these countries continue to enjoy preferential access to the UK market via EU trade agreements and preference schemes. The irony of this is that the countries for which Commonwealth linkages remain most materially important are precisely those that are accorded lowest priority in contemporary Eurosceptic Commonwealth discourse.

The UK and the Commonwealth after Brexit

There are many uncertainties about what Brexit will mean for the future of the UK and its relations with the outside world, not least because these external relations will be significantly shaped by the eventual settlement that is arrived at between the UK and the EU. In this section, I make the assumption that the UK will leave the European Single Market and Customs Union and will therefore be able to forge trade agreements with the rest of the world independently of the EU, as well as ceasing to be party to existing EU trade agreements (for a useful explainer on the implications of Customs Union membership for independent trade policy, see Stojanovic 2017). In this section, I draw a series of tentative conclusions about the likely future of relations between the UK and the Commonwealth.

At the Commonwealth Heads of Government Meeting in March 2017, UK ministers briefed the press that they were seeking to "reenergise and revitalise" the grouping (Stone 2017). Yet there are a number of reasons that it is unlikely that the Commonwealth as an institution will become a key organisational unit in global trade or that it will be possible to create a Commonwealth free trade area. The Commonwealth as it currently stands is a large, highly diverse and distant group of countries whose economic ties have dwindled to low levels over the course of the last half-century. Finding common ground amongst this diverse group of developed and developing countries would likely prove difficult – particularly given that members of the group have been on opposite sides of key cleavages within multilateral trade negotiations (see Gallagher 2007). Formal institutionalisation of the Anglosphere bloc is also unlikely given that the primary economic concerns of Canada, Australia and New Zealand lie in their own regions. In a stinging rejection of the Anglosphere idea, former Australian foreign minister Gareth Evans (2016) stated:

> Probably the hardest truth that Britain's Anglosphere dreamers must confront is that there is just no mood politically, in any of the candidate countries of which I am aware, to build some new global association of the linguistically and culturally righteous.

More likely than the creation of a Commonwealth free trade area or a formal Anglosphere association is a drive to deepen the network of bilateral ties that exist between the UK and priority members of the Commonwealth. Writing for the *Daily Express* in March 2017, Trade Minister Liam Fox (2017a) said that the UK was in trade talks with fifteen countries, amongst whom he called Australia and New Zealand "some of our closest allies." New Zealand Trade Minister Todd McClay (2017) also confirmed that he had been told by Fox that Australia and New Zealand would be the "first cab[s] off the ramp" for trade deals with the UK. Canada has also been tipped as one of the first countries with which the UK may be able to agree a trade deal, following talks between Fox and the Canadian Trade Minister Francois Philippe-Champagne in early 2017 (Leroux and Noelke 2017). Here, the existing EU–Canada Comprehensive Economic and Trade Agreement (CETA) could provide a template for a UK–Canada deal. While there remain obstacles to be overcome, all three countries have indicated their openness to a trade deal with the UK, and they appear to offer opportunities for early wins for Fox and his trade negotiating team. However, given the distances involved and small levels of existing trade, it is unlikely that these trade deals will be of huge commercial significance to either side. Other possibilities for early Commonwealth trade agreements are relatively open economies like Malaysia and Singapore (Cleverly and Hewish 2016), but again distances are very large and existing trade volumes very small.

In South Asia, the priority for the UK is clearly India – a huge and rapidly growing economy with which the UK Government sees significant room for trade expansion. On separate occasions, the UK Prime Minister and Chancellor have both visited India since the referendum. However, negotiations here are likely to prove significantly more challenging than with Australia, New Zealand or Canada. Although Eurosceptics have frequently blamed the slow pace of EU trade negotiations with India on other EU member states, reports from members of the European Parliament suggest that British offensive and defensive interests were in fact key obstacles to agreement (Boffey 2017). The two countries' different approaches to trade in services and intellectual property rights are also likely to be sticking points in any future trade negotiations. As the recipient of 3.3 per cent of Indian global exports, the UK market has some importance to India, but probably not enough to give it any huge clout in negotiations. While the UK is a more important export market for other South Asian countries, these seem so far to have been of little priority in the UK's post-Brexit trade plans.

As noted previously, as a result of continuing preferential access to the UK market under EU trade rules and agreements, certain Commonwealth countries in Africa, the Caribbean and the Pacific are amongst the most reliant on historic trade links with the UK. The UK Government has guaranteed that it will secure existing duty-free access to its market for forty-eight LDCs by replicating the EU's EBA scheme (Department for International Trade 2017a), and the necessary legislation for doing this is included in the Taxation (Cross-Border Trade) Bill 2017–19. While the government has also stated that the terms on which all developing countries trade with the UK will stay the same or improve (Coates and Leroux 2017), it is less clear how this will be achieved in the case of non-LDCs that currently have duty and quota-free access to the EU market under EPAs. It is unlikely that the government will unilaterally offer existing levels of market access to these countries because this would leave the UK open to challenge from other developing countries under World Trade Organization rules (see Stevens 2017). The UK could adopt a preference scheme similar to EBA but with eligibility expanded to include all middle-income developing countries, but by including large economies like India, this would erode the advantages of preferences for the existing beneficiaries. The government indicates in its 2017 trade white paper that its preferred option for a trade policy–independent UK is to seek to replicate the existing EPAs between the EU and ACP countries (Department for International Trade 2017c: 32). The task of renegotiating these reciprocal free trade agreements could be complicated by a number of factors, including varying levels of dependence on trade with the UK amongst ACP countries and the complexities of ACP regional configurations (Murray-Evans 2017). If the government is to avoid "being in the odd position of having worse trading terms with these Commonwealth countries than the EU does" (Fraser 2017), then action needs to be taken to address these complications immediately. Given that DIT's focus seems largely to be elsewhere in the Commonwealth, it is not clear that this will happen, although pressure from UK development NGOs and ACP Commonwealth countries them-selves, as well as a forthcoming inquiry into trade with Commonwealth developing countries by the House of Commons International Trade Committee (HOC International Trade Com-mittee 2017), may help to force the issue. In this way, the countries accorded least attention in Eurosceptic Commonwealth discourse will need to become more central if Britain is to avoid not only damaging its reputation within the group but also causing material harm to a number of its members.

Conclusion

The Commonwealth was a prominent feature of Eurosceptic discourse in the lead-up to and aftermath of the June 2016 referendum on UK membership of the EU. The contemporary Eurosceptic narrative about the Commonwealth blends two central strands. The first is nostalgia for the old ties of Empire and in particular Britain's perceived affinities and friendship with the old dominions, especially Australia, New Zealand and Canada. The second is a forward-looking agenda that seeks to identify economic opportunities for Britain that would apparently come from rediscovering ties of history, language, culture and institutions with important markets around the world. These aspects of the discourse have shaped a selective geographic focus, which centres on the old dominions and larger, relatively developed or emerging Commonwealth economies that are thought to present good economic opportunities as export markets for the UK. This, in turn has shaped DIT's priorities in seeking to create new trade links with Com-monwealth countries.

This geographic focus, however, belies material changes in Commonwealth economic rela-tionships that have taken place since decolonisation and UK accession to the EEC. Trade ties between the UK and the old dominions have dwindled to low levels, while in all of these countries exports have become more concentrated in markets closer to home. Likewise, trade between the UK and large developing Commonwealth economies like India has fallen over this period, with only a small recent increase in UK exports to India as a result of the country's rapid economic rise since the 1990s. Meanwhile, the countries for whom old Commonwealth ties remain most materially important are those that tend to receive least attention from Eurosceptic Commonwealth enthusiasts, namely Commonwealth African, Caribbean and Pacific countries that currently receive preferential access to the EU market and that continue to rely on these preferences for exports in certain key sectors.

Future UK relations with the Commonwealth are therefore likely to be shaped by both the imaginaries of the Commonwealth that animate aspects of the Eurosceptic agenda and by the material realities of the historical trajectories of economic relations with the Commonwealth. Close political ties and a shared liberal economic outlook – plus prioritisation by DIT – may make the negotiation of free trade agreements with Canada, Australia and New Zealand relatively quick wins. Yet given the low levels of existing trade between the UK and these partners and the huge distances involved, such deals will not compensate for new trade barriers with Europe that may emerge as a result of Brexit. Negotiations with key emerging markets like India are likely to be significantly more difficult. The decline of the UK's significance as an export market means that it has nothing like the material leverage in relation to India that it once did, while major differences over key trade issues would have to be overcome to reach a deal. Given the low priority accorded to the Commonwealth countries of Africa, the Caribbean and Pacific, the UK has yet to engage fully with the complexities that will need to be addressed in order to avoid a loss of market access for these countries as a result of Brexit. In the light of the threat of material damage to these economies, however, the government may yet be forced to sit up and take notice.

Notes

1 For reasons of space, I concentrate here on three main groups of Commonwealth countries – the old dominions, the South Asian Commonwealth countries, and the African, Caribbean and Pacific countries.
2 All trade data gathered from Simoes and Hidalgo (2011).

References

Adler-Nissen, R., Galpin, C. and Rosamond, B. (2017) Performing Brexit: How a Post-Brexit World Is Imagined outside the United Kingdom. *British Journal of Politics and International Relations* 19(3): 1–19. New York: SAGE Journals.

Andrews, K. (2017) Building Brexit on the Myth of Empire Ignores Our Brutal History. *The Guardian*, March 7. Available at: www.theguardian.com/commentisfree/2017/mar/07/building-brexit-on-myth-of-empire-ignores-history-at-our-peril [Accessed November 5, 2017].

Bagehot's Notebook (2011) The Ultimate Eursceptic Fantasy: Putting Faith in the Commonwealth. *The Economist*, October 30. Available at: www.economist.com/blogs/bagehot/2011/10/britain-and-eu-3 [Accessed January 18, 2017].

Bell, D. (2017) The Anglosphere: New Enthusiasm for an Old Dream. *Prospect*, January 19. Available at: www.prospectmagazine.co.uk/magazine/anglosphere-old-dream-brexit-role-in-the-world [Accessed January 18, 2017].

Blitz, J. (2017) Post-Brexit Delusions about Empire 2.0. *Financial Times*, March 7. Available at: www.ft.com/content/bc29987e-034e-11e7-ace0-1ce02ef0def9 [Accessed January 18, 2017].

Boffey, D. (2017) Brexit Could Help EU Strike Free Trade with India, MEPs Believe. *Guardian*, February 23, 2017. Available at: www.theguardian.com/politics/2017/feb/23/brexit-could-help-eu-strike-free-trade-deal-india-meps [Accessed January 18, 2017].

Bounds, A. (2016) UK Entering a Post-Geography Trading World' says Liam Fox. *Financial Times*, September 29. Available at: www.ft.com/content/e456c008-8642-11e6-8897-2359a58ac7a5 [Accessed January 18, 2017].

Cleverly, J. and Hewish, T. (2016) Reconnecting with the Commonwealth: The UK's Free Trade Opportunities. *Free Enterprise Group*, January 10, 2017. Available at: www.tralac.org/news/article/11055-re-connecting-with-the-commonwealth-the-uk-s-free-trade-opportunities.html [Accessed November 5, 2017].

Coates, S. and Leroux, M. (2017) Ministers Aim to Build 'Empire 2.0' with African Commonwealth. *The Times*, March 6. Available at: www.thetimes.co.uk/article/ministers-aim-to-build-empire-2-0-with-african-commonwealth-after-brexit-v9bs6f6z9 [Accessed November 5, 2017].

Commonwealth Secretariat (2016) Brexit and Commonwealth Trade. *Commonwealth Trade Policy Briefing*. London, November. Available at: http://thecommonwealth.org/sites/default/files/news-items/documents/BrexitPolicyBrief18112016.PDF [Accessed November 5, 2017].

Davis, D. (2016) Brexit: What Would It Look Like? Speech on Brexit at the Institute of Chartered Engineers. Available at: www.daviddavismp.com/david-davis-speech-on-brexit-at-the-institute-of-chartered-engineers/ [Accessed August 9, 2016].

Department for International Trade (2017a) Government Pledges to Help Improve Access to Uk Markets for World's Poorest Countries Post Brexit. Available at: www.gov.uk/government/news/government-pledges-to-help-improve-access-to-uk-markets-for-worlds-poorest-countries-post-brexit [Accessed August 9, 2016].

Department for International Trade (2017b) Lord Price Visits Africa to Build Shared Trading Links. Available at: www.gov.uk/government/news/lord-price-visits-africa-to-build-shared-trading-links [Accessed August 9, 2016].

Department for International Trade (2017c) Preparing for Our Future UK Trade Policy. Available at: www.gov.uk/government/publications/preparing-for-our-future-uk-trade-policy [accessed December 30, 2017].

Dilley, A. (2016) The Commonwealth Is Not an Alternative to the EU for Britain. *The Conversation*, April 8. Available at: http://theconversation.com/the-commonwealth-is-not-an-alternative-to-the-eu-for-britain-57009 [Accessed August 12, 2016].

Evans, G. (2016) Brexit: Anglosphere Dreamers Are Wrong to Dump Europe. *The Australian*, February 23. Available at: www.theaustralian.com.au/opinion/brexit-anglosphere-dreamers-are-wrong-to-dump-europe/news-story/28508435d2f7496c1543c68836bfbcbc [Accessed January 18, 2018].

Fox, L. (2017a) Britain Is the Champion of Free Trade and I'm in Talks with 15 Countries. *Daily Express*, March 27. Available at: www.express.co.uk/comment/expresscomment/784073/great-britain-trade-agreements-global-free-liam-fox-comment [Accessed January 18, 2018].

Fox, L. (2017b) Commonwealth Trade Ministers Meeting: Towards a Free Trading Future. Speech at the First Commonwealth Trade Ministers' Meeting, March 9. London.

Fraser, S. (2017) Bracing Ourselves for Brexit. *Chatham House*, April and May. Available at: www.chathamhouse.org/publications/twt/bracing-ourselves-brexit [Accessed July 18, 2017].

Gallagher, K.P. (2007) Understanding Developing Country Resistance to the Doha Round. *Review of International Political Economy* 15(1): 62.

The Guardian (2016) The Guardian View on the EU Debate: It's about Much More Than Migration. June 1. Available at: www.theguardian.com/commentisfree/2016/jun/01/the-guardian-view-on-the-eu-debate-its-about-much-more-than-migration [Accessed January 18, 2018].

Hannan, D. (2015) Forget the EU: Let's Take on the World with Our True Friends. *Daily Mail*, January 23. Available at: www.dailymail.co.uk/news/article-2922715/Forget-EU-let-s-world-TRUE-friends-Greek-elections-threaten-shatter-Europe-DANIEL-HANNAN-says-Britain-s-destiny-lies-booming-Commonwealth.html [Accessed January 18, 2018].

Heron, T. and Murray-Evans, P. (2016) Regional Encounters: Explaining the Divergent Responses to the EU's Support for Regional Integration in Africa, the Caribbean and Pacific. *Third World Thematics* 1(4): 470–489.

Heron, T. and Murray-Evans, P. (2017) Limits to Market Power: Strategic Discourse and Institutional Path Dependence in the EU–ACP Economic Partnership Agreements. *European Journal of International Relations* 23(2): 341–364.

HOC International Trade Committee (2017) *International Trade Committee Launches Inquiry into Trade with Developing Countries*. Available at: https://www.parliament.uk/business/committees/committees-a-z/commons-select/international-trade-committee/news-parliament-2017/trade-and-the-commonwealth-developing-countries-launch-17-19/ [Accessed December 30, 2017].

Kenny, M. and Pearce, N. (2015) The Rise of the Anglosphere: How the Right Dreamed Up a New Conservative World Order. *New Statesman*, February 10. Available at: www.newstatesman.com/politics/2015/02/rise-anglosphere-how-right-dreamed-new-conservative-world-order [Accessed January 18, 2018].

Kenny, M. and Pearce, N. (2017) The Empire Strikes Back. *New Statesman*, January 23. Available at: www.newstatesman.com/politics/uk/2017/01/empire-strikes-back [Accessed January 18, 2018].

Leroux, M. and Noelke, P.D. (2017) Canada Tipped as First Brexit Trade Partner. *The Times*, February 15, 2017. Available at: www.thetimes.co.uk/article/canada-tipped-as-first-brexit-trade-partner-5bq9606xf [Accessed January 18, 2018].

May, T. (2017) The Government's Negotiating Objectives for Exiting the EU. *PM Speech*, January 27.

McClay, T. (2017) Pleased to Confirm with @LiamFoxMP NZ along with Australia Will Be First Counties to Get FTA with UK Following Brexit. Available at: https://twitter.com/toddmcclaymp/status/840306636107390976 [Accessed July 26, 2017].

Murray-Evans, P. (2016) Myths of Commonwealth Betrayal: UK–Africa Trade before and after Brexit. *The Round Table* 105(5): 489–498.

Murray-Evans, P. (2017) Brexit Risks Harming African Economies That Trade with the UK. *Sheffield Political Economy Research Institute*, July 27. Available at: http://speri.dept.shef.ac.uk/2017/07/27/brexit-risks-harming-african-economies-that-trade-with-the-uk/ [Accessed July 27, 2017].

Office for National Statistics (2017) Commonwealth Trade in Focus as UK Prepares for Brexit. Available at: http://visual.ons.gov.uk/commonwealth-trade-in-focus-as-uk-prepares-for-brexit/ [Accessed July 14, 2017].

Rachman, G. (2017) Brexit Reinforces Britain's Imperial Amnesia. *Financial Times*, March 27. Available at: www.ft.com/content/e3e32b38-0fc8-11e7-a88c-50ba212dce4d [Accessed January 18, 2018].

Ravenhill, J. (2004) Back to the Nest? Europe's Relations with the African Caribbean and Pacific Group of Countries. In: Aggarwal, V.K. and Fogarty, E.A. (eds.), *EU Trade Strategies: Between Regionalism and Globalism*. London: Palgrave Macmillan.

Richardson, H.J. (1936) *British Foreign Economic Policy*. New York: MacMillan.

Roberts, A. (2016) CANZUK: After Brexit, Canada, Australia, New Zealand and Britain Can Unite as a Pillar of Western Civilisation. *The Telegraph*, September 13. Available at: www.telegraph.co.uk/news/2016/09/13/canzuk-after-brexit-canada-australia-new-zealand-and-britain-can/ [Accessed January 18, 2018].

Ross, T., McCann, K. and Holehouse, M. (2016) Michael Gove and Boris Johnson Tell David Cameron: You've Deceived Public on Economy. *The Telegraph*, June 5. Available at: www.telegraph.co.uk/news/2016/06/04/michael-gove-and-boris-johnson-tell-david-cameron-youve-deceived/ [Accessed November 6, 2017].

Simoes, A.J.G. and Hidalgo, C.A. (2011) The Economic Complexity Observatory: An Analytical Tool for Understanding the Dynamics of Economic Development. Workshops at the Twenty-Fifth AAAI Conference on Artificial Intelligence 2011.

Stevens, C. (2017) Poor Country Trade with the UK: Brexit Winners and Losers. *Shaping Policy for Development*, April 5. Available at: www.odi.org/comment/10507-poor-country-trade-uk-brexit-winners-and-losers [Accessed July 18, 2017].

Stojanovic, A. (2017) Five Things to Know about a Customs Union. *Institute For Government*, July 5. Available at: www.instituteforgovernment.org.uk/blog/five-things-know-about-customs-union [Accessed July 17, 2017].

Stone, J. (2017) Theresa May to Use Commonwealth Meeting Months before Brexit to Push Closer Trade Ties. *The Independent*, March 13. Available at: www.independent.co.uk/news/uk/politics/eu-brexit-commonwealth-free-trade-meeting-2018-uk-london-chair-a7625791.html [Accessed July 18, 2017].

Tharoor, I. (2017) Brexit and Britain's Delusions of Empire. *Washington Post*, March 31. Available at: www.washingtonpost.com/news/worldviews/wp/2017/03/31/brexit-and-britains-delusions-of-empire/ [Accessed July 18, 2017].

Wellings, B. (2016) Our Island Story: England, Europe and the Anglosphere Alternative. *Political Studies Review* 14(3): 368–377.

Wellings, B. (2017) The Anglosphere in the Brexit Referendum. *Revue Française de Civilisation Britannique* 22(2): 1–14.

Wellings, B. and Baxendale, H. (2015) Euroscepticism and the Anglosphere: Traditions and Dilemmas in Contemporary English Nationalism. *Journal of Common Market Studies* 52(1): 123–139.

Winand, P., Vicziany, M. and Datar, P. (2015) *The European Union and India: Rhetoric or Meaningful Partnership*. Cheltenham: Edward Elgar.

17

BREXIT AND BRITAIN'S ROLE IN THE WORLD

Oliver Daddow

Introduction

Content analysis carried out during (Centre for Research in Communication and Culture 2016) and after (Moore and Ramsay 2017: 27) the Brexit referendum has revealed that discussion about Britain's world role, including the foreign and defence implications, played out on the margins of the campaign. Economic considerations drove the arguments on each side. The Remain campaign's 'project fear' (Daddow 2016) came up against the Leave campaign's desire to 'take back control'. Both, however, put financial matters at the heart of their discourse. 'Britain Stronger in Europe' accented the benefits membership of the Single Market gave Britain in terms of trade, jobs and prices, plus workers' rights (Britain Stronger in Europe 2016). VoteLeave, famously, publicised on the side of its battle bus that Britain could spend £350 million per week more on the National Health Service if it left the EU. This was nested within arguments about border control, immigration, sovereignty and global trade prospects beyond Europe, particularly with the Commonwealth (Vote Leave 2016).[1]

This reflected a long, historically constituted tradition of many in Britain seeing Europe not so much as an ideal to be cherished but as an arena purely for safeguarding vital British interests (Liddle 2014). The instrumentalist vision of European integration dominated British discourse right back to the period when Britain joined the European Economic Community (EEC) in 1973 (for instance CMND. 4715 1971: 7–11). Governments through the 1980s, 1990s and 2000s continued to sell 'Europe' to the British public on economic grounds (Daddow 2011). This, along with a short and often acrimonious 2016 referendum campaign, meant that even at a turning point in British history, many key issues, such as Britain's world role, were skated over. The period since the referendum has, by contrast, offered up ample opportunity for people to engage with the issues in a more sustained manner. What was below the surface before the election (for instance Foreign Affairs Committee 2016; Kleine 2016) suddenly gained in prominence because Brexit posed all sorts of unexpected policy dilemmas. In terms of the world role, the challenge was to explain how Britain would fulfil its historically destined great power role *outside* the EU instead, as after 1973, from inside. Brexit thus prompted the May government to espouse a new ambition for a 'Global Britain' (hereafter without speech marks) that would bring to fruition decades of global economic potential stymied by membership of the European club. The origins, nature and contestations around the concept of Global Britain provide the focus for this chapter.

The chapter opens by analysing the key ruling narrative of British foreign policy – Winston Churchill's 'three circles' model – which it pinpoints as, still, the first port of call for elite thinking on Britain's world role because it gets to the heart of a long-running debate between supporters of 'limited liability' and proponents of 'continental commitment'. Next, it explores the idea of Global Britain, which responds to Brexit – withdrawal from the Europe circle – by scaling up British involvement in the Commonwealth and Anglosphere circles. The synergies with the Churchill model, it is suggested, are plainly evident. Finally, it identifies two waves of criticism that were levelled against Global Britain: one dealing with the desirability of Global Britain, the other with its achievability, especially on trade, defence and security. The argument pursued is that 'leaving' the Europe circle has not encouraged much in the way of novel policy thinking, despite the branding. May has rebadged British foreign policy for the Brexit age, but beneath the rhetoric lies an aspiration to greatness and exceptionalism (on which Tilford 2017) of a much older vintage (for more on exceptionalism, see Chapter 11). Global Britain is, and will remain, a highly contested ambition for Britain's future world role, if it can be realized at all. Articulated at a particularly febrile time in British history, even a fully thought through articulation of Global Britain would have elicited strong opposition. When the terms of Britain's exit from the EU are not yet even known, such a proposition seems speculative at best (see Wintour 2018).

Part 1: Churchill's three circles and Britain's world role

There is a wealth of literature exploring the theory and concept of a nation's 'world role', detailed consideration of which is beyond the remit of this chapter (usefully, McCourt 2014: 19–57). Three features of that literature help us grasp the connections between world role thinking and Brexit. First, a role is constructed through foreign policy practices, which have two components. One is material: the output of foreign policy decisions contained in legislation, diplomacy, including the Brexit negotiations in Brussels, multilateral bargaining and, sometimes, 'hard' interventions or invasions. The other component is ideational: the accompanying narratives that explain and legitimize the exercise of state agency by defining the identity and interests of the people on whose behalf the nation is acting. These are found in statements, press conferences, policy speeches, policy documents and other official communications, in which Britain is constituted and branded as an international actor (Daddow 2011).

Second, a state's foreign policy practices can reveal a lot about the identity a state is trying to express internationally. This is the 'negotiated' aspect of a nation's role. It encompasses 'expectations about Britain's likely and appropriate behaviour in international politics', which are evident in Britain's 'institutional membership, alliance commitments, and the specific forms these take' (McCourt 2011: 34). Brexit represents a choice to opt out of a previously settled – if not wholly unchallenged – 'European' role, bringing with it material as well as ideational dilemmas. Third, foreign policy narratives support current policy choices by blending past, present and future in complex ways. They are often strongly positioned, normatively speaking, affording salience to some episodes over others, (in Britain's case, the memory of 'Dunkirk', for instance). As we shall see in what follows, thinking on the nation's world role combines aspects of what Britain *has been* as a global actor, reflections on what Britain *is* as a global actor and finally what Britain *should* be in the future.

To explore the impact of world role thinking on British foreign policy practices, this section foregrounds the iconic figure of Winston Churchill, wartime leader 1940–1945 and peacetime Prime Minister 1951–1955. In making this selection, the chapter draws on research not only in Britain but also in the United States and globally (Toye 2008; Daddow and Gaskarth 2014) that has repeatedly demonstrated that Churchill has been and remains a touchstone source of thinking on Britain's world role (for instance Deighton 2002; Hill 2010; Harvey 2011). The year 2017 alone saw the release of two major cinema films about Churchill. His three circles model of British foreign policy 'set the context for British foreign policy in the decades after the war' (Wallace 1992: 432). It is assumed in this chapter that Churchill's model has been 'the accepted conceptual prism through which Britain's external relations are thought about, deliberated upon and executed' by the British foreign policy establishment since its elaboration in 1948 (Daddow and Gaskarth 2011: 13). This section will therefore put the case that there was good reason why Churchill featured heavily in the Brexit referendum: he is the source of thinking on British foreign policy for many elites and in civil society alike.

First elaborated at the Conservative Party conference in 1948, Churchill's idea was that Britain occupied an exceptional position in world affairs because it operated at the intersection of three great circles of power and influence. The first circle, 'naturally', was the British Commonwealth and Empire, which he described as 'the foundation of our [Conservative] Party's political belief'. The second circle was 'the English-speaking world in which we, Canada, and the other British Dominions play so important a part'. This was, in effect, the Anglosphere circle, including countries such as the United States, Australia and New Zealand. The third circle – note the ordering – was 'United Europe' (Churchill 1948: 153).

There are two connections to be drawn between Churchill's three models and Brexit. First, Churchill's model wrestled with two historical traditions, which competed for dominance over British foreign policy from the sixteenth century onward. One tradition was that of 'limited liability', whereby Britain would act as a balancer to continental threats by operating outside European structures. As the European balancer for several centuries, England/Britain sought to 'to prevent others from disturbing the peace and endangering the security of states' (Giovanni Botero, quoted in Wright 1975: 20). Moreover, it kept 'a Cyclopean eye to her own aggrandizement' (Richard Cobden, quoted in Wright 1975: 113). In other words, the balance was struck for both economic and security reasons. The rival tradition was exemplified by those propounding a firmer 'continental commitment' to Europe, which would see Britain involve itself in the machinations of European diplomacy from within. As scholars of British foreign policy have found, historically, the former position had won out more often than the latter (Crowson 2011; Grob-Fitzgibbon 2016: 49). Brexit in this light can be interpreted as the latest victory for the 'limited liability' approach to British foreign policy, following decades of a 'continental commitment'.

The second point is much less well noticed, let alone discussed. It is that Churchill wrote an essential ambiguity about Britain's approach to Europe directly into his three circles model. He was comfortable about Britain operating actively at the heart of the two other circles: Empire and the English-speaking peoples. By contrast, things in the European circle were not so clear-cut. He extolled the virtues of a United Europe *and* held the view that the British should not be constrained by operating fully inside that European entity. As he said in 1930: 'we have our own dream and our own task. We are with Europe, but not of it. We are linked but not comprised. We are interested and associated but not absorbed' (quoted in Crowson, 2011: 31). Responding to Robert Schuman's 1950 proposal to create a European Coal and Steel Community (ECSC), the newly elected prime minister reminded his Cabinet that: 'Our attitude is that we help, we dedicate, we participate, but we do not merge and we do not forfeit our insular or Commonwealth character'. Churchill's view was, crucially, shared by large swathes of the elite and public at this time. The consensus included the top echelon of the Labour Party, which was as suspicious as Churchill was of making a continental commitment in the 1950s. For example, discussing the ECSC in 1950, Labour Foreign Secretary Ernest Bevin remarked that Britain had a different 'character' from European nations, making it 'fundamentally incapable of wholehearted integration with them' (quoted in Grob-Fitzgibbon 2016: 116).

In many ways, the untold story of Brexit is the struggle by British elites to reconcile the ambiguous place occupied by 'Europe' in Churchill's model of British foreign policy. Churchill's model actively avoided resolving the dilemma between 'limited liability' and 'continental commitment'. The point, though, is that it *seemed to* have resolved it. It gave something to both proponents and opponents of a place for Britain at the heart of a supranational Europe. Read one way, Churchill was the 'authentic' voice of British Conservatism who viewed continental entanglements with distaste (Holmes 1994). Led by Leave big hitter and biographer of Churchill, Boris Johnson, it was a simple step for Leave campaigners to co-opt Churchill to their side as someone who fought for British democracy and the 'special relationship' outside the confines of Europe (notably Johnson 2016). As the *Express* showed with its article of 2 June 2017: "'We are with them, but not of them!" Even Sir Winston Churchill opposed membership of EU'. Churchill's 'with but not of' quotation was used to introduce a story about the former prime minister on his hospital bed in 1962. Asked by Montgomery of Alamein whether he would have taken Britain into the European Economic Community (EEC), the ailing Churchill reportedly said, 'No!', accompanied by some colourful language (Maddox 2016).

Read another way, however, Churchill was a supporter of a United States of Europe and the European Movement more widely (Daddow 2004: 78–79). Remainers, therefore, mobilized Churchill's memory to caution against Brexit. In response to Boris Johnson's article just discussed, David Cameron warned about the dangers of Britain slipping into isolation. Churchill, Cameron said, had 'argued passionately for Western Europe to come together' (Cameron 2016). In a helpful piece of choreography, Cameron was followed a day later by Churchill's grandson Nicholas Soames saying his grandfather would have backed Remain (Watt 2016).

To draw this section to a close, the polarized memories of Churchill summoned up during the Brexit referendum reflects the fact that British policy towards the Europe circle was always the most ambiguous, both in Churchill's own mind and in the practice of British foreign policy going back centuries. The exercise of British agency in all the circles has been contested at different points in time as anti-colonial views and criticisms of Britain's 'slavish' subservience to the United States both attest. However, the Europe circle has been the subject of most dispute. Even inside the EEC/EU from 1973, British leaders never managed to convince the British public of the merits of a European future. It may not be sufficient to explain the Brexit vote alone, because so much else went on during the campaign. Yet, thinking on British exceptionalism provided important background framing for the identity, economic and sovereignty concerns that dominated the debate at the level of rhetoric. The next section will explore how the vote to leave Europe impacted on thinking about Britain's role in the world via May's concept of Global Britain.

Part 2: From Churchill's three circles to May's Global Britain

Winston Churchill's three circles model provided an elegant account of Britain's supposedly unique world role after the Second World War. It appealed to generations of Britons literally schooled on Britain's status as the globally pre-eminent imperial power in the nineteenth century and then the closest ally of the United States from the middle of the twentieth century. After the Second World War, Europe was held at arm's length to promote Britain's freedom of movement in the other two circles. This was not simply a Churchill or Conservative 'thing'. Labour leaders from Attlee onward accepted that Britain should stand apart from Europe, mainly to protect British sovereignty. In this, they were in line with British public opinion (Grob-Fitzgibbon 2016: 75). Some changes of tone aside, there was little substantive difference between Labour and the Conservatives on the main points of European integration. As a result, Britain was kept on the fringes as a powerful but largely disinterested observer of Europe's early attempts at unity. Within the space of a few years, however, Europe had became the sine qua non of consolidating Britain's status as a great global power. The period around Britain's initial decision to join the EEC is thus highly telling. It will be studied now, prior to an elaboration of May's Global Britain, enabling a comparison to be made between discourse and practice at two historical turning points in British foreign policy.

As early as 1956 – prior to the Suez debacle, which compelled an even more thoroughgoing overhaul – Conservative Prime Minister Anthony Eden had initiated an official review of Britain's world role. Its objective was to discover how to sustain for Britain 'an effective role in world affairs'. At this point, Eden still judged Empire to be, unequivocally, the source of Britain's global prestige. By contrast, Foreign Secretary Selwyn Lloyd downgraded Empire below 'co-operation with Western Europe' (cited in Grob-Fitzgibbon 2016: 208–209 and 221). Within Cabinet, proponents of 'limited liability' were already locked in a battle with those supporting the 'continental commitment'. The decisive shift in the direction of the latter approach did not come until Eden's successor as Conservative Prime Minister Harold Macmillan delivered his 'wind of change' speech at Cape Town in February 1960. The speech reflected on the growth of 'national consciousness' and independence movements around Africa, as well as the ways in which British foreign policy could more effectively take account of them (Macmillan 1960).

Shortly after the speech, Macmillan asked the Treasury – tellingly, still the lead department making British European policy – to review the fundamentals of British European policy. Its report 'caused the cabinet to seriously debate British entry into the EEC for the first time' (Grob-Fitzgibbon 2016: 257). The first British application to the EEC was launched in July 1961 on the back of the Treasury's evidence that Western Europe was booming, the Commonwealth was in decline and, not least, the United States strongly favoured a British move on Europe. Washington elites had been communicating this behind the scenes for many years. Occasionally they went public, very painfully as far as British sensibilities were concerned (Brinkley 1990). US backing became yoked to Whitehall's discovery of the materiality of British economic decline to push the Europe circle to the forefront of British Government thinking.

When Macmillan addressed the Conservative Party conference at Llandudno in autumn 1962, he was adamant: 'Britain in Europe will have a double influence, both as a European country and one of world-wide interests. Britain's power and value to the other Commonwealth countries, old and new, will be greatly enhanced' (quoted in Grob-Fitzgibbon 2016: 295). Macmillan's successors continued to use a scaled-up European circle as a prop to Britain's great power pretensions. The list is a long one, including more pro-European leaders such as Edward Heath and Tony Blair (Daddow 2011: 217–229), along with more reluctant but pragmatic Europeanists such as Harold Wilson (Daddow 2003), Margaret Thatcher and David Cameron (Daddow 2013). The crux – and a marked point of comparison with May's Global Britain – is that the emphasis on Britain's global leadership ambitions survived what in all other regards was a major turning point in British foreign policy in 1973. EEC entry was, indeed, sold as 'more of the same but in a new setting': strategic continuity necessitating a tactical shift in the ordering of the three circles was the mantra. As Heath proclaimed in a speech marking Britain's signature of the EEC accession treaty in January 1972, British values chimed with European values. 'Britain, with her Commonwealth links, has also much to contribute to the universal nature of Europe's responsibilities' (Heath 1972). In Europe, Heath assured his audience, Britain could fulfil the role assigned to it by Churchill.

Just as at the point of entry, the pattern repeated it at moment of departure, even if we might have expected Brexit to stimulate an even more fundamental review of Britain's role in the world. Perhaps because of the confusion over the precise form and content of Brexit, however, the May government did not seize the opportunity to bring vision in line with policy reality. Elite rhetoric fell back on the tried and trusted trope of continuity, the aim being to buttress Britain's global leadership role, now by 'taking back control' of Britain's borders and political economy. In this respect, the mirror image in terms of *tactic* should not cloud the fact that the *strategy* remained consistent. Heath argued that Britain's global influence would best be attained through a leadership role in Europe (Europe as modernity and the future), while May argued that Europe was now holding Britain back from achieving that same destiny (Europe as anachronistic past). Her view was encapsulated in the idea of Global Britain as the 'new' route for Britain to maintain an elevated world role.

May spelled out her plans for Global Britain in a speech at Lancaster House, London, on 17 January 2017 (all quotes in this paragraph from May [2017]). For May, Brexit meant the UK will be 'best friend and neighbour to our European partners, but a country that reaches beyond the borders of Europe too'. The UK, she said, would go 'out into the world to build relationships with old allies and new friends alike'. May implicitly agreed with Churchill, that Britain was 'with but not of' Europe: 'It remains overwhelmingly and compellingly in Britain's national interest that the EU should succeed'. However, there were irreconcilable differences marking Britain apart from the EU. First, many in Britain felt European immersion came at the expense of Britain's global connections, especially 'free trade with the wider world'. Second, Britain's political traditions differed too much. The British had a suspicion of written constitutions and a strong concern with sovereignty, were befuddled by the idea of coalition government (ironically perhaps, given the recent history of the Coalition Government, 2010–2015), and viewed the EU's supranational institutions with distaste because they 'sit very uneasily in relation to our political history and way of life'. The prime minister spent the rest of the speech outlining her twelve-point plan for Brexit, which at the time of writing remains up for grabs. The negotiations are covered elsewhere in this volume and will therefore not be covered here.

Top members of the Conservative Cabinet fleshed out the Global Britain idea in a series of speeches that expanded on May's Lancaster House speech. For example, then Secretary of State for International Development Priti Patel told Commonwealth Trade Ministers on 9 March 2017 that 'it is time for Britain to rediscover our place as a champion of global trade'. For Patel, Britain's promotion of free trade went hand in hand with its mission to enhance global development, alleviate poverty and enhance national self-determination. The political corollary of free trade came at the end of the speech. Patel subscribed to the theory that '[t]rading nations are less likely to be warring nations'. Much as the Europeanists spoke about the EU as creating a liberal zone of peace in Europe, Patel felt the Commonwealth could perform the same function, using economic ties to bind states together in cooperative webs of relations (all from Patel 2017).

Earlier the same day, Secretary of State for International Trade Liam Fox told Commonwealth ministers that Brexit represented an opportunity for Britain to realize its free trade vision dating back to the eighteenth century. The Commonwealth was a central plank in the strategy because it was home to 'a vast pool of talent and resources that can help transform the world'. Like May and Patel, Fox spoke against protectionism and universalized British values. Significantly for this chapter, he suggested: 'There is not only an economic but a moral dimension to our mission' (Fox 2017). Poverty reduction and the sharing of wealth within the Commonwealth were, for Fox, the platforms on which Britain could 'provide the leadership' required to safeguard 'our own security and prosperity'.

Between them, the words of May, Patel and Fox show how Global Britain blended elements of altruism with hard-headed concerns to secure British interests, economically, politically and strategically. Where Heath justified EEC entry as Britain's route to the future, the May government depicted EU exit as the precursor to Britain rediscovering its *true* world role, one of a much older, Churchillian vintage. The next section will review the main arguments made against the concept of Global Britain as a post-Brexit role in the world for Britain.

Part 3: 'Slightly smaller than Oregon': critical assessments of Global Britain

Criticism of Global Britain has come in two waves. Although there are elements of overlap between them we will split them up for the purposes of analysis. It is also important to point out that we are focusing here on the criticisms, but some commentators, not to mention the government proponents previously considered (for example, Fox 2018), remain extremely positive about the future for Britain's global trade options outside the EU (*The Spectator* 2017). There was a certain breezy optimism on the part of prominent Leavers such as Boris Johnson and David Davis, who maintained throughout the Brexit negotiations that Global Britain would be achieved and that it would make Britain more prosperous (Winders 2016). Brexit, in the official view, represented a 'golden opportunity to forge a new role for ourselves in the world' (Fox 2016).

The first wave of criticisms crystallized after the 2016 referendum, when it became known that Whitehall civil servants were, cynically, referring to Global Britain as 'Empire 2.0'. For first wave critics, the question was, '*Should* Britain be doing this?' Writing in *The Guardian*, David Olusoga called May's foreign policy vision a 'dangerous nostalgia' built on 'neo-colonial fantasy' (Olusoga 2017). Boris Johnson's paean to a benign, 'force for good' Empire could not gloss over the fact that, for many, Empire was and still is experienced as a place where Britain exercised coercive, repressive power. Imperial greatness was, in this interpretation, built on 'murder and plunder', an uncomfortable counter-narrative not well publicized in Britain (Kappal 2017; Tilford 2017). In a widely quoted radio interview, Indian MP Shashi Tharoor said that any plan resembling 'Empire 2.0' would 'go down like a lead balloon' in countries such as India, which would be vital to the success of the Global Britain strategy (quoted in Dale 2017). India, argued Simon Tilford (2017), was 'bemused' by Britain's post-Brexit plan to lead the Commonwealth.

What was more, English-speaking and former African colonies had found new markets that would be difficult for the UK now to penetrate (Olusoga 2017). It would not be as simple as Britain picking up where it left off in the 1950s, bringing 'all its former colonies back into the fold of a warm, free-trade loving family' (Kappal 2017). Interviewed at the Festival of Finance in July 2016, many business leaders from around the Commonwealth spoke coolly about the prospects for Britain substituting EU trade with Commonwealth trade. Leavers' optimism on this account was described as 'excessive' (Sivathasan 2016). During the referendum, prominent leaders of the fifty-three Commonwealth states had expressed the view that Britain should Remain. Their support was rooted in pragmatic concerns around future trade prospects, rights for Commonwealth citizens and worries that vital UK aid and development spending might decline in the event of a Brexit-inspired economic downturn (Onslow 2016). Economists also judged the complexity of forging new Commonwealth trade deals to be enormous. On the one hand, Britain would have to ask around three-quarters of its Commonwealth partners for new trade deals to replace what it already gleaned through the EU. For the remaining one-quarter, new deals would be required. Given the economic benefits to Britain from EU–Commonwealth trade agreements, 'there's no certainty that UK exports to the Commonwealth would gain from Brexit' (Peers 2015).

Some Commonwealth voices in favour of Brexit, for example from New Zealand (Heffer 2016), did surface during and after the referendum. However, these tended to be rather more isolated than Global Britain enthusiasts would have wished. For example, in November 2016, the Commonwealth published a report identifying potential economic advantages of Brexit to Commonwealth countries. The document was replete with caveats and warnings and had nothing on how Britain would benefit (The Commonwealth 2016). A return to Commonwealth leadership was, in the main, held to be ethically dubious and, in any case, a poor substitute for British membership of the EU (Blitz 2017), fraught with peril in terms of optics and substance.

Cold water was also poured onto the idea of scaling up the Anglosphere circle to compensate for withdrawal from the EU. Proponents of Brexit on the Eurosceptic political right had touted the Anglosphere as an alternative to EU membership for some years (see Wellings and Baxendale 2015a). As Britain's crunch point with Europe loomed large, they channelled their inner Churchill (from Bell 2017) to promote the CANZUK union of English-speaking peoples (Canada, Australia, New Zealand and the United Kingdom), to be constructed through free trade deals and military cooperation (notably Bennett 2016; Roberts 2016). Updating 'Third Force' thinking from the early Cold War years (see Daddow 2004: 123–133), historian Andrew Roberts suggested that CANZUK 'would be easily the largest country on the planet, have a combined population of 129 million, the third biggest economy and the third biggest defence budget' (quoted in Bell 2017). CANZUK supporters believed that, in time, the Anglosphere could develop into a 'third pillar' of Western civilization alongside Europe and the United States.

In one of the most trenchant first-wave criticisms, Duncan Bell argued that the Anglosphere, like 'Empire 2.0', was 'a reheated version of arguments forged when Victoria reigned'. Furthermore, there was no consensus on the core features of the Anglosphere: its constitutional arrangement, economic organization or where the globe's pre-eminent superpower, the United States, fitted in (Bell 2017). Britain would according to this line of argument be leaving the confines of the EU and launching on a journey into destination unknown based on a Conservative 'fantasy of going back decades – or, in some cases, centuries' (Keegan 2017). Critics of the Anglosphere suggested that global political connections and economic forces had mutated dramatically over time, making it very difficult to see how an already amorphous concept could be realized institutionally and certainly was 'unlikely to be realised anytime soon' (Wellings and Baxendale 2015b). Although some cultural links might still resonate, countries such as Australia (as we shall see), had come to look to the United States and China for their export markets (Olusoga 2017) and as their security guarantors (Levin 2016).

On security, indeed, Brexit and the closer Anglo-American 'special relationship' it presaged were argued to be destabilizing for EU security and NATO cohesion as a whole. That the strongest military power in Europe should leave the EU should, wrote Daniel Keohane (2016), make it 'self-evident' that 'Brexit would damage EU security and defense policies' by straining relations with France and Germany. Keohane went on to argue that, prior to the referendum, the EU and NATO had been working more closely than ever on threats such as cybersecurity, on which cross-institutional cooperation was vital. De-aligning London from Paris and Berlin would only make such co-operation more difficult to achieve. Brexit would, experts cautioned, lead to Britain becoming even more of a junior partner to the United States, as well as diminishing its influence in NATO. 'A scenario may therefore develop whereby the UK winds up as less influential on security debates within Europe (replaced by a Franco-German pole) and both more subservient to the US and less valued by it' (Street and Reeve 2016). The Brexit distraction for the Civil Service and diplomats could even weaken Britain's ability to shape UN decision-making on international crises (ibid.).

Put simply, leaving the EU was predicted to have a big ripple effect on the entirety of Britain's bilateral and multilateral relationships in Europe and the wider world. Ideologically committed Leavers may not see any damage from Britain losing influence over EU foreign and defence policies. The argument was either that 'they can form a European Army if they wish' (Adu 2017) or that bilateral cooperation between Britain and key allies could continue outside of European structures and/or in NATO, as on Libya in 2011 (Lenarz 2017). Crucially, though, Britain 'will also lose EU membership as a platform to encourage EU action on issues in its own national interests', such as on Ebola in 2014 or sanctions against Russia (Lain and Nouwens 2017). Almost entirely absent from the referendum debate itself, the security angle is thus an interesting one, but mostly because it was absent from mainstream campaigning. The financial and 'sovereignty' gains from Brexit should ideally have been weighed against the potential damage to Britain's ability to achieve its national interests in areas where collective EU action was vital to the pursuit of those interests. The future form of British–EU relations in the realm of CSDP will go a long way to determining Britain's continued capacity to secure its interests in both harder and softer security matters.

First-wave debates thus spanned economics, ethics and the security implications of Brexit. After May triggered Article 50, the economic, political and legal practicalities of actually 'doing' Brexit hove into view. The intense scrutiny that came with them fuelled a second wave of criticism against Global Britain, with economics very much to the fore. The question for this wave of writers was, '*Can* Britain do this?' (see Blitz 2017). Before we begin, it is worth noting that May herself did not think much about the prospects for an economic Global Britain before she became prime minister. As she said, when home secretary, in a speech on behalf of the Remain campaign: 'It is tempting to look at developing countries' economies, with their high growth rates, and see them as an alternative to trade with Europe'. However, May (2016; emphasis added) continued:

> We export more to Ireland than we do to China, almost twice as much to Belgium as we do to India, and nearly three times as much to Sweden as we do to Brazil. *It is not realistic to think we could just replace European trade with these new markets.*

The irony of May's U-turn was not lost on second-wave critics.

To grasp the fundamentals of second-wave criticisms of Global Britain, it is necessary firstly to hear from opinion formers among Britain's key global partners. Some of them are, it transpires, critical of the whole Brexit agenda. For example, Justin Trudeau of Canada – a CANZUK leader, note – said that after the referendum Britain seemed to be 'turning inward', going in a different direction from his country (quoted in Oppenheim 2017). This hardly sounded like an enthusiastic endorsement of Global Britain as the regeneration of the Anglosphere. Even if the will were to exist, there were also process issues to be catered for. No trade deals can be signed until Britain has left the EU: 'only the vaguest expressions of future interest can be made so long as the terms of the divorce remain unknown' (Crace 2017). Fox and his team could put in place some groundwork before 2019 but little more. Britain 'may be able to start discussions, but our counterparts will want to know what our future relationship with the EU is going to be before they can negotiate meaningfully' (Corbett 2017). As Prime Minister Malcolm Turnbull said of the Australian position: 'we stand ready to enter into a free trade agreement with the UK', but a deal with the EU would have to come first (Mason 2017; Green 2017). New Zealand more than intimated that it would go down the same path: 'it seems more likely that an EU–NZ free trade agreement could be brokered than a UK–NZ agreement' (Jacotine and Bale 2017).

By contrast, Brexit-supporting President Donald Trump responded positively to the prospect of a UK–US trade deal, talks about which began in Washington on 24 July 2017 (Agerholm 2017). Speaking at the G20 Summit in July 2017, Trump said it would be a 'powerful' agreement, concluded 'very, very quickly' (BBC News 2017). That said, there were some thorny issues to be resolved in any such deal, particularly involving financial regulation and food standards (Ward and Ryan 2017). David Allen Green argued, furthermore, that 'a quick deal with the United States would just mean that the UK was capitulating' on a range of issues, 'which would not go down well' (Green 2017; see also Kettle 2017a). The immense power balance between the two countries did not bode well either. As the CIA *World Factbook* laconically put it, the UK is 'slightly smaller than Oregon' (quoted in Kettle 2017b). Finally, even the US president could not circumvent the sequencing issue. Ireland's Prime

Minister Leo Varadkar drew attention to this facet: 'I can't see a scenario where Britain could remain a member of the EU, even in a transitional period, and then negotiate other trade deals on their own' (quoted in Oppenheim 2017). Warm words were, wrote Green, not enough: 'Trade agreements between Britain and the US and Australia are not "in the bag". They are nowhere near the bag. The bag is not in sight, and it may never be' (Green, quoting Digby Jones, 2017).

For precisely these reasons, some of May's own Cabinet ministers expressed doubts about the extent to which the rhetoric of Global Britain could be turned into reality. For example, Justice Secretary David Lidington warned that even a wide-ranging deal with a country such as the United States would not offset the many economic negatives caused by Brexit (Kentish 2017). Chancellor of the Exchequer Philip Hammond went further by stressing that 40 per cent of British exports are services, not goods. This is an unusually high figure, the point being that services would not be covered by free trade agreements. 'Much of our trade with the world is service trade, where free trade agreements won't make any particular difference', Hammond surmised. It seems that the critical voices from within government surfaced on the back of unpublished papers studying the prognosis for Britain's economy post-Brexit: 'Last autumn [2016] the Treasury produced an unpublished internal paper that concluded that the costs of hard Brexit far outweighed any potential gains from Liam Fox's free trade agreement strategy' (Kettle 2017b).

Ministerial doubts resonated with academic economists such as John Ravenhill and Jeff Huebner, who studied the relationships among the ten largest economies in the Anglosphere: Australia, Canada, India, Malaysia, New Zealand, Nigeria, Singapore, South Africa, the UK and United States. They found that UK trade patterns have shifted dramatically towards the EU and away from the Anglosphere since the Second World War. Journalists such as Martin Kettle agreed with this analysis: 'UK trade with the Anglosphere nations has massively declined from its pre-1914 peak' (Kettle 2017a). Labour Member of the European Parliament, Richard Corbett (2017), also remarked that 'only 15 per cent of UK trade is with countries that are not in the EU or covered by an EU trade agreement that is either in force or under negotiation'. Moreover, with regional blocs now the pre-eminent mode of organizing international trade (Ravenhill and Huebner 2017: 5), Brexit would disrupt Britain's economic relationships that have been developing in line with global patterns for decades. Ravenhill and Huebner concluded that, although it is nigh on impossible to predict the impact of Brexit on Britain's future trading prospects:

> what is of relevance . . . is how Brexit will affect the UK's attractiveness as a trading partner. And on this specific dimension, developments suggest that it is highly unlikely that Brexit will have a positive impact. Brexit, rather, will reinforce the trend of the UK having diminished significance in the global economy.
>
> *(Ravenhill and Huebner 2017: 15)*

By way of summarizing this section, second-wave criticism about the practical obstacles in the way of fashioning a free trade Global Britain fanned the flames of the ideological attacks popularized by first-wave writers. An array of policymakers, commentators and professional economists showed themselves to be none too optimistic that Global Britain would be realized in such a way as to enhance Britain's economy or world standing, despite the rhetorical flourishes of May and her team.

Conclusion

The 2016 Brexit referendum was partly about the kind of global actor Britain used to be, partly about the kind of global actor Britain had become and partly about the kind of global actor Britain aspired to be. This chapter has therefore suggested that Brexit was the latest act in a long-running national drama in which proponents of 'limited liability' have fought for supremacy with exponents of the 'continental commitment'. The vote in favour of Brexit was the latest victory for the former over the latter. The chapter further argued that, to understand the ideational fault lines in the Brexit referendum, one must appreciate the ambiguities and inconsistencies running through Winston Churchill's thinking on Britain's world role. A vocal advocate of the United States of Europe, Churchill's three circles model never envisaged a role for Britain at the heart of the Europe circle. Britain, he maintained, should instead be proactively involved only in the Empire and Anglosphere circles. British entry to the EEC in 1973 did nothing to resolve this quandary for British pro-Europeans. Nor did the 1975 referendum that produced a 2:1 vote in favour of continued EEC membership. Pressure for another 'reckoning' on British European policy built year on year, fuelled by a combination of a lack of coherent pro-European leadership, a blame-the-EU political culture and a rabid UK media treatment of European integration (Daddow 2012).

Supporters of Global Britain responded to Brexit by rehashing Churchill for the modern age, as the second part of the chapter explained. Above, we recounted the two waves of criticism that have crashed against the idea of Global Britain, one questioning its desirability, the other its viability. At the time of writing, we do not yet know whether Brexit will happen at all, although the signs are that it will be happening in some form. We still know little to nothing about the length or nature of a transitional deal and how far that will affect Britain's ability to negotiate trade deals after 2019. With the leaders of Australia, Canada, India and New Zealand none too optimistic, and the American president offering warm words and even the prospect of a trade war the author is rather more pessimistic than optimistic about the prospects for a strong consensus being built behind a Global Britain that eventually materialises in the range of trade deals envisaged by Liam Fox. We end, therefore, with the observation that, insofar as Britain's world role links to the exercise of British power, the idea of 'taking back control' sounded better in theory than in practice: 'Brexit means finding oneself alone, separate from a now reinvigorated European club – a molecule cast around by random colliding forces' (Nougayrède 2017).

Note

1   To keep things simple, the campaigns are referred to in this chapter as Remain and Leave, respectively.

References

Adu, A. (2017) There WILL Be an EU Army: German Official Claims 27 European Militaries Will UNITE. *Express*, June 20. Available at: www.express.co.uk/news/world/819033/Brexit-article-50-EU-army-Germany-defence-Hans-Peter-Michael-Fallon-Theresa-May [Accessed August 11, 2017].

Agerholm, H. (2017) EU Chief Mocks UK's Brexit Ambitions with Comparison to Limbless Monty Python Knight. *Independent*, July 5. Available at: www.independent.co.uk/news/brexit-monty-python-knight-uk-eu-chief-mocks-trade-ambitions-a7826181.html [Accessed August 11, 2017].

BBC News (2017) G20: UK-US Trade Deal to Happen Quickly, Says Trump, July, 8. Available at: www.bbc.co.uk/news/uk-politics-40540340 [Accessed August 11, 2017].

Bell, D. (2017) The Anglosphere: New Enthusiasm for an Old Dream. *Prospect*, January 19. Available at: www.prospectmagazine.co.uk/magazine/anglosphere-old-dream-brexit-role-in-the-world [Accessed August 11, 2017].

Bennett, J.C. (2016) *A Time for Audacity: How Brexit Has Created the CANZUK Option*. London: Pole to Pole Publishing.

Blitz, J. (2017) Post-Brexit Delusions about Empire 2.0. *Financial Times*, March 7. Available at: www.ft.com/content/bc29987e-034e-11e7-ace0-1ce02ef0def9 [Accessed May 22, 2017].

Brinkley, D. (1990) Dean Acheson and the 'Special Relationship': The West Point Speech of December 1962. *The Historical Journal* 33(3): 599–608.

Britain Stronger in Europe (2016) You and Your Family Are Stronger In. Available at: www.strongerin. co.uk/#UuaU6dHJu2rQOeGy.97 [Accessed June 30, 2017].

Cameron, D. (2016) Speech on the UKs Strength and Security in the EU, May 9. Available at: www.gov.uk/ government/speeches/pm-speech-on-the-uks-strength-and-security-in-the-eu-9-may-2016 [Accessed June 29, 2017].

Centre for Research in Communication and Culture (2016) Media Coverage of the EU Referendum (Report 5), June 27. Available at: http://blog.lboro.ac.uk/crcc/eu-referendum/uk-news-coverage-2016-eu-referendum-report-5-6-may-22-june-2016/ [Accessed June 20, 2017].

Churchill, W. (1948) Speech to Conservative Party Conference. Official Proceedings of Conservative Party Conference. Bodleian Library Special Collections, Shelf Mark NUA 2/1/56: 149–156.

CMND.4715 (1971) *The United Kingdom and the European Communities.* White Paper, July. Available at: www. cvce.eu/en/obj/white_paper_presented_by_the_uk_government_to_the_uk_parliament_july_1971-en-8cf072cb-5a31-46f6-b04f-cb866be92f72.html [Accessed June 20, 2017].

The Commonwealth (2016) Brexit and Commonwealth Trade. *Commonwealth Trade Policy Briefing,* November. Available at: http://thecommonwealth.org/sites/default/files/news-items/documents/Brexitand CommonwealthTrade.pdf [Accessed August 10, 2017].

Corbett, R. (2017) Brexit and Trade: Another Ticking Timebomb, July, 16. Available at: www.richard corbett.org.uk/another-ticking-timebomb/ [Accessed June 20, 2017].

Crace, J. (2017) Liam Fox and His British-Made Tie: Wrapping Brexit Up in Knots. *The Guardian.* Available at: www.theguardian.com/politics/2017/jul/06/liam-fox-and-his-british-made-tie-wrapping-brexit-up-in-knots [Accessed July 7, 2017].

Crowson, N.J. (2011) *Britain and Europe: A Political History Since 1918.* Abingdon: Routledge.

Daddow, O. (2003) Introduction: The Historiography of Wilson's Bid to Join the EEC. In: Daddow, O. (ed.), *Harold Wilson and European Integration: Britain's Second Application to Join the EEC.* London: Frank Cass, pp. 1–36.

Daddow, O. (2004) *Britain and Europe since 1945: Historiographical Perspectives on Integration.* Manchester: Manchester University Press.

Daddow, O. (2011) *New Labour and the European Union: Blair and Brown's Logic of History.* Manchester: Manchester University Press.

Daddow, O. (2012) The UK Media and 'Europe': From Permissive Consensus to Destructive Dissent. *International Affairs* 88(6): 1219–1236.

Daddow, O. (2013) Margaret Thatcher, Tony Blair and the Eurosceptic Tradition in Britain. *British Journal of Politics and International Relations*, Special Issue: Interpreting British Foreign Policy 15(2): 210–227.

Daddow, O. (2016) Project Fear versus the Positive Vase for 'Bremain'. *The UK in a Changing Europe, ESRC*, March 15. Available at: http://ukandeu.ac.uk/project-fear-versus-the-positive-case-for-bremain/ [Accessed July 7, 2017].

Daddow, O. and Gaskarth, J. (2011) Introduction: Blair, Brown and New Labour's Foreign Policy, 1997–2010. In: Daddow, O. and Gaskarth, J. (eds.), *British Foreign Policy: The New Labour Years.* Basingstoke: Palgrave Macmillan, pp. 1–27.

Daddow, O. and Gaskarth, J. (2014) From Value Protection to Value Promotion: Interpreting British Security Policy. In: Bevir, M., Daddow, O. and Hall, I. (eds.), *Interpreting Global Security.* London: Routledge, pp. 73–91.

Dale, I. (2017) Former Indian Minister: 'Empire 2.0 Will Go Down Like a Lead Balloon in India', March 6. Available at: www.lbc.co.uk/radio/presenters/iain-dale/empire-20-will-go-down-like-a-lead-balloon-india/ [Accessed May 25, 2017].

Deighton, A. (2002) The Past in the Present: British Imperial Memories and the European Question. In: Müller, J.-W. (ed.), *Memory and Power in Post-War Europe: Studies in the Presence of the Past.* Cambridge: Cambridge University Press, pp. 100–120.

Foreign Affairs Committee (2016) Implications of Leaving the EU for the UK's Role in the World. Available at: https://www.parliament.uk/business/committees/committees-a-z/commons-select/foreign-affairs-committee/inquiries1/parliament-2015/referendum-result-16-17/publications/ [Accessed June 20, 2017].

Fox, L. (2016) Speech at Manchester Town Hall, September 29. Available at: www.gov.uk/government/speeches/liam-foxs-free-trade-speech [Accessed June 20, 2017].

Fox, L. (2017) Speech at Commonwealth Trade Ministers Meeting, March 9. Available at: www.gov.uk/government/speeches/commonwealth-trade-ministers-meeting-towards-a-free-trading-future [Accessed July 6, 2017].

Fox, L. (2018) Speech, 'Britain's trading future', London, 27 February. Available at: https://www.gov.uk/government/speeches/britains-trading-future [Accessed 14 March, 2018].

Green, D.A. (2017) Brexit: The Ballad of Digby Jones. *Financial Times*, July 12. Available at: http://blogs.ft.com/david-allen-green/2017/07/12/brexit-the-ballad-of-digby-jones/?mhq5j=e2 [Accessed July 13, 2017].

Grob-Fitzgibbon, B. (2016) *Continental Drift: Britain and Europe from the End of Empire to the Rise of Euroscepticism.* Cambridge: Cambridge University Press.

Harvey, M. (2011) Perspectives on the UK's Place in the World. *Europe Programme Paper*, December. London: Chatham House.

Heath, E. (1972) Speech in Brussels, January 22. Available at: www.cvce.eu/content/publication/2001/9/14/45bb74bd-554c-49d4-8212-9144ce2e8c1d/publishable_en.pdf [Accessed June 20, 2017].

Heffer, G. (2016) Ex-New Zealand Minister Says Brexit Is Chance to 'Heal a Rift' with Commonwealth, February, 25. Available at: www.express.co.uk/news/politics/647528/New-Zealand-Winston-Peters-Brexit-heal-rift-Commonwealth-free-trade [Accessed August 9, 2017].

Hill, C. (2010) Tough Choices. *The World Today*, April, pp. 11–14.

Holmes, M. (1994) The Conservative Party and Europe. *Bruges Group*. Available at: www.brugesgroup.com/media-centre/papers/8-papers/807-the-conservative-party-and-europe [Accessed June 20, 2017].

Jacotine, K. and Bale, T. (2017) Brexit: The Big Uncertainty. *Pacific Outlier*, July 14. Available at: https://pacificoutlier.org/2017/07/14/brexit-the-big-uncertainty-jacotine-and-bale/ [Accessed July 14, 2017].

Johnson, B. (2016) UK and America Can Be Better Friends Than Ever Mr Obama . . . If We LEAVE the EU, April 22. Available at: www.thesun.co.uk/archives/politics/1139354/boris-johnson-uk-and-america-can-be-better-friends-than-ever-mr-obama-if-we-leave-the-eu/ [Accessed June 29, 2017].

Kappal, B. (2017) Why Brexiteers Need to Update Their Reading of Colonial History. *New Statesman*, March 17. Available at: www.newstatesman.com/politics/brexit/2017/03/why-brexiteers-need-update-their-reading-colonial-history [Accessed July 13, 2017].

Keegan, W. (2017) Election Euphoria Won't Last Long If Labour Doesn't Foil Brexit Folly. *Guardian*, July 17. Available at: www.theguardian.com/politics/2017/jul/16/labour-must-foil-brexit-folly-save-economy-youth-vote [Accessed July 17, 2017].

Kentish, B. (2017) UK Trade Deal with the US Will Not Make Up for the Damage Caused by Brexit, Justice Secretary David Lidington Says. *Independent*, July 9. Available at: www.independent.co.uk/news/uk/politics/uk-us-trade-deal-brexit-negotiations-david-lidington-donald-trump-theresa-may-g20-andrew-marr-show-a7831621.html [Accessed August 9, 2017].

Keohane, D. (2016) European Defense and Brexit: A Tale of Three Cities. *Carnegie Europe*, March 1. Available at: http://carnegieeurope.eu/strategiceurope/?fa=62922 [Accessed August 11, 2017].

Kettle, M. (2017a) Here Is Britain's New Place in the World: On the Sidelines. *Guardian*, July 6. Available at: www.theguardian.com/commentisfree/2017/jul/06/britain-world-sidelines-brexit-trump-theresa-may-g20 [Accessed August 11, 2017].

Kettle, M. (2017b) Reject the Chancers and Their Fantasy Visions of Post-Brexit Trade. *Guardian*, July 13. Available at: www.theguardian.com/commentisfree/2017/jul/13/post-brexit-trade-deals [Accessed August 14, 2017].

Kleine, M. (2016) Britain's Role in World Affairs Will Be Dwarfed Post-Brexit. *LSE Brexit Blog*, March 11. Available at: http://blogs.lse.ac.uk/brexit/2016/03/11/britains-role-in-world-affairs-will-dwarf-post-brexit/ [Accessed June 20, 2017].

Lain, S. and Nouwens, V. (2017) The Consequences of Brexit for European Defence and Security. *RUSI Occasional Paper*, August 2017. Available at: https://rusi.org/sites/default/files/201704_08_rusi-fes_brexit_defence_and_security_lain_and_nouwens.pdf [Accessed August 11, 2017].

Lenarz, J. (2017) Even after Brexit, Europe Will Need Britain's Military: That's What the New Pact with Germany Is All About. *Telegraph*, March 20. Available at: www.telegraph.co.uk/news/2017/03/20/even-brexit-europe-will-need-britains-military-new-pact-germany/ [Accessed August 11, 2017].

Levin, S. (2016) Beyond Shared Values: Reassessing the Australia-US Alliance. *The Policy Space*, November 22. Available at: www.thepolicyspace.com.au/2016/22/155-beyond-shared-values-reassessing-the-australia-us-alliance [Accessed May 25, 2017].

Liddle, R. (2014) *The Europe Dilemma: Britain and the Drama of European Integration.* London: I.B. Tauris & Co.

Macmillan, H. (1960) The Wind of Change. *Speech at South African Parliament*, February 3. Available at: www.africanrhetoric.org/pdf/ayor%206.2%205%20Harold%20MacMillan%20-%20The%20wind%20of%20change.pdf [Accessed July 4, 2017].

Maddox, D. (2016) 'We Are with Them, But Not of Them!' Even Sir Winston Churchill Opposed Membership of EU. *Express*, June 2. Available at: www.express.co.uk/news/history/676022/Winston-Churchill-EU-European-Union-Brexit [Accessed June 29, 2017].

Mason, R. (2017) Australia Ready to Do Post-Brexit Trade Deal: But EU Comes First. *Guardian*, July 10. Available at: www.theguardian.com/politics/2017/jul/10/australia-ready-to-do-post-brexit-trade-deal-but-eu-comes-first [Accessed July 11, 2017].

May, T. (2016) Speech on Brexit, April 25. Available at: www.conservativehome.com/parliament/2016/04/theresa-mays-speech-on-brexit-full-text.html [Accessed July 11, 2017].

May, T. (2017) Speech at Lancaster House, January 17. Available at: www.telegraph.co.uk/news/2017/01/17/theresa-mays-brexit-speech-full/ [Accessed July 6, 2017].

McCourt, D. (2011) The New Labour Governments and Britain's Role in the World. In: Daddow, O. and Gaskarth, J. (eds.), *British Foreign Policy: The New Labour Years*. Basingstoke: Palgrave Macmillan, pp. 31–47.

McCourt, D. (2014) *Britain and World Power since 1945: Constructing a Nation's Role in International Politics*. Ann Arbor: University of Michigan Press.

Moore, M. and Ramsay, G. (2017) UK Media Coverage of the 2016 EU Referendum Campaign. Centre for the Study of Media, Communication and Power, King's College London, May. Available at: www.kcl.ac.uk/sspp/policy-institute/CMCP/UK-media-coverage-of-the-2016-EU-Referendum-campaign.pdf [Accessed June 20, 2017].

Nougayrède, N. (2017) After the G20 Summit, Brexit Britain Looks Increasingly Adrift and Friendless. *Guardian*, July 10. Available at: www.theguardian.com/commentisfree/2017/jul/10/g20-summit-brexit-britain [Accessed July 12, 2017].

Olusoga, D. (2017) Empire 2.0 Is Dangerous Nostalgia for Something That Never Existed. *Guardian*, March 19. Available at: www.theguardian.com/commentisfree/2017/mar/19/empire-20-is-dangerous-nostalgia-for-something-that-never-existed [Accessed May 20, 2017].

Onslow, S. (2016) What Brexit Means for the Commonwealth. *The Conversation*, July 7. Available at: http://theconversation.com/what-brexit-means-for-the-commonwealth-61941 [Accessed August 10, 2017].

Oppenheim, M. (2017) Justin Trudeau: Canadian PM Takes Swipe at UK over Brexit and Argues It Is 'Turning Inward'. *Independent*, July 5. Available at: www.independent.co.uk/news/world-0/justin-trudeau-brexit-latest-news-uk-turn-inward-g20-summit-canada-leave-eu-prime-minister-a7824561.html [Accessed July 12, 2017].

Patel, P. (2017) Speech on Commonwealth Trade, March 9. Available at: www.gov.uk/government/speeches/priti-patel-commonwealth-trade-speech [Accessed June 6, 2017].

Peers, S. (2015) The Commonwealth and the EU: Let's Do (Trade with) Both. *LSE Brexit Blog*, December 10. Available at: http://blogs.lse.ac.uk/brexit/2015/12/10/the-commonwealth-and-the-eu-lets-do-trade-with-both/ [Accessed August 10, 2017].

Ravenhill, J. and Huebner, J. (2017) The Political Economy of the Anglosphere' Conference: The Anglosphere and Its Others: The English-Speaking Peoples in a Changing World Order. Forthcoming in Proceedings of the British Academy. London: British Academy, June 15–16.

Roberts, A. (2016) CANZUK: After Brexit, Canada, Australia, New Zealand and Britain Can Unite as a Pillar of Western Civilization. *Telegraph*, September 13. Available at: www.telegraph.co.uk/news/2016/09/13/canzuk-after-brexit-canada-australia-new-zealand-and-britain-can/ [Accessed July 13, 2017].

Sivathasan, N. (2016) The Commonwealth's View on Brexit. *Financial Times*, July 1. Available at: www.ft.com/video/d36ac277-23ee-3400-8bb0-f8970da3a0cb [Accessed August 8, 2017].

The Spectator (2017) The Quiet Successes of Brexit, July 8. Available at: www.spectator.co.uk/2017/07/the-quiet-successes-of-brexit/ [Accessed July 12, 2017].

Street, T. and Reeve, R. (2016) Brexit: Whither UK Defence and Foreign Policy? *Oxford Research Group*, July 15. Available at: www.oxfordresearchgroup.org.uk/publications/briefing_papers_and_reports/brexit_whither_uk_defence_and_foreign_policy [Accessed August 11, 2017].

Tilford, S. (2017) The British and Their Exceptionalism. *Centre for European Reform*, May 2. Available at: https://issuu.com/centreforeuropeanreform/docs/insight_st_3.5.17 [Accessed July 20, 2017].

Toye, R. (2008) The Churchill Syndrome: Reputational Entrepreneurship and the Rhetoric of Foreign Policy Since 1945. *British Journal of Politics and International Relations* 10(3): 364–378.

Vote Leave (2016) Why Vote Leave. Available at: www.voteleavetakecontrol.org/why_vote_leave.html [Accessed June 30, 2017].

Wallace, W. (1992) British Foreign Policy after the Cold War. *International Affairs* 68(3): 423–442.

Ward, J. and Ryan, C. (2017) Business Casts Doubt on UK–US Post-Brexit Trade Deal. *Fin24*, July 11. Available at: www.fin24.com/Economy/business-casts-doubt-on-uk-us-post-brexit-trade-deal-20170711 [Accessed July 10, 2017].

Watt, N. (2016) EU Referendum: Churchill Would Back Remain, Soames Says. *BBC News*, May 10. Available at: http://www.bbc.com/news/uk-politics-eu-referendum-36253224 [Accessed June 29, 2017].

Wellings, B. and Baxendale, H. (2015a) Euroscepticism and the Anglosphere: Traditions and Dilemmas in Contemporary English Nationalism. *Journal of Common Market Studies* 53(1): 123–139.

Wellings, B. and Baxendale, H. (2015b) The Power of the Anglosphere in Eurosceptical Thought. *LSE Brexit Blog*, December 10. Available at: http://blogs.lse.ac.uk/brexit/2015/12/10/anglosphere-is-the-other-side-of-the-eurosceptic-coin-a-conception-of-britains-identity-and-place-in-the-world/ [Accessed July 13, 2017].

Winders, S. (2016) *Brexit and Free Trade: Would a Post-Brexit UK be Better Able to Sign Free Trade Agreements with the Rest of the World?* London: Bruges Group, May 9. Available at: www.brugesgroup.com/images/papers/brexitandinternationalfreetrade.pdf [Accessed June 29, 2017].

Wintour, P. (2018) 'Foreign Office policy of Global Britain is "superficial rebranding"'. Guardian, 12 March. Available at: https://www.theguardian.com/politics/2018/mar/12/foreign-office-policy-of-global-britain-is-superficial-rebranding [Accessed 14 March, 2018].

Wright, M. (1975) *Theory and Practice of the Balance of Power 1486–1914*. London: Dent.

18

BREXIT AND THE EU AS AN INTERNATIONAL ACTOR

Henrik Larsen

Introduction

British membership of the European Union comprises participation in the Union's actions on the international stage. This chapter looks at the effects of Brexit on the EU as an international actor. As the UK is a major member state that has taken part in the creation of central decision-making structures and the establishment of *acquis politiques* in this field for more than forty years, we would expect Brexit to be important for the EU as an international actor. But the question is how important and in what ways? Most literature on the subject mentions the dualism that, on the one hand, Brexit will lead to a reduction in the means available for the EU on the international stage. On the other hand, the departure of the UK (which is sceptical towards aspects of European foreign policy) will also facilitate more advanced and ambitious EU foreign policy decisions. The chapter examines the general thrust of the literature on the subject.

The impact of Brexit is arguably played out along three dimensions: first of all, the implications for strength and capacity for the EU as an international actor; secondly, the bearings on the ways decisions are made in the EU and the ways they are carried out; and, finally, the consequences for the policies of the Union towards the outside world. In addition, the EU's international policies can be looked at as covering three sub-areas: trade policy and related areas, the Common Foreign and Security Policy (CFSP) and the Common Security and Defence Policy (CSDP) (see also Chapters 7 and 19).

The assessment of the impact of Brexit will need to be based on an understanding of the nature of EU foreign policy before Brexit. The chapter therefore starts out by presenting its understanding of the main features of European foreign policy. This understanding is that European foreign policy cooperation is institutionalized in such a way that it is more than the lowest common denominator amongst the member states at any given point in time. There are substantial *acquis politiques*, and these have been extended to a degree where the EU has stances on most issues in world politics. The chapter then goes on to presenting the likely changes arising from Brexit. The focus here is primarily on the direct effects of Brexit for EU foreign policy. The last section broadens the perspective and considers the implications of the wider processes that may combine with Brexit or that Brexit may reflect.

The EU as an international actor

The main features of the EU as an international actor can be divided into three interlinked dimensions: the EU as an economic actor, as a political actor and as a security actor. The EU is the largest economy in the world in terms of GDP. It is the world's biggest exporter of manufactured goods and accounts for 16 per cent of world exports and imports (Commission 2014). The Union is a trading bloc of global significance in all areas of trade. It is a major player in negotiations about the environment, including in the climate negotiations where the EU has played an important role over the years. The EU and its member states are the biggest providers of development aid – in total more than 50 per cent of all global aid.

It is a central political player in and around Europe, and, by its mere existence, its attraction to prospective members and its diplomacy, it shapes European security. The EU is engaged in diplomacy in or with most parts of the world. It issues declarations and statements on most geographical and functional issues in world politics. There is a high degree of EU coordination in the United Nation's General Assembly, where the EU has "enhanced observer" status and the EU's high representative can take the floor in the United Nation's Security Council (UNSC), but cannot vote. Since 2002, the Union has had access to military means. The military operations that the EU has engaged in have – with the exception of the anti-pirate operation, Atalanta, off the Horn of Africa – mainly been related to peacekeeping, protection of civilians or training of military forces. The EU has limited military planning capacity on its own. It mainly draws on national headquarters, and it is also able to draw on NATO's planning capacities. The biggest military operation so far has been EUFOR in Tchad 2007–2009 which deployed 3,700 ground forces. The Common Security and Defence Policy (CSDP) has comprised more non-military operations than military ones (European External Action Service 2016).

The EU has formalized executive functions that allow the EU to speak with one voice where the member states and institutions have come to an agreement – the high representative, the president of the European Council, the Commission and, on certain issues, the rotating presidency. According to Keukeleire and Delreux (2014), the decision-making procedures in EU foreign policy fall in three categories, each with its dynamics: first of all, Commission-steered foreign policy, then EEAS- (European External Action Service)-steered foreign policy, and, finally, foreign policy steered by informal divisions of labour (ibid.: 104–107). Commission-steered foreign policy dominates in trade and related areas where the Commission has the monopoly on representing the Union internationally. Here, decisions can be made by qualified majority voting, even if attempts to reach consensus are much more common (Lewis 2016). EEAS-steered logic is prominent in the CFSP where the high representative represents the Union, sets the agenda (but has no monopoly) and chairs the foreign ministers' meetings. Decision-making procedures are, for all practical purposes, formally intergovernmental in line with British wishes right from the beginning of European Political Cooperation (EPC) in 1973 (Nuttall 1992). Informal divisions of labour are also important in the CFSP. In foreign policy steered by an informal division of labour, one or more member states may conduct or drive policy on behalf of the EU and report back to the EU. It follows from EEAS-steered and informally steered foreign policy that when member states disagree, there is no European foreign policy, a clear example being the lack of a common position on the Iraq War in 2003. However, this does not mean that EU foreign policy is usually the lowest common denominator. Many policy areas are shaped according to the median principle rather than the lowest common denominator (ibid.: 311; White 2001: 78). Also, the differing intensities of national preferences across policy areas mean that many member states will not block decisions even if they are in less than full agreement (Keukeleire and Delreux

2014: Chapter 3). Moreover, there is a "coordination reflex" amongst the EU member states with regard to major foreign policy decisions, meaning that they find it natural to consult with the EU partners prior to any major foreign policy decision (Smith 2004: 94, 122). The consultation reflex is inscribed in the Lisbon Treaty article 32. EEAS-steered foreign policy, and informal division of labour has also been the central mechanism in the CSDP.

The implications of Brexit

In the following, I will present the likely implications in these three fields of European foreign policy: trade and related areas, the CFSP and the CSDP. The focus in this section is on the direct effects of Brexit.

Trade and related areas

As it looks at the time of writing, the UK will not stay in the internal market or be part of the Customs Union (with the important caveat that the Labour Party wants the UK to stay in the Customs Union). Given the considerable size of the UK economy (16 per cent of the EU GDP) (Eurostat 2017), Brexit will mean a loss of economic strength and leverage for the EU in multilateral and bilateral contexts (even if the UK is not part of the Eurozone). There is no EU coordination in the IMF and the World Bank, so Brexit will not have immediate effects here (Aktipis and Oliver 2011: 86). But if EU coordination occurs in these fora in the future, it will be without the economic weight of the UK. Moreover, Brexit happens at a time when trade agreements are being contested all over the world (Dullien 2017). Trade agreements will be hard work for EU negotiators – if they are concluded at all. The energy used on trade negotiations with the UK cannot be used on negotiating other complex agreements that will weaken the EU's negotiation capacity.

Within the EU, the UK has been an ardent proponent of international trade liberalisation in opposition to more protectionist countries like France. Even if the British views on trade are shared by many member states in Northern Europe, including Germany, Brexit will move the centre of gravity towards the more protectionist countries in the EU and hence, all other things being equal, mean a more protectionist EU. However, the impact of Brexit might be difficult to separate from the current sceptical sentiment towards free-trade that is also affecting the other EU countries. On the issues of the negotiation and entry into force of the Transatlantic Trade and Investment Partnership (TTIP) and the Comprehensive Economic and Trade Agreement (CETA), the UK is not the decisive country; whether TTIP and CETA will pass has more to do with the publics in Germany and France (and the United States) than with the UK (Weilandt 2016). Concerning the impact of procedures, the UK has since 2010 on some occasions con- tested the Commission's exclusive right to negotiate on behalf of the EU on certain aspects of trade, also when it agreed with the policy position taken by the Commission (ibid.). As Britain is the member state that has challenged the Commission's exclusive right to negotiate in this field the most, the pressure on the Commission is likely to ease after Brexit.

Brexit will weaken the role of the EU in international development aid. The UK is the world's third largest donor of development aid in absolute terms and the third biggest contributor to the European Development Fund (EDF) (European Parliament 2017: 11). If EU development aid (through the EU budget and EDF) is reduced in line with the loss of the British contributions after Brexit, EU development aid will diminish by 15 per cent (ibid.: 26). However, following Brexit, the EU institutions and the member states will still be providing more than 50per cent of total overseas development aid at the global level (OECD 2016).

The UK is one of the key drivers in the fight against climate change in the EU. So here the balance will move towards the more sceptical countries, even if a radical change is not to be expected due the path dependency of policy in this field. Moreover, the role of the UK diplomats on the side of the global climate negotiations will be missed.

UK has traditionally been a key driver of enlargement. However, since 2013, it has become much more reticent towards enlargement out of concern for the possible new immigration of workers to the UK (Milevska 2013). So the absence of the UK will not bring a more reticent EU view on enlargement as the UK has already moved in that direction. In any case, EU enlargement is not a pressing concern at the moment.

Thus, the indications are that the EU will lose economic and diplomatic power within these fields. The EU's positions are also likely to be affected if only slightly in most fields.

The Common Foreign and Security Policy

There is broad agreement that Brexit will weaken the hard and soft power of the EU as a foreign policy actor in a number of ways. First of all, the numerous British links to, engagements in and institutional knowledge about its former colonies and the Commonwealth countries will no longer be brought into EU foreign policy (see also Chapter 16). Second, the well informed and efficient British diplomatic service will cease to share information with the EU on a day-to-day basis and take part in the preparation and implementation of EU foreign policy. This will not just be a loss of passive power resources. The UK (together with France and, to a lesser extent, Germany) contributes a strong impetus towards global foreign policy action that comes from its history of global engagement and shaping of international society (Whitman and Tonra 2017: 6; Whitman 2016: 2–3). However, the latter has been of diminishing importance for EU foreign policy after 2010 when the UK started to become less engaged in EU foreign policymaking. Third, there will be only one member state on the UN Security Council after Brexit. Fourth, the loss of a major member state is a blow to the prestige and power of attraction of the EU. Brexit gives rise to questions whether the EU will be able to deal with dissent in the future and about whether the EU is heading towards dissolution. This debate contributes to reducing the prestige of the EU (ibid.). Moreover, if the EU is no longer attractive to one of its own larger members, this also weakens the EU's ability to promote its own model of integration internationally, together with its norms and values. For many, the EU's attraction and status have already suffered as a result of its inadequate reactions to the problems in the Eurozone and, later on, the refugee and migrants issue. Brexit will further hurt the EU's soft power, which is a source of international influence (Weiland 2016). Last but not least, diplomatic resources will be needed to sort out the new relationship between Britain and the EU at all levels even after Brexit. This will divert political and administrative energy away from substantial EU foreign policymaking in the short term (Demsey 2017; Oliver and Williams 2016: 559). Taken together, there will be an EU loss of both softer and harder kinds of power as a consequence of Brexit. However, the loss for the EU will be reduced if – as expected – the UK is associated with EU foreign policy in some way. The more institutionalised and intense the association, the less the loss of power.

At the same time, there is also broad agreement that there are ways in which EU foreign policymaking will be strengthened as a result of Brexit. First of all, there will be less challenging of the status of the EEAS and the high representative in the conduct of EU foreign policy. For example, the British have been the main opponents of issuing statements in the name of the EU only, preferring instead "the EU and its member states". This has been a permanent point of controversy in the UN after 2010 (Weilandt 2016). The background to this is that the British governments have not in recent years seen the EU's foreign, security and defence policy ambitions as central to their own ambitions (Whitman and Tonra 2017: 6). The EEAS can be expected to gain more room of manoeuvre after Brexit.

In the United Nation's General Assembly (UNGA) the EU member states often vote together. Britain and France are the two countries that diverge the most from the EU majority, mostly on questions that have to do with nuclear weapons and disarmament. The two countries vote together with the EU in 84 per cent and 89 per cent of all UN resolutions, respectively (Aktipis and Oliver 2011: 86). With the departure of the UK, the level of joint EU voting in the UNGA can be expected to go up slightly as the UK votes less with the EU than the other member states.

Second, after Brexit, the staunchest supporter of intergovernmental decision-making in the CFSP will no longer be there. Britain played a founding role in the creation of the formally intergovernmental European Political Cooperation (EPC) in the early 1970s and has been active in the shaping of these structures ever since (Nuttall 1992: Smith 2004). However, the effect of Brexit is not likely to be a total change in decision-making structures. The formally intergovernmental structures in the CFSP have the support of many member states, including France. Countries that have previously sheltered behind the UK's position on intergovernmentalism are likely to speak up for themselves more strongly post-Brexit. France has also been very active in shaping the EEAS structures and in controlling the room for manoeuvre of the EEAS since its creation. So, while Brexit will clearly weaken the group of member states that support formal intergovernmentalism and a very restricted room for manoeuvre for the EEAS and the high representative in European foreign policy, it is not likely to lead to a fundamental change in the workings of the CFSP (Weilandt 2016).

The substantial impact of Brexit on the CFSP foreign policy depends on which policy area we are looking at. Here, I will present some of the central areas. Britain has a well known Atlantic orientation in its foreign policy (see, for example, Aktipis and Oliver 2011 or Chapter 11). The UK has played a role as interlocutor in connecting European policy initiatives to Washington, and when the United States has aired its disquiet about EU initiatives, notably on defence, the UK has, on several occasions, worked to reassure Washington about the bona fide nature of the EU initiatives. This was, for example, the case with the establishment of the European Security and Defense Policy (ESDP) following the Saint Malo process from 1998 and the modification of the ESDP structures in 2003. With the absence of the UK, it may be more difficult to map out a European grand strategy in the world with the United States (Whitman and Tonra 2017: 6). The group of countries with strong Atlantic sympathies will be considerably weakened with the departure of the *Atlanticist par excellence*. But a weakening does not mean disappearance; most Eastern European member states, Denmark, Portugal, the Netherlands and Germany with Atlantic sympathies will remain (about Germany, see Whitman and Tonra 2017: 7). Parallel to this, the UK has been amongst the hardliners when it comes to reactions against Russia's policy in Europe, including EU sanctions (Smith 2017). Here again, the hardliners will be weakened with Brexit, but they will not disappear. The weakening may, however, be sizeable enough to affect the level of EU sanctions against Russia, which are renewed every six months. In any case, France and in particular Germany have been at the forefront of the EU's response to the Ukrainian crisis rather than the UK, so there is not going to be a huge change with Brexit in this respect. There are a number of other foreign policy issues where the UK's views are closer to the United States' views than many other EU member states and where Brexit might therefore weaken the side that leans against the line taken by the United States. This is, for example, the case with regard to the lifting of the weapons embargo against China, the support of Israel vs. Palestine in the Middle East conflict and the emphasis on the fight against ISIS.

The Common Foreign and Defence Policy

The CSDP is the area in European foreign policy where the individual states have the biggest say. The literature distinguishes between two interrelated areas on which Brexit may have an impact: first of all, the CSDP governance model that represents the framework for decisions and where CSDP structures are made; and, second, the content of the decisions made within this framework.

With respect to CSDP governance, Britain and France have been the main architects in the CSDP since the Saint Malo meeting in 1998. Because of the British and French traditions and capacity for global military engagements, they play a key role in shaping the structures of the CFSP. Due to their capacities in this field, they have de facto veto power on the way the CSDP governance structures develop – both at the intergovernmental conferences and between them (Whitman and Tonra 2017: 6; Aktipis and Oliver 2011: 83–84). Britain and France are two out of the five EU countries that spend more than 2 per cent of their GDP on defence, and they have nuclear weapons. Since 2010, the UK has been very sceptical towards any further integration in this area. For example, it has gone against the introduction of Permanent Structured Cooperation in this area, and it has held back budgetary resources for the European Defence Agency, the creation of which it supported in 2004 (Faleg 2016; Weilandt 2016). Thus, it has exercised its veto. At the same time, other countries have also been sceptical towards the further development of the CSDP. The 2010 Franco-British Lancaster House Treaties, which laid the ground for a closer Franco-British defence relationship, were aimed at greater burden sharing in the EU and NATO but were not an initiative within the CDSP (Whitman and Tonra 2017: 8). France has viewed cooperation with Britain as a necessity for progress in the CSDP (Whitman 2016: 2–3). With Brexit, France will be left as the sine qua non for any further integration in CSDP. The most likely partner to take the place of the UK is Germany. There are indeed signs that Germany may adopt this role: the German white paper on defence attributes an important role to European defence, and France and German acted together with a joint proposal on European defence in September 2016 after the British no (Rettman 2016).

As the UK has acted as a veto player on any further integration in the field of defence, Brexit may be a context for increased EU integration in this field. EU High Representative Frederica Mogherini stated at the Foreign Affairs Council 18 May 2017, "We will go on with the Permanent Structured Cooperation (PESCO), with the use of Battlegroups" (Mogherini 2017). On 11 December 2017, the Council established Permanent Structured Cooperation in the field of defence. The central elements were the joint development of defence capabilities and a commitment to regularly increase defence expenditures. A political declaration on seventeen common projects to be undertaken under PESCO was also issued (European Council 2017a). On the background of Brexit and the increase in Eurosceptic votes in many European countries, the declaration at the 60th anniversary of the Union in March 2017 stated that the Union had to strengthen its common security and defence structures (European Council 2017b). Apart from the substantive reasons for enhancing European defence structures (i.e. compensation for the possible diminishing interest of the United States in European security, the stronger military role of Russia and the loss of the UK defence capacity in the EU), the choice of defence as an area for European initiatives was undoubtedly due to the positive view on European defence held by Europeans in opinion polls such as Eurobarometer compared with other policy areas (Eurobarometer 2017). So Brexit may play a role for the development of European defence in that proposals in this field are a safe way for the Union to show that it is alive and kicking after Brexit. However, there are still sceptical states that can be expected to become more outspoken when the British shelter in the CSDP disappears. It is also an open question how Germany will act with France in the CSDP as Germany has previously put more emphasis on civilian crisis management than both France and Britain (Faleg 2016).

When it comes to providing personnel and capacity for CSDP operations, Brexit will not make a big difference in the conduct of present operations. The UK's participation in CSDP operations since the Cameron governments 2010 has been limited. In 2016, it ranked fifth amongst the contributors to EU military operations and seventh for civilian operations. In total, it provides 4.19 per cent of the personnel deployed by the member states (ibid.; Weilandt 2016). So, in spite of the UK's importance for the development of the area, it has not played a significant military role in the EU for many years since it has redirected its efforts towards NATO and bilateral cooperation (Faleg 2016). But the EU will be losing a contributor who could, if political power changed in Westminster, have contributed more.

Brexit will therefore weaken the EU's potential as a military actor more than its actual capacity. It is possible that further integration will take place in this field following Brexit. Absence of the UK may make it easier to take new initiatives in this field. In any case, the absence of the UK will be only one piece in the jigsaw puzzle. The general focus on the CSDP as a possible area for more EU dynamism in the years to come makes it likely that we will see new initiatives in this field. At the same time, other factors, such as the developments in NATO and the United States and the EU's surroundings, different views within the EU and the role of Germany, will be decisive for whether the easier ride provided by the absence of the UK will lead to different CSDP structures. There is no reason to expect that new endeavours in this field will be aiming at hard military balancing of the United States solely as a consequence of a different configuration of forces resulting from Brexit (Oliver and Williams 2016: 565). In any case, the UK may continue to take part in some EU military or civilian operations through the EU's Framework Participation Agreement (FPA) as a third country or within a special framework adapted to the UK. Cooperation relating to the defence industry may also continue since this is already taking place outside the EU treaty framework (Faleg 2016).

Concluding remarks and broader perspectives

Brexit has bearings on the means available for European foreign policy and hence its power potential, EU foreign policy decision-making procedures and the content of EU policies. The most clear-cut impact is the reduction of economic means available in EU foreign and development policy and the absence of Britain's long-standing engagement in world affairs and efficient diplomatic service. But, after Brexit, the EU will still be a very important trade bloc and provider of overseas development aid, a significant player in environmental diplomacy and a central actor in European and, in many cases, international diplomacy (Whitman 2016: 4).

Whether EU decision-making procedures will change in the aftermath is by no means obvious as other member states share the British Governments' view on the decision-making procedures in EU foreign policy. But the EEAS, the high representative and the Commission are likely to get a higher profile and more leeway after Brexit. The content of the EU's foreign policy may change slightly as a consequence of Brexit, but whether and how much depends on the policy area. Dramatic changes in foreign policy decision-making procedures and policies do not seem likely as a direct consequence of Brexit.

However, there may be significant indirect effects in the longer term as far as the central players are concerned: with Britain out of the regular threesome coordination with France and Germany in European foreign policy, the Franco-German couple will play an even more significant role in shaping European foreign policy. France will be the closest there is to a de facto EU representative with voting rights in the United Nations Security Council. Germany's foreign policy role in the EU has increased with the crisis in the Ukraine, and its role will be even more salient in EU foreign policy – and indeed EU integration in general – after Brexit. German understandings about how to act in that role will be increasingly important after Brexit. It is possible that foreign economic aims will be more central for Germany in the EU than foreign policy aims (Oliver and Williams 2016: 563). With Brexit, the EU's political centre of gravity will shift eastward as France and Germany become more central. Eastern Europe and Russia are likely to become even more important concerns (ibid.: 560). It has been argued that the EU has lost the memory of war and communist tyranny that once helped drive it forward (Korteweg 2015; Oliver 2017: 136). Whether this is true or not (President Donald Tusk's letter, mentioned below, which makes reference to both, suggests that it is not), it is an open question whether Brexit will weaken or strengthen this narrative of the EU as a means of breaking with war and the communist past. A stronger role for the Franco–German axis would seem to strengthen the narrative of the EU as a means against war, a narrative that is, if anywhere, rooted in these two countries. The departure of the UK will not weaken this narrative – if anything, the opposite. Within the British Conservative Party and Labour, there has always been a sizeable group who did not see the EU as an insurance against war in Europe (Larsen 1997). In the Conservative Party, this group has increased very considerably over the last decades (Larsen 1999; Allen 2013).

Brexit in itself does not appear to have the potential to bring about a fundamental change in EU foreign policy – let alone the end of the EU as a foreign policy actor. However, at the present moment, there are other challenges to EU foreign policy, and Brexit will add to the pressures on the EU foreign policy at a time when challenges for European foreign policy are in no short supply. President of the European Council Tusk's letter to the heads of state and government prior to the meeting of the European Council on the future of the European Union in Malta (3 February 2017) entitled "United We Stand, Divided We Fall" strikes a tone of hitherto unseen crises and threats for the EU, including the EU as an international actor (Tusk 2017). In 2015, Rem Korteweg mentioned four horsemen circling Europe (Korteweg 2015): Brexit, the Greek debt crisis, Russian destabilisation of Eastern Europe and the challenge of immigration. Brexit can be taken as a broader metaphor for the increasing Eurosceptic challenge to the European project in its present form. The election of Donald Trump as president of the United States is a potential fifth horseman (Oliver 2017: 132). The increasing Eurosceptic sentiment, the Greek debt crisis (and other member states' economic problems) and increased immigration are not direct challenges to European foreign policy (although the latter has an important foreign policy component). But a significant unravelling of internal European integration will affect the EU as an international actor as well, both because many internal policies are intertwined with external actions and because the lack of trust and uncertainty associated with an unravelling of parts of European integration will most likely not be restricted to internal affairs.

The remaining two horsemen, the election of Trump as president and the Russian destabilisation of Eastern Europe, are closely linked to what kind of actor the EU will be in the emerging multipolar world order. While the United States has for a long time preferred a united Europe to a disintegrated one, the signals of President Trump suggest that the US preferences (or at least his preferences) are now the opposite. Brexit would under all circumstances complicate EU relations with the United States but would not seriously upset them. But the new emphasis in the United States (if it lasts) will have the potential to drive the EU and the United States apart (Oliver and Williams 2016: 565). This may contribute to a split in EU foreign policy, where some member states will try to hang on to the United States at all costs. But it could potentially also contribute to reinforcing European foreign policy. Russia might likewise contribute to tearing European foreign policy cooperation apart, with some countries increasingly siding more with Russia. In the long term, the EU will be surrounded by Europe's most populous states: Turkey, Russia and the UK (Germany will in the long term have a smaller population than the UK)!

It could become divided between the US and Asian power (Oliver and Williams 2016: 560). But this could in the long term also have the opposite effect of reinforcing EU cohesion and foreign policy cooperation.

References

Aktipis, M. and Oliver, T. (2011) Europeanization and British Foreign Policy. In: Wong, R. and Hill, C. (eds.), *National and European Foreign Policies: Towards Europeanization*. London: Routledge.

Allen, D. (2013) The United Kingdom: Towards Isolation and Parting of the Ways? In: Bulmer, S. and Lequesne, C. (eds.), *The Members of the European Union*. Oxford: Oxford University Press.

Commission (2014) EU Position in World Trade. Last updated October 2, 2014. Available at: http://ec.europa.eu/trade/policy/eu-position-in-world-trade/ [Accessed August 8, 2017].

Demsey, J. (2017) Judy Asks: Is Brexit a Distraction from EU Foreign Policy? *Carnegie Europe*, March 29, 2017. Available at: http://carnegieeurope.eu/strategiceurope/?fa=68441 [Accessed August 15, 2017].

Dullien, S. (2017) Britain Steps into a Deglobalising World. *European Council on Foreign Relation*, February 20, 2017. Available at: www.ecfr.eu/article/commentary_britain_steps_into_a_deglobalising_world_7238 [Accessed August 15, 2017].

Eurobarometer (2017) Designing Europe's Future: Security and Defence: Special Eurobarometer 461. *European Commission*, April, 2017. Available at: http://ec.europa.eu/commfrontoffice/publicopinion/index.cfm/Survey/getSurveyDetail/instruments/SPECIAL/surveyKy/2173 [Accessed August 15, 2017].

European Council (2017a) Defence Cooperation: Council Establishes Permanent Structured Cooperation (PESCO), with 25 Member States Participating, December, 11. Available at: www.consilium.europa.eu/en/press/press-releases/2017/12/11/defence-cooperation-pesco-25-member-states-participating/ [Accessed August 15, 2017].

European Council (2017b) The Rome Declaration, March 25, 2017. Available at: www.consilium.europa.eu/en/press/press-releases/2017/03/25-rome-declaration/ [Accessed August 15, 2017].

European External Action Service (2016) Military and Civilian Missions and Operations, May 6, 2016. Available at: https://eeas.europa.eu/headquarters/headquarters-homepage_en [Accessed August 15, 2017].

European Parliament (2017) Possible Impacts of Brexit on EU Development and Humanitarian Policies. *Directorate-General for External Policies*. Available at: www.europarl.europa.eu/RegData/etudes/STUD/2017/578042/EXPO_STU(2017)578042_EN.pdf [Accessed August 15, 2017].

Eurostat (2017) Share of Member States in EU GDP, April 4, 2017. Available at: http://ec.europa.eu/eurostat/web/products-eurostat-news/-/DDN-20170410-1 [Accessed August 13, 2017].

Faleg, G. (2016) The Implications of Brexit for the EU's Common Security and Defence Policy. *CEPS*, July 26, 2016. Available at: www.ceps.eu/publications/implications-brexit-eu%E2%80%99s-common-security-and-defence-policy [Accessed August 15, 2017].

Keukeleire, S. and Delreux, T. (2014) *The Foreign Policy of the European Union*. London: Palgrave Macmillan.

Korteweg, R. (2015) Beware the Four Horsemen Circling Europe: Greece, Russia, Migrants and the Brexit. *The Independent*, June 24, 2015. Available at: www.independent.co.uk/voices/comment/beware-the-four-horsemen-circling-europe-greece-russia-migrants-and-the-brexit-10343447.html [Accessed August 15, 2017].

Larsen, S. (1997) *Discourse Analysis and Foreign Policy: France, Britain and Europe*. London: Routledge.

Larsen, S. (1999) British and Danish European Policies in the 1990s: A Discourse Approach. *European Journal of International Relations* 5(4): 451–484.

Lewis, J. (2016) The European Council and the Council of Ministers. In: Cini, M. and Borrágan, N. (eds.), *European Union Politics*. Oxford: Oxford University Press.

Milevska, T. (2013) UK No Longer Advocates for EU Enlargement. *Euroactiv*, December 21, 2013. Available at: www.euractiv.com/section/enlargement/news/uk-no-longer-advocates-for-eu-enlargement/ [Accessed August 15, 2017].

Mogherini, F. (2017) Remarks by Federica Mogherini upon Arrival at the Foreign Affairs Council (Defence). *EEAS*. Brussels, May 18, 2017. Available at: https://eeas.europa.eu/headquarters/headquarters-homepage_en [Accessed August 15, 2017].

Nuttall, S. (1992) *European Political Cooperation*. Oxford: Clarendon Press.

OECD (2016) *Development Finance Data*. Available at: www.oecd.org/dac/financing-sustainable-development/development-finance-data/ [Accessed August 15, 2017].

Oliver, T. (2017) The EU Falling Apart? Theoretical Discussions of Brexit, Grexit and Other Scenarios. In: Grimmel, A. and Ciang, S.M. (eds.), *Solidarity in the European Union*. Cham: Springer International, pp. 131–144.

Oliver, T. and Williams, M.J. (2016) Special Relationships in Flux: Brexit and the Future of the US–EU Relationship. *International Affairs* 92: 547–567.

Rettman, A. (2016) France and Germany Propose EU Defence Union. *Eurobserver*, September 12, 2016. Available at: https://euobserver.com/foreign/135022 [Accessed August 15, 2017].

Smith, K.E. (2017) Implications of Brexit for the UK, the EU and the International System: A Summary of the 2016 Lecture Series. *London School of Economics*, Department of International Relations Blog, January 11, 2017. Available at: http://blogs.lse.ac.uk/internationalrelations/2017/01/11/implications-of-brexit-for-the-uk-the-eu-and-the-international-system-a-summary-of-the-2016-lecture-series/ [Accessed August 15, 2017].

Smith, M. (2004) *Europe's Foreign and Security Policy: Institutionalization of Cooperation*. Cambridge: Cambridge University Press.

Tusk, D. (2017) *United We Stand, Divided We Fall*. Letter by President Donald Tusk to the 27 EU Heads of State or Government on the Future of the EU before the Malta Summit, February 3, 2017. Available at: www.consilium.europa.eu/en/press/press-releases/2017/01/31-tusk-letter-future-europe/ [Accessed August 15, 2017].

Weilandt, R. (2016) Brexit's Trifling Impact on EU External Affairs. Friends of Europe, August 4, 2016. Available at: http://www.friendsofeurope.org/publication/brexits-trifling-impact-eu-external-affairs [Accessed February 14, 2018].

White, B. (2001) *Understanding European Foreign Policy*. Basingstoke: Palgrave Macmillan.

Whitman, R. (2016) After the 'Leave' Vote: The UK's European Year Zero. *Chatham House*, March 10, 2016. Available at: www.chathamhouse.org/expert/comment/after-leave-vote-uk-s-european-year-zero [Accessed August 15, 2017].

Whitman, R. and Tonra, B. (2017) Western EU Member States Foreign Policy Geo-Orientations. In: Hadfield, A., Manners, I. and Whitman, R. (eds.), *Foreign Policies of EU Member States: Continuity and Europeanization*. London: Routledge.

19

BREXIT AND EUROPEAN DEFENCE

Why more defence does not equal more integration

Mikkel Vedby Rasmussen

Introduction

Defence has been made a priority issue in Brussels in response to Brexit. From an integration perspective, the initiatives on defence seem to confirm the notion that crisis can be an impetus for further integration. From this perspective, Brexit opened an area for integration that had hitherto been resistant to efforts to realise synergies between European defence establishments. However, one should be careful accepting the rhetoric of the Commission and certain member states that presented defence initiatives as proof that the Union would become stronger because of Brexit. If one changes perspective from the high politics of integration to the defence domain, it becomes clear that Brexit occurred in the middle of a new dynamism in defence. From this perspective, the integration efforts are but one element in a process of European rearmament that began before Brexit and will end on terms that are not decided in the EU but rather in national capitals. Of these, Berlin is probably the most important one. In the German case, the two perspectives merge because the German Government has found it convenient to dress up its own reinvestment in defence and forging of a European network of military cooperation in the garb of European integration.

This chapter is structured around the integration and the defence perspective, focusing on events in the EU. It is important to note that this focus serves to identify important issues and how they are addressed rather than being an argument for EU having usurped the European defence agenda after the June 2016 referendum. On the contrary, the Brussels focus demonstrates the very real limits of the EU's, especially the Commission's, influence on this issue and thus serves to demonstrate the way in which Brexit policy is very much an issue of the national governments. Of these, the German Government has been the key player, and Berlin's position is thus very much in focus in this chapter. This focus on the hard realities of defence policy serves to put in perspective the ambitions of the European Commission and others who see defence as an integration area that will save the Union after Brexit.

The Berlin-based researchers Claudia Major and Christian Mölling have to a large extent shaped the research agenda on Brexit and defence. They argue that it is difficult to assess Brexit's impact on security and defence because of (1) causality – is the increase in defence spending, for example, caused by Trump or Brexit? – and (2) the uncertainty of the policy position of the key players (most notably Germany, France and the UK) because of 'the uncertain political environment of key European players'. The uncertain economic prospects after Brexit adds to this uncertainty, they argue – is the increase in defence budgets sustainable? (Major and Mölling 2017: 4). For a handbook of Brexit to provide any guide to events under such circumstances, one approach is to focus on core issues and then describe how these issues have been addressed in a European context. These are central issues for European defence that this chapter will focus on.

Strategic outlook and strategic culture

Brexit takes place at a time when terror, migration and Russian challenge some of the assumptions that have underwritten European security and defence policy since the end of the Cold War. Especially, the EU's self-image as a normative power focused on soft security issues is being challenged. In this debate, the views and strategic cultures of the participating governments become hugely important. Claudia Major and Christian Mölling argue that, in the wake of Brexit, 'a reduced strategic outlook without the UK's strategic culture might inhibit the CSDP but also the wider foreign policy power of the EU' (ibid.: 6).

Technological development and industrial base

The current procurement of new platforms – from aircraft carriers to drones – reflects that European governments have come to a point where Cold War materiel is finally completely replaced by the platforms and technologies of a new era. Given that military technology is currently developing rapidly and decisively, this presents a unique set of challenges and opportunities. European military capabilities for years to come are being established by the current generation of procurement, and this in turn determines the future for much for the European industrial base. The fact that European investments are no longer large enough to underpin global defence producers puts a certain perspective on this.

Renationalisation of defence

After a period of integration when the enlargement of NATO and the reintegration of France into NATO's military command structure, the fact that only a number of allies were willing and able to engage in operations in Afghanistan and elsewhere meant a renationalisation of defence where bilateral and multilateral defence cooperation takes place within the NATO framework but not directed by Brussels. The increased cooperation between the EU and NATO might be regarded as a way for organisations that have been increasingly hollowed out by cooperation arrangements between their member states to reassert themselves.

After describing how defence came to be an important part of the European agenda after the UK referendum, this chapter focuses on these three issues in turn: strategic outlook and strategic culture, technological development and industrial base and the renationalisation of defence. They thus serve as focus points to guide the narrative of how the EU and its members have developed defence cooperation after the UK referendum resulted in Brexit. It is important to put these events in the proper context, and, in order to do so, we start with the sea trials of an aircraft carrier.

A renaissance in European defence

HMS *Queen Elizabeth* left Rosyth for sea trials on 27 June 2017. The *Queen Elizabeth* is the first of two 65,000-ton carriers ordered by the Royal Navy. The carrier had to leave port at midnight in order to hit the low tide that would just allow its masts to pass below the Forth Bridge. At 280 metres long and 70 metres wide, the carrier was not only a potent piece of military hardware but to UK Defence Minister Sir Michael Fallon a powerful symbol also: 'For the next 50 years she will deploy around the world, demonstrating British power and our commitment to confronting the emerging challenges from a dangerous world' (BBC 2017). The *Queen Elizabeth* is but one of a number of defence investments that will dramatically increase European military capabilities in the years to come. The F-35s that are to take off from the flight deck of the *Queen Elizabeth* is part of the order for 344 F-35s placed by a number of European nations. European defence spending is increasing, and while it might not seem impressive that the spending is just crawling back to 2010 levels, it is worth noting that the new funds are being used for investment in equipment like the UK carriers or F-35s. Investment in defence equipment in European NATO countries has increased from US\$42 billion in 2010 to US\$47 billion in 2016. While this may not seem like a huge increase, the new money in defence has been spent on procurement, resulting in an increase in procurement from 15 per cent of defence budgets to 19.7 per cent of defence budgets. This means that, on average, NATO has almost realized the goal of 20 per cent of defence budgets in investments. This is arguably a much more important target than the notorious 2 per cent of GDP (NATO 2017).

If one adds the new capabilities acquired by the European nations individually, then one might argue that a renaissance in European defence is underway. After a couple of decades where either operational requirements (Iraq, Afghanistan) or austerity budgets have undercut investment in new platforms and technologies, the European countries are now investing in top-of-the-line military capabilities. The question remains how one is to add up those new capabilities. Brexit has put this question in the forefront of European defence debates – so much in front that Brexit might be taking attention away from the real story: the new European commitment to and investment in security and defence. After the British electorate decided to leave the European Union, the question became whether one should subtract HMS *Queen Elizabeth* and other UK military capabilities from the European roster or whether the UK was still to be counted as a part of European defence. The consequence of Brexit was to question the European defence arrangements. Thus, the issue was not only the EU's defence arrangement but also those of NATO and how the two organisations interact. This is no idly theoretical matter. The UK contribution to European security was quickly made a political issue, a card to be played in the Brexit negotiations. In her letter activating Article 50, UK Prime Minister Theresa May thus warned that 'in security terms a failure to reach agreement would mean our cooperation in the fight against crime and terrorism would be weakened' (Deean and Jones 2017). Where Prime Minister May argued that the remaining EU member states would need to accommodate the UK in order to maintain current levels of security, Federica Mogherini (the EU's high representative on foreign affairs) argued that the fact the UK was leaving the Union made it possible for the remaining EU members to get serious about defence integration by leaving the protection of national defence industries and national armed forces behind in favour of truly European defence investment and common military operations (Banks and Foster 2016).

Five days before the HMS *Queen Elizabeth* began her sea trials, the European Council of foreign and defence ministers met in Brussels. In the run-up to the meeting, Commission President Jean-Claude Juncker argued that 'we have reached a point where progress is the only option. The only question is the speed' (Juncker 2017). The challenge for anyone following European defence in a time of Brexit is to be able to deal simultaneously with the issue of European defence from an integration, or EU, perspective, a national perspective and a capabilities perspective. Because while these perspectives constitute distinct logics, they often operate at the same time, most crucially in the case of Germany. Germany is set to increase defence spending by €130 billion over the next five years, which among other things means an investment in naval vessels and an increased number of Leopard II tanks from 225 to 320 (Fiorenza 2016). German rearmament is a consequence of the changes in the European security environment following the Russian intervention in Ukraine and US pressure to increase defence spending. These causes operate independently from Brexit. However, the way Germans go about this increase in defence spending is heavily influenced by Brexit because defence has become a way to prove the continued ability of the EU to increase integration. Yet one should be careful not to buy all the rhetoric of integration because Berlin has insisted on the EU adopting a method for defence cooperation that in reality makes it a bi- or multilateral project independent of Brussels. Thus, one might even argue that defence cooperation proves that power and initiative are moving away from Brussels and back to national capitals and thus that EU policy on defence actually confirms the fragmentation of the EU of which Brexit is the most dramatic example.

A new strategic concept: timing is everything

If David Cameron had decided to hold the referendum in February or December, would defence then have become a major integration effort? There is reason to argue that defence would have become a major issue anyway. The Juncker Commission was committed to redoubling the Union's efforts on defence. Defence had for some time been identified as the most promising terrain for new integration efforts. In July 2014, Juncker set the agenda for his Commission, arguing that 'even the strongest soft powers cannot make do in the long run without at least some integrated defence capabilities'. Juncker's predecessor had made much of the Union's 'normative' power perfecting the image of the Union as a foreign policy actor of a different kind from traditional great powers. This fitted the Union's narrative of constituting a new type of international relations that left the type of foreign policy doctrines that had produced two world wars behind in favour of an approach to international affairs based on negotiation and institutionalisation (Manners 2002). Even if Juncker did not break completely with that narrative, he spoke for an important constituency that argued that the Union could not do with soft power alone. High Representative Federica Mogherini was tasked to revise the Union's strategic concept for the first time since 2003. Especially in Berlin, there were great expectations of Mogherini's new text.

To Chancellor Angela Merkel's government, the new strategic concept was to coalesce the European governments in a united front against Russia after years of haggling over the response to Russian bellicosity in Ukraine and elsewhere. Such a united front would serve to legitimise an increase in German defence spending, which the Social Democrats in Merkel's grand coalition were highly sceptical about. Mogherini failed decisively to deliver on German ambitions, delivering a document that focused on the unique, soft nature of the Union's power and that had a focus on the South rather than the East, which was uppermost in the German mind. Had the high representative delivered this document before Brexit, Berlin and London would surely have come together in criticising it and setting a new an agenda, but she crucially did not hand in the document before the referendum, and in that sense, it did matter that Cameron decided that the referendum should be held in June. By withholding publication until after the referendum, Morgehini had ensured that the new strategic concept for the EU would either set the agenda for a Union reconfirmed in its purpose by a UK decision to remain or offer a new agenda for the remaining members of the EU. With Britain's decision to head for the exit, the defence portfolio became an integration issue, and the ability to deliver on it a test of the Union's ability to function and set a new course after Brexit. Mrs Morgehini even argued that defence integration was made possible by Brexit (Banks and Foster 2016).

The timing of the new security strategy and the referendum thus became crucial to the way the defence brief was handled, but that does not mean that Brexit caused defence integration.

On the contrary, the initial German reaction was to double down on producing initiatives on defence that went much further than Mrs Morgehini had suggested. To the German Government, the main attraction of Morgehini's strategy was the timing of its publication. In terms of content, the strategy was remarkable for its inability to meet the needs of the governments in Berlin and Paris. They were not overly impressed with a document that sought to encompass the very different ambitions on security and defence by emphasising the uniquely civilian nature of European power. Even if President Juncker tried to toughen up the message, arguing in his State of the Union Address in 2016 that 'even though Europe is proud to be a soft power of global importance, we must not be naïve. Soft power is not enough in our increasingly dangerous neighbourhood' (Juncker 2016). The initiative had moved from Brussels to Berlin where the German foreign ministry cancelled the holiday of its key defence people who worked through the summer of 2016 to be able to present a package of defence initiatives.

However, the first event of the European calendar after the referendum was neither in Brussels nor in Berlin but at the NATO Summit in Warsaw in July. As Richard Whitman notes, 'The NATO Warsaw Summit commitment to deepen the EU–NATO relationship sees a subtle evolution of the UK's position from a participant on both sides of that relationship to an outsider in the EU's deliberations' (Whitman 2017: 522). The European Council and Commission president was invited to Warsaw and, together with the NATO secretary general, they stated that 'we believe the time has come to give new impetus and new substance to the NATO–EU strategic partnership' (NATO-EU 2016a). Instead of 'North Atlantic community', which is NATO jargon, they refer to the 'Euro-Atlantic community', thus pointing to Europe as an independent and unitary partner. NATO–EU relationship should be 'ambitious and pragmatic' (European Council 2016b: para. 1). In this statement, Juncker's ambition for a tougher EU approach to defence and security met secretary general Jens Stoltenberg's ambition for integrating the EU more in NATO's affairs. Stoltenberg's key message when he took over as secretary general from Anders Fogh Rasmussen was to increase NATO–EU cooperation. To the European Parliament he outlined an agenda for cooperation on hybrid, strengthened deterrence for East and South, as well as defence investment that foreshadowed the agenda adopted after Brexit (NATO 2015).

In December 2016, the EU council, as well as the NATO Council, decided on forty-two areas in which to increase capabilities. It is worth noting that these initiatives concern cyber and hybrid threats; in other words, the organisations are cooperating on new missions, meaning that cooperation is focused on issues that are currently the main investment area of new funds. This demonstrates a seriousness of purpose that the two organisations are not fighting over new funds but actually sharing them. It also reflects a realisation that neither the member states nor the EU and NATO can afford duplication of missions – which is another step in the direction of genuine cooperation because it addresses completion between the two Brussels institution in a manner much more forthright and business oriented than has hitherto been the case (2016b). Staff exchange and interaction are a very important part of this new cooperation, and so is the inclusion of the EU in the NATO Defence Planning Process (NDPP) and the Partnership for Peace Planning and Review Process (PARP). The acronyms describe what is arguably the most enduring, long-term effect of Alliance membership because the defence planning processes ensure a continuous alignment of procurement and planning in the individual countries with Alliance priorities. The reason why NATO members can engage in joint operations is because they invest in capabilities that enable them to do so and train in doing so. By allowing the Union to be part of that process, NATO is transforming the very foundation of the Alliance from an exclusive arrangement between members to a defence planning process that is truly European in the sense that it includes EU priorities and neutral EU members as well. The fact that EU and NATO realise that they are engaging in organisational transformation is apparent in the

June 2017 progress report on EU–NATO cooperation that concluded that 'we have witnessed a change in the culture, quality and dynamics of our engagement' (NATO–EU 2017). Since strategic culture, or the lack thereof, has continuously been described as one of the key obstacles for the development of a defence dimension in the EU, as well as an important stumbling block in EU–NATO cooperation, this is an important finding. It also constitutes an important 'not to self' on the part of the EU; the future success of defence cooperation also depends on the ability of Brussels to approach defence issues in new ways. The fact that Britain is less engaged in the EU might work against such new thinking, Major and Mölling (2017) argue, because Britain has contributed operational experience and hard-nosed realism to the European debates. A reconfiguring of the NATO–EU relationship offers the UK the opportunity to use active engagement in NATO to influence the EU because closer integration between the two institutions also makes it possible for the UK to have a voice from beyond Brexit.

From this perspective, it is crucial that the EU introduces a coordinated annual review on defence (CARD) as an NDPP 'lite' (European Council 2017). For the first time, EU capability generation constitutes a genuine military planning process instead of a political process where the good news for the communique far too often dictated decisions. On the conceptual level, this is a clear indication of a departure from the notion that guided the Barroso commission as well as Mogherini's strategic concept that the EU should be a different kind of power from traditional, defence-focused nation states. In Brussels, this is often described as reluctance within the Commission to engage with hard security issues. From this perspective, Juncker's call for the EU 'to toughen up' (Juncker 2016) is also an HR exercise by which the Commission president instructs his people to embrace a more military agenda. It is this farewell to soft power that really changes the EU's relationship to NATO. It influences the way individual civil servants and military officers are supposed to work together, but it also stipulates that this work should be seen as a coherent effort. The notion of a Euro-Atlantic area is a clear signal that the EU has a contribution to make. In planning terms, this is translated to the single-set-of-forces concept – 'the Council underlines that Member States have "a single set of forces" which they can use in different frameworks' (NATO–EU 2016b). The single-set-of-forces framework is crucial for future defence cooperation because it for the first time recognises the need for coherent planning and action rather than regarding defence in terms of individual initiatives. It forces the Commission to think in terms of effects rather in terms of the politics of integration. It also recognises that European defence is European rather than EU or NATO. This approach undermines Morgehini's argument that Brexit makes further EU defence integration possible. On the contrary, the de-emphasising institutions means that the UK, as well as Germany and France, can engage in joint operations and procurement cooperation with each other and clubs of like-minded nations that increasingly structure European defence cooperation on terms where concrete cooperation is much more important than individual membership of the EU or NATO. This opens the possibility for the UK to continue to play a pivotal role in European defence, but it also makes this role much more contingent on taking initiatives on defence. The UK no longer has the option of shaping European defence policy by blocking EU initiatives. London will have to outperform the Commission in terms of creativity and coalition building.

Capability development: jobs or tanks?

The realisation of the post-Brexit defence agenda is thus heavily dependent on integration between the EU and NATO. The single-set-of-forces-concept presents European defence as truly European, as does the notion of Euro-Atlantic defence cooperation. This demonstrates the new meaning that 'European' is gradually taking on as Brexit becomes reality. Europe can no longer be a shorthand for the EU when Britain is not a member. Neither the EU nor NATO can speak in Europe's name, but paradoxically this means that the need for cooperation on equal terms becomes more evident. It also undermines the effort to understand defence cooperation exclusively in integration terms. One might actually argue that the EU has left its anti-NATO stands and that this has been the main trigger of integration. To argue that Brexit was necessary for this to happen is hardly convincing, but it does demonstrate the extent to which defence cooperation in the EU had developed into trench warfare between 'integrationists' and 'atlantics'. By leaving the field, the British made it possible for the 'integrationists' to accept the British argument without giving in to Britain. Now, the EU is striving for 'capacity to act autonomously when and where necessary and with partners wherever possible' (European Council 2017). Capability development is thus a crucial part of the EU approach to defence (Biscop 2016).

In the Council conclusions of March 2017, the ministers state that they intend to:

> enhance the effective of the CSDP and the development and maintenance of Member States' capabilities, supported by a more integrated, sustainable, innovative and competitive European Defence Technological and Industrial Base (EDTIB), which also contributes to jobs, growth and innovations across the EU and can enhance Europe's strategic autonomy, strengthening its ability to work with partners.
>
> *(European Council 2017)*

The language of this paragraph illustrates the issues. The paragraph opens with a strong statement that implicitly recognizes the lacklustre state of security and defence cooperation while explicitly promising new action. Capabilities are to be developed, and a plan for doing so by developing not only military capabilities but also the industrial capabilities to support this is presented. This strong opening is immediately diluted, however, when the next sentence makes the contribution to jobs, growth and innovation a rival purpose for building capabilities. These capabilities, the next sentence informs us, should be sufficient to support an autonomous policy – this is no small ambition given the current state of affairs, but the purpose of the sentence is immediately diverted by the emphasis that this increase in capabilities should also strengthen the Union's ability to work with partners; in other words, the capabilities are not to be all that autonomous after all.

Previous EU efforts in defence cooperation have been hampered by the fact that EU planners neither recognised a concept of a single set of forces nor seemed to be able to connect capability development with realistic mission planning. The EU's rapid reaction force was thus declared operational or partly operational several times without that declaration seeming to reflect neither the real state of readiness of the forces nor a genuine desire to actually use the force – which has yet to be deployed in a real-life mission. The discussion of level of ambition is thus crucial to European defence efforts. The EU has imported this discussion from NATO where it was central to the discussions around the last strategic concept when the Alliance was asking itself how to prioritise resources after the mission in Afghanistan had had the highest priority for a number of years. The EU is defining its defence ambitions in terms of the capability to respond to external conflicts and crisis. The Union is cautiously moving beyond the so-called Petersberg tasks stating a willingness to engage in the whole spectrum of crisis management in rapid and decisive ways (European Council 2016a: para. 7.a). This is potentially a large commitment, especially as the commitment to a single set of forces means that such operational capability should be prioritised in relation to other commitments. The EU thus acknowledges the need to discuss priorities – which opens the discussion between France and Germany on whether to prioritise deterrence missions in the East or out-of-area operations in the South. The legacy from the security strategy lives on in a continued focus on capacity building of partners, training, security sector reform, but this is supplemented with a focus on border control and other in-area issues. The list of caveats to these commitments is so long, however, that it would be fair to say that the EU has acknowledged that there is a discussion to be had rather than actually having the discussion. Neither capability nor mission come cheap, so a discussion of the budget level follows from any discussion of level of ambition. The Union is cautiously open for 'financial solidarity and burden sharing' on the basis of the allies having a 'sufficient level of defence expenditure'. With the NATO discussion as backdrop, this sounds like a lite version of the 2 per cent commitment in NATO (ibid.: para. 9). The level of discussion on ambition will be a pivotal site for future discussions of European defence because it defines the framework for the budget level and the force level, thus setting the scene for the rest of the issues. It is also here that the European element in '*Euro*-Atlantic' defence cooperation becomes most significant because the debate between the Trump administration and its allies on the proper level of defence investment to a large extent depends on different perceptions of how large defence establishments the current security situation calls for.

Structured cooperation: the renationalisation of defence

The level of ambition and the focus of those ambitions differ among the member states. To the frustration of the Merkel government, Mogherini tried to get around that issue by adopting a lowest common denominator in the strategic concept, Berlin immediately set out to make the strategic concept a starting line for further and more military-focused cooperation. In 2014, well before Brexit, President Juncker had argued that Permanent Structured Cooperation (PESCO) on defence would enable the willing and able to cooperate without permitting the more reluctant members of the Union to stand in the way. Juncker revisited this point in his 2016 State of the Union: 'The Lisbon Treaty enables those Members States who wish, to pool their defence capabilities in the form of a permanent structured cooperation. I think the time to make use of this possibility is now' (Juncker 2016). In this, as in many other matters, President Juncker's beliefs seem to reflect those of Chancellor Merkel. The German Government has worked hard to make PESCO the structuring principle in EU defence cooperation. In March 2017, the Council decided on:

> the possible projects and initiatives that Member States are willing to pursue through PESCO including in a modular way and while making use of ongoing projects and making new commitments in the area of defence investment, with a view to tackling recognized shortfalls and addressing EU and Member States' priorities in the field of capabilities; improving the deplorability and operational availability of their armed forces; and increasing their interoperability by polling and sharing existing capabilities.
> *(European Council 2017: para. 7)*

The concept of PESCO puts an end to any idea of a European Army. It underlines the concept behind a single-set-of-forces that defence is a national capability that can be developed and utilised for joint effort on the basis of cooperation between national governments. The council thus 'notes that any capabilities developed through PESCO will remain owned and operated by Member States. It recalls that Member States have a single set of forces that they can use in other frameworks' (European Council 2017: para. 6).

PESCO places the initiative with member states rather than with the Commission. PESCO thus codifies the renationalisation of defence that has defined European defence policy for the last ten years. After a period of integration when the enlargement of NATO and the reintegration of France into NATO's military command structure, the fact that only a number of allies were willing and able to engage in operations in Afghanistan and elsewhere meant a renationalisation of defence where bilateral and multilateral defence cooperation takes place within the NATO framework, but it is not directed by Brussels. The UK has been at the forefront of this development by establishing a joint expeditionary force (JEF) that commits a number of Northern European countries to operate together in the framework of a UK task force. PESCO allows Germany to do something similar. Berlin has made arrangements for the integration of Czech and Dutch units into the Bundeswehr, as well as a number of capability development projects – from a submarine development programme with Norway to the agreement on developing a new fighter with France. As Christian Mölling has described it, German is increasingly a hub for defence cooperation with neighbouring states that can contribute with either technology or manpower with considerable marginal effects for German military capability. PESCO allows this to take place within an EU framework that gives the crucial legitimacy that opens the way for support in the Bundestag for increased defence spending and, in time, more assertive defence posturing. Chancellor Merkel thus follows the traditional German recipe for operating 'in Europe's name' (Ash 1994). While in London the politics of Brexit is to a large extent determined by the infighting in the Conservative Party, it is the workings of the coalition government that determine the politics of Brexit in Berlin. The social democrats in the coalition would not accept increased defence spending if it was done unilaterally and with reference to Russia. Defence spending as a means to reinvigorate European integration after Brexit is a completely different issue, however. Chancellor Merkel carefully secured a European framework for increased defence spending but defined this European framework in ways that enabled Berlin to invest in national defence rather than in pan-European structures.

Having established that European defence is the responsibility of the national governments who can use NATO and the EU to further the development of a single set of forces, the second act begins. Now, the crucial question becomes to what extent Britain and British companies will be included in PESCO-based consortia. Germany has created the optimal conditions for Britain to take part in European defence, even if the UK is not member of EU, but it is by no means certain that these conditions will be utilised. It is equally possible that Germany and the UK will compete for smaller European states to take part in their coalitions and consortia. This places France in a rather difficult position. While the French Government found the German approach to defence much too focused on procedure, Paris recognised the political realities in Berlin, allowing the PESCO decisions to be made. The Macron administration's decision to cut defence spending with €850 million (Rubin 2017) means that France is not able to invest in new PESCO initiatives in the way Germany will be. France was decided to defence spending from 2019, peaking at 3 percent of GDP in 2023, so in the longer term France will be able to make investments with Germany. At the same time, France is much more focused on overseas interventions and not quite as focused on deterrence in the East as Germany is. This difference in perception and priority means that it is a real possibility that the current defence initiatives will be largely left to Germany while France will look to the UK for joint cooperation on overseas missions and the like. The result of this might be that the Saint Malo agreement will be a much better guide to Anglo-French cooperation than the Brexit treaty (Black et al. 2017: 27; Pannier 2017). A French military that faces new cuts under President Macon will have to choose its partners carefully, and many French security priorities are much better served in cooperation with Britain than with Germany.

Conclusion: an army of metaphors

The concept of a European army is a mobile army of metaphors, in Nietzsche's words, rather than an actual military force. The notion of a European army is either a metaphor for the continued ambition to create an ever closer Union or a conceptual reminder of the dark days of the world wars, which continue to be the starting point for the narrative of European integration. Then again, the notion of a European army conjures up the many instances in which military integration has failed. Either way, the concept of a European army is a curious anti-vision because military integration has failed before and will probably fail again. But even if people recall Jacques Poos's boast in 1991 that 'the hour of Europe has dawned', talking about an army that will never be opens the possibility for imaging other ways to engage in European integration – in the military as well as in civilian terms. Thus, a European army or, more broadly defined, defence integration becomes a metaphor of grand historical purpose and little else. And purpose was exactly what Brussels needed in the wake of the UK referendum. As defence cooperation moves beyond integration rhetoric, it confirms the renationalisation of defence that has characterised security and defence in Europe for a number of years. Current efforts for defence integration is more than anything else defined by the German need to put rearmament in a European context. However, security is a much larger concern in all European electorates than it has previously been, and that means that making initiatives on defence address clear and imagined fears in the electorate, which will keep political attention on the area in ways that have not been the case previously.

The notion of a European army also falls short of describing the real challenges that Europe faces beyond its borders – in North Africa, the Middle East and on border with Russia. The concept of a European army describes military capability as something that Europeans can achieve on their own if only they are willing and able to pool their resources. The fact remains that European security depends heavily on US military capabilities. What the Europeans are actually discussing is the ways in which their forces are to be cooperating with American forces. That is why EU–NATO integration is so important – it links the EU closer to the United States in operational terms. Even in the instances where Europeans might operate on their own, they will depend on close cooperation with local forces. The way the Italians and others have tried to stabilise Libya in order to prevent a continued flow of refugees across the Mediterranean is a case in point. The Commission has emphasised security cooperation and capacity building of partners, but this falls far short of a coherent strategy of engagement with partners in order to increase capability and security. This European perspective also limits the geographical scope: can European security be defined only in terms of the European neighbourhood at a time when Asia becomes increasingly strategically important?

The fact that more money is being invested in defence means that the EU has a real possibility in succeeding with the collaboratory investment plans that NATO failed at with its Smart Defence Initiative during Anders Fogh Rasmussen's time as secretary general. With more money to go around, the appetite for cooperation is simply greater today than five years ago. It is important to note that the PESCO approach will put national governments front and centre. Much will depend on how the German Government will chose partners and on what kind of operational and technological innovation the German Government will encourage. The Franco-German decision to develop a next-generation fighter aircraft is one important decision that will shape force structure and operations but also potentially mean a considerable drain on investment resources. Even if Europeans are reinvesting in defence, the funds are still comparatively modest. Capabilities are developed slowly and with an eye constantly on the costs. From that perspective, organisational affiliations mean much less than actual ability to procure and eventually deploy capabilities. That is why it is more important for Britain's role in European defence that HMS *Queen Elizabeth* has begun sea trails than the fact that the government in London has started Brexit negotiations.

References

Ash, T.G. (1994) *In Europe's Name*. London: Vintage.

Banks, M. and Foster, P. (2016) Europe Forges Ahead with Plans for 'EU Army'. *The Telegraph*, September 6. Available at: www.telegraph.co.uk/news/2016/09/06/europe-forges-ahead-with-plans-for-eu-army/ [Accessed September 6, 2017].

BBC (2017) HMS Queen Elizabeth Sets Sail from Rosyth for Sea Trials, June 27. Available at: www.bbc.com/news/uk-scotland-edinburgh-east-fife-40402153 [Accessed August 29, 2017].

Biscop, S. (2016) All or Nothing? The EU Global Strategy and Defence Policy after Brexit. *Contemporary Security Policy* 37(3): 431–445.

Black, J., Hall, A., Cox, K., Kepe, M. and Silfversten, E. (2017) Defence and Security after Brexit: Understanding the Possible Implications of the UK's Decision to Leave the EU: Overview Report. *RAND Corporation*. Available at: www.rand.org/pubs/research_reports/RR1786z1.html [Accessed August 31, 2017].

Deean, A. and Jones, J. (2017) Brexit Begins: UK Triggers Article 50 to Begin EU Divorce. *CNN*, March 29. Available at: http://edition.cnn.com/2017/03/29/europe/article-50-brexit-theresa-may-eu/index.html [Accessed July 8, 2017].

European Council (2016a) Council Conclusions on Implementing the EU Global Strategy in the Area of Security and Defence, November 14. Brussels.

European Council (2016b) Council Conclusions on the Implementation of the Joint Declaration by the President of the European Council, the President of the European Commission and the Secretary General of the North Atlantic Treaty Organization, December 6. Brussels.

European Council (2017) Council Conclusions on Progress in Implementing the EU Global Strategy in the Area of Security and Defence, March 6. Brussels.

Fiorenza, N. (2016) Germany to Invest €130 Billion in Defence. *Shephardmedia*, February 3. Available at: www.shephardmedia.com/news/defence-notes/germany-invest-130-billion-defence/ [Accessed July 8, 2017].

Juncker, J.-C. (2016) State of the Union Address 2016: Towards a Better Europe: A Europe That Protects, Empowers and Defends. Strasbourg, September 14. Available at: http://europa.eu/rapid/press-release_IP-16-3042_en.htm [Accessed September 6, 2017].

Juncker, J.-C. (2017) Speech at the Defence and Security Conference Prague: In Defence of Europe. Prague, June 9. Available at: http://europa.eu/rapid/press-release_SPEECH-17-1581_en.htm [Accessed September 6, 2017].

Major, C. and Mölling, C. (2017) Brexit, Security and Defence: A Political Problem, Not a Military One. *Ulbrief* No. 3. Stockholm: Swedish Institute for International Affairs.

Manners, I. (2002) Normative Power Europe: A Contradiction in Terms? *Journal of Common Market Studies* 40: 235–258.

NATO (2015) Secretary General: NATO and the EU Can Achieve More If We Work More Closely Together. *Nato.int*, March 30. Available at: www.nato.int/cps/en/natohq/news_118367.htm [Accessed September 6, 2017].

NATO (2017) Defence Expenditure of NATO Countries (2010–2016). *Nato.int*, June 29. Available at: www.nato.int/cps/en/natohq/news_145409.htm [Accessed July 8, 2017].

NATO–EU (2016a) Joint Declaration by the President of the European Council, the President of the European Commission, and the Secretary General of the North Atlantic Treaty Organization. Warsaw, July 8. Available at: http://europa.eu/rapid/press-release_STATEMENT-16-2459_en.htm [Accessed September 6, 2017].

NATO–EU (2016b) President of the European Commission and the Secretary General of the North Atlantic Treaty Organization, December 6. Available at: www.consilium.europa.eu/en/press/press-releases/2016/12/06/eu-nato-joint-declaration/ [Accessed October 29, 2017].

NATO–EU (2017) Progress Report on the Implementation of the Common Set of Proposals Endorsed by NATO and EU Councils on 6 December 2016, June 14. Available at: https://eeas.europa.eu/sites/eeas/files/170614-joint-progress-report-eu-nato-en-1.pdf [Accessed September 6, 2017].

Pannier, A. (2017) The Anglo-French Defence Partnership after the 'Brexit' Vote: New Incentives and New Dilemmas. *Global Affairs* 2(5): 481–490.

Rubin, A. (2017) France's Top General Resigns in Dispute over Military Spending. *The New York Times*, July 19. Available at: www.nytimes.com/2017/07/19/world/europe/france-general-pierre-de-villiers-macron-military-budget.html?mcubz=1 [Accessed September 6, 2017].

Whitman, R.G. (2017) Epilogue: European Security and Defence in the Shadow of Brexit. *Global Affairs* 2(5): 521–525.

20

BREXIT AND EU FINANCIAL REGULATION

Lucia Quaglia[1]

Introduction

Brexit will have far-reaching implications for financial integration and regulation in the European Union (EU), as well as for the financial sector in the United Kingdom (UK). Although the policy implications of Brexit will depend on the deal eventually agreed by the EU and the UK, it is possible to discuss the most likely effects on the basis of past trends and ongoing developments (for a comprehensive legal analysis, see Alexander et al. 2017; for an economic analysis, see Batsaikhan et al. 2017). In the past, the UK's market-making approach to financial regulation contributed to boosting financial integration in the EU and made EU financial regulation more market-friendly and open to third countries than it would have been otherwise. After Brexit, financial integration between the EU27 and the UK will diminish, EU financial regulation will become more market-shaping, and the access of third country entities and products to the EU financial markets will be more strictly regulated. At the same time, the UK will strive to increase its (already significant) influence in international standard setting so as to compensate for the loss of (direct) influence on EU financial regulation.

With reference to financial integration, the UK has a very large financial sector that is strongly interconnected to the financial sector in the rest of the EU. London is the main financial centre internationally, well ahead of other financial centres in the EU27. After Brexit, the degree of financial integration between the EU and the UK will diminish, mainly because of the loss of the so-called passport, which will only partly be compensated by 'equivalence' and possibly other ad hoc legal mechanisms. The predominance of London as the main international financial centre might be challenged (see also Chapter 5). At the same time, the size of the EU27 financial services sector will shrink substantially.

With reference to EU financial regulation, the UK's market-making approach left a strong imprint in the rules adopted by the EU prior to the international financial crisis and was important in 'calibrating' the EU's regulatory response post-crisis. After Brexit, the UK will no longer have a direct influence in the making of EU financial regulation. Hence, future EU financial regulation is likely to become more market shaping and less open to third countries, as compared to the past. Indeed, the UK's market making contributed to opening up the Single Market in finance to third-country entities and products and acted as their point of entry into the EU. At the same time, the UK is likely to become more of a 'rule-taker', even though UK regulators (e.g. Carney 2017b) explicitly rejected this idea.

Finally, the UK has traditionally been a major player in international standard setting, often adopting positions close to those of the United States rather than the rest of the EU. After Brexit, the UK will have more room for manoeuvre to take positions not aligned with the EU in international regulatory fora. Moreover, UK policymakers will seek to promote international standards as an indirect way to influence EU legislation.

In order to elaborate these points, this chapter proceeds as follows. Section 2 outlines the configuration of the financial sector in the UK and its interconnections to the EU. This section also briefly discusses the positions of the UK-based financial industry in the Brexit debate. Section 3 discusses the influence of the UK in the development of the single financial market and its regulation. Section 4 focuses on the UK and the external dimensions of the Single Market in finance, including relations with third countries and international standard-setting bodies. Each of these sections discusses the state of play prior to Brexit and the most likely policy implications of Brexit.

The financial sector in the UK and financial integration in the EU

The UK has a very large financial sector in absolute terms and compared to the rest of the national economy. London is ranked as the world's leading financial centre, just ahead of New York and significantly ahead of other EU cities (see more in Chapter 5). The London Stock Exchange is by far the largest in Europe and the second largest in the world in terms of stock market capitalisation and daily trading turnover. The UK has the second largest banking sector in the EU. The UK is, after France, the second location for managed collective investment funds in the EU and is the prime location for alternative investment funds, first and foremost, private equities and hedge funds, in the EU. The UK hosts four-fifths of hedge funds managers in the EU, and internationally it is the second main location for hedge fund managers, after the United States. About 70 per cent of the EU's foreign exchange trading and 40 per cent of global trading in euros takes place in the UK. London is the main centre for clearing euro-denominated securities, despite being outside the euro area. Over 90 per cent of the £440 billion of euro-denominated swaps, options and other derivatives traded each year are cleared in London. Finally, the British insurance sector is the largest in the EU and the third largest in the world. The UK has half of EU pension assets and international insurance premiums. Lloyds is the largest reinsurance market worldwide (TheCityUK 2015; Burrows and Low 2015).

Certain parts of the financial industry, first and foremost banking, reinsurance and clearing of derivatives, are highly concentrated and have strong ties with the rest of the EU, as well as with third countries. Foreign banks mainly deal with wholesale investment banking, whereby the UK serves as point of entry for many non-EU banks, first and foremost US investment banks (but also Swiss, Chinese and Japanese banks), which have subsidiaries and branches in London and from there operate across the EU (Schoenmaker 2013). Half of EU investment bank activity is based in the UK. Lloyds dominates the reinsurance market, and the London Clearing House (LCH), which is owned by the London Stock Exchange, dominates derivatives clearing. Reinsurance and derivatives clearing are really global business.

The financial services sector contributed more than 7 per cent of UK GDP. The financial sector in the UK employed an estimated 1 million people. The number of employees reached nearly 2 million when related professional services were added (House of Lords 2016). The consultancy Oliver Wyman (TheCityUK 2016b) calculated the annual financial revenues at around £200 billion, £90–95 billion of which was domestic business, £40–50 billion related to the EU, and £55–65 billion related to the rest of the world. Around a quarter of revenues in banking and asset management and nearly half of revenues in market infrastructure and others were related to the EU. The UK net exports of financial services were the largest in the world: $71 billion, contributing to decrease the large deficit in the UK balance of payments. The EU was the biggest market for UK exports of financial services: the UK's exports to the EU were £26 billion; the UK's imports from the EU were £3 billion (2015).

Given the fact that the UK-based financial industry had greatly benefited from the Single Market in the past, in the run-up to the referendum, most of the UK-based financial industry campaigned in favour of remaining in the EU. However, the City was internally divided on this issue (Lavery 2017). For example, some hedge fund bosses were major contributors to Vote Leave, the main pro-Brexit campaign (James and Quaglia 2017). After the referendum, the British financial industry called for the preservation of as much market access as possible (TheCityUK 2016a, 2016b). The City also asked for a long transition period out of the Single Market. The strategy adopted by the UK-based financial industry was to point out that it provided a variety of services to 'customers' across Europe and that those services were necessary and could not be easily switched to other locations. Moreover, restrictions imposed on British financial services to access the Single Market or to clear euro-denominated assets would result in higher costs and more risk for customers across the EU.

Depending on the final deal agreed by the EU and the UK, some of these financial activities and the revenues they generate will be at risk, albeit the size of the losses will depend on the new arrangements set in place between the UK and the EU. The report by Oliver Wyman predicted that in the worst-case scenario of low Single Market access, up to 50 per cent of EU-related activity (£20 billion in revenue) and an estimated 35,000 jobs could be at risk in the UK, along with £5 billion of tax revenues per annum. Furthermore, the knock-on impact on the ecosystem would result in an estimated further £14–18 billion of revenue, up to 40,000 jobs and £5 billion in tax revenue per annum (TheCityUK 2016b).

Particularly important will be the loss of passporting, whereby a firm authorised in a European Economic Area (EEA) country is entitled to carry on permitted activities in any other EEA country by either exercising the right of establishment (of a branch and/or agents) or by providing cross-border services (Howarth and Quaglia 2017). The loss of passport will imply that UK financial firms will have to relocate part of their activities to the EU in order to continue to enjoy unrestricted access to the Single Market. Moreover, third-country entities will also have to relocate some of their activities to the EU, as they will no longer be able to use the UK as a point of access to the EU (Sapir et al. 2017; TheCityUK 2016a). Equivalence, a legal concept shortly discussed, will only be able to partly compensate for the loss of passport.

On the one hand, it is true that London was a major financial centre prior to well before the establishment of the EU. Yet, over the last two decades, the development of the Single Market significantly contributed to the expansion of the financial services sector in the UK (Djankov 2017; Lanoo 2016). In turn, the UK's market-making approach contributed to boosting financial integration in the EU. In the wake of the Brexit referendum, the main financial centres on the continent actively mobilised to attract business away from the UK, seeking to exploit their comparative advantages in specific financial sectors (Sapir et al. 2017; Schoenmaker and Véron 2017). Thus, Frankfurt and Paris were well positioned to attract investment banking and derivatives clearing. Luxembourg, Dublin and Amsterdam were well positioned to attract asset managers (see Lavery 2017).

On the other hand, according to some commentators and policymakers (see, for example, the evidence given to the House of Lords 2016; House of Commons 2016a, 2016b), only a limited amount of activities would relocate to the EU as a result of Brexit; others might relocate outside the EU (e.g. United States or Asia) or disappear altogether (Carney 2017b; Djankov 2017). The Bundesbank president did not 'expect a mass exodus from London', and then German Finance

Minister Wolfgang Schäuble (Reuters 2017) recognised that 'London offers financial services in a quality that is not found on the continent, albeit that would change a bit after a split'. Some parts of the financial industry, mainly hedge funds, claimed that London as an international financial centre would actually thrive outside the EU (Reuters 2016).

Although financial integration between the UK and EU27 will diminish after Brexit, the magnitude of this shift is unclear. At the same time, the existing high degree of financial integration and sheer size of the UK financial sector can cause havoc in the EU in case of a disorderly or too hard Brexit. Governor of the Bank of England Mark Carney (2017a) described the UK as 'Europe's investment banker'. He pointed out that the EU relied on the UK for three-quarters of its hedging activities, three-quarters of its foreign exchange activity, half of its lending and half its securities transactions' (Carney 2017b). Yet the European Central Bank (2017), the Bundesbank (Dombret 2017), the Banque de France (La Tribuna 2017) and other national central banks and regulatory agencies explicitly downplayed and/or challenged concerns about the implications of Brexit for financial stability or credit provisions in the EU27. The French authorities – in both the public sector and banking sector – were generally unwilling to raise the prospect of EU-wide financial instability caused by Brexit (Asimakopoulos and Wright 2017: 11). Be that as it may, financial interdependence and the dependency of the EU on the City as 'Europe's investment banker' are incentives to a suitable compromise, which is, however, to be part of the broader Brexit negotiations and the politics surrounding it.

The UK and EU financial regulation

The UK, the City of London and the most competitive part of the financial industry on the continent were the main driving forces for further financial market integration because they would mostly benefit from it (Macartney 2010; Mügge 2010; Posner and Véron 2010). The further integration of the Single Market in financial services, which regained momentum with the Financial Services Action Plan in 1999, was characterised by the presence of two competing coalitions: the market-making one, which was led by the UK and included Ireland, the Netherlands, Luxembourg and the Scandinavian member states, and the market-shaping one, which focused upon re-regulating the market at the EU level and which included France, Germany, Italy, Belgium and the other Mediterranean countries (Quaglia 2010). Pre-crisis EU financial regulation was strongly influenced by the UK – as suggested by the prevailing market-making content of the four so-called Lamfalussy directives in securities markets, the Solvency II directive in insurance and the Payment Systems directive – even if certain provisions of these pieces of legislation could be described as market shaping.

What accounts for the UK's influence on financial market integration and pre-crisis EU financial regulation? First, the UK was the second or third largest EU member state in terms of GDP. Second, the UK had voting power: under qualified majority voting rules in the Council, the four largest member states (Germany, France, the UK and Italy), together with any other EU member state, had sufficient votes to block any proposed pieces of legislation on finance. Most importantly, though, the UK financial sector was by far the largest in the EU, and the City of London was the largest financial centre in Europe and the second largest in the world. Given the size of the financial sector – in particular when compared to the rest of the economy (Macartney 2010) – British authorities had considerable subject-specific expertise on matters related to finance and were regarded by many policymakers and stakeholders as providing state-of-the-art regulation (Mügge 2010). Moreover, British policymakers invested a considerable amount of technical and human resources in order to shape the regulatory debate in the EU (Posner and Véron 2010; Quaglia 2010). In addition, the UK hosted large banks, including large US banks, that had the resources to lobby policymakers both domestically and at the EU level (Baker 2010). For example, in most of the consultations held by the Commission on proposed EU financial regulation, the majority of the responses came from financial institutions located in the UK.

In the wake of the international financial crisis, the UK's influence on EU financial regulation waned somewhat, at least in the short term. Unlike the period prior to the international financial crisis, most EU regulation from 2009 was market shaping rather than market making. Hence, the UK was often a foot dragger, for example concerning the legislation on hedge funds, rating agencies and the financial transaction tax (Pagliari 2011, Quaglia 2012). These pieces of legislation were resisted by the UK, in line with its market-making approach, on the grounds that they would impose unnecessary costs, damage the competitiveness of the financial industry in Europe and reduce the attractiveness of European financial centres as a result of regulatory arbitrage. The concern about international 'regulatory arbitrage' was at the forefront of policymakers' minds in Britain, given the fact that London hosted many non-British-owned financial institutions and successfully competed with other financial centres worldwide to attract business (Quaglia 2010). The main exception were capital requirements, whereby the UK authorities called for stricter EU legislation (i.e. higher capital requirements) (see James 2016).

The UK was by and large supportive of Banking Union and specifically the Single Supervisory Mechanism (SSM) for euro area member states, notably as a way to tackle the sovereign debt crisis distressing the euro area periphery and to ensure financial stability therein. However, the British Government had no intention of participating in Banking Union because of domestic political and political economy considerations. Banking Union implied a considerable pooling of power at the EU/Banking Union level – first and foremost the supranationalisation of banking supervision – which was politically unacceptable in the UK. Moreover, the institutional and decision-making framework of Banking Union was primarily designed for euro area members (Howarth and Quaglia 2016).

During the negotiations on Banking Union, British policymakers feared that a euro area majority would be able to impose its rules on non-euro area members in the European Banking Authority (EBA) – the body of national bank supervisors that sets supervisory standards for the entire EU. Hence, the British demanded and eventually obtained an EBA voting reform, whereby any decision by the Authority had to be approved by a 'double majority' of member states inside and outside Banking Union, thus effectively giving veto power to a small number of non-euro area member states (Ferran 2017; Moloney 2016). The end of the UK's membership of the EU is likely to weaken the bargaining position within the EBA of those supervisors from member states outside of Banking Union. Brexit is also likely to strengthen the powers of the European Supervisory Authorities (Moloney 2017b) because in the past the UK was the main member state that had opposed the expansion of the remit and powers of these authorities, which would have implied further centralisation in the EU.

Finally, the UK was strongly supportive of Capital Markets Union (CMU), which was in line with the UK's market-making approach that promoted financial market integration over the previous two decades (Quaglia et al. 2016). First, a British national, Jonathan Hill, was chosen to lead the CMU project at the European Commission and was appointed as commissioner 'for Financial Stability, Financial Services and Capital Markets Union' (Hill 2015) – one of the few examples in EU history where a commissioner's job title matched that of a specific project. Second, UK policymakers and stakeholders engaged extensively in the agenda-setting process on CMU. Third, of all EU Member States, the UK had the most potential to benefit from the financial liberalisation and diversification promised in the CMU project, given the diversity of its financial sector and, in particular, the high concentration of wholesale market activity, private equity and hedge funds in the City (Véron and Wolff 2015). Given the fact that the UK was one of the main cheerleaders of CMU, the UK's departure is likely to have negative implications for this project. However, some commentators would argue that Brexit might be an incentive for the EU to move ahead with CMU so as to compensate for the more limited access to Europe's investment banker (the UK) (Moloney 2016).

After Brexit, future EU financial regulation is likely to be somewhat less market making, albeit this will be subject to several caveats (cf. Moloney 2017a). Indeed, this trend towards more market-shaping EU regulation will be mitigated by the formation of ad hoc alliances between the UK and like-minded EU member states (i.e. the countries that mostly align with the UK on financial issues), as a way to preserve the UK's indirect influence on EU financial regulation post-Brexit. There are coalitions of common interests that the UK can work with in the future; notable examples concern the financial transactions tax, which some EU/euro area member states oppose; the EBA double majority voting, which non-euro area member will be keen to keep; all the equivalence provisions in various pieces of EU legislation concerning third-country access, which third countries will be keen to safeguard.

As for UK financial regulation post-Brexit, UK regulators will continue to have powerful incentives to maintain broad equivalence with EU financial regulation in banking rather than engage in a deregulatory 'race to the bottom', so as to avoid undermining domestic financial stability. After the international financial crisis, the Bank of England in particular has been a strong advocate of higher capital requirements, new resolution rules and bank structural reforms (James 2016). In the non-banking sector, however, there is perhaps much greater scope for UK regulators to seek to strengthen the competitiveness of the private equity, hedge fund and venture capital sectors through the pursuit of increasingly lax regulation (James and Quaglia 2017).

The UK and the external dimension of the Single Market in finance

The UK had a strong influence in maintaining the EU market open to third countries (Pagliari 2013; Quaglia 2015), consistent with the UK's market-making approach. This was done first and foremost through the so-called equivalence rules, which were the cornerstone of the post-crisis regulatory approach of the EU towards third countries in finance. Several pieces of financial markets legislation adopted from 2009 contained 'equivalence clauses', as detailed shortly. These clauses stipulate that unless third-country rules are equivalent to EU rules, foreign firms providing services in the EU or doing business with EU counterparts will be subject to EU regulation in addition to their home country regulation. Without equivalence, foreign firms failing to respect EU regulations would be blocked from accessing the Single Market (Ferran 2016; Moloney 2017a).

For policymakers in countries such as France and Germany, which embraced a market-shaping regulatory paradigm, the equivalence clauses were first and foremost intended to prevent the 'import' into the EU of financial instability from third countries. These clauses were also seen as instrumental in seeking to align third-country rules with EU rules. By contrast, British policymakers worried about the potential risk of closing the EU market to third-country entities and products, as well as the detrimental effects that the new EU equivalence rules could have on the competitiveness of the financial sector in the EU. For British policymakers, loose equivalence rules were needed above all to ensure the access of third-country financial entities and products managed from London to the EU market. The UK was particularly concerned about the equivalence clauses, given the strong financial transatlantic ties of the City of London (Quaglia 2015).

There are currently nearly forty equivalence requirements in place in total. The Commission decides on the equivalence of third countries on the basis of advice from the European

Supervisory Authorities – the EBA, the European Securities Markets Authority (ESMA) and the European Insurance and Occupational Pension Authority (EIOPA). It is somewhat ironic that equivalence, which was in part a British invention to ensure that the single financial market remained open to third countries, is considered as one of the main legal mechanisms to keep the EU market open to UK financial entities and product post-Brexit (Ferran 2016).

However, EU's equivalence only covers a narrow range of services; it can be withdrawn at any time; and its approval is generally a political rather than a technical process. Furthermore, in 2017, the European Commission (2017) announced the intention of tightening up equivalence for non-EU jurisdictions. At the same time, the UK authorities, first and foremost the Bank of England, advocated a different mechanism to decide on equivalence, one that would give a greater say in the process to third countries. In this way, the UK would not be a rule-taker, as is currently the case for third countries in the process of achieving equivalence (Carney 2017b). Furthermore, post-Brexit, the UK authorities are likely to engage intensively in international standard setting, as an indirect way to influence EU legislation. Indeed, the EU is bound to incorporate the international standards it subscribes to into EU legislation.

The UK has traditionally been an influential player in international standard setting, given the size and degree of internationalisation of the UK financial sector (Fioretos 2010; James 2015). Moreover, in finance, unlike, for example trade policy, the member states or at least main member states including the UK remain key players for several reasons (Mügge 2014; Quaglia 2014). The EU does not have exclusive legal competences, hence the main supranational institution of the EU, the European Commission, does not have the exclusive power to represent the EU and its member states in international regulatory fora. Moreover, the mechanisms for the international representation of the EU and its member states vary across financial services: in several cases, the Commission participates as an observer, together with representatives from the member states. The main change in terms of external representation of the EU (to be precise, the euro area) in international financial fora was a consequence of the setting up of Banking Union, whereby the European Central Bank (ECB) and SSM became full members of the Basel Committee on Banking Supervisions (BCBS).

In the international standard setting over the last decades, the UK sometimes sided with the rest of the EU, as in the case of insurance solvency requirements in the 2000s. Other times, it sided with the United States, as in the case of the (non-)regulation of hedge funds and rating agencies prior to the crisis, and capital requirements for banks (pre- and post-crisis), whereby the United States and the UK completely reversed their position. Pre-crisis, in the making of the international accord on capital requirements for banks (Basel II in 2004), the United States and the UK had favoured lower capital requirements for banks, whereby post-crisis called for strict capital and liquidity rules in the negotiation of Basel III in 2010 (James 2016). Depending on where the UK sat in the international standard setting, it either strengthened the EU's ability to shape those standards, if the UK sided with the rest of the EU, as in the case of insurance. Or it weakened it, when the UK sided with the United States, as in the case of Basel I, Basel III and pre-crisis self-regulation for hedge funds and rating agencies (Quaglia 2014).

On the one hand, the EU's external influence will be weakened by Brexit, given the size of the financial sector in the UK and fact that the City of London is the only real international financial centre in Europe. Market size is an important asset in the international standard setting (Drezner 2007). On the other hand, the cohesiveness of the EU in international regulatory fora is likely to increase, coalescing around the preferences of the euro area, especially in banking regulatory fora in which the ECB and SSM are full members, such as the BCBS. In the past, EU's cohesiveness was weakened by the fact the UK often sided with the United States rather than with the rest of the EU (first and foremost, France and Germany, which are the main continental players) in the negotiations taking place in international regulatory. The cohesiveness of a jurisdiction, like its market size, is often (but not always) an asset in international negotiations (Conceição-Heldt and Meunier 2014; Moschella and Quaglia 2016). As for the UK, its position in international financial fora will move closer to the position taken by the United States on several financial issues, and UK policymakers will not be restrained by the quest for a common EU 'denominator'.

Conclusion

The implications of Brexit for the single financial market and the UK financial sector will depend on the transitional provisions and the final deal agreed between the EU and the UK. At the time of writing, the Brexit negotiations are ongoing. In February 2017, the UK Government (2017) made clear that the UK would not seek Single Market membership after Brexit. Yet the UK's plan highlighted 'a legitimate interest in mutual cooperation arrangements that recognise the interconnectedness of markets' in finance. However, the political guidelines for the Brexit negotiations agreed by the European Council (2017) in April 2017 ruled out any special deal for finance. They restated, 'Preserving the integrity of the Single Market excludes participation based on a sector-by sector approach'. In December 2017, the UK and the EU issued a joint report on the first stage of the negotiations on the UK's withdrawal from the EU and decided that sufficient progress had been made to move ahead with the second stage of the negotiations concerning future relations between the UK and the EU.

The most disruptive outcome for the financial sector, especially for the activities based in the UK, would be a no-Brexit deal. Hence, the new relations between the UK and the EU would be regulated by the rules set by the World Trade Organization, albeit this possibility has receded, after the agreement of December 2017. The least disruptive outcome for finance would be something resembling the current level of Single Market access, which until recently seemed to be unfeasible from a political point of view, given the hard Brexit option chosen by the British Government. However, the joint UK–EU document of December 2017 makes reference to the possibility of 'regulatory alignment' between the UK and the EU in the future. The duration of the transition period and the content of the transition rules are also important to secure financial stability and smooth the adjustment that will take place in the financial sector. Be that as it may, Brexit will reduce the integration of the UK financial sector with the rest of the EU and will make EU financial regulation more market shaping; also, concerning the access of third-country entities and products, Brexit is also likely to alter relations with third countries and diminish the EU's clout in international fora.

Note

1   Orcid.org/0000–0001–8816–0583. This piece was partly written while Lucia Quaglia was a research fellow at the Scuola Normale Superiore, Florence.

References

Alexander, K., Barnard, C., Ferran, E., Lang, A. and Moloney, N. (2017) *Brexit and Financial Services Law and Policy*. Sydney: Hart Publishing.
Asimakopoulos, P. and Wright, W. (2017) What the Rest of the EU Thinks about Brexit and the City of London. *New Financial*, April. Available at: http://newfinancial.eu/what-the-rest-of-the-eu-thinks-about-brexit-the-city/ [Accessed September 6, 2017].
Baker, A. (2010) Restraining Regulatory Capture? Anglo-America, Crisis Politics and Trajectories of Change in Global Financial Governance. *International Affairs* 86 (3): 647–663.

Batsaikhan, U., Kalcik, R. and Schoenmaker, D. (2017) Brexit and the European Financial System: Mapping Markets, Players and Jobs. *Bruegel Institute, Policy Contribution* (4). Available at: http://bruegel.org/wp-content/uploads/2017/02/PC-04-2017-finance-090217-final.pdf [Accessed July 3, 2017].

Burrows, O. and Low, K. (2015) Mapping the UK Financial System. *Bank of England Quarterly Bulletin* Q2. Available at: https://www.bankofengland.co.uk/quarterly-bulletin/2015/q2/mapping-the-uk-financial-system [Accessed September 6, 2017].

Carney, M. (2017a) Speech: The High Road to a Responsible, Open Financial System. *Bank of England*, April 7, 2017. Available at: www.bankofengland.co.uk/publications/Documents/speeches/2017/speech973.pdf [Accessed September 6, 2017].

Carney, M. (2017b) Treasury Committee Oral Evidence: Bank of England Financial Stability Reports. Bank of England, January 11.

TheCityUK (2015) Key Facts about the Financial Industry. Available at: www.thecityuk.com/assets/2015/Reports-PDF/Key-Facts-about-UK-financial-and-related-professional-services-2015.pdf [Accessed September 6, 2017].

TheCityUK (2016a) *Brexit and the Industry*. September, 7. Available at: www.thecityuk.com/research/brexit-and-the-industry/ [Accessed March 10, 2017].

TheCityUK (2016b) Brexit Impact on the UK-Based Financial Services Sector, October, 5. Available at: www.thecityuk.com/news/the-impact-of-the-uks-exit-from-the-eu-on-the-uk-based-financial-services-sector/ [Accessed September 6, 2017].

Conceição-Heldt, E.D. and Meunier, S. (2014) Speaking with a Single Voice: Internal Cohesiveness and External Effectiveness of the EU in Global Governance. *Journal of European Public Policy* 21(7): 961–979.

Djankov, S. (2017) The City of London after Brexit. *LSE Discussion Paper* No. 762. London, February.

Dombret, A. (2016) What Does Brexit Mean for European Banks? Keynote Speech at a Conference of the Association of German Banks Center for Financial Studies, Goethe University Frankfurt, July 13. Available at: www.bundesbank.de/Redaktion/EN/Reden/2016/2016_07_13_dombret.html [Accessed June 12, 2017].

Drezner, D. (2007) *All Politics Is Global: Explaining International Regulatory Regimes*. Princeton, NJ: Princeton University Press.

European Central Bank (ECB) (2017) Financial Stability Review, May. Available at: www.ecb.europa.eu/pub/pdf/other/ecb.financialstabilityreview201705.en.pdf?ce0cddcde1256fb5f6653e8aedf2ebd7 [Accessed June 2, 2017].

European Commission (2017) EU Equivalence Decisions in Financial Services Policy: An Assessment. Brussels, February 27. Available at: https://ec.europa.eu/info/sites/info/files/eu-equivalence-decisions-assessment-27022017_en.pdf [Accessed January 18, 2018].

European Council (2017) Special Meeting of the European Council (Art. 50) (29 April 2017): Guidelines. EUCO XT 20004/17, BXT 10, CO EUR 5, CONCL 2. Brussels, April 29. Available at: www.ecb.europa.eu/pub/pdf/other/ecb.financialstabilityreview201705.en.pdf?ce0cddcde1256fb5f6653e8aedf2ebd7 [Accessed June 24, 2017].

Ferran, E. (2016) The UK as a Third Country Actor in EU Financial Services Regulation. *University of Cambridge Faculty of Law Research Paper* No. 47.

Ferran, E. (2017) European Banking Union: Imperfect, but It Can Work. *University of Cambridge Faculty of Law Research Paper* No. 30/2014.

Fioretos, O. (2010) Capitalist Diversity and the International Regulation of Hedge Funds. *Review of International Political Economy* 17(3): 696–723.

Hill, J. (2015) For a Financial Sector That Promotes Investment. Speech to the City of London Corporation Policy Committee. London, July 15. Available at: http://europa.eu/rapid/press-release_SPEECH-15-5380_en.htm [Accessed February 1, 2017].

House of Commons (2016a) *Brexit Transitional Arrangements*. London: Treasury Select Committee.

House of Commons (2016b) Equipping the Government for Brexit. Report of the Foreign Affairs Committee. Available at: www.publications.parliament.uk/pa/cm201617/cmselect/cmfaff/431/43102.htm [Accessed October 31, 2017].

House of Lords (2016) Brexit: Financial Services. EU Committee. London, December.

Howarth, D. and Quaglia, L. (2016) *The Political Economy of Banking Union*. Oxford: Oxford University Press.

Howarth, D. and Quaglia, L. (2017) Brexit and the Single European Financial Market. *Journal of Common Market Studies Annual Review* 55: 1. Available at: http://onlinelibrary.wiley.com/doi/10.1111/jcms.12589/abstract [Accessed October 31, 2017].

James, S. (2015) The UK in the Multilevel Process of Financial Market Regulation: Global Pace-Setter or National Outlier? In: Maynz, R. (ed.), *Multilevel Governance of Financial Market Reform*. Cologne: Max Planck Institute, pp. 121–137.

James, S. (2016) The Domestic Politics of Financial Regulation: Informal Ratification Games and the EU Capital Requirement Negotiations. *New Political Economy* 21(2): 187–203.

James, S. and Quaglia, L. (2017) Brexit and the Limits of Financial Power in the UK. Working Paper, University of Oxford. Available at: www.geg.ox.ac.uk/brexit-and-limits-financial-power-uk [Accessed October 31, 2017].

Lanoo, K. (2016) Brexit and the City. *CEPS Policy Paper.* Available at: www.ceps.eu/publications/brexit-and-city [Accessed October 31, 2017].

La Tribuna (2017) Brexit: selon le gouverneur de la Banque de France, Paris a 'toutes ses chances' pour accueillir les banques de la City. *Europe1,* May 29. Available at: www.europe1.fr/economie/brexit-selon-le-gouverneur-de-la-banque-de-france-paris-a-toutes-ses-chances-daccueillir-les-banques-de-la-city-3344810 [Accessed November 1, 2017].

Lavery, S. (2017) Frankfurt, Paris and Dublin: Post-Brexit Rivals to the City of London? *SPERI Global Political Economy Brief* No. 6. Sheffield: University of Sheffield.

MaCartney, H. (2010) *Variegated Neoliberalism: EU Varieties of Capitalism and International Political Economy.* London: Routledge.

Moloney, N. (2016) Institutional Governance and Capital Markets Union: Incrementalism or a 'Big Bang'? *European Company and Financial Law Review* 13(2): 376–423.

Moloney, N. (2017a) Brexit, the EU and Its Investment Banker: Rethinking 'Equivalence' for the EU Capital Market. *LSE Legal Studies Working Paper* No. 5. London.

Moloney, N. (2017b) EU Financial Governance and Brexit: Institutional Change or Business as Usual? *European Law Review* 42(1): 112–128.

Moschella, M. and Quaglia, L. (2016) To Agree or Not to Agree: The EU in the G20. *Journal of European Public Policy* 23(6): 906–924.

Mügge, D. (2010) *Widen the Market, Narrow the Competition: Banker Interests and the Making of a European Capital Market.* Colchester: ECPR.

Mügge, D. (ed.) (2014) *Europe and the Governance of Global Finance.* Oxford: Oxford University Press.

Pagliari, S. (2011) Who Governs Finance? The Shifting Public–Private Divide in the Regulation of Derivatives, Rating Agencies and Hedge Funds. *European Law Journal* 18(1): 44–61.

Pagliari, S. (2013) A Wall around Europe? The European Regulatory Response to the Global Financial Crisis and the Turn in Transatlantic Relations. *Journal of European Integration* 35(4): 391–408.

Posner, E. and Véron, N. (2010) The EU and Financial Regulation: Power without Purpose? *Journal of European Public Policy* 17(3): 400–415.

Quaglia, L. (2010) *Governing Financial Services in the European Union.* London: Routledge.

Quaglia, L. (2012) The 'Old' and 'New' Politics of Financial Services Regulation in the European Union. *New Political Economy* 17(4): 515–535.

Quaglia, L. (2014) *The European Union and Global Financial Regulation.* Oxford: Oxford University Press.

Quaglia, L. (2015) The Politics of 'Third Country Equivalence in Post-Crisis Financial Services Regulation in the European Union. *West European Politics* 38(1): 167–184.

Quaglia, L., Howarth, D. and Liebe, M. (2016) The Political Economy of European Capital Markets Union. *Journal of Common Market Studies Annual Review* 54(1): 185–203.

Reuters (2016) London Still Top Finance Centre, but Brexit May Change That Survey, September 26. Available at: https://uk.reuters.com/article/uk-britain-eu-financial/london-still-top-finance-centre-but-brexit-may-change-that-survey-idUKKCN11W1I0 [Accessed November 1, 2017].

Reuters (2017) Germany's Schaeuble Wants 'Reasonable' Brexit Deal for London, February 4. Available at: http://uk.reuters.com/article/uk-britain-eu-germany/germanys-schaeuble-wants-reasonable-brexit-deal-for-london-idUKKBN15J0GL [Accessed November 1, 2017].

Sapir, A., Schoenmaker, D. and Véron, N. (2017) Making the Best of Brexit for the EU27 Financial System. *Bruegel Policy Brief* Issue 1. Brussels, February 2017.

Schoenmaker, D. (2013) *Governance of International Banking: The Financial Trilemma.* Oxford: Oxford University Press.

Schoenmaker, D. and Véron, N. (2017) *Making the Best of Brexit.* Brussels: Bruegel. Available at: http://bruegel.org/wp-content/uploads/2017/02/Bruegel_Policy_Brief-2017_01-060217.pdf [Accessed October 31, 2017].

UK Government (2017) The United Kingdom's Exit from, and New Partnership with, the European Union White Paper, February 2. Available at: www.gov.uk/government/publications/the-united-kingdoms-exit-from-and-new-partnership-with-the-european-union-white-paper [Accessed July 27, 2017].

Véron, N. and Wolff, G.B. (2015) *Capital Markets Union: A Vision for the Long Term.* Brussels: Bruegel Policy Paper.

21

BREXIT AND THE EUROPEAN UNION

Hanging in the balance?

Mads Dagnis Jensen and Holly Snaith

Introduction

When on 23 June 2016 a majority voted in favour of the United Kingdom (UK) leaving the European Union (EU), it generated a host of unknowns. Prior to the referendum, scholars had already started to anticipate the implications of a potential Brexit from different perspectives, including considering the legal (Cardwell 2016; Łazowski 2016; Butler et al. 2016), political (Kroll and Leuffen 2016; Oliver 2016; Freedman 2016) and economic (Jensen and Snaith 2016) implications. After the referendum, studies have begun to address the reasons for the Brexit vote (Hobolt 2016; Clarke et al. 2017) and its potential consequences. This chapter will add another piece to the Brexit jigsaw by focusing on the impact upon the EU itself. To do so, it first develops an analytical framework to study the shifts in power that may occur because of Brexit, using an approach that tackles in turn the micro, meso and macro levels of analysis (focussing alternately on changes within the institutions, between the institutions and outside of the institutions). It afterwards outlines a brief introduction to Britain's historically fractious relationship with the EU as a means of demonstrating where key policy divisions lie and suggesting where Britain's exit will leave the greatest strategic vacuums. The subsequent analysis centres on the actors that will likely win and lose from the UK's exit from the Union.

Analysing power in UK–EU relations

Power is central to any understanding of the EU. It is a system that has not only been built on the pre-existing power of the member states but also one in which the main purpose is to transform the exercise of this power. Power in the EU can be divided into three dimensions that correspond to the three analytical levels that must be considered when estimating the effects of Brexit. At the micro level is the intra-institutional level, which is concerned with the power distribution within the institutions, such as member states in the Council and members of the European Parliament. At the meso level is the inter-institutional level, which focuses on the balance of power among the EU institutions, for example the European Council, the Council, the European Parliament, the Commission and the Court. Finally, at the macro level, the EU is seen as an aggregate actor whose position might change in the international system because of Britain's departure (see Table 21.1).

Table 21.1 A taxonomy for measuring the impact of Brexit on the balance of power in the EU

Level	Theory	Research questions
Micro	Wallace's (2005) many faces of power in EU intra-institutional decision-making	What will the impact be within the different institutions?
Meso	Theories and models about power in inter-institutional decision-making and on the overall balance of power in the EU	How is the balance of power likely to shift among the institutions? Will the EU become more supranational or more intergovernmental?
Macro	Theories about the EU as a global actor	How will the EU's position change in the world?

Brexit will certainly influence power distribution across all three levels in the EU, but estimating exactly how is highly challenging due to the interlinked nature of the dimensions. To wit, an example: a change in the power distribution (let us say among the member states in the Council) should be anticipated by the actors concerned and consequently lead to a change in the power balance between the institutions (let us say from supranational to intergovernmental decision-making), which again could influence the EU's position in the international scene. The following is therefore written under a *ceteris paribus* assumption.

For each of the three dimensions or levels, we need to define what types of power we scrutinize with regard to Brexit. At the micro level, Wallace (2005) reminds us of the many different forms power can take, ranging from hard power, such as veto rights, to soft powers, such as trust generation or providing appealing ideas. This broad understanding of power embraces both the realist (material) and the constructivist (ideational) approaches. At the meso level, scholars have focused on the distribution of power among the different EU institutions, where two key questions have been addressed: how powerful are the institutions in shaping policy outputs, and to what extent do the intergovernmental or supranational institutions dominate (Marks et al. 1996; Tsebelis and Garrett 2000; Thomson and Hosli 2006; Hix and Hoyland 2011; Thomson 2011)? At the macro level, we draw on Manners' (2002) concept of 'normative power Europe' to help illustrate the ways in which the EU is likely to seek to exercise global influence in the post-Brexit era. In particular, we focus on the debate on the EU's power in economic spheres, such as global trade, but we also consider possible changes to its ability to transform its surroundings through military intervention (Manners 2002; Hyde-Price 2006).

Past and current studies of Brexit generally face the challenge that they are dealing with a moving target, where the consequences will materialise slowly and may change over time. To address this challenge, this study will use the behaviour and impact of the UK's more than forty years of membership of the EU as proxy for what will happen when taking it out of the EU 'equation'. In other words, this chapter uses the past as a predictor of the future by looking at studies that have directly or indirectly addressed the UK's historic impact with regard to the three dimensions/levels. It thereby engages in discussing empirically founded counterfactuals, but it also applies secondary simulations of what would have happened in the EU without the UK. These estimations are combined with empirical evidence, to the extent that it has already emerged in the wake of the Brexit vote, to judge the impact.

Britain's historic contribution to the EU

The following section outlines how the UK's membership to date has proven significant in shaping both the material and ideational terrain of the EU. Right from the beginning, Britain's membership of the EU has been fractious: the UK held its first referendum on membership in 1975, a mere two years after it had eventually joined in 1973. In a series of events that proved eerily similar to the 2016 referendum, the 1974 Labour majority was won partly on the back of a manifesto promise to deliver a renegotiation on the terms of, followed by a vote on, continued membership. The outcome of the negotiations was an agreement with the other eight member states on the introduction of the Community's regional policy and creation of a budgetary correction mechanism (Miller 2015) – on which basis, the government advocated continued membership. The referendum was won with a Remain vote of 67 per cent, but the terms of the debate have shaped the narrative in Britain ever since: core areas of concern included the Common Agricultural Policy (CAP), the UK contribution to the budget, the nascent goal of the Economic and Monetary Union, the harmonisation of the value-added tax (VAT) and national sovereignty in pursuing regional, industrial and fiscal policies (ibid.). On all of these topics, the UK has been vocal.

Britain's economic priorities have been significant in shaping the policy direction of the Union. The differences in the UK's economic structure from the original six, especially where agriculture was concerned, were so significant that they prevented Britain's initial applications for membership in 1963 and 1967 from being accepted. The UK's farming sector was markedly smaller than that of the other members (Ackrill 2000); consequently, the UK has long been in favour of minimising CAP support, helping to drive changes such as the MacSharry reforms and Agenda 2000. The relative paucity of the UK's CAP receipts was a significant factor in the budgetary correction mechanism negotiated in 1975, in the rebate granted in 1984 at Fontainebleau (which in turn was responsible for initiating a web of other rebates across the rest of the EU's members) and in the creation and corresponding expansion of the regional policy that accompanied these moves. The UK, with its depressed post-industrial regions, was initially a substantial recipient; it has worked to promote the expansion of regional policy, which has since evolved to become the biggest area of spending in the EU. The UK's exceptional status has therefore played a significant part in generating the economic policies of the contemporary EU.

The UK has pursued ideational leadership in a number of areas, manifesting particularly in a desire to advance market liberalism and minimal regulation. It has also historically been a liberalizing force concerning external trade, with the signing of the Lomé Convention in 1975 driven primarily by the need to accommodate the Commonwealth countries with preferential trade deals. (One of the major planks of the 1975 renegotiation deal concerned market access for New Zealand dairy products) (Miller 2015). The Single European Act is likewise an example of Britain's role in shaping the EU's internal ideational direction. This programme to complete the Single Market originated in the white paper of Lord Cockfield, the British commissioner for the Internal Market, Tax Law and Customs, and culminated in Margaret Thatcher's belligerent stance on market opening during the final negotiations. The UK later opted out of the 'social chapter' agreed at Maastricht, by which Jacques Delors intended to provide an antidote to the liberalising policies of the SEA. In line with this historically market-based approach to European integration, the UK has been key in providing expertise and policy leadership in a number of cognate fields at the EU level, such as in financial regulation (Moloney 2017) or the Lisbon strategy. Most recently, the British fought to gain the newly created Financial Stability, Financial Services and Capital Markets Union brief within Jean-Claude Juncker's commission. The appointee, Lord Hill, initially attracted a critical reception from MEPs but later proved dynamic in the role, particularly with respect to providing impetus for the Capital Markets Union.

The UK has also exercised influence in order to shape the emergence of particular institutional arrangements, which then in turn tilts the playing field upon which power is exercised. Negotiations over the Single European Act, for example, resulted in the European Parliament being awarded greater powers as a corollary (although this was more of a side effect than a conscious strategy by the UK). The UK has also helped to shape the Commission's functioning, for example through the so-called Kinnock reforms (spearheaded by the former Labour leader), which, in the wake of the Santer scandal, reorganized strategic policy setting, human resources and financial management. By 2003, it was reported that eighty-four of the ninety-three task areas had been actioned or completed (Peterson and Birdsall 2008). These reforms were also designed to prepare the Commission for the 2004 enlargements – of which the UK was a key supporter, not least because it would disrupt the existing alliances of EU policy agreement and move the Union closer towards being a loose alliance of states rather than a federation.

Brexit and the changing distribution of power in the European Union

In light of Britain's historic role, the remainder of this article goes on to estimate which members and institutions within the organisation that emerges (the EU27) will be best able to benefit from the strategic vacuum created by Brexit, by deploying the micro, meso and macro frameworks outlined in the previous section.

The micro level: power balance within the institutions

The Council of Ministers and the European Council

According to Wallace (2005), of the different ways power can be gauged in the EU, the first and the most obvious is 'political weight', which in accordance with the voting rules is determined by population size. As a big member state comprising nearly 65 million citizens (amounting to 12.74 percent of the EU's population) the UK is a significant actor. However, when looking at the voting record in the Council, the UK was in the period 2009–2015 the member state that was most frequently on the losing side (12.3 per cent of the time) (Hix et al. 2016). The UK found itself on the losing side more often when it came to 'budgetary policies, foreign and security policy, and international development' whereas it was more commonly on the majority side in areas such as 'international trade, industry, environment, transport, legal affairs, economic and monetary union and internal market policies' (ibid.: 5). However, an important caveat is in order: being outvoted in the Council is very much a political strategy, which is used to signal dissent to voters 'back home' (Goetz and Meyer-Sahling 2008: 9). In other words, there might be member states whose preferred policy is further away from the Council compromise than the UK but who nonetheless decide not to create antagonism by voting against a proposal. In terms of coalition partners, the UK voted most often together with Sweden, the Netherlands and Denmark, which are likely to lose an important ally when it leaves the EU (Hix et al. 2016).

It is also possible to project the systemic impact that the removal of the UK will have. Utilizing the Shapley–Shubik power index, Kóczy (2016) has calculated the power distribution in the EU with and without the UK, through which the following pattern emerges. In general, the big member states are going to win greater power by virtue of Brexit, whereas the small member states are going to lose out. The reasoning is as follows: majority and blocking minority coalitions usually comprise a mixture of big and small member states. However, with the UK leaving, the small member states have fewer big member states to cluster around when forming coalitions, which, everything else being equal, diminishes the small member states' influence. Looking at the power index, the cut-off point based upon population size is around 5.4. million (corresponding to states the size of Finland and Slovakia). Member states with populations smaller than this will experience a loss of power, whereas member states with larger populations will gain. The member state benefiting the most according to the study is Spain, with 44.4 million inhabitants, which will move from being the 5th to the 4th most populous member state. Dividing the member states into other groups according to factors such as their accession time (old vs. new) and geographical clustering (North, South, East, Centre) suggests that the central and old member states, such as Germany and France, will gain the most from Brexit.

The second aspect concerns the 'economic weight' exercised by member states. The UK is a major economy and net contributor to the EU's budget (Stenbæk and Jensen 2016). As shown in the previous section on Britain's historic contribution to the EU, the country has been very active in creating items in the budget from which it would benefit (such as regional policy), cutting spending on items to which it was/is a net contributor (such as the CAP) and securing itself a rebate, as an overall net contributor to the budget. With the UK gone, the coalition of 'better spending', which comprises net contributors to the budget, has lost its most vocal and hardest fighting member in the Council (ibid.).

The third source of power is 'compelling demands'. The UK has historically as well as recently been a so-called demandeur when it comes to policies related to or impacting upon the internal market, as illustrated in the previous section. It has, for instance, forcefully defended non-Eurozone member states' rights to have a say on decisions taken by the Eurozone member states, if these will have impact on the functioning of the internal market (for example, over the signing of the fiscal compact and on banking union) (Miller 2012). With Brexit, non-Euro member states such as Sweden (which for technical reasons does not fulfil the accession criteria, operating a de facto derogation by refusing to join the ERM) and Denmark, which has a formal opt-out, will be in a weaker position to defend these rights vis-à-vis the Eurozone member states.

The fourth power asset is 'persuasive ideas'. Taking the UK out of the decision-making equation, the EU will lose a powerhouse when it comes to launching market-related ideas. This will certainly be an advantage for member states in the South advocating regulation of markets (market shaping), whereas member states in the North, in favour of market-creating polices (market making, who therefore share an accord with the UK) (Quaglia 2010), are expected to lose out. In particular, the loss of UK influence over Capital Markets Union and trade deals such as the Transatlantic Trade and Investment Partnership (TTIP) may be keenly felt by member states enthusiastic to achieve them.

The last source of power and influence, according to Wallace (2005), is 'credibility and consistency'. Historically, the UK has been seen as a member state with great negotiating capital because of its credible and consistent behaviour in the Council, which is not least due to its extremely well functioning internal coordination system (Bulmer and Burch 2001). However, the UK diminished a lot of its negotiation capital during the preceding two governments headed by David Cameron (Rasmussen 2015; Jensen 2017), whose strategy surrounding first the fiscal compact and subsequently the renegotiation of Britain's membership atrophied goodwill towards the UK. Despite this, the UK's loss is likely to be deeply felt, as it performs two significant functions. First, the UK is important for structuring negotiations in the Council, as it has been the initiator of different coalitions such as 'friends of better spending' and groups of like-minded member states (Stenbæk and Jensen 2016). Second, the UK provides an information-sharing function in the Council, as it over the years has proven extremely capable at gathering and disseminating information both about the potential consequences of different legislative solutions and other member states' positions. With the UK out of the picture, it might be more difficult to find compromises due to lack of information and the restructuring of political conflict.

The European Parliament

The European Parliament is structured according to ideology rather than territory, which makes it more difficult to apply the faces of power suggested by Wallace (2005). Nonetheless, Hix et al. (2016) show that proposals for legislation are likely in future to be less focused on decreasing regulatory burdens for businesses and defending property rights by running simulations of voting in the European Parliament without the members from the UK. According to the study, the influence of UK members of the European Parliament has been decreasing in recent years, due to a self-created distance from the institution (ibid.). A related example of this is the Conservative Party's decision in 2009 to leave the dominant centre-right block, the European People's Party, and join the newly created European Conservatives and Reformists. With the UK out of the equation, representation of the European Conservatives and Reformists will be significantly reduced, implying diminishing influence on legislation from an already low baseline. Of the UK's seventy-three members of European Parliament (MEPs), nineteen are currently Conservatives affiliated with the European Conservatives and Reformists, which has forty-five MEPs in total; furthermore, twenty-four UK MEPs are from UKIP, contained in the Europe of Freedom and Direct Democracy alliance, which is chaired by Nigel Farage and has seventy-three MEPs in total. With the UK gone, the right wing in the European Parliament will therefore be weakened, especially since it in several cases has won votes due to a higher turnout of members when compared to the left wing. The groups most likely to benefit from this will be the two largest groups, the European People's Party and the Socialists and Democrats.

Occupying central positions in the Parliament is another way of exercising power because it enables the individual MEP to be an agenda setter, which can be used both in a realist sense to assert one's preferences or in an ideational sense to frame issues. Here a distinction can be made between leadership positions and rapporteurship. Looking at the former data indicates that taking the UK's size into account, its MEPs have quantitatively been somewhat less successful in securing important positions in the European Parliament when compared to other big member states, which might be due to self-distancing, as described in the previous section (ibid.). Qualitatively, however, UK members of the European Parliament have taken on key positions. Since 2004, two vice-presidents, three quaestors and four political group leaders, as well as a number of committee chairpersons including one from the important internal market committee, have come from the UK (Hix and Benedetto 2016).

In addition to occupying leadership positions, MEPs from the UK have also been successful in getting rapporteurships on many significant legislative proposals when compared to other big member states. Getting a rapporteurship implies writing up a report on a legislative proposal for a committee. Though this report should reflect the preferences of the committee members as a whole, it can be an important vehicle for influence because of information asymmetry. The key question is then how Brexit will influence the daily work of the European Parliament when these different posts are taken over by MEPs from other nationalities (and who will benefit?). This process is already beginning, with the midterm reshuffle being used as an opportunity to shift the British out of these key positions. The most likely winners will be MEPs from big member states such as Germany and France, who are best placed to exploit the uncertainty generated. As these MEPs can be expected to favour less internal market and deregulation, it will reinforce the tendencies from the voting simulations.

The Commission

The UK has (as with the Council and the Parliament) mostly defended a deregulatory approach in the Commission, which will in consequence be ideationally weakened due to Brexit. However, given that this has been an ongoing agenda within the Commission for some time (with

José Manuel Barroso's establishment of the Impact Assessment Board in 2006, subsequently replaced by Juncker in 2015 with the Regulatory Scrutiny Board), it is unclear how materially affected this platform will be in the absence of the UK. What is certain is that EU agencies based in London, such as the European Medicines Agency and the European Banking Authority, will be moving, resulting in disruption to their staffing structures and the potential loss of institutional memory. Other member states are looking to benefit from this process. Nineteen countries applied to host the European Medicines Agency, and eight vied for the European Banking Authority. The Netherlands won the European Medicines Agency and Paris the European Banking Authority, both determined by drawing lots after a draw in the Council.

Though Commissioners do not formally represent the interests of their member states, they are nevertheless an important vehicle for injecting national preferences into the work of the executive (Hooghe 2002). Historically, Commissioners from the UK have occupied portfolios related to the internal market and regional policy. With the UK leaving, many senior positions will be up for grabs by other member states. As of 1 January 2017, only 3.2 per cent of all Commission staff are from the UK (compared to 10.3 per cent from the greatest contributor, France). However, they are disproportionately likely to be senior: the percentage of British officials at the so-called administrative grades (AD 5 to AD 16) is 4.02 per cent, and British citizens compose 6.5 per cent of officials at the top two grades (AD 15 and 16).[1] Regardless, the Commission would appear to be the least threatened of the three institutions, not least because there appears to be no immediate intention to offload the British staff that are currently incumbent, with Juncker reassuring British officials that 'you are "Union officials." You work for Europe. You left your national "hats" at the door when you joined this institution and that door is not closing on you now'.[2] It should be noted, however, that staff on secondment from British institutions working on sensitive dossiers in DG FISMA have been sent back, and this may presage wider moves. In general, however, the status quo is more likely to be preserved than in the European Parliament and Council, where the ejection of British influence will be immediate.

Power balance between the institutions

Turning to the inter-institutional balance, one should expect, *ceteris paribus*, the EU to become more supranational as a consequence of the UK leaving, as it over the years has defended an intergovernmental approach and blocked federal aspirations. However, Brexit could also cause the EU to become *more* intergovernmental by causing more decisions to be shifted to the European Council. In other words, the UK's egress could be the cause of two possible, contradictory outcomes – one of which empowers the European Council and one the Commission. There are several aspects to this uncertainty. First, one 'diagnosis' of Brexit is that increasing Euroscepticism is at least partly caused by the EU's inability to deliver viable solutions to significant challenges such as the euro and refugee crises. According to this argument, solutions to such problems cannot be delivered at the systemic level but require the political power of heads of states and governments at the super-systemic level in the EU. This implies that decisions could be moved from the Council to the European Council. Such a move would also accordingly weaken the European Parliament, Commission and the Court, as these institutions play a less significant role when decisions are reached through intergovernmental means.

Second, although Germany and the UK are the member states voting together least in the Council (Hix et al. 2016), the two have shared interests in many areas such as the internal market and the budget. With the UK gone, Germany fears that the way will be paved for more protectionism and higher spending in the EU – and, with Angela Merkel weakened in the most recent German elections, Germany may be keen to preserve influence wherever possible.[3] Therefore,

Germany and the other Northern European member states, such as the Netherlands and Denmark, will have an interest in shifting decision making from the Council, which in many areas uses qualified majority voting, to the European Council, which reaches decisions with unanimity. By doing so, Germany and its allies can veto decisions that run counter to their interests. Given Germany's current status as the economic 'primus inter pares' (Bulmer and Paterson 2013), its interests in this sphere should not be discounted. However, Germany's dominance is treated by some authors as symptomatic (along with Brexit) of a broader legitimacy crisis in the EU, where domestic populations are increasingly sceptical of the EU as a vehicle for positive change. The need to manage domestic pressures may also cause member states opposed to Germany (particularly in the Southern periphery) to fight for more repatriation of powers via the European Council.

However, the story of member state disagreements and domestic politics could yet spin both ways. The Commission might, paradoxically, be a key beneficiary of the centrifugal forces unleashed by Brexit. The political process of negotiations under Article 50 has involved both the Commission and the European Parliament nominating representatives (Michel Barnier and Guy Verhofstadt, respectively). In the initial phase after the vote, many of the interventions shaping the possible terrain of Brexit have come from member states themselves, whose different interests are competing and may yet prove irreconcilable. But the Commission's receipt, after the triggering of Article 50, of a set of guidelines from the European Council, followed by negotiating directives from the Council of Ministers has shaped the potential for the Commission to take charge of the negotiations and to act as a conduit for conflicting member states.

One key way in which the Commission could leverage Brexit for its own benefit is if it is able to mobilise uncertainty over the budget. On the revenue side, the UK may have to pay if it wants future access to the internal market (depending on the terms of such access). Regardless of whether continued contributions are negotiated, Brexit will leave at least a shortfall, which could mean that net recipients from the budget receive less – or that net contributors (especially Germany) have to pay more. We are already witnessing the contours of this shift, as the drop in the value of the pound following the Brexit vote left a €4 billion hole in the EU's funds for 2017, which was partially filled by letting the EU temporarily keep the money it collects in corporate fines (€1.1 billion) instead of remitting them to the member states (via a draft amending budget). Negotiations on how to resolve the rest of the shortfall are ongoing.

The upshot of the budgetary uncertainty is that it will probably lead to some kind of wholesale revision of the budget come the next Multiannual Financial Framework (MFF), for the period after 2020, which is due to be negotiated by 2019. Several other member states have rebates that are dependent on the UK's (including Germany, Austria and Denmark), and this web of different allowances is likely to unravel post-Brexit, an eventuality considered by the EU's High Level Group on Own Resources (HLGOR), which published its findings in December 2016.[4] Brexit could lead the EU to get some kind of direct or indirect taxing powers future, either in addition to or as a replacement for its existing own resources (drawn from VAT and customs levies), which are prone to fluctuation and which now constitute a mere 20 per cent of its revenues. More stable and autonomous revenue streams could potentially empower the Commission, if it is able to capitalize on the uncertainty generated by Brexit.

The external dimension

In a number of respects, the UK's exit will shape the EU's external policies going forward. Key areas of external policy include trade (involving the Common External Tariff, CET) and security and defence (falling under the Common Security and Defence Policy, CSDP). In evaluating the external impact of Brexit, we draw on Manners' (2002) ideas on the EU is a normative power.

The core of this approach specifies that the EU's power lies not only (or even primarily) in its civilian or military capacity but rather in its ability to shape conceptions of what is normal in international relations. This has the benefit of allowing us to think broadly about the possible axes along which the EU's influence may be redefined post-Brexit. Uncertainty, not least, is a threat: the possibility of disintegration will itself diminish the EU's ideational status with regard to the rest of the world, and the EU is likely to fight hard to project a more positive image.

Concerning material influence, the key variable is trade. Here, much depends on what kind of Brexit is agreed – in particular, which elements of the package of Single Market (including services) and common external tariff (including the EU's external trade policy) it retains: current UK Government policy is to leave both. Other association agreements have demonstrated that to an extent these elements are separable (such as the EEA, which does not include the CET), although it is unlikely that freedom of movement will be one of the options available à la carte. If the UK leaves the CET and ceases to be subject to the EU's trade policy – which seems likely, given the creation of a Department for International Trade – major ongoing deals like the TTIP could be called into question The UK is, as of 2014, the second largest EU destination for US exports, behind Germany,[5] which could make the deal less appealing to the United States (indeed, the Trump presidency appears to have cooled on TTIP, but this may reflect internal vacillation as much as an externally coherent policy shift). One possible outcome of TTIP would be to set global standards for trade (Siles-Brugge and De Ville 2015), the loss of which would mean a diminution in potential global normative impact for the EU. The recently signed CETA agreement demonstrates the difficulty of garnering agreement amongst the EU27, and, without the UK as a driving force, it may be that appetite for further deals diminishes both within the EU and amongst potential external partners (at least for deals following the same mixed agreement model). Of course, the converse is also possible: that the EU views the UK's exit as a catalyst for further initiatives, with the recent Japanese agreement as a precedent.

With the UK out of the picture, the EU will also lose one of its strongest military forces measured on a number of indicators,[6] corresponding to almost 25 per cent of all military spending in the EU (Guzelyté 2016). Together with France, the UK has been important in terms of promoting the view that the EU should also be able to use military force. In 1998, the British Prime Minister Tony Blair and French President Jacques Chirac agreed on the Saint Malo declaration. The declaration, which was a response to the EU's failure to prevent the atrocities committed in the armed conflicts in Kosovo in the late 1990s, stipulated that the EU should have its own military capabilities so that something similar could not happen in the future. Though the UK and France have disagreed over key military issues, such as the second Iraq War, both countries have emphasized the importance of backing up the EU's soft power with hard power. Although Britain has indicated that it has common interests with the EU when it comes to military issues, Brexit means that a strong advocate for hard power will disappear from the EU.

The EU would not only lose out in terms of hard power but also in soft power – its main tool – as the UK commands a strong diplomatic corps and network (Patel and Reh 2016). Together with pressure from the United States for Europe to contribute more, this may force the EU as a whole to advance its military capacity. This in turn could prove an opportunity for Germany to replace the UK as the choice of strategic partner for the United States in Europe, as, *ceteris paribus*, the United States would prefer a member state of the EU to a non-member state. Another perhaps more likely alternative would be that France increases its military capacity significantly in exchange for concessions from Germany with regard to economic issues. However, the outcome of both elections may yet prove to reshape the Franco-German axis and make predictions difficult to render. Macron will wish to stamp his authority on the Élysée, not least by delivering on his promises to take a bold stance on Europe. Meanwhile, the rise of the AFD in Germany may limit Merkel's room for manoeuvre and limit her capacity to act as an honest broker in international affairs. However, for the EU as a whole, Brexit could also mean an opportunity for the EU to develop a stronger military arm under the CSDP: the UK, despite being in favour of supplementing soft power with hard power, has to date vetoed attempts in that direction, which it perceived as being supranational rather than intergovernmental in orientation. It is therefore possible that Brexit may prove either a divisive force amongst the military powers of Europe or conversely a chance to bolster the reach of the EU itself.

Conclusion

This article has sought to provide an estimate of how the UK's intention to leave the EU is likely to affect power relations within the Union. Both material and ideational factors have been significant in conditioning the UK's relationship – and occasional culture clashes – with the EU. The UK has played an important role in shaping the politics of the Union, and thus its removal will generate significant legacies. We have mapped these potential legacies by deploying a framework detailing the micro-, meso- and macro-level shifts likely to occur. Our major findings are threefold. Firstly, in terms of administrative and political arrangements within the institutions, the Parliament and Council are likely to be significantly more affected than the European Council or Commission. Secondly, in terms of the balance of power among institutions, one of these two latter institutions is most likely to be the principal beneficiary of the uncertainty created by Brexit, although this is likely to be zero sum, and it is impossible at this stage to determine which will benefit more. Finally, the changes within the EU will undoubtedly have implications for the organisation's place in the world. Whether Brexit will prove to be a geopolitical threat or opportunity for the EU as a whole remains to be seen.

Notes

1. European Council, Commission Staff. Available at: http://ec.europa.eu/civil_service/docs/europa_sp2_bs_nat_x_grade_en.pdf [Accessed February 16, 2018].
2. Tara Palmieri and Carmen Paun, EU Leaders to UK Staff: We'll Try to Protect You after Brexit, *Politico*, June 24, 2016. Available at: www.politico.eu/article/eu-leaders-to-staff-well-try-to-protect-you-after-brexit-eu-referendum-consquences-uk-leave-europe/ [Accessed February 16, 2018].
3. The shape of any potential alliance with Emmanuel Macron may also prove critical.
4. Future Finacing of the EU: Final Report and Recommendations of the High Level Group on Own Resources, December 2016. Available at: http://ec.europa.eu/budget/mff/hlgor/library/reports-communication/hlgor-report_20170104.pdf [Accessed February 16, 2018].
5. Atlas, What Did United States of America Export in 2014? n.d. Available at: http://atlas.cid.harvard.edu/explore/tree_map/export/usa/show/all/2014/ [Accessed February 16, 2018].
6. GFP, European Powers Ranked by Military Strength Ranking, n.d. Available at: www.globalfirepower.com/countries-listing-europe.asp [Accessed February 16, 2018].

References

Ackrill, R. (2000) *The Common Agricultural Policy*. Sheffield: Sheffield Academic Press.

Bulmer, S. and Burch, M. (2001) The 'Europeanization' of Central Government. In: Schneider, G. and Aspinwall, M. (eds.), *The Rules of Integration: Institutionalist Approaches to the Study of Europe*. Manchester: Manchester University Press, pp. 73–96.

Bulmer, S. and Paterson, W.E. (2013) Germany as the EU's Reluctant Hegemon? Of Economic Strength and Political Constraints. *Journal of European Public Policy* 20(10): 1387–1405.

Butler, G., Jensen, M.D. and Snaith, H. (2016) Slow Change May Pull Us Apart: Debating a British Exit from the European Union. *Journal of European Public Policy* 23(9): 1278–1284.

Cardwell, P. (2016) The 'Hokey Cokey' Approach to EU Membership: Legal Options for the UK and EU. *Journal of European Public Policy* 23(9): 1285–1293.

Clarke, H., Goodwin, M. and Whiteley, P. (2017) *Brexit: Why Britain Voted to Leave the European Union.* Cambridge: Cambridge University Press.

Freedman, L. (2016) Brexit and the Law of Unintended Consequences. *Survival* 58(3): 7–12.

Goetz, K. and Meyer-Sahling, J.-H. (2008) The Europeanisation of National Political Systems: Parliaments and Executives. *Living Reviews in European Governance* 3(2): 4–30.

Guzelyté, S. (2016) National Defence Data 2013–2014 and 2015 (est.) of the 27 EDA Member States. *European Defence Agency*, June. Available at: https://eda.europa.eu/docs/default-source/documents/eda-national-defence-data-2013-2014-(2015-est)5397973fa4d264cfa776ff000087ef0f.pdf [Accessed January 18, 2018].

Hix, S. and Benedetto, G. (2016) UK Influence Series: Do British MEPs Win Key Positions of Power in the European Parliament? London School of Economics and Political Science, *europpblog*. Available at: http://blogs.lse.ac.uk/europpblog/2016/02/05/uk-influence-series-do-british-meps-win-key-positions-of-power-in-the-european-parliament/ [Accessed January 18, 2018].

Hix, S., Hagemann, S. and Frantescu, D. (2016) Would Brexit Matter? The UK's Voting Record in the Council and the European Parliament. *Tech. Rep. VoteWatch Europe.* Brussels, April. Available at: http://eprints.lse.ac.uk/66261/1/Hix_Brexit%20matter_2016.pdf [Accessed January 18, 2018].

Hix, S. and Hoyland, B. (2011) *The Political System of the EU.* Hampshire: Palgrave.

Hobolt, S.B. (2016) The Brexit Vote: A Divided Nation, a Divided Continent. *Journal of European Public Policy* 23(9): 1259–1277.

Hooghe, L. (2002) *The European Commission and the Integration of Europe.* Cambridge: Cambridge University Press.

Hyde-Price, A. (2006) Normative Power Europe: A Realist Critique. *Journal of European Public Policy* 13(2): 217–234.

Jensen, M.D. (2017) Exploring Central Governments' Coordination of European Union Affair. *Public Administration* 95(1): 249–268.

Jensen, M.D. and Snaith, H. (2016) When Politics Prevails: The Political Economy of a Brexit. *Journal of European Public Policy* 23(9): 1302–1310.

Kóczy, L.Á. (2016) How Brexit Affects European Union Power Distribution. Óbuda University, Keleti Faculty of Business and Management, Working Paper Series, No. 1601. Available at: http://uni-obuda.hu/users/vecseya/RePEc/pkk/wpaper/1601.pdf [Accessed November 3, 2017].

Kroll, D. and Leuffen, D. (2016) Ties That Bind, Can also Strangle: The Brexit Threat and the Hardships of Reforming the EU. *Journal of European Public Policy* 23(9): 1311–1320.

Łazowski, A. (2016) Unilateral Withdrawal from the EU: Realistic Scenario or a Folly? *Journal of European Public Policy* 23(9): 1294–1301.

Manners, I. (2002) Normative Power Europe: A Contradiction in Terms? *JCMS: Journal of Common Market Studies* 40(2): 235–258.

Marks, G., Hooghe, L. and Blank, K. (1996) European Integration from the 1980s: State-Centric v. Multi-Level Governance. *JCMS: Journal of Common Market Studies* 34(3): 341–378.

Miller, V. (2012) The Treaty on Stability, Coordination and Governance in the Economic and Monetary Union: Political Issues. House of Commons Library Research Briefings, Research Paper 12/14.

Miller, V. (2015) The 1974–75 UK Renegotiation of EEC Membership and Referendum. Commons Briefing Papers CBP-7253.

Moloney, N. (2017) Extracting the UK from EU Financial Services Governance: Regulatory Recasting or Shadowing from a Distance? In: Dougan, M. (ed.), *The UK after Brexit: Legal and Policy Challenges.* Cambridge: Intersentia, pp. 135–158.

Oliver, T. (2016) European and International Views of Brexit. *Journal of European Public Policy* 23(9): 1321–1328.

Patel, O. and Reh, C. (2016) Brexit: The Consequences for the EU's Political System. *UCL Constitution Unit Briefing Paper.* Available at: www.ucl.ac.uk/constitution-unit/research/europe/briefing-papers/Briefing-paper-2 [Accessed November 3, 2017].

Peterson, J. and Birdsall, A. (2008) Enlargement as Reinvention? In: Best, E. Christiansen, T. and Settembrini, P. (eds.), *The Institutions of the Enlarged European Union: Continuity and Change.* Cheltenham: Edward Elgar, pp. 54–82.

Quaglia, L. (2010) Completing the Single Market in Financial Services: The Politics of Competing Advocacy Coalitions (2010). *Journal of European Public Policy* 17(7): 1007.

Rasmussen, M.K. (2015) Heavy Fog in the Channel: Continent Cut Off? British Diplomatic Relations in Brussels after 2010. *JCMS: Journal of Common Market Studies* 54(3): 709–724.

Siles-Brugge, G. and De Ville, F. (2015) *TTIP: The Truth about the Transatlantic Trade and Investment Partnership.* Cambridge: Polity Press.

Stenbæk, J. and Jensen, M.D. (2016) Evading the Joint Decision Trap: The Multiannual Financial Framework 2014–20. *European Political Science Review* 8(4): 1–21.

Thomson, R. (2011) *Resolving Controversy in the European Union: Legislative Decision-Making before and after Enlargement.* Cambridge: Cambridge University Press.

Thomson, R. and Hosli, M. (2006) Who Has Power in the EU? The Commission, Council and Parliament in Legislative Decision-Making. *JCMS: Journal of Common Market Studies* 44(2): 391–417.

Tsebelis, G. and Garrett, G. (2000) Legislative Politics in the European Union. *European Union Politics* 1(1): 9–36.

Wallace, H. (2005) Exercising Power and Influence in the European Union: The Roles of Member States. In: Bulmer, S. and Lequesne, C. (eds.), *The Member States of the European Union.* Oxford: Oxford University Press, pp. 25–44.

22

BREXIT AND SMALL STATES IN EUROPE

Hedging, hiding or seeking shelter?

Anders Wivel and Baldur Thorhallsson[1]

Introduction

'There are two kinds of European nations', Danish Finance Minister Kristian Jensen told the audience including the British Ambassador to Denmark at a Brexit conference in the Danish Parliament in June 2017. 'There are small nations and there are countries that have not yet realized they are small nations' (Boffey 2017). Jensen's remarks, provoking a spirited response from the British ambassador, signalled the bafflement – rather than disappointment or anger – from a small European state, which had allied closely with the United Kingdom on numerous issues concerning security, transatlantic relations, economic and political freedom and the institutional development of the EU. The Danish finance minister was not the only prominent representative from a small state trying to make sense of the British decision. Economic policymakers from small states inside and outside the EU were 'consistently pessimistic about Brexit', noting the experience of small EU outsiders having to limit their scope for domestic policymaking considerably in order to benefit from EU integration (O'Sullivan and Skilling 2017).

The aim of this chapter is to unpack how Brexit influences small states in Europe. The main argument is that, while all small states are negatively affected by the British decision to invoke Article 50 of the Treaty of Lisbon and thereby to effectuate the outcome of the British 2016 referendum on EU membership to leave the European Union, some small states are considerably more affected than others. As a result, small states are likely to pursue different strategies to meet the challenges following from Brexit. The most prominent among these strategies are hedging, hiding and seeking shelter.

The chapter proceeds in four steps. First, we identity the shared challenges and opportunities of small European states following from Brexit. Second, we zoom in on the variations in consequences of Brexit for different clusters of small states. Third, we discuss the strategic responses of small states to Brexit. Finally, we sum up our analysis and conclude the chapter.

Small states in Europe after Brexit:
do the dark clouds have a silver lining?

The decision of British voters to leave the European Union marks a turning point in the history of European integration. The European integration process has never before been rolled back to such an extent. Already in the early 1960s, Britain had given up on its initiative to create an alternative form of cooperation in Europe, the European Free Trade Area (EFTA), and sought full participation in the European project. In 1973, two small states followed Britain into the Union, and the remaining EFTA states (Austria, Norway, Portugal, Sweden, Switzerland and Iceland) signed free trade agreements with it. Britain has always been a champion of widening of the EU and trade liberalisation in Europe, in general. Nowhere was this more evident than in the EU's enlargement processes after the end of the Cold War. Britain helped to push small states across Europe through the entrance gate of the Union. Small European states saw Britain as the main advocate of free trade, allowing them the market access necessary for growth in their small economies and an important part of the security and defence mechanism of the EU. Accordingly, Brexit poses a serious challenge for small European states inside and outside of the EU.

A small state is by definition 'the weaker part in an asymmetric relationship, which is unable to change the nature or functioning of the relationship on its own' (Wivel et al. 2014: 9). In absolute and relative terms, they lack capabilities. Consequentially, scholars and policymakers typically regard small states as vulnerable and with a more limited action space than great powers in the interactions with other states (Browning 2006; Hey 2003; Neumann and Gstöhl 2006). Thus, small states 'are stuck with the power configuration and its institutional expression, no matter what their specific relation to it is' (Mouritzen and Wivel 2005: 4). In particular, small states are vulnerable to international change and crisis because of their smaller margin of time and error due to lack of (economic, military, diplomatic) resources (Jervis 1978: 172f). Consequentially, small state foreign policies tend to be risk averse and status quo oriented, aimed primarily at reducing dependence and increasing action space with limited resources, in particular by working through international organisations (Toje 2011).

International organisations formalize interstate relations, thereby levelling the playing field by requiring all states to play by the same rules. Even though power politics persist and powerful actors may continue to circumvent or even break the rules, institutionalisation increases the cost for them to do so because they need to argue why this is legitimate, and the use (and abuse) of power is more visible than without the rules (Neumann and Gstöhl 2006: 20). For this reason, 'small states generally prefer multilateralism as both a path to influence and a means to restrain larger states' (Thorhallsson and Steinsson 2017).

To most small states in Europe, the EU has offered a particularly useful tool for simultane-ously maximizing influence and binding the larger member states (Bunse 2009; Goetschel 1998; Panke 2010; Steinmetz and Wivel 2010; Thorhallsson 2011). The EU provides a shelter for small states against multidimensional security challenges, including military hard security, non-state violence and societal security challenges and economic volatility (Bailes and Thorhallsson 2013). Couched in the language of the small states literature, the EU increases the 'margins of time and error' for small states by supplying an institutional cushion against external shocks backed up by the combined capabilities of the member states, including the continental great powers. At the same time, EU integration has replaced military balancing between competing European power centres with a single centre by channelling 'national security concerns' and has replaced rivalry among competing power centres with cohesion around a single power centre, symboli-cally located in Brussels but actually in the Franco-German coalition (Wæver 1998: 47). Thus, to the small EU member states, the EU provides a shelter against global shocks as well as great intra-European power rivalry. At the same time, the EU provides a platform for European and global influence for small states, even though '[s]ize is an advantage in EU negotiations, since bigger states are simply in a position to do more' (Panke 2015: 69) because of their financial and diplomatic resources, as well as more votes in the Council and parliamentarians in the Euro-pean Parliament. These shelter and platform effects are partly due to the reconstruction of the European political space, which has transformed the fundamental problematic of small EU and

NATO members from a 'survival problem' to an 'influence problem' (Løvold 2004). Free from worrying about a military attack from nearby great powers and embedded in a complex network of European and Euro-Atlantic institutions, small states have the opportunity to seek influence. Moreover, they have a strong incentive to do so in order to maximize their influence and action space in the highly institutionalized European political space (Björkdahl 2008; Grøn and Wivel 2011; Jakobsen 2009; Nasra 2011; Panke 2015).

Although these functions are most pertinent to small EU member states, they have important spillover effects for small non-members. Thus, rather than a question of either/or, EU integration affects small European states on a continuum. At one end, we find core member states (the Benelux countries as well as member states from Central and Eastern European and the Mediterranean joining through the EU enlargements in 2004, 2007 and 2013). These are the small states affected most by EU integration in the sense of having their action space most severely limited by EU rules and regulations but also enjoying the best chance of influencing the EU through multiple formal and informal channels. Moving along the continuum, we find member states with opt-outs (Sweden and Denmark), EFTA/EEA states (Norway, Iceland, Lichtenstein, Switzerland) and finally EU and EFTA/EEA outsiders (Serbia, Bosnia and Herzegovina, Former Yugoslav Republic of Macedonia, Albania, Kosovo, Montenegro, Moldova, as well as the micro states Andorra, Monaco, San Marino, Vatican City). While this last group of small states have very limited means of influencing EU policymaking, they still enjoy the benefits of political stability and economic growth (favourable access to the EU market), as well as access to specific EU programmes (e.g. Moldova is covered by the European Neighbourhood Policy (ENP), and Albania is part of the Euro-Mediterranean Partnership).

In this context, Brexit poses a quadruple challenge to small European states. First, the decision of the United Kingdom to leave the EU has deepened the post-Euro crisis debate on whether the EU is now experiencing a crisis, which is existential, multidimensional and unprecedented and potentially transforming differentiated integration into differentiated disintegration (Dinan et al. 2017: 373).

Second, while this process may by itself undermine the shelter and platform benefits of EU integration for small European states, the potential solution could add even further to the small states' post-Brexit conundrum. Solving an extraordinary crisis demands extraordinary leadership, and Germany and France have used the British activation of Article 50 to reconfirm their strong coalition ties. Thus, Brexit leaves small states in Europe with an increasing risk of a German-Franco 'cooperative hegemony' preconditioned on 'a capacity for power-sharing vis-à-vis smaller states in a region, for power aggregation on the part of the predominant regional state(s) and for commitment to a long-term regionalist policy strategy' (Pedersen 2002: 684). Although rarely a constructive player in the European integration process, Britain has played the important role of jester to the Franco-German court: questioning the rationale and good intentions of the two dominant powers of the integration process and pointing to potentially negative consequences of deepened integration. By doing this, the United Kingdom has provided a shelter for small states that may not agree with all British arguments but that have still benefitted from the UK bearing the costs of balancing Germany and France.

Third, Brexit is likely to result in a recalibration of the transatlantic relationship. While the United Kingdom and the United States will preserve a 'special relationship', it is likely that a second special relationship will develop between the United States and the Franco-German axis (Foundation Robert Schuman 2016). This development will limit the action space of small European states as close informal ties between the United States and a Franco-German cooperative hegemony will leave little room for the influence of other actors. The ability of small EU member states to have a say on the joint decision-making of these powers will depend on the strength of the EU institutions and the possibility of small states to influence decisions taken within them.

Finally, small states share with other European states a number of practical challenges regarding their citizens' right to life and work in Britain and access to the British market when Britain leaves the EU. However, because of their limited size and ties to the United Kingdom, a number of small states with strong political or economic affiliations with the United Kingdom are likely to be hit particularly badly by the fallout from a hard Brexit. Consequentially, Sweden, the Netherlands, Lithuania, Latvia, Ireland, Estonia, Denmark and Cyprus are proponents of a soft Brexit. They have more to lose from looser trade, investment and security ties with Britain than other member states, which demand a costly withdrawal (Economist Intelligence Unit 2017).

Taken together, these four challenges threaten to undermine some of the most fundamental benefits from European integration that small states have enjoyed for more than half a century. However, the dark clouds gathering over European small states after Brexit may not turn out to be an inevitable thunderstorm for three reasons.

First, Brexit may be seen as the logical conclusion of a long history of British self-marginalisation in the EU, beginning with the election of Margaret Thatcher as British prime minister in 1979, intensified since the election of David Cameron as Prime Minister in 2010 and concluded by the 2016 referendum (see also Chapter 11 on British historical exceptionalism). This process has gradually decreased the value of the United Kingdom as an ally of small states even when they – e.g. in the case of Denmark – shared a scepticism towards supranationalism, an Atlanticist foreign and security policy and an agenda of free trade. Consequently, for some traditional small state allies of the UK, such as Malta, the EU has outperformed Britain as a shelter against external challenges and as a platform for influence and growth (Follain et al. 2017). Thus, the political cost of Brexit to small EU member allies of the United Kingdom is significantly lower than it would have been two decades ago.

Second, the explicit British focus on maximizing national benefits from European integration has helped legitimize not only increased intergovernmentalism but also large member states flexing their muscle to push for special treatment even when this risked circum-passing or undermining European institutions. For this reason, continued British membership of the EU could have had the effect of undermining the shelter and platform benefits of EU integration for small states.

Finally, although a Franco-German cooperative hegemony, with Germany as the prime leader, poses several challenges to small European states, as previously noted, Germany has built its power and legitimacy on being a European power safeguarding and developing the institutionalisation and stabilisation of the European political space with non-coercive means. Paradoxically, the most powerful state in Europe may serve as the best guarantee against undermining the benefits of EU integration for small states. Moreover, Germany's greater assertiveness within the EU has been evident in the last few years, such as regarding its response to and leadership role in the financial and migrations crises, long before the Brexit referendum.

Variations on a theme: clusters of small states in post-Brexit Europe

Brexit is likely to change the EU's balance of power in the long term. In addition to strengthening the Franco-German axis into what might in effect be a Franco-German hegemony with Germany as the main leader, small states are likely to be part of losing or winning clusters of this rebalancing depending on their economic and political affiliations with the United Kingdom (Patel and Reh 2016).

One set of small state clusters pertains to the European security order. France and Germany are the two strongest military powers in a post-Brexit EU. Following the British referendum, the remaining twenty-seven member states have already committed to strengthening the EU's security and defence policy. The EU's new security strategy was published only a week after the British referendum in June 2016 and stressed the need for hard security instruments. At the European summit in December 2016, member states approved a package focusing on capability development, military planning and research, and, in June 2017, the European Commission launched the European Defence Fund in order to underpin collaboration on research, development and acquisition. This will potentially affect Atlanticist small EU members such Denmark, the Netherlands and the Baltic states, which stand to lose their most important ally in the EU in regard to transatlantic relations and national security, when the United Kingdom leaves the EU. With the United Kingdom pushing for a stronger role for NATO in Europe post-Brexit and with Germany and France eager to develop the EU as a security actor, these states may find themselves caught in the middle with little influence on institutional developments, while facing demands for contributions from both organisations. On the other hand, small states in favour of strengthening the EU's security and defence policy, such as Finland and Sweden, may gain from stronger EU defences.

Another set of small state clusters pertain to the political economy of the EU. The small states in the Northern liberal cluster (including Sweden, Denmark, Finland, the Netherlands and the Baltic states) have most to lose from Brexit. Germany and Britain are the most powerful members of the cluster, and, with Britain's departure from the EU, the weight of the cluster will decline. Germany is already seeking to rekindle relations with France and is more likely to seek leadership of the EU as a whole than of one cluster of states within the Union. In contrast, the Southern protectionist cluster (including the small states Greece, Portugal and Cyprus along with France, Italy and Spain) is likely to be strengthened as a consequence of Brexit. At present, both clusters have a blocking minority in the Council, but Britain's withdrawal from the EU will mean that the Northern liberal cluster will lose its blocking minority. Sweden, Denmark and the Netherlands are the main allies of Britain in the Council in terms of voting most often with it. Germany is least likely to vote with Britain according to VoteWatch data (cited in Patel and Reh 2016). Thus, Germany's position might become stronger within the Union after the withdrawal of Britain. This is a worry for some of the small states, which are concerned about German domination but at the same time could strengthen the small states' ad hoc alliances with Germany in the Council (Patel and Reh 2016).

To be sure, there are strong national variations within the Northern liberal cluster and the Southern protectionist cluster of small states reflecting the national challenges and opportunities following from Brexit. A KPMG study on the consequences of Brexit for EU member states found that the negative economic implications of Brexit were cutting across the two clusters: Ireland, Cyprus and Malta are the biggest losers, while small member states such as Sweden, Finland and Slovenia are among those state least affected (Gilchrist 2017). Also, the specific type of consequences varies. Portugal will mainly feel the effect on its export of wine and port to the United Kingdom (Spindler 2016). Malta will feel the effect on both imports and exports, as well as in regard to the large number of Maltese citizens living in the EU and the large number of British citizens living in Malta (Haig 2016). For small Central and Eastern European EU member states, a main concern will be the future of their many citizens working in the UK and sending home a substantial part of their income. Thus, in Latvia, Lithuania, Hungary and Croatia more than 3 per cent of GDP comes from remittances from citizens working abroad, typically in another EU country and many of them in the UK (Gilchrist 2017).

Also, opportunities for small EU member states stemming from Brexit cut across the two political economy clusters and reflect national economic, political and administrative structures. For instance, Greece may welcome a less liberal Europe but resent a Europe with an even wider action space for the 'ordoliberal' agenda-setting powers of Germany (Nedergaard and Snaith

2015). At the same time, the Greek Government is working to take advantage of new opportunities resulting from Brexit by persuading shipping companies and shipping insurance companies based in London to move their EU headquarters to Greece (Tugwell and Nikas 2017). Likewise, Denmark may be losing an important ally, but at the same time, the Danish Government and financial sector see opportunities in attracting banks, brokers and insurance companies located in London to Copenhagen with the aim of creating a Scandinavian financial hub. Also, the Danish Government saw opportunities in strengthening the Copenhagen area 'Medicon Valley', for example by attracting the European Medicines Agency now located in London with a staff of 900 and estimated economic effects of several billion Danish kroner (Sørensen and Wivel 2017). However, Denmark lost its bid to host the agency after a fierce competition with a number of small member states including the eventual winner, the Netherlands. Malta may be set to suffer heavily from Brexit because of the strong economic, historical and cultural ties to the UK. However, at the same time, the Maltese Government sees important opportunities in attracting the EU headquarters of multinational companies located in Britain pointing to the advantages of English as its official language, a British educational system and work ethic and – as a bonus – a Mediterranean quality of life (Haig 2016).

The three small EFTA/EEA states constitute a third post-Brexit small state cluster in addition to the clusters based on the European security order and the political economy of the EU. They face the same general challenges from Brexit as the small EU member states previously identified, but in addition they face a number of challenges and opportunities following from their EFTA/EEA status (e.g. see EFTA 2017a; Thorhallsson and Gunnarsson 2017). The UK–EFTA trade (including Switzerland) is significant. In 2015, total UK–EFTA trade in goods and services was higher than trade between UK and France (Phinnemore and Najy 2017). In 2016, export from the four EFTA states to the UK was worth €27.625 million and import from the UK to EFTA states €9.481 million (EFTA 2017b). Consequentially, Brexit is the 'highest priority' in the Icelandic Ministry for Foreign Affairs (Guðmundsson 2017), which has identified a number of issues of concern for Iceland, such as eviction of landing rights of Icelandic airlines in Britain (Þórðarson 2017).

Britain's exit from the EU is likely to change the geopolitics and geo-economics of the North Atlantic, the UK's immediate regional setting. Brexit will add to the list of states (Norway, Iceland, Canada and the United States) and entities (Greenland and the Faroe Islands) in the region that are not part of the EU. This creates uncertainty in relation to what role Britain will require for itself in the region, for example in regard to the opening of the Arctic Ocean. In the wake of the Brexit negotiations, Britain has decided to withdraw from the London Fisheries Convention from 1964, which allows countries to fish near one another's coasts (McHugh 2017). The Icelandic Government has raised concerns over having yet another state/actor taking part in negotiations over common fish stocks in the North Atlantic making the negotiations even more complex than they are at present, and Norway and Denmark have raised concerns about the future of fishing rights (FishUpdate 2017; Guardian 2017). Also, Brexit means that a new powerful actor, Britain, will get a seat at the negotiation table in the North Atlantic concerning policy sectors, such as environmental protection and sailing/shipping. Moreover, Norway and Iceland follow closely the Scottish debate on independence in relation to Britain's departure from the Union since it could create a new situation in the North Atlantic (Þórðarson 2017).

On the other hand, Brexit may create opportunities for the North Atlantic region. For instance, after the Brexit referendum, Icelandic President Ólafur Ragnar Grímsson claimed that Brexit was good news for the region, stating that the states' relations in the region, on both sides of the North Atlantic, would undergo positive changes (Iceland Monitor 2016b). Although more cautious and stressing the continued importance of the EU, leading Danish politicians emphasized that Brexit signalled a legitimate and necessary call for reforms of the EU (Larsen 2016). Britain is likely to campaign for a stronger NATO after its withdrawal from the Union and, in light of growing disputes between the West and Russia, might seek to strengthen its security and defence ties with states in the region. This move would be highly welcomed by the small Atlanticist states such as Denmark, Norway and Iceland (e.g. see Thorhallsson and Gunnarsson 2017).

Responding to Brexit: Hedging, hiding or seeking shelter?

Small European states are likely to pursue three different strategies when seeking to limit the costs and maximizing the potential benefits from Brexit: hedging, hiding and seeking shelter. Traditionally, small states have sought either to 'opt out' of international relations by pursuing so-called hiding strategies, that is, signalling that they do not take sides in the overall struggle between great powers or to seek economic, military and societal shelter from great powers and international organisations (Bailes and Thorhallsson 2013; Fox 1959; Smed and Wivel 2017; Vital 1967). For the majority of small European states, a combination of hiding and seeking shelter will be the logical strategic response to Brexit. This is true for the small states that remain outside the EU/ EFTA/EEA. It is also true for small member states in Central and Eastern Europe and the Mediterranean without specific historical, political and economic ties to the United Kingdom. Like other EU member states, they face questions of their citizens' right to life and work in Britain and access to the British market, but they have little incentive to spend any political capital on the issue. Thus, these small states are likely to 'hide' from Brexit by only stating vaguely (or not at all) their preferences on Brexit negotiation issues and seek shelter from the EU. In sum, they are pursuing a classical small state approach of staying out of trouble and freeriding on the order negotiated by the great powers.

For the small states affected directly by Brexit, because they are part of one or more of the three clusters identified in the previous section, the cost–benefit analysis is different. These states have a common interest in a soft Brexit with continuing strong economic and political ties between the EU and the United Kingdom and between the individual states and the United Kingdom. Because of their close ties with the United Kingdom, they may also have particular policy interests not only in a soft Brexit but also on the specific content of a soft Brexit. For these states, a combination of hiding and shelter seeking will be insufficient. They are likely to pursue a hedging strategy seeking to spread their bets by taking shelter from the EU and its big member states, whenever necessary but seeking to form coalitions with like-minded states on specific aspects of a Brexit deal, as well as on the timetable and format of the Brexit process. In turn, these coalitions may serve as post-Brexit caucuses within the EU, even though small states 'are unlikely to risk undermining EU cohesion' (Economist Intelligence Unit 2017).

One example of an emerging small states coalition/caucus is Ireland, the Netherlands and Denmark. These three countries share an Atlanticist, free trade agenda and a relatively intergovernmentalist approach to EU integration, as well as close economic and political ties with the United Kingdom (Sørensen and Wivel 2017). In April 2017, Irish Prime Minister (Taoiseach) Enda Kenny – meeting with his Dutch and Danish counterparts, Mark Rutte and Lars Løkke Rasmussen, for a Brexit mini-summit in the Hague – stressed that the EU needed to consider the concerns of small states and work towards fair and pragmatic solutions in a Brexit deal (Minihan 2017). He noted that 'we have similar interests of a very common nature and we wanted those reflected in the ground rules being set out by the European Council' (ibid.). Prime Minister Rutte noted that the three countries focused on concerns about EU citizens' European businesses based in the United Kingdom. The three prime ministers were keen to stress that they did not constitute a breakaway group or intra-EU alliance, but, as noted by Naomi O'Leary (2017) of *Politico*:

> The three have much in common. They are all big exporters to the U.K. They have all been on London's side in the past in EU negotiations, tending toward a liberal, trade-friendly vision of the bloc. With the U.K.'s departure, they are all losing an ally in the internal politics of the EU.

This may be the beginning of an inner circle of small like-minded states seeking to influence not only the Brexit process but also the EU in general. Only a few weeks before the mini-summit, Danish Foreign Minister Anders Samuelsen went on a trip to Lisbon, Vienna and Prague with an explicit aim of seeking partners to balance Franco-German leadership in the EU. The Danish minister saw opportunities, for example, for cooperating with Portugal on stabilizing NATO and strengthening transatlantic free trade and cooperating with Austria on reducing red tape in EU practices (Sørensen and Wivel 2017).

For the EFTA/EEA states, Brexit may prove an efficient way of hedging by integrating the United Kingdom into EFTA, while maintaining strong ties with the EU and its member states. Thus, the current Icelandic foreign minister, just like his predecessor (Reid 2016), has taken the lead in approaching Britain to apply for membership in EFTA (Chan 2017). The Foreign minister has emphasized the possibility of Iceland and the other EFTA states following the British lead and making free trade agreements with states around the globe (Tryggvason 2017). Potentially, this could result in a better trade deal with Britain than they enjoy at present (Iceland and Norway still pay tariffs on some of their marine export to the other EEA states) (Helgason and Sigurfinnsson 2017). On the other hand, the governments in Norway and Switzerland have been cautious about the possibility of Britain joining EFTA. They fear that Britain might take over their leadership role in the organisation and that the current tension between Britain and the EU might damage the good working relationship between EFTA and the EU (Phinnemore and Najy 2017).

Conclusions: missing the bull in the China shop?

Brexit is a challenge for small European states. The post-Brexit rebalancing of the EU and recalibrating of the transatlantic relationship are likely to strengthen the Franco-German axis, potentially leading to a cooperative hegemony over Europe with Germany as the principal leader. This will limit the foreign policy action space of small states in Europe. Even though Britain was routinely mocked for acting as the bull in the china shop, many small states benefitted from somebody else breaking the china, when EU member states disagreed over institutional reforms and policy development. Thus, Britain provided small states with an often overlooked shelter against Franco-German dominance and a critical interrogation of new developments useful in any democratic political space. The ability of the small states to deter the supremacy of Germany and France will depend on the strength of the EU institutional framework in limiting their unilateral scope of action within the Union.

To the majority of small EU member states, Brexit will lead to few new policy initiatives, as they will seek shelter from Germany and France in the negotiations with the United Kingdom and the institutional reforms that follow. A group of North European Atlanticist, free trade small states with a predominantly intergovernmentalist approach to EU integration will see their strongest political and economic ally leave the EU. Others, such as Portugal or Austria, will find themselves in opposition to Germany and France on selected issue areas. Not surprisingly, these states have already begun to hedge their diplomatic bets seeking informal negotiations and creating a loosely bound small state coalition. On the other hand, the small states that will follow the France and German policy preferences and align themselves with their visions of deeper European political and economic integration may benefit from the reinforcement of the Franco-German powerhouse.

For the EFTA/EEA states, Brexit entails opportunities as well as challenges. Iceland and Norway may become less dependent on the EU if they manage to utilize Brexit in their advance and develop closer security, trade and cultural relations with Britain in a post-Brexit world. This might in particular become the case if Britain rejoins EFTA, as already suggested by some politicians and academics. For instance, Phinnemore and Najy (2017) have suggested that Britain considers joining EFTA in order for it to ease the complex challenges it faces concerning Brexit and to maintain some continuity in its trade relations with the EFTA states and the thirty-eight states with whom EFTA has concluded free trade agreements. They claim that Britain would be much more at ease with EFTA membership than EU membership, legally, politically and financially. On the other hand, they identify EFTA commitment to free movement of persons as the main hindrance of British membership. Hence, they propose that Britain seeks an association with EFTA (UKEFTA) – a similar arrangement Finland had with EFTA (FINEFTA) from the early 1960s to the mid-1980s (ibid.). British membership or association with EFTA would transform the organisation and its relations with the EU – even though Britain would not join the EEA – and firmly place it on the political and economic map in Europe and around the globe. This could provide the current small member states of EFTA with several new opportunities in Britain and in relations with their trade dealings with states outside Europe. However, Brexit has created great uncertainty for the relations between the EFTA states and Britain, and there are no guarantees that the states' relations will triumph after Britain leaves the EU; at present, Britain has not signalled its intention to join or seek association with EFTA, and Norway and Switzerland are sceptical about such a scenario.

Brexit has had a limited impact on national politics across the EU member states, especially when compared with the Eurozone and the migration crises. However, it has 'dramatically *reduced* party-based Euroscepticism in Ireland 'due to: economic uncertainty, the opportunities it presents for Irish "reunification" and for Ireland to act as a bridge between the UK and EU, and its association with English nationalism' (Szczerbiak and Taggart 2017: 2). In addition, Brexit 'definitely changed the public debate in terms of redefining Euroscepticism' in posing a more pressing question on the EU's future (Exadaktylos et al. 2017: 1). For example, Szczerbiak and Taggart's (2017) surveys indicate that Brexit has had an impact on the EU debate in small EU member states such as Denmark, Greece and Austria. Most likely, Britain's withdrawal from the EU will make it much harder for pro-Europeans to sell membership to the already Eurosceptical public in Norway, Switzerland and Iceland. Brexit has already influenced the EU debate in Iceland and firmly *frozen* its EU accession negotiations, which have been on hold since 2013 (e.g. see Iceland Monitor 2016a). In contrast, the impact of Brexit has been relatively modest in the Netherlands.

It remains to be seen how Brexit will affect Euroscepticism in small European states in the long run, but evaluations of the pros and cons of EU membership are likely to be influenced by British successes and failures in relation to Brexit. If Brexit is generally seen as having negative effects on Britain, it may lead to greater support for the Union. And if life outside the Union will turn particularly bad for the British, this might even convince the pro-European side in Iceland to start again to campaign actively for membership – more is needed for that to happen in Norway and Switzerland. If British economy is flourishing after its departure from the EU and its political influence is maintained or even increased, this will have an impact the EU debate in states such as Denmark, Sweden and Finland and be near impossible to sell EU membership in the EFTA states.

All European states may be small states, as argued by the Danish finance minister in the beginning of this chapter. However, some European states are smaller than others. The United Kingdom has – because of its size and capabilities and being a leading proponent of Atlanticism, free trade and intergovernmentalism – played a pivotal role in EU integration, balancing the Franco-German coalition and providing a shelter for like-minded small states. Without the United Kingdom, these states have started to hedge their diplomatic bets by creating new coalitions, while continuing to signal their support for EU integration and avoiding direct opposition to Germany and France. The success of these coalitions, in combination with British success or failure to create a new shelter outside the EU, will affect not only the future of small European states after Brexit but EU integration in general.

Note

1 We would like to thank Peter Nedergaard for useful comments on an earlier draft.

References

Bailes, A.J. and Thorhallsson, B. (2013) Instrumentalizing the European Union in Small State Strategies. *Journal of European Integration* 35(2): 99–115.

Björkdahl, A. (2008) Norm Advocacy: A Small State Strategy to Influence the EU. *Journal of European Public Policy* 15(1): 135–154.

Boffey, D. (2017) Brexit Broadside: British Officials Bristle at Danish Scorn. *The Guardian*, June 14. Available at: www.theguardian.com/politics/2017/jun/14/road-to-brexit-is-paved-with-amusement-danish-and-brave-faces-british [Accessed August 22, 2017].

Browning, C. (2006) Small, Smart and Salient? Rethinking Identity in the Small States Literature. *Cambridge Review of International Affairs* 19(4): 669–684.

Bunse, S. (2009) *Small States and EU Governance: Leadership through the Council Presidency*. Basingstoke: Palgrave Macmillan.

Chan, S.P. (2017) Iceland Opens Door for UK to Join EFTA, July 15. Available at: www.telegraph.co.uk/business/2017/07/15/iceland-opens-door-uk-join-efta/ [Accessed September 4, 2017].

Dinan, D., Nugent, N. and Paterson, W.E. (2017) Conclusions: Crisis without End. In: Dinan, D., Nugent, N. and Paterson, W.E. (eds.), *The European Union in Crisis*. London: Palgrave, pp. 360–375.

Economist Intelligence Unit (2017) The Brexit Negotiations: Hard or Soft Europe? Available at: http://country.eiu.com/article.aspx?articleid=1865298170&Country=United%20Kingdom&topic=Politics&subtopic=Forecast&subsubtopic=International+relations [Accessed September 4, 2017].

EFTA (2017a) Norwegian EEA Minister: Norway Should Be Included in UK–EU Brexit Deal on Internal Market. An Interview with Frank Bakke-Jensen Norway's Minister of EEA and EU Affairs. *The EFTA Newsletter*, December 2016. Available at: www.efta.int/About-EFTA/news/Norwegian-EEA-Minister-Norway-should-be-included-UK-EU-Brexit-deal-Internal-Market-502111 [Accessed September 4, 2017].

EFTA (2017b) Trade between EFTA and the United Kingdom. Available at: http://trade.efta.int/#/country-graph/EFTA/GB/2016/HS2 [Accessed September 4, 2017].

Exadaktylos, T., Guerra, S. and Guerrina, R. (2017) Public Euroscepticism after the British Referendum. *The European Parties Elections and Referendums Network (EPERN)*, July 17. Available at: https://epern.wordpress.com/2017/07/17/public-euroscepticism-after-the-british-referendum/ [Accessed September 4, 2017].

FishUpdate (2017) Norwegian Fishing Leaders in Brexit Talks. *FishUpdate*, May 9. Available at: www.fishupdate.com/norwegian-fishing-leaders-brexit-talks/ [Accessed August 29, 2017].

Follain, J., Stearns, J. and Navarra, K.N. (2017) Goodbye and Good Luck: U.K. Gets Brexit Message from Old Friend. *Bloomberg Politics*. Available at: www.bloomberg.com/news/articles/2017-02-06/u-k-gets-brexit-message-from-its-old-friend-malta-goodbye-and-good-luck [Accessed September 5, 2017].

Foundation Robert Schuman (2016) Transatlantic Relations after Brexit. *European Issue*, No. 409. Paris: Foundation Robert Schuman. Available at: www.robert-schuman.eu/en/european-issues/0409-transatlantic-relations-after-brexit [Accessed August 25, 2017].

Fox, A.B. (1959) *The Power of Small States Diplomacy in World War II*. Chicago: University of Chicago Press.

Gilchrist, K. (2017) Ireland, Cyprus, Malta and Luxembourg to Be Hardest Hit by Brexit: KPMG Report. *CNBC*, March 1. Available at: www.cnbc.com/2017/03/01/ireland-cyprus-malta-and-luxembourg-to-be-hardest-hit-by-brexit-kpmg-report.html [Accessed September 5, 2017].

Goetschel, L. (1998) The Foreign and Security Policy Interests of Small States in Today's Europe. In: Goetschel, L. (ed.), *Small States Inside and Outside the European Union*. New York: Springer, pp. 13–31.

Grøn, C. and Wivel, A. (2011) Maximizing Influence in the European Union after the Lisbon Treaty: From Small State Policy to Smart State Strategy. *Journal of European Integration* 33(5): 523–539.

Guardian (2017) Denmark to Contest UK Efforts to 'Take Back Control' of Fisheries. *Guardian*, April 18. Available at: www.theguardian.com/politics/2017/apr/18/denmark-to-contest-uk-efforts-to-take-back-control-of-fisheries [Accessed August 29, 2017].

Guðmundsson, H. J. (2017) Þetta er í algerum forgangi. *Mbl.is*, January 18. Available at: www.mbl.is/frettir/innlent/2017/01/18/etta_er_i_algerum_forgangi/ [Accessed August 29, 2017].

Haig, A.S. (2016) *Effects of Brexit on UK Expats in EU Malta–BBC: Rights for Maltese Citizens Set to Endure, Opportunities for Malta as an EU Financial Centre*. Valetta: Chetcuti Cauchi Advocates. Available at: www.ccmalta.com/news/effects-of-brexit-on-uk-expats-in-malta?lang=hu-HU [Accessed September 5, 2017].

Helgason, R.M. and Sigurfinnsson, H.Ö (2017) Miklir hagsmunir undir, líka fyrir Ísland. *RÚV*, March 29. Available at: www.ruv.is/frett/miklir-hagsmunir-undir-lika-fyrir-island [Accessed August 29, 2017].

Hey, J.A.K. (2003) Introducing Small State Foreign Policy. In: Hey, J.A.K. (ed.), *Small States in World Politics: Explaining Foreign Policy Behaviour*. Boulder: Lynne Rienner, pp. 1–11.

Iceland Monitor (2016a) Brexit: The Idea of Iceland in the EU an Even More Distant Reality. June 24. Available at: http://icelandmonitor.mbl.is/news/politics_and_society/2016/06/24/brexit_the_idea_of_iceland_in_the_eu_an_even_more_d/ [Accessed August 29, 2017].

Iceland Monitor (2016b) Brexit Is Good News Says the President of Iceland. June 25. Available at: http://icelandmonitor.mbl.is/news/politics_and_society/2016/06/25/brexit_is_good_news_says_president_of_iceland/ [Accessed August 29, 2017].

Jakobsen, P.V. (2009) Small States, Big Influence: The Overlooked Nordic Influence on the Civilian ESDP. *Journal of Common Market Studies* 47(1): 81–102.

Jervis, R. (1978) Cooperation under the Security Dilemma. *World Politics* 30(2): 172–173.

Larsen, J.B. (2016) Danske politikere om Brexit: Ualmindeligt sørgeligt, fantastisk modigt – og 'åh, nej!'. *Danmarks Radio*, June 24. Available at: www.dr.dk/nyheder/politik/overblik-danske-politikere-om-brexit-ualmindeligt-soergeligt-fantastisk-modigt-og [Accessed April 25, 2017].

Løvold, A. (2004) Småstatsproblematikken i internasjonal politikk. *Internasjonal Politikk* 62(1): 7–31.

McHugh, M. (2017) UK's Withdrawal from Fishing Deal Is 'Unwelcome and Unhelpful' – Says Government. *Independent*, July 2. Available at: www.independent.ie/irish-news/politics/uks-withdrawal-from-fishing-deal-is-unwelcome-and-unhelpful-says-government-35886609.html [Accessed July 4, 2017].

Minihan, M. (2017) EU Should Prioritise Concerns of Small Countries, Says Kenny. *The Irish Times*, April 21. Available at: www.irishtimes.com/news/politics/eu-should-prioritise-concerns-of-small-countries-says-kenny-1.3056781 [Accessed August 27, 2017].

Mouritzen, H. and Wivel, A. (2005) Introduction. In: Mouritzen, H. and Wivel, A. (eds.), *The Geopolitics of Euro-Atlantic Integration*. London: Routledge, pp. 1–11.

Nasra, S. (2011) Governance in EU Foreign Policy: Exploring Small State Influence. *Journal of European Public Policy* 18(2): 164–180.

Nedergaard, P. and Snaith, H. (2015) As I Drifted on a River I Could Not Control: The Unintended Ordoliberal Consequences of the Eurozone Crisis. *JCMS: Journal of Common Market Studies* 53(5): 1094–1109.

Neumann, I.B. and Gstöhl, S. (2006) Introduction: Lilliputians in Gulliver's World? In: Ingebritsen, C., Neumann, I.B., Gstöhl, S. and Beyer, J.C. (eds.), *Small States in International Relations*. Seattle: University of Washington Press, pp. 3–36.

O'Leary, N. (2017) Northern European Mini-Summit Seeks to Soften Brexit Blow. *Politico*, April 20. Available at: www.politico.eu/article/northern-european-mini-summit-seeks-to-soften-brexit-blow-denmark-ireland-netherlands/ [Accessed August 27, 2017].

O'Sullivan, M. and Skilling, D. (2017) Brexit View: From Great Britain to Little England. *Euronews*, March 31. Available at: www.euronews.com/2017/03/31/view-from-great-britain-to-little-england-theresa-may [Accessed August 22, 2017].

Panke, D. (2010) *Small States in the European Union: Coping with Structural Disadvantages*. Farnham: Ashgate.

Panke, D. (2015) Small States in EU Decision-Making: How Can They Be Effective? In: Keating, M. and Baldersheim, H. (eds.), *Small States in the Modern World*. Cheltenham: Edward Elgar, pp. 59–72.

Patel, O. and Reh, C. (2016) Brexit: The Consequences for the EU's Political System. UCL Constitution Unit Briefing Paper, No. 2. London: UCL Constitution Unit Briefing Paper. Available at: www.ucl.ac.uk/constitution-unit/research/europe/briefing-papers/Briefing-paper-2 [Accessed August 22, 2017].

Pedersen, T. (2002) Cooperative Hegemony: Power, Ideas and Institutions in Regional Integration. *Review of International Studies* 28(4): 677–696.

Phinnemore, D. and Najy, C. (2017) The Option of Association: The United Kingdom Post-Brexit and the European Free Trade Association. Zurich and Geneva: Foraus-Policy Brief, June. Program Europe.

Reid, H. (2016) Iceland Would Welcome Britain into EFTA after Brexit – Iceland Foreign Minister. October, 19. Available at: http://uk.reuters.com/article/uk-iceland-eu-britain/iceland-would-welcome-britain-into-efta-after-brexit-iceland-foreign-minister-idUKKCN12J2EA [Accessed August 4, 2017].

Smed, U.T. and Wivel, A. (2017) Vulnerability without Capabilities? Small State Strategy and the International Counter-Piracy Agenda. *European Security* 26(1): 79–98.

Sørensen, C. and Wivel, A. (2017) Danmark efter Brexit: Business as usual eller en ny begyndelse for dansk europapolitik? *Internasjonal Politikk* 75(2): 117–130.

Spindler, K. (2016) *How Brexit Might Affect the UK and Portugal*. Lisbon: British-Portuguese Chamber of Commerce. Available at: www.bpcc.pt/spotlight-arch/256-spotlight-117.html [Accessed September 5, 2017].

Steinmetz, R. and Wivel, A. (2010) *Small States in Europe: Challenges and Opportunities*. Farnham: Ashgate.

Szczerbiak, A. and Taggart, P. (2017) How Has Brexit, and Other EU Crises, Affected Party Euroscepticism across Europe? *The European Parties Elections and Referendums Network (EPERN)*, May 16. Available at: https://epern.wordpress.com/2017/05/16/how-has-brexit-and-other-eu-crises-affected-party-euroscepticism-across-europe/ [Accessed August 4, 2017].

Thorhallsson, B. (2011) Domestic Buffer versus External Shelter: Viability of Small States in the New Globalised Economy. *European Political Science* 10(3): 324–336.

Thorhallsson, B. and Gunnarsson, P. (2017) Island og Brexit: 'Icexit' fra sóknaden om EU-medlemskap? *Internasjonal Politikk* 75(2): 167–179.

Thorhallsson, B. and Steinsson, S. (2017) Small State Foreign Policy. In: Thies, C. (ed.), *Oxford Research Encyclopedia of Foreign Policy*. Oxford: Oxford University Press. Available at: http://politics.oxfordre.com/view/10.1093/acrefore/9780190228637.001.0001/acrefore-9780190228637-e-484 [Accessed August 29, 2017].

Toje, A. (2011) The European Union as a Small Power. *Journal of Common Market Studies* 49(1): 43–60.

Tryggvason, T.P. (2017) Nýr utanríkisráðherra sér tækifæri í útgöngu Breta úr ESB. *Vísir*, January 11. Available at: www.visir.is/g/2017170119742/nyr-utanrikisradherra-ser-taekifaeri-i-utgongu-breta-ur-esb [Accessed December 15, 2017].

Þórðarson, G.Þ (2017) Foreign Minister's Report on Foreign Policy and International Affairs. *Iceland: The Althingi*, May. Available at: www.althingi.is/altext/pdf/146/s/0671.pdf [Accessed July 6, 2017].

Tugwell, P. and Nikas, S. (2017) Greece Seeks to Lure U.K.-Based Shipowners, Brokers on Brexit. *Bloomberg.com*, May 31. Available at: www.bloomberg.com/news/articles/2017-05-30/greece-seeks-to-lure-u-k-based-shipowners-brokers-on-brexit [Accessed September 5, 2017].

Vital, D. (1967) *The Inequality of States: A Study of the Small Power in International Relations*. Oxford: Clarendon Press.

Wæver, O. (1998) Integration as Security: Constructing a Europe at Peace. In: Kupchan, C. (ed.), *Atlantic Security: Contending Visions*. New York, Council on Foreign Relations, pp. 45–63.

Wivel, A., Bailes, A. and Archer, C. (2014) Setting the Scene: Small States and International Security. In: Archer, C., Bailes, A. and Wivel, A. (eds.), *Small States and International Security: Europe and Beyond*. London: Routledge, pp. 3–25.

23

BREXIT AND THE EU'S AFFILIATED NON-MEMBERS

John Erik Fossum

Introduction

Over its six decades of existence, the European Union (hereafter EU) has grown from six to twenty-eight members. The functional and territorial reach of the EU does not, however, end at its borders but extends deep into many of the states in Europe that are *not* EU members. In the broad category of 'affiliated non-members', we find at one extreme states that have incorporated EU rules and norms to such an extent as to raise questions as to whether they are inside or outside the EU, and at the other extreme are states that have developed narrow and/or far less committed affiliations with the EU.

Brexit will place the UK in a new category of state in Europe – that of an EU ex-member state (Lord 2015), and an important question that is currently wrestled with is what type of future affiliation that will be. Will the UK end up in a new category, with a distinct UK–EU relationship; if so, will others join it? Or will the UK join a (group of) state(s) in an off-the-shelf form of affiliation, such as for instance the European Economic Area agreement (EEA)? The question of what form of future EU affiliation the UK ends up with is not only important for the UK and the EU; it is vitally important for most affected non-members, as well.

We need to know what kind of relationship the UK establishes with the EU in order to understand the implications for the affiliated non-members, not the least because the EU's affiliated non-members are not directly involved in the Brexit negotiations.

The main purpose of this chapter is to explore the possible implications of Brexit for the EU's affiliated non-members. I start by outlining the types of affiliations that the EU has with its non-members. Focus is on what distinguishes each affiliation and on how binding they are for each party to the agreement. I assess the most Brexit-relevant EU association arrangements in terms of how they grapple with the trilemma pertaining to state sovereign control, democratic self-governing and market access (legally regulated and predictable relations with the EU) (Featherstone 2017; Rodrik 2011). Particular emphasis is placed on the so-called sovereign democrats (Eriksen and Fossum 2015), namely those states that qualify for EU membership but have decided not to become EU members. These states are the ones that most likely will end up in close affiliation with the UK.

In the second part, I seek to establish the UK's preferred mode of EU affiliation, including a brief assessment of how realistic that is. The UK Government has explicitly stated that it wants assured market access without being included in the EU's internal market or Customs Union. It seeks a new form of relationship. The question is whether the EU will accept that or whether the UK will end up having to choose among one of the off-the-shelf options that are available or an arrangement that looks different but in practice works similarly. Of importance to the overall assessment is whether these will be permanent or temporary arrangements.

In the third part, I present and discuss several scenarios for the effects of Brexit on affiliated non-members. The assessment needs to take into consideration the nature and dynamics of the triangular relationship between the EU, the UK and the EU's affiliated non-members.

The final part holds the conclusion.

The EU's non-members: forms of affiliation

The EU has developed a broad range of affiliations with non-members. There are so many and so diverse states bordering the EU that this diversity is almost bound to shape the EU's external relations (geographically speaking, the United States has only two states directly bordering upon it). The EU's member states play a fundamental role in shaping the EU's external relations, and they are not only culturally and institutionally diverse, they have (often deep historical) links that span across continents and in all kinds of directions (ranging from former intercontinental empires to nation states and even former colonies such as Cyprus). In addition, the Union has itself expanded greatly in size and depth at a rapid albeit uneven pace. There are therefore historical and structural reasons for expecting that the overall picture of the EU's relations to the world beyond its membership will be complex and composite. Managing its external relations is an intrinsic part of the EU's efforts to manage its internal relations and dynamics.

The EU's openness to its surroundings is apparent in the fact that it is open to membership for all European states (even if it is readily apparent that some long-term applicants such as Turkey are unlikely ever to become members), but EU membership is conditional on compliance with a range of criteria, notably the so-called Copenhagen criteria.[1] The question of conditionality and compliance with EU rules and norms does, however, not stop at the EU's borders; states can operate in accordance with EU rules and norms without being EU members. The implication is that in the EU, we need to consider borders on the one hand in terms of formal membership and on the other with reference to variegated territorial functionality. The territorial reach of functions varies, and the same applies to the functional breadth of a given territorial configuration.[2] Consider the differences in territorial reach of, respectively, the Euro-area, the EEA, the EU's Customs Union, and Schengen (see Figure 23.1).

In an EU context, therefore, the issue of borders and bordering differs from how we are conditioned to think of borders as per the classical conception of state sovereignty (not the reality of existing states), which induces us to think of borders as a manifestation of territorial and functional *contiguity*. Since the EU has such an extensive system of arrangements with non-members, it is useful to consider EU conditionality as an intrinsic element of how to think about borders and bordering. In the extension of that, the following three features depict how the EU constitutes its relations to its members and *affiliated* non-members. First is that formal EU membership provides the member states with *direct access* to all the relevant decision opportunities within the complex EU structure (the core ones are a seat in the European Council, direct representation in the Council of Ministers formations, direct representation in the European Parliament, and direct presence in the system of comitology). That right is reserved for EU members (EEA members have a limited form of non-decision-relevant access, see Fossum 2015). Second is that non-members may incorporate EU norms and rules insofar as there is reciprocity that will be subject to EU-made conditionality and compliance requirements. Third is what appears to be the underlying principle, namely that the closer the

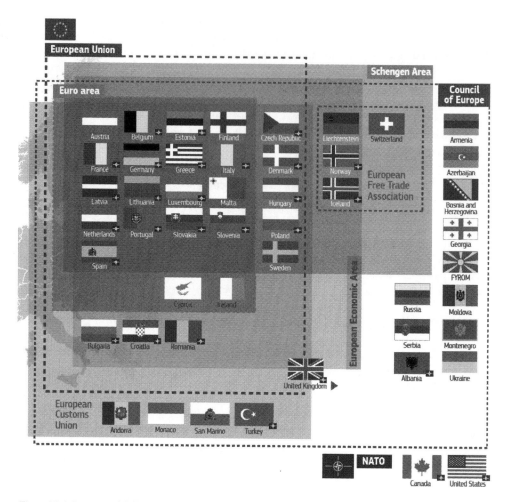

Figure 23.1 Patterns of differentiation in the EU

Source: European Commission (https://ec.europa.eu/commission/sites/beta-political/files/white_paper_on_the_future_of_europe_en.pdf)

affiliation (in breadth and depth terms), *the stricter the requirements*. This last point serves to underline that the EU's relationship to affiliated non-members is all but voluntaristic. States that seek an affiliation with the EU cannot unilaterally determine their relationship to the EU; the EU sets down quite explicit conditions for the relevant types of access (to what functions and territories) and insists on mechanisms to ensure that states operate in accordance with what they have committed themselves to do in relation to the EU. Another way of putting this is to say that the EU is concerned with avoiding its external relations – forms of affiliation with non-members – undermining internal coherence and weakening policy consistency. The non-members face the need for balancing ensured access to the EU's internal market and the other policies that the EU regulates, on the one hand, and retaining domestic control of what is taking place within their territories (and beyond) on the other. The basic considerations that animate actors differ considerably. Structurally speaking, the EU on its part will seek to limit the non-members' room for manoeuvre, harmonize and unify the various relations it has with the external world, and ensure that those affiliated fulfil their obligations, whereas the affiliated states will seek to maximize their room for manoeuvre, obtain special treatment, and minimize external controls.

To sum up thus far, the EU has shifted the equation among state sovereign control, national democracy and assured market (and other forms of) access. There is an important shift in the equation for affiliated states, but it is not the same as for members, and it varies across types of affiliated non-members.

In the following, I will briefly introduce each of the forms of EU affiliation with non-members and thereafter clarify the core issues and concerns of relevance for the discussion of Brexit and the EU's non-members. When discussing these affiliation arrangements in relation to Brexit, we need to keep in mind that there is an important distinction between those non-member states that *qualify* for EU membership but have declined membership (or have failed to apply for it) and those states that *do not qualify* for EU membership. The latter category will include states that may become future EU members, as well as states that may never be. The UK being 'EU-encoded' through forty-five years of EU membership will definitely belong to the former category, not the least given that the UK will pass the European Union (Withdrawal) Bill 2017–19, which, apart from repealing the 1972 European Communities Act, also incorporates much of present EU legislation into UK law. The other reason is that the EU is more willing to give unqualified access to states that qualify for EU membership.

EU-affiliated states that do not qualify for EU membership

In this category, following Sieglinde Gstöhl (2015), we find four main forms of affiliations. These are the European Neighbourhood Policy (ENP), Turkey's Customs Union, the position of the European small-sized countries, and sectoral multilateralism such as the Energy Community Treaty. The two latter are clearly not relevant in a Brexit context. Neither is the EU's Neighbourhood Policy, which was initiated in 2004. It provides Eastern and Southern Mediterranean countries with enhanced preferential trade relations; they receive financial and technical assistance and 'the prospect of a stake in the EU Internal Market based on legislative and regulatory approximation, the participation in a number of EU programmes and improved interconnection and physical links with the EU' (ibid.: 18). Even if the Mediterranean countries thus become subject to a comprehensive market access conditionality, there is no presumption that this will lead to future EU membership (in contrast to what may be the case for Eastern European countries). The Turkey model has been discussed in the UK setting in connection with Brexit (HM Government 2016). Turkey is both an EU candidate country (since 1999) and has participated in a Customs Union with the EU since 1995. This model appears to be less than well suited for the UK because it gives Turkey only selective access to the EU's internal market, which does not include services, provides no say on the decisions affecting it, and lacks reciprocity with regard to EU trade agreements with third countries. As the UK Government position paper notes (ibid.: 30):

> [W]e would lose our decision-making power over the UK's external tariffs, because we would be part of the Customs Union. Instead, we would be forced to open our borders to countries with which the EU had agreed trade deals, without necessarily being able to secure reciprocal access. Such a situation would put the UK economy at a substantial disadvantage.

None of the options available for affiliated states that fail to qualify as EU members appears relevant for the UK. These states are also less closely affiliated with the UK than are those that qualify for EU membership. The assessment of the effects of Brexit will therefore be confined to this group of states.

EU-affiliated states that qualify for EU membership

All the four states in this category are EFTA members. Switzerland, after a negative referendum, turned down EEA membership in 1992 and has instead established a set of bilateral agreements with the EU. Iceland applied for EU membership in July 2009, but in 2015 the Icelandic Government approached the EU Commission with the following request: 'Iceland should not be regarded as a candidate country for EU membership'.[3] Norway has applied twice for EU membership, in 1972 and in 1994, but has had to withdraw each application after negative popular referendum results.

In the following, I will briefly present the two main arrangements, what in the UK context is referred to as the Swiss model and the Norwegian model, respectively, and then discuss similarities and differences and how they handle the trilemma previously listed.

The main difference between these two models is that Switzerland's EU relationship is bilateral, whereas the most important and extensive portion of the Norwegian model, the EEA Agreement, is multilateral. What the two models, the Swiss and the Norwegian, share is that each is based on a broad range of agreements.

Switzerland's EU relationship is based on two sets of bilateral agreements, which are labelled Bilateral I (entered into force in 2002) and Bilateral II (signed in 2004 and gradually implemented since). These are, formally speaking, *static sectoral agreements*, which add up to twenty main and over 100 secondary agreements, without an overarching structure binding them together. Switzerland's EU relationship is, however, quite dynamic, not the least since Swiss authorities have since the late 1980s operated with the doctrine of *autonomer Nachvollzug*, which refers to autonomous adaptation and represents a policy of voluntary alignment with the EU. This doctrine 'stipulates that each new piece of legislation is evaluated with respect to its compatibility with EU norms' (Lavenex 2009: 552). In a similar manner, Alfred Tovias (2006: 215) noted ten years ago that 'Switzerland has had an EC reflex for more than a decade now and tries to shadow EU moves autonomously. Because this process is invisible and silent, it is frequently but wrongly ignored'. Leaked documents from the ongoing EU–Swiss negotiations reveal that the EU seeks to impose much stricter legal obligations on Switzerland (Piris 2017).

The EEA countries have assured access to the EU's internal market even if they are not part of the EU's Customs Union (that is also the case with Switzerland). In contrast to Switzerland's (broad range of) sectoral bilateral agreements, the EEA Agreement is a broad and dynamic multilateral agreement between the (still) twenty-eight EU member states and the three EFTA states of Iceland, Liechtenstein, and Norway. It is based on a two-pillar structure with bridging institutions and includes a court and a surveillance body (see Figure 23.2).

The EEA Agreement came into effect in 1994 (Lichtenstein's took effect 1 May 1995) and was intended to include the remainder of the European Free Trade Association (EFTA[4]) states in the EU's internal market. When the EEA Agreement took effect, the EEA countries had to incorporate all relevant EU legislation that was in effect at the time of signing the agreement. In line with what was previously said about EU conditionality, the EEA Agreement is intended to ensure legal homogeneity within the entire thirty-one-member EEA. The EEA Agreement is therefore a dynamic agreement: new relevant EU legislation is incorporated in the agreement in an ongoing manner, albeit subject to specific decision procedures.

How do the EEA states handle the trilemma of reconciling state sovereign control, democratic self-governing and market access? With regard to market access, the fact that the agreement is dynamic is intended to minimize the problems of market access. There is a matter of compliance, which is closely monitored by the EFTA Surveillance Authority (ESA). There has been considerable expansion into related flanking areas, such as for example environmental and social affairs.

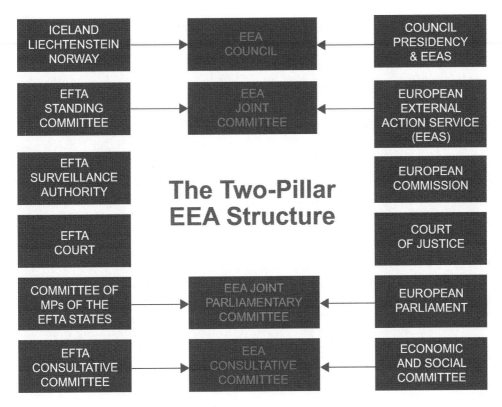

Figure 23.2 The institutional structure of the European Economic Area Agreement

Source: © EFTA Secretariat, 2014 (www.efta.int/eea/eea-institutions)

In addition, the dynamic nature of the EEA Agreement makes it difficult for a state to prevent areas that have been explicitly excluded from the agreement being subsequently pulled into its orbit. For Norway, a telling example is agriculture. It is politically very sensitive and was *explicitly excluded* from the initial EEA Agreement. At present, 40 per cent of the rules and regulations that Norway incorporates are in the field of agriculture. Important reasons for inclusion were the need for market access for fish and the sheer dynamics of horizontal expansion. These provisions are not confined to border-crossing activities but cover internal affairs: 'In practice today, this body of regulations makes up the main portion of all public regulation pertaining to production, sale, labeling, hygiene and so forth with regard to fish and agriculture in Norway and to a large extent sets the standards in both these sectors' (Official Norwegian Report NOU 2012: 2, 646–647, author's translation). This is not simply a matter of trading-off market access and state sovereign control. It shows how the affiliated non-member loses control over an issue area that it explicitly sought to *remove* from the trade-off equation. A further problem that illustrates the dilemmas of trading-off different considerations under circumstances of close and dynamic EU rule adoption is the fact that '[t]he EEA has no mechanism to formally update its rules as a follow-up to such changes in the EU' (Graver 2016: 818). Insofar as the EEA rules are subsequently changed through legal interpretation, 'this means that legislation is changed without any collaboration from the EFTA countries' (ibid.).

An open market in goods, services, persons and capital requires low-threshold access and passage. That is one of the reasons why the EEA–EFTA states have signed Schengen association agreements, which in effect locate them within the EU's external borders and systems of border controls. If we look more closely at Norway, it has signed a number of additional parallel agreements with the EU, including agreements on asylum and police cooperation (Dublin I and II) and on foreign and security policy – Norwegian troops are at the disposal of the EU's battle groups. The Norwegian Official Report that produced the largest ever assessment of the EEA Agreement estimated that around 75 percent of all of EU's laws and regulations apply to Norway (Official Norwegian Report NOU 2012: 2).

This dense form of affiliation generates its own pressures for contiguity in norms, rules and interpretations, which show up in how domestic institutions operate. Two telling examples pertain to how the Norwegian Supreme Court in the rulings *Nye Kystlink* and *Bottolvs* voluntarily adapted to EU law and did so in issue areas that were *not* regulated by the EEA Agreement (Fredriksen 2015). In a situation of tight regulation coupled with 'regulatory gaps', rule contiguity becomes important. The institutions within a closely associated non-member will feel strong domestic pressures for filling in whatever 'gaps' there are between the different agreements that the country has signed with the EU.

The EEA countries have hardly any access to those bodies that member states use to forge decisions in common in the EU, notably the European Council, the Council and the European Parliament. The critical issue is that they are excluded from any decisional impact. It is a matter of taxation without representation.

These observations suggest that the EEA countries relate to the trilemma of state sovereign control, democratic self-governing and market access by ensuring market access at the expense of the other two, not formally speaking but in actual practice. In addition, these countries, as the Norway example testifies to, have not proven capable of (or not even been willing to) confine the incorporation to market-related issues. It is therefore not simply a matter of market access but of incorporation in the broader legal and socio-economic order that the EU has been constructing over time. The distinctive feature of the form of affiliation that they have chosen is akin to voluntary hegemonic submission (Eriksen and Fossum 2015). The EU is not set up to be a hegemon, but some of its relations to (non-)members resonate well with hegemony.

The question is whether the unique Swiss form of sectoral bilateralism provides Switzerland with more scope for retaining state and popular sovereignty in return for a weaker form of market access. An obvious difference is that the Swiss EU affiliation is less hierarchical since there is no set of supranational arrangements that regulates it. Analysts have, however, noted that 'Swiss bilateralism – while apparently more tailored – does not necessarily imply that the EU exerts less influence on Swiss policies than it does in the formally more constraining EEA' (Lavenex and Schwok 2015: 49). There are significant functionalist pressures that emanate from close patterns of interdependence. The Swiss–EU relationship, it has been shown, is quite dynamic (Vahl and Grolimund 2006).

In the next section, we focus on the UK Government's objectives and stances on Brexit, with emphasis on whether or the extent to which the UK's future EU relationship will resemble that of the so-called sovereign democrats.

The UK debate on Brexit: options

The UK referendum produced a Yes vote to leave the EU, but the binary yes/no question did not provide a set of clear instructions as to the type of relationship that the UK would have to the EU post-Brexit. In a comprehensive report issued prior to the referendum, the government discussed three main alternatives to continued EU membership: the Norway model, bilateral negotiated agreements, and a World Trade Organization-only model (HM Government 2016).

The government did not discuss any of these as part of a plan B because it did not expect to lose. In effect, after the referendum, it took a long time before the May government started coming clear on what it wanted. It was really only well over six months after the referendum, in Prime Minister Theresa May's Lancaster House speech on 17 January 2017 that the range of options was narrowed down (May 2017).[5] The UK Government stated that it would not seek to retain full access to the EU's internal market and Customs Union because that entailed reneging on control of immigration. The government underlined the need for a set of bespoke agreements across the relevant policy areas and wanted a set of parallel negotiations that would cover the terms of Brexit *and* the UK's future relationship with the EU. The EU, on the other hand, preferred to settle the terms of separation first and only thereafter discuss the terms of the UK's future EU relationship (Renwick 2017).

Taking stock of the situation at the end of 2017, the EU's preferred procedure won out (Eeckhout and Patel 2017). Being barred from the ability to negotiate the terms of the UK's future EU relationship, the UK Government found itself under an evermore pressing time constraint, which, combined with a range of other pressures, had bearing on the terms of separation: the UK's position has moved substantially towards the EU's position. In addition, the UK Government has recognized that it needs a period of transition in order to avoid a cliff edge. The European Union (Withdrawal) Bill 2017–19 is intended to help prevent that, but this unilateral act does not unto itself provide any assurance that market actors will have the same future operating conditions. The question remains unresolved as to how the UK will balance sovereign control with EU access. As a recent report from the Institute for Government notes (bold in original): '**The UK can't escape a fundamental choice: the more access it has to the Single Market, the more obligations it must accept**' (Owen et al. 2017: 2, author's underlining).

With regard to the period of transition, a recent paper by Eeckhout and Patel (2017) presents five options: (1) extension of the EU *acquis communautaire*, without membership, (2) an extension of the Article 50 withdrawal negotiations, (3) remaining in the internal market via the EEA Agreement, (4) remaining in the internal market by negotiating a new agreement modelled on the EEA Agreement, and (5) entering into a customs union agreement with the EU Customs Union. The first four of these options bear some semblance to the situation of the EFTA states, whether in terms of being rule-takers without access to the rule-making forums or through being subject to similar institutional arrangements (option 3). The period of transition therefore appears to be one akin to a 'soft' Brexit. Other factors that seem to push the UK in the same direction are the terms of the separation agreement, especially the Northern Ireland border question.

Nevertheless, it is notable that one and a half years after the referendum result, the UK Government 'is clear on what it does not want – but has failed to articulate what it does. The UK must put forward a concrete proposal on the relationship it wants with the EU and the Single Market as a basis for negotiations with the EU' (ibid.). There is a short window even here: the EU is expected to have its position hammered out by March 2018; if the UK Government still does not have a clearly articulated position it risks a repeat of the separation negotiations.

Possible implications of Brexit for the EU's affiliated non-members

What then are the possible implications for the EU's affiliated non-members? We need to discuss possible effects by considering a triangular relationship: the non-members (EEA and Switzerland), the UK and the EU. Why is that necessary? The affiliated non-members are not present in the negotiations between the UK and the EU on the terms of UK exit and on the terms of the UK's future association with the EU. Their future terms of negotiations with the UK will be determined by the agreement that the UK strikes with the EU. The dynamics of the UK's negotiation process with the EU will also likely spill over to the non-members in the sense that the more conflictual these become, the greater the pressure on the non-members to take sides. In addition, it is important to keep in mind that even if there is no UK–EU agreement, the UK will have incorporated the better of well over 12,000 EU provisions in UK law through the European Union (Withdrawal) Bill 2017–19. Finally are the strong two-way bonds involved. For instance, are Norway's economic bonds to the EU stronger than its bonds to the UK, even if over 20 per cent of Norway's total exports of goods and services go to the UK? The UK is Norway's single largest trading partner in goods, and Norway provides 40 per cent of the UK's consumption of natural gas.[6]

In the following, I will briefly outline and discuss four possible scenarios in terms of possible effects of Brexit on affiliated non-members. Some of the scenarios are close to the transition scenarios; other ones deviate considerably.

Four possible scenarios

Scenario 1: No EU–UK association agreement

Under this scenario, the UK would revert back to World Trade Organization (WTO) rules, but since the UK has been a member of the WTO through being an EU member, it is not entirely clear as to whether it at Brexit would have to negotiate the specifics of its WTO membership, which would take time. For the EU's non-members, this would mean that they would face the prospect of tariffs at the moment of Brexit (a fear that the Norwegian Business Association (NHO) has voiced in several instances. The non-members will have to negotiate their terms of trade and access with the UK, most likely on a bilateral basis. The effects will depend on the extent to which the UK would set in motion a race to the bottom in social and environmental terms.[7] Another source of uncertainty pertains to the role of non-member states' citizens in the UK and UK citizens in the affiliated non-member states. There are pressing areas such as developing a proper system for fisheries management. This serves to show that it is not simply a matter of negotiating access but that it may be necessary to redesign entire regulatory regimes.

Scenario 2: UK association agreement with the EU outside the context of the EEA

None of the off-the-shelf alternatives that are available under this rubric will work for the UK. The EU is not willing to grant a Swiss-type option to the UK. If the EU changed its position, it would likely have wanted arrangements akin to those that Piris refers to in the leaked document (previously mentioned), but these would not be acceptable to the UK. The Turkey model is highly unsatisfactory for the UK. The only remaining option under this scenario is to forge some new type of arrangement, which is what the UK Government wants. For such an arrangement to come into place, it is necessary for there to be a modicum of trust and goodwill on both sides. Those seem in short supply: The UK is criticizing the EU for lack of flexibility, whereas the EU is criticizing the UK for lack of progress in negotiations; lack of coherent strategy and preparedness; and internal divisions.

For the EU's non-members, it is very unclear what this option will entail. It likely matters a lot whether the arrangement is temporary or permanent. If it is similar to the EEA, then it may mean that non-members can organize their relations to the UK within the EU context and therefore will not need to work out bilateral agreements. Such an agreement may give rise to claims that the UK has gotten a better deal and generate pressure for renegotiating existing arrangements. There are actors in Norway that see Brexit as an opportunity to renegotiate or do away with the EEA agreement.

Scenario 3: UK association agreement with the EU within the context of the EEA

The UK cannot continue in the EEA after Brexit because EEA membership requires membership in EFTA. Each EFTA country has a veto on whether to accept the UK as a member, but it is unlikely that any of them would deny membership to the UK, in EFTA or in the EEA. There are several options under this scenario. One is that the UK may become a formal member of EEA on a permanent or temporary basis. Another perhaps, politically speaking, more likely option is that the UK develops a slightly different arrangement that has the appearance of being different but in reality mimics much of the EEA. A third option is that the UK may become a member of EFTA and have access to some of the EFTA institutions as an interim agreement (one proposal is that it replaces the CJEU with the EFTA Court). A final option is that of partial incorporation, for instance if Scotland (either as an independent country or in a form of internal UK differentiation) were to join the EEA, whereas the rest of the UK did not.

For the EU's non-members, a temporary UK arrangement is easier to manage but postpones some of the problems of working out the triangular EU–UK–non-members relationship. There are three reasons why a temporary UK membership may be easier for the non-members to handle than a permanent UK relationship. First is that the UK's significantly greater size and global influence will make the EEA very lopsided. Second are differences in interests and priorities. The EEA is not tailored to the UK's interests. It, for instance, excludes agriculture, which the UK would want. The EEA countries are not in the EU's Customs Union, which matters far more to the UK. Finally, is the problem of politicisation. The EEA countries have de-politicised their EU relations; the UK will politicise these and likely render the arrangement much more precarious and volatile.

Scenario 4: A two-tiered EU with the UK in the outer tier

This scenario underlines that we need to consider Brexit in light of the discussions that are currently unfolding in the EU about further EU consolidation. The EU's crises have exhibited a structural weakness in the Eurozone that is only partly addressed.

The European Commission's White Paper (2017) lists five different options, with the third option the one most akin to a two-tiered EU, or polity differentiation – in other words a system with a hard core and a periphery. A weaker version is policy differentiation, which refers to differences in access in various policy areas.

Either version could be a way for the EU of addressing Brexit – by locating the UK in the outer tier if there is a hard core or by including it in some policies if there is greater policy differentiation. An important question is where the EU's closely affiliated non-members will be. Would the non-members be inside or outside the outer tier? An important determining factor would be how strong the divide between tiers would be. If they were left outside the two tiers, the non-members could easily be forgotten and lose out on market access. It is therefore reasonable to assume that they would want to be inside the second tier, but even there they are small states and could easily find themselves at the mercy of cantankerous large states.

Conclusion

This chapter has assessed possible implications of Brexit for the EU's affiliated non-members. This issue is rendered more complex due to the fact that the EU reconfigures sovereignty and the terms of territorial control in Europe. Or, to put it differently, the EU deviates from the traditional notion of sovereignty as based on territorial–functional contiguity. The main feature that distinguishes EU members from affiliated non-members is not subjection to EU rules and norms but access to those EU decision-making institutions and procedures that determine the rules. The feature that is shared among members and non-members alike is EU conditionality, which operates on the basis of compliance with EU norms and rules – across the membership divide. The more closely associated a non-member, the greater the onus on homogeneity. This onus on homogeneity plays a central role in the EU's efforts at reconciling the centrifugal pressures that it faces internally and in its complex and composite external relations. In the context of Brexit, the EU's insistence on the indivisibility of the four freedoms can be construed as another means for curtailing centrifugal pressures.

With regard to Brexit, the question is how these concerns are to be worked out in relation to the UK's internal pressures for 'taking back control'. Precisely what EU relationship the UK will end up with is still shrouded in uncertainty. The affiliated non-members face significant cross-pressures given that they are squeezed between the EU and the UK. Many options are still under debate, which hinge on what turns the UK and the EU take. The EU and UK are contested entities with numerous internal and external pressures that can drive developments in different directions. I discussed four different scenarios because it is not even clear in what overall direction developments will unfold. Some of the relevant considerations are time frame, legal framework, interest congruity (or not), basic patterns of trust (or mistrust), and politicisation vs. depoliticisation. We know that the effects of the decisions will be momentous; we do not know when they will occur and in what direction they will take us. At the time of writing, a cautious assessment would suggest that scenario 2 (agreement formally outside the context of the EEA agreement) appears the most likely because there is a significant UK pressure for a 'soft' Brexit and significant opposition to the type of relationship that the EEA represents. There might, however, be scope within this option for arrangements that are formally different yet quite similar in practice. At the same time, we cannot rule out the no-agreement scenario; neither can we rule out that Brexit may never actually occur.

Notes

1 See EUR-Lex, Glossary of Summaries. Available at: http://eur-lex.europa.eu/summary/glossary/accession_criteria_copenhague.html [Accessed February 16, 2018].
   There is an important debate on conditionality in connection with EU enlargement. See for instance Schimmelfennig and Sedelmeier (2004) and Steunenberg and Dimitrova (2007).
2 Phillippe Schmitter (2000) has discussed such scenarios extensively. His notion of *condominio* is the most radical option.
3 European Commission, European Neighbourhood Policy and Enlargement Negotiations, n.d. Available at: https://ec.europa.eu/neighbourhood-enlargement/countries/detailed-country-information/iceland_en [Accessed February 16, 2018].
4 EFTA was established in 1960 and has now four members: Iceland, Liechtenstein, Norway and Switzerland. Three of these countries are members of the EEA but not Switzerland.
5 See also HM Government White Paper Cm 9417.
6 Regjeringen.no, Britisk uttreden fra EU: Innledende kartlegging – enkelte momenter, 6 March 2017. Available at: www.regjeringen.no/no/dokumenter/brexit_norge/id2541874/?q=kartlegging [Accessed February 16, 2018].
7 Speech by Michel Barnier. Available at: http://europa.eu/rapid/press-release_SPEECH-17-4765_en.pdf [Accessed January 20, 2018]:

> The UK has chosen to leave the EU. Does it want to stay close to the European model or does it want to gradually move away from it? The UK's reply to this question will be important and even decisive because it will shape the discussion on our future partnership and shape also the conditions for ratification of that partnership in many national parliaments and obviously in the European parliament. I do not say this to create problems but to avoid problems.

References

Eeckhout, P. and Patel, O. (2017) Brexit Transitional Arrangements: Legal and Political Considerations. *Brexit Insights*, UCL, November.

Eriksen, E.O. and Fossum, J.E. (eds.) (2015) *The European Union's Non-Members: Independence under Hegemony?* London: Routledge.

European Commission (2017) White Paper on the Future of Europe: Reflections and Scenarios for the EU27 by 2025. COM(2017)2025. Available at: https://ec.europa.eu/commission/sites/beta-political/files/white_paper_on_the_future_of_europe_en.pdf [Accessed November 1, 2017].

Featherstone, K. (2017) The EU and Its Neighbours: Reconciling Market Access, Governance, and Democracy. *Dahrendorf Forum*, September 1.

Fossum, J.E. (2015) Representation under Hegemony? On Norway's Relationship to the EU. In: Eriksen, E.O. and Fossum, J.E. (eds.), *(ÅRSTAL) The European Union's Non-Members: Independence under Hegemony?* London: Routledge, pp. 153–172.

Fredriksen, H.H. (2015) The EEA and the Case-Law of the CJEU: Incorporation without Participation? In: Eriksen, E.O. and Fossum, J.E. (eds.), *The European Union's Non-Members: Independence under Hegemony?* London: Routledge, pp. 102–117.

Graver, H.-P. (2016) Possibilities and Challenges of the EEA as an Option for the UK after Brexit, *European Papers* 1(3): 803–821.

Gstöhl, S. (2015) The European Union's Different Neighbourhood Models. In: Eriksen, E.O. and Fossum, J.E. (eds.), *The European Union's Non-Members: Independence under Hegemony?* London: Routledge, pp. 17–35.

HM Government (2016) *Alternatives to Membership: Possible Models for the United Kingdom outside the European Union.* London: Crown.

Lavenex, S. (2009) Switzerland's Flexible Integration in the EU: A Conceptual Framework. *Swiss Political Science Review* 15(4): 547–575.

Lavenex, S. and Schwok, R. (2015) The Swiss Way: The Nature of Switzerland's Relationship with the EU. In: Eriksen, E.O. and Fossum, J.E. (eds.), *The European Union's Non-Members: Independence under Hegemony?* London: Routledge, pp. 36–51.

Lord, C. (2015) The United Kingdom, a Once and Future(?) Non-Member State. In: Eriksen, E.O. and Fossum, J.E. (eds.), *The European Union's Non-Members: Independence under Hegemony?* London: Routledge, pp. 211–229.

May, T. (2017) Brexit Speech, Lancaster House, January 17, 2017. Available at: www.telegraph.co.uk/news/2017/01/17/theresa-mays-brexit-speech-full/ [Accessed October 31, 2017].

Official Norwegian Report NOU (2012:2) Outside and Inside: Norway's Agreements with the European Union. Delivered to the Norwegian Ministry of Foreign Affairs, January 17.

Owen, J., Stojanovic, A. and Rutter, J. (2017) Trade after Brexit: Options for the UK's Relationship with the EU. *Institute for Government*, December 18. Available at: www.instituteforgovernment.org.uk/summary-trade-after-brexit [Accessed January 20, 2018].

Piris, J.-C. (2017) The UK and Europe: Why the UK Will Not Become an EEA Member after Brexit. *Connect.* Available at: https://esharp.eu/debates/the-uk-and-europe/why-the-uk-will-not-become-an-eea-member-after-brexit [Accessed October 31, 2017].

Renwick, A. (2017) *The Process of Brexit: What Comes Next?* UCL Working Paper Series.

Rodrik, D. (2011) *The Globalization Paradox: Democracy and the Future of the World Economy.* Oxford: Oxford University Press.

Schmitter, P.C. (2000) *How to Democratize the European Union . . . and Why Bother?* Lanham, MD: Rowman & Littlefield.

Tovias, A. (2006) Exploring the 'Pros' and 'Cons' of Swiss and Norwegian Models of Relations with the European Union: What Can Israel Learn from the Experiences of These Two Countries? *Cooperation and Conflict* 41(2): 203–222.

Vahl, M. and Grolimund, N. (2006) *Integration without Membership: Switzerland's Bilateral Agreements with the European Union.* Brussels: Centre for European Policy Studies.

24

BREXIT AND THE FUTURE OF EU THEORY

Christian Lequesne

Introduction

For EU studies, Brexit represents an epistemological breach. Most of the theories available in the toolbox of EU theories start from the assumption that the EU is developing through a process of integration. Crises are not absent from EU theories, but in most cases they are considered unavoidable moments to move forward the integration process. Many courses on EU politics taught the students for years that leaving the EU was an issue that member states could never experience because of strong interdependence. It is exactly the opposite that took place with Brexit, and it has become a strong incentive for EU scholars to rethink their theoretical accounts of EU, from neo-functionalism to liberal intergovernmentalism and multilevel governance (Saurugger 2014). EU is now confronted with disintegration trends (Zielonka 2014). Brexit demonstrates that crises do not always lead to compromises that allow the EU to bounce back and move forward. They can also be disruptive in the sense of a renationalisation of EU competences. Brexit is also an incentive to insert more the domestic politics of the member states in the EU theory. Too many theoretical works have neglected the role of domestic politics in their modelling. EU theories have been for five decades too EU-centric. The reason is that it has been easier to concentrate on the central deals in European institutions than opening the black box of the member states. Of course, opening the black box of twenty-eight (or twenty-seven) member states is not an easy task for scholarly research. It requires making comparative work in the capitals of the member states, not only in Brussels, and mastering several national politics and languages. Domestic politics in EU member states is still delivered in national languages, and EU scholars cannot expect any progress in their work if they do not go into this diversity. Brexit shows forcefully that there is no other choice for EU scholars than going back to a detailed study of national polities and politics if they have the ambition to renew EU theories.

This contribution develops four questions conceived as an invitation for further debate. First, it presents Brexit as an event that has restored the role of domestic politics in EU theory. Second, it demonstrates the limits of EU theories that focus on a purely rationalist approach of interests. Third, it considers Brexit as an incentive to think more about the de-politicisation/re-politicisation dialectics in the EU. Finally, it shows that Brexit is an incentive to integrate into EU theories new social cleavages that have penetrated domestic politics of the member states politics since the Treaty of Maastricht.

Restoring the role of domestic politics in EU theory

In 1983, Simon Bulmer was among the first scholars to claim a domestic politics approach to the EU, which was still called at this time the European Community (Bulmer 1983). Bulmer insisted on two assumptions that have come back to the front of research with Brexit. First, we must not forget that 'the national polity is the basic unit' of the EU, and second, each national polity has a 'different set of social and economic conditions that shapes its national interests and policy content' (ibid.: 354). In this 'youthful' publication, Bulmer had no ambition to compete with existing integration theorists. His argument was mostly analytical and empirical, as his detailed knowledge of German EU politics showed. Bulmer's intuition that domestic politics of the member states remains the basic determinant of the EU pinpointed a dimension that was missing or not developed enough in most EU theories: structure vs. agency. As Bulmer and Joseph rightly explained thirty-four years after Bulmer's seminal article, EU theories have devoted a lot of importance to macro structures – something that is perfectly legitimate – but have not elaborated enough about the relations between macro structures and agents who remain national for their most part in the EU (Bulmer and Joseph 2016). Political choices made by agents at the national level, as David Cameron's decision to organise in June 2016 a referendum on Brexit under the pressure of his own Conservative Party, can totally change the nature of the EU macro structure. Since the end of the 1980s, national agency has been taken into consideration by scholars who studied the Europeanisation of public policies but not enough by those who reflected on the EU as a polity. It is a lack that Brexit will not allow to be perpetrated anymore. Let's examine the EU theoretical landscape a bit more in detail.

One of the most developed theoretical frameworks for exploring the role of the member states in the EU remains liberal intergovernmentalism (Moravcsik 1998). Assuming a demarcation from IR neorealists, Andrew Moravcsik has developed a framework to explain preference formation at the domestic level. This framework is not very sophisticated: it starts from the assumption that member states' governments define national interests that are the outcomes of democratic debates between the executive, the legislative and national interest groups at each national level. Then, member states have to bargain among themselves to find a compromise between their various national interests. Liberal intergovernmentalism has always been more interested in the nature of interstate deals produced by national governments at the EU level than the nature of the relationships between the EU and the member states. As Bulmer and Joseph write, if liberal intergovernmentalism can be persuasive to explain Brexit negotiations between the United Kingdom and the twenty-seven, it is rather poor value to understand why a majority of the UK people decided to quit the EU and changed with this decision the whole course of the EU political project (Bulmer and Joseph 2016).

New intergovernmentalism, as it has developed in the last ten years, takes more systematically into consideration the influence of domestic politics on the EU polity (Bickerton et al. 2015). But again, new intergovernmentalism has a strong tendency to focus on the nature of institutional dynamic at the EU level (the role of the so-called *de novo* institutions) but is not a systemic attempt to explain how and why domestic politics frames the EU polity.

The literature on theory of Europeanisation, which has been vast since the beginning of the 2000s, has concentrated a lot of efforts on understanding how the EU has introduced change into national polities (Featherstone and Radaelli 2003; Bulmer and Lequesne 2013) and how this change has sometimes to cope with resistance at the national level (Saurugger and Terpan 2016). But again, Europeanisation studies have much less studied the influence of domestic politics on the EU structure. They are not very helpful to understand how and why Brexit has destabilised the whole project of EU in challenging its core principles (in particular free movement), has given legitimacy to national agents tempted to follow the same path in other member states (Frexit, Cexit, Nexit etc.) and has opened the door of disintegration (Webber 2014).

As Bulmer and Joseph observe, it is among scholars who used the theory of governance or multilevel governance that the impact of domestic politics on EU integration has been the most seriously studied. Liesbet Hooghe and Gary Marks (2009), in their 'post-functionalist theory' of EU integration, understood before the financial and refugee crises that the elite–society relationships at the national level have become a crucial determinant of EU integration. One weakness in Hooghe and Marks's approach is a tendency to generalise too quickly the trends coming from domestic politics without exploring enough national diversity. For instance, Ivan Krastev (2017) has recently demonstrated that the relationships between elites and societies are still not the same in West European and in Central and East European member states and that these differences explain different patterns of relationship with the EU polity.

Brexit is an invitation to rethink European integration theories in assuming firmly that national agents, in their diversity, remain the driving motors of the structure that operates at the EU level. It is far insufficient to say, as liberal intergovernmentalists do, that the drive of the EU results from the nature of compromises built between national governments in Brussels (Schimmelfennig 2015). We must assume that concrete elements of domestic politics, like the choice of British Prime Minister Cameron to organise a referendum on his country's membership, can change the course of European integration as a whole. Many other examples outside Brexit can be found to confirm the restoration of domestic politics as a serious variable. The choice of a majority of French and Dutch voters in 2005 to refuse the ratification of the European Constitutional Treaty is an example. The two negative referendums have completely changed the macro project of European integration. For too many years, scholars thought that the relevant agents that shape the EU were transnational (Sweet and Sandholtz 1996), when they remain first and foremost national.

Any interesting theoretical account of the EU must then assume the assumption: national politics → EU polity → national politics. As Europeanisation studies have shown for policymaking, there is a retroactive causality between national politics and EU polity. Going back to Brexit, controversial debates inside the Conservative Party have an influence on Theresa May's ability to negotiate Brexit with the twenty-seven, which has in turn an effect on Theresa May's legitimacy as the Prime Minister of the UK (see more in Chapter 13). What needs to be theorised, in the vein of the agent–structure debate, introduced by Bulmer and Jones in their critical integration theory, is the impact of domestic politics and national agency on the transformation of the EU polity (Bulmer and Joseph 2016).

The inadequacy of rationalist theories of EU integration

Liberal intergovernmentalism, neo-functionalism and multilevel governance are all rationalist accounts of EU integration focusing on actors' interests. Liberal intergovernmentalism assumes the relevance of national interest for EU integration, when neo-functionalism insists on transnational interests and multilevel governance introduces a more diffuse and disaggregated notion of interest (political parties' interests, subnational governments' interests etc.).

These rational accounts are far too restrictive to catch the relationships between domestic politics of the member states and the EU. Strong elements of domestic politics in the member states, which strongly influence the EU structure, have little to do with the rationality of interests. The debate about Brexit in the UK has been and still is an excellent example of how emotions and other irrational variables in domestic politics impact the EU (Howarth and Andreopouli 2017). There is a literature on the politicisation of the EU that demonstrates quite rightly that, since the Treaty of Maastricht, EU issues are a full part of political controversies and party competition at the national level, as well as challenge the notion of 'permissive consensus' that Inglehart (1970) introduced to characterise the pre-1990s period. 'Permissive consensus' has been a right concept to describe general trends in the member states towards EU integration for decades but with noticeable limits. If we examine past events as the French debate on the European Defense Community in 1954 or the British debate on the first EC referendum in 1975, doubt is permitted about the full accuracy of Inglehart's argument (Dinan 2014).

Going back to Brexit, the main arguments used during the referendum campaign by the Brex-iteers (UKIP, Eurosceptic group inside the Conservative Party and Brexit campaign lobbyists) stress the importance of defending national identity against the EU. Identity in this case manifests a glorification of 'English history', parliamentary democracy and heroic resistance to external threats – especially during the Second World War (see also Chapter 11). The consolidation of this English identity (*Englishness*) in the context of devolution is another element that influences the relationship of the UK to EU (see Chapter 12). It is not by chance that a majority of English voters supported Brexit when a majority of Scottish voters did exactly the opposite. Even controversial debates about the British contribution to the EU budget reflect a certain identity of many Brits regarding money whose foundations are not purely rational. It is a very interesting research topic for anthropologists and social psychologists.

In their 'post-functionalist approach' of EU integration, Liesbet Hooghe and Gary Marks (2009) make the clear argument that the identity of national publics is an element that engages EU inte-gration. They do not push too far the argument, as their analysis was pre-Brexit and even pre-EMU crisis. What Hooghe and Marks demonstrate is that identity is a full part of the politicisation process at the national level. Brexit shows that they are absolutely right but with one footnote: identity is not to be approached as a rational variable that contributes to the formation of national preference. There is a rational dimension to identity, like the one materialised in being the holder of a certain nationality passport. But identity has also to do with representation of 'your' relationship with a national history that goes beyond rationality. The belief expressed by some Brexiteers that 'we Brits are stronger when we go it alone!' is a non-rational element of identity. It feeds UK domestic pol-itics, which in turn influences the EU macro project. Exceeding rational accounts of politics is a challenge for EU theorists, who must absolutely integrate more the contribution of anthropologists and sociologists to their understanding of EU politics (Favell and Guiraudon 2011).

The de-politicisation/re-politicisation process

Peter Mair was one of the first scholars to make an explicit argument about the relationships between a de-politicisation process in the member states and the very project of European integra-tion. As Mair (2013) writes: The EU 'has been a project that has been pursued without becoming politicised and without seeking to generate any fanfare. . . . In the spirit of the so-called Monnet method, the EU-building process was almost always kept clear of conventional adversarial politics and public political debate' (p. 113f). With such an argument, Mair is acknowledging Inglehart's observation that 'permissive consensus' has characterised the building of an EU polity for decades and that this phenomenon has materialised in a number of political practices at the national level: no strong controversial debates about the EU inside the mainstream political parties; acknowl-edgement by the governing elites that there is no alternative to the implementation of EU public policies; growing role of non-majoritarian and regulatory institutions in the member states and in the EU (Majone 1996); reluctance of the governing elites to make Europe explicit in their programmes. As Hooghe and Marks (2009) stress, the foundations of de-politicisation start to be seriously destabilised with the Treaty of Maastricht in 1992, which generated controversies and conflicts about the future of core policies as monetary policy and police cooperation. The growing use of referendum by national governments for the ratification of EU reforms can interestingly be considered as a full part of the de-politicisation process (Qvortrup 2014). It is because mainstream political parties refuse to address the EU issue inside their own structures and governing leaders decide to use direct consultation. The political treatment of negative referendums on EU reforms also exemplifies de-politicisation, as the people's decision was several times bypassed by governing leaders. After the Danish referendum on the Maastricht referendum in June 1992, a renegotiation was organised between the Danish Government and the eleven European partners to have a partial implementation of the reforms (Siune 1993). In 2002 and 2009, Irish voters were invited twice to vote again on the same texts they had rejected a year ago: the Treaty of Nice and the Treaty of Lisbon. In both cases, the second referendum was positive. In 2005, the rejection of the European Constitutional Treaty by the Dutch and French voters did not prevent the two governments from accepting the integration of a huge part of the institutional provisions in the Treaty of Lisbon, ratified in 2009 by their national parliaments (Lequesne 2008). All these elements, referring to a de-politicisation of national politics on the EU issue have not really been included in new theories of European integration. Simon Hix had already observed in 1994 that comparative politics had to be more mobilised to understand the EU polity, but he did not insist on the need for a systemic link between national politics and the EU polity (Hix 1994). Hooghe and Marks at the end of the 2000s and Mair at the beginning of the 2010s made steps forward in their research.

De-politicisation of the EU goes together with re-politicisation. As Cees van der Eijk and Mark Franklin (2004: 47) wrote, the EU issue becomes 'ripe for politicisation' after the Treaty of Maastricht. Re-politicisation can be observed and measured in the influence the EU exerts 'on the parties and their modes of competition' in national elections (Mair 2013: 115). This trend includes the development of political parties, which are openly anti-EU or Eurosceptic (Leconte 2010). Brexit is one example of this re-politicisation of the EU issue at the national level, which has to be included into any new EU theory. In UK politics, the long period going from Thatcher to Cameron (1990–2016) has been characterised by a policy of minimalist engagement in the EU (Bulmer and James 2017). It has been true for labour as for conservative governments and even for the conservative/liberal democrat government between 2010 and 2015. Cameron was the last prime minister who wanted to continue the commitment in the Single Market without engaging the country too much far in political integration. As a member of the Conservative Party said in 2011: 'David Cameron's dream is to manage the UK membership to the EU without having to say a single word about it'.[1] But the re-politicisation of the EU issue did not make this situation anymore possible. The creation of UKIP and the development of a strong Eurosceptic line inside the Conservative Party were elements of re-politicisation, which forced the prime minister to ask the risky question about UK membership in the June 2016 referendum (Glencross 2017). The outcome (52 per cent in favour of Brexit) had consequences not only for the UK but also for the EU polity.

The dialectics between de-politicisation and re-politicisation of EU issues in the national debates has a direct impact on the evolution of the EU polity and must be included in theoretical frameworks. Competition around the EU issue in national elections and controversies inside and between political parties at the national level are independent variables that influence the EU macro project. They must be considered seriously by theorists of the European union. The study of electoral politics and party politics at the national level cannot remain the monopoly of comparatists who produce works about electoral convergence and divergence in domestic political arenas. They are variables that EU scholars must have a good knowledge of in order to theorise the EU polity.

New social cleavages in the member states

Peter Mair's (2013) excellent analysis of the future of democracy in Europe still gives a lot of importance to political parties, even if Mair's main message is the decrease of legitimacy of mainstream and mass political parties in all EU member states. Hooghe and Marks stress that the state of public opinion in the member must be taken seriously into account. They are right even if public opinion is a very broad variable, which is not easy to identify empirically (Hooghe and Marks 2009).

In EU theory, accounts must be given to new social cleavages and new forms of polarisation at the national level, which bypass the classic left/right opposition. In the domestic politics of all member states, globalisation concomitant to the end of the Cold War has created a new cleavage between citizens who are prepared to accept the impact of an 'open world' on their individual status and those who, at the opposite end, refuse this impact, considering they are the 'losers of the opening'. In general, the first group has a higher level of education and qualification and lives in big cities when the second group, who has a lower educational background and lives in small cities and rural areas. For the Brexit referendum, polls show clearly that a majority of citizens from England with a university degree voted for Remain when a majority of those with an elementary degree voted for Leave. Of Londoners, 59.9 per cent of the inhabitants of Manchester 60.4 per cent voted for Remain, whereas 66,3 per cent of people from North Lincolnshire voted for Leave (BBC 2016).

Studies on new cleavages must, of course, not tend to be reductive and must consider differences from one domestic political context to another. Let's take the case of United Kingdom Independence Party (UKIP) voters: they are supporting free trade for the UK and a closing of borders to foreign migration (UKIP 2015). It is different from Alternative für Deutschland in Germany or Front National in France, whose voters are both in favour of trade protectionism and against foreign migrants. But Brexit shows also that the new cleavages are not fixed and stabilised, especially inside mainstream political parties. The Conservative Party in the UK is an interesting case on economic issues. If there is inside the party a large group of militants defending a neoliberal 'Global Britain', there is also another group, called by Bulmer and James 'national conservatives', who are in favour of protecting British industries from outside competition. In her address to the Conservative Party on 5 October 2016, Theresa May spared carefully this second group when she declared that she wants 'markets for working people' (May 2016).

New social cleavages at the domestic level, built upon acceptance or resistance to the impact of globalisation on individual status, determine not only domestic politics but also the evolution of the European polity. Scholars cannot draw any EU theory if they do not consider new forms of social polarisation that frame domestic politics at the national level. It fits with the rehabilitation of domestic politics in the study of EU: New social cleavages → national politics → EU polity. Other issues can be added to the analytical framework. For instance, how far are government leaders – as French President Emmanuel Macron – able to bypass new social cleavages in the construction of a voluntarist macro project for Europe? Such a political strategy creates immediately forms of resistance at the national level. It is for this very reason that Emmanuel Macron is using, on the one hand, the argument of a more integrated EU (project supported by the part of French society that is not afraid of an 'open world') and, on the other hand, is asking for amendments to the Service Directive organising detached work in the EU (a message to the part of French society that considers the EU as a conveyor of social dumping against their jobs and social status). EU theory has no other choice than taking into consideration these elements of domestic politics to catch the evolution of EU polity and poltics as a whole.

Conclusion

Brexit has destabilised the EU but also research on the EU, especially the theoretical component of EU studies. It is not possible anymore to theorise the EU by focusing exclusively on transnational agency and on the nature of the deals made by transnational agents at the EU level. To understand the future of EU, theorists must mobilise explicitly the variable of domestic politics in their model (political regimes, political parties, social cleavages). Because agents who influence the development of EU polity/structure with their personal choices remain mainly national, theoretical modelling must start from the assumption that domestic politics influences EU polity, which in return influences domestic politics. It is time for EU scholars to reinvest in a systemic manner the comparative study of domestic politics in the member states to explain the macro change in EU polity. It is also time to abandon the normative term of 'integration theory' and to use more the term 'EU theory'. Brexit shows that the impact of domestic politics on the EU does not produce only integration. It can also bring disintegration, which cannot be considered equivalent to dilution or dislocation. The EU will survive the exit of the UK, but it will be a different polity, and EU theory will also be different.

Note

1   Conversation of the author with Maurice Fraser, Professor in Practice at the London School of Economics and member of the Conservative Party, 2011.

References

BBC (2016) EU Referendum: The Result in Maps and Charts. Available at: www.bbc.com/news/uk-politics-36616028 [Accessed November 15, 2017].

Bickerton, C., Dermont, H. and Puetter, U. (2015) *The New Intergovernmentalism: States and Supranational Actors in the Post-Maastricht Area*. Oxford: Oxford University Press.

Bulmer, S. (1983) Domestic Politics and European Community Policy-Making. *Journal of Common Market Studies* 21(4): 349–364.

Bulmer, S. and James, S. (2017) Managing Competing Projects: Unpacking the Domestic Politics of Brexit. UACES Conference, Krakow, September 4–6.

Bulmer, S. and Joseph, J. (2016) European Integration in Crisis? Of Supranational Integration, Hegemonic Projects and Domestic Politics. *European Journal of International Relations* 22(4): 725–748.

Bulmer, S. and Lequesne, C. (eds.) (2013) *The Member States of the European Union*. Oxford: Oxford University Press.

Dinan, D. (ed.) (2014) *Origins and Evolution of the European Union*. Oxford: Oxford University Press.

Favell, A. and Guiraudon, V. (eds.) (2011) *Sociology of the European Union*. Houndmills: Palgrave MacMillan.

Featherstone, K. and Radaelli, C. (eds.) (2003) *The Politics of Europeanization*. Oxford: Oxford University Press.

Glencross, A. (2017) *Why the UK Voted for Brexit? David Cameron's Great Miscalculation*. Basingstoke: Palgrave Macmillan.

Hix, S. (1994) The Study of the European Union: The Challenge to Comparative Politics. *West European Politics* 17(1): 1–30.

Hooghe, L. and Marks, G. (2009) A Postfunctionnalist Theory of European Integration: From Permissive Consensus to Constraining Dissensus. *British Journal of Political Science* 39(1): 1–23.

Howarth, C. and Andreopouli, E. (eds.) (2017) *The Social Psychology of Everyday Politics*. London: Routledge.

Inglehart, R. (1970) Public Opinion and Regional Integration. *International Organization* 24(4): 764–795.

Krastev, I. (2017) *After Europe*. Philadelphia: University of Pennsylvania Press.

Leconte, C. (2010) *Understanding Euroscepticism*. Basingstoke: Palgrave Macmillan.

Lequesne, C. (2008) *La France dans la Nouvelle Europe: Assumer le Changement d'Echelle*. Paris: Presses de Sciences Po.

Mair, P. (2013) *Ruling the Void: The Hollowing of Western Democracy*. London: Verso.

Majone, G. (1996) *Regulating Europe*. London: Routledge.

May, T. (2016) May's Keynote Speech at Tory Conference in Full. *Independent*, October 5. Available at: www.independent.co.uk/news/uk/politics/theresa-may-speech-tory-conference-2016-in-full-transcript-a7346171.html [Accessed November 28, 2017].

Moravcsik, A. (1998) *The Choice for Europe*. Ithaca, NY: Cornell University Press.

Qvortrup, M. (ed.) (2014) *Referendums and the World: The Continued Growth of Direct Democracy*. Basingstoke: Macmillan.

Saurugger, S. (2014) *Theoretical Approaches of European Integration*. Basingstoke: Palgrave Macmillan.

Saurugger, S. and Terpan, F. (2016) Resisting New Modes of Governance through Policy Instruments. *Comparative European Politics* 14(1): 53–70.

Schimmelfennig, F. (2015) Liberal Intergovernmentalism and the Euro Area Crisis. *Journal of European Public Policy* 53(4): 177–195.

Siune, K. (1993) The Danes Said No to the Maastricht Treaty: The Danish EC Referendum of June 1992. *Scandinavian Political Studies* 16(1): 93–103.

Sweet, A.S. and Sandholtz, W. (eds.) (1996) *European Integration and Supranational Governance*. Oxford: Oxford University Press.

UKIP (2015) UKIP 2015 General Election Manifesto. Available at: www.ukip.org/ukip_manifesto_summary [Accessed November 16, 2017].

van der Eijk, Cees, E. and Franklin, M. (2004) Potential for Contestation in European Matters as European Elections in Europe. In: Marks, G. and Steenbergen, M.R. (eds.), *European Integration and Political Conflict*. Cambridge: Cambridge University Press.

Webber, D. (2014) How Likely Is That the EU Will *Disintegrate*? A Critical Analysis Approach of Competing Theoretical Perspectives. *European Journal of International Relations* 20(2): 341–365.

Zielonka, J. (2014) *Is the EU Doomed?* Cambridge: Polity Press.

INDEX

Note: Page numbers in italic indicate a figure on the corresponding page; page numbers in bold indicate a table on the corresponding page.

A2 countries/residents 124
A8 countries/residents 123–124
academics 105–108, 113, 180, 274
acquis communautaire 285
acquis politiques 223
affiliation 10, 242, 269, 278–281, 284; affiliated non-members 278–282, 284–288
Afghanistan 234–235, 239, 241
Africa 8, 197, 199–205, 212; African colonies 214; Horn of Africa 224; North Africa 9, 242; South Africa 198, 200, 202, 217
agriculture 4, 6, 41, 46, 70, 92–101, 105, 122, 164, 256, 283, 287; agricultural policy 6, 28, 43, 92, 95–96, 98–101, 170; Agriculture Act, 1947 93, 95; Agriculture and Horticulture Development Board (AHDB) 97; farmers 6, 35, 43, 92–96, 99–101
Albania 104, 268
Algeria 97
alliance 7, 9–10, 32, 148, 165, 169, 171–172, 174, 199, 209, 237, 239, 249, 257, 259, 270; alliance commitments 209; economic alliance 199; Franco-German alliance 9; intra EU-alliance 273
All-Island Civic Dialogue 35
Alterative for Germany/Alternative für Deutschland 184, 295
ambiguity 8, 19, 34, 167, 174, 210; 'constructive ambiguity' 167
Amsterdam 129, 246
Andorra 268
Anglosphere 4, 7–8, 153–155, 163, 198–199, 203, 209–210, 215–217; Anglosphere circles 209–210, 215–217; Anglosphere tradition 7
anti-dumping 81

anti-imperial 211
anti-politics 8, 10, 179–185, 187–188; anti-political sentiment 179–180, 182–185, 187, 189–191; *see also* populism
aristocratic 50
Armenia 104
army 9, 137–138, 140, 215, 240–242; *see also* European Union, European army
Article 50 10, 16, 18, 35, 45, 85–86, 88, 126, 136, 161, 216, 235, 261, 266, 268, 285
ASEAN 80
Ashfield 187
Asia 9, 80, 109, 111, 124, 200–201, 203, 231, 242, 246
Atlanticism 7, 10, 163
Atlanticist states 272
Attlee, C. 169, 211
Australia 88, 97, 110, 129, 154, 163, 198–201, 203–205, 215–218
authority 15, 18, 40, 50, 52, 70, 87, 138, 168, 262
Aviva 59
Azevêdo, R. 84

backbenchers 158, 161
Balfour Declaration, 1926 198
Bangladesh 201
bank 68, 71, 139, 245, 248–249
Bank of America Merrill Lynch 59
Bank of England 49–55, 57, 69, 73, 247, 249–250
Banque de France 247
Barclays 55, 57, 59
Barnier, M. 36, 106, 113, 261
Barroso, J. M. 42, 238, 260
Basel Committee on Banking Supervisions (BCBS) 250

Belfast 18, 20–21; Belfast Agreement, 1998 27, 29, 31, 33, 36; *see also* Good Friday Agreement
Belgium 216, 247
Belize 202
Berlin 60, 129, 215, 233, 236–237, 240–241
Berlin, I. 138
Bevin, E. 169, 210
Bexley 21
bilateral(ism) 20, 28, 83, 98, 111, 113, 198, 203, 215, 225, 229, 234, 241, 282, 284, 286; bilateral agreements 86, 113, 282; bilateral cooperation 111, 215, 229; bilateral I 282; bilateral II 282
biodiversity 94
Blair, T. 70, 111, 119, 142, 151, 158, 167, 169–171, 183, 212, 262
Bleanau Gwent 21
blocking minority 257, 270
Bologna Declaration, 1999 104
Bolsover 21
border 5, 7, 29, 30–36, 43, 46–47, 62, 75, 85, 87, 99, 119–122, 128–129, 154, 164, 174, 185, 203, 208, 213, 240, 242, 246, 278–279, 283–285, 295; border control 33, 208, 240; cross-border 29–31, 87, 126, 203, 246; hard border 30, 32–33, 36, 87, 174; soft border 38; *see also* Northern Ireland border
Bosnia–Herzegovina 104, 268
Botswana 202
Bradford & Bingley 55
Brazil 88
Brexit: Brexit bill 62 or 'divorce bill' 164; Brexiteers 2, 23, 37, 43–44, 47, 61, 95, 129, 153–154, 164, 188, 293; Brexit mandate 42; Brexit negotiations 3, 10, 33, 35, 44, 81, 114, 121, 127, 141, 168, 174, 188, 209, 214, 242, 247, 251, 271, 278, 291; Brexit option 251; Brexit process 3–4, 6–8, 10, 24, 38, 67, 74, 157, 160, 164–165; Brexit vote 5–9, 42, 59, 84, 89, 105, 118, 120, 123, 126, 128, 148, 180, 187–188, 200, 211, 254–255, 261; hard Brexit 9, 59, 61, 75, 96, 188–189, 217, 247, 251, 269; no deal 9, 85, 99, 175–176; Plan for Britain 162; post-Brexit 1, 5, 30, 34, 36, 60–62, 76, 83, 87, 98, 108–109, 112–113, 118, 127–129, 154, 164, 187, 203, 213–214, 217, 227, 238, 249–250, 255, 261–262, 268–274, 284; soft Brexit 10, 73, 85, 96, 162, 165, 168, 174–175, 177n1, 269, 272; *see also* Leave supporters
British Election Study 148–149, 173
British Empire 140–141, 149, 198
British European policy 212, 218
British-Irish relationship 27–30, 38
Britishness 24, 40, 149–150, 152–153; *see also* Englishness
Brown, G. 53–54, 122, 142, 152
Brussels 35, 106, 189, 209, 233–238, 241–242, 267, 290, 292

Bulgaria 98
Bundesbank 246–247

Cabinet 15, 29, 35, 61, 73–74, 144n21, 154, 160, 170, 210, 212–213, 217
Callaghan, J. 169
Cambridge 114, 187
Cameron, D. 118, 125–126, 134, 142, 152, 199, 211–212, 229, 236, 258, 269, 291–292, 294
campaign 2, 7, 15, 22, 32, 41–43, 74–75, 94–95, 107, 121, 125, 134, 136, 149–150, 153–154, 159–160, 162–164, 170, 172–174, 180, 184–186, 188, 190, 198–199, 208, 216, 218n1, 246, 272, 274, 293; Brexit campaign 128, 153, 190, 293; Leave Campaign 74, 107, 153, 162, 164, 185, 190, 208, 211; referendum campaign 22, 32, 41–42, 94–95, 154, 159, 163, 172–173, 199, 208, 293; Remain campaign 42, 125, 134, 216
Canada 45, 87–88, 109–110, 129, 154, 163, 198–202, 203–205, 210, 215–218, 271
CANZUK 163, 215–216
capabilities 113, 228, 234–235, 236–237, 239–240, 242, 262, 267, 275; defence capabilities 228, 236; military capabilities 234–235, 239, 242, 262
Cape Town 212
capitalism 3–6, 49–50, 66–75, 77, 126, 171, 180–181; British capitalism 49–50, 66–67, 70; UK's model of capitalism 3–6, 66–72, 74
Cardiff 18, 20
Caribbean 8, 197, 199–201, 203–205
Catalonia 43
Central Europe 119
Chamberlain, J. 198
Chevening Global Award Programme 109
Chief Trade Negotiation Adviser 81
China 4, 60, 71, 88, 105, 107–111, 171, 201, 215–216, 227, 273
Chirac, J. 262
Churchill, W. 8, 140, 209–213, 215, 218; three circles model 209–212, 217
Citigroup 59
citizens 4, 15–16, 21, 24, 30–31, 49, 85, 87, 92, 104–105, 120, 123–127, 134, 136–137, 148–150, 172, 183, 185, 188, 190–191, 214, 257, 269–270, 272, 286, 295; British citizens 49, 124, 128, 260, 270, 272; citizenry 24; citizenship 105, 125–126, 149–150, 183; EU citizens 85, 87, 92, 120, 123–124, 127, 272
CityUK 62, 73
Civil Law 135
civil society 35, 42, 210
Clarke, K. 158
class society: capitalist class 50, 138; entrepreneurs 123, 139; merchant class 139; middle class 55, 189; nobility 136, 138–139; working class 50, 119, 129, 139, 153; *see also* social groups
cleavage 10, 24, 28, 186, 203, 290, 295–296

climate change 94, 100–101, 106, 226
clusters: Northern liberal cluster 270; small states clusters 266, 269–270; Southern protectionist cluster 270
coalition 9–10, 55, 69, 72–76, 125, 158–159, 164, 168, 173–174, 189, 199, 213, 236, 238, 241, 247, 249, 257–258, 267–268, 272, 274–275
Cold War 92, 215, 234, 267, 295
collaboration 29, 104–105, 109, 111–112, 114, 134, 143n3, 270, 283
colonies 135, 139, 141, 197, 199–200, 202, 214, 226, 279
Common Law 135
Common Travel Area (CTA) 30, 35, 121
Commonwealth 3, 8, 80, 88, 140–141, 149, 154, 169, 197–205, 209–210, 212–214, 226, 256; Asian Commonwealth 200–201, 205n1; Commonwealth countries 3, 8, 197–205, 212, 226, 256; Commonwealth enthusiasts 198–200, 204; Commonwealth Secretariat 202
competition state 6, 68–69, 74, 76
competitiveness 62, 67, 75, 94, 97, 101, 104, 107, 163, 248–249
compliance 47, 94, 121, 279, 282, 288; compliance requirements 94, 279
conflict 10, 16, 20, 27–29, 33–34, 36, 67, 70, 75, 114, 140, 142, 143n11, 157, 161, 163–164, 227, 239, 258, 261–262, 286, 294
consensus 37, 42, 45, 48, 58, 100, 119, 141, 161, 176, 187, 210, 215, 224, 293
Conservative Party 7, 22, 32, 69, 74–76, 118, 134, 142, 157–165, 168, 170, 174, 176, 184, 189, 210, 212, 230, 259, 291–296; Conservative statecraft 157, 163; Parliamentary Conservative Party (PCP) 158
Conservatives 7, 15, 42–44, 48, 125, 141, 144n32, 151–152, 157–165, 167, 173, 176–177, 186, 189, 259, 295
constitution 3, 16–20, 24–25, 40, 45, 48, 136, 138, 141, 213; constitutional arrangement 16; constitutional settlement 1, 38; constitutional statutes 18
convention 20, 44–45, 48, 83; Dublin convention 121; European Convention on Human Rights 18, 41; Lomé Convention 200–201, 256; Sewel Convention 45–46; Vienna Convention on Succession of Copenhagen 82
co-operation 212, 215, 229, 231, 240–242
Copenhagen criteria 279
Corbett, R. 217
Corbyn, J. 8, 15, 61, 76, 150, 164–165, 168, 172–176, 188–189
Coveney, S. 32
Croatia 270
Customs Union 1, 5, 16, 33–34, 38, 46–47, 85, 87, 98, 103, 161–162, 164–165, 169, 174–175, 177n1, 202, 225, 279, 281–282, 285
Cyprus 269–270, 279

Danish People's Party 184
Darling, A. 54
Davis, D. 86, 154, 198–199, 214
deadlock 85, 127
defence 9, 37, 51, 137, 147–151, 153, 155, 167, 170, 208–209, 215, 223–224, 226–229, 233–242, 261–267, 270, 272; Coordinated Annual Review on Defence (CARD) 238; defence industry 229; defence policy 9, 223–224, 226, 228, 233–234, 238, 240, 261, 270; defence spending 233, 235–236, 241; deterrence 237, 239, 241; European Defence Technological and Industrial Base (EDTIB) 239; Nato Defence Planning Process (NDPP) 237–238; Partnership for Peace Planning and Review Process (PARP) 237; post-Brexit defence 238
deficit 69, 71, 76, 153, 183, 246; budget deficit 69; democratic deficit 153, 183
de Gaulle, C. 135
Delors, J. 41, 69, 173, 256
democracy 2, 8, 24, 62, 120, 125, 140, 142–143, 152–153, 170, 179–180, 182–183, 188, 190–191, 198, 211, 281, 293, 295; democratic 2, 7, 16, 21–22, 42, 44, 46, 118, 120, 138, 148, 153, 157, 161, 171–172, 176, 179–183, 187–190, 273, 282, 284, 291; parliamentary democracy 293; party democracy 24; representative democracy 8, 153, 188
Democratic Unionist Party (DUP) 32, 46, 161
demography 120, 174
Denmark 121, 140, 143n4, 227, 257–258, 261, 266, 268–272, 274–275
Department for Business, Energy and Industrial Strategy (BEIS) 23
Department for Environment, Farming and Rural Areas (Defra) 99
Department for Exiting the European Union (DExEU) 80–81, 199
Department for International Trade (DIT) 80–81, 112, 199, 262
dependence 69, 72, 75, 96, 202, 204, 267
depoliticisation 288
de-politicisation 290, 293–294
deregulation 5, 49, 56, 61, 74, 164, 259
Deutsche Bank 59
devaluation 71–72, 76
developing countries 197, 199–200, 202–204, 216
devolution 5, 16–24, 38n1, 40–42, 45–48, 66, 100, 148–149, 152–153, **181**, 293; devolution settlement, 1999 19, 42, 46, 48, 66, 148–149, 153
digital communication 199
diplomacy 37, 209–210, 224, 229; British diplomatic service 226; diplomatic power 226; environmental diplomacy 229; European diplomacy 210
directive 17, 70, **181**, 247, 261, 295; Service Directive 295

discourse 3, 7–9, 56, 125, 152, 171, 186, 197–200, 202, 204, 208, 212; Commonwealth discourse 199, 202, 204; Eurosceptic discourse 8–9, 197–200, 204; political discourses 3; public discourse 56, 186
discrimination 120, 121, 126, 128–129
distrust 2, 15–16, 21
divide 61, 160, 162, 164, 176, 287–288; cultural 187; geographic 187
division 4, 5, 15–16, 21, 24, 28, 33, 50, 84, 148, 152, 158–162, 164, 168, 170, 172, 175, 187, 224–225, 254, 286; party division 164; political division 4; social division 5
doctrine 17, 40, 45–46, 84, 135, 142, 236, 282
domestic business 245
domestic policy 19
Doncaster 187
Dublin 5, 59, 121, 246

economics 56, 75, 111, 162, 208, 216; macroeconomics 71
economy 1–6, 15–17, 22–23, 27–30, 34–35, 49–52, 56, 57, 60–62, 66–68, 70–76, 80, 100, 107–108, 118, 120, 122–129, 138–139, 142, 151, 161–164, 169, 181, 183, 187, 202–203, 214, 224–225, 245, 247–248, 258, 270–271, 274; British economy 15, 22–23, 49–52, 60–61, 71, 80, 108, 122–123, 125, 128–129, 151, 169, 171, 175–176, 217, 225; Irish economy 29–28, 34
Edinburgh 18, 20, 187
education 6, 21, 62, 69, 86, 103–114, 123, 127, 152, 186–187, 295
Education Select Committee (ESC) 108
election 2, 7–8, 15, 22, 32–33, 43, 47, 76, 96, 134, 141, 143n5, 144n34, 150–154, 158–165, 167–168, 170, 173–174, 184, 187–189, 208, 230, 269; election system 140; UK's 2015 general election 152–153, 187; UK's 2017 general election 150, 167, 173–174, 188; *see also* referendum
elites 2, 66–67, 71, **73**, 147–148, 150, 162, 210–212, 292–293
empire 8, 41, 51, 129, 137, 140–142, 149–150, 153, 198, 200, 202, 204, 210, 212, 214, 217
employment 4, 52, 68–70, 72, 74, 76, 97, 104, 121, 123–124, 128, 168, 173, 183; employment policy 69–70
energy 29, 225–226
Engels, F. 139
England 19–24, 41–43, 45–48, 50, 112, 135–137, 139–140, 147–155, 173–174, 189, 210, 295
Englishness 22, 24, 148–152, 155, 293; *see also* Britishness
English Votes for English Laws (EVEL) 19, 148
Erasmus programme 103–104, 106, 113
Estonia 269
Eurobarometer 228
Euro-caution 167, 169–170

Euro-fanaticism 167
Europe: Continental Europe 7, 135, 137, 143, 171, 199; Eastern Europe 9, 107, 122, 230, 272; Northern Europe 225; Southern Europe 125; Western Europe 119, 187–188, 190, 211
European Union: budget 6, 92–93, 100–101, 105, 113–115, 158, 170, 225, 258, 261, 293; Capital Markets Union (CMU) 70, 248–249, 256, 258; Common Agricultural Policy (CAP) 6, 28, 43, 92–95, 98, 100–101, 170, 256, 258; Common Commercial Policy (CCP) 81, 84; Common Consolidated Corporate Tax Base (CCCTB) 37; Common Security and Defence Policy (CSDP) 216, 223–225, 228–229, 234, 239, 261, 263; Court of Justice of the European Union (CJEU) 18, 86–87, 287; Directorate General for Trade (DG Trade) 81; Eastern/EU Enlargement 122, 134, 226, 267, 288; Economic and Monetary Union (EMU) 162, 256–257, 293; Economic Partnership Agreements (EPAs) 201, 204; EU decision-making 9, 229, 288; EU law 16–18, 41, 45–46, 75, 82, 86–88, 98, 104, 174, 284; EU presidency 224; Euro-area 55–56, 279; Euro-Mediterranean Partnership 268; European army 9, 137–138, 215, 240–242; European Banking Authority (EBA) 204, 248–250, 260; European Banking Union 55, 248, 250, 258; European Central Bank (ECB) 54, 58, 70, 247, 250; European Coal and Steel Community (ECSC) 210; European Commission 4, 9, 36, 42, 94, 100, 104, 113, 121, 126, 188, 224–225, 229, 233, 235–238, 240, 242, 248, 250, 254, 256–257, 259–261, 263, 270, 282, *283,* 287; European Communities Act (ECA), 1972 17–19, 21, 24, 281; European Community (EC) 92, 167–169, 171–172, 176, 282, 291, 293; European Council 9, 33, 35, 83, 86, 224, 230, 235, 237, 251, 254, 257, 260–261, 263, 272, 279, 284; European Council of Ministers 46, 235, 257, 261, 263, 279; European Defence Agency 228; European Defence Fund 270; European Defense Community 293; European Development Fund (EDF) 225; European Economic Area (EEA) 10, 16, 32, 43, 46–47, 87, 98, **104**, 108, 113, 175, 246, 262, 268, 271–274, 278–279, 282–288; European Economic Community (EEC) 28, 41, 66, 81, 151, 157, 197–198, 200–201, 204, 208, 211–213, 218; European Institute of Technology (EIT) 105; European Insurance and Occupational Pensions Authority (EIOPA) 250; European Medicines Agency 174, 260, 271; European Neighbourhood Policy (ENP) 121, 268, 281, 288n3; European Parliament 4, 35, 60, 137, 150, 152, 158, 176, 183, 203, 217, 225, 237, 254, 257, 259–261, 279, 283–284; European People's Party 158, 259; European policy 106,

158, 161, 168, 170, 172, 176, 212, 218, 227; European Political Cooperation (EPC) 224, 227; European Research Area 103, 105; European Research Council 106; European Securities and Markets Authority (ESMA) 250; European Students Union (ESU) 103; European Supervisory Authorities (ESAs) 55, 248; Eurozone 37, 54, 76, 162, 225–226, 258, 274, 287; EU sanctions against Russia 215, 227; EU's external relations 279–280, 279; EU's Framework Participation Agreement (FPA) 229; EU's High Representative 224, 226–229, 235–236; EU studies 2, 290, 296; Foreign Affairs Council 228; Impact Assessment Board 260; Multiannual Financial Framework (MFF) 261; Permanent Structured Cooperation (PESCO) 228, 240–242; post-EU future 163; Regulatory Scrutiny Board 260

Europeanisation 121, 291–292
European University Association 103, 106
Europe of Freedom and Direct Democracy alliance 259
Euroscepticism 2, 7, 18, 118–119, 147–154, 157–159, 161–163, 167, 171–172, 260, 274; Eurosceptics 40, 152, 154, 159, 163–164, 198–199, 203
EU theory 290–296; integration theory 292, 296; liberal intergovernmentalisme 290–292; multilevel governance 290, 292; neo-functionalism 290, 292; 'post-functionalist theory' 292; *see also* theory
exceptionalism 7, 49, 50–51, 61, 121, 134–143, 147, 269
exchange rate 53, 56, 67–68, 71
export 69, 71, 76, 81, 88, 95, 97, 99, 108, 200–205, 215–216, 270, 271, 273; export markets 88, 202, 204, 215; net exports 246
external relations 198, 202, 210, 279–280; *see also* European Union, EU's external relations

Falconer, C. 81
Fallon, M. 137, 235
Farage, N. 15, 74, 118–120, 128, 148, 159, 164, 184–186, 259
Faroe Islands 104, 271
Fianna Fáil 34
Fiji 202
finance 35, 51–52, 54, 60–61, 67–68, 70–72, 76, 123, 137, 173, 214, 244–247, 249–251; finance curse 67, 70–72; financial centre 6, 55, 59, 61–62, 67, 71, 76, 244–247, 250; financial crisis 8, 49–53, 55, 66, 123, 152, 183, 244, 248–249; financial market 143, 245, 247–248, 250–251; financial services 5, 7, 30, 54–55, 57–60, 69, 99, 134, 244–248, 250, 256; Financial Services Action Plan, 1999 247; Financial Services

Authority (FSA) 55; fiscal austerity 76; revenue 53, 68, 246, 261
Fine Gael 34
Finland 258, 270, 274–275
First World War 140
Fischlerler, F. 93
fishing 29, 271
Florence 106
food 92–94, 96–97, 98–100, 216; food security 92–93, 96
Foot, M. 169
foreign affairs 32, 44, 208, 228, 235, 271
foreign policy 1–3, 8–9, 66, 172, 209–212, 214, 223–231, 234, 236, 273; British foreign policy 209–212; European foreign policy 223–225, 227–230
fossil fuels 94
Fox, L. 80, 86, 154, **160**, 197–199, 203, 213, 216
France 9–10, 22–23, **53**, 54, 97, 100–101, 106–107, 121, 123, 136, 140, 143n8, 144n31, 170, 184, 215, 225–230, 233–234, 238–239, 241, 245, 247, 249–250, 258–260, 262, 268–271, 273–275, 280
Franco-German axis 230, 262, 268–269, 273
Frankfurt 59, 129, 246
Freedom Party, Austria 184
free movement 7, 29, 42, 47, 69, 75, 86–87, 113, 118, 120–123, 127, 129, 150, 162, 172, 183, 274, 291; free movement of capital 129, 162; free movement of people 7
French Revolution 140
Future of England Survey (FoES) 149

G20 81, 216
Gaitskell, H. 169
Generalised System of Preferences (GSP) 200
geopolitics 271
Georgia 104
Germany 9–10, 22–23, **53**, 54, 97, 100, 106–107, 121–122, 140, 170, 184, 215, 225–231, 233, 235, 238–239, 241, 247, 249–250, 258–262, 268–270, 273, 275, 295
Gibraltar 126
Glasgow 139
Global Innovation Initiative Fund 109
globalisation 2, 5, 49–50, 55–59, 61–62, 68–69, 89, 148, 153, 158, 171–172, 186, 295
global markets 5, 92
Golden Dawn, Greece 184
Goldman Sachs 59
Good Friday Agreement 5, 31, 34–36; *see also* Belfast, Belfast Agreement
Gove, M. 154, 160
Gramscian 50
Grayling, C. 160
Great Britain 7, 19
Great Depression, 1930s 22, 198
Great Repeal Bill 136, 143n13; *see also* withdrawal bill

Great Yarmouth 187
Greece 43, 184, 270–271, 274; Greek debt crisis 230
Grieve, D. 164
Gross Domestic Product (GDP) 29, 80, 99, 101, 144n36, 201, 224–225, 228, 245, 247, 270
Gulf States 71, 88

Hague, W. 154, 158, 272
Hammond, P. 61, 162, 217
HBOS 54, 57
health 25, 94, 100, 123, 126–127
Heath, E. 157, 212–213
hegemony 49–51, 55, 62, 162, 268–269, 273, 284
higher education (HE) 6, 103–114, 123, 295
Hill, J. 70, 248
Hix, S. 129, 259, 294
HM Treasury 69, **73**
HMS *Queen Elisabeth* 234–4, 242
Hobbes, T. 120, 138
Hong Kong **53**, 61
Horizon 2020 103–104, 106, 109, *110*, 113, 174
House of Commons 33, 85, 137–138, 141, 143n14, 162–163, 168, 175, 177, 189, 204
House of Lords 17, 20, 31, 137, 246
Howard, M. 158
HSBC 59
human capital 7, 120, 123

Iceland 16, 54, 87, 104, 154, 267–268, 271–274, 282, *283*
identity 2, 5, 7, 16, 21–22, 30–31, 40, 113, 120, 147–155, 183, 209, 211, 266, 293; English identity 7, 22, 147–155, 293; European identity 113; national identity 21–22, 149, 183, 293
ideology 50, 154–155, 157, 162, 190, 259
immigration 7, 42, 111, 118–129, 149–151, 154, 161, 163, 170–171, 174–176, 183–186, 188, 190, 208, 226, 230, 285
implementation period 86
import 46, 62, 249, 271
income 21–22, 51, 53, **54**, 67–69, 72, 96, 100, 183, 187, 204, 270
independence 5, 7, 19–20, 34, 41–48, 74, 152, 170, 173, 198, 212, 271; British 7, 74, 152; Scottish 5, 20, 34, 41, 173, 271
India 8, 80, 88, 107–111, 144, 171, 199–200, 203–205, 214, 216–218
industrialisation 139–140
industrial revolution 138–139, 183
industrial strategy 16, 23–24, 103, 108, 112
inequality 25, 67, 69, 72, 148, 183, 185–186
inflation 69–70, 72, 142
infrastructure 24, 58, 60–62, 71, 112, 126, 138, 245
Innovate Finance 59–60
instability 5–6, 27, 38, 247, 249
Institute of Economic Affairs (IEA) **73**, 74
institution 138, 143n7, 199, 202, 237, 250, 259–260

institutionalisation 104, 203, 236, 267, 269
integration 1–2, 9–10, 41–42, 49, 56, 69–70, 89, 108, 110, 121, 127, 136, 138, 147–149, 150–152, 154, 161–163, 167–169, 171, 176, 208, 218, 226, 228–230, 233, 235–236, 238–242, 244–245, 246–248, 251, 256, 266–269, 272, 275, 290–294, 296; defence integration 235–236, 238; disintegration 262, 292; economic integration 274; European (EU) integration 1–2, 10, 41, 69–70, 138, 147–148, 150–152, 154, 158, 162–163, 167–169, 171–172, 176, 208, 218, 228, 230, 233, 241–242, 256, 266–269, 272–273, 275, 292–295; financial integration 9, 244, 246–248; market integration 56; monetary integration 169, 172; political integration 176, 294
integrationists 239
interdependence 247, 284, 290
intergovernmentalism 9–10, 227, 269, 275, 290–292
internal market 4, 164, 225, 256–261, 279–282, 285; *see also* Single Market
internal relations 279
international political economy 56–57
international relations 1, 4, 56, 107, 112, 163, 236, 262
investment 30, 35, 51, 53, 58–62, 68–69, 72, 75–76, 80–81, 88–89, 100, 109, 121, 139, 225, 235, 237, 240, 242, 245–247, 249; European investments 234; investment funds 245
Iran 15
Iraq War 154, 170, 234–235, 262
Ireland 5, 16, 19, 24, 27–38, 46–47, 59, 85, 87, 95–98, 112, 121–122, 143n4, 161, 174, 216, 247, 269, 272, 274, 285
Irvine, D. 149
ISIS 227
Islington 187
Israel 15, 104, 227
Italy 97, 140, 184, 247, 270

Japan 53, 80, 245, 262
Jobbik, Hungary 184
Johnson, B. 15, 129, 143n12, 148, 154, 198–199, 211, 214
Jørgensen, T. 106
journalism 15
judge 16–18, 24, 31, 135, 255
Juncker, J. C. 36–37, 70, 235–238, 240, 256, 260

Kenny, E. 35, 272
Kenya 154, 202
Keynes, J. M. 23
Kinnock, N. 169, 257
Knowledge and Information Centres (KICs) 105
Kosovo 262, 268

labour 6, 30, 58, 61–62, 66–72, 76, 93, 95, 97–98,
    118, 121–124, 126, 128–129, 150, 162–164,
    169, 171–172, 224–225, 309; British labour
    market 121, 124; labour market 6, 61, 66–72,
    76, 118, 121–124, 126, 128–129, 163; *see also*
    workers
Labour, England 7–8, 15, 19–21, 41, 75, 93, 119,
    121–122, 138, 141–142, 151, 158–160, 164–165,
    167–177, 186, 188–189, 210–211, 217, 225, 230,
    256–257; Blue Labour 150; Labour government
    151–152, 165, 169, 174–176; New Labour 69,
    123, 151–152, 176; Parliamentary Labour Party
    (PLP) **73**, 74, 172
Labour, Scotland 42, 48, **73**, 74
Lancaster House Speech 213, 285
Latvia 269–270
law 4, 16–20, 35, 41, 44–46, 62, 68, 72, 75, 82–83,
    85–88, 98, 104, 120–121, 124, 127–128, 135–136,
    142, 174, 176, 281, 284, 286
leadership 28, 44, 52, 74–73, 89, 101, 109, 111, 113,
    157–161, 163–164, 167–168, 171–174, 176, 197,
    212–213, 218, 256, 259, 269–270, 273; party
    leadership 75–76, 157–158, 164, 169
Leadsom, A. 160
Least Developed Countries (LDCs) 201
Leave supporters 15 / voters 119, 128–129,
    153, 174
legislation 1, 17–18, 20–21, 41, 68, 70, 138, 149,
    161, 164–165, 168, 203, 209, 245, 247–250,
    259, 281–283; legal framework 125, 288; legal
    jurisdiction 19; legal system 17, 135–136, 143;
    Legislative Consent Motions (LCM) 20
legitimacy 7, 17, 135–136, 148, 160, **181–182**, 190,
    241, 261, 269, 292, 295; legitimacy crisis 261
Liberal Democrats 73–74, 158–160, 173
liberalisation 5, 7, 49, 56–57, 62, 70, 161, 201, 225,
    248, 267
liberalism 129, 141–143, 161–162, 164, 198, 256
liberals 5, 49, 59, 62
liberty 138, 154
Libya 215, 242
Lidington, D. 217
Liechtenstein 16, 87, 104, 282–283, 288n4
Lisbon Agenda 104, 170, 256
Lithuania 269–270
living standards 7, 28, 67–68, 72, 172, 183
Lloyds 54, 59, 245
lobby 73, 94, 106, 162, 248; agribusiness lobby 94;
    business lobbyists 162; lobby groups 73
Locke, J. 138
London 5–6, 9, 20, 22–23, 30, 42, 49–63, 67, 69–71,
    73, 110, 119, 123, 137, 139, 152, 161–162, 164,
    213, 215, 236, 238, 241–242, 244–250, 260, 271,
    273, 295
London Clearing House (LCH) 245
London Stock Exchange 59, 245
Luxembourg 17, 172, 246–247

Macmillan, H. 169, 212
Macron, E. 107, 113–114, 241, 262, 263n3, 295
MacShane, D. 138
Magna Carta 136, 138
Major, J. 40, 69, 151
majority 2, 15, 18, 24, 31–32, 34, 41, 54, 92, 95,
    97, 109, 119, 123–124, 134, 140–141, 144n32,
    151–152, 161–162, 164, 168, 173, 176, 185, 248,
    254, 256–257, 272–273, 291–293, 295
majority voting 69, 141, 161, 224, 247, 249, 261
Malaysia 108–110, 199, 203, 217
Malta 101, 230, 269–270, 271
Manchester 295
Mansfield 187
manufacturing industry 23, 139
marginalization 179
Marie Sklodowska-Curie Programme (MCSP) 105
market 8–9, 24, 28, 31, 41, 52, 54, 60–62, 71, 75,
    88, 93–95, 97, 100, 110, 121–122, 141–143, 162,
    198, 200–205, 244–251, 256, 258, 267–269,
    278–279, 281–285, 287; market access 41, 70,
    86, 95, 162, 200, 204–205, 246, 251, 256, 267,
    278–279, 281–284, 287; market-friendly 9, 244;
    market prices 93
Marx, K. 138
Marxist 51
Mauritius 202
May, T. 15, 23, 32, 36, 61, 80, 88–89, 106, 122,
    127–128, 136, 141, 144n37, 160–165, 168,
    175–176, 188, 199, 208–209, 212–217, 235, 285,
    295; May Government 168, 175, 208, 285
McClay, T. 203
McDonnell, J. 168, 174–175
McShane, D. 174
media 3, 24, 124, 171, 173, 176, 186, 218
Mediterranean 242, 247, 268, 271, 281
Mercosur 80
Merkel, A. 236, 240–241, 260, 263
Middle East 9, 201, 227, 242
military 137, 140, 215, 224, 228–229, 233–235,
    238–242, 255, 262–263, 267–270, 272; military
    operations 224, 229, 235; military power 215;
    military technology 234
Miller case 18, 44–45; *see also* Supreme Court
Milne, S. 173
minister: Cabinet minister 160; finance minister
    173, 266, 275; foreign minister 43, 203, 273;
    prime minister 15, 32, 35, 80, 88–89, 103, 106,
    108, 111, 118, 122, 125, 134, 159–160, 162, 165,
    168–170, 176, 185, 188–189, 203, 209–213,
    216, 235, 262, 269, 272, 285, 292, 294; trade
    minister 203
modernisation 5, 28, 104, 158, 170
Modi, N. 111
Mogherini, F. 228, 235–236, 238, 240
Moldova 104, 268
Monaco 172, 268

monetary policy 54, 56, 69, 294
money 51, 54–55, 58, 100, 106, 185–186, 235, 242, 261, 293
Montenegro 104, 268
Moravcsik, A. 291
Moray 21
Morgan Stanley 59
Morocco 97
mortgage 52, 57
multicultural(ism) 150, 152
multilateral(ism) 83–84, 203, 209, 215, 225, 234, 236, 241, 267, 281–282; multilateral defence cooperation 234, 241
mutual recognition 69, 112–113

Namibia 200
nation 6, 80, 88, 120, 129, 135, 143, 148, 154, 157, 161–162, 199, 238, 279
National Assembly for Wales 21, 46
National Front, France 184 / Front National 295
nationalism 5, 7, 24, 147–155, **181**, 190, 274; English nationalism 7, 147–155, 274; Scottish nationalism 150; *see also* patriotism
nationality 120–121, 126, 128, 149, 152, 293
national unions of students (NUS) 103
NATO 9, 137, 172, 215, 228–229, 234–235, 237–242, 268, 270, 272–273; anti-NATO 239; EU-NATO relationship 237–238; NATO-EU strategic partnership 237; NATO Summit, Warsaw 237
Neil, A. 43
neoliberalism 141, 162; *see also* liberals
Netherlands 97, 106, 121, 123, 140, 227, 257, 260–261, 269–272, 274
New Asia Strategy 201
Newton Fund 109
New York 52, 58, 144n20, 245
New Zealand 81, 88, 97, 154, 163, 198–201, 203–205, 210, 214, 216–218, 256
Nigeria 108, 202, 217
non-discrimination 104, 121, 126
Northern Ireland 5, 16, 19, 24, 28–38, 46–47, 95–96, 161, 174, 285; Northern Ireland Assembly 32–33, 38n1; Northern Ireland border 28; Northern Ireland Executive 32–33
Northern League, Italy 184
Northern Rock 55
North Lanarkshire 21
North Lincolnshire 295
Norway 16, 43, 87, 98, 104, 113, 154, 241, 267–268, 271–274, 282–284, 286, 288n4; Norwegian solution 98 / model 282, 284; Norwegian Supreme Court 284
Norwegian Business Association (NHO) 286
nuclear weapons 227–228

Obama, B. 55, 88, 154
OECD 68, 106, 225
Oireachtas, Ireland 34, 36
opt-out 70, 121, 125, 258, 268
Oxford 114

Pacific 8, 111, 197, 199–205
Pakistan 144n28, 200–201
Palestine 237
Paris 54, 60, 215, 237, 241, 246, 260
parliamentary 2, 15, 17–21, 24, 40, 44–46, 74–75, 137–138, 141, 143, 151–152, 158, **160**, 164, 168, 176, 293
party system 4, 16, 21, 37, 168, 189; intra-party divisions 159, 164; party politics 184; political parties 2, 4, 15–16, 21, 24, 29, 31, 34, 37, 74, 161, **181**, 190–195
passport 59–60, 244, 246, 293
Patel, P. 15, 213, 262, 269, 285
patriotism 7, 141–143, 150, 186; *see also* nationalism
peace 5, 27, 29–38, 46, 141, 209–210, 213, 224, 237
People's Party, Switzerland 184
pesticides 94–95
plurilateral agreement 82
Poland 104, 122–123, 140
political culture 7, 168, 199, 218
political mobilisation 148, 151
political opinion 42
political volatility 76
politicians 10, 15, 21, 24, 28, 35, 47, 62, 76, 134, 140, 152, 168, 172–173, **181–182**, 182–186, 190–191, 271
politicisation 7, 148–149, 287–288, 290, 292–294
politics 1–4, 6–10, 15, 17–18, 20, 22–24, 28, 31, 33, 55, 57, 67–68, 70, 76, 84, 88, 119–121, 129, 138, 148, 150–155, 157–164, 167–168, 172, 176, 179–191, 209, 223–224, 233, 238, 241, 247, 261, 263, 267, 271, 273–274, 290–296
polity 1–4, 7, 50–51, 125, 148, 287, 291–296; European polity 295; national polity 291
polls 15, 34, 95, 159, 163, 173, 189, 228, 295
populism 8, 75, 179, **181**, 187–191; *see also* anti-politics
Portugal 227, 267, 270, 273
Position Paper on Northern Ireland and Ireland 33
Powellism 151
power: agenda-setting powers 270; decentralisation of power 142–143; great powers 236, 267–266, 272; hard power 255, 262–263; normative power 234, 255, 261; power blocs 67, 72–73, 75–76; power distribution 254–255, 257; powerful actor 9, 271; power index 257–258; power politics 267; relative power 9; soft power 226, 236–238, 262–263; *see also* military, military power
pragmatic adaptation 49–53, 55, 59, 61–62

productivity 16, 22–24, 58, 61, 68, 71, 76, 93, 158, 163
pro-European 7, 41, 158, 167, 169–174, 176, 212, 218, 274
protectionism 89, 172, 198, 200, 213, 295
Prudential 59
public administration 1–2, 4, 15–17, 22–23
public opinion 34, 42, 114, 118–119, 177, 211, 295

qualified majority voting 69, 161, 224, 247, 261

race 59, 121–122, 172, 176, 199, 249, 286
Rasmussen, A. F. 242
Rasmussen, L. L. 272
ratification 88, 151, 158, 170, 288, 292, 294
referendum: Brexit referendum 2, 8, 15, 19, 21, 42–43, 118, 148, 152, 185–188, 208, 210–211, 218, 246, 269, 271, 295; 'referendum lock' 158; Scottish independence referendum 5, 20, 34, 41–48, 173; UK referendum 27, 234, 242, 284; *see also* campaign
reform 5–6, 19, 75, 92, 94, 101, 135, 140, 148, 170, 240
refugee 121, 226, 242, 260, 292; refugee crisis 121, 260, 292
regional policy 256, 258, 260
regulation 9, 51–52, 55, 58–60, 68, 72, 86, 95, 100, 112, 121, 159, 162, 171, 216, 244–251, 256, 258, 283–284; banking-sector regulation 55; financial regulation 9, 55, 216, 244–251; regulatory gaps 284; regulatory regimes 66, 286
regulatory convergence 69, 86
Remain supporters 43, 98 / voters 8, 22, 95, 152, 164, 174
retail 29, 70
Richmond 187
rights 18, 24, 28, 31, 41, 47, 59–61, 69, 84–85, 87, 105, 107, 110, 121, 125–128, 138–140, 164, 168, 172–174, 183, 186, 203, 208, 214, 229, 255, 258–259, 271; fishing rights 271; human rights 18, 24, 31, 41, 127; Human Rights Act, 1998 18; property rights 84, 107, 110, 138–140, 203, 259; voting rights 126, 140, 229
Romania 98, 101, 123, 128
Rompuy, H. V. 42
Rotherham 187
Rousseau, J. 138
Royal Bank of Scotland 54
Royal Navy 137, 140, 234
Russia 4, 9, 71, 106, 171, 215, 227–228, 230–231, 234, 236, 241–242, 272
Rutte, M. 272
Ryan Air 122

Saint Lucia 202
Samuelsen, A. 273
San Marino 268

Santander 59
Scandinavia 123, 247, 271
Schäuble, W. 247
Schuman, R. 210, 268
science 2–4, 7, 21–22, 55, 86, 103, 105–107, 110, 118, 179
Scotland 5, 16, 19, 22, 24, 40–48, 54, 95–96, 139, 148, 151–152, 173, 287; Scotland Act, 1999 41, 44–45; Scottish Parliament 20, 40–41, 43–46, 48
Scottish National Party (SNP) 19, 34, 41, 152, 173
Seasonal Agricultural Workers Scheme (SAWS) 98
Second World War 41, 92, 140–141, 151, 167, 169, 197, 200, 211, 217, 293
Secretary for International Trade, UK 80, 112, 197, 199, 213
sectors 27, 29, 35, 57–58, 66–70, 72, 76, 86, 95–97, 99, 101, 105, 123, 202, 205, 246, 249, 271, 283; arable sector 93; banking sector 52, 54–55, 58, 245, 247, 249; dairy sector 92, 97; financial sector 9, 50–53, 55, 57, 59, 67, 72–73, 142, 162, 244–245, 247–251, 271; manufacturing sector 68; services sector 5, 68, 244–246; university sector 103, 114, 123
security 4–5, 9, 31, 33, 37, 86, 92–93, 105, 121, 148, 170, 209–210, 213, 215–216, 223–224, 226–229, 233–242, 261, 266–267, 259, 270–274, 284; European security 170, 224, 227–228, 234–236, 242, 269, 271; security policy 4, 223, 226, 269, 284; security strategy 236, 239, 270
self-determination 40, 213
self-governing 278, 282, 284
separatism 148
Serbia 104, 268
services 5–7, 19, 23, 29–30, 47, 51, 53–56, 58–62, 63n23, 66, 68–70, 75–76, 84, 86, 89, 99–100, 114n1, 122–123, 126, 128–129, 134, 190, 203, 217, 244–250, 256, 262, 271, 281, 283, 286
Seychelles 202
Sillars, J. 43
Singapore *53*, 61, *73*, 74, 76, 86, 109–110, 144n20, 154, 176, 199, 217
Single Farm Payment (SFP) 93–94, 96, 100
Single Market 1, 5, 16, 29, 33–34, 38, 41, 43, 46–47, 66, 69–72, 74–75, 80, 85–87, 96, 98, 103, 113, 120, 134, 139, 152, 161–163, 173–176, 177n1, 202, 208, 244–247, 249, 251, 256, 262, 285, 294
Sinn Féin 32–34, 28n1
Slovenia 270
small states 10, 266–270, 272–275, 287
Smith, A. 138–139
Smith, I. D. 158
Social Democratic Party (SDP) 168
social democrats 236, 241; Socialists and Democrats 259
social dumping 295
social Europe 41, 69–70, 151
social groups 179; *see also* class society

socialism 19, 62, 63n1, 151, 171
Social Mobility Commission 16
South Africa 198
South Holland 21
South Korea 110
sovereignty 5, 7, 17–18, 20–21, 37, 40–41, 44–46,
    48, 85, 89, 95, 119, 120, 147–151, 153, 155,
    163, 169, 172, 176, 179, 208, 211, 213, 216,
    256, 278–279, 284, 287; British sovereignty
    7, 119, 147–151, 153, 155, 172, 211; national
    sovereignty 37, 41, 120, 163, 172, 256;
    Parliamentary Sovereignty 17–18, 21, 44–46,
    151; 'sovereign democrats' 278; 'sovereignty
    pooling' 169, 176, 179; state sovereign control;
    state sovereignty 279
Soviet Union 140
Spain 43, 97, 121, 126, 137, 258, 270; Spanish 43,
    128, 137, 142
special status 32
Sri Lanka 201
stability 30, 33–35, 37, 56, 62, 82–83, 140, 164,
    247–248, 251, 256, 268
stakeholder 3, 103–104, 247–248
Standard Life 59
Starmer, K. 174–175
State of the Union Address 237
Stoke-on-Trent 187
Stoltenberg, J. 237
Sturgeon, N. 42–43
subsidies 43, 92–93, 95–96, 99–100
supranational Europe 211
Supreme Court 16–18, 21, 24, 44–47, 284
sustainable development 86
Sweden 121–122, 184, 216, 257–258,
    267–270, 275
Sweden Democrats 184
Switzerland 98, 104, 113, 267–268, 271, 273–274,
    282, 284–285, 288n4; Swiss solution/model 98,
    113, 282, 286
Syria 121

Taoiseach 27–29, 35–36, 38
tariff 47, 61–62, 69–70, 84, 93, 96–99, 164, 198,
    261–262, 273, 281, 286; Common External
    Tariff (CET) 98–99, 261–262; non-tariffs
    barriers 69, 97, 99
tax 5, 37, 62, 68–69, 72, 74, 76, 137, 139, 164, 172,
    189, 246, 248–249, 256; Financial Transactions
    tax 249; income tax 68, 72; taxpayer 54–55; tax
    revenue 68, 246
Tchad 224
technological change 58
territorial configuration 279
territorial constitution 3, 16, 19–20, 24
territory 23, 82, 99, 120, 148, 259; territorial
    governance 19
terrorism/terror 234–235

Thatcher, M. 40, 61, 69, 122, 141, 151, 157, 161,
    212, 256, 269, 294; Thatcher era 61, 122, 157,
    161; Thatcherism 19, 161
theory 22, 49, 56, 83, 107, 123, 180, 185–186, 209,
    213, 218, **255,** 290–292, 294–296
third way 151
Tokyo 58
Tourism 35, 96, 124, 128
trade 6, 8, 80–81, 84–87, 89, 173, 197, 202–204,
    216, 218, 223, 225, 250, 258, 262, 273;
    Agreement on Trade-Related Aspects of
    Intellectual Property Rights (TRIPS) 84; EFTA
    Surveillance Authority (ESA) 87, 282–283;
    EU-Canada Comprehensive Economic and
    Trade Agreement (CETA) 87, 203, 225,
    262; EU-NZ free trade agreement 216–217;
    EU-Singapore FTA 86; European Free Trade
    Area (EFTA) 16, 24, 85, 87, 98, 113, 267–268,
    271–275, 282, *283,* 285, 287, 288n4; EU-UK
    FTA 81, 86–87, 99; free trade agreement (FTA)
    43, 81, 86, 97, 99, 112, 154, 216–217; trade deal
    86, 203, 216, 218, 273; trade policy 6, 8, 80–81,
    84–85, 87, 89, 197, 202, 204, 223, 250, 262;
    Trade Remedies Organization 81; Trade Union
    Congress (TUC) 173; Transatlantic Trade and
    Investment Partnership (TTIP) 89, 225, 258, 262
transport 86, 138, 257
treaty 10, 17, 69, 82, 85–86, 93, 103, 105, 151, 158,
    170, 200, 212, 225, 229, 240–241, 266, 281,
    290, 292–294; European Constitutional Treaty
    294; Lisbon Treaty/Treaty of Lisbon 10, 170,
    225, 240, 266, 294; Maastricht Treaty 69, 103,
    151, 290, 293; Treaty of Amsterdam 103; Treaty
    of Nice 294; Treaty of Rome 93, 200; Treaty
    on the Functioning of the European Union
    (TFEU) 82
the Troubles (Ireland) 27
Trump, D. 2, 9, 48, 184, 216, 230, 233, 240, 262
trust 21, 152–153, 230, 255, 286, 288
Tunisia 104
Turkey 98, 104, 231, 279, 281, 286; Turkey model
    281, 286
Turnbull, M. 216
Turner, A. 52
Tusk, D. 35, 125

UK Civil Service 16, 81
UK India Education & Research Initiative
    (UKIERI) 111
UK Parliament 20, 44, 46; *see also* Westminster,
    Westminster Parliament
Ukraine 104, 230, 236; Ukrainian crisis 227
UK-US Trade and Investment Working Group 80
unionism 5, 38, 153
United Kingdom Independence Party (UKIP) 7,
    73–75, 118–119, 124–125, 143n5, 150, 152–153,
    159, 162–164, 180, 183–189, 259, 293–295

United Kingdom/UK 1, 4, 15, 19, 21, 28, 35–36, 42–44, 47, 74, 80–83, 89, 107, 109, 111–112, 143n5, 147–150, 152–154, 162, 197, 215, 244, 254, 266, 268–270, 272–273, 275, 295
United Nation 224, 227, 201, 215, 226–227; General Assembly (UNGA) 224, 227; Security Council (UNSC) 224, 226, 229; UN resolutions 237
United States 2, 4, 9, 22–23, 53–55, 60, 74, 80, 88, 97, 105, 107–111, 129, 140, 154, 170–171, 184, 199, 201, 209, 211–212, 215–217, 225, 227–231, 236, 242, 245–247, 250–251, 262–263, 268, 271, 279
University of London International Programmes 110
urban areas 4, 6, 103, 106–110, 112, 114, 123, 295

Varadkar, T. L. 27–28, 36, 38, 217
Varoufakis, Y. 173
Vatican City 268
Verhofstadt, G. 168, 261
Veto 43, 84, 113, 135, 170, 228, 248, 255, 261, 263, 287
visas 105, 108, 110–111, 121, 128
von Hayek, F. 142

wage 61, 67–70, 72, 172; low wage 70; wage disparities 72; wage growth 70; wage pressure 70
Wales 19, 21–22, 42, 44–47, 95–96, 112, 129, 151–152, 187
Wall Street 54–55, 68
Washington 54, 216, 227
wealth 22, 67, 134, 148, 152, 209, 213

welfare state 5, 62, 123, 125; national health service 62, 69, 208; welfare provision 69
West Lothian Question 149
Westminster 5, 15, 17–22, 24, 32–33, 38, 40–41, 44–48, 73, 141, 149, 185, 189, 229; Westminster Acts 19; Westminster parliament 5, 18, 21, 48, 141; *see also* UK Parliament
white paper 34–35, 87–88, 204, 228, 256, 287; White Paper on exiting the EU 35; White Paper on Irish Unification 34; Trade White Paper 87, 204
West Somerset 21
Whitehall 18–20, 23–25, 212, 214
Wilson, H. 169, 173, 212
withdrawal bill 46, 48; *see also* Great Repeal Bill
workers 47, 52, 60–61, 66, 68, 70–71, 75, 98, 120–125, 128–129, 140, 172, 183, 186, 208, 226; skilled workers 60, 70, 123; unskilled labour 57; workforce 52, 68, 97; *see also* labour
World Bank 225
world order 9, 230; multipolar world order 9, 230
World Trade Organisation (WTO) 17, 24, 81–82, 84–86, 88, 99, 109, 113, 175, 204, 251, 284, 286; General Agreement on Tariffs and Trade (GATT) 82, 84, 201; tariff-rate quotas (TRQs) 84, 99; Uruguay Round 93; WTO Government Procurement Agreement 82; WTO option 84; WTO schedules 84, 88, 99

xenophobia 15, **181**

Zaghari-Ratcliffe, N. 15